Karl Wohlmuth, Chicot Eboué,
Achim Gutowski, Afeikhena Jerome, Tobias Knedlik,
Mareike Meyn, Touna Mama (Eds.)

Africa – Commodity Dependence, Resource Curse and Export Diversification

AF831961

African Development Perspectives Yearbook

Edited by the

Research Group on African Development Perspectives Bremen:
Karl Wohlmuth, Chicot Eboué,
Achim Gutowski, Afeikhena Jerome, Tobias Knedlik,
Mareike Meyn, Touna Mama

Vol. XII

LIT

Karl Wohlmuth, Chicot Eboué,
Achim Gutowski, Afeikhena Jerome, Tobias Knedlik,
Mareike Meyn, Touna Mama (Eds.)

Africa – Commodity Dependence, Resource Curse and Export Diversification

LIT

Bibliographic information published by the Deutsche Nationalbibliothek
The Deutsche Nationalbibliothek lists this publication in the Deutsche Nationalbibliografie; detailed bibliographic data are available in the Internet at http://dnb.d-nb.de.

ISBN 978-3-8258-0256-1

A catalogue record for this book is available from the British Library

© LIT VERLAG Dr. W. Hopf Berlin 2007
Ziegelstr. 30
D-10117 Berlin

Auslieferung:
LIT Verlag Fresnostr. 2, D-48159 Münster
Tel. +49 (0) 2 51/620 32 - 22, Fax +49 (0) 2 51/922 60 99, e-Mail: lit@lit-verlag.de

Distributed in the UK by: Global Book Marketing, 99B Wallis Rd, London, E9 5LN
Phone: +44 (0) 20 8533 5800 – Fax: +44 (0) 1600 775 663
http://www.centralbooks.co.uk/acatalog/search.html

Distributed in North America by:

Transaction Publishers
New Brunswick (U.S.A.) and London (U.K.)

Transaction Publishers
Rutgers University
35 Berrue Circle
Piscataway, NJ 08854

Phone: +1 (732) 445 - 2280
Fax: + 1 (732) 445 - 3138
for orders (U. S. only):
toll free (888) 999 - 6778
e-mail:
orders@transactionspub.com

Contents

Unit 2: Commodity Dependence and Export Diversification. Towards New Strategies and Policies for Nigeria

Edited by Afeikhena Jerome, Karl Wohlmuth and Mareike Meyn

Unit 3: Escaping the Primary Commodities Dilemma by Pro-active Policies: The Case of Cameroon

Edited by Chicot Eboué, Touna Mama, Karl Wohlmuth and Tobias Knedlik

Unit 4: Book Reviews and Book Notes

edited by Achim Gutowski and Mareike Meyn

Unit 5: Profiles, News and Information

edited by Mareike Meyn

The Research Group on African Development Perspectives in Bremen

The aggravating social, political and economic crisis of the African continent forces institutions, organisations, researchers, development practitioners, ad hoc working groups and networks on Africa, and all others involved in African development affairs to intensify the analytical and conceptional work on alternative development visions and designs for Africa. There is a growing number of plans and programmes, conceptions, researches, and ideas being published worldwide focussing on the peculiarity of the African crisis, the chances for structural adjustment, the issue of planning development beyond adjustment, and on the necessary responses to the globalisation trend. The discussion referring to Africa's development problems and perspectives is widening. However, it is difficult to get an overall view of the different approaches and proposals and, subsequently, to make the discussion useful for the programming and co-ordinating of development policies. So there is a need for a comprehensive publication that compiles, evaluates, and analyses the scattered and often not easily available sources.

To fill this gap, the *Research Group on African Development Perspectives* at the University of Bremen is presenting the *African Development Perspectives Yearbook*, being published since 1989. Research activities of group members comprise country studies, macroeconomic policies, aspects of labour market policies and informal sector activities, human development policies, food security policy, environmental policy, promotion of small-scale industries, private sector development policies, entrepreneurship development, assessments of structural adjustment policies, trade and regional integration policies, as well as economic diversification options.

The *African Development Perspectives Yearbook* is the first English-speaking periodical published in Germany relating to development problems in Africa. African, European and North-American experts from universities, international and regional organisations, and from non-governmental and donor organisations report on problems and possible solutions, on new political approaches, on economic programmes, and on visions for alternative African development paths.

Africa's future will depend on both, on its economic and political connections with the international community at the Pan-African, regional, national, and sectoral levels, and on local projects and development efforts at the micro level. Most important are own African development visions, programmes, strategies and policies. The *African Development Perspectives Yearbook* contains information and analyses with regard to these various dimensions. Global analyses, regional and country studies, sectoral studies and project evaluations are published in the *African Development Perspectives Yearbook*, as well as declarations of international conferences, important documents of African organisations and states, and programmes of civil society organisations and self-help groups.

Beside the analytical and documentary character of the *African Development Perspectives Yearbook*, the editors successfully established an extensive network for the exchange of news and information and are so relating and connecting development organisations and research institutions that are working in and for Africa. The members of the *Research Group on African Development Perspectives* are interested to deepen the contacts with partners that are sharing similar objectives.

The *African Development Perspectives Yearbook* is targeted to decision-makers in development policy and to experts in project consultancies, media, research and development, aid institutions, and to all others that are interested in Africa's development. It offers comprehensive analysis and information about recent developments with regard to the African continent.

Thus, the *African Development Perspectives Yearbook* is reporting on

- visions and conceptions with regard to long-term development strategies for Africa;
- strategies that emphasise a longer-run planning process that goes beyond conventional structural adjustment policies;
- successful projects and programmes concerning countries, regions, institutions, or specific sectors of African economies, by analysing the conditions of their success;
- resourceful and creative activities of socio-economic interest groups, local development initiatives and NGOs, which could serve as models for other regions;
- innovative strategies for and prospects of regional integration in Africa; and on
- economic, social, and political trends in Africa's sub-regions, nation-states, provinces, towns and local communities.

The *African Development Perspectives Yearbook* takes into account sources and information from all relevant levels of action, planning, discussion, and research, i.e. from international, regional, and national organisations and institutions, committees, working groups, and NGOs, but with particular emphasis given to those ideas and approaches originating from Africa.

Address:
Research Group on African Development Perspectives
c/o Prof. Dr. Karl Wohlmuth, Coordinating Editor
University of Bremen
Department of Economics (FB 7)
Institute for World Economics and International Management (IWIM)
P.O. Box 330 440
D-28334 Bremen
Germany

Telephone:	+49-421-218-3074/ -3429/ -2138
Fax:	+49-421-218-4550
E-mail:	iwim@uni-bremen.de (regarding the administrative issues of the Research Group and the Yearbook) wohlmuth@uni-bremen.de (regarding the scientific work of the Research Group and the editorial issues of the Yearbook)
Internet:	http://www.iwim.uni-bremen.de

Acknowledgements

This Volume 12 of the *African Development Perspectives Yearbook* has again benefited from many contributions, from various inputs and from important donations. The great number of contributions from all over the world and especially from Africa was made possible because of the continuing support from African and international organisations, from numerous research and development institutions, and from individual experts. International and regional organisations, such as the African Development Bank (AfDB), the United Nations Economic Commission for Africa (UNECA), the OECD Development Centre and the NEPAD Secretariat, have contributed with information and encouragement. We are always interested in their advice and guidance so as to structure the future work on the *African Development Perspectives Yearbook*. Many other institutions have contributed with news, information, publications, and encouragement. Further regional and international organisations, like the World Bank, UNCTAD, UNDP, IMF, UNIDO, ILO and various others, continue to support our effort by sending us timely their new strategy documents and their researches for publication and review. Furthermore, we would also like to thank all these institutions by informing so many others about our work for Africa.

Special thanks go to Dr Afeikhena Jerome from the NEPAD Secretariat in Midrand, South Africa who provided as editor of Unit 1 and Unit 2 of this Yearbook valuable support in the revision of contributions, and who provided as author insights into Nigeria's economic and political system.

We would also like to express our deep gratitude to Prof. Chicot Eboué, Prof. Touna Mama, Dr. Ernest Bamou and Dr. Alexandre Magloire Schouamé from the University of Yaoundé II in Cameroon who led the research team that edited Unit 3 of this Yearbook. Their continued endeavours were essential for the successful finalisation of this important Unit about Cameroon's economic diversification attempts.

We also have to thank all supporters and contributors of the *African Development Perspectives Yearbook* for their hard work, their steady encouragement and their continuous assistance. The valuable input from leading African research institutions and experts has contributed over the years to the success of the *African Development Perspectives Yearbook*. We are also grateful to the World Institute for Development Economics Research (WIDER) of the United Nations University (UNU-WIDER), and especially our friend Adam Swallow, for promoting the Yearbook at numerous events and workshops.

Various institutions have over the years made donations and have funded allocations to the Yearbook, especially to mention the Bremer Gesellschaft für Wirtschaftsforschung and the University of Bremen, Germany. These donations have helped us to research on African development issues, to distribute the various volumes of the Yearbook to African universities and to major African research institutions, and to invite research scholars from leading African research institutions to work with us in Bremen.

Many others have given support, advice, and encouragement; others have helped with frank and critical assessments. However, the responsibility for the final product remains with the editorial team of the *Research Group on African Development Perspectives* in Bremen.

Yixin Lu as an editorial assistant has contributed to the final layout of this volume, and has thereby given valuable support to the editorial team so as to make possible a timely publication of the Yearbook. The various staff of the Institute for World Economics and International Management (IWIM) of the University of Bremen has encouraged the work of the Research Group continually and actively.

In the name of the Editorial Team:

Prof. Dr. Karl Wohlmuth

List of Contributors

Aka, Bédia Francois., Associate Professor, Department of Economics and Development, University of Bouaké, Côte D'Ivoire and Researcher, Centre de Recherche en Économie Appliquée, University of Luxembourg, Luxemburg.

Aigbokhan, Bernard E., Professor, Department of Economics, Ambrose Alli University, Ekpoma, Nigeria.

Ailemen, Moses, Researcher, Department of Economics, Ambrose Alli University, Ekpoma, Nigeria.

Alabi, Reuben A., Ph.D., Research Fellow, Department of Agricultural Economics, Ambrose Alli University, Ekpoma, Nigeria.

Arvidson, Anders, Project Manager, Stockholm Environmental Institute (SEI), Stockholm, Sweden.

Bamou, Ernest, Faculty of Economics and Business Administration, University of Yaoundé II and Department of Economic Affairs, Ministry of Economics and Finance, Yaoundé, Cameroon.

Coulibaly, Adama, Economist, Middle East and North African Region, World Bank, Washington D.C., USA.

Eboué, Chicot, Professor, Head of the Economics Department, University of Nancy 2, France.

Etogo Messomo, Mireille, Ph.D. Research Fellow, Department of Economics, University of Yaoundé II, Cameroon

Fongue, Joseph Ndeffo, Ph.D., Researcher, Karlsruhe, Germany.

Gutowski, Achim, Ph.D., Research Fellow, Research Group on African Development Perspectives, Institute for World Economics and International Management, University of Bremen, Germany.

Jerome, Afeikhena, Ph.D., Consultant and Senior Lecturer, NEPAD/African Peer Review Mechanism Secretariat, Midrand, South Africa.

Johnson, Francis X., Research Fellow, Climate and Energy Resources Programme, Stockholm Environment Institute (SEI), Stockholm, Sweden.

Knedlik, Tobias, Ph.D., Research Fellow, Halle Institute for Economic Research (IHW), Halle, Germany.

Kouassi, Bernard, Ph.D., Executive Director, NEPAD/African Peer Review Mechanism Secretariat, Midrand, South Africa

Menck, Karl Wolfgang, Ph.D., Senior Researcher, Hamburg Institute for International Economics, Hamburg, Germany.

Meyn, Mareike, Ph.D., Research Fellow, Research Group on African Development Perspectives, Institute for World Economics and International Management, University of Bremen, Germany.

Ndedi, Alain A., Founding Member of YENEPAD (Young Entrepreneurs for the New Partnership for Africa's Development), University of Pretoria, South Africa.

N'Donga, Célestin, Research Fellow, Department of Economics, University of Yaoundé II, Cameroon.

Okoh, Rosemary N., Ph.D., Senior Lecturer and Research Fellow, Department of Agricultural Economics, Delta State University, Abraka, Nigeria.

Olutayo, Akinpelu O., Research Fellow, Department of Sociology, Faculty of the Social Sciences, University of Ibadan, Nigeria.

Omobowale, Ayokunle O., Research Fellow, Department of Sociology, Faculty of the Social Sciences, University of Ibadan, Nigeria.

Ongolo Zogo, Valérie, Ph.D., Research Fellow, Department of Economics, University of Yaoundé II, Cameroon.

Schouamé, Alexandre M., Senior Lecturer, Department of Economics, University of Yaoundé II, Cameroon.

Seebaluck, Vikram, Lecturer, Department of Chemical and Sugar Engineering, Faculty of Engineering, University of Mauritius, Reduit, Mauritius.

du Toit, Charlotte, Professor, Department of Economics, University of Pretoria, Pretoria, South Africa.

Touna Mama, Professor, Department of Economics, University of Yaoundé II, Yaoundé, Cameroon and Lead Adviser of the Prime Minister, Republic of Cameroon.

Ujah, Oliver C., Researcher, African Institute for Applied Economics, Enugu, Enugu State,Nigeria.

Uzochukwu, Amakom, Lecturer, Department of Economics, Nnamdi Azikiwe University, Awka, and Researcher, African Institute for Applied Economics, Enugu, Enugu State, Nigeria.

Uzor, Osmund O., Researcher, Institute for World Economics and International Management, University of Bremen, Germany.

Watson, Helen Kerr, Ph.D., Senior Lecturer, Department of Geographical and Environmental Sciences, School of Life and Environmental Sciences, University of Kwazulu Natal, Durban, South Africa

Wohlmuth, Karl, Professor, Research Group on African Development Perspectives, Co-ordinating Editor of the African Development Perspectives Yearbook, Director, Institute for World Economics and International Management, University of Bremen, Germany.

Woods, Jeremy, Ph.D., Research Fellow, Centre for Energy, Policy and Technology (ICCEPT), Imperial College, London, UK.

Abbreviations

Abbreviations for Unit 1

ACP	African, Caribbean and Pacific
AfDB	African Development Bank
AGOA	African Growth and Opportunity Act
ASCCI	Association of SADC Chambers of Commerce and Industry
ASPB	Advisory Service for Private Business
BIT	Bilateral Investment Treaty
CDG	Carl Duisberg Foundation
CCIM	Mauritius Chamber of Commerce and Industry
CMA	Common Monetary Area
COMESA	Common Market for Eastern and Southern Africa
COMREG	COMpany REGisters
COSSE	Committee of SADC Stock Exchanges
CTB	Contributions to Trade Balance
DBSA	Development Bank of Southern Africa
DPRU	Development Policy Research Unit
DRC	Democratic Republic of Congo
DTT	Double Taxation Treaty
EPA	Economic Partnership Agreement
EPZ	Export Processing Zone
EU	European Union
FDI	Foreign Direct Investment
FISCU	Finance and Investment Sector Coordinating Unit
FTA	Free Trade Area
GDP	Gross Domestic Product
GTZ	German Technical Cooperation (Deutsche Gesellschaft für Technische Zusammenarbeit GmbH)
HIV/AIDS	Human Immune Deficiency Virus/Acquired Immune Deficiency Syndrome
ICASA	Independent Authority of South Africa
ILO	International Labour Organisation
JSE	Johannesburg Stock Exchange

ICM	SADC's Integrated Committee of Ministers
InWent	Internationale Weiterbildung und Entwicklung gGmbH (Capacity Building International, Germany)
ITC	International Trade Centre
IMF	International Monetary Fond
KAS	Konrad-Adenauer-Foundation
LDC	Least Developed Country
M&A	Mergers and Acquisition
MCCI	Malawi Chamber of Commerce and Industry
MCCCI	Malawi Confederation of Chambers of Commerce and Industry
MDC	Maputo Development Corridor
MEPC	Malawi Export Promotion Council
MERCOSUR	Mercado Común del Sur (Southern Common Market)
MoU	Memorandum Of Understanding
NEPAD	New Economic Partnership for Africa's Development
NER	National Electricity Regulator
NIC	Newly Industrialised Country
ODA	Official Development Assistance
OECD	Organisation for Economic Cooperation and Development
PPP	Public-Private Partnerships
PTA	Preferential Trade Agreement
RAPID	Regional Activity to Promote Integration through Dialogue and Policy Implementation
RCA	Revealed Comparative Advantages
RETOSA	SADC Charter of the Regional Tourism Organisation of Southern Africa
RSA	Republic of South Africa
RTA	Regional Trade Arrangement
SABN	Southern African Business Network
SACOB	South African Chamber Of Business
SACU	Southern African Customs Union
SADC	Southern African Development Community
SADCC	Southern African Development Coordination Conference
SAFTA	SADC Free Trade Area
SAFTO	South African Foreign Trade Organization
SAIIA	South African Institute of International Affairs
SDI	Spatial Development Initiative
SEDCO	Small Enterprise Development Corporation
SITCD	SADC Industry and Trade Coordination Division
SME	Small and Medium-sized Enterprise

SNC	SADC Nation Committees
SOE	State Owned Enterprise
SPA	SADC Programme of Action
TNC	Transnational Company
TAZARA	Tanzania-Zambia Railway Authority
TIFI	SADC's directorate of Trade Industry, Finance and Investment
TNC	Transnational Company
TNF	Trade Negotiating Forum
UNCTAD	United Nations Conference on Trade and Development
UNDP	United Nations Development Programme
UNECA	United Nations Economic Commission for Africa
UNIDO	United Nations Industrial Development Organization
USA	United States of America
USAID	United States Agency for International Development
WTO	World Trade Organization
ZCC	Zambia Competition Commission

Abbreviations for Unit 2

ABCDE	Annual Bank Conference on Development Economics (of the World Bank)
ACP	African, Caribbean and Pacific Countries
ACP-EU	African/Caribbean/Pacific Countries negotiating with the European Union
ADLI	Agricultural Demand Led Industrialization
ADPs	Agricultural Development Projects
AEC	African Economic Community
AER	American Economic Review
AFSPC	Agriculture and Food Security Policy Commission
AGOA	African Growth and Opportunity Act
BBC	British Broadcasting Corporation
BC	Bankers Committee (of the Central Bank of Nigeria)
BoI	Bank of Industry
BPE	Bureau for Public Enterprises
CAP	Common Agricultural Policy
CAPAN	Cassava Processors Association of Nigeria
CARICOM	Caribbean Community and Common Market
CBN	Central Bank of Nigeria

CDC	Commodity Dependent Countries
CED	Cassava Enterprise Development Project
CET	Common External Tariff
CGA	Cassava Growers Association
CIAT	International Centre for Tropical Agriculture
CIC	Cassava Initiative Committee
CIL	Cocoa Industry Limited
CMD	Cassava Mosaic Disease
COSCA	Collaborative Study of Cassava in Africa
CRIN	Cocoa Research Institute of Nigeria
CSAE	Centre for the Study of African Economies
CU	Customs Union
DC	Developing Countries
DFID	Department for International Development of the United Kingdom
DG	Directory-General
DTI	Department of Trade and Industry
ECOWAP	Agricultural Policy of the Economic Community of West African States
ECOWAS	Economic Community of West African States
EEC	European Economic Commission
EME	Emerging Market Economics
EPA	Economic Partnership Agreements
EPCC	Economic Policy Coordinating Committee
EPTD	Environment and Production Technology Division
EPKEA	Enugu Palm Kernel Extraction Association
EPZ	Export Processing Zone
ETLS	ECOWAS Trade Liberalization Scheme
EU	European Union
FAMAD	A New name for Bata Shoes Manufactures
FAO	Food and Agriculture Organization
FAS	Foreign Agricultural Service
FDI	Foreign Direct Investment
FDLPCS	Federal Department of Livestock and Pest Control Services
FG	Federal Government
FGN	Federal Government of Nigeria
FIIRO	Federal Institute of Industrial Research, Oshodi
FMANR	Federal Ministry of Agriculture and Natural Resources
FMARD	Federal Ministry of Agriculture and Rural Development
FMF	Federal Ministry of Finance
FMST	Federal Ministry of Science and Technology

FOS	Federal Office of Statistics
FTA	Free Trade Agreement
FTZ	Free Trade Zone
Ha	hectares
Hg	hectogram
GATS	General Agreement on Trade and Services
GATT	General Agreement on Tariffs and Trade
GCC	Global Commodity Chain
GDP	Gross Domestic Production
GSP	Generalised System of Preferences
GTZ	German Technical Cooperation
GVC	Global Value Chain
IATPP	Intra-African Trade Promotion Programme
IBRD	International Bank for Reconstruction and Development
ICP	Integrated Cassava Project
IDC	Industrial Development Council
IDEAA	Initiative for Development and Equity in African Agriculture
IDRC	International Development Research Centre
IFAD	International Fund for Agricultural Development
IFC	International Finance Corporation
IFPRI	International Food Policy Research Institute
IGAD	Intergovernmental Authority on Development
IITA	International Institute of Tropical Agriculture
ISO	International Standards Organisation
ITC	International Trade Centre
LDC	Least Developed Country
LEEDS	Local Economic Empowerment and Development Strategy
LSEs	Large Scale Enterprises
MFN	Most Favoured Nation
MSEs	Medium Scale Enterprises
MSG	Monosodium Glutamate
Mt	metric tons
N	Naira (Nigerian currency)
NACB	Nigerian Agricultural and Cooperative Bank
NAP	Nigerian Agricultural Policy
NACRDB	Nigerian Agricultural Cooperative and Rural Development Bank
NAFDAC	National Food and Drugs Administration and Control
NCAM	National Centre for Agricultural Machinery
NCDC	National Cocoa Development Committee

NCE	National Certificate of Education
NBFIs	Non-Bank Financial Institutions
NEDLAC	National Economic and Development and Labour Council
NEEDS	National Economic Empowerment and Development Strategy
NEI	Nucleus Estate Initiative
NEIB	Nigerian Export-Import Bank
NEP	Nigerian Export Policy
NEPA	National Electricity Power Authority
NEPAD	New Partnership for Africa's Development
NEPC	Nigeria Export Promotion Council
NEPZA	Nigerian Export Processing Zones Authority
NESG	Nigerian Economic Summit Group
NEXIM	Nigeria Export Import Bank
NFP	National Focal Point on Multilateral Trade Matters
NGN	Nigerian Naira
NGO	Non Governmental Organisation
NIFOR	Nigerian Institute for Oil Palm Research
NIPC	Nigerian Investment Promotion Commission
NIYAMCO	Nigerian Yeast and Alcohol Manufacturing Company
NLDB	The Nigeria Local Development Board
NPC	National Planning Commission
NRCRI	National Root Crops Research Institute
NTC	Nigerian Tanning Council
OECD	Organisation for Economic Co-operation and Development
OFN	Operation Feed the Nation
OPEC	Organisation of Petroleum Exporting Countries
OND	Ordinary National Diploma
PACI	Pan-African Cassava Initiative
PBN	Peoples Bank of Nigeria
PKC	Palm Kernel Cake
PKO	Palm Kernel Oil
PPP	Public-Private Partnership
PRODA	Project Development Agency
PTA	Preferential Trade Agreement
RAIDS	Rural Agro-Industrial Development Scheme
R&D	Research and Development
RBS	This is not an abbreviation; it is the name of a firm as found in the reference. Advice: delete from here.
RMRDC	Raw Materials Research Development Council
RTEP	Root and Tuber Expansion Programme

RUSEP	Rural Sector Enhancement Programme
SATRA	South African Telecommunications Regulatory Authority
SAP	Structural Adjustment Programme
SDT	Special and Differential Treatment
SE	South Eastern
SEEDS	State Economic Empowerment and Development Strategy
SED	Small Enterprises Development
SEDI	Scientific Equipment Development Institute
SFI	Soil Fertility Initiative
SME	Small and Medium Enterprise
SMIEIS	Small and Medium Scale Industries Equity Investments Scheme
SON	Standards Organization of Nigeria
SPFS	Special Programme for Food Security
SPS	Sanitary and Phytosanitary Standards
SSE	Small Scale Enterprise
S&T	Science and Technology
TCB	Trade Capacity Building
TCC	Trade Compliance Centre
TDCA	Trade, Development and Co-operation Agreement
TMS	Tropical Manioc Selection
TPN	Trade Policy of Nigeria
TRIPS	Agreement on Trade Related Aspects on Intellectual Property Rights
UNCED	United Nations Conference on Environment and Development
UNCTAD	United Nations Conference on Trade and Development
UNIDO	United Nations Industrial Development Organisation
UNSTATS	United Nations Statistics Division
USAID	United States Agency for International Development
US	United States
USA	United States Of America
USDA	United State Department of Agriculture
VSA	Volunteers Service Agency
WAEMU	West African Economic and Monetary Union
WBES	World Bank Enterprise Survey
WIPO	World Intellectual Property Organisation
WRDB	The Western Region Development Board
WRPDB	Western Region Production Development Board
WTO	World Trade Organization

Abbreviations for Unit 3

ADB	African Development Bank
AERC	African Economic Research Consortium
AFD	Agence Française pour le Développement
AfDB	African Development Bank
ALUCAM	Cameroon Aluminium Smelting Company
AU	African Union
BCD	Cameroon Development Bank
BEAC	Bank of Central African States
BEL	Belgium
BOT	Built-Operate-Transfer
BTP	Building and Public Works
BVMAC	Central Africa Stock Exchange Market
CAF	Central African Republic
CAMSUCO	Cameroon Sugar Company
CAPME	Support Centre for Small and Medium Size Enterprises
CAR	Central African Republic
CARBAP	Centre Africain de Recherches sur Bananiers et Plantains
CARICOM	Caribbean Common Market
CBC	Commonwealth Business Council
CBN	Central Bank of Nigeria
CCIMA	Chambers of Commerce, Industry, Mines, and Handicraft
CDC	Cameroon Development Corporation
CEMAC	Economic and Monetary Community in Central Africa
CET	Common External Tariff
CFA	African Monetary Community
CFAF	French African Financial Community
CIF	Cost, Insurance and Freight
CIRAD	Centre for International Cooperation in Agronomic Research for Development
CHE	Switzerland
CHN	China
CICAM	Cameroon Cotton Industry
CIL	Cocoa Industry Limited
CIP	Competitive Industrial Performance Index
CIPCC	Inter-Professional Cocoa and Coffee Board
CIRAD	French Agricultural Research Centre for International Development
CNCE	National Centre for Foreign Trade

CNIC	Cameroon Shipyard and Industrial Engineering Ltd.
CPI	Consumer Price Index
CRA	Central Africa Republic
CRIN	Cocoa Research Institute of Nigeria
CTA	Technical Centre for Agricultural and Rural Cooperation
CU	Customs Union
DAE	Department of Economic Affairs
DC	Developing Country
DFID	Department for International Development of the United Kingdom
DP	Direction de la Prévision (Economic Planning Directorate)
DRC	Domestic Resource Costs
DSCN	Direction de la Statistique et de la Comptabilité Nationale (National Accounts and Statistics Directorate)
DSDRE	Development Strategy and Economic Recovery Declaration.
DSX	Douala Stock Exchange
ECA	Economic Commission for Africa
ECOWAP	Agricultural Policy of the Economic Community of West African States
ECOWAS	Economic Community of West African States
EDI	Export Diversification Index
EPA	Economic Partnership Agreement
EPCC	Economic Policy Coordinating Committee
EPIP	Export Promotion Industrial Policy
EPKEA	Enugu Palm Kernel Extraction Association
ESP	Spain
EU	European Union
FAO	Food and Agricultural Organisation
FCFA	Francs Communaute Francais Afriquain
FCP	Financial Capital Profitability Ratio
FDI	Foreign Direct Investment
FED	Fonds Européen de Développement
FF	French Francs
FL	Finance Law
FOB	Free on Board
FOGAPE	Support Fund and Credits to Small and Medium Size Enterprises
FRA	France
FTA	Free Trade Area
FYP	Five Year Plan

GBR	United Kingdom
GDP	Gross Domestic Product
GICAM	Cameroon Employers' Union
GRP	Green Revolution Programme
GRSDS	Global Rural Sector Development Strategy
GTZ	German Technical Cooperation (Deutsche Gesellschaft für Technische Zusammenarbeit GmbH)
HIPC	Highly Indebted Poor Countries
IBRD/WB	International Bank for Reconstruction and Development /World Bank
ICCO	International Cocoa Organization
IFOAM	International Federation of Organic Agriculture Movements
IIS	Industries Import Substitution
IITA	International Institute of Tropical Agriculture
IMF	International Monetary Fund
INS	National Institute of Statistics
ISO	International Standard Organisation
ITA	Italy
ITC	International Trade Centre
LDC	Least Developed Country
MAGZI	Industrial Park Management Mission
MDG	Millennium Development Goal
MECAM	Association of Cameroon Enterprises
MINEFI	Ministry of Economy and Finance
MINADER	Ministère de l'Agriculture et du Développement Rural (Ministry of Agriculture and Rural Development)
N	Naira (Nigerian currency)
NAIRU	Non-Accelerating Rate of Unemployment
NAFDAC	National Agency for Food and Drug Control
NAFPP	National Accelerated Food Production Programme
NCDC	National Cocoa Development Committee
NCE	National Certification of Education
NEDLAC	National Economic and Development and Labour Council
NEPAD	New partnership for African Development
NEPC	Nigeria Export Promotion Council
NEXIM	Nigeria Export Import Bank
NFP	National Focal Point on Multilateral Trade Matters
NGN	Nigerian Naira
NGO	Non Government Organisation
NICTs	New Information and Communication Technologies
NLDB	Nigeria Local Development Board

NIC	Nicaragua
NLD	Netherlands
NTB	Non Tariff Barrier
OECD	Organisation for Economic Co-operation and Development
OFN	Operation Feed the Nation
OHADA	Organization for the Harmonization of Business Law in Africa
OSIC	One Stop Investment Center
PCS	Primary Commodities' Share
PKC	Palm Kernel Cake
PKO	Palm Kernel Oil
PREBAP	Programme de Reconversion Economique de la Filiere Banane Plantain
PRSP	Poverty Reduction Strategy Paper
PSVA	Public Sector Value Added
RC	Republic of Cameroon
REA	Real Exchange Rate
RSDS	Rural Sector Development Strategy
RTAs	Regional Trade Agreements
RZFI	Free Zone Regime
SAP	Structural Adjustment Programme
SIFIM	Intermediary Financial Services Indirectly Measured
SITRASS	Solidarité Internationale sur les Transports et la Recherche en Afrique Sub-Saharienne
SMEs	Small and Medium Enterprises
SMIs	Small and Medium Industries
SMIEIS	Small- and Medium-Scale Industries Equity Investments Scheme
SNI	National Investment Corporation
SOCATRAL	Cameroon Aluminium Rolling Mill Company
SOCAPALM	Cameroon Oil Company
SODECAO	Cocoa Development Corporation
SODECOTON	Cotton Development Company
SON	Standard Organisation of Nigeria
SONARA	National Refining Company Ltd
SONEL	National Electricity Corporation
SPS	Sanitary and Phytosanitary Specifications
SSA	Sub-Saharan Africa
SSATP	Sub Saharan Africa Transport Program
SSE	Small-Scale Enterprise
STCP	Sustainable Tree Crops Program

STF	Special Telecommunications Fund
STR	Road Transporters' Union
SYNDUSTRICAM	Union of Cameroon Industries
S&T	Science and Technology
TCB	Trade Capacity Building
THA	Thailand
TPG	Taxe Progressive Généralisée
TRIP'S	Trade Related Aspects of Intellectual Property
TSP	Transport Sectoral Project
UR	Uruguay Round
UDEAC	Union Douanière et Economique de l'Afrique Centrale (Central African Customs and Economic Union)
UNECA	United Nations Economic Commission for Africa
UN	United Nations
UNCTAD	United Nations Conference on Trade and Development
UNDP	United Nations Development Program
UNIDO	United Nations Industrial Development Organisation
UNSTATS	United Nations Statistics
USA	United States of America
USAID	United States Agency for International Development
VSA	Volunteers Service Agency
WAEMU	West African Economic and Monetary Union
WB	World Bank
WRDB	Western Region Development Board
WRPDB	Western Region Production Development Board
WTO	World Trade Organization

Abbreviations for Unit 4

AISA	Africa Institute of South Africa
GDP	Gross Domestic Product
HIPCs	Heavily Indebted Poor Countries
HIV/AIDS	Human Immune Deficiency Virus/Acquired Immune Deficiency Syndrome
ERF	Economic Research Forum
ES	Environmental Security
EU	European Union
IDC	Industrial Development Council

IMF	International Monetary Fund
ISO	Organization of Standardization
OECD	Organization for Economic Co-operation and Development
MDG	Millennium Development Goals
NEPAD	New Economic Partnership for Africa's Development
NGO	Non Government Organisation
NIFOR	Nigerian Institute for Oil Palm Research
PRODA	Project Development Agency
RMRDC	Raw Materials Research Development Council
SD	Sustainable Development
SEDI	Scientific Equipment Development Institute
TICAD III	Third Tokyo International Conference on African Development
UEMOA/CEMAC	Central African Economic and Monetary Community
UK	United Kingdom
UNIDO	United Nation Industrial Development Organization
UNU	United Nations University
UNU-WIDER	World Institute for Development Economics Research at the United Nations University
US	United States
VAT	Value Added Tax
WTO	World Trade Organization

Abbreviations for Unit 5

ACBF	The African Capacity Building Foundation
ACP	African, Caribbean and Pacific Countries
AFRINEM	The African Institute for Economic Modelling
AFRITAC	Africa Regional Technical Assistance Center
APRM	African Peer Review Mechanism
AU	African Union
AUA	Agricultural University of Athens
BEE	Black Economic Empowerment
BIG-GT	Biomass Gasifier/Gas Turbine system
BPO/IT	Business Processing Outsourcing and Information Technology
BUN	Biomass Users Network
CAMEL	Capital adequacy, Asset quality, Management, Earnings, and Liquidity

CARENSA	The Cane Resources Network for Southern Africa
CEEEZ	Centre for Energy, Environment, and Engineering, Zambia
CENBIO	National Reference Centre for Biomass
CEST	Condensing Extraction Steam Turbine
CIRPS	Interuniversity Research Centre on Developing Countries
CRT	Country Review Team
CODESRIA	Council for the Development of Social Science Research in Africa
CSD	The Commission for Sustainable Development
DG TREN	Directorate General for Energy and Transport
EAC	East African Community
EC	European Commission
ECOWAS	Economic Community of West African States
EU	European Union
EUEI	The European Energy Initiative
FAO	Food and Agricultural Organisation
GDN	Global Development Network
GDP	Gross Domestic Product
GHG	Greenhouse gas
GPRS	Ghana Poverty Reduction Strategy
HILCS	High Impact, Low-Cost and Scalable solutions
HIV/AIDS	Human Immune Deficiency Virus/Acquired Immune Deficiency Syndrome
HSGIC	Heads of State and Government Implementation Committee
ICT	Information and Communication Technologies
ICCEPT	Centre for Energy, Policy and Technology
IDEP	African Institute for Economic Development and Planning
IEE	The Intelligent Energy Europe
IMF	International Monetary Fund
ISO	International Sugar Organisation
ISO	International Organization of Standardization
kW	kilowatt
MDG	Millennium Development Goals
MEFMI	The Macroeconomic and Financial Management Institute of Eastern and Southern Africa
MOU	Memorandum of Understanding
MTEF	Medium Term Expenditure Framework
MW	Megawatt
NGO	Non Governmental Organisations
NEPAD	The New Partnership for Africa's Development
OECD	Organization for Economic Co-operation and Development

PGGA	the Pretoria Good Governance Academy
PRS	Poverty-reducing Strategies
PRSPs	Poverty Reduction Strategy Papers
SA	South Africa
SADC	Southern African Development Community
SC	Steering Committee
SEI	Stockholm Environmental Institute
SWOT	Strengths, Weaknesses, Opportunities and Threats
tc	steam/cane
UNDP	the United Nations Development Programme
UNISA	University of South Africa
U.S.	United States
USD	United States Dollar
WII	Winrock International India
WTO	World Trade Organisation
YENEPAD	YOUNG ENTREPRENEURS FOR NEPAD

Foreword and General Introduction

This Volume 12 of the *African Development Perspectives Yearbook* deals - in the form of country cases and country units - with African countries' state of commodity dependence, their efforts for export diversification, and their vulnerability to crises and disasters. These problems are considered in the context of the continent's abundance of natural resources, especially the strategic oil resources. Volume 12 of the *African Development Perspectives Yearbook* is complementary to Volume 11, which discusses African countries' options to escape the primary commodities dilemma, to diversify their exports of products and services, to upgrade production and processes in order to serve markets for higher valued goods and services, and to improve Africa's position in the international global value chains.

African countries' high dependency on a few primary export goods is one of the reasons for their vulnerability to conflicts. In this volume of the *African Development Perspectives Yearbook*, the focus is on the vulnerability of resource-rich, mainly oil-exporting, African countries. Strategies of export diversification, options how to overcome political instabilities that impede investment, and strategies how to work towards reconstruction and sustainable economic and political development are discussed by highlighting examples from various resource-rich countries. It is analysed how these countries can manage to escape from the primary commodities dilemma by proactive economic policies and especially by solving political conflicts that have arisen from resource rents. Resource curse problems are discussed in various contributions, focussing on Cote d'Ivoire, Angola, Sudan, Democratic Republic of Congo, and Nigeria. Full country cases for Nigeria and Cameroon highlight the export diversification issues by product and function. The implications for the required policy changes of overcoming the resource curse problems are analysed at national, regional and sub-regional level.

Book Reviews and Book Notes are included and News and Information inform the reader with up-to-date entries regarding the overall topic of Volume 12. The relevance of these issues for Africa's development has increased tremendously in view of the repercussions of the globalisation trend on Africa.

This volume of the *African Development Perspectives Yearbook* is a joint effort by many contributors and editors who have presented analytical essays, country studies, and informative reports on necessary policy changes in Africa as well as case studies of successful diversification strategies in specific sectors. The issue how to overcome the resource curse in commodity dependent African countries and how to stimulate diversification attempts was carefully considered by referring to policy areas and to action levels, such as national economies, sub-regional entities, local communities, and social groups. References were also made to the relevant strategic positions of regional organisations in Africa that have highlighted in policy and research papers Africa's future perspectives. Volume 12 of the Yearbook comprises five Units in total.

Unit I presents, first of all, a frame for the analysis of vulnerability, instability, crises and conflicts in Africa. It is argued that for the purpose of strategy formulation the various sources of vulnerability have to be identified. Only then it becomes possible to design strategies to overcome the problems emanating from vulnerability. Resource-rich countries in Africa, and especially the oil-exporting countries, are obviously especially vulnerable.

It is also argued in Unit 1 that resource control at the local level is imperative for any attempt to attack the conflicts that are attached to the problems of abundance of raw materials. The cases of Cote d' Ivoire and Nigeria are presented as resource-rich countries with high risk of conflicts, crises and post-conflict problems. After a period of rapid growth spanning from 1960 to 1979, Côte d'Ivoire experienced a slow down in the GDP growth rate until the 1990s. Since September 19, 1999 Côte d'Ivoire has been experiencing political turmoil and social crises that had started with a first coup in 1999, followed by a second one in 2002 and a war that has not ended yet. It is however also assumed that the current crisis situation is transitory, and that the country could regain a new growth path based on its endowments in physical and human resources as well as its economic infrastructure, all of which might help the country to break away from its dependency on agricultural raw material exports. Some strategies are presented to reach this new growth path.

Nigeria is emblematic of the 'oil curse' or the failure to utilize oil wealth prudently. Despite earning a cumulative revenue estimated at about US$ 350 billion over a 35-year period, Nigeria continues to rank low on all development indicators with an alarming increase in the incidence of poverty. The country unfortunately provides some of the most egregious examples of rent seeking and corruption that undermine good governance, and has also become a global reference point for the irresponsible management of oil wealth.

It is argued that there are new management techniques available with regard of oil revenues in Nigeria that offer practical solutions for lifting the oil curse. Based on the reality on ground, the study on Nigeria recommends a holistic approach in the management of the oil rent. Despite these important reforms being proposed, Nigeria will in the foreseeable future continue to be highly dependent on oil and this calls for diversification as an urgent strategy. Some crucial elements of such a new strategy are outlined.

Resource-rich Nigeria has suffered from oil-induced conflicts, especially in the Niger Delta. Such conflicts include revenue allocation-induced conflicts, conflicts because of inter-communal claims to ownership of land where oil wells are situated, and many other sources of conflicts such as emanating in the area of environment. Politics revolves however mainly around the distributive concerns generated by the expenditure of the oil wealth, which induce riots, disputes, killings and protests. It is argued that there is a need to address the renewed or heightened wave of conflicts in the nation over oil resources and the suffering of the people of the Niger Delta in the midst of the oil wealth of the country. There is also a need to revisit the system of compensation payments for the damages done in oil-producing regions to the people and their assets. A greater commitment to fight against corruption in the country is also necessary. The study also emphasizes the respective roles of government at all levels, oil companies, non-governmental organizations, civil societies, oil-producing communities and donor agencies in reducing conflict in Niger Delta.

Because of the obvious coexistence between the abundance of raw materials and crises in Africa, it is argued that the behaviour of the different actors that are involved in the "Raw material – Crisis" system in Africa have to be articulated This is done exemplary with regard of the DR of Congo. It is considered as important to focus on the profile of African leaders. A "Vagabonds in Power"/ "Vagabonds in Rebellion" (VIP/VIR) framework is proposed to explain the resource curse in Africa. The obvious co-existence between abundance of raw materials and high levels of poverty in Africa is analysed in the frame of "raw materials games", in which the African leaders in power (VIP) or in Rebellion (VIR) cooperate with other agents (multinational corporations in America, in Europe and in Asian Countries, and companies/individuals in neighbouring countries) in order to exploit the mineral resources to the detriment of the welfare the population. The study also proposes actions and strategies to react to this situation by national and international policies. There is a role for actors in Africa that are interested to pursue endogenous development strategies, and there is a role for actors that are supporting equitable and fair international standards and policies towards resource-rich African countries and towards the global markets and value chains for raw materials. It is part of the analysis to show that there is a potential to change policies and strategies towards this end.

There is a need for a new international order to avoid the crises and the conflicts that are related to the resource abundance. In resource-rich economies, when being exposed to a crisis, export earnings are spent in a manner that discriminates parts of the population and supports initiatives by violent actors to reverse the situation by military means. The impact of trans-national companies is also ambiguous: they provide technology and marketing skills to explore the resource stocks and to provide the resource earnings, but they are also part of the mechanism that generates the crises and conflict. A strong co-operation between the companies and the elites is perceived by the public to divert income in a manner that strengthens the violation of human rights in the respective countries. The companies however do not serve as substitutes for "failed states" by providing important services. The availability of incomes from natural resources is often also a means to destabilise neighbouring countries or to invite them to start cross-border operations being determined to gain access to the commodities.

Actions at the international level are therefore recommended to interrupt the access of potentially violent actors to funds, equipment and staff by "cutting off the market", by enhancing transparency on the spending of commodity revenues, and by creating an adequate frame for the co-operation with trans-national companies. Furthermore, regional collaboration may provide for joint activities to stop smuggling and illegal trafficking of primary commodities. Developed countries are also requested to grant inputs to a peaceful development mainly by strengthening social sectors such as education, health, housing, water and sanitation. Good governance, ownership of the development process, and the strengthening of the civil society are furthermore proposed to remove internal sources of conflicts. The analysis of conflict generation and conflict dynamics in resource-rich African countries underlines that internal and international efforts have to be considered as interrelated. It has to be seen that those individuals and groups that benefit from the lack of control over resources and traded primary commodities will not contribute to those activities that may help to make international regulations more effective. The control of illegal transactions through international regulations requires an additional administrative capacity that extends far beyond the current staffing and funding opportunities in resource-rich African countries.

The so far proposed actions to control raw materials markets and to increase transparency of resource sectors are however not sufficient to eliminate the sources of conflict in resource-rich African countries. The links between the commodity markets and the patterns of conflict generation were ignored for too long. Security and stability in commodity-exporting African countries have to be considered as public goods in terms of supply and demand on a national, regional and even a global scale. Therefore, joint actions have to be undertaken to provide for long-term supplies of raw materials under a regime of open markets – towards the benefit of economically, socially and politically stable commodity-exporting African economies as well as to the benefit of commodity-importing states. International agreements have to be implemented, and destructive actions should not be permitted what necessitates sanctions. Development co-operation is supposed to act as a means to contribute to peaceful development, to lead to an environment conducive to an internal consensus in the supplying countries, and to contribute to the diversification of the economic structure there. Thereby it is possible to enhance growth and social welfare and to secure a long-term and continuous supply of commodities at prices that are to the mutual benefit of sellers and purchasers.

Unit 2 of the African Development Perspectives Yearbook explores primary commodity dependence and export diversification strategies in Nigeria. The contributions appraise various important strategic aspects of exports diversification in Nigeria with an emphasis on policy. Nigeria has made substantial progress in designing and implementing a new development strategy since the advent of democratic rule in 1999, albeit being fragile. A common thrust in the contributions is that much more is needed to orientate towards a new economy. The Unit identified various strategic elements for a revitalisation of the Nigerian economy. These are: a creative response to the globalisation trends; a coherent strategy to overcome the overt dependence on primary commodity exports; and the development of the agricultural sector so that a broad-based industrialisation, an export diversification and an exploitation of the globalisation chances open to the country become feasible. A new set of policies and institutions is also required to make for coherence in all strategic elements and policies. This is the first systematic attempt to analyse deeply how to embark on this challenge.

The problems of primary commodity dependence and resource curse are discussed on the example of Nigeria, the eight largest oil exporter in the world and one the potentially richest countries in Africa. The case of Nigeria is a teaching example for the curse of mineral resources. Revenues from oil exports account for the bulk of government income and have resulted in the negligence of other economic sectors and activities. The relevance of non-oil products for export revenues has declined over the past decades until Nigeria has almost become a single commodity exporter. However, the country is not only rich on oil but has also vast other potentials, such as in agricultural production and in human capital. These other potentials are under-utilised so far and wait for exploitation in an increasingly global world economy.

The authors in the Unit discuss how Nigeria can escape the status quo and use its potentials so as to reduce its dependency on oil exports and to diversify economic activities towards agriculture, manufacturing and services. Four case studies (on oil palm production, cocoa, cassava, and leather products) discuss in detail the necessity to improve quality, to upgrade production and to enter new markets. The authors analyse the role of the various stakeholders in the Nigerian society and economy and draw policy recommendations what needs to be done to diversify the Nigerian economy successfully. Thereby, it is not only the different interest groups within Nigeria but also various external actors that are considered. The relevance to integrate Nigeria better into international trade is indisputable. What is however disputed is how this could be achieved. It is therefore necessary to discuss in great detail the internal and external constraints of Nigeria's improved participation in the globalisation process, such as diverse supply-side constraints in the country and non-tariff barriers in relevant export markets. Policy recommendations are given how these export barriers (on the supply-side and on the demand-side) can be overcome. The reader gets a comprehensive overview on the problem of commodity dependence for Nigeria and which policies and strategies are necessary for the country to escape its resource curse by effective export diversification strategies.

In Nigeria the leather sector is a viable sector with tremendous potentials. Nigeria has the potential to diversify its economy through the export of leather and leather products. Presently finished leather exports constitute more than 30 percent of non-oil exports, and over US$ 300 million were realized through the export of finished leather in 2004. Yet, evidence has shown that most of the products are wasted and consumed locally due to a low export patronage. The study on leather export potentials therefore tries to find the bottlenecks of the sector, which - if tackled - could bridge the lacuna between export and waste. Top on the list of constraints, as perceived by leather firms, are inadequate infrastructure, high utility prices, official corruption, bureaucratic burdens (including red tape and rent seeking), and missing access to affordable credits. Other constraints include regulations for new businesses/business expansion as well as tax regulations/high taxes. The study on leather recommends therefore improvements in infrastructure like electricity, water, communication, etc, and the refocusing of the development banks to enable them to provide affordable credits. Moreover, the harmonization of policies between the three tiers of government and the involvement of stakeholders are recommended to make national, state and local policies effective.

Given the high instability of Nigeria's mono-product economy, the country has made frantic efforts (in principle, but not with commensurate actions) to diversify the economy. Agriculture, particularly cassava, has been identified as a diversification option. In order to make the strategy on agriculture effective, an Agricultural Demand-Led Industrialization (ADLI)-based strategy is recommended for Nigeria. This is enunciated at least partly in Nigeria's current development model, the National Economic Empowerment and Development Strategy - NEEDS. The main aim of this policy, with respect to cassava, is to realise the exportation of cassava worth about US$ 3 – 5 billion by 2007. Currently, Nigeria is neither an importer nor an exporter of fresh cassava tubers, but the exportation of cassava-based products is expected to begin next year.

Within the context of the NEEDS and given the important role of agriculture in the Nigerian economy, there is the need for deep analyses of the incentives (prices, subsidies, etc); trends of production, yield, cultivated and harvested areas; export values; technologies; constraints and/or leakages in the "cassava pipeline" (including iack of information on informal trade and market exchanges, especially across the boarders). This is critical given cassava's prospects for food security and poverty alleviation. It is therefore important to identify the constraints and opportunities for cassava production, processing, storage and marketing considering the policies in place at macro-, meso- and micro-levels. Like this, a cassava-induced diversified economy can be achieved and a strategy to maximise the cassava potential for income and employment generation and poverty alleviation can be applied.

In this unit also the perspectives of other important agricultural subsectors in Nigeria, namely cocoa and palm-oil, are discussed. There are chances to revitalise cocoa production and to increase palm-oil production by volume, quantity and processing level. However, all these successes will depend on a thorough implementation of the NEEDS and ADLI-type strategies in Nigeria. Also, the strengthening of local capabilities for processing and marketing is important as well as the synchronisation of efforts of government tiers, donor organisations and non-governmental organizations. Although these sectors are in the moment uncompetitive in terms of international values, comprehensive policy packages based on strategies as outlined in the unit could change the situation quickly to the better. The main message of the Unit is that the resource curse in Nigeria is not a fate, but can be politically overcome.

Unit 3 aims at answering some of the up-cited questions in the case of Cameroon. The key findings of the Unit are very important for a new strategic orientation and give lessons for required policy changes. It is analysed how the country could organize its economic policy so as to go beyond the structural adjustment programmes (SAPs) and to cope with the new and tremendous challenges of the Millennium Development Goals (MDGs), especially to achieve economic growth, poverty alleviation and income redistribution for sustainable development. Cameroon's past SAPs are assessed and it is concluded that they failed to boost growth and development. A new route for the country to achieve sustainable development is mainly based on: 1) the improvement of governance and the combat of corruption; 2) the reduction of legal and judicial insecurity for investment; 3) the compensation of the absence of a fiscal system that is adapted to specific sectors of activity; 4) the upgrading of local enterprises hampered by outdated equipment and underutilization of their capacities; 5) the improvement of infrastructure, such as roads, ports, airports, railways, energy, telecommunications and storage facilities; 6) the decentralisation of government coupled with reconstructed governance; and, 7) the diversification of exports towards products with comparative advantages. Rationalization of resource utilization, reaching the achievement point of the Highly Indebted Poor Countries (HIPC) initiative, and financial deepening are proposed as main sources to finance these activities.

In the Unit we find analyses how to promote exports and regional trade in the Economic and Monetary Community in Central Africa (CEMAC) through improvements of the transport infrastructures. After outlining various barriers to trade, among which transport costs are the main, the direct and indirect benefits of a new road linking Yaoundé to Libreville are assessed. It is shown that the direct benefits for Cameroon are fiscal and trade-related, since the country is a net exporter within CEMAC. Indirect benefits are also accruing to Gabon, giving the 'inter-closing' of markets at the border with Cameroon. To finance the new road in a period of budget limitations, preference is given to a public financing mode. The possibility to couple public finance with private finance, through the Built-Operate-Transfer (BOT) system, is also envisaged. The Unit therefore presents a case where regional cooperation can have very positive repercussion and interaction effects.

The Unit also presents analyses of the challenges and prospects of investments and industrialization in Cameroon. After giving a detailed history of the industrialization policy reforms in Cameroon since 1960 and their impact on the sequencing of development of the country, it is argued that priority has to be given to industrial development in order to meet the MDGs. Competitive products and industries are then envisioned. It appears that bauxite-aluminium, forest-timber, cotton-textile, energy, and food industry are interesting sub-sectors despite the intense competition on the world market. However, to boost the related industries, an appropriate institutional frame and an enabling economic environment have to be put in place as well as a new shape of the public-private sector partnership model.

Also for Cameroon an industrialization strategy of an ADLI-type has some relevance. The Unit comprises an analysis how to achieve efficient diversification of agricultural exports with reference to food production and non-food agriculture supply. Considering the world's demand, there is much room to promote local supply of natural rubber, palm oil and Arabic gum. Looking at the sub-regional market (CEMAC), a diversification through food crops, vegetables, fruits and biological products can enable the country to increase its exports to oil-producing countries like Chad, Congo/Brazzaville, Gabon, and Equatorial Guinea. The success of such a diversification policy requires however multi-dimensional actions, including the reform of the agricultural development strategy, its institutions and policies so as to increase the yields and to adapt the structure of the production to the bio-ecological diversity of the country, and improving the sub-regional trade policy frame to allow the private sector to respond favourably to non-price incentives. Primary commodities and raw materials of developing countries are facing negative trade effects due to the volatility of world prices. As suggested by many authors, primary commodity producers must find other ways for development. The diversification of agricultural production in order to improve export performance appears to be one way. Three objectives for a successful and sustainable policy change are then targeted: 1) identifying new markets which can support an export-led agricultural diversification policy; 2) identifying agricultural products for which Cameroon has a comparative advantage in exporting; and 3) making some inferences for policy considerations at the various policy levels.

New developments in the agricultural sector are key for sustainable development. Several products of the sector have been identified with comparative advantage due to contextual factors (agro-climatic conditions, competitive agro-industries, etc.) and other factors (like a strategic geographic position in the sub-region). It appears that for traditional export crops (cocoa, logs, etc.), Cameroon has a natural potential, but the country has also potentials for the development of new promising sub-sectors like pepper, horticulture, and organic farming. Three types of promising products have been analysed: selected traditional export crops (natural rubber, palm oil, Arabic gum, and cocoa) selected food crops (cassava, plantains, corn or potatoes); and selected fruits and vegetables (pineapple, avocado, mangoes, papayas, banana, etc.). Geo-climatic conditions, abundant reserves of land, and experienced producers with low cost production systems constitute the main advantages. However, lacks of investment, of storage facilities, and of rural infrastructures are among the obstacles that hinder the utilization of Cameroon's advantages. Considering Cameroon's potential for agricultural production, two diversification paths are presented in detail, concerning cocoa and plantains.

However, public action is needed in the form of a "pro-active" growth strategy. Although already initiated by the Cameroonian government, there is much room for improvement, and there is a need to emphasize even more the new public/private partnerships that are now established. It is revealed however that concrete policies in Cameroon remain embryonic, because the strategy is limited with regard to two main points: for some areas of production, the externalities are too weak to promote the diversification; and some crops are neglected despite their opportunities. Obviously, Cameroon has a great potential to increase food and export production, but it has to make up a real strategy for export diversification in order to sustain economic growth when facing trade shocks. The success of this strategy is conditioned by many constraints. Among other things, there are the effectiveness of governmental action, the efficiency of the private sector, and the continued support of development partners for such programmes.

In *Unit 4*, relevant books, magazines and documents dealing with the topics of primary commodities dependence, resource curse and diversification strategies, as well as other important publications about socio-economic developments in African countries are discussed in book reviews and book notes. It is interesting to see how many research institutes, international organisations and development policy institutions add to the knowledge in this field by presenting new books, seminar reports and discussion papers on various issues. More and more editors, authors and publishers send their publications for review to the Review Editor of the *African Development Perspectives Yearbook*, and the Yearbook Editors hope that this trend will continue.

In *Unit 5* Profiles, News and Information are presented. In this Unit information on new initiatives for Africa, new research projects, and new networks on and for Africa are presented with a special focus on conflict resolution and diversification options. Reports about new researches and documents on key issues for Africa's development are coming in from institutions and persons that are part of the global network that was created already in 1988/1989 by the *Research Group on African Development Perspectives* in Bremen. These reports and documents are of great importance because they are proof of the collective will and effort of African people to change their situation by determined action. It is also part of the editorial policy of the *African Development Perspectives Yearbook* to broaden and to deepen its research network and to make most important documents, reports and researches from the continent available to the public, giving authentic proof of

African intentions, plans and objectives for the development of the African continent.

The theme of the current *Volume 12* of the *African Development Perspectives Yearbook* is of great importance for Africa's future, as it is now more and more pressing to overcome conflict potentials associated with the abundance of resources, and to develop long-term sustainable strategies of economic diversification. In order to realise this objective, the combined efforts of African governments, civil society and enterprises, of international donors, and of the international community are necessary.

Also the complementary *Volume 11* of the *African Development Perspectives Yearbook* with the title *"Africa – Escaping the Primary Commodity Dependence"* highlights the discussion on how to revitalise and ultimately transform African economies. Volume 11 addresses firstly, successful cases of diversification; secondly, strategies to improve African countries' position in international trade and production; and thirdly, diversification efforts of commodity producers in the SADC region.

With now 12 volumes, the *African Development Perspectives Yearbook* has become an important source on Africa, and we look back to a highly successful working period of the *Research Group on African Development Perspectives* in Bremen. The work on *Volume 13* with the title *"New Growth and Poverty Alleviation Strategies for Africa"* is underway. The forthcoming volume 13 will discuss how the recent experience of accelerated growth in African countries can be made sustainable and how economic growth can be made more poverty alleviating. The national and regional growth experiences in African countries are quite different, as well as the effects of growth on poverty alleviation. There are models that contain positive growth acceleration and poverty alleviation strategies that can form the basis of best practise case studies. We will present country cases as well as local and sub-regional cases of new growth and poverty alleviation strategies and lessons that can be learned from these cases. The forthcoming vol. 13 titled *"New Growth and Poverty Alleviation Strategies for Africa"* will be published in 2008.

In the past 12 volumes of the *African Development Perspectives Yearbook* the *Research Group on African Development Perspectives* discussed such important themes as the human dimensions of structural adjustment; the role of agriculture for industrialisation; the role of new energy policies; the importance of active labour and employment policies; the role of regional labour and employment strategies; the issue of good governance for African development; economic and social empowerment strategies and policies; the options and problems of Africa's reintegration into the world economy; the issue of African entrepreneurship and private sector development; the problem how private and public sectors can be successfully balanced in African countries; the strategies and policies to escape the primary commodities dilemma in Africa; and, with this newly available volume of the Yearbook, the central issues of primary commodity dependence, resource curse and diversification efforts in African countries.

With these volumes of the *African Development Perspectives Yearbook* that were presented over the years to an international readership we have covered central issues of African development and have also formulated innovative strategies how to cope with these relevant problems. This may help to shape in a future-oriented way the fabric of the economies and societies in Africa by analyses and projections that are telling us what has to be achieved during the next decades. In future we will continue to focus on the necessary changes of economies and societies in Africa and on the new role of Africa in the world economy and society, especially in the context of the global informational and technological revolution. Thus, the views of the Research Group on African Development Perspectives in Bremen are focussed on a future vision for Africa that is based on a fair global order, on principles of sound political and economic governance, and on an African society that is reflecting the demands for and the opportunities of the globally emerging knowledge society.

For the Research Group on African Development Perspectives:

Karl Wohlmuth

Professor for Comparative Economic Systems, and
Co-ordinating Editor of the African Development Perspectives Yearbook
University of Bremen, Faculty of Economics, IWIM Bremen, Germany

Bremen, January 2007

Unit 1: Abundance of Natural Resources and Vulnerability to Crises, Conflicts and Disasters

edited by Karl Wohlmuth and Afeikhena Jerome

Abundance of Natural Resources and Vulnerability to Crises, Conflicts and Disasters – An Introduction

Karl Wohlmuth

1 The Issues

Vulnerability and Growth: Dimensions and Relevance for Africa

Vulnerability in this context means that countries and their economic actors are exposed to shocks, conflicts, risks and uncertainties so that growth rate and stability of growth rate are negatively affected. Growth in Africa is highly vulnerable, most of all in natural resource-rich countries. Growth is highly unstable could not be sustained for long (Wohlmuth 2004; IMF 2005a). Growth is dependent on raw materials cycles and on raw materials sector developments (see Warner 2000). Growth is highly related to and interconnected with conflicts. Conflicts impede growth, and unfavourable growth conditions affect the spread and dynamics of conflict (see UNCTAD 2004).

There are however significant differences among African countries. Land-locked and natural resource-rich countries are more vulnerable than coastal countries and areas and than resource-poor countries (see UNIDO 2004; Wohlmuth 2004). This natural resource curse-phenomenon is given various explanations – economic, political, and social ones. Resource-rich countries differ in their ability to manage the revenues from exports for productive development (see Auty 1998, 2001; Collier 2003). Many African countries that are exporters of natural resources are considered to be failed according to the Failed States Index 2006 (see FFP 2006). However, successful cases and strategies can also be identified in resource-rich African countries (see Wohlmuth 2006, Fosu/O'Connell 2006).

Growth in Africa is also very dependent on external factors like terms of trade fluctuations, changes in the position in the global value chain, but also changes of official development assistance (see Collier/Gunning/Associates 1999; Gibbon/Ponte 2005, UNCTAD 2002, 2004). Changing financial market situations, external debts and changing imperatives, priorities and conditions of donors contribute to dependence and vulnerability of African countries. Furthermore, growth in Africa also dependent on the economic and political situation in neighbouring countries, affecting investment and monetary conditions and transmitting shocks. Risks and uncertainties affect investment and growth, and to a large extent also political stability.

Growth in Africa has not been sustainable at rates that would allow a continuous reduction of poverty, and many countries are far away from the envisaged 7 per cent growth rates necessary to realise the Millennium Development Goals (Asche 2006). Income inequality and poverty also negatively affect growth rates.

Growth is also vulnerable because of the slow adaptation of African countries to globalisation trends, depending on the state of political and economic governance and on the prevalent types of development management.

There are some few African countries that are exceptions to this broad picture. However, the episodic character of African growth is evident and leaves only few countries with an outstanding performance. Often mentioned is Botswana with a period of more than 40 years of growth, implying that it could avoid excesses of negative growth incentives (see Fosu/O'Connell 2006).

In order to combat the general malaise of poor growth rates in Africa, international and regional organisations as well as independent commission work hard on new strategies to make growth in Africa more stable (see Asche 2006). The new Action Plan for Africa of the World Bank reminds us again that not only drivers of growth are important but also growth sharing so as to reach stable growth rates. Growth drivers matter (such as an export push strategy, closing the infrastructure gap, making regional integration more effective, creating a knowledge base for an internationally competitive economy, creating the conditions for a better management of shocks, and making agriculture a key sector of growth) but they are not sufficient to sustain growth. The "drivers of growth" perspective is therefore combined with a "shared growth" perspective, i.e. developing and strengthening social sectors and improving the access to production factors and markets for the poor. Most of these ideas are not new, and more important than the identification of guiding principles for strategy formation is their translation to country-specific conditions so as to realise ownership as a base for effective policy regimes.

Vulnerability is to a large extent related to the severe economic and corporate governance situation in Africa (see UNECA 2005, AfDB 2005). The exploitation of its vast resources is therefore related to improvements of governance (Wood 2003). However, the issue of governance is not clearly defined. There is a huge gap in interpretations as governance can be related to the main functions of a developmental state or simply to technical prerequisites for governing. However, the new interest in Africa to deepen and broaden the discussion on governance, especially in resource-rich African countries, gives hope that new and sustainable growth and development patterns can be approached.

The vulnerability of resource-rich African countries and their exposure to crises, conflicts, civil wars, and humanitarian disasters is the topic of Unit 1 in Volume 12. There is urgent need to look for effective national, regional and international policies and strategies to make growth more sustainable in resource-rich African countries.

Instability, Uncertainty and Slow Growth in Africa

Instability is a major issue in Africa's development and a factor of the overall vulnerability to which African countries are exposed. Instability is a major factor hampering investment, growth, and export performance and also affects human capital formation and regional integration and cooperation negatively. Two groups of instability have to be considered, namely political and economic instability. Moreover, interrelationships of political and economic instability need to be considered.

Economic instability is a major factor that impedes investment, domestic as well as foreign private investment. Also public investment is affected because of the effects of volatilities, uncertainties, risks and shocks on public revenues, public expenditures and the level of budget deficits. There are different and overlapping definitions and interpretations of economic instability. According to Azam et al. (2002) it is necessary to distinguish various factors to explain the unsatisfactory growth performance in Africa. The six factors are 1) an adverse macroeconomic policy environment; 2) macroeconomic instability and policy reversibility; 3) external shocks affecting the economy; 4) insignificant exploitation of human capital; 5) negative spillover effects and underexploitation of positive regional spillover effects; and 6) institutional, bureaucratic and political instability.

In natural resource-rich countries all these factors play a role and culminate into specific problems in economic policy labelled as resource curse. The macroeconomic policy environment is an issue because unsustainable fiscal deficits, inflation and uncompetitive levels of real exchange rates raise complex macroeconomic management problems. Unsustainable fiscal deficits imply problems for monetary authorities and result in crowding out problems for investors. As a result, macroeconomic uncertainty and deficits increase, negatively affecting the level of investment and the balance between public and private investment.

Macroeconomic uncertainty and policy reversibility are further factors that determine investment. Uncertainty and risk come in as factors that determine the levels and patterns of investment. Two major forms of macroeconomic uncertainty have to be identified (Azam et al. 2002, p. 183): firstly, the volatility of economic variables such as terms of trade, inflation rate and real exchange rate since these variables determine the risk and risk assessment of investors and the overall level of instability. Another form of macroeconomic uncertainty is the probability of reversing macroeconomic and trade policies. Obviously, both groups of uncertainty and risk factors matter in natural resource-rich countries because of the generation and distribution of resource rents. In such countries low credibility of economic policy and low reputation of economic institutions matter even more (Collier/Gunning 1999; Wohlmuth 2004). Risk and uncertainty in such an environment lead to a restriction, to a postponement and to an increasing volatility of investment. Therefore, capital instability/investment instability is an important factor inhibiting growth and exports, but also human capital formation. In natural resource-rich countries capital instability (instability of capital formation process) and export instability (due to high terms of trade fluctuations) can become major problems for growth and development (see Fosu 2002c). Concerning human capital spillover effects, investment may be affected by all these volatilities, uncertainties and instabilities, and so human capital turns out as a most important factor in explaining slow growth. It is important to think about human capital deficits especially in resource-rich countries that are affected by instability, violence, civil war, and other types of conflicts and uncertainties.

Regional spillover effects can be positive and negative for investment and growth. There is a robust link between regional spillover effects and variations in growth and investment between countries (Azam et al. 2002, p. 186). Credibility and flexibility of regional cooperation policy is therefore important so as to prevent negative neighbourhood effects on investment and economic performance. This links up with the last factor mentioned that causes slow growth in Africa – political and institutional instability. However, institutional, bureaucratic and political instability need to be analysed isolated for analytical purposes. Political instability ranges from government turnover, violence and civil war to the erosion or even collapse of institutions for state integration and economic policy formation (Azam et al. 2002, pp. 188-189). One can distinguish between macro insecurity (collapsing institutions) and micro insecurity (negative effects on individuals). Also the distinction between political, institutional and bureaucratic instability makes sense (Azam et al. 2002). Other categorisations also matter. Fosu (2002a, 2002b, 2003) added important dimensions to the debate on the consequences of political instability for growth and development in Africa. Political instability can take the form of elite political instability (the frequency of coups d'État in Africa), and this type of political instability has proven negative effects on human development, growth and export performance. Fosu (2002a) went even further and distinguished between growth effects of successful and aborted coups d'État and of coup plots. Political instability of this type may be even more harmful to exports than to growth.

Altogether the impact of instability and insecurity on private, public and foreign investment is severe, and the repercussions on human capital and regional spillover effects add to negative overall effects. Taking natural resource-rich countries as a special case, we can see that all these factors matter and enhance the dangers for the development process – coming from an adverse macroeconomic environment, from macroeconomic uncertainty and external shocks, and from all forms of political, institutional and bureaucratic instability. The instability of investment and of growth in African resource-rich countries and the resource curse phenomenon are highly interrelated problems. In an equilibrium model for growth and political stability (Azam et al. 2002, pp. 209-210) it is easy to prove that a comprehensive development strategy requires both - growth boosting strategies and polity-stabilising measures. However, to date the various types of vulnerability resource-rich African countries face have not been adequately considered when assessing African growth problems.

Civil Wars, Conflicts and Humanitarian Disasters in Africa: Greed, Grievance, Scarcity, and other Responsible Factors

The fact that civil wars have increased in the past two decades in Africa (Yartey 2004, p. 93), but fallen in other regions means that the causes and consequences of civil wars in Africa have to be investigated more deeply in order to reconstruct political and economic governance. As all civil wars are associated with humanitarian disasters (refugees, displaced people) and increasing levels of poverty, the economics of civil war tries to explain the initiation, dynamics and options to terminate end civil wars.[1] When assessing the causes of civil wars and humanitarian emergencies we observe that economic decline, income inequality and pervasive rent seeking by ruling elites (threatening the survival income of the population), a weakening state, and competition for the control of mineral exports matter (see Nafziger/Auvinen 2002). We also observe that there are quite robust explanations of civil wars in terms of poverty levels, slow growth rates, abundance of primary com-

---

1 See especially the collections of essays by Fosu/Collier, Eds., 2005; Clement, Ed., 2004; and Marysse/Reyntjens, Eds., 2005; and the contributions on the economic theory of civil war by Collier 1998; Collier/Hoeffler/Söderbom, 2001; Collier/Hoeffler, 2002a, 2002b; Yartey 2004; Azam 2001; Nafziger/Auvinen 2002. For more specific studies on violence and civil wars affecting political and economic performance, see Mohamoud 2006; Humphreys 2003; Alesina/La Ferrara 2003.

modities, peace duration, large populations, difficulties in developing strong institution, and high levels of corruption (see on such determining factors the analysis by Yartey, 2004). Other insights of analysis show a) that countries that trade and cooperate with each other are less likely to be involved in civil wars; b) that short-term economic fluctuations do not matter in the generation of (international) conflict; c) that domestic investment is negatively affected long after the end of conflicts; d) that health infrastructure is extremely hit by violence and wars, retarding development in the long run; e) that economic sectors depending on capital and transport logistics are affected particularly severe; f) that wars are prolonged by illegal trading illegal commodities; g) that civil wars last longer in poorer countries; and h) that aid is effective in post-conflict situations (see Humphreys 2003).

These analytical insights can be used for reconstructing political and economic governance after civil wars in order to prolong the period of peace, as the duration of peace itself is a supportive factor preventing future civil wars. However, it is useful and necessary to distinguish first of all the types of conflicts. In Ethiopia for instance three categories of conflicts can be identified: firstly, competition for positions of power, understood as intra-elite struggles referred to earlier as elite political instability; secondly, popular revolts against those in power, understood as struggles between ruling elites and the people; and thirdly, conflicts among the impoverished people over resources (see Geda/Degefe 2005). This categorisation provides a good frame for analysis not only for Ethiopia but also for natural resource-rich countries. In these countries violent conflicts and civil wars are caused by elites that are competing for resource rents; by elites that claim for ownership of resources against the people that live in resource-rich areas; and by conflicts that arise because the environment, the land availability and the water resources are affected by the exploitation of natural resources. These three types of conflict intermingle and culminate in the case of natural resource-rich countries.

Another categorisation comes in when starting to analyse the civil wars of the post-Cold War period and when arguing that there must be new causes and therefore "new wars". Leopold (2005) mentions four approaches that matter now in the international discussion: firstly, "Malthus with guns", meaning that war is caused by competition over scarce resources needed for survival; secondly, "New Barbarism", implying that the end of the Cold War had unleashed long-suppressed ethnic, religious and other conflicts; thirdly, "Greed, not Grievance", implying that economic motivations and calculations are important in determining violence and civil wars; and fourthly, "Ethnographic History", with the view that an ethnographic perspective is necessary as common patterns of civil wars are not easy to detect, and that the start, the continuation, the dynamics, and the end of wars have to be investigated by having in mind all these mono-causal explanations (see Leopold 2005, pp.

686-687). Also this categorisation of conflict causes is important for reconstructing political and economic governance after civil wars, as the solutions are more open, requiring multi-dimensional approaches. For resource-rich countries, this categorisation is important as civil wars and their associated regional and international dimensions show elements of all these explanations of "new wars".

Other explanations refer to the militarization of societies and economies and the role of the military and the militia in politics, economics and trade. This militarization is seen as a legacy of the Cold War period with destructive long-term effects (see De Waal 1996 on militarization and Möller 2006 on the role of militias). In the case of mineral resources and other natural resources these explanations based on the militarization of societies and economies are relevant. The effects of resource exploitation on the structure of the society and its elites, on the environment, land and water, on long-suppressed conflicts, and on greed are severe in African countries. However, there is need to consider the specific dynamics of wars and their regional and international implications, as it is the cases in the Democratic Republic of Congo (DRC) and the Sudan. The case of the oil-rich Bakassi peninsula in Cameroon shows that even in complex border conflict situations balanced solutions can be found, and that border conflicts and economic border interests can even help to increase economic opportunities for both sides (see Konings 2005). Such cases reveal the important economic perspective for maintaining peace.

Important conclusions emerge for African countries, especially for resource-rich countries. Economic policies for reconstructing economic policy and governance in resource rich African countries have to be very specific in terms of peace consolidation, social and economic reconstruction, and in terms of the political economy agenda of reforms (see Collier 2005). These agendas, following the analysis of violence and civil wars, have core issues that need to be considered by policymakers: preventing new wars; assisting wisely and massively post-war countries so as to prolong and to consolidate peaceful conditions; reducing primary commodity dependence and preventing illegal commodity trade; and developing high-quality institutions (see Yartey 2004, pp. 117-121 and Humphries 2003, pp. 20-22). These insights are highly relevant for local, national, regional and international politics, and for economic policy reconstruction and reconstruction of economic governance at all levels. We know that fiscal policy has to adapt creatively to the conditions of peace consolidation, and there are enough instruments available to work on this route (see Addison/Roe, Eds., 2004). Improving and balancing public expenditure management and public expenditure policies are key requirements. Fiscal policy must have a clear poverty alleviation focus in post-conflict situations. The levels of public expenditures and public revenues matter for peace consolidation as well as the structure of the public expenditures and the timing of public revenues. Also important for peace consolidation are the level, the timing and the structure of aid and debt relief and the transition towards a democratic developmental state in order to sustain peace (see Addison/Roe, Eds., 2004, p. 297).

Resource Curse and Managing Resource Rents at the National Level

Countries with abundance of natural resources, especially in Africa, suffer from vulnerabilities that have to do with the mismanagement of resources, including the exploration, production, servicing, processing, and marketing of resources. In fact, sophisticated public action is needed to deal with the complexities of making use of natural resource endowments. Either the public sector is too weak to deal with these issues properly or the multinational corporations involved in the production and distribution of natural resources do not work in a transparent and accountable way. We know from the theory of foreign investment that multinational corporations depend on three groups of advantages to be successful as foreign investors: Firstly, they need ownership advantages such as technology and competence in various areas and must be able to exploit them; secondly, they need location advantages such as cheap factor costs and favourable factor supplies which can be assessed properly; and thirdly, they need internalisation advantages such as the ability to minimise transaction costs by finding internal rather than market solutions. Multinational corporations that deal with natural resources can use these advantages by minimising governmental control and by ignoring public interest. This is not only common for Western multinationals but also for those from Eastern regions, e.g. from China, India, Malaysia, and South Korea.

"Resource Curse" is often identified with the Dutch Disease effects, implying that, because of currency appreciations and wage increases, international competitiveness declines and tradable sectors shrink so that the country becomes very dependent on natural resource exports. However, there are many more channels to explain the phenomenon of resource curse (see Basedau/Mehler, Eds., 2005; and Basedau 2005). Most important, and increasingly emphasised in the debate, is the evolution of institutional arrangements which is likely to be negatively affected by abundant natural resources (see Basedau/Mehler, Eds., 2005, p. 15). If economic and political institutions are poorly developed and if the state becomes more and more involved in the distribution of revenues based on resource rents, the psychology of windfall gains comes in and has to be handled politically successful in order to avoid further harm to national and local institutions (see Basedau/Mehler, Eds., 2005, p. 18). Thus, many areas of policy are affected by the resource curse and the respective transmission channels. Natural resources can definitely enhance growth, but only if the negative effects on corruption on investment, on openness to trade, and on human capital formation can be controlled. A rich agenda for pro-active government policies is therefore necessary to contain the potentially negative effects of natural resources abundance on manufacturing output and the export sectors (see especially Papyrakis/Gerlagh 2004).

In order to address the negative effects of Dutch Disease and the resource curse, the macro-economic effects of aid also have to be envisaged carefully. An ineffective management of natural resources and an ineffective handling of aid flows can culminate in additional vulnerabilities of resource-rich economies. A proper management of natural resources and of aid flows are for many African countries tasks that have to be achieved simultaneously. There-fore, institutional development needs to be addressed for both policy areas (see UNECA 2004, and Gupta/Powell/Yang 2006).

However, we also know that Resource Curse is not inevitable, neither in economic nor in political terms. Resource Curse can be avoided by pro-active policies. Increasingly we notice the importance of such strategies to overcome the dangers of natural resources abundance, though many countries in Africa, such as the new petroleum states, give the impression that the lessons have not been learned. However, the Resource Curse depends very much on the type of resources and on the specific conditions of resource-rich countries. Most important, resource types can differ according to production technologies, rent dispersion, potential of forward and backward linkages, rent appropriation through state institutions, and long-term trends in prices and price volatilities (see Basedau/Mehler, Eds., 2005, and especially the contribution by Lay/Mahmoud 2005). Whatever the differences are, institutional quality and sound economic policies are considered as the main factors to avoid and to overcome a Resource Curse. This analysis is quite similar to the observed risks of civil conflicts. We know that the risks decline with a higher quality of institutions and with improved economic and social policies. It is therefore important to emphasise that institutional reforms and policy reforms may help to reduce the risks of civil war and at the same time the dangers of a Resource Curse.

More recent studies on the strategies and policies to overcome the Resource Curse, drawing on worldwide comparative studies and experiences, show that key lessons can be derived for policy makers to take action in terms of forward planning for the resources sector, policy sequencing in resource-rich countries, resource revenues management, democratic governance, and the synchronisation of aid and resource revenues management (see ODI 2006). Moreover, governing the access to resources by following appropriate rent and revenue management policies and by improving the mineral policy design and policy implementation are regarded as important as well as the diversification of the economy and the creation of human and social capital in resource-rich countries (see UNECA 2004). Last but not least, policies that mainstream mineral wealth in growth and poverty reduction policies are crucial (see Pedro 2004). There are many options for African countries endowed with minerals to achieve these objectives by concerted action. Pedro (2004) recommends to improve the public participation in mineral resources development, to improve the management of resources sectors by including poverty alleviation strategies and by fostering a minerals cluster development policy, and to improve the sustainability of artisanal and small-sale mining communities. Other studies see the necessity of more far-reaching and radical reforms (see Sala-i-Martin/Subramanian 2003). They argue that it would be the best way to avoid a Resource Curse by "expropriating" the state in oil-rich and natural resource-rich countries – by an equal distribution of resource proceeds to the people and by a state that has to compete for resources by a transparent and effective taxation system so as to finance the provision of public goods. Such an equal share of resource revenues, if distributed to the people, could force the state and the bureaucracy to tax equitably, efficient and effectively and to handle public expenditures transparently and accountably. Since the quality of public institutions has to be improved in most resource-rich countries, a strategy to deny the government a prior and uncontested share of resource revenues may be quite effective. This strategy could also contribute to enhance the quality of private institutions as rent seeking and corruption would diminish. Moreover, positive effects on income distribution and poverty alleviation would be likely and the risks of civil wars and of conflicts between regional and ethnic groups would diminish if all people benefit equally from resource rents. Like this, countries could reduce economic and social gaps if the state looses the discretionary powers to privilege certain ethnic groups and regions on the basis of resource revenues. International research shows that practical action can be taken to avoid a Resource Curse by good governance (see IMF 2005b; IMF Survey 2005a; Katz et al. 2004). Good governance in this context means clarity of roles and responsibilities; public availability of information; open budget preparation, execution, and reporting; and giving assurances of integrity to all those that may be affected by the resource sector (IMF 2005b). Other practical aspects concern fiscal policy aspects of the management of petroleum/natural resource revenues, which are crucial (see especially Katz et al. 2004). The core areas for action are: Macroeconomic policy consistency and fiscal policy formulation; generation of persistent fiscal surpluses and the accumulation of budgetary reserves; related exchange rate regimes to achieve and maintain international competitiveness; appropriate institutional oversight of the oil/natural resource sector; and relevant transparency requirements. However, the requirements in terms of democratic and development governance are too often not mentioned when presenting such practical guidelines and agendas for action.

Not only African countries, also countries like Russia have to work on the dangers of a Resource Curse to sustain growth (see Hishow 2004, and Ahrend 2006). The problem for Russia and other emerging countries is it that a regulating and strong state is needed to develop and integrate the resource sector into a modern economy. The state should not favour specific interest groups, sectors or regions and should not overtax enterprises and consumers. In fact, democratic governance is a condition to avoid the Resource Curse. The accumulation, appropriation, taxation and distribution of resource rents are therefore crucial to govern developmentally resource-rich countries. A more balanced economy that also favours industrial and agricultural development can be supported by an appropriate taxation of resource rents and an appropriate spending of the revenues (see Hishow 2004).

Fiscal policy has to be effective in taxing resource rents at such levels and in such a structure that other sectors of the economy have incentives to develop. Competition policy is complementary to fiscal policy in resource-rich countries in order to avoid monopolies. Therefore, privatisation is not enough but however an important step to reduce state intervention. It is then replacing direct forms of resource control by indirect forms of resource sector regulation and guidance - taxing the resource sector and the resource rents adequately and speeding up the institutional development to the point of organising an adequate control of the resource sector (see on these issues also Ahrend 2006). Demands for more transparency and accountability at the regional and international levels are however not sufficient. The experiences with transparency guidelines and proposals initiated by the IMF and the World Bank reveal that much more is needed to achieve a positive change in resource-rich countries. We can see this when looking at the experiences of Norway with its democratically controlled oil fund as a basis for future-oriented projects (IDW 2005). Other conditions that matter in resource management are to take environmental concerns into account; to empower and include the populations; and to improve the toolkits for resource sector control so as to avoid and overcome the Resource Curse and related conflicts, tensions and civil wars in African countries (see e.g. Basedau 2005).

Resource Control at the Local Levels

Resource control at the local level is another important factor in sustainable development. Lack of resource control at the local level leads to conflicts, tensions, and even to violence and civil war. Without sufficient local resource control, resource-rich countries are exposed to additional sources of vulnerability. It is necessary to consider two aspects of resource control that are highly interrelated: First, abundance of natural resources is often geographically concentrated, and therefore local entities and communities are affected by exploration and production. These "point resources" such as oil and diamonds have to be distinguished from dispersed natural resources like agricultural products, which can however also result in vulnerabilities if multinational corporations or marketing boards intervene with policies and strategies that negatively affect the local population. The second aspect of resource control relates to the problem of scarcity for land, water, forests, and wildlife, but also in terms of environmental quality and infrastructure, as well as institutional capacities to organise complex production issues. We can see that in richly endowed regions important economic factors – especially when based on abundant point resources – may conflict with the scarcity of other very important factors. In such situations various dilemmas can arise. The concentration of central and corporate power affects the economic and social situation in local entities as there is increasing competition for access to scarce resources and severe pressure for their control. The scarce resources are depleted fast, especially if the natural resources management is not working properly. The replenishment of these scarce factors is difficult or even impossible. The situation in local entities is aggravated if ethnic minorities are affected by the production of point resources, and these minorities may be exposed to pressure arising from the conflicts between using the abundant and the scarce factors. These conflicts are for instance prevalent in the Niger Delta region where oil is produced. People in the oil-producing areas have lost control over the abundant and the scarce resources. The lack of resource control and the loss of citizenship rights then lead to forms of ethnic citizenship rights agitation (see Dibua 2005). This explains also the "oil paradox", which is referred to as the phenomenon that oil abundance is associated with rich wealth and power but also with deep poverty, violence and hopelessness (see Obi 2004, pp. 5-6).

Local governments come in as important actors to manage the abundant and the scarce factors properly. This requires the establishment of a functioning governance regime based on adequate forms of decentralisation, devolution of power, availability of competencies, and building of required capacity to govern. This means that an effective local governance regime, either in a centralised state or in a system of working federalism, also needs to establish full resource control at local levels. It is not enough to co-administer the resources at the local levels, which can be clearly seen with respect to the escalating crisis in the Niger Delta (see the most recent assessment for the Niger Delta by ICG 2006).

The local security situation in resource-rich regions is fundamentally related to issues of resource control and participation in all aspects of resource use (see ICG 2006 on the payments for security that have resulted in more violence). Studies on the "politics of plunder" in Nigeria show that social movements among young people and security concerns are highly interrelated with resource control issues (see Gore/Pratten 2003). Militant youth movements in Nigeria are seen as the product of the economic crisis and as forms of collective youth action in response to denied access to resources and to inequities in the distribution of power. Their actions are obviously a result of top-down forms of governance that ignore the demands for resource control at local levels; bottom-up forms of disorder are the consequence of the inappropriate governance regime (Gore/Pratten 2003). Violence and disruption are also a reaction of the resource curse dilemmas that unfold at local levels, like corruption, inflation, and mismanagement. In terms of micro-politics these new social movements, emerging at local levels, represent new forms of governance that are further undermining social cohesion and institution building (Gore/Pratten 2003, p. 240). Ethnic dimensions are coming in on the basis of these imbalances and inequities and tremendously increase as it is the case in the Niger Delta (see ICG 2006, p. i). Ethnic issues come in even in case of potential resource as the debate about the diamonds search in the game reserves of Botswana showed, where the indigenous San are threatened by forced removals (see Taylor/Mokhawa 2003, and Basedau/Mehler, Eds., 2005, pp. 105-120, and pp. 305-323). Considering the limited employment effects of diamond production in Botswana, the indirect effects of diamonds production on ethnic groups and indigenous people are heavily discussed. Also, in countries and regions with potential oil discoveries (such as in Darfur, Sudan and in Gambella, Ethiopia) the observed and discussed potentials lead to conflicts and tensions.

The interrelationship between resource abundance and resource scarcity becomes especially severe in terms of conflict intensity when scarce resources are affected by increasing demand because of population increases and/or by decreasing supply because of degradation processes.[2] Conflicts at the level of individuals and between generations are then easily trans-formed into conflicts between governments and local people, especially if the central government intervenes for resource-seeking purposes. Natural resources abundance and the associated resource curse effects then transform local conflicts about scarce natural resources into sub-regional and national conflicts so as to get fair shares of revenues from abundant re-sources and also compensation for the effects of raw materials production.

Strategies to cope with scarcity problems have to be transformed since traditional responses to conflicts fall apart in situation of resource abundance (see Baechler/Spillmann/Suliman, Eds., 2002, pp. 19-21). The effects on land, water, and other scarce factors are severe. Also local conflict resolution mechanisms may break down, even in situations where natural resources like oil are not yet explored but expected to be found (like in Darfur and in the

---

2 This is investigated for countries such as Ethiopia, Sudan, and Eritrea by Baechler/Spillmann/Suliman, Eds., 2002.

Nuba Mountains in Sudan and in Gambella in Ethiopia). This is a case in point where conflicts over natural resources between ethnic groups are created by governments in the context of resource-seeking attitudes (see Baechler/Spillmann/Suliman, Eds., 2002, pp. 163-183).

The transformation of resource conflicts into ethnic conflicts by government actions is the main problem. The longer the conflicts last, the greater is the probability that it is transformed from a classical resource conflict to an ethnic conflict (as to be seen in Darfur and in the Nuba Mountains in Sudan).

If natural resource abundance is geographically concentrated (point resources), facilitating access to these resources at a government level gives the central governments another incentive to transform the traditional conflicts into ethnic conflicts. Oil discoveries or even expected oil discoveries influence the local conflict resolution mechanisms fundamentally because the central government's economic interest overshadows these established forms of conflict resolution by the expectation of appropriating increasing shares of resource rents. In the case of environmental conflicts that are created and aggravated by natural resources exploitation, the local institutions will no longer be able or become sufficiently empowered to solve such conflicts. New forms of empowerment at the local levels are then necessary to solve conflicts on resource use. Resource control at the local level has therefore to consider all resources (scarce and abundant ones). Not only natural resources but as well social resources (such as justice, fairness, equitable sharing, and equal development) have to be considered for conflict prevention and resolution (Baechler/Spillmann/Suliman, Eds., 2002, pp. 163-164). Based on the local availability of abundant natural resources such as oil the danger is great that the neutral role of traditional conflict mediation institutions is diminished in their dealings with conflicts between ethnic, religious and social groups. Resource competition changes the working style of these institutions and their working basis becomes violated. The central/regional state comes in as an interested party and destroys quickly the mediating role of traditional mechanisms for conflict resolution.

Not only in case of resource abundance, conflicts and conflict resolution mechanisms are transformed. Conflicts between production systems such as between peasant production and livestock husbandry are easily transformed into ethnic conflicts, even when people from the same tribe fight for resources (as it is the case in Ethiopia; see Baechler/Spillmann/Suliman, Eds., 2002, p. 329). We are reminded by many scholars that also "failed modernisation" affects conflict resolution mechanisms like the tribal peace conferences in Sudan. As a result, underdevelopment feeds tribal and ethnic conflicts that need more and deeper forms of conflict resolution (Baechler/Spillmann/Suliman, Eds., 2002, p. 379). In a model for assessing the efficacy of tribal peace conferences three determinants are revealed as relevant: first, the degree of homogeneity of the ethnic political class; second, the degree of central government intervention; and third, the degree of conflicts on land and other resources (see Atta El-Battahani in Baechler/Spillmann/Suliman, Eds., 2002, especially pp. 431- 443). All three elements matter for local conflict resolution: Homogeneity of the political class; neutrality of central government intervention; and a degree of land-related disputes below a threshold level. These conflicts are transformed when natural resources like oil come on the scene. The political class becomes less homogenous, the central government intervention becomes less neutral, and the conflicts on the use of land and other resources are escalating in many forms. Development strategies and political strategies on the local level are required for conflict resolution. This refers to the use of all resources involved. Development strategies matter especially if water rights are concerned (see Baechler/Spillmann/Suliman, Eds., 2002, pp. 451- 476). Local resource control in this case requires a concerted action of producers, entrepreneurs and government officials to meet the challenges of various production systems in terms of water. New regulatory regimes in the context of functioning local governance structures are necessary in order to synchronise them with new development strategies associated with increased resource use. Participatory approaches in the traditional sense are loosing their importance for natural resource management and for conflict management if abundant natural resources come into the picture. As resource management and resource conflict management are highly intertwined areas, the concept of resource conflict transformation comes in, meaning that a new mechanism is needed to achieve both – the management of natural resources and the conflict resolution with regard of natural resources by transforming resource conflicts in time and functionally adapted to the environment in a developmental way (see Baechler/Spillmann/Suliman, Eds., 2002, pp. 527-555). Transforming resource conflicts in case of abundant and scarce natural resources and also with regard to scarce political and social resources at local levels are new and important tasks for local and national governance.

Though there is no easy solution in sight some answers relating to "democratic decentralisation" and to "local development governance" might be given (see on a survey of the issues Larson/Ribot 2004). Natural resource management is considered as an important objective of democratic decentralisation so as to base natural resources management on democratic structures and human rights. However, the reality is different. In terms of natural resources, democratic forms of decentralisation are difficult to find and the results are quite diverging (see Larson/Ribot 2004, p. 4). Evidence shows that central governments fear that national control over natural resources is lost or constrained by decentralisation (see the case studies mentioned in Larson/Ribot 2004). Arguments for deconcentration and decentralisation like efficiency, transparency and participation are compromised by emphasising national interest on the side of the central governments. Decentralisation cannot be effective to solve resource conflicts if natural resource-related competencies and powers are not effectively transferred to local entities. Resource control, resource politics and resource planning are extremely limited at local levels so that the discovery of new natural resources brings new risks to the local people in terms of civil conflict, rent-seeking, degradation of environment and poverty (what we observe now in Nigeria, in Sudan and in Ethiopia but also in many other African countries). Resource control is however also becoming increasingly important countries that are richly endowed with agricultural resources (as the conflict in Cote d'Ivoire shows). However, though the abundance of natural resources complicates the process, conditions of democratic governance and local empowerment leading to pro-poor local economic development strategies are feasible (see Africa Insight, December 2005).

Experiences of the Old and the New Petroleum-Economies in Africa

Africa started with very great hopes into its oil future (see Baker 1977). It was even expected that Nigeria and Algeria could reach a sustainable development path on the base of its oil. The situation turned however the other way round (see the various essays in Basedau/Mehler, Eds., 2005). Africa's oil has in the meanwhile become part of a strategic game (see Ellis 2003; Traub-Merz 2003), and the situation differs considerably among the oil-exporting African countries (AfDB 2006; Wurthmann 2006). Most of the African Atlantic coast areas are involved in oil production and/or exploration. Established oil producers like Nigeria, Angola, Cameroon, Congo and Gabon give examples of the experiences and mechanisms how oil rents are generated, distributed and used, and how the resource curse works from which conflicts arise and are proliferated. Now there is great interest in the situation of the new petroleum economies like Equatorial Guinea, and Chad, Sao Tomé E Principe. Old and new petroleum countries are compared regarding their development potentials, probability of resource curse, and dangers of violence and civil conflict.

There are new initiatives to secure peaceful oil exploitation in African countries by regional cooperation and transparency campaigns that aim to control the public oil revenues and to create oils funds for generating savings for the future (see Traub-Merz 2003, pp. 403-407; AfDB 2006; Wurthmann 2006). However, the reality of the old and new petroleum economies is quite different and careful reviews of country cases show that all these efforts are more actions for publicity than for creating a new reality. None of these instruments for controlling the oil sectors and especially the public oil revenues has been effective yet.

The case studies of the old petroleum economies (Nigeria, Angola, Cameroon, Congo Republic, and Gabon) show how the resource curse works through the economy and the society (see especially the essays in Basedau/Mehler, Eds., 2005). The case of the Congo Republic is of great interest (see Clark 2002,2005) as it becomes clear that the democratic development in the country is deeply connected with the oil sector. The Congo Republic could manage a democratic transition but failed in the consolidation of its democratic process. The case of Gabon shows the importance of external factors in maintaining a patronage system of rent distribution that is broad-based and associated with a strong public sector (Basedau/Lacher 2006, pp. 20-22).

The cases of the new petroleum countries show that old and new destructive factors combine in producing the resource curse. The case of Equatorial Guinea (see Frynas 2004; Wood 2004; Basedau/Lacher 2006, pp. 17-20) is instructive as it becomes clear how external and internal factors work together to bring forth the type of resource curse that the country experiences now (despite of huge per capita oil incomes that could be used for human development and economic diversification). The case of Chad reveals how easy and quick pro-active public interventions can be eroded that aims to overcome the resource curse and to develop regulatory institutions (see Guyer 2002; Pegg 2006). The case of Sao Tomé E Principe (see Frynas et al. 2003; Seibert 2005) highlights the problems associated with the transformation towards an oil sector that is controlled by a local elite which is inexperienced in handling negotiations and businesses with the international oil industry and is completely dissociated from the peasantry and the poor in the country. What can we learn from the experiences of the old petroleum-economies? Obviously, the research interest is growing as the many researches on Nigeria and the case of the Niger Delta in this Yearbook show. International considerations of the African oil industry are further enhanced by new strategic objectives. We know much more about the resource curse issues, the governance issues with regard of oil sectors, the domestic and international actors in oil sectors, and about the whole set of interests, relations, capacities, resources and strategies that are part of a deep analysis of oil and development. In order to assess the local and regional effects of oil production and oil rents distribution, much more is needed than looking at the local capacities and the local problems. A complex strategic analysis of interests, actors, resources, capacities and strategies is needed to identify the real causes of conflicts in oil-producing countries and regions (this is done in an exemplary case study by Engel 2005 for the Niger Delta region so as to identify the country-wide factors and processes in Nigeria being responsible for the resource curse and violence/civil war phenomena).

We also know much more about the relation between resources abundance, relative wealth and dependency of oil-rich/resource-rich states. The "oil paradox" (see Obi 2004), which implies huge oil revenues and increasing poverty in oil, can be partly explained when looking at the per capita oil income rather than on the degree of oil revenues/export dependency of these countries. A country like Nigeria has a high export dependence on oil but the per capita income derived from oil is rather low so that the potential for large-scale distribution of funds is quite limited and patronage networks dominate (see Basedau/Lacher 2006). The "paradox of plenty" is solved when we distinguish between countries: first, those countries that are relatively rich endowed with oil resources/revenues and can therefore invest in security and human development; and second, those countries that are less richly endowed with oil and invest mainly in patronage networks so as to stabilise the regime's power. Nigeria as an old petroleum economy and Sudan as a new petroleum economy are both dependent on oil for revenue but - considering the number of inhabitants - the per capita oil income and the per capita value of oil reserves are small (see Basedau/Lacher 2006; AfDB 2006). Oil producing countries with a per capita oil income of more than US $ 1000 can obviously keep political stability and organise some social change by a combination of security and distribution measures, while countries below this threshold cannot invest that much in security and distribution systems. As a result, they have a higher propensity to conflict and rely on other forms of political control, thus limiting social change (Basedau/Lacher 2006). However, even relatively rich endowed countries like Equatorial Guinea and Gabon can see their social and economic changes fundamentally blocked because of pre-oil societal configurations and/or external interventions. The new oil economy of Equatorial Guinea shows that pre-oil conditions still matter, such as unsustainable logging, dumping of toxic waste, arms and dugs trafficking, and illegally taxing entrepreneurs (see Basedau/Lacher 2006, pp. 17-20). The old oil economy of Gabon is an example of neo-colonial interventions where forces of social and political change are blocked (see Basedau/Lacher 2006, pp. 20-22).

The case of Sudan - as a new petroleum economy that is relatively less endowed on a per capita basis - is especially interesting as the "compromised peace" of January 9, 2005 brought with it a sharing of oil revenues between the government and the former rebel movement. This signals a modification of the oil rents distribution which is however still based on autocratic political systems in the North and in the South. In fact, a local resource control is not expected.

It is obvious that the resource curse and resource control issues of the oil countries are different in forms and mechanisms and complex with regard of natural resources management and public intervention.

2 The Contributions

The five papers of Unit 1 deal with these important issues in great detail. The paper by *Bedia F. Aka* and *A. Coulibaly* considers the road from growth to crisis and the way out in Cote d`Ivoire, an agricultural commodity dependent country. The paper by *A. Jerome* deals with the case of Nigeria, a country that has yet to go the long way towards managing the oil rents for sustainable growth. Related to this paper is the study by *B. Aigbokhan*, *R. A. Alabi* and *M. Aileman* that analyses the conflicts in the Niger Delta based on oil production. These countries highlight the particular situation of agricultural and mineral raw material producers, explain how the crises emerged and developed, and what can be done to escape the environment of conflict and crisis.

Broader is the outlook in the paper by *J. Ndeffo* as there is an attempt to relate the wide array of problems of African raw material producers to the abundance of raw materials and to the greed of Vagabonds in Power/Vagabonds in Rebellion (VIP/VIR). He aims to link it with the debate on greed or grievance as the central factors leading to conflict in Africa. Since years this debate has influenced policy discussions and prescriptions for conflict-prone areas in Africa.

The last paper by *K. W. Menck* attempts to provide a systematic frame for a new international order that is capable of creating incentives for conflict prevention and resolution of conflicts arising from raw materials abundance and raw materials trade.

From Economic Miracle to Conflict and Restarting again in a Resource-Rich Country: Learning from Failures to Adjust to Globalisation (The case of Cote d'Ivoire)

How to explain the economic decline of a country that was celebrated as "economic miracle" for decades? *Bedia F. Aka* and *A. Coulibaly* analyse the economic and political path of Cote d'Ivoire from an African economic miracle to a country with crises prevalent until today.

The causes of the 1999 crisis are elaborated in detail. The multi-dimensional facets of the crisis in Cote d'Ivoire and the failure of the past economic regime are considered. According to the assessment of the authors, there are signs that the crisis is only transitory. There are chances because of potentials and endowments to re-establish the state functions and the productive system of the country. However, the authors make clear that this optimistic account is based on leaders' ability to learn from the past failures – the failures to respond adequately to internationalisation and globalisation and to adjust adequately to the new requirements of the economy and society.

It is considered to be important to look at the history of failures, to realise the decline of public infrastructure and the growth reduction, but also the weaknesses and failed experiments of reform policy, such as the split of the national marketing boards into five uncontrollable entities. The authors look carefully at the effects of globalisation and openness and also make a differentiation between short-term and long-term effects of globalisation and openness. The basic outcome of the study is that Côte d'Ivoire opened its economy but did not react properly to the requirements of globalisation. It is important to note that not all strategies to open up the economy have proved to be developmental and that the strategies were not guided by an understanding of the economic policy demands of globalisation.

Most important, the authors look at the history of economic policy choices in times of increasing internationalisation and globalisation. They focus on "choices" that the country and the leadership had, and they relate the "choices" to the "potentials" and "options" the country has. Abundance of raw materials is a key factor in addition to Côte d'Ivoire's geographic location, the human capital factors, etc. The central questions are: What were the concrete choices after Côte d'Ivoire's independence? Was at that time a coherent policy to overcome commodity dependence at work? By such an analysis weaknesses and failures with regards to political and economic choices can be understood. Such "choices" of production and export patterns have intensified pressures on land, exacerbated over-dependence on few agricultural products, led to a severe concentration on few trading partners, and led to specific production methods that implied accelerated labour migration and environmental degradation. Most important, in terms of failures of the past, there was a lack of a coherent export development strategy. On the production side, there was a tendency towards exploitation and underutilisation of scarce land, an increasing use of migrant labour in production, and severe pressures on the environment. All these trends produced increasing conflicts among people. The economic, political, social and ecological consequences of these "choices" and "development paths" are analysed by the authors. Moreover, institutional choices were part of these unfavourable development paths. Marketing boards under government control, public corporations and parastatals invited corruption and mismanagement and cemented the failures and choices of the past. Later, when liberalisation, deregulation and privatisation policies failed to deliver economic benefits to the people the crises conditions were there and the severe crisis emerged.

The country case of Cote d'Ivoire shows that responding timely to globalisation demands with adequate reform policies is necessary but will only be successful if the state capacity is there to enact appropriate economic and political choices. State capacity and capacity building are the factors that condition the implementation of required choices that matter for Cote d'Ivoire. Confronting with the demands of globalisation, international choices matter for the country. It is important to have a ready concept for avoiding highly concentrated trade structures in product and partner terms, and it is important to solve the problems of windfall profits accruing from primary commodities. It is important to work on the proper management of excess resources, and it is important to be active in creating strategic partnerships for raw materials of importance to the country, such as the International Cocoa Organisation (ICO). Obviously, the country has failed to make such international choices in time. Also with regard of internal choices mistakes were made. The crises will aggravate if the country fails to develop new models of development. This refers to regional policies, migration policies, reform policies related to market organisations, but also to technological and human capital policies. Additionally, more specific policies are part of a new development path that is conducive to respond timely to the demands of globalisation. New regulations to improve the marketability of products are important so that quality and international standards can be reached. Research and Development are needed to transform agricultural products and raw materials into processed goods. Forms of branding that are adapted to the agricultural products of the country, development of agro-tourism, and productivity partnerships to increase agricultural productivity are needed so as to transform the agricultural base of the country. Moreover, spatial changes and movements that are generated by new policies and appropriate incentives are needed because the relation between the local production base and the location of the people is unbalanced which has lead to economic, social and ecological problems and even to ethnic conflicts. Many examples by the authors highlight the necessary changes in agriculture regarding labour and land use and regarding of a much-needed introduction of new varieties. The resulting chances from implementing such changes are obvious and illustrate the potentials of resource-rich countries in Africa.

Institutional reforms at various levels are needed so that the country can become again a regional hub and a place for regional and international investments. The Ivorian Diaspora can play a positive role in this regard and can contribute to a success of these reforms in various ways, especially by building a platform for political and economic dialogue and networks for technical and financial support. This requires new forms of institutional development. Also the service sector can play an important role by improving infrastructure and institutional capacities and help the country to become a regional hub again. A comprehensive export development strategy will also be needed. Part of all these developments should be a much stronger role of the country in international and regional organisations. Côte d'Ivoire can emerge by the time also as a financial centre and as a centre for specific futures markets for the region, and over the years the country might reclaim its importance as an economic powerhouse in the region.

However, it is elaborated clearly in the paper that more fundamental reforms are needed to follow such a path, such as a reconstruction of the state in its capacity to provide economic and social development functions, to serve all the provinces and communities, to provide the key public goods and services, and to design and implement an agricultural reform strategy that is broad enough to encompass policy components on incomes, incentives, infrastructure, information, innovation, and ecology. Such a rearticulated state has also to design and implement legal, administrative and financial reforms, especially by policies on land and land use, and on financial sector developments. A New Social Contract is proposed to ease political, economic, social, and ethnic conflicts. A rearticulated state is required to address the manifold problems and to make internal and external choices for adjusting to globalisation trends.

All in all, the paper presents a comprehensive analysis of the crisis as a consequence of inappropriate public choices and draws a comprehensive strategy how Cote d'Ivoire can become a dynamic economy again. The case shows that a raw material exporter such as Cote d'Ivoire can benefit from globalisation if certain requirements are met, and if appropriate economic policy and institutional choices are undertaken. It is obvious that countries with abundant natural resources such as Cote d'Ivoire are vulnerable to crises, conflicts, civil war, and humanitarian disasters even after decades of rather successful economic development. However, adequate policy reactions will make the economy less vulnerable and Cote d'Ivoire can show that chances exist to overcome the high degree of vulnerability.

Formulating New Objectives and Strategies to Overcome the Resource Curse and Experimenting with New Instruments to Manage Effectively the Resource Rents (The Case of Nigeria)

The paper by *A. Jerome* deals with Nigeria as a case of an economy that is abundant with resources and highly vulnerable to internal and external shocks. The paper is not limited to a thorough analysis of the crucial relation between abundance and vulnerability but also looks at the various aspects of managing natural resource rents (oil rents) in innovative and rather unconventional ways in order to achieve a sustainable growth path. Practical steps and concrete modalities for reform actions are outlined. No other African country has seen such high hopes and later disappointments associated with its natural resource wealth.

The focus of the paper is on the discussion of feasible strategies to revive the non-oil economy by managing properly the oil revenues of the country. The author argues that any attempt to develop a sustainable non-oil economy means that one has to consider the coalition of interests to exploit the oil in Africa and particularly in Nigeria (the roles of African governments, multinational companies, foreign governments and international finance companies and organisations).This understanding of the coalition of interests may allow to explain the poor outcome decades of oil production in Nigeria had on economic development (with increasing poverty, political instability, probability of conflict, etc.). It is obvious that any change with regard of revenue management has to consider the current coalition of economic and political interests.

Governance is considered as the central variable in explaining the oil resource curse and the negative effects of the resource wealth on the rate and variability of growth. It is clear from the analysis that the abundance of oil resources, the coalition of interests, poor governance, and the high propensity to conflict are interrelated phenomena, and that such an economy is trapped into increasing vulnerability at governmental, provincial and local levels, including the macro and micro levels. Resource revenues have insulated the country from pressures for institutional reform and modernisation so that the chances of globalisation could not have been realised. Political and economic elites, bureaucrats and unproductive classes have become more and more autonomous and non-responsive to demands for change because of the secured access to revenues. The outcome is an underdevelopment of the whole system: political, social, economic, ecological, cultural, and in terms of ethnic balance.

However, the author reminds us that it is necessary to distinguish carefully between types and systems of governance when handling the resource management issues. There are quite different groups of oil-exporting countries when political regimes and revenue management regimes are considered. Therefore, any attempt to formulate new strategies for resource revenue management requires abstaining from generalisations. Because of quite different regimes (by political control of natural resources, access to resources, transparency with regard of the resource sector, and the participation of stakeholders in decisions about the production chain and the revenues) an assessment of the regime properties is the first task for the design of new strategies for effective oil revenues management. Most important, technical solutions will only work in the process of implementation if the type of the underlying regime is evaluated and correctly assessed, so that the modalities along the production marketing chain of oil resources are known. Technical solutions will work if the regime properties are understood and if they are reformed accordingly. Reform and transparency proposals of international organisations often lack this perspective and are only concerned with financial aspects of controlling the revenue streams. Taking the example of the oil funds of Norway, such instrument would need to be designed differently to work in Nigeria. However, such oil funds can play a positive role in Nigeria but at a different level and with a different background.

Technical solutions to mange oil and other resource revenues need to be adapted. Autocratic and democratic political systems cannot apply these instruments, such as fiscal rules, resource funds, transparency guidelines, accounting rules, etc in the same way. Paternalistic and predatory autocratic regimes versus fractional and mature democracies have to be distinguished regarding the frame they give to national resource management. The author assesses the regime characteristics in Nigeria and the role of the country at the regional level. Most important, the paper highlights the interrelation of revenue management policies and political stability at national, sub-regional and state levels. Internationally we find a wide acceptance of new transparency initiatives to push for transparency and accountability of resource revenues. However, even if such initiatives are politically supported, as it seems to be the case now in Nigeria, they will work on the basis of the current regime characteristics. Nigeria is on a transition path, but far away from a mature democracy, so that a Norway-type oil fund solutions will not work. Institutional reforms, political and administrative reforms, an aware civil society, and steps towards the application of transparency and accountability at all state levels have to be undertaken. Only then, the technical solutions to the revenue management problem are embedded in the context of the political regime and the dynamics of political and economic change.

The author also assesses carefully the political changes since 1999, the moves towards democracy, and the new development and poverty alleviation strategies. These strategies emphasise growth based on the non-oil economy (manufacturing, agriculture and related services) to make the economy less dependent on oil production and exports. Although little progress has occurred since 1999, some visions were developed in the form of programmes to address the problems of the country. Because the bulk of government funds is still based on the (fluctuating) oil revenues and the Nigerian manufacturing and agricultural sector continues to lack international competitiveness, it becomes more and more pressing to implement reforms in the oil and non-oil economy. Obviously the translation of visions into strategies, programmes and projects is largely imperfect. Investment activity is too low to perform structural changes and the agricultural sector is still neglected with respect to all spheres of policy formulation and execution, and regarding the public goods and infrastructure supplies that are needed for a new direction of the economy. The land tenure system, to take just one example, does not encourage agricultural sector rehabilitation.

Reforms require first of all that the seriousness of the situation is understood. According to the author, the Nigerian agrarian society was transformed into a rent-accumulating and -distributing society, which makes its now necessary to transform this society into a productive economy based on agriculture, manufacturing and services activities. Elements of such a new path are analysed in Unit 2. However, the presented cases of cassava, leather and leather products, cocoa, and palm-oil production as forms of production and export diversification show that successes depend on the progress made in the management of oil revenues. Income and asset concentration in Nigeria is extreme, in horizontal and in vertical terms, and the high export earnings concentration on oil and the regional concentration of oil exploration within the country are associated with weak bureaucracies and policies, and with corruption and capital flight. Despite some recent anti-corruption efforts by the government, the credibility and the outreach of such measures are limited. Reactions from certain groups to fight misery and corruption then lead to civil conflicts, to violent action, to organised theft of oil and thereby to a financial base for sustaining conflicts in the oil-producing provinces and regions of Nigeria. The low level of investment in the non-oil economy is therefore directly related to this high degree of political instability.

Managing oil wealth is therefore a central issue in such a serious situation. The author starts discussing the whole array of problems by firstly defining objectives and options. While the basic objectives for management are quite clear (generating savings for future generations, avoiding boom/burst cycles, dealing with uncertain revenues, and spending revenues for high quality projects), the management task is more difficult. Controversial is the discussion of feasible options and the assessment of concrete options for required changes of policies and institutions to deal with the revenues, such as privatisation, centralisation, and democratisation of oil revenues. How can this work in a society with an unorganised civil society, with a serious lack of democratic institutions, with a lack of control over private monopolies, with a lack of budgetary accounting and control mechanisms, and with hitherto unresolved fiscal relations problems at the various federation levels? These questions are answered to a large extent in the paper. *A. Jerome* proposes a rather "holistic approach" to change the situation of Nigeria's resource management. All relevant stakeholders have to be involved in strategy formulation and in executing the programmes at all levels for action; transparency has to be institutionalised; international actors and donors have to be mobilised; and adequate public finance management programmes have to be improved by local, national, regional and international action. It will be important to elaborate this approach further - for the case of Nigeria and for other African "petroleum-states".

Instituting transparency requires that constitutional changes and new fiscal relations within the federation are established since the institutions at all state levels need to improve their fiscal rules and adopt new control procedures to guarantee a proper management of oil revenues. A holistic approach also needs to involve multinational corporations, and the governments of industrial and developing oil-importing countries. New types of national oil and savings funds should be developed and implemented in order to realise stabilisation and development objectives. Improving participatory decision-making by involving the relevant national and international stakeholders is imperative to ensure workability of such a fund. Otherwise, the gap between new objectives and implementation modalities and the reality of implementation will remain huge. In order to sustain the necessary changes of a holistic reform package a real coalition of interests would need to be created. The political economy for change in resource-rich states is not yet fully outlined. According to the assessment of the author civil society formation may be the most important element of the revenues management equation. Again, this paper shows that oil abundance can be made manageable and that oil resources and revenues can be controlled by politics. The resource curse is not a fatality and can be overcome by vision, strategy and integrated and decisive action.

Identifying Local Sources of and Actors in Resource Conflicts and Developing New Instruments to Overcome the Resource Dilemma at National and Local Levels (The case of the Niger Delta, Nigeria)

The paper by *B. Aigbokhan, R. A. Alabi* and *M. Aileman* considers the varied consequences of the abundance of raw materials at the regional level in the Niger Delta. Moving from the national and federal level to the regional and provincial level means that more specific social and economic interests have to be considered. The distribution of benefits from abundant raw materials that are found in the region comes in as a crucial policy issue. In this case it is oil, a highly strategic commodity because of international and domestic uses, the involvement of multinational actors, and its importance as revenue source. The relevant questions are: 1) how can the Niger Delta benefit from the revenue and what has to be changed at various polity levels? 2) How can the local actors interact successfully with the federal state in order to maximise regional effects in terms of value added, taxes, public expenditures, livelihoods and employment? 3) How can the ecological repercussions of raw materials exploration and production adequately be considered?

The Niger Delta region is largely underdeveloped in the Nigerian context, despite its vast oil resources. As all socio-economic indicators show unsatisfactory ratios – economic, social, ecological, and in infrastructure – there is a strong pressure for quick changes from the people and the interest groups in the region. The developmental impact of oil production was extremely low, as well as the income and employment effects. The question then arises how the region can benefit from its resources. The region is also affected by the flaring of gas that is not used in the process of oil production and by other detrimental ecological consequences of oil production. However, the region is also affected by severe underdevelopment of legal provisions and the judicial system to allow an exploration and production of resources according to standards and laws that aim to protect the environment.

Moreover, the mono-cultural production structure and the decline of other production activities than oil affect the region negatively. It is therefore important to analyse carefully the costs of this extreme concentration of production activity, and to propose and to implement strategies to counterbalance this situation. The tendency of an increasing vulnerability of the production structure, the ecological structure and the livelihoods situation of the people is aggravated by the low share of allocation of budgetary funds from the federal state. Small regional and local funds allocated from the central government do not mirror the resource wealth and lack accountability. This has led to mistrust on the side of the local inhabitants and the local politicians. The lack of development spending for public investments leads to a decline of the social and economic infrastructure in a region that is producing most of the export revenues of the federation.

The authors discuss a wide variety of oil sector-induced conflicts. Such conflicts arise from fluctuating earnings, the use of funds, the direct and indirect effects from oil production, the distribution of funds between actors at the local and regional levels, and the distribution of funds between federal level, the central government, and local levels. Conflicts about resource allocation are important in Nigeria and the principle of allocation (derivation formulae) was often debated and revised. However, a democratic debate involving all levels of government about the allocation of funds principles has never taken place so that the use of funds could not be organised in a developmental way. Decade by decade the "derivation formulae" was changed but always late and not in a development-oriented way.

Conflicts about environmental damages from oil production and from vandalism affecting oil pipelines increased in scope and effects. The lack of transparency about these events and their real causes led to mistrust among the people and to high economic losses. Further conflicts were induced by the oil price fluctuations and various political processes related to such changes. Political failures to respond adequately to the oil price fluctuations led to social unrest and strikes, to riots, and to violent demands for social safety measures. Inappropriate pricing of petroleum products at the national and local level and the inability to anticipate market development trends led to widespread black market activities and to parallel market activities that affected many people and distorted income distribution further. In a country richly endowed with oil, the petroleum price became a political price and a symbol for income inequality and unequal access to resources. The mass of people is constantly affected by shortages and price increases of petroleum products.

The authors also present their views on the causes of corruption affecting the economic, social, legal, cultural, and security system, not only in the Niger Delta, but also in the rest of the country. The whole system of public finance and public revenue sharing leads to corruption and the developmental impact of the resource sector is low because of this corrupt system. Systemic solutions can help to change the situation but need more than symbolic action, which is however a widespread tendency to act in Nigeria.

Again it has to be emphasised that abundance is not associated forever and inseparable with resource curse. A democratic organisation of government and a democratic control of the oil industry are requirements to dissociate the resource sector from the current reality of resource curse. This implies that action is necessary at the federal level, the state and local levels of administration to avoid the reoccurrence of the negative impacts of the oil economy. Also this study shows that the resource curse can be overcome by determined action from government and the civil society. Weak and overlapping government institutions and organisations (especially so in environmental protection, in law enforcement, and in regulatory activities) create administrative problems, lack of transparency, and result in societal mistrust. Inappropriate legal systems lead to the inability of assessing damages resulting in a major source of local conflict. There are minimum conditions to avoid a resource curse, and in these abovementioned fields there is urgent action needed.

This contribution is important because the authors also design a strategy to minimise conflicts in the Niger Delta. Enhancing the participation of people and communities in local decision-making is critical for this strategy. It is argued that more and qualified representation of the local civil society in developmental and ecological commissions and agencies for governing the oil sector is crucial. The role of the various state levels in governing the oil sector has to be defined and the collaboration of the multinational oil companies has to be organised in a new way, including all levels of action towards improving the governance system for the oil sector. Despite some recent changes, the progress of reforms is low. The low rate of success of development projects initiated by multinational companies should lead to a new strategy for their integration into the development process. A holistic approach is needed that involves all stakeholders in the region at all state levels, involves the multinationals and the large state-owned companies, the civil society, and donors. So far, all laudable initiatives to change the internal governance system of the oil sector, to reorganise the distribution of revenues, and to make the oil companies behave more developmental seem to be retarded and ineffective.

The authors also go ahead to design a programme of measures to improve the local and regional situation in the Niger Delta by defining a specific set of concrete measures for a concerted action in the short-term, in the medium-term and in the long-term. Actions to improve the governance system of the oil sector and the institutionalisation of appropriate and effective rules and regulations are part of the programme. Part of the programme is also the initiation of long-term production and export diversification at the regional level. Especially at the regional level it is important to diversify the economy of the Niger Delta and to build-up appropriate institutions for economic governance.

The study highlights the current situation, the sources of conflicts, the means to mitigate the conflicts, and the concrete actions needed to overcome the resource curse. It is a case that gives lessons for other resource-rich African countries. It is also shown that action demands first of all an analysis of the causes and types of conflicts. Only then it is possible to design a political economy-centred strategy to mitigate the conflicts and to rearrange for the long-term by institutions that are capable to overcome the resource curse.

Identifying the Real Actors Present in Resources Sectors and Causing Resource Conflicts, and Assessing their Strategies in Resource Conflicts

In his paper *Joseph Ndeffo Fongue* argues that the level of abundance of raw materials in Africa invites players from all over the world to act according to their personal benefits. This goes so far that these actors initiate and sustain conflicts within and between African countries to get access to natural resources. These "raw materials games" are played more or less without any explicit reference to a background ideology. Ideology only matters to get fast access to natural resources. The author's approach on "Vagabonds in Power/Vagabonds in Rebellion" (VIP/VIR) is based on research regarding raw materials games played by domestic and foreign politicians, companies, military and security people, and other external actors. The author gives a detailed analysis based on various examples. His work is also based on a detailed mapping of Africa's raw materials abundance.

The author goes on to contrast the relevance of various causes of conflicts in Africa (ethnic, religious, environmental, etc.) with his approach that raw materials games take place for personal profit and that these actors exploit systematically conflicts for their personal gain. The results of these games are measurable and visible in the forms of low growth and low ad uneven social and human development in African countries. The abundance of raw materials makes these games lucrative, thus creating mechanisms that lock in countries and people in a desperate way. This lock-in process creates a downward spiral in African countries that are endowed with abundant raw materials. The rents from raw material exploitation are acquired by small elites which are neither development-oriented nor development-minded. Although these small elites are steadily rearranging and redistributing their shares and positions regarding the appropriation of rents, they are homogenous in their actions and motives. The political changes after the end of civil wars may just lead to the emergence of new groups of beneficiaries from the rents but do not imply development. Oil-rich countries in Africa are cases of raw material games as well as some countries richly endowed with diamonds, timber, and scarce minerals and metals.

The author starts his analysis with information on the geological structure of the African continent. The abundance of all types of raw materials makes Africa so attractive for VIPs and VIRs. The more recent interest of Asian raw materials exploration companies in Africa comes after the long history of European and American companies being active in Africa. These new actors follow similar strategies and give substance to the thesis that the abundance of resources in countries without appropriate political institutions is associated with foreign-dominated exploitation and private appropriation of rents.

The author relates the weak state/weak institutions hypothesis to the abundance of raw materials thesis (that incorporates such important explanations of underdevelopment in resource-rich countries as the Dutch disease, the political corruption, and the institutional weakening). The abundance of raw materials approach in the context of the VIP/VIR actors is broader and more powerful as an explanatory device. The detrimental effects of abundance under VIP/VIR conditions on the tradable sectors and the productive capacities of the African countries are analysed in a deeper context.

The mapping and surveying of African natural resources makes clear that the situation may become worse for some African countries s the number and the volume of exploitable strategic materials is large and growing. New strategic minerals such as coltan in the Democratic Republic of Congo (DRC) lead to new interest groups and to new alliances that may intensify the VIP/VIR dilemma. Although oil and diamonds are crucial among the strategic and conflict minerals, other minerals like coltan emerge as strategic mineral conflicts that lead to national and regional conflicts.

The author distinguishes carefully between different causes of conflicts and wars and comes to the conclusion that the major cause for conflict in Africa is abundance of natural resources, and less so ethnicity and environmental scarcity. Thus, the VIP/VIR-approach reminds us that the controversy about greed or grievance as causes of conflicts and wars is not yet settled. The abundance thesis gives some support to the greed explanation. Abundance of strategic and conflict resources means that transactions are easier and less costly, that accessibility and tradability of resources bring in relevant actors, that there is an easy way of financing the fighters for governments and rebel movements, and that established international trading networks emerge quickly so that the appropriation and accumulation of rents is easy. The abundance thesis shows the opportunities for financing a continuation of conflict and the risks of a re-emergence of conflicts that may exist even when the civil war ended and post-conflict strategy has been developed. Abundance creates opportunities that make the dynamics of conflicts more independent from the real situation of the people. This may impede post-conflict recovery strategies as the window of opportunities can be easily closed. A policy implication is that "development" is important to avoid a re-occurrence of conflict. However, such a development policy is not enough and has to be related to a strategy that destroys the VIP/VIR framework. The coalition of African governments, local and international companies, foreign governments, finance institutions, soldiers and militias, and of interested individuals remains solid even after a peace agreement had been reached. This is the case because the coalition is based on a global production, financing and trading network, as it is the case regarding coltan in the Democratic Republic of Congo (DRC).

The author applies his analytical concept to the case of the *Democratic Republic of Congo (DRC)*, a country affected by internal and cross-border conflicts of which some experts even argue that it is the place of an African world war. The DRC is the prototypical case of an African resource-abundant country that could not manage its resources properly. This case is of interest when analysing the relation of abundance and rent appropriation within the VIP/VIR framework. "Vagabonds in Power" and "Vagabonds in Rebellion" are individuals and groups that act unilaterally and in alliances and have only private monetary interest to exploit the raw materials of the country. The VIP/VIR approach is helpful to understand the operations of actors who are dissociated from the living situation of the people and who have no concept and vision of development (despite using propaganda that they act for development and poverty alleviation). The approach also allows it to discuss more deeply the foundations of developmental states in Africa - how they can be built, who could be involved, and what has to be done to create governance structures and incentives that allow the sustainable exploitation of abundant resources in a productive manner.

The author's analytical approach reminds us that the current form of globalisation is visible in global value chains. However, not all global value chains have a productive base and not all are developmental. Some of the chains are even destructive when financing wars and conflicts, sustaining and prolonging instability, and systematically distorting the foundations of production capacities in African countries. The approach also gives hints how to intervene more successfully in African resource sectors. It is obvious that not only national but also regional and international measures have to be coordinated and forcefully pursued so as to control such exploitative activities effectively.

Referring to the Bakassi Peninsula conflict between Cameroon and Nigeria the author shows that there are possibilities to find peaceful solutions for inter-African conflicts and to build even regions of cross-border trade and growth out of conflict zone.

The author comes up with a programme for endogenous development strategies and some policy recommendations how to escape the VIP/VIR-dilemma. Such a new development strategy goes beyond national endogenous development; there is the need for a new relationship to the customers of raw materials (in Europe, America and Asia) and for a new commitment at the regional African level to counteract exploitative structures. In fact, the development cooperation at all levels and in all forms needs a new focus. To date, donors' development strategies have not adequately considered the complex interrelations of resource abundance, mismanagement of revenues, and propensity to war and conflict. Investing in political stability is an important investment into growth. Endogenous development requires that the strategic factors of political stability, poverty alleviation and growth are seen as complementing factors and that policy has to consider the VIP/VIR-framework. Therefore, endogenous development strategies have to be based on a new international order for raw materials producers and users affecting trade and finance channels that sustain war and conflict in Africa.

Towards a New International Order for Raw Materials Production and Trade that is Compatible with Peace and Development

The paper by *K. W. Menck* complements the analysis of the country cases (Cote d'Ivoire and Nigeria) and the case of a specific conflict area (Niger Delta). It also complements the political-economic context of the VIP/VIR-approach applied to the DRC. The paper identifies the gaps in the international surveillance of raw materials markets that avoid a developmental exploitation, production and trade of commodities. The formulation of principles that should guide the international community in reforming the modalities of these markets is art of the work in this paper. The modalities of the new global scheme should be designed in such a way that the generation, appropriation and use of revenues by developing countries, especially in Africa, do not give incentives to finance unproductive expenditures, wars and civil conflicts.

A new international order for raw materials markets would then complement the hitherto unfinished agenda of international organisations as these markets and the trans-national corporations as the main actors are so far not internationally controlled and guided. The "abundance of raw materials syndrome" has a lot to do with market failures. To correct these market failures a new world order must be based on a framework that incorporates international, regional and national levels of actions: international and regional organisations, governments of raw materials producing and consuming countries, multinationals involved in commodity production and related finance and services, civil society organisations, etc. The main objectives for a new global order should be principles such as equity and equality, growth and development, and security and peace. Especially for resource-abundant and least developed countries this new global approach is important. Moreover, such a new global order will improve the guarantee of raw materials supplies so that there may be a convergence of interests between producers and users in a long-term framework. Indeed, a new global order that creates more stable, equitable and more developmental regulations for raw materials markets will benefit all market partners.

The author highlights these issues by referring, first of all, to three country cases (*Angola, DRC and Sudan*). Although these cases are quite different in terms of raw materials abundance, forms and actors of exploitation, dependency on primary commodity exports, social and economic characteristics, and dynamics of conflict and post-conflict recovery, it can nonetheless be made clear that the global economy and society can benefit from a new global framework for raw materials markets. The cases of DRC and Sudan are so important because these countries are part of complex inter- and intra-state conflict configurations. Also Angola was part of a geo-political conflict configuration and still suffers from the legacy of these patterns. These three cases are also important because strategic and conflict minerals, such as oil, coltan and diamonds play a prominent role. The economic interest in raw materials is inseparably interwoven with a complex history and reality of economic, social, ethnic, religious, and environmental conflicts.

The author makes clear that a new order for global raw materials markets can only be built if there is concerted action that changes the behaviour of trans-national companies and African governments that have to incorporate codes of behaviour as part of their strategy. Governmental and supra-governmental regulations, controls and codes of conduct for production and surveillance of financing and trading channels of raw materials need to be enforced. Regional effects of the abundance of raw materials also need to be considered because resource-poor neighbouring countries are often attracted by the wealth of the abundant regions and countries and intervene accordingly. This can be seen in all three cases considered by the author.

Part of such a new global framework is also the consideration that countries can learn from best-practice cases of revenues management, public spending and raw materials exploitation (say from the revenues management of Botswana or the functioning of the oil fund in Norway).

The main argument by the author is based on the assumption that there is a common global interest to stabilise the raw materials markets and the political economy in resource-abundant countries. It is also argued that state failure should not be mixed up with the incapacity of public institutions; some state institutions work obviously effectively regarding the exploitation of resources for private profit. It is part of a new global order to build up functioning states in resource-abundant countries by transforming effective public institutions so that they work towards the interest of development.

The author designs elements of a new International Commodity Agreement (ICA) that include 1) trade liberalisation for all raw materials markets and final products markets in order to eliminate rents and make the processing of raw materials profitable; 2) newly designed international commodity agreements that may help to overcome the specific dilemma of strategic and conflict commodities by introducing regulations for the whole commodity chain; 3) control of trans-national corporations that goes beyond the codes of conduct and are more transparent.

Trade liberalisation and all efforts to open restricted markets create competition and improve the access to markets, thus influencing corrupt stakeholders. Important elements of a new order are also investment agreements that allow investments under clear and transparent conditions. Regulations of national governments should not impede investment. Development cooperation should also become part of such new arrangements by facilitating the process of re-regulation of investments and by promoting steps towards export diversification. This is the best strategy to reduce the dominant role of raw materials exports as main source of income, employment and foreign exchange. The newly designed ICAs should therefore be based on elements of a general strategy and elements of a specific strategy for each commodity. The ICAs should be designed in such a way that they impact directly on the specific international commodity chains by controlling more effectively strategic and conflict commodities. Some elements of a new international order for raw materials markets are already emerging such as the Extractive Industries Transparency Initiative or the IMF Guide for Resource Management. There is a focus on transparency and accountability but less on initiating binding guidelines for trans-national companies to act in line with good corporate governance. It has not become clear yet how and to what extent all relevant actors in raw materials markets can be reached by such initiatives and guidelines.

Ownership of development strategies and good governance are still the main topics when discussing development acceleration in African countries. Local and provincial ownership strategies are recommended in addition to national strategies so that broader population groups can benefit from the resources. Important is also the issue how conditionality in development cooperation can work in countries with large revenue inflows from raw materials. How can a new global order be built if local and international actors build a coalition of interest to exploit the resources at any price in terms of equity, environment and stability? Still, there is the urgent need for raw materials purchasing and supplying countries to define global trading rules and trading and financing standards so as to apply international and national policies to exploit and use strategic resources in a development-oriented way. NEPAD can play a relevant role in this perspective, particularly its peer review mechanism. The author proposes a holistic approach, and it is time to follow up such ideas in global politics.

These five papers discuss important aspects of resource-rich economies, especially with regard of handling crises, conflicts and vulnerabilities. Important policy lessons from these five papers can be summarised as follows.

3 The Strategy

Resource-rich African countries can do a lot to prevent a resource curse and to transform potentially violent conflicts into non-violent forms of conflict resolution. This Unit shows that local, national, and international actors (governments and non-governmental organisations) can implement and support such a strategy.

What are the policy lessons from the contributions of this Unit? We see that the vulnerabilities that affect African economies, and especially those with abundant natural resources, have various sources. We also see that these countries often experience a high intensity of conflict leading even to civil wars and to inter-state wars. The contributions of this Unit try to categorise and analyse the causes and trends. National policymakers, international finance institutions and donors do often not sufficiently consider the various sources and forms of instability, uncertainty, risks and propensities to conflict and civil war. However, growth policies can only work if the sources and forms of instabilities are ascertained and built into growth and poverty alleviation strategies. Growth-boosting and stability-enhancing strategies have to be combined. Growth-boosting strategies for countries with abundant natural resources have to consider the resource curse problems from the outset.

Fiscal policy plays a key role to manage the resource sector. Moreover, a balanced development policy for the other productive sectors of the economy is crucial. In case of resource-rich countries that were affected by civil war much more is needed to consolidate growth policies. It is necessary to lay the foundations for a broad-based economic reconstruction by giving incentives to all productive sectors and to human capital accumulation. Part of such a strategy is the reconstruction of economic, corporate and political governance.

In this introduction to the Unit we identified the main forms and contexts of vulnerability and instability that have to be considered in a new growth and poverty alleviation strategy for resource-rich African countries. However, we see that much more is needed in order to consolidate growth in resource-rich countries such as a new international order to assist countries that are affected by resource curse, violence and civil war.

Five important policy lessons follow for such future-oriented strategies:

Lesson 1: Learning from Failures to Adjust to Globalisation

We see that also resource-rich countries with agricultural exports like Cote d'Ivoire are affected by civil war and instability. The most important lesson is that these economies have to learn from failures to adjust to the globalisation trend. These countries can learn from successful adapters like Mauritius and East and South East Asian countries. The failure to adjust to globalisation implies that structural changes come too late if they come at all. Natural-resource rich countries in Africa lack institutional capacities to adjust, and might even lose existing institutional capacities as a result of their resource abundance. Institutional changes and adaptations are however needed to consolidate growth and poverty alleviation strategies. Such countries have to look at newly designed stability-enhancing strategies and institutional renewal strategies. Institutional reforms relate to market-supporting institutions, to fiscal policy and fiscal decentralisation institutions, to economic policy institutions, to political and judicial institutions, and especially to institutions for conflict resolution and for avoiding a resource curse. New types of marketing boards and of oil/resource funds can become the base of a new institutional infrastructure that is responsive to the globalisation trend. Such a new institutional infrastructure can be built by private-public partnerships and has to be controlled democratically at all government levels.

Lesson 2: Formulating New Objectives and Strategies to Overcome the Resource Curse and Experimenting with New Instruments to Manage Resource Rents Effectively

We see that resource-rich countries can identify the resource curse effects and the associated risks of violence as well as the political and institutional causes. Resource-rich countries can formulate new objectives and strategies to overcome the resource curse and they can develop new instruments to manage the resource rents. This is also the case for post-civil war countries. Again, fiscal policy, fiscal decentralisation and fiscal administrative reforms play a crucial role. As part of a new growth and poverty alleviation strategy such policies and instruments may help to avoid economic policy failures, inefficiencies and instabilities, thus reducing the probability of conflict and civil war. The case of Nigeria shows that the implementation of reforms is weak and needs to be based on new forms of governance and democratic developments.

Experimenting with new instruments towards accountability and transparency of resource sectors is relevant but obviously these instruments work best in the context of long-term development strategies, broad-based economic sector strategies, and comprehensive institutional reforms. A fiscal reform and decentralisation strategy is needed that allows for local resource control. So far, decentralisation has not gone far enough to accommodate also fiscal and natural resource issues. Also devolution of political and economic powers and an improved upward and downward accountability are required.

Lesson 3: Identifying Local Sources of and Actors in Resource Conflicts and Developing New Instruments to Overcome the Resource Abundance Dilemma at National and Local Levels

It is evident that the role of local actors in resource conflicts and the sources of local resource conflicts need to be investigated deeply, and that local rehabilitation and development strategies have to become part of national growth and poverty alleviation strategies. In the context of such policies a transformation of resource conflicts can take place – from violent forms to non-violent forms of conflict resolution.

When analysing the Niger Delta crisis we have seen that the various local sources of conflicts have to be investigated carefully, such as the competition over scarce local resources, the imposition of resource control by the central government, the lack of local political and economic governance, the lack of local powers to guide and control natural resources management, and the absence of a local growth strategy. The local competition over scarce resources such as land, pastures, forests and water is intensified by the exploitation of abundant resources such as oil.

New instruments are available to control and to transform these local resource conflicts but are however not sufficiently used. Fiscal policy measures, growth policies and poverty alleviation for regions and local communities can be used and combined. A localised resource curse can be avoided by a combination of national and local policies. Such a strategy can also be supported by donor organisations to help to transform resource conflicts in a timely and constructive manner. This requires that the local actors are involved and empowered and that participatory governance is given a chance.

Lesson 4: Identifying the Main Actors being Present in Resources Sectors and Assessing their Strategies in Resource Conflicts

In order to develop sustainable and effective growth and poverty alleviation strategies for natural resource-rich countries it is imperative to identify the main actors that are present in the resources sectors and that are causing conflicts. Knowledge about strategies and operations of these international, national and regional/local actors is necessary to manage newly designed and effective strategies to transform resource conflicts to non-violent conflict solutions. The identification of these actors (multinational corporations, state-owned enterprises, marketing boards, private/public conglomerates etc.) and of the relevant regulatory, standard-setting and law-making institutions is of key importance. Also all fiscal institutions that deal with resource revenues have to be identified as well as off-budget forms of revenues accumulation and use.

Moreover, the beneficiaries of resource rents and those groups that are - economically, environmentally, socially, legally, and politically -negatively affected by the production in the resource sectors need to be identified. Governance of the resource sector requires also that a careful assessment of the production system and its international linkages is made, and that the system of revenues distribution changes as part of a comprehensive programme. Such a programme has to deal with actors in various forms and to renegotiate all important elements of resource contracts. This requires capacity building activities. Furthermore, the redesign of policies to manage the resource sectors effectively needs to be based on a careful investigation of the role of actors in the whole production chain and a careful review of the economic, environmental, judicial, and social effects of their operations in local production areas. The strategies of actors in resource conflicts have to be assessed and correcting action should follow, which can be supported by international organisations and donors. Growth-boosting and stability-enhancing national strategies require democratic control and reconstructing political, economic and corporate governance means that these actors become controlled and embedded by renewed and more effective institutions.

Lesson 5: Creating a New International Order for Raw Materials Production and Trade that is Conducive to Peace and Development

It is necessary to develop an international order for raw materials production and trade so that countries endowed with natural resources are protected and consumer countries have reliable supplies. It is not a novelty to make international agreements on raw materials so that production and trade can be controlled to the benefit of producers and consumers. Because of the importance for peace and development of controlling global raw materials sectors the debate about a new international order is revived. Up to now, we do not even have a concept or a strategy for such an international order as most of the international commodity agreements have collapsed without any substitute in place. We have only few guidelines and codes of conduct that are limited to some commodities and/or corporations.

Much more is needed to ensure that trade, competition, investment, access to international markets and technology transfers are brought into an international arrangement. Part of such a strategy is it to give incentives for a peaceful exploitation and production of resources and disincentives to use resources for financing and prolonging conflicts and civil wars. Disincentives to those responsible for resource conflicts can be given in the form of sanctions, embargoes and financial restrictions. Such actions and restrictions should affect greedy behaviour and grievance as resource conflicts increase the misery of the population.

So far we have only policy recommendations what should be done in terms of empowerment, formation of capabilities, local resource control, transparency, and accountability. A new international order for raw materials should help to balance such incentives and disincentives towards a better functioning of markets and a transformation of resource conflicts towards non-violent forms of conflict solutions.

Especially the situation in petroleum-exporting countries in Africa shows that such an international order is necessary. The new petroleum-exporting countries show tendencies of severe political, economic and social distortion that affect peace in the whole region. The probability of violent conflicts has increased since the bulk of revenues is channelled to small groups of rent-seekers. Weak states and weak governments on the one side and huge international commercial and economic actors on the other side are unequal partners. Often, neither the governments nor the people know about local, cross-border and international transactions of resource rents.

Oil is a special resource that does not only generate national resource curse effects and conflicts but also regional and international distortions and conflicts. Important lessons can be drawn from the case of Nigeria and the Niger Delta crisis for other petroleum-exporting countries. However, the case of the Bakassi conflict between Nigeria and Cameroon also shows that international mediators can be supportive to a peaceful solution of border and resource conflicts. This gives hope that we can learn from such positive examples of peace and development initiatives in oil-rich regions.

References

Addison, Tony and Alan Roe, Eds. (2004): "Fiscal Policy for Development, Poverty, Reconstruction and Growth", United Nations University/World Institute for Development Economics Re-search, Houndmills, Basingstoke, Hampshire, UK/New York, USA: United Nations University/Palgrave Macmillan.

AfDB (African Development Bank) (2005): "African Development Report 2005, Public Sector Management in Africa", published For The African Development Bank, Oxford/New York: Oxford University Press.

AfDB (African Development Bank) (2006): "High Oil Prices and the African Economy", Concept Paper for the 2006 AfDB Annual Meetings, Ouagadougou, Burkina Faso.

Africa Insight (2005): "Special Issue: Decentralisation, Paving the road to local development?", in: *Africa Insight*, Volume 35, no. 4, December 2005, Published by Africa Institute of south Africa, Pretoria.

Ahrend, Rüdiger (2006): "How to Sustain Growth in a Resource Based Economy? The Main Concepts And Their Application To The Russian Case", Economics Department Working Papers no. 478, Paris: OECD, February 2006.

Alesina, Alberto and Eliana La Ferrara (2003): "Ethnic Diversity and Economic Performance", Discussion Paper Number 2028, December 2003, Harvard University, Cambridge, Mass.: Harvard Institute of Economic Research.

Asche, Helmut (2006): "Der Afrika-Aktionsplan der Weltbank: neue Aktionen? Analysen und Stellungnahmen", Deutsches Institut für Entwicklungspolitik (DIE), 3, 2006, Bonn: DIE.

Auty, R. M. (Ed.) (2001): "Resource Abundance and Economic Development", UNU-WIDER (The United Nations University/World Institute for Development Economics Research) Studies. In: Development Economics, Oxford: Oxford University Press.

Auty, R. M. (1998): "Resource Abundance and Economic Development, Improving the Performance of Resource-Rich Countries", Research for Action 44, Helsinki: UNU/WIDER (The United Nations University/World Institute for Development Economics Research).

Azam, Jean-Paul (2001): "The redistributive state and conflicts in Africa", Working Paper Series WPS/2001-3, Oxford: Centre for the Study of African Economies, University of Oxford.

Azam, Jean-Paul, Augustin Fosu and Njuguna S. Ndung'u (2002): "Explaining Slow Growth in Africa", pp. 177-220, in: *African Development Review*, Volume 14, issue 2, 2002.

Baechler, Günther, Kurt R. Spillmann and Mohamed Suliman (Eds.) (2002): "Transformation of Resource Conflicts: Approach and Instruments", Bern et al.: Peter Lang.

Baker, Jonathan (1977): "Oil and African Development", pp. 175-212, in: *The Journal of Modern African Studies*, Volume 15, Issue 2, 1977.

Basedau, Matthias (2005): "Context Matters - Rethinking the Resource Curse in Sub-Saharan Africa", Working Papers Global and Area Studies No. 1, Hamburg: DÜI/Deutsches Übersee-Institut, May 2005.

Basedau, Matthias and Wolfram Lacher (2006): "A Paradox of Plenty? Rent Distribution and Political Stability in Oil States", GIGA Working Papers No. 21, Hamburg: GIGA German Insti-tute of Global and Area Studies/Leibniz-Institut für Globale und Regionale Studien, April 2006.

Basedau, Matthias/ and Andreas Mehler (Eds.) (2005): "Resource Politics in Sub-Saharan Africa", Hamburg African Studies 14, Hamburg: Institut für Afrika-Kunde, Hamburg 2005.

Clark, John F. (2002): "Resource revenues and political development in sub-Saharan Africa", Congo Republic in comparative perspective, pp. 25-41, in: *afrika spectrum*, Volume 37, Issue 1, 2002.

Clark, John F. (2005): "Petroleum Revenues and Political Development in the Congo Republic: The Democratic Experiment and Beyond", pp. 121-144, in: Basedau/Mehler, Eds., 2005, op. cit.

Clement, A. P. (Ed.) (2004): "Post-conflict Economics In Sub-Saharan Africa, Lessons from the Democratic Republic of the Congo", Washington D.C.: International Monetary Fund.

Collier, Paul (1998) "The Political Economy of Ethnicity", Working Paper Series WPS/98-8, April 1998, Oxford: Centre for the Study of African Economies, University of Oxford

Collier, Paul (2003): "Primary Commodity Dependence and Africa' s Future", pp. 139 ff, in: Boris Pleskovic/Nicholas Stern, Eds., The New Reform Agenda, Annual World Bank Conference on Development Economics 2003, World Bank, Washington D.C. and Oxford University Press, New York.

Collier, Paul (2005): "Economic Policy in Post-Conflict Societies", pp. 45-56, in: Fosu/Collier, Eds., 2005, op. cit.

Collier, Paul and Anke Hoeffler (2002a): "Greed and Grievance in Civil War", Working Paper Series/WPS 2002-01, Oxford, UK: Centre for the Study of African Economies, 2002.

Collier, Paul and Anke Hoeffler (2002b): "On the Incidence of Civil War in Africa", in: *Journal of Conflict Resolution*, vol. 46, No. 1, February 2002, pp. 13-28.

Collier, Paul, Anke Hoeffler and Mans Söderbom (2001): "On the Duration of Civil War", September 2001, Paper for the World Bank/University of California Workshop on Civil Wars and Post-Conflict Transitions, May 2001.

Collier, Paul and Jan Willem Gunning (1999): "Explaining African Economic Performance", pp. 64-111, in: *Journal of Economic Literature*, Vol. XXVII (March 1999).

Collier, Paul, Jan Willem Gunning and Associate (1999) "Trade Shocks in Developing Countries", Volume 1: Africa, Oxford: Oxford University Press.

De Waal, Alex (1996): "Contemporary Warfare in Africa, Changing Context, Changing Strategies", pp. 6-16, in: *IDS Bulletin*, Volume 27, Number 3, July 1996, Theme: War And Rural Development In Africa.

Dibua, J. J. (2005): "Citizenship and resource control in Nigeria: the case of minority communities in the Niger Delta", pp. 5-28, in: *afrika spectrum*, volume 39, 1, 2005.

Ellis, Stephen (2003): "Briefing: West Africa And Its Oil", pp. 135-138, in: *African Affairs*, Volume 102, Number 406, January 2003.

Engel, Ulf, (2005): "The Niger Delta Region - A Strategic Conflict Analysis of Conflicts Around Oil", pp. 191- 221, in: Basedau/Mehler, Eds., 2005, op. cit.

FFP (The Fund for Peace) (2006): Failed States Index 2006, online: http://www.fundforpeace.org/programs/fsi/fsindex2006.php.

Fosu, Augustin Kwasi (2002a): "Political Instability and Economic Growth, Implications of Coup Events In Sub-Saharan Africa" pp. 329-348, in: *The American Journal of Economics and Sociology*, vol. 61, January 2002, No. 1.

Fosu, Augustin Kwasi (2002b): "Transforming Economic Growth to Human Development in Sub-Saharan Africa: The Role of Elite Political Instability", pp. 9-19, in: *Oxford Development Studies*, Vol. 30, No. 1, 2002.

Fosu, Augustin Kwasi (2002c): "Economic Volatilities And Growth In Latin America: Comparative Evidence With Sub-Saharan Africa On Export Versus Capital Instability", pp. 1-16, in: *Economia Internazionale/International Economics*, Volume LV, number 1, 2002.

Fosu, Augustin Kwasi (2003): "Political Instability and Export Performance in Sub-Saharan Africa", pp. 68-82, in: *The Journal of Development Studies*, Vol. 39, No. 4, April 2003.

Fosu, Augustin Kwasi and Paul Collier (Eds.) (2005): "Post-Conflict Economies in Africa", International Economic Association, Houndmills, Basingstoke, Hampshire, UK and New York, N.Y., USA

Fosu, Augustin Kwasi and Stephen A. O'Connell (2006): "Explaining African Economic Growth: The Role of Anti-Growth Syndromes", pp. 31- 66, in: World Bank, Annual World Bank Con-erence on Development Economics 2006, Washington D.C.: The IBRD/The World Bank.

Frynas, Jedrzej George (2004): "The Oil Boom In Equatorial Guinea", pp. 527-546, in: *African Affairs*, volume 103, number 413, 2004.

Frynas, Jedrzej George,Geoffrey Wood and Ricardo M. S. Soares De Oliveira (2003): "Business And Politics In Sao Tome E Principe: From Cocoa Monoculture To Petro-State", pp. 51-80, in: *African Affairs*, Volume 102, Number 406, January 2003.

Geda, Alemayehu and Befekadu Degefe (2005): "Conflict, Post-Conflict and Economic Performance in Ethiopia", pp. 125-142, in: Fosu/Collier, Eds., 2005, op. cit.

Gibbon, Peter and Stefano Ponte (2005): "Trading Down, Africa, Value Chains, and the Global Economy", Philadelphia: Temple University Press.

Gore, Charles and David Pratten (2003): "The Politics Of Plunder: The Rhetorics Of Order And Disorder In Southern Nigeria", pp. 211-240, in: *African Affairs*, Volume 102, Number 407, April 2003.

Gupta, Sanjeev, Robert Powell and Yongzheng Yang (2006): "Macroeconomic Challenges of Scaling Up Aid to Africa, A Checklist for Practitioners", Washington D. C.: International Monetary Fund.

Guyer, Jane I. (2002): "Briefing: the Chad-Cameroon Petroleum And Pipeline Development Project", pp. 109-115, in: *African Affairs*, Volume 101, Number 402, January 2002.

Hishow, Ognian N. (2004): "Resource Curse und ökonomische Entwicklungsoptionen Russlands", pp. 81-105, in: Osteuropa-Wirtschaft, 49. Jhg., 1, 2004.

Humphreys, Macartan (2003) "Economics and Violent Conflict, February 2003, Printed Memo), Harvard: Harvard College, Harvard University.

ICG (International Crisis Group) (2006): "The Swamps of Insurgency: Nigeria's Delta Unrest", Africa Report No. 115, 3 August 2006, Brussels et al.: International Crisis Group.

IDW (Informationsdienst des Instituts der deutschen Wirtschaft Köln) (2005): Jg. 31, 10, März 2005, S. 6-7, Rohstoffe, Reich und doch arm.

IMF (International Monetary Fund) (2005a): "Regional Economic Outlook, Sub-Saharan Africa", World Economic and Financial Surveys, Washington D.C.: IMF, May 2005.

IMF (International Monetary Fund) (2005b): "Guide on Resource Revenue Transparency", Washington D. C.: IMF, June 2005, 77 pages.

IMF Survey (2005a): February 7, 2005, Vol. 34, No. 2, pp. 22-23: "A guide to avoiding the 'resource curse'"; and p. 19: Africa's oil wealth raises the stakes for transparency, Washington D. C.: International Monetary Fund.

IMF Survey (2005b): March 7, 2005, Vol. 34, No. 4, pp. 60-62: "Democratic Republic of the Congo: Lessons from the ashes of conflict", Washington D. C.: International Monetary Fund.

Katz, Menachem, Ulrich Bartsch, Harinder Malothra and Milan Cuc (2004): "Lifting the Oil Curse, Improving Petroleum Revenue Management in Sub-Saharan Africa", Washington DC: International Monetary Fund.

Konings, Piet (2005): "The Anglophone Cameroon-Nigeria Boundary: Opportunities and Conflicts", pp. 275-301, in: *African Affairs*, Volume 104, Number 415, April 2005.

Larson, Anne M. and Jesse C. Ribot (2004): "Democratic Decentralisation through a Natural Resource Lens: An Introduction", pp. 1-25, in: *European Journal of Development Research*, Vol. 16, No. 1, Spring 2004.

Lay, Jann/Toman Omar Mahmoud, 2005, The Resource Curse at Work: A Cross-Country Perspective with a Focus on Africa, pp. 45-71, in: Basedau/Mehler, Eds., 2005, op. cit.

Leopold, Mark (2005): "Violence In Contemporary Africa Reassessed, Review Article, pp. 685-695", in: *African Affairs*, Volume 104, October 2005, Number 417.

Marysse, Stefaan and Filip Reyntjens (Eds.) (2005): "The Political Economy Of The Great Lakes Region in Africa, The Pitfalls of Enforced Democracy and Globalization", Houndmills, Basingstoke, Hampshire UK/New York USA: Palgrave Macmillan.

Mohamoud, Abdullah A. (2006): "African Diaspora and Post-Conflict Reconstruction in Africa", DIIS Brief, February 2006, Copenhagen: Danish Institute For International Studies (DIIS).

Möller, Björn (2006): "The Role of Militias and other Paramilitaries in African (Un) Civil Wars", DIIS Working paper no. 2006/23, Copenhagen: Danish Institute For International Studies (DIIS).

Nafziger, E. Wayne and Juha Auvinen (2002): "Economic Development, Inequality, War, and State Violence", pp. 153-163, in: *World Development*, Vol. 30, No. 2.

Neumann, Lutz (2005): "Oil in Sub-Saharan Africa", pp. 25-44, in: Basedau/Mehler, Eds., 2005, op. cit.

Obi, Cyril I. (2004): "The Oil Paradox: Reflections on the Violent Dynamics of Petro-Politics and (Mis) Governance in Nigeria's Niger Delta", University of Leipzig Papers on Africa No. 73, Politics And Economics, Leipzig: Institut für Afrikanistik, Universität Leipzig/ University of Leipzig, 2004.

ODI (Overseas Development Institute) (2006): "Meeting the Challenge of the "Resource Curse", International Experiences in Managing the Risks and Realising the Opportunities of Non-Renewable Natural Resource Revenues", Prepared for the Bureau for Resources and Strategic Partnerships (BRSP), United Nations Development Programme (UNDP), January 2006, 82 pages.

Papyrakis, Elissaios and Reyer Gerlagh (2004): "The resource curse hypothesis and its transmission channels", pp. 181-193, in: *Journal of Comparative Economics*, Volume 32, Number 1, March 2004.

Pedro, Antonio M. A. (2004): "Mainstreaming Mineral Wealth in Growth and Poverty Reduction Strategies", ECA Policy Paper No. 1, Sustainable Development, Addis Ababa: UNECA, December 2004.

Pegg, Scott (2006): "Can Policy Intervention Beat The Resource Curse? Evidence from the Chad-Cameroon Pipeline Project", pp. 1-25, in: *African Affairs*, Volume 105, issue 418.

Warner, A. M. (2000): "African Economies without Raw Materials", pp. 60-65, in: WEF (World Economic Forum), The Africa Competitiveness Report 2000/2001, New York/Oxford: Oxford University Press.

Sala-i-Martin, Xavier and Arvind Subramanian (2003): "Addressing the Natural Resource Curse: An Illustration from Nigeria", IMF Working Paper WP/03/139, Research Department, July 2003, Washington.

Seibert, Gerhard (2005): "Sao Tome e Principe: The Difficult Transition from International Aid Recipient to Oil-Producer", pp. 223- 250, in: Basedau/Mehler, Eds., 2005, op. cit.

Taylor, Ian and Gladys Mokhawa (2003): "Not Forever: Botswana, Conflict Diamonds And The Bushmen", pp. 261-283, in: *African Affairs*, Volume 102, Number 407, April 2003.

Traub-Merz, Rudolf (2003): "Kurzbeitrag/Report: Öl-Boom im Golf von Guinea", pp. 399-407, in: *afrika spectrum*, 2003, Volume 38, Issue 3.

UNCTAD (United Nations Conference On Trade And Development) (2002): "The Least Developed Countries Report 2002", New York and Geneva: United Nations

UNCTAD (United Nations Conference On Trade And Development) (2004): "The Least Developed Countries Report 2004", New York and Geneva: United Nations

UNECA (United Nations Economic Commission for Africa) (2004): "Managing Mineral Wealth, Training Materials", September 2004, Addis Ababa, Ethiopia: UNECA.

UNECA (United Nations Economic Commission for Africa) (2005): "African Governance Report 2005", Addis Ababa, Ethiopia: UNECA.

UNIDO (United Nations Industrial Development Organization) (2004): "Industrialization, Environment and the Millennium Development Goals in Sub-Saharan Africa, The new frontier in the fight against poverty", Vienna: UNIDO.

Wohlmuth, Karl (2004): "The African Growth Tragedy: Comments and an Agenda for Action", Berichte aus dem Weltwirtschaftlichen Colloquium der Universität Bremen Nr. 91, Bremen: University of Bremen, IWIM, October 2004, 56 pages.

Wohlmuth, Karl (2006): "Are Successful Strategies Feasible?, An Introduction", pp. 3-25, in: Karl Wohlmuth/Philippe Burger/Achim Gutowski, Mohammed N. Hussain/Tobias Knedlik/Mareike Meyn, Eds., Africa - Escaping the Primary Commodities Dilemma, Vol. XI, Hamburg and Münster, Lit-Verlag.

Wood, Adrian (2003): "Could Africa Be Like America?", 163 ff, in: Boris Pleskovic/Nicholas Stern, Eds., The New Reform Agenda, Annual World Bank Conference on Development Economics 2003, World Bank, Washington D.C. and Oxford University Press, New York.

Wood, Geoffrey (2004): "Business and Politics In: A Criminal State: The case of Equatorial Guinea", pp. 547-567, in: African Affairs, Volume 103, number 413

Wurthmann, Geerd (2006): "Ways of Using the African Oil Boom for Sustainable Development", Economic Research Working Paper no. 84, March 2006, Tunis: African Development Bank

Yartey, Charles Amo (2004): "The Economics of Civil War in Sub-Saharan Africa", pp. 87-128, in: A. P. Clement, Ed., op. cit.

Globalisation and Growth in Côte d'Ivoire: From Miracle to Crisis

Bédia F. Aka and Adama Coulibaly

1 Introduction

Côte d'Ivoire (CI) is one of the youngest former French colonies that acceded to independence in 1960 (see maps 1 and 2 in the annex). The country made headlines with its economic performance in a bid to replicate the Japanese miracle (Amin, 1967). Since the early years of its sovereignty the country developed a growth strategy based on openness. This model of growth heavily relied on the rest of the world (ROW) to (i) provide skilled labour; (ii) provide manufactured goods and capital; and to (iii) buy raw materials from the country's primary sector that is dominated by forest products, where cocoa and coffee represented about 45% of the total exports in 1995. Exports of cocoa beans and processed cocoa accounted for more than 30% of Côte d'Ivoire's export earnings, while coffee and forest products made up 5% each. At the peak of its economic prosperity the GDP grew at an average annual rate of 5.7% from 1960 to 1979. Some observers named this period of sustained growth "the Ivorian Miracle". By the end of 1979, the growth process of the country had slowed down due to the drop in the export prices of its main agricultural products, and this tendency was exacerbated by both the 1973 and 1978 oil crises coupled with the deterioration of terms of trade. Since then, the country's option for openness was amplified by the globalisation phenomenon, including trade liberalisation initiatives under regional integration arrangements, such as the Economic Community of West African States (ECOWAS) and WAEMU (West African Economic and Monetary Union) as well as broader trade agreements such as the multilateral trade system (MTS) agreements and the WTO. In effect the MTS and WTO assessments contain several rules which aim at creating a favourable environment, which could enhance international trade and prosperity of participating countries by increasing the potential of export for firms and the economic growth of these countries (see Centre du Commerce

International CNUCED/OMC/CCI, 1999). But indeed, the impacts could be diversified from one country to another according to their specificities.

Several issues related to governance, widespread corruption, rent seeking, mismanagement, and political rivalries culminated to the September 1999 Coup which was followed by a war that faltered the socio-political climate ever since. The crisis appears to be multidimensional (economic, social, political). In fact, the roots of the current crisis could be found in the socio-economic system erected by the previous regimes with the blessing of the former colonial master (France). The choice to export selected agricultural products was made to fit the needs of the metropolis (France and other industrialised European countries). The choice of import substitution industries was made to allow the same countries to invest in selected industrial sectors. While the system brought economic growth and welfare early on and for a limited period of time, it was not sustainable to heed for the needs of a growing population that was faced with inadequate infrastructure and increasing income distribution disparities. The state failed to implement policies that could decrease the income gap between socio-economic groups, the perception of growing regional disparities, the mismanagement of public funds, and so the governance issues led to this socio-economic and political crisis. As a result, the GDP growth rate fell to 1.58% in 1999 and plummeted consecutively to –2.47% in 2000, and to –3.77% in 2003 (WDI database 2003). Despite the ongoing political and social crises, this paper assumes that the current situation is transitory and the country could quickly regain a new growth path based on its endowments in physical and human resources as well as its existing economic infrastructure, all of which might help it to escape from its dependency on agricultural raw material exports. Escaping from the crisis situation supposes, first of all, the re-establishment of the power of the state, and then the reorganization of the productive system to address the socio-economic needs of the local population. The strategy of producing and exporting commodities without transforming and consuming a significant part of them should be phased out. In that regard, the paper examines several issues including (i) the relationship between the growth strategy adopted at the early years, openness/globalisation, and the current crisis; (ii) alternative policies and the perspectives to escape the primary commodity export dilemma; and (iii) policy recommendations with an agenda for recovery.

The following Section 2 of the paper presents a brief overview of Côte d'Ivoire's economic history, including sectoral growth, economic performance, the structure of external trade, as well as the social and institutional conditions underlining the economy. Section 3 focuses on the relationship between the growth strategy adopted in the early years and globalisation, highlighting their links with the current crises. The choices facing the country to break away from the commodity dependency and heading for new perspectives of export diversification are presented in Section 4. Finally, section 5 presents the policy recommendations and the conclusion.

2 Overview of Côte d'Ivoire's Economic History

2.1 Overview of Sectoral Growth and Economic Performance

Côte d'Ivoire's (CI's) economy was characterised by a relatively long period of growth during 1960-1979 (see Chart 1). In 1969, services represented 51% of the GDP while agriculture and industry only represented 34% and 15% respectively. In 1998 the relative share of industry grew to 28%, so exceeding the share of agricultural value added in GDP. The share of services in GDP still remained predominant around 44%. The agricultural value added fell to 21.99% of GDP in 1999 but rose thereafter to 24.22% in 2000, 24.75% in 2001, 26.19% in 2002 and 27.65% in 2003. During the same period, industrial and services value added fell from 24.18% in 1999 to 20.77% in 2003 and from 53.83% in 1999 to 51.58% in 2003 respectively (WDI database 2003). The growth process slowed down by the end of 1979 due to the decline in the prices of agricultural products. Since the early 1980s the macroeconomic situation worsened, and the emergence of persistent budget deficits constrained the government to reduce its investment efforts for development programmes that were previously initiated in several sectors such as health and education. As an example, while education represented 35.6% of the budget and 6.3% of the GDP in 1992, these shares dropped to 15.5% of the budget and to 4.1% of GDP in 1997. Public investment fell to 3.6% of GDP in 2003 (AfDB/OECD 2004). The economic policy choice during 1970-1979 was the diversification and modernisation of the agricultural sector in order to diversify the export revenue base (see Ministère du Plan, République de Côte d'Ivoire, 1971). Unfortunately, the end of the decade was marked by an economic crisis, the deterioration of the terms of trade, and by structural adjustment programs.

The decrease of government revenue combined with demographic growth (natural and migration) reduced the efficiency of the existing public infrastructure (education and health).

Chart 1: Economic and Political Chronology of Côte d'Ivoire: 1960-2006

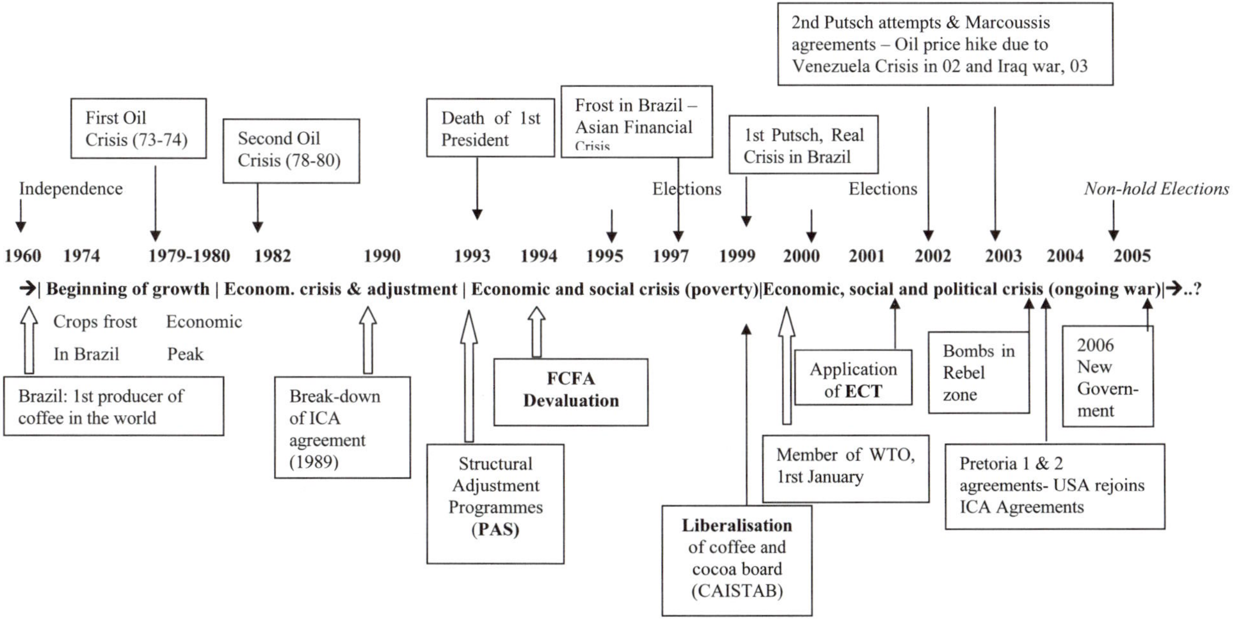

Note: *The chronological chart by the authors shows up the main economic and political shocks on Côte d'Ivoire since its independence in 1960.*

Overall in the history of the growth process of Côte d'Ivoire (see Chart 1) the period spanning from 1960 to 1980 could be considered as the beginning of growth followed by the economic crisis and adjustment period from 1980 to 1990. During the 1990-1999 period the economic crisis is combined with social crisis and to increase in poverty. This economic and social crisis worsened and culminated in the political crisis with the ongoing war since 19 September 2002.

2.2 External Trade Structure and Commodity Dependency

The economic structure described in the previous section led to a growth in agricultural exports and revenues that were managed then by the CAISTAB[1] (see Awudu and Philippe 2002, Fosu 1990a, Fosu 1990b). These revenues and the huge debt accumulated then by the government helped to undertake various investment programmes in all sectors of the economy. Total investments represented more than 15% of GDP and grew at a rate of 20% on average over the period 1960-1979. In more recent years there was a decline as total investment represented 13.12% of GDP in 1999 and decreased steadily to 10.12% of GDP in 2003. The liberalization policy urged by international financial institutions to mitigate the economic crisis led to the dismantlement of the CAISTAB into five entities including the ARCC (Autorité de Régulation de Café et Cacao), FRC (Fonds de Régulation de Café et Cacao), BCC (Bourse du Café et du Cacao), FGCCC (Fonds de Garantie des Coopératives Café – Cacao), and FDPCC (Fonds de Développement et de Promotion des Activités des Producteurs de Café et de Cacao).

Total exports remained nearly constant around 43% of GDP on average from 1999 to 2003, and total imports represent 31% of GDP during the same period (WDI database 2003). As shown, these exports are mostly composed of primary commodities (cocoa, coffee). The export revenues represent the building block of the financial system of Côte d'Ivoire.

Côte d'Ivoire's external trade (exports and imports) was and remains geographically oriented towards Europe, which absorbed more than 50% of the trade flow from 1995 to 2003. Almost 66.3% of exports and 59.6% of imports in 1995 and 54.1% of exports and 54.2% of imports in 2003 are in direction of Europe (see, Direction Générale des Douanes for the period 1995-2000, period

---

1 Caisse de Stabilisation et de Soutien du prix des produits agricoles (public marketing boards).

2001-2002 computed from UNCTAD Handbook of Statistics 2003, 2004). Nevertheless an increasing part of trade was and still is conducted with other African countries as the second destination with 24.8% of exports in 2003, 22.2% of exports in 1995 and 32% of exports in 2000, and provider with 20.2% of imports in 2003, 17% of imports in 1995 and 31% of imports in 2000. America, which absorbs 5.1% of CI's exports in 1995, is the third destination of the country exports and has an increasing share with 10.72% of exports in 1996, 17.7% of exports but only 8.2% of exports in 2003, while Asia is the third provider with 13.6% of imports in 1995 and 14.8% in 2003, but absorbs only 5.6% of exports in 1995 and 6.5% in 2003.

2.3 Social and Institutional Conditions

Faced with a persistent decline in the international prices of agricultural products and thus with the decline of terms of trade[2] effects, the government was engaged in Structural Adjustment Programmes (SAPs) that lasted throughout the 1980s and were financed by the World Bank (WB) and the International Monetary Fund (IMF), in an attempt to restore macroeconomic equilibrium, improve the efficiency of the economy and foster growth (see Azam and Morisson, 1994). In effect the terms of trade, which were positive from 1960 to 1970, became negative in 1972 and 1975 and definitively negative from 1980 to now (WDI 1999). These programmes as they were done failed to restore the health of the economy and instead worsened the economic situation of the country.

In the beginning of the 1990s, the international financial institutions and their partners in development cooperation urged the privatisation of several public enterprises and a freeze in the wage bill. In addition, they imposed the liberalisation of the agricultural sector, mainly the sub-sectors cocoa and coffee, which represented the heart of the country's finances (see Cogneau and Mesplé-Somps, 2003). In the meantime the Franc CFA was devalued by 100% in 1994 January the 12th (while one needs 50 Franc CFA to get 1 French Franc before, after devaluation he needs 100 Franc CFA to get 1 French Franc, which is 100%[3]),

---

2 Define as the capacity to import less exports of goods and services in constant prices.

3 The rate of devaluation is computed as follows: (100 FCFA - 50 FCFA)/50FCFA=1*100=100%. Note that the Franc CFA is linked to Euro through the French Franc with parity 1 euro= 655.957 FCFA, as 1 euro= 6.559 French Franc.

followed by the suppression of the CAISTAB in January 1999, just 4 months before the first Coup.

The economic decline (a -1.23% GDP decrease in average from 1999 to 2003) combined with an average demographic growth of 3.3% per annum between 1988 and 1998 (last census) as well as with the negative consequences of structural adjustment policies that led to a sharp decrease in government revenues. By the same token, income per capita and personal consumption plummeted and poverty increased sharply during the period. Consumption (total, private and public) decreased from 1979 to 1993 and increased in 1994 only by the effects of the 1993 devaluation of the CFA franc. According to the National Statistical Institute (INS) survey, poverty in CI increased from 10% in 1985 to 32.3% in 1993 and to 33.6% in 1998. The Human Development Index (HDI) for CI has declined: country ranked 154th out of 174 countries in 1998 versus 163rd out of 177 countries in 2004.

With the drop in government revenues the institutions of the state were eroded, and it seems that the country has not moved from a system of one political party to a multiparty system. In the education sector, for example, since the 1990s intolerance and next violence are installed as a rule for regulation in the only one new students organisation (FESCI). There was a replacement of the former students organisation (MEECI) by the new one, giving room for ongoing-armed conflict.

In the political area in general, following the first president (Félix Houphouet Boigny, who governed from independence to 1993), the second one (Henry Konan Bédié, from 1993 to the 1999 coup) missed the opportunity to change the former system that regulated ethnic group antagonism, and was replaced by the third (Robert Guéi), following a 1999 military coup that marked the end of political stability in Côte d'Ivoire and brought political rivalry in the country. Following the push, the new president (Robert Guéi) was urged by political parties and international partners to organise elections in October 2000. The actual president (Laurent Gbagbo, FPI) was the winner of these controversial elections, as the main political parties (PDCI, RDR) did not fully participate because of the exclusion of two major candidates (Allassane Dramane Ouattara of the RDR and Henry Konan Bédié of the PDCI). In September 19th, 2002 a group of soldiers organised a push without success but gained control of the northern part of the country, and since the country is still cut in two parts (see conflict situation map 3 in the annex) and the normalization of the situation appears to be an optimistic view of the current situation. The real end of the crisis could only be expected with the holding of the October 2005 presidential elections; but initial phases of demobilization, disarmament and social reintegration of all belligerents (included in the Marcoussis Agreements in 2003, and reaffirmed by the Pretoria agreements in April 2005) should be completed before the displaced population (estimated at 1.5 million people) is reinstated, government services are restored, the economy is jumpstarted, and before reconstruction really begins. Unfortunately the last political developments are pessimistic concerning the disarmament and the elections of October 2005. The second Pretoria agreements have urged the protagonists to accelerate the move towards peace but unfortunately the last political pessimistic developments (see International Crisis Group, 2005) concerning the disarmament and elections of October 2005 were confirmed.

As the October 2005 elections could not take place due to the unsolved problem of disarmament, reunification and identification of populations, International partners agreed to keep the actual president (Laurent Gbagbo) in place for one more year along with the nomination of a 'consensual' new Prime Minister (Charles Konan Banny, the Governor of the WAEMU common regional Central Bank). Recently, following the information by GTI[4] (Groupe de Travail International) concerning the dissolution of National Assembly, 10 civil persons were killed in Guiglo (in the western part of the country) during violent manifestations against United Nations representatives in 16 to 19 January 2006.

The next section examines how the country moved from the most stable and attractive in the region to chaos.

3 Relationship between Growth Strategy, Openness/ Globalisation and the Current Crisis

3.1 Openness, Globalisation and the Current Crisis in Côte d'Ivoire

The growth strategy adopted by the country implies export of raw materials; import of manufactured goods, import of labour and of capital. The GDP growth could be seen as a function of openness as measured by several authors (see Baldwin 2003, Batra 1992, Batra, and Slottje 1993, Edwards 1992, Harrison 1996, Grossman, and Helpman 1992, Randolph 2001, Solow 1957, Terra 1998,

---

4 Composed of representatives of United Nations, African Union, European Union, International Organization of Francophonie, International Monetary Fund, World Bank, South Africa, Benin, Ghana, Guinea, Niger, France, United Kingdom and United States of America.

Romer 1993, Yanikkaya 2003) with the share of imports in the GDP, and as a function of globalisation as measured by the share of imports plus exports in the GDP. It is clear that alternative measures of globalisation exist (see Randolph 2001, Rodriguez and Rodrik, 2001, Stiglitz 2003, Subramanian and Tamisira 2003, Zywietz 2003). The practical difficulties in assessing globalisation using other factors in the context of Côte d'Ivoire led us to retain trade as the only proxy variable to measure the phenomenon. This paper uses GDP growth rates expressed as a function of openness and globalisation growth rates[5] so as to analyse the effects of these independent variables on output growth.

A simple estimation of the log relationship between the 3 variables gives the impacts of the independent variables on the GDP growth rate[6] (see the econometric results in Table 1 using PcGive 10, Hendry and Doornik (2001)).

The static long run analysis (bottom left panel of Table 1) indicates that while globalisation has a positive impact on growth, openness negatively impacts on growth. The results of our dynamic analysis (bottom right panel) show that previous globalisation efforts have a positive impact on future GDP growth rates, as a 1% increase in globalisation efforts leads to a 0.74% GDP increase. On the other hand, previous efforts to increase openness seem to have an adverse effect on future GDP growth rates; a 1% increase in openness resulted in a 0.34% decrease of GDP growth rate. It appears however that the immediate increase of openness and globalisation has a positive impact on the GDP growth rate.

The empirical dynamic analysis (see Table 1 on the next page) reveals that increasing globalisation has positively affected Côte d'Ivoire's economic growth. On the other hand increasing openness has had a mixed impact on CI's economic growth. Overall, the results indicate that the short run effect of openness and globalisation are positive, while the openness effect in the long run is negative, while the globalisation effect is positive in longer horizons.

5 $GDP_t = F(OP_t, GLOB_t)$.

6 This relation can be further disaggregated in sectoral value added (agriculture, industry and services): $VAD_{it} = F(OP_t, GLOB_t)$.

Table 1: Econometric Results

Static Modelling by OLS (sample: 1973 to 2001):

LGDP	Coefficient	t-value
LGDP_1	1.503	10.6
LGDP_2	-0.53	-3.76
LOPENNESS_4	-0.284	-3.28
LGLOB	0.706	5.4
LGLOB_1	-0.874	-4.46
LGLOB_2	0.405	2.66

Sigma 0.056 RSS 0.072

log-likelihood 45.73 DW 2.07

Dynamic Modelling by OLS (sample: 1974 to 2001):

DLGDP	Coefficient	t-value
DLGDP_1	0.494	3.86
DLOPENNESS_3	0.525	3.13
DLGLOB	0.738	6.22
DLGLOB_1	-0.227	-1.6
ECM_1	-0.029	-2.88

Sigma 0.055 RSS 0.07

log-likelihood 44.16 DW 2.1

Solved static long run equation for LGDP

	Coefficient	t-value
LOPENNESS	-11.28	-4.87
LGLOB	9.42	1.58

Long-run sigma = 2.23157

ECM = LGDP + 11.27*LOPENNESS - 9.42*LGLOB;

WALD test: Chi^2(2) = 160.747 [0.0000] **

Dynamic Equation

$$
\begin{aligned}
DLGDP_t = {} & 0.5DLGDP_{t-1} + 0.53DLOPENNESS_{t-3} \\
& + 0.74DLGLOB_t - 0.23DLGLOB_{t-1} \\
& - 0.03LGDP_{t-1} - 0.34LOPENNESS_{t-1} \\
& + 0.28LGLOB_{t-1}
\end{aligned}
$$

Notes: 1. LGDP, LOPENNESS, LGLOB indicate the logarithm of the GDP, Openness and Globalisation respectively.
2. DLGDP, DLOPENNESS, DLGLOB indicate the first difference of the log of the GDP, Openness and Globalisation respectively.
3. X_i variable indicates that the variable X is lagged i period.
4. ECM_1 is the Error correction term one period lag.
5. All variables are significant regarding the t-values.

The major result that emerges from this analysis on CI's economy is consistent with the findings of Jang (2000) for the East Asia's fast growing countries about the relationship between openness and growth. In fact, our results concerning the CI's economy show that the relationship between openness and growth does not contradict the new growth theory assessment where increasing openness positively impacts on the long-run growth of the economy through its effects on technological change, in the sense that the new growth theory is pessimistic regarding the ability of developing countries to catch up despite their openness. The results of globalisation on CI's economic growth are also consistent with the forecasts of the WTO (World Trade Organization) and MTS (Multilateral Trade

System) assessments about the expected long run benefits about increasing the dynamism of economic growth. However, these results need to be taken with a certain degree of caution because the real definition of globalisation goes far beyond the simple notion captured here by the GDP share of imports and exports.

While openness usually refers to the extent to which a country trades with the rest of the world, globalisation is a much broader concept including the growing integration of the world's economies with the undeniable implications in terms of political, social, cultural, environmental, and judicial influences - accelerated by the movements of people and capital, as knowledge and technological advances are spread around the globe at ever-increasing speed, thanks to faster means of transportation and communication devices. This paper aspired to only address the economic aspects of globalisation. In the context of a global economy, no national economic policy decision should be made regardless of what is happening around the world, and more importantly in countries that emerge as potential competitors to Côte d'Ivoire. In that regard, the next sub-sections will review the main choices made by the country both on the national and international stages in conjunction with the international economic environment in order to assess their effect on the national economy and the current crisis.

3.2 National Choices and the Current Crisis in Côte d'Ivoire

The national growth strategy led to the influx of huge numbers of foreign workers and to the export of agricultural primary commodities. There were impressive results, but the strategy had mixed consequences. Can the current crisis be attributed in part to the national choices made since the early years? During the 1980s, the opposition claimed for more democracy but not for the change of the economic system background. The system of production was not really disputed. The current crisis could be seen as a crisis generated by the model relying on the export of raw crops and import substitution industrialisation, resulting in the crisis of the state that was unable to regulate the various interest groups (national ethnics, migrant population groups, the former colonial partner, other international financial partners) in the country (see Conte, 2004). This led to an erosion of state capacity by the diminution of its authority with serious political consequences.

3.2.1 The Choice of Perennials and Loose Immigration Laws

Just following the first years of its independence, the country deliberately chose to generate most of its export revenues from primary commodity exports, mainly coffee and cocoa. The country's choice of perennials[7] (Coffee and Cocoa, their types and methods of production, etc.) and its loose immigration policy have had serious implications on the current situation. Early on, the country established itself as the world leader in cocoa production, and ranked among the first five producers of coffee. However, it should be noted that Côte d'Ivoire made a questionable choice to break away from the crowd and to specialize in the production of a variety of coffee called Arabusta (A hybrid from genetically combining Arabica - which has the most favoured quality - and Robusta - which is the strongest but has much lower quality). This choice for mainly a single variety of coffee has had far-reaching demand-side implications.

In developing cocoa and coffee production, the country selected extensive agricultural methods using labour-intensive techniques. This resulted in (1) the aggressive use of huge forest areas with total disregard to land-ageing processes and to the need to maintain biological diversity, and (2) the increasing need for human labour to help till in the growing number of coffee and cocoa plantations. The choice of exporting primary commodities while importing manufactured goods made the country vulnerable to deteriorating terms of trade. Sub-Saharan Africa (SSA) in general and Ivory Coast in particular seriously suffered from declining terms of trade. According to World Bank estimates, declining terms of trade cost non-oil-exporting countries in Africa the equivalent of 119 percent of their combined annual gross domestic product (GDP) in lost revenues between 1970 and 1997. Exports never grew enough to cover this loss. Later during the 1970s, diversification efforts led to the development of other export crops (pineapple, cotton, timber, rubber, palm oil, etc.), but manufacturing and industrial activities remained quite weak. The abusive deforestation that fuelled timber exports drastically affected the country's climate and endowment in arable land; and it remains to be seen whether the country ever designed a sound program to reduce its dependency on agricultural primary commodities and to start developing both its manufacturing and industrial sectors in order to reduce the devastating effects of the deteriorating terms of trade. The ageing of productive land in areas previously located in the Eastern region of the country led to an inter-regional migration of population from the Central and South

---

7 Perennial crops are agricultural plants, which last and produce more than one-year season.

Eastern regions to the South Western region (see maps 1 and 2 in the annex). This migration movement put more pressure on agricultural lands in the South Western region, which became the new cocoa and coffee land.

The arable land used decreases from 0.43 hectares per person in 1961 to 0.21 hectares per person in 1996 (WDI 1999). In the same time the land used under permanent crops (mainly coffee and cocoa) production increases from 3.14% of land area in 1961 to 13.52% of land area in 1996 (WDI 1999) and the land used under cereal production increases from 471,000 hectares in 1961 to 1,504,000 hectares in 1996 (1999), the remaining land for other usage decreases from 91.57% of land area in 1960 to 77.36% of land area in 1996 (WDI 1999).

The rapid economic expansion in the early years following the country's independence prompted for the need of workers at all levels in all sectors (public and private administrations, teachers, nurses, tillers, etc.). It appears that the country deliberately loosened its immigration policy at some point in order to attract the required human resources immediately needed, and to use them to build the needed national capacity in the process. The first president (Houphouët-Boigny) even introduced at some point a referendum (which was overturned by Ivorians) to allow any member of the Economic Community of West Africa (CEAO) to become a citizen of Côte d'Ivoire. The country's open-door immigration policy actually allowed millions of people from around the world (Europe and Middle-East), but mainly from neighbouring countries (Burkina Faso, Mali, Guinea, and Ghana) to migrate to Côte d'Ivoire (the foreign population is estimated to 36% in the 1998 census according to INS).

The rapid growth of the migrant population in the short and medium run led to considerable pressure on diminishing arable lands and to past and recent conflicts between local and migrant populations in the Western part of the country, as in Duekoue where estimated more than 50 persons were killed in two villages during June 2005. In effect 47 persons from the Guere ethnic group were killed during the night of the 1rst of June 2005 in Guitrozon (a village 5 km from Duekoue the main area town) and in Petit-Duekoue (another village near Duekoue). The day after during the night of the 1rst to 2 of June 2005, 10 persons form Dioula ethnic group (originating mainly from northern part of the country) were killed in Duekoue downtown. None of the killers have been arrested. It seems that these massacres were due to worsening land conflicts between migrant populations (from other part or from outside the country) working in cocoa and coffee farms and local populations (see Chauveau, 2000).

3.2.2 The Choice of Marketing Boards, and the Parastatals

The over-reliance on primary commodity exports could be captured through the huge share of labour and businesses involved in the production and trade of perennials, mainly coffee and cocoa. Consequently, price swings of these few commodities were bound to having significant multiplier effects on employment and incomes all over the economy, particularly with declining prices having devastating macroeconomic and microeconomic implications. The country established a marketing board (CAISTAB/Caisse de Stabilisation et de Soutien des Prix des Produits Agricoles) to keep part of the revenue windfall during price hikes and to guarantee a minimum price to farmers during price declines. Parastatals that were established to administer agricultural development programs for specific crops quickly became riddled with corruption and also collapsed one after the other. Policies designed to remedy the demise of the economy proved to have been either inappropriate or ill conceived. The liberalisation policies implemented to restore growth through the suppression of Marketing Boards (e.g. CAISTAB), and the privatisation policy aimed at reducing the monopoly of State Owned Enterprises (SOEs) did not generate the expected results. The stability of the country eroded even further with the increasing prevalence of inequality in income distribution, macroeconomic imbalances, and a growing social malaise. The combination of these various factors appears to have contributed tremendously to the current crisis.

It seems that countries willing to reap the benefits of globalisation should improve their macroeconomic stability, observe financial soundness, open their economies, observe transparency, and promote good governance. Maybe the efforts by the Ivorian government were not enough due to the fact that the revenue generated by the CAISTAB was diminishing along with the erosion of the power of the state. But, could it be that the current crisis results from international choices the country made since the early years of its emergence?

3.3 International Choices and the Current Crisis in Côte d'Ivoire

The demise of the Ivorian economy cannot be analysed without considering a combination of factors that contributed to an unfavourable international economic environment: (i) declining prices of agricultural raw materials (mainly cocoa and coffee), (ii) oil price shocks, (iii) increasing external debt, appreciation of the US dollar and the level of interest rates on external debt, (iv) deterioration of the terms of trade, (v) declining foreign aid, and (vi) diversion of foreign investment - huge increases of FDI diverted to Asia, as the NICs emerged and the Tigers followed in their footsteps. More importantly, the liberalisation of the economy imposed by international partners (IMF, WB, France, etc.) had a huge impact on the country's situation since the 1990's and resulted in the current crisis, which could also be seen as a consequence of the globalisation process in which the country is involved.

3.3.1 The Choice of Trading Partners and External Financial Resources

The historical ties between Côte d'Ivoire and its former Colonial Master (France) have seriously influenced the country's trade relations with the Rest of the World for a long time until recently. As a member of the CFA Franc zone, the conversion of the national currency on international markets has been guaranteed by the French Treasury; and most - if not all - international trade transactions have been channelled through the 'Compte des Operations', thereby shunning the country from the positive effects of direct windfalls in hard foreign currencies. For a long time, the country did not create new partnerships to diversify its trading partners around the world and to explore areas for new business activities. The country confined itself in the role of exporting primary commodities to partners who have been making more money by processing these commodities for the end users.

The relative political stability of the regime and the revenue windfalls from coffee and cocoa price hikes on world markets during the mid 1970s facilitated the country's access to external financial resources of all kinds at both fixed and variable interest rates. It appears that the external debt stock doubled between 1982 and 1997. Between 1971 and 1993 the value of the external debt stock increased in nominal terms more than 36 times. The total debt service, which was 47,700,000 current US dollars in 1971, culminated to 1,539,800,064 current US dollars in 1982 and fluctuates between 1,000,000,000 and 1,400,000,000 current US dollars from 1983 to 1997 (WDI 1999). The combination of external debt and revenue windfall provided a cushion to the Ivorian economy against the oil crises of 1973-74 and 1979-80 that inflicted relatively limited economic damage to the country. However, the mismanagement of these excess resources and the deterioration of the terms of trade set the stage for a profound economic crisis triggered by the collapse of coffee and cocoa prices. Unable to sustain the huge burden of its debt service, Côte d'Ivoire then joined the Heavily Indebted Poor Countries (HIPC) initiative. In 1991, the External Debt/GDP ratio almost reached 182%, while the External Debt/Export of Goods and Non-factor Services ratio reached 592%. Government ran chronic fiscal deficits during the 1980s and the 1990s, and foreign debt seemed to be the means to finance this deficit. Finally, the economic crisis combined with widening economic disparities among social and ethnic groups what led to a social malaise that finally culminated to a political crisis.

3.3.2 The Choice of Strategic Partnerships

While Côte d'Ivoire has been member of most international organisations created to defend the interest of producers of coffee, cocoa etc. the country does not seem to have done enough to protect its interest and that of its people in general, and particularly of its farmers. With the country exporting about 40% of the world cocoa and ranking among the first 5 coffee producers, its hard to believe that Côte d'Ivoire did not do more to prevent the collapse of the ICO in 1998 (FAO Commodity Market Review 2003-2004), and did not rally buyers and producers together to help device a scheme to prevent the devastating price trends that have been experienced in recent years. The example of OPEC should have inspired coffee and cocoa producers to engage in strong producer/buyer agreements with more chances to contain price-swings within a certain limit for relatively long periods of time.

While export earnings of coffee producing countries have fallen drastically as demonstrated by the price drop (actually from US$ 10-12 billion in the early 1990s to US$ 5-6 billion currently, FAO Commodity Market Review 2003-2004), the value of retail sales of coffee has increased over the same period from around US$ 30 billion to around US$ 70 billion. In Côte d'Ivoire in particular, the price paid to growers has had a declining trend, while during the same period the average retail price of coffee in the US, in the UK and in Switzerland kept increasing. Coffee prices declined sharply from 1977 to 1982, from 1986 to 1993, and from 1998 to 2002 where they dropped to their 1973 level (even lower than their 1963 level for Robusta, ICO Statistics, Historical data).

The next section presents some alternative approaches to break away from the primary commodity dilemma. The model of growth in Côte d'Ivoire is reproducing this dilemma; it is - as shown above - inherited from the former colonial power interests, the interests of international partners, and the strategies of trans-national actors which result in more openness amplified by globalisation.

4 Alternative Policies to Escape from the Primary Commodity Dilemma

4.1 Increasing the Value Added of Agricultural Products

It clearly appears that the system of production is oriented towards exports of raw materials in developed countries where the processing industries are installed. Thus, the potential value added, investments, and job creation opportunities in the economy are transferred abroad. In the national Ivorian economy local industries belong to international capital through French interest in the country. The challenge consists in finding an alternative model but the successive governments after president Félix Houphouet-Boigny failed to develop such a new strategy.

4.1.1 New Regulations for and Investments in Efficient Processing, Packaging, and Marketing of Agricultural Products

While Ivorian exports have overwhelmingly been comprised of primary agricultural products, efforts in the past were made to package goods in ways that facilitate their access to world markets. In that regard, companies like SONACO (Société Nationale de Conditionnement), which manufactured packages for banana, and FILTISSAC (Filature et Tissage), which manufactured coffee and cocoa bags, helped to generate substantial amounts of income and jobs. As the country expanded its diversification policy, the list of such companies stretched with, inter alia, COTIVANA (Côte d'Ivoire Ananas), involved in the processing and packaging of pineapples, and COTIVO (Compagnie du Textile Ivoirien), involved in textiles. Processing and packaging companies are often created in response to market demands, but may well be intended to provide increased accessibility to local or foreign markets for products that were previously struggling to benefit from such an opportunity. In addition, efficient processing and packaging of perishable goods prolong their conservation, thereby reducing the health hazards related to their handling throughout their journey from the producer to the consumer. Every year, the economy is hurt by huge losses due to products that perish because they are not appropriately and time-effectively shipped where they are needed.

New regulations could help to improve the way some perishable goods are processed and packaged in order to provide incentives for new investments and job creation in those areas. These regulations should be designed to require a certain level of processing to be performed on selected agricultural products, at least to promote their healthy handling, their accessibility to markets, their identification, and the correct presentation of production and expiration dates, etc. Lots of agricultural products are still being sold regardless of such considerations, thereby hindering their marketability beyond the status quo.

4.1.2 Investing in Research and Development to Transform Agricultural Products into Processed Goods

Only a limited number of agricultural products available in Côte d'Ivoire are actually processed. In most cases these products are still sold in their primary condition. While some efforts have been made to process (partially) the most dominant export commodities (coffee, cocoa, palm oil, pineapples, etc.), too many more crops remain outside the scope of research to improve their marketability. More investments are needed for research to process these products in ways that can facilitate their conservation, transportability and safe consumption. In the past a research centre ITIPAT (Institut pour la Transformation et l'Industrialisation des Produits Agricoles Tropicaux) was created in 1962, replaced in 1982 by CIRT (Centre Ivoirien de Recherches Technologiques) and now CNRA (Centre National de Recherche Agronomique, created in 1998) for the transformation of agricultural products. Among its many discoveries were ethanol generated from cassava. The full extent of the therapeutic value of products such as kola nuts and cashew nuts still remains unexplored while it has been mulled that these nuts could well be used to generate medical products. However, most of the findings seldom got promoted. The lack of political will and of government commitment to get the most out of these discoveries discouraged any hope for necessary investments.

So far, investments in fisheries have been insufficient despite the availability of natural wetlands throughout a country stripped with 5 rivers and endowed with seashore all along the coastal south riddled with lagoons. Government should encourage much more investments, particularly in fish farms and in food crop processing, drawing on lessons from international experience and best practices in other parts of the world.

4.1.3 Increasing Visibility and Awareness by Promoting Therapeutic Virtue or Other Usages of Agricultural Products, and Developing Agro-tourism

Many agricultural products have limited visibility even on local markets due to ill-spread knowledge of both the nutrients they contain and their healing power. The lack of efficient research conducted on these products keeps them in the dark, thereby providing no incentive to either promote them or to invest in efficient ways to produce and to market them. Efforts could be directed towards linking some processed agricultural goods with the name of the country, as Tequila is reminiscent of Mexico, Vodka for Russia, Camembert and Beaujolais for France, etc.

Côte d'Ivoire is endowed with the necessary infrastructure to attract tourists from around the world. The country owns several natural parks, one of which has been declared a World Wildlife Reserve. The variety of ethnic groups, each one having its own cultural habits, provides a mosaic of lifestyles, dishes and rituals that can be effectively used to successfully promote and develop Agro-tourism.

4.1.4 Encouraging Partnerships to Promote Higher Yields and Profitability of Agricultural Production

While Côte d'Ivoire still ranks first in the world for cocoa production (with about 40% of the world production), and ranks fourth or fifth for coffee production, the country has favoured labour-intensive production over higher yields and productivity from capital-intensive agricultural production. This choice was certainly made because of the availability of surplus labour (about 80% of the labour force is involved in agricultural production), a significant share of which came from neighbouring countries. However, with the swift degradation of the land used in the production of the main two export crops (coffee and cocoa), production areas have moved from the Eastern part of the country to the Southwest. The income implications of such a move have somewhat exacerbated lend-tenure issues among some ethnic groups on the one hand, and between local farmers and some of their foreign workers on the other hand. Most farmers own small lands, too small to allow for an efficient production. While in the past small farmers have been encouraged to regroup through cooperatives, more needs to be done in order to significantly increase the productivity levels. It is very important however that measures be taken to discourage expansion of coffee or cocoa farms beyond their current levels (representing 60% of all cultivated areas). For these products, the focus should now turn from labour-intensive agricultural production on large cultivated areas to high-yield capital-intensive agricultural production on even reduced cultivated areas. Such a move could gradually free a growing share of the surplus labour to be re-trained for other manufacturing and service jobs, e.g. processing and packaging activities and agro-tourism as advocated earlier. In addition, the reduction of coffee and cocoa farms could allow the introduction/promotion of new varieties of agricultural products or high income-generating products, such as flowers etc.

4.2 Institutional Reforms to Create a Market-friendly Environment and to Attract FDI

4.2.1 Improving the Investment Climate (Infrastructure, social, political, and institutional) and Crafting Agreements that Promote and Protect FDI/ Businesses

The various political moves taken and policies promoted by successive governments following the death of President Houphouët-Boigny and the political instability that followed the 1999 coup have affected negatively the investment climate in a country once among the most stable, peaceful, and prosperous of the African continent. When peace is recovered, the country will still be in desperate need for institutional reforms to create a market-friendly and a business-friendly environment so as to be able to attract foreign direct investment (FDI) and to facilitate business activity. On the basis of the existing infrastructure that can easily be brought back to first class operation levels and a relatively well-educated human resource base the country can spring again from the current economic slum. Several bilateral agreements could then be concluded with foreign businesses in targeted areas where the country has a comparative advantage. When government provides the necessary regulatory framework and the institutional support to ensure business security, accountability and a due process for law enforcement or disputes settlement, authorities will then also be able to tap the growing and vibrant Ivorian Diaspora to encourage them not only to invest or to do business in Côte d'Ivoire, but also and more importantly to promote and to expand market shares for Ivorian products and businesses in Africa and around the world. In that regard, all administrative barriers to business creation and development should be systematically identified and promptly removed; and fiscal incentives such as tax concessions/holidays for new businesses (mainly SMEs) should be put in place. The government could present a token of appreciation to the increasing weight of remittances made by Ivorians living abroad to specified types of Bank accounts inside the country. This token could be anything from reduced financial charges or increased interest on deposits to reduced taxes on material costs for the construction of residential homes (or reduced financial charges on housing loans etc.).

4.2.2 Creating Industrial and Free Zones

During the mid-seventies and early eighties, Côte d'Ivoire was perceived as a focal point for international conferences in Africa. Most major cultural events used to take place there, and Abidjan quickly became the cradle for most emerging African artists of all kinds. The burgeoning web of specialized schools was attracting students from all neighbouring countries and even beyond. The national Radio and TV broadcasting network became the training ground for TV anchors and hosts from West and Central Africa. While consecutive economic and political crises have hampered such trends, a renewed interest and a new political commitment could quickly transform the country in a regional hub for the Arts, Trade, Information Technology, and Services, etc. by 2015. These goals can be achieved through the relentless pursuit of focused policies and well-designed strategies that would promote the values of excellence, integrity, as well as individual and organizational performance.

Government should strengthen institutions so that they create a levelled playing field where business operations are simplified but secure, economic agents are well informed and accountable for their deeds, security becomes a priority, and hospitality a virtue. Such an environment could be fostered in a Free Zone (FZ[8]) to attract foreign investments. The spillover effects of FDIs in terms of foreign capital, knowledge, technology, and jobs etc have proved to be growth-accelerating in cases where FZs have been effectively set up. These free trade zones, if located in the Northern part of the country and in the South-Western port city of San Pedro, could provide tremendous business opportunities around the country and to land-locked countries such as Mali, Burkina Faso, and Niger. In line with the core of our suggestion the Ivorian government unveiled this May 2005 its plans to create the Gandhi Free Zone for Information and Communication Technology in Grand Bassam (in the South-Eastern region of the country).

4.2.3 Reducing input costs (Electricity, Water, and Communications in particular)

As much as electricity and water availability and costs can be strong deterrents to investments in production operations, communications and information technology availability and costs can also be strong deterrents to investments in the service sector. Thus, it is of utmost importance that electricity, water, and communications costs be reduced to a level that makes it possible for businesses to compete on the global scale. Electricity in the country is generated through gas, hydroelectric, and thermoelectric plants. Since 1995, gas-fired electricity

---

8 Depending inter alia on the objectives, sector-focus and market targets, FZs can take the form of Free Trade zones, Technology Parks, Special Economic Zones, Industrial Zones or estates, Exports Processing zones, and Enterprise Zones, etc.

plants have increased, transforming the country into a net energy exporter to neighbouring Ghana, Togo, Benin, Mali, and Burkina Faso. An additional connection to Guinea is being studied. Electricity production rises continuously from 58,800,000 kilowatt-hours in 1971 to 3,015,000,064 kilowatt-hours in 1996 with a decrease in 1983 and in 1992. Electricity generation totalled 4.6 billions kilowatt-hours in 2001. While this production was 76.36% based on oil source and 23.64% based on hydroelectric in 1971, the relative share evolved to 37.91% based on oil and 62.08% hydroelectric-based in 1996.

Cote d'Ivoire is a leading proponent of the development of the West African Power Pool (WAPP), which was formed by an agreement between ECOWAS Energy Ministers in November 1999, in a bid to interconnect the power networks of all the mainland ECOWAS nations. The power and water sector as well as the telecommunications sector were run by state-owned monopolies until the early 1990s when government decided to privatise them. Unfortunately, the changes moved them from one monopoly to another since the Compagnie Ivoirienne d'Electricité (CIE, 51% owned by a French private business group) has a monopoly on water and electricity supply. Having become an oil exporter, Côte d'Ivoire should be in a better position to significantly reduce power costs in order to improve the competitiveness of businesses that heavily depend on it. The development of wireless telecommunication technologies has opened the door to competition and has removed the bottleneck created by the inability of Côte d'Ivoire Telecom to respond to the exponentially increasing demand for fixed phone lines, although a large part of the wireless companies belong to French private groups also.

4.3 Developing the Services Sector, the Export Orientation Strategy, and the World Markets

4.3.1 Supporting and Promoting the Services Sector (Marketing, Standards, Quality, Regulatory Framework)

The Ivorian economy is predominantly based on the production of services, accounting for about 53% of GDP in 2002, well above agriculture and industry representing about 26% and 21% respectively during the same year. However, agriculture employs about 80% of the labour force. With the appropriate support and promotion efforts, the services sector could grow even stronger and should be able to absorb a great deal of surplus labour that is freed from agricultural production. However, a regulatory framework should be created to provide guidance for marketing rules, quality and standard requirements, etc. for all services activities.

With a government committed to making the country a services hub, major efforts could be redirected at providing and improving targeted skills that enable the efficient use of performance/productivity enhancing tools and techniques. Well-designed education programs could provide the necessary support needed to transform a growing share of cohorts of young and energetic college graduates into emerging entrepreneurs, service workers, scientists, teachers etc. according to the country objectives. Government could invest more substantially in the development of extension services for farmers, entrepreneurs, and even SMEs in other sectors.

4.3.2 Expanding the Export Orientation Strategy

It is imperative to figure out the answers to the following question: Where can we export the goods we either currently produce or where we could have or could develop comparative advantage in producing? The answers to this question are crucial to both the further development of the country's export diversification strategy and to client-base enlargement. However, this requires a thorough analysis of global market trends and provision of information to determine which countries are buying what? Who are they buying these products from? What else could they be interested in buying? What types of partnerships could we get involved in, in order to create a niche in a specific area? After finding answers to these questions and more, Côte d'Ivoire will have to select carefully the countries that will compose its client-base or where to build/strengthen its partnerships, in order to put in place a well-designed strategy to penetrate better-targeted markets. Foreign regulations, customer preferences etc. should be analysed to identify arrangement options that could mitigate existing obstacles to export expansion.

A strategy to promote export diversification by way of introducing new products and some level of processing for existing agricultural products could address as well the situation of backward linkages in order to provide policy instruments that will unleash the full potential of the domestic market. Tariff and non-tariff barriers should be either eliminated or brought to non-prohibitive levels in light of WTO requirements. Productivity- and performance-enhancing technologies should be introduced more effectively in the production and processing of agricultural products in particular, and in exports in general.

Efforts to improve the performance of the Ivorian export sector in order to generate increased revenues, business opportunities, and job-creation will have to be initiated through policy measures and instruments that are carefully designed to meet interim and final objectives.

The importance of institution strengthening and regulatory frameworks should be stressed for the successful implementation of all the reform initiatives needed to support the export expansion and the diversification strategy. The required regulations and the role of all the institutions that may be involved at one point or another in the activities of the export sector should be clearly defined and shared among all participating economic agents.

A particular emphasis should be put on creating low-rate credit facilities, rural/farm insurance coverage, and extension services for farmers. Government could use an input (seeds and fertilizers) subsidy policy to promote cooperatives and partnerships in agricultural production, and investment grants targeted at land development/irrigation systems for the production of selected products. In addition, farms should have access to safe drinking water, sanitation, and appropriate health services, etc.

Government should promote investments in research, training, and extension services. Moreover, marketing and processing firms should be given tax holidays/concessions.

4.3.3 Integration into Regional and World Markets

Côte d'Ivoire is a member of several regional organizations (AU, ECOWAS, WAEMU, Conseil de l'Entente, and the Franc Zone). The country can build upon its membership to these organisations to grow as an economic powerhouse in the African continent.

In spite of the creation of marketing boards in the exporting countries and other forms of commodity price stabilization schemes as, for example, provided by the EU under the Lomé Convention (now replaced by the Cotonou Convention), farmers have almost always been exposed to devastating price fluctuations. While the creation of regional markets could help organize better all information about supply and demand for all agricultural products both at the local and national levels, producers of export products (cocoa, coffee, cotton, etc.) could be better off with the creation of a regional futures market. The creation of all these markets could in return translate into additional job-creation.

It is imperative that all infrastructures be upgraded and scaled up in order to provide convenient first-class service to users both within and outside the country. The country already has one of the longest quality networks of roads (about 82,000 km of classified roads) in the entire continent. Every region of the country is accessible by airplane and by car with a network of more than 8,000 miles of paved roads (8.7% of roads were paved in 1990 and 9.7% in 1996; WDI 1999). The port of Abidjan is one of the biggest, well-equipped and busiest ports in Africa. Its capacity could easily be doubled with the construction of an additional terminal. The port of San Pedro could easily be upgraded in order to handle all freight for free-trade areas and land-locked neighbouring countries. The telecommunications sector has expanded rapidly since the opening of the sector to private Mobile telephony licence operators (Orange, Telecel, and Comstar) and the privatisation of Côte d'Ivoire Télécom in 1997. Every city in the country is already accessible by phone. With the development of the telecommunications sector, Internet providers and users have also increased substantially.

5 Policy Recommendations and Conclusions

As international efforts to mend the socio-political pieces and to bring the country back to normalcy seem to be paying off, several policies will be needed to jump-start the economy. They include but are not limited to the following:

1. Restoring the power of the state - by strengthening all institutions with the aid of the UN and international partners - could be considered as the first requirement for recovery. Further decentralisation of the state apparatus will be needed for more effectiveness in the development and maintenance of infrastructures (road network, airports, ports, ICT, transport system, schools, hospitals, sports facilities, etc…) that is essential to facilitate the expansion of social and business activity. In that regard, government should create a fully computerized "one-stop shop" to (i) issue business licenses to prospective investors in record time, and to (ii) provide guidance on request to help resolve legal matters. In a smaller scale, this could be implemented in areas established as FZs (Free Zones) and could be part of government initiatives under the New Partnership for Africa's Development (NEPAD). The government should take the lead in delineating milestones for the economic recovery, and defining new growth objectives in a new development plan that features a timeline to break away from primary commodity dependency.
2. Promoting agricultural reforms. This calls for (1) the creation of a well established framework for legal property rights; (2) an incentive system with fiscal incentives (including tax reductions) and financial incentives (including loans, investment grants, insurance systems, input subsidies, etc.) to encourage diversification, new production and conservation techniques/methods, cooperatives and other partnerships in the operation of agricultural activities; (3) substantive investments in research & development in agriculture with specific goals for maximising biological diversity with on-farm experiments to study various combinations of trees to create

a shade canopy, favourable soil characteristics, crop genotypes, and yields. An optimal combination should generate revenues from such a diverse pattern of agricultural production that a huge production of a single crop would become needless. In such a scheme, extension services should provide assistance to farmers until they reach a self-sufficient level of operation.

3. Developing legal and financial procedures to value farm assets as collateral so as to facilitate access to credit on local financial markets. This requires the existence of marketable land/property rights well crafted for this purpose, and a reliable legal system to enforce it.
4. Establishing a new social contract between government and all economic agents based on agreed principles of respect, trust, accountability, responsibility, civil rights, moral ethics, etc. at all levels of society. This should re-affirm the choice of economic liberalism and promote policies rewarding individual performance while punishing corruption, cheating, robberies, and all other forms of crimes against the living and the environment.

In this paper we show that the strategy of openness adopted by Côte d'Ivoire and amplified by the globalisation phenomenon has positively affected the short-run economic growth in Côte d'Ivoire. In the long run however, based on the current setting, openness is expected to have a negative effect while globalisation is expected to have a positive effect on the country's economy. More importantly, we find that the current crisis situation could be attributed in part to the national choices made by the country during the early and later years of its development, but also to international factors that affected the national economy. Fundamental institutional and economic reforms are necessary to bring about changes that are necessary to turn the country around, with policies that encourage more consumption of local products, and production systems that help process the majority of primary commodities before exporting them.

References

Amin, Samir (1967): Développement du capitalisme en Côte d'Ivoire, Paris, Les éditions de minuit.

African Development Bank / OECD (2004): African Economic Outlook, Paris: OECD and AfDB: Abidjan.

Awudu, Abdulai and Jaquet, Philippe (2002): Export and Economic Growth: Cointegration and Causality Evidence for Côte d'Ivoire, in: African Development Review vol. 14 (1), pp. 1-17.

Azam, Jean-Paul and Christian Morisson, 1994, La faisabilité politique de l'ajustement en Côte d'Ivoire et au Maroc, OCDE, Paris.

Baldwin, Robert E. (2003): Openness and growth: what's the empirical relationship? NBER Working Paper No. 9578 (March).

Barro, Robert (1991): Economic growth in a cross section of countries, Quarterly Journal of Economics 106 (2), 407-443.

Batra, Ravi (1992): The fallacy of free trade", Review of International Economics, 1(1), pp. 19-31.

Batra, Ravi and Slottje, Daniel J. (1993): Trade policy and poverty in the United States: theory and evidence, 1947-1990, in: Review of International Economics, 1(3), pp. 189-208.

CCI (Centre du Commerce International CNUCED/OMC) (1999): Guide à l'intention des entreprises: Le système commercial mondial, 2ème éd. Genève: CCI/CS, 1999.xxvi, pp. 348.

Chauveau, Jean-Pierre (2000): Question foncière et construction nationale en Côte d'Ivoire, Politique africaine, n. 78, pp. 94-125.

Cogneau, Denis and Sandrine Mesplé-Somps (2003): Les illusions perdues de l'économie ivoirienne et la crise politique, Africaine contemporaine, n 206, pp. 87-104.

Conte, Bernard (2004): Côte d'Ivoire: clientélisme, ajustement et conflit, DT/101//2004, CED, Université Bordeaux IV, France.

Edwards, Sebastian (1992): Trade orientation, distortions, and growth in developing countries, in: Journal of Development Economics, 39(1), pp. 31-57.

FAO, 2003: Commodity Market review (2003-2004): Food and Agriculture Organization of the United Nations, Rome, Italy.

Fosu, Augustin Kwasi (1990a): Export Composition and the Impact of Exports on Economic Growth of Developing Economies, in: Economic Letters, 34, pp. 67-71.

Fosu, Augustin Kwasi (1990b): Export and Economic Growth: The African Case, in: World Development, 18 (6), pp. 831-835.

Grossman, Gene M. and Helpman, Elhanan (1992): Innovation and Growth: Technological Competition in the Global Economy, Boston: MIT Press.

Harrison, Ann (1996): Openness and growth: a time-series, cross-country analysis for developing countries, in: Journal of Development Economics, 48(2), pp. 419-447.

Hendry, F. David and Doornik, A. Jurgen (2001): Empirical Econometric Modelling Using PcGive, Timberlake consultant Press, London.

International Crisis Group, 2005: Côte d'Ivoire: Le pire est peut être à venir, Rapport Afrique N°90, 24 mars 2005.

Jang, J. Jin, 2000: Openness and Growth: an interpretation of empirical evidence from East Asian Countries, in: Journal of International Trade and Economic Development, 9(1), pp. 15-17.

Ministère du Plan, République de Côte d'Ivoire, 1971: Plan quinquennal de développement économique, social et culturel 1971-1975, Imprimerie R. Royer, Paris.

Randolph, Jan, 2001: G-Index 'globalization measured...', World Markets Research Centre, August 2001, pp. 33.

Rodriguez, Ferdinand and Rodrik, Dani (1999): Trade policy and economic growth: a skeptic's guide to the cross-national evidence, NBER Working Paper w7081.

Romer, David (1993): Openness and Inflation: Theory and Evidence, in: Quarterly Journal of Economics 108(4), pp. 869-903.

Solow, M. Robert (1957): Technical change and the aggregate production function, in: Review of Economics and Statistics, 39, 312-20.

Stiglitz, E. Joseph (2003): Globalisation and growth in emerging markets and the new economy, in: Journal of Policy Modelling, 25(5), pp. 505-524.

Subramanian, Arvind and Tamisira, T. Natalia (2003): Is Africa Integrated in the Global Economy?, in: IMF Staff Paper, 50(3), pp. 352-371.

Terra, Cristina (1998): Openness and Inflation: Theory and Evidence, in: Quarterly Journal of Economics, 113(2), pp. 641-652.

UNCTAD (2003): Handbook of Statistics, Geneva: United Nations, 2003.

UNCTAD (2004): Handbook of Statistics, Geneva: United Nations, 2004.

WDI (World Bank Development Indicators) (1999): World Development Indicators, Washington D.C.: World Bank.

World Bank (2003): World Development Indicators database 2003, Washington D.C.: The World Bank.

Yanikkaya, Halit (2003): Trade openness and economic growth: a cross-country empirical investigation, in: Journal of Development Economics, 72(1), pp. 57-89.

Zywietz, Daniel (2003): Measuring Globalisation, constructing a modified indicator, International Centre for Integrative Studies (ICIS), Faculty of General Sciences, Maastricht University, p. 71.

Annex

Map 1: Vegetation Map of Côte d'Ivoire and Neighbouring Countries

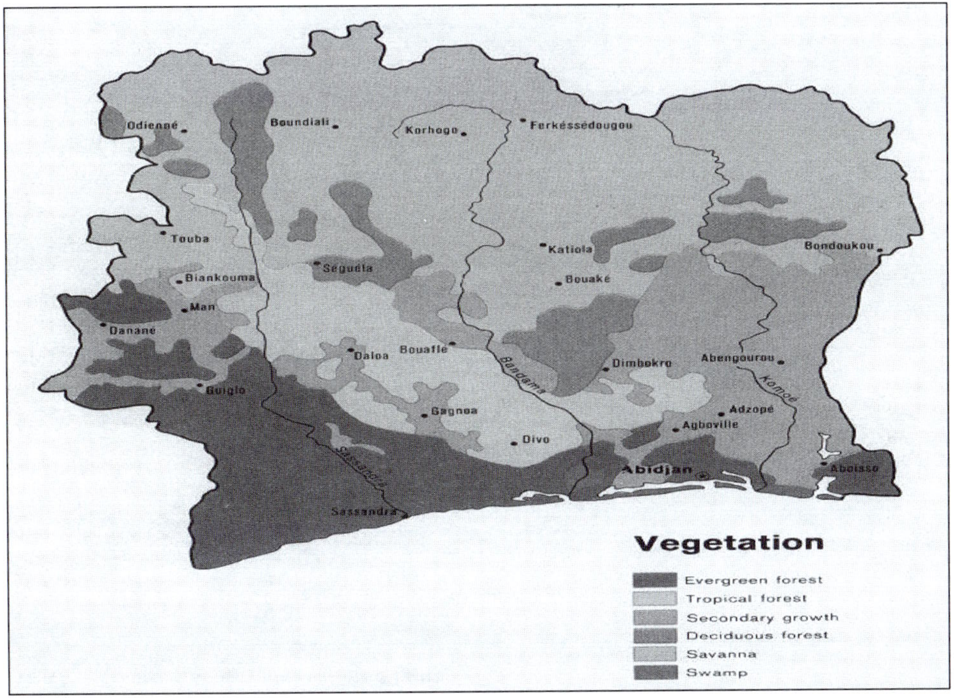

Source: *Perry-Castañeda Library Map Collection,* http://www.lib.utexas.edu/maps/cote_d'ivoire.html.

Map 2: Economic Activity Map of Côte d'Ivoire

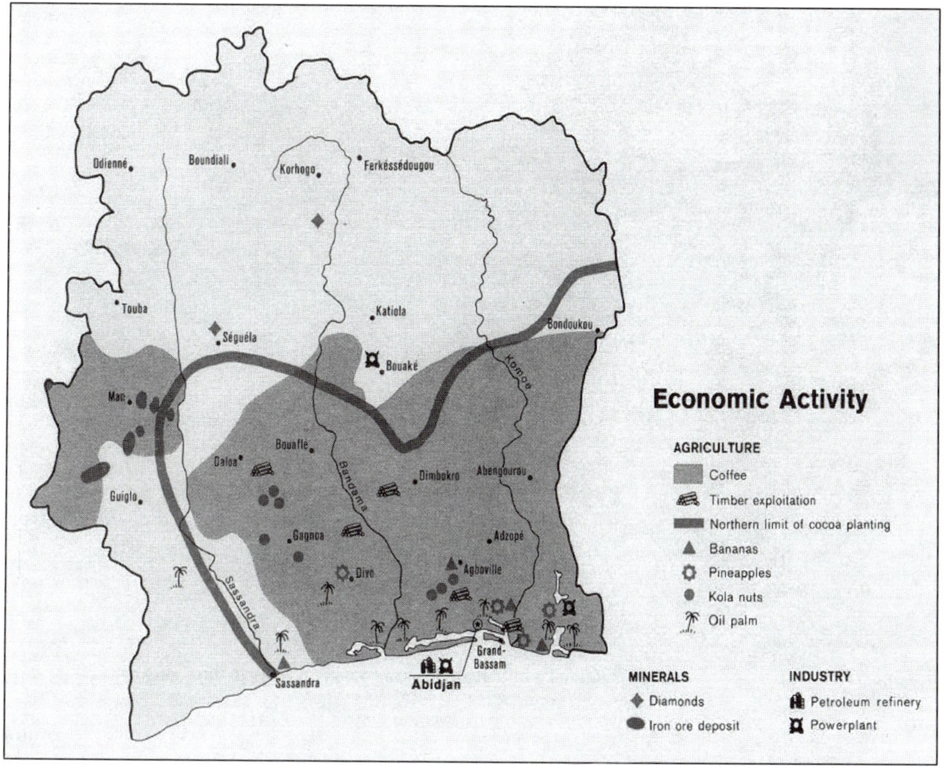

Source: *Perry-Castañeda Library Map Collection, http://www.lib.utexas.edu/maps/cote_d'ivoire.html.*

Map 3: Conflict Situation Map

Averting Anarchy in Nigeria: Practical Proposals for Lifting the Oil Curse

Afeikhena Jerome[1]

1 Introduction

Nigeria presents key challenges for development practitioners. When she attained political independence in 1960, there was a latent optimism regarding the attainment of sustained and rapid growth, poverty reduction and improvement in living standards. Unfortunately, the development trajectory has largely been unstable. Despite its bountiful oil resources (ranking tenth in oil and gas reserves, and being the sixth biggest exporter in the world) and a cumulative value of revenues estimated at about US$350 billion over a 35-year period (Sala-i-Martin and Subramanian, 2003), Nigeria's economic performance has been startlingly poor. Between 1970 and 2000, the number of Nigerians living in poverty on less than a dollar a day had risen to 70 percent from 36 percent, and inequality widened considerably. Per capita income has suffered significant erosion since the peak in the early 1970s that occurred, not coincidentally, when oil prices were at a historic high - per capita income fell from $1,113 in 1974 to $780 in 1980 and to $300 in 2002 (Jerome, 2004).

What then can be done to alter the trajectory of a country that, along with South Africa, holds the key to the elusive African renaissance? This is rendered more urgent by the recent upsurge in the price of crude oil in the international market that has revived the debate on how to manage Nigeria's "excess oil revenue". Furthermore, Nigeria is on the cusp of consolidating its

1 The comments of participants at the Workshop on "Africa- Escaping the Primary Commodity Dilemma", held at the University of Bremen, Germany, from November 17-19, 2004 are gratefully acknowledged. I am grateful to Adam Swallow for useful suggestions and materials. Discussions with Karl Wohlmuth have also been very helpful.

democratic transition with the successful completion of a second consecutive democratic election that is unprecedented in Nigeria's history. Moreover, over the last decade, the Atlantic Ocean off the coast of Western and Southern Africa has become one of the most promising oil exploration areas in the world. A convergence of interests between African governments, multinational oil companies, International Financial Institutions, and Northern governments is propelling the rush to exploit Africa's oil reserves (Gary and Karl, 2003). Six countries in the region, namely Nigeria, Angola, Gabon, Equatorial Guinea, São Tome, Cameroon and, more recently, Chad and Sudan have become key players in the world's energy stake and more are likely to join their ranks in the near future.

The oil curse is by no means unique to Nigeria. For many oil-producing developing countries and countries in transition, petroleum revenues make up a substantial share of gross domestic product, national and state budgets, and foreign exchange earnings. The potential to utilize oil revenue to create wealth is tremendous but, more often than not, it is mismanaged. Controlling for income level, countries that are highly dependent on revenues from oil and other minerals score lower on the United Nations Human Development Index (HDI), exhibit greater corruption, have a greater probability of conflict in any five-year period, and have larger shares of their population in poverty (Palley, 2003). Birdsall and Subramanian (2004), for example, estimated that of the 34 less developed countries that have substantial oil and natural gas reserves, 12 of them have annual per capita income that is below $1500, and up to half of their population live on less than $1 per day. Historically, countries rich in natural resources tend to be blighted by corruption, conflict, poor economic growth, low public spending, and poor human rights. Natural resource income has been associated with economic stagnation, the destruction of other export activities (Gelb, 1988; and Sachs and Warner, 2001), and violent conflict (Collier and Hoeffler, 2004).

Clearly, Nigeria exhibits all the symptoms of the malaise of the oil curse. Sala-I-Martin and Subramanian (2003: 12) noted that:

> "Nowhere are all the pathologies associated with oil as clearly manifest as in Nigeria. ...Its 'pirates in power' have plundered Nigeria's oil wealth to a tune of perhaps $100 billion. The explosion in windfall-financed expenditures has also provided opportunities for kickbacks. All these forces have contributed to poor economic growth and other staggeringly malign results."

While Nigeria is emblematic of many oil-producing developing countries, the country provides some of the most egregious examples of rent seeking and corruption that undermine good governance. Oil has so far exerted a negative and non-linear relationship on growth through its deleterious impact on institutional quality. Proper management of petroleum revenues depends on a number of factors, including institutional capacity, and more importantly, the quality of governance. Where governance is poor, there is little chance that sound policies will be implemented. Furthermore, in weak institutional environments, petroleum revenues are associated with the further erosion of governance.

Against this background, this study appraises the paradoxical links between oil and the development crisis in Nigeria, and how oil can contribute to sustainable development and poverty reduction. Drawing from the literature and best practices elsewhere, it focuses on positive, practical and achievable approaches that key actors, including government, extractive companies, and the civil society can use to lift the 'resource curse' and to improve the developmental impact of oil in Nigeria.

The study contends that oil dependency and the allure it generated of great wealth through government contracts spawned several economic distortions of unprecedented proportion in Nigeria, including corruption, which has become endemic in recent years, with the oil boom and busts distorting the incentive structure. The use of oil resources to finance large-scale public expenditure programmes introduced large-scale corruption in Nigeria. More than the Dutch disease, waste of resources and poor institutional quality stemming from oil appear to have been primarily responsible for Nigeria's poor long-run economic performance. The current global push for transparency in the oil industry is desirable but not sufficient. Even if governments are committed to transparency, translating revenues to tangible benefits remains a formidable task.

The paper is structured in six sections. Apart from this introductory Section, Section 2 presents the analytical framework, while section 3 presents an overview of the Nigerian Economy. The debilitating effect of oil is evaluated in Section 4, and section 5 appraises practical solutions for lifting the oil curse in Nigeria, and then section 6 concludes.

2 Analytical Framework

A recurring theme in the theoretical and empirical literature is that, counter-intuitively, the discovery of a natural resource can lead to a decrease in the rate of economic growth and development. On average, countries with a large endowment of natural resources perform worse than countries that are less well endowed. This phenomenon has variedly been described as oil curse, resource curse, or paradox of plenty (Karl, 1997). The failure of resource-led growth has been extensively investigated in the literature. The empirical regularity however owes much to research by Sachs and Warner (1995) that, so far, has presented the most comprehensive evidence worldwide. Based on standard cross-section growth regressions, they demonstrated that countries with exports concentrated in the natural resource sector in 1970 tended to grow relatively slowly, on average, by about 1 percent per year during the period 1970–89. The results are robust even after controlling for institutional quality, initial income levels and trade policies, among other variables (Sachs and Warner, 1995). Variations of this basic result can be found in Leite and Weidmann (1999) and in Bravo-Ortega and De Gregorio (2001). Case studies presented in Auty (1990) and Gelb (1988) also show the adverse effects of resource abundance on growth. However, some of these studies have been challenged. Lederman and Maloney (2003) raised doubts about the robustness of the Sachs and Warner findings while Hausman and Rigobon (2003), in spite of supporting the generally inverse relationship, point out that oil-rich countries performed well economically in the 1980s when oil was doing well-contrary to the prediction of these studies.

Understanding its causes has not been a straightforward task. Sachs and Warner (1995) and Leite and Weidmann (1999) attempt to unravel the potential channel of causation, but without great success. More recently, de Soysa (2002) and Collier and Hoeffler (2004), using new models of conflicts, have shown that natural resources considerably increase the chances of civil conflict in a country. Collier and Hoeffler (2004), for instance, demonstrated that the effect of natural resources on conflict is strong and non-linear. A country that has no natural resources faces a probability of civil conflict of 0.5 percent, whereas a country with a natural resources-to-GDP share of 26 percent faces a probability of 23 percent. Sala-i-Martin and Subramanian (2003) use cross-section analysis to demonstrate that stunted institutional development - a catch-all for a range of related pathologies, including corruption, weak governance, rent seeking, plunder, etc. - is a problem intrinsic to countries that own natural resources such as oil or minerals. The empirical evidence on causality remains however weak as these studies are mainly suggestive.

The theoretical literature has been much more successful at demonstrating causality. It identifies several channels of causation from natural resource abundance to lower growth. Natural resources generate rents that lead to rapacious rent seeking (the voracity effect), whose adverse manifestation on long-term growth is felt through political economy effects (Lane and Tornell, 1995) and increased corruption (Mauro, 1995 and Leite and Weidmann, 1999).

The study by Isham et. al. (2003) provides an excellent summary of the mechanisms of causation identified in both economics and political science literature. In the latter, emphasis is placed on the "rentier" effects, whereby large revenues from natural resources allow governments to mollify dissent and to avoid accountability, insulating governments from pressures for institutional reform and modernization. Rentier states tend to be autonomous in the sense that natural resource rents allow them to be more detached and less accountable since they do not need to levy taxes. Mahdavy (1970), Yates (1996) and Karl (1997) use this argument to explain the lack of pressure (from below) for democratic change in the Middle East. However, Wantchekon (1999) is of the persuasion that the "state autonomy" argument lacks empirical support and predictive power. First, the lack of pressure from below for democratic change is common to most developing countries (Diamond, Linz and Lipset, 1989). Thus petroleum-rich states are no exception. Second, Okruhlik (1999) suggested that throughout the Middle East and North Africa, in both oil and non-oil states, there are demands for social justice and political reforms. He cited the case of Saudi Arabia, where political opposition to the ruling family is fuelled by the fact that prosperity of private citizens is dependent upon the acquisition of government wealth, with access to contracts, information, jobs in the public sector, or infrastructure governed by family relations, friendship and religious affiliation. Finally, natural resource ownership makes countries susceptible to fluctuating revenues and the Dutch disease. Prices of natural resources are very volatile, causing macroeconomic difficulties in the management of large and fluctuating resources in the absence of export diversification.

The Dutch disease[2] is the tendency for the real exchange rate to appreciate overtly in response to positive shocks, which in turn leads to a contraction of the tradable sector. The deindustrialization of a nation's economy occurs when the discovery and exploitation of a natural resource raises the value of that nation's currency, making manufactured goods less competitive with other nations, increasing imports and decreasing exports. While the Dutch disease model explains the sectoral shifts in the economy that often result from a natural resource boom, it neglects the importance of governance and of political regimes in this process.

---

[2] The phenomenon was first observed in the Netherlands in the 1960s, when large reserves of natural gas were first exploited in the adjoining North Sea. The Netherlands, after its discovery of North Sea gas and oil, found itself plagued with growing unemployment and workforce disability (many of those who could not get jobs found disability benefits to be more generous than unemployment benefits).

Oil-exporting countries differ considerably with respect to the relative importance of oil to their economies, the level of oil production and the reserve base, the maturity of the oil industry, the ownership structure and control, taxation, the stage of development of the non-oil sector, and the political structure (Ojemeruaye, 2004). Thus, using such categories as political stability, party systems, legitimacy of government, transparency, stability and quality of policies, political freedom and the role of civil society organizations, Eifert, Gelb, and Tallroth (2003) have classified oil-exporting countries into five main groups: mature democracies (Norway, the state of Alaska in the United States, and the Canadian province of Alberta); factional democracies (Venezuela, Ecuador, Colombia, and Nigeria 1979-1983 and post-1999); paternalistic autocracies (Saudi Arabia, Kuwait and Oman); predatory autocracies (Iraq pre-2004, Gabon, and Nigeria pre-1999); and reformist autocracies (Indonesia, Libya, and Iran). Table 1 presents a characterization of these groups.

Table 1: Political Economy Classification of Oil Exporters

Political features	Institutional implications	Economic implications
Mature democracy • Stable party system • Range of social consensus • Strong, competent, insulated bureaucracy • Competent, professional judicial system • Highly educated electorate	• Long-term policy horizon • Policy stability, transparency • High competitiveness, low transaction costs • Strong private/traded sector, pro-stabilization interests vis-à-vis pro-spending interests	• Saving likely • Expenditure-smoothing, stabilization • Rents transferred to public through government providing social services and insurance or direct transfers
Factional democracy • Government and parties often unstable relative to interest groups • Political support gained through clientelistic ties and provision of patronage	• Short-term policy horizon • Policy instability, nontransparency, high transaction costs • Strong state role in production	• Saving very difficult • Procyclical expenditure; instability

Continuation on next page.

Continuation of table 1 from previous page.

Political features	Institutional implications	Economic implications
Factional democracy • Wide social disparities, lack of consensus • Politicized bureaucracy and judicial system	• Strong interests attached directly to state expenditures; politically weak private non-oil sector and pro-stabilization interests	• Rents transferred to different interests and to public through subsidies, policy distortions, public employment
Paternalistic autocracy • Stable government; legitimacy originally from traditional role, maintained through rent distribution, strong cultural elements of consensus, clientelistic, and nationalistic patterns • Bureaucracy provides both services and public employment	• Long-term horizon • Policy stability, non-transparency • Low competitiveness, high transaction costs • Strong state role in production • Strong interests attached directly to state expenditures • Weak private sector	• Procyclical expenditure, mixed success with stabiliza-tion • Risk of unsustainable long-term spending trajectory leading to political crisis • Little economic diversification
Reformist autocracy • Stable government, legitimized by develop-ment • Social range of consensus toward development • Constituency in non-oil traded sectors • Insulated technocracy	• Long-term horizon • Policy stability, non-transparency • Drive for competitiveness, low transaction costs • Strong constituency for stabilization and fiscal restraint	• Expenditure-smoothing, stabiliza-tion • State investment complementary to competitive private sector • Active exchange rate management to limit Dutch disease
Predatory autocracy • Unstable government, legitimized by military force • Lack of consensus-building mechanisms • Bureaucracy exists as mechanism of rent capture and distribution; corrupt judicial system • Little or no civic counterweight	• Short-term horizon • Policy instability, non-transparency • Low competitiveness, high transaction costs • Spending interests strong vis-à-vis private sector or pro-stabilization interests	• No saving • Highly procyclical expenditure • Very high government consumption, rent absorption by elites through petty corrup-tion and patronage, capital flight

Source: Eifert, Gelb, and Tallroth (2003).

Apart from mature democracies, ensuring cautious use of oil income has been a continuing struggle. While traditional and modernizing autocracies have demonstrated their ability to sustain long decision horizons and to implement developmental policies, resistance to transparency and the danger of oil-led spending and expenditure commitments becoming the major legitimizing force behind the state may pose risk to the long-term sustainability of their current development strategies. In contrast, little positive effect can be expected from the politically unstable predatory autocracies, which typically have very short policy horizons and sometimes show the characteristics of "roving bandit" regimes. Factional democracies, with weak political parties and highly personalized politics, present particular challenges because they lack a sufficiently effective political system to create a consensus among strong competing interests. Special attention will be needed to increase transparency and to raise public awareness in these countries. And oil rent makes it more difficult to sustain a constituency in favour of sound, longer-run economic management because it weakens incentives for agents to support checks and balances that impinge on their individual plans to appropriate the rents. Thus, technical solutions such as the establishment of oil stabilization funds and budgetary reforms to enhance transparency and efficiency in the use of oil rents will not work well unless constituencies can be developed in support of such measures.

The oil industry in Africa is currently at the epicenter of corruption charges amidst international efforts to bring greater transparency to the continent's resource exploration. This is vividly illustrated in Angola, where an International Monetary Fund fiscal audit has been unable to account for hundreds of millions of dollars of oil revenues (International Monetary Fund, 2003). In Nigeria, Cameroon, and the Republic of the Congo, oil wealth has failed to generate development and has instead generated deep-seated corruption that retards growth. Sudan is marked by strife over oil. Conspicuously poor governance in Nigeria and in Angola, as well as in second-tier emergent producers, such as São Tome and Principe, Equatorial Guinea, and Chad, undermines both national and regional stability (Jerome, Adjibolosoo and Busari, 2005).

In an effort to combat corruption in the oil industry, a push for transparency and liberalization has increased pressure on international oil operators to open their books. The "Publish What You Pay" (PWYP) campaign, sponsored by George Soros' Open Society Institute, and Global Witness, supported by over 130 NGOs, has called on international extraction companies to publish net taxes, fees, royalties, and other payments made so that the civil society can more accurately assess the amount of money misappropriated and can lobby for full transparency in local government spending.

Underlining the effort, British Prime Minister Tony Blair announced the Extractive Industries Transparency Initiative (EITI), endorsed by a coalition of institutional investors during the World Summit on Sustainable Development in Johannesburg in September 2002. Concurrently, civil-society organizations demand budget transparency and monitor spending on the national level. In the case of the Chad-Cameroon oil pipeline project, such initiatives integrate stakeholders at the national level and international institutions such as the World Bank, the latter being involved in financing the project.

Observers hope that this new transparency will lessen corruption and will enable citizens of these countries to have greater insight in how their governments spend national oil wealth. In the ongoing debate, it must be noted that full disclosure is not sufficient. Weak institutional capacity precludes host countries from using information effectively, regardless of how complete and accessible it may be.

3 Country Background Information

Nigeria is a country of paradox. The country is richly endowed in material and human resources. Aside from its immense mineral wealth, of which its oil and gas resources are currently the most prominent, the country is also endowed with rich agricultural lands capable of sustaining a wide variety of crops, and with one of the best human resource bases in the developing world, in addition to the domestic market potentials which its demographic advantage confers (Institute for Democracy and Electoral Assistance, 2001: 152).

With a GDP of $58.4 billion and a population of 136.5 million in 2003 (World Bank, 2005), Nigeria is the fourth largest economy in Africa and by far Africa's most populous country (every fifth person in Sub-Saharan Africa is a Nigerian). In global terms, Nigeria is said to constitute 2 per cent of the world population and is expected to be among the five or six most populated countries in the world by 2025 (UNDP, 2001).

Proved oil reserves are estimated to 35.876 billion barrels[3] in January 2006. With a daily production of 2.55 million barrels per day in 2004, Nigeria is currently ranked as the twelfth major oil producer in the world. As well the country is an influential member of the Organization of Petroleum Exporting Countries (OPEC). With natural gas reserves of 184.660 Trillion Cubic Feet in January 2006, the tenth largest in the world, Nigeria is poised to become a major exporter of natural gas. Nigeria has numerous solid mineral deposits including coal, bitumen, and gypsum that have barely been harnessed.

Several years of economic mismanagement and corruption have restricted economic growth, leaving Nigeria's GDP per capita at $350 in 2003, and placing the nation amongst the 20 poorest nations in the world (World Bank, 2005). The GDP grew by an average of just 1.6 percent throughout the 1980s, 2.8 percent in the 1990s (leaving the per capita growth rate at zero (Iwayemi, 1994), and 3.6 per between 1999 and 2003 (with a per capita growth rate of 0.8 percent per annum, which is far lower than the 4.2 percent per capita growth rate needed to significantly reduce poverty (Jerome, 2004). Relative to its own history and in comparison with other countries in Africa and in Asia (especially Indonesia, which is comparable to Nigeria in many aspects), its level of economic development over the decades became more and more disappointing (Jerome, 2004). There is also spatial and sectoral unevenness in the distribution of the GDP. The real sector is still dominated by the primary production sector — agriculture (41%), which is predominantly peasantry with low and declining productivity, and crude oil (13%), while the secondary sector, especially manufacturing, has stagnated at 5 - 7% of GDP, making Nigeria one of the least industrialized countries in Africa (Central Bank of Nigeria, 2000).

Nigeria is highly indebted (external and domestic debt amounts to about 70 percent of GDP), and relations with donors are periodically strained, chiefly over the government's persistent refusal to clear the external debt stock, which stood at $33.9 billion in 2003 (World Bank, 2005), largely as a result of borrowing heavily in the 1970s on the back of high oil prices by successive military leaders. In November 2005, Nigeria received Paris Club approval for a historic debt-relief deal that by March 2006 should eliminate

---

3 All petroleum and gas data are sourced from United States Energy Information Administration EIA hompeage www.eia.doe.gov (Accessed 23/03/06). Proved reserves of crude oil are the estimated quantities which geological and engineering data demonstrate with reasonable certainty can be recovered in future years from known reservoirs, assuming existing economic and operating conditions.

$30 billion worth of Nigeria's total $34 billion external debt. The deal first requires that Nigeria repay roughly $12 billion in arrears to its bilateral creditors. Nigeria would then be allowed to buy back its remaining debt stock at a discount. The deal also commits Nigeria to more intensified IMF reviews.

Nigeria continues to rank low on most development indices, with an alarming increase in poverty incidence over the last twenty years. The UNDP Human Development Report (2004) ranked Nigeria as 152nd out of 175 countries in its Human Development Index for that year, down from 148 out of a total of 173 in 2003. Life expectancy is only 44.9 years, while combined gross enrolment is an atrocious 45 per cent. Latest estimates of income poverty by Ali-Akpajiak and Pyke (2003) suggest that about two- thirds of Nigerians, more than 80 million people, survive on less than $1 per day (from a headcount of approximately 28% nationally in 1980, poverty incidence has risen to about 66%, equally among the urban and rural population). A relatively short period of increase in economic growth during the 1980s did result in a temporary decrease in poverty during that time. But this was followed by a sharp increase and a relative stagnation of the level of poverty incidence during the 1990s. Nigerian poor currently account for 6 per cent of the world's total poor (Jerome, 2004).

Across the country, the poor are not a homogeneous group. With 78% of the population living in rural areas, the rural poor represent the largest overall segment of the poor (Ali-Akpajiak and Pyke, 2003). While all the three geographic zones of the South had much lower poverty incidence in the 1980s, relative to the North, regional variations have now largely disappeared (World Bank, 2004). A particularly worrisome feature of poverty in Nigeria is the high and growing youth unemployment with estimates for urban areas ranging between 40 and 60 percent (Central Bank of Nigeria, 2000).

Nigeria is composed of about 250 ethnic groups, with diverse languages and religious faiths. The largest ethnic groups are the Hausa-Fulani in the North, the Igbo in the Southeast, and the Yoruba in the Southwest. Regional, ethnic, and religious differences have contributed to the country's instability, and Nigeria's development will depend on advancing a political formula that accounts for the country's diverse characteristics. Table 2 presents Nigeria's key economic indicators.

Table 2: Nigeria: Key Indicators

	1999	2002	2003
People			
Population, total (million)	123.9	133.2	136.5
Population growth (annual %)	2.5	2.4	2.4
Life expectancy (years)	47.5	45.3	44.9
Fertility rate (births per woman)	..	5.7	5.6
Infant mortality rate (per 1,000 live births)	..	..	98.0
Prevalence of HIV, total (% of population aged 15-49)	..	..	5.4
Literacy rate, adult male (% of males ages 15 and above)	71.0	74.4	..
Literacy rate, adult female (% of females ages 15 and above)	54.3	59.4	..
Primary completion rate, total (% age group)	..	82.0	..
Primary completion rate, female (% age group)	..	73.0	..
Environment			
Surface area (thousand/sq. km)	923.8	923.8	923.8
Access to improved water source (% of total pop.)	..	60.0	..
Access to improved sanitation (% of urban pop.)	..	48.0	..
Energy use per capita (kg of oil equivalent)	697.9	718.3	..
Electricity use per capita (kWh)	69.2	68.2	
Economy			
GNI, Atlas method (billion current US$)	32.7	39.6	47.5
GNI per capita, Atlas method (current US$)	260.0	300.0	350.0
GDP (billion current $)	34.8	46.7	58.4 n
GDP growth (annual %)	1.1	1.5	10.7
GDP implicit price deflator (annual % growth)	12.3	3.9	21.0
Value added in agriculture (% of GDP)	36.6	31.2	26.4
Value added in industry (% of GDP)	35.2	43.8	49.5
Value added in services (% of GDP)	28.2	25.0	24.2
Exports of goods and services (% of GDP)	36.9	40.8	50.0
Imports of goods and services (% of GDP)	41.1	41.0	40.9
Gross capital formation (% of GDP)	23.4	26.1	22.7
Technology and infrastructure			
Fixed lines and mobile telephones (per 1,000 people)	4.4	19.2	32.5
Personal computers (per 1,000 people)	6.4	7.1	..
Internet users (per 1,000 people)	0.5	3.5	6.1
Paved roads (% of total)	30.9	..	..
Aircraft departures	8,400	10,800	9,000

Continuation on the next page.

Continuation of table 2 from the previous page.

	1999	2002	2003
Trade and finance			
Trade in goods as a share of GDP (%)	64.5	48.5	53.3
Trade in goods as a share of goods GDP (%)	88.5	64.0	69.8
Foreign direct investment, net inflows (billion current US$)	1.0	1.3	1.2
Present value of debt (billion current US$)	..	31.5	33.9
Total debt service (% of exports of goods and services)	6.9	..	..
Short-term debt outstanding (billion current US$)	6.5	2.3	3.4
Aid per capita (current US$)	1.2	2.4	2.3

Note: *".." indicates not available.*
Source: *World Bank (2005).*

The return to civilian rule in 1999 has given rise to new hopes that Nigeria will finally begin to fulfill the task to exploit its enormous economic potential. President Obasanjo's ambitious economic reforms aim to combat entrenched corruption and to reduce poverty while establishing macroeconomic stability. The government has made an expeditious start on an ambitious program of reforms. In 2004, the government put forth a comprehensive strategic vision for addressing the country's deep-rooted macroeconomic instability and structural bottlenecks.

The National Economic Empowerment and Development Strategy (NEEDS), the equivalent of a home-grown Poverty Reduction Strategy Paper (PRSP), covering the four-year period 2004 to 2007, aims to make the private sector the engine of growth, through privatisation, deregulation and liberalisation, accompanied by infrastructure development, especially in electricity and transport. It sets a growth objective of 6 per cent per annum, led by the agricultural and manufacturing sectors, rather than oil.

Largely as a result of the oil price increases, real GDP growth picked up strongly to 10.7 percent in 2003 and was estimated to have reverted to 4 per cent in 2004 (AfDB/OECD, 2005). So far, however, little progress has been achieved in overcoming obstacles to private sector development, such as unreliable electric power, lack of access to financing for small and medium enterprises, and a pervasive climate of strife and insecurity.

4 The Debilitating Effects of Oil in Nigeria

The issue of economic regress in Nigeria has evolved considerable discussion in the literature (Faruquee, 1994; Iwayemi, 1994; Central Bank of Nigeria, 2000; and Jerome, 2004). Oil wealth is perhaps the main cause of the pervasiveness of rent-seeking activities and corruption in Nigeria. Oil dependency, and the allure it generated of great wealth through government contracts, spawned several economic distortions.

The performance of the Nigerian economy is inextricably linked with the performance of its oil sector. The oil sector accounts for 20 percent of the gross domestic product (GDP), 95 percent of total foreign exchange earnings and more than 80 percent of the governmental revenue base (Central Bank of Nigeria, 2000 and UNDP, 2001). Thus, the capacity of the government to support the process of economic development depends crucially on public revenues from the oil sector. There is a strong relationship between macroeconomic performance and the events in the petroleum market. The Nigerian economy experienced a robust real income growth in the 1970s during the oil boom period, but it contracted when oil prices weakened. The boom period was characterized by sharp improvements in the balance of trade, increases in public sector investments, and also increases in foreign borrowing. The increased availability of foreign credit has - via monetary effects on the balance of payments - reinforced the expansionary impact of the oil boom.

The inherent softness of the international oil market, the attendant collapse of oil prices especially since the early 1980s, and the lack of effective inter-sectoral balance pushed the economy into deep recession. The post-boom period witnessed a sharp contraction of the Nigerian economy, with internal and external imbalances. Nigeria was forced in the 1980s to adjust to two dramatic external shocks that produced real income contractions hardly seen anywhere in the developing world. Oil exports, which reached almost US$26 billion (at current prices) in 1980, declined to a level that oscillated between US$10.4 billion and US$12.6 billion in 1983-85 (Iwayemi, 1994). Again in 1986, oil exports fell to half their 1985 value and remained depressed until the outbreak of the Iraq war. Increased foreign borrowing during the boom period, facilitated by the willingness of international creditors to lend on expectations that the oil price increase was permanent, resulted in a large debt overhang.

Poor quality public sector investments made during the boom period failed to enhance the productive capacity of the economy. In the 1970s and in the early 1980s, high oil prices and high public revenues helped finance large public enterprises. Nigeria did not have adequate implementation capacity to manage sudden bursts of investment expenditure. Project selection criteria and procedures were lax, and most of the projects have turned out to be a drain on the economy. Due to the country's high propensity to import, about 80 per cent of government expenditure was recycled into foreign exchange (Faruquee, 1994). Cheap consumer imports, resulting from a chronically overvalued Naira, coupled with excessively high domestic production costs, due in part to erratic electricity and fuel supply, have pushed down industrial capacity utilization to less than 30 per cent (Central Bank, 2000). Many more Nigerian factories would have closed except for relatively low labour costs. Domestic manufacturers, especially of pharmaceuticals and textiles, have lost their ability to compete in traditional regional markets. Along with the endemic malaise of Nigeria's non-oil sectors, the economy continues to witness a massive growth of "informal sector" economic activities, estimated by some to be as high as 75 per cent of the total economy (Abumere, et. al. 1998).

At independence in 1960, the Nigerian economy was essentially agrarian. The configuration of the Nigerian economy was tilted in favour of production of exportable agricultural produce. Beginning from the 1970s, the fairly broad-based agricultural economy became considerably less diversified as the oil sector dominated production and trade structures. Oil became the dominant sector of the economy, accounting for more than 90 per cent of exports. Between 1972 and 1974, federal revenue from oil increased fivefold, constituting 80 percent of total revenue (Iwayemi, 1994).

Nigeria's new wealth radically affected the scope and the content of investment, production, and consumption patterns, the government's approach to economic management, and the policies and programmes that were implemented. Federal expenditures increased rapidly, doubling between 1973 and 1974, and again doubling between 1974 and 1975. Much of this increase in government expenditures went to investment. Measured at 1984 prices, the share of investment in GDP increased from less than 12 percent in 1971 to more than 25 percent in 1977 (Faruquee, 1994). The rapid growth of the public sector - and the construction boom that accompanied the massive investment program - led to the classic 'Dutch disease' syndrome in Nigeria, including the contraction of agriculture (the principal non-oil tradable sector), the appreciation of the real exchange rate, and the loss of the international competitiveness of agricultural exports. Although the appreciation of the exchange rate was an inevitable response to the oil boom, the use of oil resources to finance large-scale public expenditure programmes introduced large-scale political corruption in Nigeria. The perennial fuel crisis in Nigeria (the world's sixth largest producer of crude oil) can be attributed to corrupt practices, including hoarding, smuggling and willful damage to government-owned refineries. The country has been on a downward spiral since the last 20 years, even in the face of global economic prosperity. The 2004 Millennium Development Goal (MDGs) progress report for Nigeria indicates that it is unlikely that the country will be able to meet most of the goals by 2015, especially the goals relating to eradicating extreme poverty and hunger, reducing child and maternal mortality and combating HIV/AIDS, malaria and other diseases (Federal Republic of Nigeria, 2004).

The largely subsistence-based agricultural sector has suffered from years of mismanagement, inconsistent and poorly conceived government policies, and the lack of basic infrastructure. The oil boom of the 1970s led to the benign neglect of its strong agricultural base, and an unhealthy dependence on crude oil was created. The agricultural sector has failed to keep up with rapid population growth, and Nigeria, once a large net exporter of food in the early 1990s, became an importer of more than US$2 billion per year in foodstuffs a decade later (Central Bank of Nigeria, 2000).

Nigeria is no longer a major exporter of cocoa, groundnuts (peanuts), rubber, and of palm oil. Cocoa production, mostly from obsolete varieties and over age trees, is stagnant at around 180,000 tons annually compared to 300,000 tons 25 years ago (Iwayemi, 1994). An even more dramatic decline in groundnut and palm oil production also has taken place. Once the biggest poultry producer in Africa, corporate poultry output has been slashed from 40 million birds annually to about 18 million (Iwayemi, 1994). Import constraints limit the availability of many agricultural and food processing inputs for poultry and other sectors. Fisheries are poorly managed. Most critical for the country's future, Nigeria's land tenure system does not encourage long-term investment in technology or modern production methods and does not inspire the availability of rural credit.

Arguments over the distribution of oil wealth precipitated the end of the civilian rule in 1966 and the descent into civil war in 1967 and 1968, following the failed secession of Biafra. The Biafran Civil War, contested largely by Ibo secessionists and Nigerian federalists, was one of the bloodiest disputes over the control of oil revenues experienced in human history. Sources estimate 500,000 - 2 million casualties, mainly civilian deaths resulting from disease and starvation created by the conditions of war (Lacina and Gleditsch, 2005: 159). The federal government's response was to divide the rebellious region into small administrative units. This was done with the backing of many small southern minorities, such as the Adonis, one of Nigeria's approximately 250 linguistic minorities, who did not benefit locally from petroleum revenues dominated by the regional Ibo majority.

The transition from an agrarian economy to a "rentier economy" also translated into an increased centralization of administration and decision-making. This process was reinforced by military rule that resulted in the federal state assuming a position of unprecedented and disproportionate pre-eminence. Since gaining its independence from Britain in 1960, Nigeria has been controlled for twenty-eight of the last forty-five years by a succession of military governments. In May 1999, the democratically elected government of President Olusegun Obasanjo assumed power, and was re-elected to a second term in May 2003. The new democracy, albeit fragile, is threatened by recurrent political tension and heightened communal, religious and ethnic violence in the quest for access to economic resources and political power.

More than ever before, control of federal power conferred enormous power of patronage and influence, with consequences for the intensity of the struggle for access to, and the control for resources. Since independence in 1960, Nigeria has witnessed one civil war, six violent changes of government, substantial economic mismanagement, and widespread and persistent poverty. A World Bank report mentioned in the revenue fact sheet of the Organisation of Petroleum Exporting Countries (OPEC) has disclosed that about 80 per cent of Nigeria's oil and natural gas revenues accrue to just one per cent of the country's population.[4] The other 99 per cent of the population receive the remaining 20 per cent of the oil and gas revenues, leaving Nigeria with the second lowest per capita oil export earnings put at $212 (N 28,408) per person in 2004. The 2004 per capita earnings when compared to the $589 per person earned in 1980, the peak year for Nigerian oil export revenues (in inflation-adjusted terms), shows a decline of more than 50 per cent. The oil boom is also largely responsible for the massive capital flight such that Nigeria has in fact exported considerable amounts of its own private savings. UNIDO (2004: 7) estimated that by 1999 Nigeria had an estimated $107 billion of its private wealth held abroad. This represents about 70 percent of the total private wealth in Nigeria.

Corruption has been the bane of Nigeria's development, eroding any beneficial impact of the oil wealth. It has become endemic in recent years, with the oil boom and busts distorting the incentives structure. Many construction projects, financed by the revenues from the oil boom, were ruined through the use of inferior cement. Buildings would collapse and roads would wash away because of the use of poor materials and products. Although Nigeria earns billions of dollars every year from exporting crude

---

4 For details, see United States Energy Information Administration (2005).

oil, its domestic refineries have been laid waste by corruption and mismanagement, and so the country relies on expensive imports of refined fuels. Traditionally, governments have subsidised retail sales of petrol, diesel and kerosene to their people, more than three-quarters of whom live in abject poverty. It may take 146 years for Nigeria to wipe out corruption from its system going as revealed by the Transparency International (TI) Corruption Perceptions Index 2004[5] which ranked the country as the third most corrupt country in the world after Bangladesh and Haiti. This represents a marginal improvement on the 2003 report when Nigeria was ranked on the second worst position. Anecdotal evidence on the magnitude of corruption in Nigeria can be found in media sources and in proceedings of various tribunals set up to investigate cases of alleged financial impropriety on the part of government officials. The most prominent case perhaps is the looting of US $4 billion by the Abacha regime, a case in which the UK Financial Services Authority indicated that 15 British banks (Jerome, Adjibolosso, and Busari, 2005) were involved. A former Nigerian President was alleged to have awarded a $1 billion oil bloc in the nation's most prized oil-producing zone to his wife's hairdresser (Jerome, Adjibolosso, and Busari, 2005).

Ethnic conflicts around oil resources in the Niger Delta are a continued source of concern. Poor corporate relations with indigenous communities, vandalism of oil infrastructure, severe ecological damage, and personal security problems throughout the Niger Delta oil-producing region continue to plague Nigeria's oil sector. The Ijaw, Ogoni and other communities living in the oil-rich Niger Delta are up in arms against misrule from Abuja, and from the oil companies they demand a bigger share of the oil wealth. These localized conflicts are now much better financed through increasingly highly organized theft of oil from the region. Oil companies are feeling the backlash[6] from militants and other groups, which increasingly use

---

5 The Corruption Perceptions Index (CPI) is a poll of polls, reflecting the perceptions of business people and country analysts, both resident and non-resident. This year's Corruption Perceptions Index draws on 18 surveys provided to Transparency International between 2002 and 2004, conducted by 12 independent institutions.

6 The Nigerian subsidiary of San Ramon, California-based Chevron Texaco Corporation is among the companies hit hardest by Nigeria's worsening oil-related violence, suffering an estimated US$750 million in sabotage to its wells, pipelines and other facilities since March 2003. Royal Dutch/Shell, Nigeria's largest oil operations company, producing half of the 2.5 million barrels of Nigeria's exports daily, is also reeling in agony. A confidential 93-page security report commissioned by Shell in December 2003 (See Mc Kenzie, 2004) warns

sophisticated equipment to siphon off oil from pipelines. The incidence of crude oil theft is currently estimated at over 300,000 barrels per day, about 15 percent of total exports, with state officials accusing faceless highly placed Nigerians of being the masterminds (Mc Kenzie, 2004).

Nigeria also is one of the world's leaders in greenhouse gas emissions of carbon dioxide and of methane. Much of Nigeria's natural gas is burnt off through gas flaring in violation of the country's environmental laws, which require gas, if unused, to be re-injected into the ground. Natural gas flaring has contributed more emissions of greenhouse gases than all other sources in sub-Saharan Africa combined. The energy loss associated with this flaring of four billion cubic meters of natural gas annually is equivalent to 60% of the total thermal-based power generation in sub- Saharan Africa (World Bank[7], 2002). Oil pollution is forcing the death of the Niger Delta's mangrove wetlands. Moreover, pollution associated with oil industry activities in the Niger Delta has been a flashpoint for political unrest in the Delta. For example, Saro-Wiwa's protests and eventual execution emerged from some of the worst cases of environmental devastation by petroleum in the world.

5 Managing Oil Rents in Nigeria

The preceding section documents how oil revenues have shaped Nigeria's economic and political development for decades, creating a rentier state, and holding together a fragile "political coalition" of diverse ethnic and religious interests. Given the litany of woes associated with oil in Nigeria, a pertinent issue is how well oil wealth can better be managed to provide savings for future generations, to deal with uncertain revenues, to avoid "boom-bust" cycles, and to ensure that spending is of high quality, whether in the form of large investment projects, public consumption or subsidies.

Various policy options have been mooted in the literature to deal with the resource curse in Nigeria. Sala-I- Martin and Subramanian (2003) recently

that mounting attacks by criminals and ethnic militants could force the oil giant to abandon its onshore operations in the delta by 2008.

7 See Paragraph 15 of the Memorandum of the President of the International Development Association and the International Finance Corporation to the Executive Directors on an Interim Strategy Update for the Federal Republic of Nigeria, February 13, 2002, Report No. 23633-UNI

appraised three options: privatizing oil resources; creating special oil funds that limit government discretion in spending oil money; and transferring oil money directly to the people. They dismissed the first approach (privatizing oil resources), noting that it has proved disappointing, resulting in 'illiberal democracies', and tending to perpetuate the power imbalances by favoring the incumbents. Privatization has been a big part of the development agenda, pushed by the IMF and by the World Bank over the last two decades. Experience so far with large-scale privatization has been fraught with failure. The majority of assets ultimately end up in the hands of multinational oil companies as evident in Russia where the selling-off of industry created a new oligarchy, and where the state failed to get its money's worth. Privatization works best only in countries with mature institutions, and this limits its usefulness.

They also noted that the second approach (creation of special oil funds) has not been encouraging. Apart from Norway, where it has been relatively successful, oil funds seem to have insulated oil revenues from appropriation by weak or unaccountable governments. They stressed that oil funds are no substitute for public accountability or for checks and balances provided by the press and a healthy democracy.

They thus prefer the third approach - distributing oil money directly to the people, a method that has a better record, at least in few places (as the state of Alaska, and the Canadian province of Alberta) where it has been tried. In both cases, the interest earnings from oil funds, rather than the oil revenues themselves, are distributed. Such systems - by distributing oil money directly - minimize opportunities for corruption and misappropriation, since windfall revenue stays out of the hands of public officials. The direct distribution of oil revenues may instantly increase per capita income, sometimes substantially, and aid the development of home grown markets and local politics. But they cautioned that distributing oil revenues directly to the people would be difficult in poor countries with limited administrative capacity, but not necessarily impossible. The greater problem would be resistance on the part of the current beneficiaries with a vested interest in the status quo.

The implementation of this third approach is likely to be very problematic and open to serious abuse if adopted in Nigeria. The country simply does not have an effective mechanism for such a distribution. Moreover, given Nigeria's huge population, it is unlikely that the distribution of oil revenue will yield any appreciable benefit. Based on the current population of 130 million and a revenue projection of $10 billion which is the equivalent of what Nigeria earns every year from oil, distributing the full amount as citizen dividends would yield about $77 per year, while rendering all tiers of governments (federal, state and local) pro-state.

Like Iraq and other emerging oil producers that could be described as "Clean Slate" in the sense that they have an opportunity to start afresh without prejudice and when nothing bad from the past is taken into account, the systems in Nigeria are already well established and mismanagement, corruption, and weak governance are deeply rooted. Thus, a more practical proposal would be the adoption of a holistic approach, comprising a range of measures by all stakeholders, including developed nations, multilateral institutions, and Nigeria itself to increase accountability and transparency and to reach an improved management of oil revenues. These include instituting full transparency, publishing all payments made by extractive companies and received by governments, and strengthening the capacity of civil society to monitor transparency and to improve resource management. In what follows, we review our proposals.

5.1 Instituting Transparency

Transparency and accountability in resource-rich countries are critical for ensuring that wealth derived from those resources is managed for the benefit of the entire population. Perhaps, the greatest challenge is how to institute transparency in government revenue and spending, as a necessary precondition and as a first step towards establishing functioning institutions. Currently, oil revenues accrue in the first instance to the Federation Account. Through the so-called revenue allocation formula they are then distributed among the central government, the states, and the local authorities. Nigeria's past economic performance indicates that neither the central government nor the states and the local governments have managed oil windfalls soundly. On the contrary, external windfalls appear to have been wasted at all tiers of government. State and local governmental bodies demand access to this "windfall", creating a tug-of-war between the federal government, which seeks to control spending, and state governments that are desirous of augmented budgets, preventing the government from making provision for periods of lower oil prices. Over the years, state and local government demands – backed by constitutional mandates that shares of all oil proceeds be distributed to them to fund their rapidly expanding spending programs - have frustrated federal government efforts to institute a savings mechanism for oil windfall revenues.

There are encouraging developments in this regard. Nigeria, together with three other countries, is currently working with the World Bank and the UK Department for International Development (DFID) to implement the nine-point Abuja joint declaration on transparency signed in June 2003. The transparency pact is part of a wider programme of public financial management ushered in by the country's President, Olusegun Obasanjo. The disclosure agreement explicitly endorses the Extractive Industries Transparency Initiative (EITI), a UK-led campaign to promote the disclosure of payments to governments from the oil, gas and mining industries that the country formally launched in February 2004. A 28-member stakeholders working group has been inaugurated to provide leadership for EITI's implementation. The EITI requires countries to establish ongoing independent audits of extractive revenues and to publish all payments by companies in the participating country. In this regard, the Nigeria Extractive Industries Transparency Initiative (NEITI) recently engaged the Hart Group, through an international competitive tender, to conduct comprehensive and independent Financial, Physical and Process Audits of covered entities in the Nigerian oil industry for the period 1999 to 2004. The disaggregated audit reports (Financial, Process and Physical) with annexes running into more than 500 pages, which have been posted on the NEITI website (see Hart Group, 2006) revealed major discrepancies in the management of oil revenue in Nigeria, especially in payments being claimed by the oil companies and the Central Bank of Nigeria (CBN). For example, the CBN, claimed it received $55 million in 1999 less than what the oil companies allegedly paid into its accounts. But a year later in 2000, CBN had a 'surplus' of $90 million, which the oil companies, from their accounts, did not pay.

In 2001, the CBN account revealed $120 million less than allegedly receipted from the oil companies. The figure rose to $250 million in 2002, and then dropped to $10 million in 2003. Furthermore, around ten million barrels of crude were lost between the flow stations and the loading terminals over the period of five years (1999 - 2004) according to the report.

Nigeria is also participating in parallel transparency initiatives initiated by the G-8 and the New Partnership for Africa's Development (NEPAD). In 2004, Nigeria and the G-8 governments signed a compact to promote transparency and anti-corruption measures in the oil industry and in government public finance at the Summit in Sea Island in the United States.

Since 2004, Nigeria has instituted greater transparency in the nation's budget by publishing details of monthly allocations from the federation accounts to each of the 36 states and to 776 local governments. Furthermore, all three tiers of government adhered to the oil price-based fiscal rule and saved oil revenue windfall in excess of the budget reference price of US$25 per barrel in 2004. They collectively deposited about US$6 billion in oil revenue windfall in the Central Bank and, for the first time in Nigeria's history, followed a fiscal rule for the disbursement (IMF, 2005). However, Nigeria is one of the few oil-producing nations without a substantive Minister in charge of oil. There is a need to set up a new Ministry, solely in charge of the sector to handle all the matters relating to revenue derivation, development and infrastructure.

Greater transparency would equally entail multinational oil companies publishing what they pay. The main multinational oil companies in Nigeria need to endorse and should be part of the international "Publish What You Pay" (PWYP) campaign, the initiative by philanthropist George Soros and his Open Society Institute that has been working endlessly to address the problem of corruption connected with natural resource extraction. This initiative proposes legislation requiring publicly listed oil and mining companies to disclose information about payments to government, as a condition of stock exchange listing. Relevant payments that would have to be disclosed include tax payments, royalty and license fees, revenue sharing and payments-in-kind, forward sales of future revenues, and commercial transactions with the government and public sector entities. The PWYP campaign already has the support of over 130 groups from all around the world. Several large natural resource extraction companies, including BP, Shell, and Newmont Mining, have expressed positive views about it.

As part of its surveillance of country economic policies, the IMF has increasingly stressed transparency and accountability. Since the late 1990s, the International Monetary Fund (IMF) has promoted fiscal transparency in member countries through Reports on the Observance of Standards and Codes (ROSCs), including several large oil exporters (e.g., Azerbaijan, Iran, Mexico, Kazakhstan, and Russia) and mineral producers (e.g., Ghana and Papua New Guinea). Nigeria may also consider joining the IMF Resource Revenue Transparency[8] which applies the principles of the Code of Good Practices on Fiscal Transparency to the unique set of problems faced by countries that derive a significant share of revenues from natural resources, especially revenues from hydrocarbon (oil and gas) and mining, and the subsequent fiscal Report on the Observance of Standards and Codes (ROSCs) would substantially aid the quest for transparency.

---

8 The Guide on Resource Revenue Transparency was formulated in June 2005 and it is available at the IMF website (http://www.imf.org/external/pubs/ft/grrt/eng/060705.pdf). It provides a framework that covers the resource-specific issues to be considered in a fiscal transparency assessment, and contains a summary overview of generally recognized good or best practices for transparency of resource revenue management that can be used by countries themselves, as well as by the IMF, the World Bank, and by others providing technical support.

5.2 Oil Stabilization and Saving Funds

Until recently, Nigeria maintains a Stabilization Account, which is supposed to operate as a mechanism to cushion external shocks. In practice, however, its role as a stabilization tool has been negligible and it is no more than a confusing accounting device that lacks a clear objective. Except in name, the Stabilization Account is not a stabilization fund.[9]

In spite of the fact that oil funds seem to work best where oil does not dominate the local economy and where a long tradition of good governance exists, as in Norway, the Nigerian government should establish a National Oil Stabilization and Savings Fund, recognizing its putative limitations and mixed experiences so far. A number of oil producing countries or regional units has already established such oil funds.[10] Carefully designed and properly administered petroleum funds can play a very useful role in enhanced accountability and economic management by limiting government discretion in spending oil revenue and by de-linking spending from revenue.

Oil stabilization and saving funds as an accounting device provide a separate account into which oil revenues are paid. Their purpose is to shield the government budget from the revenue uncertainty and volatility, and to save for future generations given that oil is non-renewable. Such funds can make a contribution to improved governance, particularly by contributing to greater transparency of revenue flows. They can also help guard against the problem of "Dutch disease" by ensuring that some of the revenues are directed to the accumulation of foreign assets. This helps to prevent an exchange rate appreciation that undermines international competitiveness. Finally, to the extent that government spending is tied to fund revenues, they can contribute to fiscal discipline.

The literature provides clear guidance on the design of such funds (Davis, Ossowski, Daniel and Barnett, 2001). Experience indicates that effective

---

9 Nigeria deposited the oil revenue from prices above US $25 dollars per barrel in the Central Bank in 2004.

10 The list includes Norway, Alaska, Alberta, Kuwait, Oman, Venezuela, Colombia, and, more recently, Azerbaijan and Kazakhstan. Unfortunately, apart from Norway (with its strong government institutions and a healthy democracy), the experience of national oil funds has not been encouraging. In Venezuela, for example, the government has changed the rules, stipulating how money in the oil fund should be spent, six times in the last few years. As a result, the fund's resources have practically dried up, and Venezuela has not managed to ensure prudent revenue management or an improvement in the quality of spending.

stabilization funds are usually fully integrated in the budget and are not based on specific rules that determine the accumulation of assets in or their withdrawal from the fund. Instead, changes in the fund assets are derived from the difference between oil revenue and the non-oil primary balance.

5.3 Distributing Oil Revenue among the Federating Units in Nigeria

Perhaps the most protracted and controversial debate in Nigeria is the way government revenue is shared amongst the component tiers of Government in the country. This debate has its foundations in the history and evolution of the Nigerian Federation. So contentious has the matter been that none of the formula evolved at various times by a commission or by decree under different regimes since 1964 has gained general acceptability among the component units of the country. Indeed, the issue, like a recurring decimal, has painfully remained the first problem that nearly every incoming regime has had to grapple with since independence. Between 1946 and 2003, the allocation formula was changed at least eighteen times, about once every three years and each adjustment is more remembered for the controversies it generated than issues settled. The changes since 1977 are presented in Table 3. In its latest incarnation, the 1999 constitutionally-stipulated 13% derivation principle is being implemented and the Niger Delta Development Commission (NDDC) has been established and adequately funded to champion the social and economic development of oil producing States.

Table 3: Historical Outline of Revenue Allocation Formulas in Nigeria

ITEM	**Date**	**Federal Govt. %**	**State Govt. %**	**Local Govt. %**	**Special Funds %**	**Total %**
Aboyade Commission	1977	57.00	30.00	10.00	3.00	100.00
Okigbo Commission	1980	53.00	30.00	10.00	7.00	100.00
Revenue Allocation Act	1981	55.00	30.50	10.00	4.50	100.00
Pre-Supreme Court – Legal Decrees/Law	Pre-April 2002	48.50	24.00	20.00	7.50	100.00

Continuation on the next page.

Continuation of table 3 from previous page.

ITEM	Date	Federal Govt. %	State Govt. %	Local Govt. %	Special Funds %	Total %
Pre-Supreme Court – RFMAC Proposal	August 2001	41.23	31.00	16.00	11.70	100.00
Supreme Court Ruling	April 2002				Unconstitutional	
Post-Supreme Court - Executive Order # 1	May 2002	56.00	24.00	20.00	0.00	100.00
Post-Supreme Court - Executive Order # 2	July 2002	54.68	24.72	20.60	0.00	100.00
Post-Supreme Court – Revenue Mobilization and Fiscal Commission Proposal	January 2003	46.63	33.00	20.37	0.00	100.00
Latest RMFAC Proposal	Submitted to President September 20, 2004	47.17	31.10	15.21	National Priority Services Funds*: Ecology - 1.50 Mineral Devt.- 1.75 Agric Devt. - 1.75 Reserve Fund - 1.50 Total - 6.50 {joint Fed/State/LG	100.00
Presidential Proposal	Submitted to National Assembly in January 25, 2005	47.17	31.10	15.21	Ditto Fund Managers to manage 13% derivation	100.00

Note: **General Ecological Fund (1.50 per cent); Solid Minerals Development Fund (1.75 per cent); National Agricultural Development Fund (1.75 per cent) and National Reserve Fund (1.50 per cent).*

Source: *Adapted from Aluko, Mobolaji (2004).*

The major tension has been between the principle of derivation, (i.e. allocating revenue on the basis of how much of it is derived from a particular part of the country), and the principle of need, (i.e. allocating on the basis of the responsibilities of each tier of government and the financial expenditures and obligations of the various governments). In determining need, such factors as population, level of development in particular areas and equality of states have at various times been considered.

Derivation had remained the most important factor until the Binns Commission of 1964. That Commission tilted the scales sharply in favour of need on the basis that "- weight must be given to the necessity to preserve continuity, including the provisions of funds necessary to meet the minimum responsibilities of government, and that it was" - equally important that the revenues available to a less developed region shall in part, at least, help to redress the inherent balance in the Federation as a whole." In 1968 the Dina Commission restored derivation as a factor in revenue allocation but gave it lower significance than need, the maintenance of national standards and balanced national development. From then on derivation continued to lose ground to other revenue allocation factors.

In the mature federal systems of USA, Canada and Australia, there is considerable autonomy to the constituent units in the management and control of natural resources. However, in Nigeria, there is a weakening of the constituent part and centralization of resource control. The growing insurgency in the impoverished Niger River delta has intensified in recent years due to dissatisfaction with the derivation principle rattling international oil markets. The oil-producing states in the Niger Delta view their current 13 percent share of oil rents as insufficient to ensure regional development and compensate them for environmental damage, and the issue has been the subject of a legal battle as well as an unexpectedly controversial topic at last year's abortive constitutional assembly. So deep are these grievances that some activists now argue that the only permanent solution is a reconfiguration of the constitutional arrangements in Nigeria's federal state to give the oil-producing area greater control over their political and economic affairs and an increase in oil revenue allocation from the current 13% to 25 or 50%. The situation has been complicated even further by bitter disputes between various ethnic groups in the area. These ethnic disputes have very ancient roots but are often aggravated by contemporary struggles for bigger slices of political power and economic resources.

There is no magic allocation formula that will satisfy all the competing interests. The division of oil revenues is a zero-sum game in which every state and local government wants as much as it can get. Getting the derivation formula "right" is the only recipe for peace in the Niger Delta. Perhaps there is need to convey a conference of ethnic nationalities to formulate viable fiscal rules which are consistent with Nigeria's fiscal federalism, work out modalities for the involvement of host communities in managing oil rent and propose the way forward in addressing the problems of inter-generational equity.

6 Policy Implications

Nigeria is potentially Africa's richest country. As the world's sixth largest producer of crude oil, with huge reserves of mineral and agricultural riches and manpower, it should be enjoying some of the highest global living standards. But at that time it has some of the lowest living standards in Africa. The heavy dependence on oil has exposed the economy to the boom-and-burst cycles of development and has led to a concomitant, unstable revenue profile. Because of the lack of a transparent use of the oil revenues and bad governance the climate of insecurity and instability continues in Nigeria. Few nations in the world face so damaging a legacy of political corruption, repression, pollution, and destitution. So overwhelming is mismanagement and rent-seeking that Nigeria has unfortunately become virtually synonymous with corruption, and the exemplary case and reference point of irresponsible oil management globally.

There is a turnaround that gives cause for optimism and hope since the advent of a democratically elected government in 1999. Nigeria has made tentative attempts to establish more responsible and accountable practices and standards for oil development. The question remains as to how far these reforms will persist. With the transition to civilian rule on track, albeit fragile, there is a need to set a corresponding transition to economic recovery. Nigeria faces the Herculean task of institutionalizing a regime of transparency in the government and in the oil industry, as well as a prudent management of oil revenues. Timid reforms are not enough and changes are still far too limited to alter the development trajectory of Nigeria. Addressing the resource curse requires vision and boldness from all major players and far reaching reforms, the type as enunciated below. The policy implications for the various stakeholders are specific, and some suggestions are made below for the major players:

- *Government*: The primary responsibility for instituting change, and for managing Nigeria's oil wealth in a transparent, fair, and accountable way, and converting the oil wealth into broad-based poverty reduction lies with Nigerian governments, at Federal, State and Local levels. Transparency and accountability inherent in good governance are essential to warding off the natural resource curse in Nigeria.

- *International Institutions*: Multilateral institutions, including the IMF and the World Bank, have an important role to play in combating the natural resource curse in Nigeria. As important large lenders, these institutions have significant power that they can leverage to improve governance and to reduce corruption. The Fund and the Bank can both help by acting as agents of restraint, by funding technical assistance programs, and by developing standards for fiscal transparency and good fiscal practice given their significant leverage. There are already precedents, including the World Bank's groundbreaking handling of financing of the Chad–Cameroon oil pipeline, which it has made conditional on Chad's compliance with strict accounting and spending management principles. Similarly, at IMF's prodding, Azerbaijan and Kazakhstan have established national oil stabilization funds that aggregate much of their oil revenues.

  Building on these initiatives, all Fund and Bank country assistance and lending programmes, especially those connected to the oil sector, should be conditional on Nigeria's transparent reporting of its revenues. This approach should apply to all development assistance loans to Nigeria, to loans to companies by the International Finance Corporation, or to investment guarantees provided through the Multilateral Investment Guarantee Agency.
- *Oil Companies*: Oil Companies are best placed to trigger change by committing to publishing their revenues and payments to the states. In the process, they can help to generate more accountable government, an environment more attractive to appropriate investment, and an improved development outlook.
- *Civil society*: Civil Society Organizations (CSOs) are an integral part of the "revenue management equation" and may in fact be the most important part. CSOs in Nigeria should devise means of holding the government and the oil companies accountable in the management of oil revenues. This could take the form of close monitoring of budget allocation and expenditure and following its impact on development, and full engagement in national planning, including Poverty Reduction Strategy Paper processes.

  A coalition of over 45 Civil Society Organisations across Nigeria met in Port Harcourt, 16-17 February 2004, to launch the Publish What You Pay campaign in Nigeria and to discuss EITI. The coalition could contribute to the implementation of EITI in Nigeria by closely engaging with the national and international stakeholders involved in its development, and by playing an independent monitoring role over the process.

7 Conclusion

Oil extraction does not inevitably result in poor development. The example of Norway, a country that has used its North Sea oil to become the UNDP's best development performer demonstrates that if revenues are managed transparently, accountably and fairly, they can benefit citizens of oil-exporting countries. Lessons from history indicate that the management of massive influx of oil revenues poses serious challenges for any government, but especially for those without strong democratic and accountable institutions. Transparency in revenue payments is not a panacea for problems of revenue mismanagement, but rather a necessary first step for corporate and government accountability: Without improving democratic institutions and administrative capacity, it is unlikely that Nigeria will be able to use oil windfalls to fuel poverty reduction. Despite the reforms proposed in Section 5, Nigeria will in the foreseeable future continue to be highly dependent on oil. There is thus a need to promote diversification in Nigeria, an issue exhaustively discussed in Unit 2 of this yearbook.

References

Abumere, Sylvester, Ben Arimah and Afeikhena. Jerome (1998): "The role of the informal Sector in Nigeria's development process", Research Report No 1, Development Policy Centre, Ibadan.

Aluko, Mobolaji E. (2004): "The 9% fight between federal and state governments over revenue allocation", March 4, 2004, online: http://www.dawodu.com/aluko85.htm, accessed 21/04/06.

AfDB/OECD (African Development Bank and Organisation for Economic Cooperation and Development) (2005): "Country studies, African Economic Outlook 2004/2005", Development Centre of the Organisation for Economic Co-operation and Development, OECD, Paris.

Ali-Akpajiak Sofo and Toni Pyke (2003): "Measuring poverty in Nigeria", Oxfam working papers online: http://www.oxfam.org.uk/what_we_do/resources/wp_poverty_nigeria.htm, accessed 26/03/06.

Auty, Richard (1990): "Resource-based industrialization: sowing the oil in eight developing countries". Clarendon Press: Oxford, UK.

Birdsall, Nancy and Arvind Subramanian (2004): "Saving Iraq from its oil", in: Foreign Affairs, 83 (4): 77-89 (August).

Bravo-Ortega, Claudio and José De Gregorio (2001): "The relative richness of the poor? Natural resources, human capital, and economic growth", Mimeo, University of California, Berkeley.

CBN (Central Bank of Nigeria) (2000): "The changing structure of the Nigerian economy and implications for development". Lagos: Realm Communications Ltd.

Collier, Paul and Anke Hoeffler (2004): "Greed and grievance in African civil wars". London: Oxford University Press.

Davis, Jeffrey, Rolando Ossowski, James Daniel, and Steven Barnett (2001): "Stabilization and Savings Funds for Nonrenewable Resources", International Monetary Fund Occasional Paper No. 205, Washington D.C.

De Soysa, Indra (2002): "Paradise in a bazaar? Greed, creed, and governance in civil war", 1989-99, in: Journal of Peace and Security, 39 (4): 395-416.

Diamond, Larry, Juan Linz, and Seymour Lipset (1989): "Democracy in developing countries", Volume 4: Latin America, Boulder, Col.: Adamantine Press.

EIA (Energy Information Administration) (2005): Eifert, Benn, Alan Gelb, and Nils Borje Tallroth (2003): "Managing oil wealth", in: Finance and Development, 40 (1).

Faruquee, Rashid (1994): "Nigeria: ownership abandoned", in: Adjustment in Africa. Lessons from country case studies, edited by Ishrat Husain and Rashid Faruquee, Washington: The World Bank, 238-285.

FRN (Federal Republic of Nigeria) (2004): "Millennium development goals report", 2004, Nigeria, online: http://www.undg.org/documents/5430-Nigeria_MDG_Report_-_Nigeria_Profile.pdf, accessed 23/04/06.

Gary, Ian and Terry Lynn Karl (2003): "Bottom of the barrel: Africa's oil boom and the poor", Catholic Relief Services, June, online: http://www.catholicrelief.org/get_involved/advocacy/policy_and_strategic_issues/oil_report_one.cfm, accessed 08/12/04.

Gelb, Alan (1988): "Oil windfalls: blessing or curse?", New York: Oxford University Press.

Hart Group (2006): "Nigeria extractive industry transparency initiative (NEITI) final audit reports", online: http://www.neiti.org/NEITI%20Final%20Audit%20-Reports.htm, accessed 16/04/06.

Hausmann, Ricardo and Roberto, Rigobon (2003): "An alternative interpretation of the 'Resource Curse': Theory and policy implications", NBER Working Papers 9424, National Bureau of Economic Research, Inc.

Institute for Democracy and Electoral Assistance (2001): "Democracy in Nigeria, continuing dialogue(s) for nation building", Capacity-Building Series 10, International Institute for Democracy and Electoral Assistance (International IDEA), SE 103 34 Stockholm, Sweden.

IMF (International Monetary Fund) (2003): "Angola: Staff Report for the 2003 Article IV Consultation", Statistical Appendix, July 11, 2003, pp. 77-78.

IMF (2005): "Nigeria - 2005 Article IV Consultation, Concluding Statement", March 25, 2005, online: http://www.imf.org/External/Np/Ms/2005/032505.htm, accessed 07/05/05.

IMF (2005): "Guide on resource revenue transparency", June, online: http://www.imf.org/external/pubs/ft/grrt/eng/060705.pdf, accessed 07/08/05.

Isham Jonathan, Michael Woolcock, Lant Pritchett, and Gwen Busby (2003): "The varieties of the resource experience: how natural resource export structures affect the political economy of economic growth", Mimeo, World Bank, Washington, D.C.

Iwayemi, Akin (1994): "Perspectives and problems of economic development in Nigeria: 1960-1990", Center for Econometric and Allied Research (CEAR) Monograph Series No. 1.

Jerome, Afeikhena (2004): "Governance and the Development Crisis in Nigeria", in: Adigun A. B. Agbaje, Larry Diamond, and Ebere Onwudiwe (Editors), Nigeria's struggle for democracy and good governance: A festschrift for Oyeleye Oyediran, Ibadan University Press, Ibadan: 205-219.

Jerome, Afeikhena., Senyo Adjibolosso, and Dipo Busari (2005): "Addressing oil related corruption in Africa. Is the push for transparency enough?", in: The Review of Human Factor Studies, 11, (1): 7-32.

Karl, Terry Lynn (1997): "The paradox of plenty: oil booms and petro-states", Berkeley, Cal.: University of California Press.

Lacina Bethany and Nils Petter Gleditsch (2005): Monitoring trends in global combat: A new dataset of battle deaths, European Journal of Population 21: 145–166

Lane, Philip and Aaron Tornell (1995): "Power concentration and growth", Harvard Institute of Economic Research Working Papers, No. 1720, Harvard Institute of Economic Research, Harvard, Cambridge, Mass.

Lederman, Daniel and William F. Maloney (2003): "Trade structure and growth," World Bank Policy Research Working Paper 3025, April (Washington, D.C.: World Bank).

Leite, Carlos and Jens Weidmann, J. (1999): "Does mother nature corrupt? Natural resources, corruption, and economic growth", IMF Working Paper WP/99/85. Washington, D.C.: International Monetary Fund.

Mahdavy, Hossein (1970): "Patterns and problems of economic development in rentier states: the case of Iran", in: M. Cook, Ed., Studies in the Economic History of the Middle-East, Oxford, U. K.: Oxford University Press.

McKenzie Glen (2004): "Ethnic, criminal bloodletting over oil wealth has Nigeria's petroleum industry reeling", Aug 8, 2004, Associated Press Writer, online: http://agonist.org/story/2004/6/14/122041/463, accessed 23/03/05.

Mauro, Paolo (1995): "Corruption and growth", in: Quarterly Journal of Economics, 110 (3): 681-712.

Ojemeruaye, Emmanuel (2004): "Managing the Dutch disease in Nigeria", Nigerian World, online: http://www.ocnus.net/artman/publish/article_13460.shtml, accessed 03/11/04.

Okruhlik, Gwenn (1999): "Rentier states, unruly law, and the rise of opposition: the political economy of oil states", in: Comparative Politics, 31 (3): 195-315.

Palley, Thomas (2003): "Lifting the natural resourse curse", Global Policy Forum, UN Security Council, December.

Ross, Michael L. (2003): "Nigeria's Oil Sector and the Poor", Prepared for the UK Department for International Development Nigeria: Drivers of Change" program.

Sachs, Jeffrey and Andrew M. Warner (1995): Natural resource abundance and economic growth, Development Discussion Paper No. 517a, Harvard Institute for International Development, Cambridge, MA.

Sachs, Jeffrey and Andrew M. Warner (2001): "The curse of natural resources", in: European Economic Review, 45: 827-838.

Sala-i-Martin, Xavier and Arvind Subramanian (2003): "Addressing the natural resource curse: an illustration from Nigeria", NBER Working Paper 9804, June, National Bureau of Economic Research, Cambridge, MA.

Tornell, Aaron and Philip Lane (1999): "Voracity and growth", in: American Economic Review, 89: 22–46.

United Nations Industrial Development Organisation (2004): "Industrialization, Environment and the Millennium Development Goals in Sub-Saharan Africa", United Nations Industrial Development Organization, Vienna.

UNDP (United Nations Development Programme) (2001): "Nigeria 2000/2001 human development report millennium edition", Lagos.

United States Energy Information Administration (2005): "OPEC Revenues: Country Details", June 2005, EIA homepage: http://www.eia.doe.gov/emeu/cabs/orevcoun.html, accessed 23/03/05.

United States Energy Information Administration (2006): "OPEC revenues fact sheet", online: http://www.expansion.com/documentos/archivos/informe_opep.pdf, accessed 25/03/06.

Wantchekon, Leonard (1999): "Why do resource abundant countries have authoritarian governments?" Yale University Leitner Center Working Paper, 99-12.

World Bank (1994): "Nigeria: structural adjustment program, policies, implementation and impact", Report No. 13053-UNI, May 13.

World Bank (2002): "Memorandum of the president of the international development association and the international finance corporation the executive directors on an interim strategy update for the Federal Republic of Nigeria". February 13, 2002. Report no. 23633-UNI.

World Bank (2005): "World development indicators database", April 2005, online: http://devdata.worldbank.org/external/CPProfile.asp?CCODE=NGA&PTYPE=CP, accessed 05/05/05.

Yates, Douglas (1996): "The rentier state in Africa", Trenton, N. J.: World Press.

Oil Resources and Incidence of Conflicts in Nigeria

Bernard Aigbokhan, Reuben A. Alabi and Moses Ailemen

1 Introduction

Nigeria is Africa's fourth largest economy, with a Gross Domestic Product (GDP) at current price standing at \$41.5 billion in the year 2001 so coming after South Africa's GDP of \$112.9 billion, Egypt's of \$93.5 billion, and Algeria's of \$54.6 billion. Nigeria's GDP growth rate that year was 4.0%, and the country's weight in the total African GDP was 7.6% (Aigbokhan, 2003a: 16). The major source of revenue in Nigeria is crude oil. In 35 years of oil production, Nigeria has earned an estimated \$350 billion at 1995 price from oil (Gary and Karl, 2003: 4).

The Niger Delta region is the bedrock of Nigeria's crude oil production, while Bayelsa, Delta and River states in the region account for 75% of the oil production and over 50% of the gross government revenues. The other states in the region are Abia, Akwa Ibom, Cross River, Edo, Imo and Ondo. The Niger Delta is one of the world's largest wetlands, and the largest in Africa. The Nigerian economy is dependent on the oil sector. The oil resource in the nation is generally not judiciously utilized. This has resulted in oil-induced conflicts, especially in Niger Delta.

This paper attempts to demonstrate this, and to suggest some measures to address the situation. The rest of the paper is divided into nine sections; section one is the introduction of the paper. Section two examines the socio – economic development constraints in the Niger Delta; section three deals with the abundance of oil and natural gas resources in Nigeria; section four discusses the neglect of other revenue sources in Nigeria. Section five presents the conflicts associated with oil production and the use of oil wealth in Nigeria, especially in the Niger-Delta region. Section six examines the extent of corruption that is associated with use of oil wealth. Section seven presents the effects of weak political and legal institutions in the Nigerian oil industry and in the Niger-Delta region. Section eight details the efforts of the government and the oil companies in minimizing conflicts in the region, while section nine concludes the paper by presenting policy recommendations on how to minimize conflicts and on how to escape the primary commodity dilemma in Nigeria.

2 Socio-economic Development Constrains in the Niger-Delta

Despite the vast oil wealth of the oil producing areas, the Niger Delta region remains poor in terms of human capital development. Gross National Product (GNP) per capita is below the estimated national average of US $280, and is lower still in the riverine and coastal areas of the region (Aigbokhan, 2003b: 76). Unemployment in Port Harcourt, the headquarters of the region, is at least 30 percent. Education levels are below the national average and illiteracy rate is correspondingly higher (Aigbokhan, 2003a: 16). The poverty level is exacerbated by the high cost of living (Okojie and Ailemen, 2003: 25). Proper sanitation is available to less than 25 percent of the population. In Port Harcourt, the region's biggest city, there is no citywide sewage system. Water-related diseases are widespread and are probably the "central health problem in the Niger Delta." In addition, the Niger Delta is known to lack basic social amenities (e.g. health facilities, schools, electricity and other infrastructure). Even though nearly the entire oil production of Nigeria's crude oil (and by implication the revenues) comes from the Niger Delta, very little of the infrastructural effects generated by oil revenues have occurred in the region. The region remains politically unorganized and is economically one of the most underdeveloped parts of the federation (Aigbokhan, 2003a: 16).

3 Abundance of Oil and Natural Gas in Nigeria

(a) Oil

Estimates of Nigeria's oil reserves range from 16 billion to 22 billion barrels. Most of this oil is found in small fields in the coastal areas of the Niger Delta. Nigerian crude is classified as "light" and "sweet," with low sulphur content, similar in quality to the North Sea varieties, and its price is linked to the price for Brent. Nigerian crude oil production averaged 2.21 million barrels per day (bpd) for the first nine months of 1997, half a million barrels per day above the country's 1.865 million bpd quota set by the Organization of Petroleum Exporting Countries (OPEC). Nigeria's quota rose to 2.042 million bpd in 1998 as a result of the OPEC meeting of November 1997. This also increased by 0.82 million bpd in November 2004, which will give Nigeria extra revenues of $98 million as announced by the OPEC recently (Uwujaren, 2004: 52).

Table 1 shows that oil production increased from 660,559 million barrels in 1990 to 685,773 million barrels in 2002. Crude oil export declined slightly from 548,249 million barrels in 1990 to 521,973 million barrels in 2002. The percentage of the oil exported also declined from 83% to 76% during the period in consideration; the share of government revenues generated from oil declined from 73% in 1990 to 71% in 2002.

Table 1: Nigerian Oil Sector's Contribution to Output, Revenues and Exports

Year	Crude oil production (million barrels)	Crude oil exports (million barrel)	Share of export in total oil produc-tion%	Share of total govern-ment revenues %	Share of oil in total exports%
1990	660,559	548,249	83.0	73.3	97.0
1991	689,850	585,838	84.9	81.9	96.2
1992	711,340	604,300	85.0	86.2	98.1
1993	691,400	563,614	81.5	84.1	97.7
1994	696,790	578,044	83.0	79.3	97.4
1995	715,400	616,900	86.2	70.6	97.6
1996	740,190	648,690	87.6	71.0	98.2
1997	759,710	673,340	88.6	71.5	94.8
1998	776,190	687,390	88.5	70.0	95.5
1999	780,110	683,370	87.5	77.8	98.4
2000	797,880	688,080	86.2	83.3	98.9
2001	817,150	674,930	82.6	90.0	98.6
2002	685,773	521,973	76.12	71.07	94.38
2003	732,488	589,025	84.67	77.70	97.14

Source: CBN (2002): 25.

The share of oil in total exports also declined from 97% in 1990 to 94% in 2002. These declines may be attributed to efforts of the present democratic government in diversifying the economic base of the country. However, it also signifies greater domestic consumption of oil.

It is also obvious from Table 1 that revenues generated annually by government from crude oil production and exports accounted for not less than 70% of total government revenues on the average between 1990 and 2002. Table 1 indicates that, on the average, about 85% of the oil produced in Nigeria was exported between 1990 and 2002. It is also evident from the table that oil constitutes around 97% of the total exports in Nigeria. This suggests that oil is the main stay of the Nigerian economy in terms of export volumes and revenue generation. Yet, despite the contribution of crude oil to the economic activities and the government revenues in Nigeria, the developmental impacts of its crude oil endowment (income effect, welfare effect, and other socio-economic impacts) remain negligible, especially in the oil-producing region (Adewuyi, 2001:119).

(b) Gas

In addition to its oil wealth, Nigeria has an estimated 104.7 trillion cubic feet (tcf) of proven natural gas reserves, the tenth largest reserves in the world; the reserves may in fact be as high as 300 tcf. Nigeria has been described as a 'gas province' (Ogbe, 1999: 2). This huge endowment in natural gas reserves places Nigeria in the 10th position in the world and second only to Algeria on the African continent (Efe, 2003: 91). Related to Nigeria's oil production about 99% and 72% of associated gas were flared in the periods 1970 - 1974 and 1995 - 1999 respectively.

According to Uzukwa (1999: 19) gas was deliberately flared and wasted because of the following:

- Gas was not a popular energy source in Nigeria;
- There were few markets for gas in Nigeria; and
- There was little environmental awareness of the consequences of gas flaring.

Table 2 presents estimates of the financial costs of wasting associated gas. The calculated loss from gas flaring was $ 12.462 billion between 1970 and 1980, $ 16.243 billion between 1981 and 1990, $ 24.290 billion between 1991 and 1998 and $ 7.332 billion between 1999 and 2000. The result is an estimated direct financial loss of about $60.3 billion (Bankole, 2001: 534).

The significance of the cumulative loss could be appreciated by the knowledge that Nigeria's total external debt of $ 31 billion is just about 51% of the total loss (Garba and Garba, 2001:491). It is revealed in Table 2 that the percentage of gas flared between 1970 and 1980 is about 97%, a percentage that declined to about 85% between 1999 and 2000. The reduction in gas flaring may be attributed to the intensification efforts of the Nigerian Government on natural gas utilization in Nigeria. One of the efforts is the establishment of a Liquefied Natural Gas Company in Nigeria. This is also coupled with an order to oil companies to achieve a zero gas flaring level by 2005. Although the zero gas flaring level has not been achieved, the government order nonetheless had some marginal effects on gas flaring, with different oil companies seeking ways of minimizing gas flaring in Nigeria.

Table 2: Crude Oil Production and Associated Externalities (Gas Flaring)

Period	Price of crude oil ($/barrel)	Crude oil output (mb)	Gas production (mcm)	% of gas flared	CO_2 emission (mcm)	Loss from gas flared (mb)	Loss from gas flared ($ million)
1970 - 1980	12.4	695.3	20,228.3	96.6	33.4	100.5	12,462
1981-1990	21.4	533.7	19,180.4	76.9	25.3	75.9	16,243
1991-1998	18.1	722.1	33,078.2	78.2	44.7	134.2	24,290
1999-2000	35.1	647.0	23,411.7	84.7	33.7	101.3	7,332
Total	-	2598.1	95,898.6	336.4	137.1	411.9	60,327

Note: *mcm = million cubic meter, mb = million barrel.*
Source: *Adapted from Garba & Garba (2001).*

The gas flaring level is a result of past government policies and regulations in the sense that the reduction rates were an explicit response to the Associated Gas Re-injection Decree of 1979 and the Associated Gas Re-injection Amendment Decree No. 7 of 1985 (Aregbeyen, 2001: 573). Since 1985, fines have been imposed as a penalty for gas flaring, ranging from 20 kobo per thousand standard cubic feet in 1985 to 50 kobo in 1992, N10 in 1988 and N20 in 1999 (Bankole, 2001: 519). This may partially explain the reduction in gas flaring level.

4 Neglect of Other Income Sources and the Primary Commodities Dilemma

Before the advent of oil, agriculture occupied the enviable position in the Nigerian economy. Agriculture, which accounted for over 80% of the federally collected revenues in 1960, declined rapidly to account for only 1.5% in 1995. The country that used to be the world-leading producer and exporter of agricultural commodities in previous years has now become a net importer of palm oil, vegetables, wheat, rice, sugar, and other staple food items. The food import bill rose significantly from N801,967 (US$9900) in 1986 to N147.301 billion (US$1.82 billion) in 1996 (Alabi, 2004: 225). About US$ 647 million was spent only on rice in 1997 (Nigeria was 99% self-sufficient in rice in the 1960s (Carim, 2002: 48). In terms of export earnings, agriculture accounted for 86% of the total exports in 1955 -1959, for 80% in 1960 - 1964 and for 57% in 1966 - 1969. In 1970 the decline became dramatic, and this coincided with the pre-eminence of petroleum as the country's main export commodity. In 1970 - 1974 agriculture accounted for 26% of the total exports, and thereafter it accounted for less than 10%, being 5.7% in 1975-79, 2.7% and 5.6% in 1980-84 and in 1985-89 respectively. In 1990 - 1993 it nose-dived to its lowest share at 1.8%. The current figure for the year 2005 is 2% (Alabi and Ailemen, 2005: 20).

Of non-oil exports, cocoa has been dominant, and it accounted for 50% in the 1970s. For much of the 1980s it accounted for over 60%. However, since the 1990s, its share has steadily declined from 49% in 1989 to about 32% in 1998 as shown in Table 3, and the downward trend continues till date (Alabi et al, 2004: 21). Table 3 shows further that non-oil exports, of which agricultural products contribute more than 50%, constituted about 9% of the total exports in 1988, and this share has declined to about 3% in 2002. The declines in shares of major agricultural products follow the same trend. Cocoa production declined from about 54% in 1988 to about 32% in 2002. Palm produce declined from about 3% in 1988 to 2% in 2002 (CBN, 2002: 23). All these data support the fact that agriculture was relegated to the background in Nigeria.

Table 3: Nigeria's Non-oil exports (1988 - 2002)

Year	Non-oil exports (% of total exports)	Cocoa (% of non-oil exports)	Palm produce (%)	Rubber (%)	Cotton (%)	Ground-nuts (%)
1988	8.8	53.6	2.5	7.4	0.0	0.0
1989	5.1	49.2	3.8	12.6	0.0	0.0
1990	5.1	40.5	2.6	16.7	0.45	0.0
1991	3.0	42.8	1.0	14.3	5.2	0.0
1992	3.9	36.4	2.1	20.5	1.9	0.0
1993	2.1	33.7	2.8	17.5	2.4	0.0
1994	2.4	34.0	2.5	12.9	4.4	0.0
1995	1.8	27	0.5	20.4	5.7	0.0
1996	2.4	31.5	2.1	21.8	7.3	0.0
1997	4.5	26.8	4.4	14.0	11.5	0.0
1998	2.1	21.9	1.0	3.0	10.5	0.0
1999	3.7	36.1	2.3	14.6	4.5	0.0
2000	3.2	34.4	2.3	15.4	4.9	0.0
2001	3.0	32.8	2.1	15.7	5.5	0.0
2002	2.8	31.8	2.1	15.6	6.1	0.0

Source: CBN (2002): 23.

The Nigerian economy exhibits a mono-cultural production base with an over-dependence on oil. A comparison for African cocoa producing countries shows the decline in cocoa production in Nigeria, a crop that was the main export good before independence. Table 4 shows that production of cocoa fell from 218 thousand metric tons in 1965 to 165 thousand metric in 2003. The reduction in cocoa output is about 24% between the time periods, whereas cocoa production in Cote d'Ivoire and in Ghana increased by 553 % and 10% respectively over the periods. Table 4 shows further that the cocoa production was higher in Nigeria than in Cote d'Ivoire between 1960 and 1961. While cocoa production increased steadily in Cote d'Ivoire, the production either declined or stagnated during the years under consideration in Nigeria.

Table 4: Cocoa Production in Selected African Countries in thousand tons (1960 – 2003)

Year	Cote d'Ivoire	Ghana	Nigeria
1960-61	202	451	218
1962-63	202	451	218
1964-65	202	451	218
1966-67	202	451	218
1967-68	202	451	218
1969-70	202	351	218
1971-72	290	351	218
1973-74	280	351	218
1974-75	301	251	208
1976-77	302	251	208
1978-79	302	251	211
1980-81	402	251	211
1982-83	403	253	202
1984-85	403	253	212
1986-87	401	253	211
1988-89	502	253	218
1990-91	502	253	218
1992-93	602	253	138
1994-95	840	245	135
1996-97	1022	340	152
1998-99	1163	397	198
1999-00	1409	437	165
2000-01	1175	395	180
2001-02	1125	335	165
2002-03	1320	497	165

Source: Computed from ICCO (2003: 12).

The negative trend in export crop production is associated with Nigeria's over-dependence on oil as a base for income generation. Gary and Karl (2003: 3) compared the oil dependence of some African Countries. Table 5 shows that oil contributes only 4%, 60%, and 20% of Cameroon's GDP, exports, and government revenues respectively.

Table 5: Oil Dependence in African Oil-exporting Countries (2002)

Country	% of GDP	% of Exports	% Government Revenues
Nigeria	40	95	83
Angola	45	90	90
Congo-Brazzaville	67	94	80
Equatorial Guinea	86	90	61
Gabon	73	8	60
Cameroon	4	60	20

Source: Gary and Karl (2003): 3.

In the case of Gabon, oil contributes 73% to GDP, 60% to the government revenues, but it contributes only 8% to the total exports. This indicates that Gabon may have a broader export base and reduced export shocks than Nigeria where oil constitutes 40% of GDP, 95% of exports and 83% of the government revenue. This exposes Nigeria to a severe primary commodity dilemma that is associated with the reliance on single primary commodity. For example, Nigeria's crude oil, which was sold at about US$41 per barrel in early 1981, fell in price drastically to less than US$9 by August 1986. This precipitated fiscal deficits that cumulated to about N98 billion (US$1.4 billion) in the four years period (1981-1984) (Egwaikhide, 1999: 5).

The other area where the primary commodity sector affects Nigeria is in the area of the balance of payments. The pattern and the trend of external trade and the balance of payments position underscore the high degree of external dependence of the Nigerian economy. The foreign exchange content of domestic production and consumption is very high, rendering the economy highly vulnerable to external shocks. The average per capita income increased to US$1000 per capita in 1980. The collapse in the oil market in the 1980s triggered a declining trend in the economy and of the per capita incomes, which adversely affected the growth rate of the economy.

To sustain the scale of the import-dependent economic activities and the consumption pattern developed during the years of the oil boom, government resorted to excessive borrowing. This resulted in a bloated external debt volume, which stood at $27 billion in 1998, rising to US $31.8 billion in 2002 (CBN, 2003: 23). Nigeria spends one third of its budget on servicing outstanding debt, what is three times what it spends on education, nine times what it spends on health care and 7.6% of all its export earnings. The debt was incurred during the time of the oil 'burst' as opposed to the time of the oil 'boom' (CCA, 2001: 23).

Over-dependence on oil as a sole source of income generation also results in the 'Dutch disease' in Nigeria. The problem of the 'Dutch disease' shows its effect on the economy based on mineral resources production, whereby an oil windfall pushes up the real exchange rate and hampers non – oil exports of agricultural and manufacturing sectors. In Niger Delta, internally generated revenue accounts for less than 15% of the state revenues (Aigbokhan, 2003b: 76). The consequence of over-dependence of the regions on the Federation Account (centrally allocated oil revenues) is that states and local governments do not feel accountable to their citizens because they do not spend the tax payers' money but the money allocated from the international revenues. This has reduced their ability or the necessity to mobilize the stakeholders for any development projects. If tax-driven spending is important, this would suggestively make public spending more developmental.

5 Oil-induced Conflicts in the Niger Delta

5.1 Revenue Allocation as a Source of Conflicts

Fiscal Federalism, particularly the modalities of revenue allocation, has been practiced in a way that exposes the people of the Niger Delta to frustration and causes feelings of hostility due to relative deprivation. It thus provokes rivalry and conflicts (Azelama and Akpotor, 2003: 55). There have been apparent inconsistencies in the allocation of revenues to the states producing revenue in Nigeria. From 1966 - 1967, the oil-producing states got 50%, the federal government 20%, while 30% was for a distributable pool. In 1967, the share between the federal government and the producing state was 50% each. During this period the "principle of derivation" led all other principles in revenue allocation. The principle of derivation states that the proportion of revenue given to a state from centrally collected revenue (Federation Account) depends on how much of it was derived from that state. During these periods the Northern and Western regions of Nigeria got the dominant part of the federally generated revenue. These two regions produced dominant parts of the Nigerian agricultural exports. The East also got some share as a result of the exportation of coal. When the mid-West region was created in 1963 (mid-West was one of the regions created at that period) it also got a share as a result of its agricultural exports. In the 1970s petroleum fast replaced agricultural products as a major revenue earner for the country. Then the emphasis placed on the "principle of derivation" fast faded away. The derivation principle was increasingly replaced with other emphasizes such as population size and land area, and this benefited the major ethnic groups that controlled the Federal government heavily (Sagay, 2002: 16).

The oil-producing states got 1% and 3% in 1982-1992 and 1992-1999 periods respectively. Agitations from oil-producing areas led to the higher share of 13% in late 1999 for the oil-producing areas (Aigbokhan, 2003b:76), but with the offshore and on-shore dichotomy drastically reducing the allocations to the producing states. At the moment 13% of the federally collected revenue is being shared by oil producing states in Nigeria. The issue of the offshore (oil derived from land) and on-shore (oil derived from coastal area) dichotomy is a controversial issue up till date. The Niger Delta people believe that they have been used and exploited to care for the other parts of the nation, the non-oil producing areas. Whether on-shore or offshore the Niger Delta people are the worst off in terms of the negative impact of oil exploration. This explains the basis for other conflicts in the Niger Delta.

5.2 Vandalization of Oil Pipelines and Oil Spillage

The saboteurs, whose business is pipeline vandalization, siphon off petroleum product and crude oil using sometimes sophisticated facilities such as expensive barges, tankers and hoses. Research has revealed that those who engage in pipeline vandalization and who sabotage the efforts of operators in the oil industry in the Niger Delta are not only the restive youths (Aregbeyen, 2001:557). There are other culprits such as: the Nigeria National Petroleum Company (NNPC) staff, staff of oil companies, law-enforcement agents, fuel dealers, contractors to oil companies, community leaders, and even criminal syndicates that exploit the greed and bitterness of the inhabitants of the oil-producing areas in the pursuit of their lucrative business. The syndicates employ drivers, technicians, and experts from oil companies who have the technical know how to tap the pipelines at the vulnerable points.

Pipeline vandalization, a consequence of youth restiveness, has been on the increase in the Niger Delta: the number of incidents rose from seven cases in 1993 to 33 cases in 1996 and to 57 cases in 1998. There was a dramatic increase of 497 reported cases of vandalization in 1999, and over 600 cases were reported in 2000 (Okecha, 2003: 25).

In 1998, about 1000 lives were lost in Jesse village and in 1999, over 12 persons died in Ekakpamne in the Ughelli Local Government area, both in the Delta State. In the year 2000, over 50 persons were also reported killed at

Nngiji and in Umuegbede in Abia state, 60 persons died in Atlas Cove Jetty in Lagos, and 300 persons in Egborode village in Okpe Local Government area of Delta State (Okecha, 2003: 25). These series of conflicts have resulted in an estimated N70 billion (US$ 518 million) loss in oil revenues.

According to the official estimates of the Nigerian National Petroleum Corporation (NNPC), based on the quantities reported by the operating companies, approximately 2,300 cubic meters of oil are spilled in 300 separate incidents annually. Statistics from the Department of Petroleum Resources indicate that between 1976 and 1996 a total of 4,835 incidents resulted in the spillage of at least 2,446,322 barrels (102.7 million U.S. gallons), of which an estimated 1,896,930 barrels (79.7 million U.S. gallons; 77 percent) were lost to the environment (Okoh and Egbon, 1999: 405). Another calculation, based on oil industry sources, estimates that more than 1.07 million barrels (45 million U.S. gallons) of oil were spilled in Nigeria from 1960 to 1997 (Adewuyi, 2001:119). Nigeria's largest spill was an offshore well blowout in January 1980, when at least 200,000 barrels of oil (8.4 million U.S. gallons), according to oil industry sources, spewed into the Atlantic Ocean from a Texaco facility and destroyed 340 hectares of mangroves. Department for Petroleum Resources (DPR) estimates were that more than 400,000 barrels (16.8 million U.S. gallons) were spilled in this incident. Mangrove forests are particularly vulnerable to oil spills, because the soil soaks up the oil like a sponge and re-releases it every rainy season. The oil spills continue to date.

5.3 Oil Price Fluctuation-induced Conflicts

The boom and bust cycle contributed to political instability in Nigeria. There were oil-induced recessions in 1978-79 and from 1981 until the early 1990s because of the slump in the price of oil internationally. The oil price fell from around U.S.$ 32 per barrel in 1981 to approximately U.S.$ 13 per barrel in 1986, and Nigeria's Gross National Product (GNP) fell from a high of U.S.$ 99,539 million in 1980 to a low of U.S.$ 24,341 million in 1987, aided by the massive devaluation of the Naira in 1986 (Aigbokhan, 2003b: 76). The consequence of devaluation was the higher inflation witnessed during the period because consumption in Nigeria is import-dependent. In the outpaced income, and external debt more than doubled from 1980 to 1985. As a result of gross mismanagement in the economy, in January 1984 military officers put an end to the civilian rule, and installed a fresh military regime.

The price of gasoline (petrol) in the petrol stations was fixed at 11 Naira (U.S. 12¢) per litre in November 1994 (a time when it was raised from a low level of 3.25 Naira (U.S. 4¢) before), and in December 1998 it was raised to 25 Naira (U.S. 28¢) (Aigbokhan, 2003a: 76). Previous attempts to reduce the level of subsidy in recent years, prompted by negotiations with the IMF for structural adjustment lending beginning in 1986, have led to street riots, strikes and security clampdowns on several occasions. Following negotiations with the union umbrella organization, the Nigerian Labor Congress (NLC), over a threat to strike, the government announced that it would review the increase, and on January 7, 1999 the price was reduced again to 20 Naira per litre. Nevertheless, on January 4, 1999 five persons were shot dead in riots in Lagos over the fuel price rise. During fuel shortages, unofficial gasoline prices can rise many times: during a shortage in April 1997, for example, a fifty-litre can was selling for 4,000 Naira (U.S.$ 44), more than seven times the usual price; in July 1998, a litre was going for 400 Naira (US$ 4.44) on the black market (Aigbokhan, 2003a: 76).

Gasoline price in Nigeria has altered more than five times since the inception of the democratic era in 1999. Each price is always met with resistance and strikes from the masses with the attendant human and material losses (Aigbokhan, 2003b: 16). Gasoline is sold at between N53 and N60 (35 to 40¢) at present in Nigeria, and the price may still be adjusted upward because of the current deregulation of oil sector. This portends more strikes and riots for the country because the Workers Union will always resist attempts to increase the fuel price, as they believe that the huge resources realized from oil are not efficiently utilized.

6 Corruption Associated with the Use of Oil Wealth

In 1992, in the context of Babangida's transition program, the government established the Oil Mineral Producing Areas Development Commission (OMPADEC) "to address the difficulties and sufferings of inhabitants of the Oil Producing Areas of Nigeria" (Human Rights Watch, 2002: 18) and the share of federal revenue allocated specifically to oil and mineral producing communities was doubled from 1.5 to 3 percent. In February 1996, the senior management of OMPADEC was fired, amid allegations of corruption and mismanagement, and a sole administrator was appointed. The Commission was still allocated 2.042 billion (U.S.$22.68 million) in 1996. OMPADEC became moribund and was scrapped eventually. In addition, the government inaugurated the board of a new Petroleum Special Trust Fund (PSTF) in March 1995, established by decree the previous November 1994, with a mandate to use revenue from increases in the prices of petroleum products to "identify key projects in all parts of the federation so as to bring about equitable development to all our communities." The Petroleum Trust Fund (PSTF) was also accused of corruption to the tune of more than N21 billion (US$ 1.6 billion) according to international assessments (Human Rights Watch, 1999: 19).

The revenue allocation formulae do not tell the whole story of the distribution of the oil money. The Nigerian political economy has come to depend on a spectacular system of corruption, involving systematic kickbacks for the award of contracts, special bank accounts in the control of the presidency, allocation of oil or refined products to political loyalists to sell for personal profit, and sweeteners for a whole range of political favors. This system of corruption is particularly entrenched in the oil sector. It is this corruption that ensures that the oil money is sent to private foreign bank accounts rather than spent on primary health care and on education in Nigeria. The" presidential allocation" was said to amount to up to 200,000 bpd, one tenth of Nigeria's production (Human Rights Watch, 1999). A Commission of Inquiry headed by the economist Pius Okigbo estimated that US$ 12.2 billion in oil earnings had disappeared between 1990 and 1994, but nobody was brought to account for this theft. Nigeria's politics revolve around the distribution of the oil money, whether officially or unofficially.

Table 6 shows the statutory revenue allocation and the 13% derivation funds allocated to Niger Delta within the period of five years (1999 to 2003). The statutory revenue allocations are N25.6 billion (190 million US dollars), N107.3 billion (795 million US dollars), N136.3 billion (1 billion US dollars), N122.7 billion (909 million US dollars), and N168 billion (1.2 billion US dollars) in 1999, 2000, 2001, 2002, and 2003 respectively. The 13% derivation allocation was N58.1 billion (684 million US dollars), N75.8 billion (892 million US dollars), N130.8 billion (1.31 billion US dollars), and N110 billion (815 million US dollars) in 1999, 2000, 2001, 2002 and October 2003 respectively. This totalled N 934.87 billion (6.93 billion US dollars) for the five years under consideration.

Table 6 shows further that the statutory allocation to the Niger Delta increased from N 25.612 billion ($ 0.2 billion) in 1999 to N 277.972 billion in 2003 ($ 2.06 billion), what is an increase of 930%. The 13% derivation funds increased from N 58,100 billion ($ 0.43 billion) to 110.026 billion ($ 0.82 billion), what is an increase of about 91%. This increment did not result in increased development because of the high level of corruption associated with the use of oil funds.

Table 6: Statutory and 13% Derivation Fund Allocation to Niger Delta State, in Billions of Naira (1999 - 2003)

Year	1999		2000		2001		2002		2003*	
State	Statutory	13%	Statu-tory	13%	Statu-tory	13%	Statu-tory	13%	Statu-tory	13%
Abia	2.30	-	6.01	0.81	7.54	1.06	7.78	1.87	9.65	2.32
Akwa Ibom	3.32	-	18.21	12.81	7.54	16.72	11.97	6.47	9.65	16.09
Bayel	2.59	-	14.70	10.57	23.53	13.80	16.87	17.49	25.55	22.73
Cross. River	2.62	-	6.15	0.001	6.79	0.002	7.24	0.88	9.27	1.77
Delta	3.59	-	22.61	17.43	29.91	22.75	32.40	30.43	38.98	33.67
Edo	2.65	-	6.49	0.34	7.28	0.44	7.22	0.67	8.88	1.24
Imo	2.54	-	7.16	1.46	8.84	1.91	8.05	1.89	10.36	2.67
Ondo	2.67	-	9.59	4.10	12.09	5.35	8.52	2.20	11.08	3.57
Rivers	3.32	-	16.4	10.57	21.17	13.80	22.61	23.11	32.49	25.85
Total	25.61	-	107.33	58.10	136.30	75.83	122.65	130.80	167.95	110.03

Note: * *Figures are for January to October 2003.*
Source: *Federal Account Allocation Committee Files, Abuja, Nigeria.*

Corruption of different government agents relating to oil exploration and production in Nigeria has led to misuse of the large amount of oil funds generated from the Niger Delta. It has been confirmed by the present Minister of State for Finance that governors in Nigeria, especially those from oil-producing states, travel abroad every month to save or to spend their monthly allocation meant for the development of their areas.

7 Effects of Weak Political and Legal Institutions in the Nigerian Oil Industry

Governance and the political process seem to have also been weakened by the presence of oil resources. The political systems which are most conducive to stable institutions and which allow for a fair distribution and utilization of oil revenues are that of mature democracies. These systems are characterized by political stability and by institutional accountability, what encourages policy makers to think in the long term as economic performance becomes central to competition for political power. Bureaucracies are competent, and existing - relatively autonomous - professional judicial systems foster depersonalized functions of markets and a stability of rules. Policy decisions are generally based on transparent information while property rights are clearly defined. These features give the citizens the opportunity to provide a critical counterbalance to the influence of interests benefiting from government policies (Aigbokhan, 2003b: 76).

Another aspect in which oil has weakened political institutions in the Niger Delta is that it has created a predatory state, which abhors counter-pressure. In a bid to resist or to prevent counter-pressure, political repression has arisen and become a feature in Niger Delta since the days of Isaac Adaka Boro (Isaac Adaka Boro was one of the leaders of the pressure group agitating for responsible use of oil resources in Niger-Delta), a feature which later climaxed in the hanging of Ken Saro-Wiwa in 1995. The following instances, as documented by Human Rights Watch (1999: 13), exemplify weak political and legal institutions in Nigeria in general and in Niger Delta in particular. A study concluded in this context: "Most state and local government institutions involved in environmental resource management lack funding, trained staff, technical expertise, adequate information, analytical capability and other pre-requisites for implementing comprehensive policies and programmes. In the case of the oil industry, overlapping mandates and jurisdiction between Federal Environmental Protection Agency (FEPA) and the Department for Petroleum Resources (DPR) frequently contribute to counterproductive competition" (Egwaikhide and Aregbeyen, 1999: 101).

There is the lack of a properly functioning legal system that could promptly and fairly rule in cases involving compensation, pollution, or contracts. The gravity of the situation in the Delta is greatly exacerbated by the fact that the Nigerian court system is in crisis. The lack of a properly functioning court system also contributes to conflict between communities and companies because, instead of proper investigation of criminal damage or other offenses, followed by charge and trial, the police instead choose to detain and assault youths and other community members, often on an arbitrary basis as forms of collective punishment for the whole community.

The quality of judicial appointments has steadily deteriorated over the years, and the level of executive interference in court decisions has increased. Judges, magistrates and other court officers, including prosecutors (and police, who often act as prosecutors), are very poorly paid. Court facilities are hopelessly overcrowded, badly equipped, and under-funded. Interpreters may be nonexistent or badly trained. Court libraries are inadequate. There are no computers, photocopiers, or other modern equipment; and judges may even have to supply their own paper and pens to record their judgments in longhand. If litigants need a transcript of a judgment for the purposes of an appeal, they have to pay for the transcript themselves. There are long delays in bringing both criminal and civil cases to court. This financial crisis encourages the acceptance of bribes, in order to achieve the standard of living regarded as acceptable by someone with a legal qualification. Corruption is a pervasive feature of court cases, whether criminal or civil.

Compensation for pollution damage is equally plagued by problems of due process and difficulties in interpreting a series of overlapping statutes, combined with rules developed through the common law. The Petroleum Act does not explicitly refer to spills, but its requirement for oil companies to pay "fair and adequate compensation for the disturbance of surface or other rights" to the owner or occupier of any land or property affected by exploration or production has been held to apply to oil spills. There is no statutory definition of fair and adequate compensation. Even when compensation is agreed in principle at oil company rates, compensation payments rarely reflect the true value of the loss to the local community. There are constant disputes as to what is included and with regard to the rates paid. Part of the problem is that there is no independent confirmation that spillages have been caused by sabotage. Although the Department of Petroleum Resources is supposed to confirm sabotage and community members may also be invited to inspect the damaged installation, often no genuinely independent experts are present.

8 Efforts of Government and Oil Companies at Minimizing Conflicts in the Niger Delta

8.1 Efforts of Federal, State and Local Governments at Minimizing Conflicts in Niger Delta

To address the renewed and heightened wave of youth restiveness in the region, following years of neglect and underdevelopment in the midst of oil wealth, the Federal Government in December 2000 set up the Niger Delta Development Commission (NDDC). Its mandate is "to conceive, plan and implement projects and programmes for the sustainable development of the Niger Delta Area", and to undertake infrastructural development in the region. The NDDC began operation in early 2001 (Aigbokhan, 2003b: 76). The NDDC is currently funded by the Federal Government and by the oil companies. The Federal Government contributes 15% of the 13% oil revenue share allocated to the nine states, while the oil companies contribute 3% of their annual budget to the NDDC fund. Finally, 50% of the funds due to the member states from the Ecological Fund are also allocated to the NDDC. The Ecological Fund allocates the means to the federal states in Nigeria to control erosion and other environmental damages.

The Commission has developed a formula whereby 60% of its funds are spent in proportion to the amount of oil produced in each state. Although its governing board has government–nominated representatives from each of the nine states, members of the civil society (a source of counter-pressure) from the region are conspicuously absent from the board. The Commission's budget for 2001 and for 2002 was N 10 billion (74 million US Dollars) and N 14 billion (103 million US Dollars) respectively (Aigbokhan, 2003b). Since youth restiveness persists, some critics feel that the NDDC should and could do more. For example, the popular view at a recent reference workshop of stakeholders in oil-producing communities in Bayelsa state was that the NDDC has not made much impact on the development of the region. The Commission is accused of not carrying the communities along in planning development projects, and thus there is a lack of project ownership. It must also be emphasized that issues of sustainability of NDDC projects may not have received adequate attention so far. In an attempt to make its presence felt throughout the region, the NDDC may have spread its budget too thinly without paying attention to sustainability.

Local governments are also relevant in reducing conflicts in Niger Delta through provision and maintenance of infrastructures. They are - according to Obadan (1993: 3) - of assistance in protecting oil installations and pipelines.

8.2 Efforts of Oil Companies at Minimizing Conflicts in Niger Delta

In response to much protests and occupations, oil companies now have extensive programmes for community development/empowerment in host communities, make sizable payments to local and state governments, and hire youths for surveillance contracts to satisfy the employment demands. In the year 2001 the Shell Petroleum Development Company (SPDC) spent approximately US$ 52 million on community development in Niger Delta and paid out US$ 2.1 million as compensation in respect of third-party claims resulting from oil spills and construction damages. The Mobil Oil Company

(MOC), on its part, contributed US$ 12 million on development projects in the year 2001 in the region (Human Rights Watch, 2002: 18).

This strategy has not been effective in reducing youth restiveness or making a noticeable development impact in the region. For example, according to an evaluation of the SPDC's development projects undertaken in the year 2001 by independent consultants, paid for by Shell, less than one-third of 408 projects were considered fully successful (Human Rights Watch, 2002: 18). Oil Companies also pay compensation to minimize conflicts in Niger Delta. The value of total compensation paid for the acquisition of land space for oil operations had been generally low. For example, ELF paid just N 28,400 (US$ 210) for 1.4 ha of land acquired at the Obodugwa four locations in Ndokwa East local government area of Delta State in the 1980s. It also paid N 130,000 (US$ 963) as total compensation for 6.3 ha at the Obodor location, also in Delta State. In River State, the company paid N 317,400 (US$ 2351) for 11.9 ha and N 206,000 (US$ 1526) for 7.3 ha as total compensation, for land acquired at the Achiara and Ibewa locations respectively (Orubu, 2001:557). Compensation rates paid by the SPDC seem to be comparatively smaller than those paid by ELF. For example, in the 1980s, the SPDC paid N 77, 026 (US$ 571) as compensation for 23 ha of land for Okpokunu 1 location (Delta State) for all economic crops, huts, shrines, animal traps, and the loss of fishing rights. Using the basic figure above, ELF's average compensation for Delta State reduces to N 9364 (US$ 69) per hectare, and to about N 27,260 (US$ 202) for Rivers State. The SPDC average compensation for Delta State, using the Okpokunu case, reduces to about N 3349 (US$ 25) per ha. Even at constant prices, these values of compensation are, no doubt, low. It is observed that when compensation paid is based on statutory rates the value is low compared to when it is negotiated (Orubu, 2001: 557).

The fact that the SPDC considers conflict resolution important led to a commissioned study by the oil company. The study was on how the exploration and production activities in Nigeria's Niger Delta region may have contributed to conflict and the breakdown of social order in the area. According to Uwujaren (2004: 50), the study was compelled by the worsening climate of violence and insecurity in the region that has increased the risk and the cost of resource extraction. The commissioned report states that SPDC induces conflicts through a "quick fix reactive and divisible approach to community engagement expressed through different areas of policy, practice, and corporate culture" (Uwujaren, 2004: 50). Some of the "offensive policies" outlined by the report include oil spill remediation and compensation, administration of land acquisition, community representation, and contracting. The study equally captures influences of SPDC's staff that instigate bogus claimants to make claims on the company and split the proceeds with the claimants on the sly.

Perhaps more worrisome is the observation that the SPDC stands the risk of not being able to continue with on-shore resource extraction in the Niger Delta if the current conflict trend is not checked.

8.3 Efforts of Donor Agencies, Civil Societies, NGOs, and Vigilante at Minimizing Conflicts in Niger Delta

Donor organizations are of assistance in ameliorating conflicts in the Niger Delta. The case of the European Union (EU) on micro-projects finance is a good case in this regard. The programme tagged MPP3 was first introduced in Bayelsa, Delta and Rivers States. A sister project MPP6 was introduced in Abia, Cross River, Imo, Akwa Ibom, Edo and Ondo States (Aigbokhan, 2003b: 76). These schemes are expected to positively influence production activities in Niger Delta.

Community heads, Non Governmental Organizations (NGO), community vigilantee groups (night guards organized and sponsored by the community), youth organizations, and trade unions of the Niger Delta also assist in the surveillance of oil pipelines. Umebali and Ebue (2002: 183) have shown that the NGOs in their administration avoid corruption and bureaucracy, which adversely affects decision-making processes. Hence, NGOs in the Niger Delta mobilize both human and non- human resources for action, thereby enhancing rural development in oil-producing communities. NGOs and donor organizations in the host communities bring out development to the rural community through the provision of infrastructural facilities. The area where these organizations are of practical use in the Niger Delta is in the area of enlightenment campaigns about the negative environmental impact of vandalism, the need for peace and tranquility, and accountability. According to Otite (2002: 48), vigilante groups should be encouraged to secure the infrastructures of oil pipelines. The leaders of vigilante groups sometimes give public enlightenment lectures and discussions in the host communities using local dialects to target community youth leaders. All these are attempts to reduce conflicts in the Niger Delta region.

9 Policy Recommendations on How to Minimize Oil-induced Conflicts and Escaping the Primary Commodity Dilemma in Nigeria

9.1 Short Term Measures

In order to ameliorate oil-induced conflicts in the Niger Delta youths who are agents of restiveness must be empowered through training and retraining. They must be trained to be gainfully employed or self-employed. A well-supervised micro credit scheme can help in this regard. There can also be Niger Delta Fund Initiatives. This is a Trust Fund that would provide, in addition to a smaller cash dividend, funds for low interest loans for sustainable development projects in the rural areas in the region. A smaller percentage of the fund would be earmarked for funding conflicts resolution and conservation programmes. The ethnic groups resident in the oil-producing areas should be listened to. All the harassment of individuals and organizations should be stopped. Civil society concerned with the affairs of the Niger Delta should come under one umbrella and articulate their agenda for the development of Niger Delta.

Oil and gas matters should be removed from the exclusive list and placed on the concurrent legislative list. This would enhance improved relationships between oil and gas companies and their oil-bearing host communities, which are largely manipulated. Just like the recently established Bank of Industry, the Federal Government should establish a Niger Delta Development Bank. Oil and gas producing communities should participate in the equity structure of such a bank.

9.2 Medium Term Measures

The issue of sustainability of all the projects in the Niger Delta must be emphasized. This can be done by carrying out impact assessments before project execution, including socioeconomic, human rights, demographic, and geographic aspects. This can be best done using a Geographic Information System (GIS) in the impact assessment. Involving the beneficiaries in the planning and implementation of the project can also ensure sustainability of the project. Oil companies should carry out their oil exploration and exploitation with the same international standards observed in the developed countries. The oil and gas companies should either alone or in collaboration with the oil-producing communities embark upon small and medium scale industries. Such industries should be based on raw materials sourced from local areas. There should be massive skills acquisition programmes by the multinational companies as well as by local, state and federal governments. The large-scale oil and gas-based industries such as refineries, gas plants, and the oil and gas companies themselves should have indigenes of the area in which they operate to serve on their boards.

The oil and gas companies should ensure the integrity of their populace and, in times of spillage, the best industry technology should be employed to undertake and effect urgent removal of toxic waste, which is widespread in the Niger Delta. The bush surrounding the NNPC pipelines should be cleared to facilitate easy detection of vandals of pipelines. Perhaps there is need to put in place an anti-pipeline vandalization squad similar to the Federal Road Safety Corps (FRSC) to stem sabotage in the Niger Delta. Improved state of the art technology is urgently required to halt or minimize pipeline vandalization, such as the provision of facilities that could automatically shut down the flow of the crude oil and petroleum products whenever leakages occur along the pipelines.

There is need for a gas policy by the government (there is none at present as distinct from an energy policy), and such a policy should then be concerned with the establishment of the optimum penalty for gas flaring. This is defined as a penalty that would achieve a zero-flaring level (in reality, about 4% as zero flaring may be technically infeasible; 4% is the minimum gas flaring level that is achievable worldwide), and would be equal to or greater than the compliance cost of flaring to producing companies. Government needs to urgently put in place a pollution enforcement agency with their anti-pollution plans/strategy for each fiscal year. Alternatively the oil companies should be made to compulsorily embark upon a pollution insurance scheme. This option has the extra advantage of compelling oil companies to adopt up to date or modern technology that is pollution-conscious in their production processes. Otherwise they will face the option of paying a substantial amount on premium.

9.3 Long Term Measures

The federal and state governments, as well as the private investors (foreign and local) should set up industries around the communities and based on the raw materials that are obtainable in the region such as rice, fish and sharp sand. Stabilization and Special Funds should be created to handle the problem of the primary commodity dilemma. The excess oil revenues being generated now should not be shared among the three tiers of government. They should be kept in this Fund that will be used to finance agricultural production and processing for exports. This may require an element of legislation on the part of the government, by making effective laws that will make the Fund functional and be used to cushion the effects of oil price fluctuations.

In conclusion, the challenge of developing the Niger Delta region is complex but not insurmountable. Most needed is peace in the Niger Delta to recover lost ground. Government owes a moral obligation to the Niger Delta people to create an enabling environment for peace and sustainable development in the region. In return, the communities should fully cooperate with the efforts of the governments.

References

Adewuyi, A. O. (2001): "The implications of crude oil exploitation and export on the environment and level of economic growth and development in Nigeria. Natural Resources Use, the Environment and Sustainable Development". Ibadan, Nigeria. Pp. 119–146.

Alabi, R. A. (2004): "Economic efficiency of cocoa based agroforestry systems in Oyo State", Nigeria. Ph. D. Thesis submitted to the Postgraduate School, Federal University of Technology, Akure, Ondo State, Nigeria. P. 225.

Alabi, R.A., Aigbokhan, B. and M. I. Ailemen (2004): "Improving technical efficiency of Nigerian cocoa farmers through institutionalized farm credits". Paper presented at the Inaugural Symposium of the Association of African Agricultural Economists. Regency Hotel, Nairobi, Kenya, 5th - 9th, December 2004. P. 21.

Aigbokhan, B.E. (2003a): "Challenges and options for social welfare development in the Niger Delta". Report Prepared for the West African Institute for Financial and Economic Management, Lagos. P. 16.

Aigbokhan, B.E. (2003b): "Oil Resources and development in the Niger Delta", A Research Report Prepared for African Network for Environment and Economic Justice (ANEEJ), Benin, Nigeria. P. 76.

Azelama, J.U. and A. S. Akpotor, (2003): "Peace-Violent: Women activities and critical development in the Niger Delta". In: F.E. Iyoha, S. O. J. Ojo, and P.O. Oviasuyi (eds), Women, Youth Restiveness and Development in Niger Delta. Institute for Governance and Development, Ambrose Alli University, Ekpoma. Pp. 55 - 63

Aregbeyen, O. (2001): "Dealing with point-source environmental pollution in Nigeria: The case of the Niger-Delta". In: G. A. Garba (ed.), Natural Resources Use, the Environment and Sustainable Development. Ibadan, Nigeria. Pp. 557–573.

Bankole, A.S. (2001): "Incentives and regulation to abate gas flaring in Nigeria: Toward optimal gas utilization policy". In: G. A. Garba (ed.), Natural Resources

Use, the Environment and Sustainable Development. Nigerian Economic Society, Ibadan, Pp. 519–534.

Carim, A. (2002): "Analysis of economic efficiency of male and female rice farmers in Ekiti State". Nigeria, NISER Monograph Series, Ibadan, No 15. Pp. 1-48.

CCA (2001): "Common Country Assessment", United Nations Development Programme Report, Lagos, Nigeria. Pp. 23-34.

CBN/Central Bank of Nigeria (2003): "Central Bank of Nigeria Statistical Bulletin, 2003. Lagos, Nigeria. Pp. 23-34.

CBN/Central Bank of Nigeria (2002): "Central Bank of Nigeria Statistical Bulletin 2002". Lagos, Nigeria. Pp. 43-45.

CBN/Central Bank of Nigeria (2000): "Central Bank of Nigeria Annual Report and Statement of Accounts".2000. Lagos, Nigeria. Pp. 23-45.

Efe, S. I. (2003): "Effects of Gas flaring on temperature and adjacent vegetation in Niger Delta environment", International Journal of Environmental Issues, Vol. 1, No. 1, Pp. 91-101.

Egwaikhide, F.O. (1999): "Determinants of imports in Nigeria: A dynamic specification", African Economic Research Consortium Research Paper 91. Pp. 1-39, Nairobi, Kenya.

Egwaikhide, F.O. and O. Aregbeyen, (1999): "Oil production externalities in Niger Delta: Are fiscal solutions feasible?" In: B. E. Aigbokhan (ed.): Fiscal Federalism and Nigeria's Economic Development. Ibadan, Nigeria. Pp. 101-118.

Garba, A. G. and P. K. Garba (2001): "Market failure, state failure and air pollution in Nigeria: A theoretical investigation of two cases". In: G. A. Garba (ed.). Natural Resources Use, the Environment and Sustainable Development. Ibadan, Nigeria. Pp. 491-517.

Gary, I. and T. Karl (2003): "Bottom of the barrel: Africa's oil boom and the poor", Catholic Relief Service. New York. Pp. 3-4.

Human Rights Watch (2002): "Nigeria: the Niger Delta – No democratic dividend". New York. Pp. 18 - 20

Human Rights Watch (1999): "Oil and Gas in Nigeria". Human Right watch website: http://www.hrw.org/reports/nigeria. accessed 03/09/2004, New York, p. 19.

ICCO (International Cocoa Organization) (2003): "Quarterly Bulletin of Cocoa Statistics 2003".

Obadan, M. I. (1993): "Local government and rural development in Nigeria, Bulletin of the National Centre for Economic Management and Administration". Ibadan, Vol. 5, pp. 3–6.

Ogbe, M. G. (1999): "The Impacts of oil exploration and exploitation on the Niger Delta", Paper presented at the Annual Field Trip of Geography and Regional Planning Students at Oleh, Port Hacourt, River State, Nigeria. Pp. 2-7.

Okecha, S. (2003): "Flames of sabotage: The tragedy of youth restiveness in the Niger Delta". In: F. E. Iyoha, S. O. J. Ojo, and P. O. Oviasuyi (eds.), Women,

Youth Restiveness and Development in the Niger Delta. Institute for Governance and Development, Ambrose Alli University, Ekpoma. Pp. 25-30.

Okojie, E. I. and M. I. Ailemen (2003): "Oil exploration and unemployment in Nigeria: The case of women and youths in the Niger Delta". In: F. E. Iyoha, S. O. J. Ojo and P. O. Oviasuyi (eds.), Women, Youth Restiveness and Development in Niger Delta. Institute for Governance and Development, A.A.U, Ekpoma. Pp. 25–30.

Okoh, R. N. and P. C. Egbon (1999): "Fiscal federalism and revenue allocation. The poverty of the Niger Delta", in: B. E. Aigbokhan (ed.): Fiscal Federalism and Nigeria's Economic Development. Ibadan, Nigeria. Pp. 405-420.

Orubu, C. O. (2001): "Compensation programmes for the use of natural resources by oil companies in Nigeria". In: G.A Garba (ed.) Natural Resources Use, the Environment and Sustainable Development. Ibadan, Nigeria. Pp. 557-573.

Otite, A. (2002): "Vigilante groups as a check against the vandalization of oil Pipelines, NEPA and NITEL lines in Delta State". In: V. T. Jike (ed.). Ethnic Militia and Youth Rebelliousness in Nigeria, A Book of Readings. Published by the Nigeria Institute for Strategic Studies Publications, Lagos, Nigeria. Pp. 48-54.

Sagay, E. I. (2002): "Nigerian constitution: Operation of federalism and the Niger Delta", Paper Presented at the Seminar on the Niger Delta and Nigeria's Federalism. Organized by TAS and Associate Company and the Office of the Governor, Delta State, 2nd - 3rd November 2002, at Petroleum Training Institute. Pp. 16-17.

Umebali, E. E. and M. I. Ebue (2002): "Role of Non-Governmental Organizations (NGOs) in rural development: A study of Enugu State". In: O. A. Ibitoye (ed.), Rural environment and Sustainable Development. Published by the Department of Geography and Planning Sciences, University of Ado Ekiti, Ekiti State, Nigeria. Pp. 183-188.

Uzukwa, A. (1999): "National gas utilization in Nigeria", Nigeria Society Conference for Gas Employee Proceedings. Pp. 19-30.

Uwujaren, W. (2004): "A cross to bear." Tell Magazine, Number 40, pp. 50–52.

Raw Materials Games and Crises in Africa: Understanding the Economic Dilemma

Joseph Ndeffo Fongue

1 Introduction

Conflicts and various other types of crises[1] can be underlined as features of the recent history of Africa. Only in the 1990s, more that 15 African counties were in conflicts (civil wars in Ethiopia, Sudan, Chad, Liberia, Angola, Mozambique, and South Africa; clan and faction warfare in Somalia; an invasion of Rwanda by armed exiles; ethnic and separatist insurrections in Uganda, Mauritania, Senegal and Morocco; and Tuareg revolts in Niger and Mali)[2]. Many analysts try to find a historical explanation of the existing conflicts and to point out factors like ethnicity, religion or environmental scarcity[3]. However, the role of raw materials as a factor of crisis has not enough been underlined. Furthermore, the existence of conflicts has also not been enough highlighted as explaining factor of the Dutch disease (or the coexistence between raw materials and poverty) in Africa.

The present work aims to (1) highlight the abundance of raw materials (AORM) as a major factor of crisis in Africa, (2) to explain the mechanism of the "raw materials games", and (3) to make some proposals for actions to be taken in order to escape from the dilemma. The work is organized as follow:

---

1 Dictatorship, apartheid, social fragmentation, etc may be mentioned. The crisis can be either active or passive. For a survey of the typology of crises in Africa, see for instance Salim, Ahmed Salim (1999: 8-29).

2 For a survey of these conflicts, see for instance Carolyn Pumphrey, Rye Schwartz-Barcott (2003: 1-26).

3 For instance, the "Pulse Model" (i.e. ecological and climate research acts as a fundamental quality that provides the backdrop for human experience) is used as a historical explanation for the tension in Niger.

The section 2 highlights the coexistence between the abundance of raw materials (AORM) and some of the main indicators of crisis like the length of conflicts, the fatality of the conflicts, and their geographical localisation within and outside the countries in crisis. The section 3 explains (1) the behaviour of the different actors that are involved in the system "Raw material – Crisis", and (2) the interactions between them. The section 4 is an application of the section 3 with a particular reference to the DR of Congo. The section 5 proposes some directives for the actions to be taken by the different agents in the prospect of a dialectics between their different interests and the development process in Africa.

2 The Abundance of Raw Materials, Poverty and Crises in Africa: The Economic Dilemma

Given a sample of countries and of raw materials, one can define a set of indicators in order to measure (1) the intensity of the crisis in a country during a given period (one year for instance), and (2) the level of abundance of raw materials in the same country[4] and for the same period, and then use them to analyse (statistically) the nature and the importance of the relations between the two. Many empirical studies highlight the weak correlation between AORM and economic growth in many countries (see for instance Ranis, edwards 1991: 59 – 101; Auty, Richard 1997: 651 – 63; Davis, Dodaldn, 1995: 1765 – 79; Fosu, Augustin, Kuasi 1996: 465 – 75; and Winter, Nelson 1995: 35-59). An explanation of this weak correlation (sometimes related to the "Dutch disease") is provided by the so – called "staple trap model", according to which the AORM leads generally to a great propensity to the specialization in the export of raw materials at the detriment of the development of other economic sectors or activities. Furthermore, this model stresses that specialization is associated with a weak development level of both human and production capital (see for example WIDER 1998: 1-3). Without rejecting the contours and the outcomes of these useful contributions, the present work would rather like to point out the role played by the different actors in the crises in the explanation of the Dutch disease in

---

4 Many authors define three measures of the role of natural capital in economic development that are the Environmental Kuznets Curve (EKC), the stock of natural capital, and the rent from natural capital. For a brief survey, see WIDER (1998: 1).

the African countries. The present section will therefore be limited especially on highlighting the coexistence between the abundance of raw materials (AORM) and some main indicators of crisis like the length of conflicts, the fatality of the conflicts, and their geographical localisation within and outside the countries in crisis.

2.1 The Abundance of Raw Materials in Africa

In order to highlight the abundance of raw materials as a feature of the African Continent, it should be useful to say a word on its geologic structure[5]. The continent is formed of plains and plateaus intercepted by cracks. One finds in Africa the so-called 3 SAHARAs (a) of Kalahari, (b) of Congo, and (c) of the North West of the continent. The basement is formed of crystal clear rocks, dated from the KIMBERLY age. Many active and mobile bands separate the 3 SAHARAs. The first Sahara is the Kalahari that covers the majority of the areas of the southern part of Africa and contains the oldest world known rocks, as well as rocky structures formed of metal and of magnesium. These rocks are characterized by their wealth in platinum, in chromites, in vanadium, in copper, in zinc, in precious stones, and in precious metals. The second Sahara is the "plateau of Congo" that covers a large area at the centre of southern Africa, and contains many underground rocky bands in granite and in green rocks. It is rich particularly of gold. The third Sahara covers the North Western part of the continent as well as the greatest part of the areas of Western Africa, and extends from the Guinea Golf in the South up to the Atlas region in Morocco. This area is formed with granite rocks and with green stones where especially gold can be found. In all these 3 SAHARAs one finds separated rocks dated from the late age of stones. One finds sediments of sandy stones, clayey stones, stones in mud, chalky stones and stones of other blocs.

These rocks are of great importance with regard to the volume of gold that they contain. That is rich obviously in South Africa, in Ghana, in Ethiopia, and in Congo (DR). One finds diamonds in Namibia, bauxites in Guinea, and phosphates in North – Africa. The great African fissure is one of the main geologic characteristics of the continent. It is a volcanic fissure

5 For more details on the geologic structure of Africa, see especially Goudie, Adams and Orme, Andrea (1999: 15 -125), Summerfield, Anderson (1985: 281 - 294) and Minns, Williams (1984: 5 - 67).

very rich in ores and in salty marshes. The African continent is therefore an area of important mineral richness. The mineral mines cover the centre and the south of the continent, because of the existence of volcanic rocks. The African basement abounds in platinum, diamonds, chromites, cobalt, phosphates, manganese, gold, and bauxites[6]. The continent monopolises the world production of diamonds and of chromate, and contributes in a large proportion to the world production of zircon (scarce and rich metal that resembles diamond and is used as its simulant), titanium, uranium, vanadium, copper, vermiculite and gold. Africa covers 30% of world proved reserves of all mineral raw materials, and more specifically it covers 80% of the world reserves of platinum, chromites and tantalum, and 40% of the world reserves of gold, cobalt and manganese. Furthermore, the African countries realise 60% of the world diamonds production, and the world contribution of countries such as Botswana, South Africa, Congo (DR) and Angola is respectively 28%, 11 %, 2.7 %, and 10%. Five African countries (Cameroon, Gabon, Ivory Coast, Congo and Liberia) are included in the list of the six first world main exporters of wood, and Congo (DR) covers over 20% of the coltan world production. The estimation of the potential of natural resources[7] in the African countries confirms the characteristic of a "*geologic scandal*" (i.e. the high density of mineral resources in this part of the world) that is used by some scientists to describe the situation in this part of the world.

Within the framework of a study that analyses the interactions between raw materials abundance and crisis, it should be worth pointing out the role and the importance of selected African raw materials for the industrial countries. As stressed in the table 1, The African raw materials are of a great importance for the world economy (especially for the industrial countries) with regard to their role in strategic industrial activities, including the automobile industry, the aerospace industry, and the new technologies.

---

6 The African marshes are characterized by their high level of concentration and by their volume of resources, especially diamonds, platinum, gold, chromites, manganese, copper, and uranium.

7 In a technical version of this work (see Ndeffo Fongue, Joseph 2004 : 14-22), an indicator to capture the natural potential (level of abundance of raw materials) covers the total value (in currency units) of the proved reserves of all the already identified raw materials of the country.

Table 1: Selected African Raw Materials: Share of Africa in the World's Proved Reserves and Output

Raw materials	Importance	Share of Africa		Main African Producers
		In the world's proved reserves	In the world's output	
Elements of the Platinum group	Especially used in the jewellery industry, in electronics industry, and in the clinics of teethe.	89%	62%	South Africa, Zimbabwe, Botswana, Namibia, Tanzania, Uganda, Ethiopia, Sierra Leone, Congo (DR)
Diamonds	Used as trenchant element in the metal industry, and in the jewellery business.	60%	50%	Botswana, South Africa, Angola, Congo (DR), Namibia, Ghana, Central African Republic, Liberia, Sierra Leone
Chromites	Used in the production of chemical products, and of materials resisting to the cast iron.	87%	43%	South Africa, Zimbabwe, Sudan, Madagascar
Zircon	Main ore of the metal zirconium, used in metallurgic industry.	85%	28%	South Africa
Cobalt	strategic mineral, employed in many industries. Cobalt is of importance for the industry of aircraft, and for the stations of the energy production.	73,8%	42%	Congo (DR) and Zambia
Vermiculite	Used in the production of calorific insulating materials.	45%	38%	South Africa, Mozambique, Egypt

Continuation on the next page.

Continuation of Table 1 from the previous page.

Raw materials	Importance	Share of Africa		Main African Producers
		In the world's proved reserves	In the world's output	
Vanadium	Used to improve the particularities of mixed irons.	3%	39%	South Africa
Manganese	Used in the production of iron, of lead, of construction materials, machines and transportation means, of dry batteries, and of aluminium mixtures	55%	33%	South Africa , Sudan, Ghana, Morocco, Egypt
Phosphates	used to produce cement, and it is used in the chemical industry producing detergents.	4%	29%	Tunisia, South Africa, Senegal, Togo, Algeria
Titanium	Used in the dyeing and in the ceramic	32%	29%	Mozambique, Kenya
Gold	Gold is used for jewellery, in the modern industry for producing computers, communication's instruments, motors of aircraft, and special ships.	46%	23%	South Africa, Ghana, Mali, Zimbabwe, Guinea
Coltan	Used in the industry of mobile phones and in the industry of condensers.	60%	70%	Central African Republic, Congo, Ethiopia, Rwanda, Burundi, Uganda.

Source: *International Financial Statistics of the International Monetary Fund (Yearbooks 1980, 1995, 2000 and 2004) completed with data from CNUCED; Department of Energy Statistics (various issues); The columns 2, 3, 4 and 5 are from the author and based on his general knowledge on the topic. See also Zussman, Deer, Howie (1996: 22–27), Schumann, Walter (1993: 11-19), Kornprobst, Jacques (2002: 45-62), Lima, de Faria(2003: 34-56), and Walter Schumann (1992: 76-85).*

2.2 Abundance of Raw materials, Poverty and Crises

2.2.1 The Social and Economic Dilemma

The natural capital (land and raw materials) is traditionally considered as key for production and is an important growth factor, especially in the countries with limited use of technical progress. The African countries should be therefore in the position to achieve their economic and development goals on the base of their raw materials, if the latter are used properly. Raw materials and petroleum contribute to far more than 50% of the exports of many African countries. In Nigeria, for instance, petroleum and petroleum products represent 95% of the total value of exports, just like in Mauritania, Zambia and Niger where raw materials represent respectively 54%, 50% and 32 % of the revenues from external trade[8].

Unfortunately, the revenue from mineral wealth is not exploited for the development of the concerned countries and does not contribute efficiently to the achievement of the welfare of their people; the revenues from raw materials are exploited in many countries to finance war. This explains why 26 African countries belong to the 32 poorest countries[9] of the world, although Africa possesses over 30% of the world's proved reserves of raw materials. Sophisticated techniques are not needed to confirm the strong link between the abundance of raw materials and the incidence of poverty in Africa. The percentage of the population that is living under absolute poverty is generally very high in Africa (comparing to the rest of the world), and there are not significant differences to be observed between the African countries in this regard. However, the African countries with their high dependency on primary resources are quite differently endowed with specific raw materials This correlation of poverty and abundance of raw materials is analogous if one takes into account the other social and economic indicators of the African countries that are abundant of raw materials. The facts of poverty in Africa are precisely the following (see for instance Ziegler, Jean 2003: 1-4):

---

8 These percentages are computed with data from the International Financial Statistics (Yearbooks 1980, 1995, 2000 and 2004) of the International Monetary Fund.

9 Some other details can be found in Artadi, Eedwards and Sala-i-Martin, Xavier, and in Khan, Mahmood Hasan (2001: 15–42).

- 315 million people – one of two people in Sub Saharan Africa - survive on less than one dollar per day;
- 184 million people – 33 % of the African population – suffer from malnutrition;
- During the 1990s the average income per capita decreased in 20 African countries;
- Less than 50% of Africa's population has access to hospitals or doctors;
- In 2000, 300 million Africans did not have access to safe water;
- The average life expectancy in Africa is 41 years;
- Only 57% of the African children are enrolled in primary education, and only one of three children do not complete the school;
- One in six children die before the age of 5. This number is 25 times higher in Sub Saharan Africa than in the OECD countries;
- Children account for half of all civilian casualties in wars in Africa; and
- The African continent lost more than 5,3 million hectares of forest during the decade of the 1990.

Although these are some few data and indicators about the situation, they highlight the case of a continent with abundance of raw materials on the one side and huge problems for the people on the other side.

2.2.2 The Abundance of Raw Materials as a Factor of Crisis in Africa

The African countries with crises are the places where we find new forms of war in which the conflicting sides are motivated by the commercial exploitation of raw materials. In the countries in crisis, especially in Congo (DR), Liberia and Sierra Leone, the areas of intensive conflicts are also those in which one finds the most important deposits of raw materials (see map in Annex). A main feature of the political crisis affecting so many African countries since many decades is therefore the coexistence between the abundance of raw materials and the number and intensity of identified conflicts. The tables 2 and 3 highlight the coexistence of a correlation between the indicators of conflicts and abundance of raw materials in selected African countries. It is shown in the table 2 that the length and the level of the fatality of the disputes coexist with raw materials abundance, especially with regard of the strategic commodities oil and diamonds. This causal link is more relevant in the more richly endowed countries (in regard to the abundance of raw materials) than in the less endowed countries. The table 3 shows that 9 out of 14 conflicts as identified in this study (on a simple observation of facts[10]) are linked with the abundance of raw materials, while only 5 are directly caused by other factors like ethnicity or environmental scarcity; 2 conflicts out of 14 are explained by all these factors.

Table 2: Raw materials, Length and Fatality of Crises In Selected Countries

Countries	Length of crisis	Number of displaced persons	Fatality of Dispute (number of persons that have died)	Raw materials as Source of the Conflict
Angola	More than 35 years	1.5 million	4,000,000 (1/3 of the population)	Diamonds, Oil
Chad	16 years	Not available	About 20,000	Oil
Congo (DR)	Over 20 years	2,000,000 since 1998	3, 300,000 since 1998	Diamonds, Coltan, Oil
Liberia	1970s - present	2,000,000	150,000 in 7 years	Diamonds, Wood
Nigeria	4 years (Biafra war)	More than 1 million	2 millions	Oil
	1992 – now (Ogoni)	Not available	Not available	Oil
	1992 – to now (Bakassi)	Not available	Not available	Oil
Western Sahara	More than 30 years	Not available	100,000	none
Sierra Leone		2 millions (44% of the population)	75,000	Diamonds
Sudan	1983 to now	1 million	200,000	Oil

Source: *Ndeffo Fongue, Joseph (2004: 43–57): Conflits et matières premières en Afrique: un tour d'horizon; GREDPEM, Yaoundé; unpublished manus-cript.*

10 See also Pumphrey Carolyn and Schwartz-Barcott, Rye (2003: 1 - 26).

Table 3: Abundance of Raw Materials, Environmental Scarcity and Crises in the Selected Countries

Countries and types of crisis	Coexistence between Raw materials and Conflict	Coexistence between Environmental Scarcity and Conflict	Coexistence between the two Factors and Conflict	Type of raw materials as Conflict "Pay off"	Type of environmental problem (including ethnicity) as Conflict Source
Angola	Yes	No	No	Petroleum, diamonds	None
Chad	Yea	Yes	Yes	Petroleum	Desertification
Congo (DR)	Yes	No	No	Diamonds, Cobalt, Copper, Oil, coltan	None
Congo (PR)	Yes	No	NO	Wood, Oil	None
Liberia	Yes	No	NO	Diamonds, Wood	None
Nigeria	Yes	No	NO	Oil	None
Western Sahara	Yes	Yes	Yes	None	None
Sierra Leone	Yes	No	No	Diamonds	None
Sudan	Yes	Yes	Yes	Oil	Water scarcity; Religion; Worsening ecological problems
Ruanda	No	Yes	No	None	Land scarcity, with a growing population
Niger	No	Yes	No	None	Desertification
Zimbabwe	No	Yes	No	None	Land scarcity (2/3 occupied by white minorities)
South Africa	Yes	No	No	High density of mineral resources	Apartheid and Social Exclusion

Source: *Ndeffo Fongue, Joseph (2004: 66 – 82): Conflits et matières premières en Afrique: un tour d'horizon; GREDPEM, Yaoundé; unpublished manu-script.*

Well-known examples (Nigeria, Angola, Congo DR, Liberia, and Sierra Leone) are quite relevant[11]:

- (i) In *Sierra Leone*, the control and the exploitation of minerals and diamonds deposits between the conflicting actors is the main cause of the conflict. Diamonds abound in the North-West area of the country, especially in Kono and Kenema areas where the most intensive combats are taking place.
- (ii) In *Liberia*, diamonds and wood are the raw materials used to finance the war.
- (iii) *In Nigeria*, the different conflicts (Biafra war, Ogoni conflict, and the Bakassi crisis with opposing Cameroon and Nigeria) experienced since 1964 are strongly linked with the abundance of petroleum on the Cross River area and at the border with Cameroon. Nigeria is the first African oil producer. Taking into account only the Biafra war, more than 2 million persons died between 1964 and 1970, with more than 1,000,000 displaced persons. Supported by many European countries, the Nigerian government, whose aim was the control of oil and the access to the Atlantic Ocean, decided to fight against Biafra that wanted the independence for the cross-river area. It is also well known that the Ogoni crisis is strongly linked to the environmental problems surrounding the extraction of oil. In the Bakassi crisis, the dispute relates essentially to the question of sovereignty over the Bakassi Peninsula, a territory of approximately 665 sq. km. lying between Cross River and the Rio del Rey, the Republic of Cameroon's title that is contested by the Federal Republic of Nigeria. In so doing, the government of the Republic of Nigeria is contesting the long-established frontier between the two countries. Since the end of 1993, this contestation has taken the form of an aggression by the Federal Republic of Nigeria, whose troops are occupying several Cameroonian localities in the Bakassi peninsula. Moreover, the maritime boundary between the two states has been the subject of several delimitation agreements, from the agreement of 11 March 1913 to the

11 In Sudan, petroleum is partly a main cause of the civil war, just like wood and petroleum have been at the base of the conflict in Congo (PR). Western Sahara has not only an important geo-political position but is also rich in raw materials. Petroleum and to some extent uranium have been at the base of the civil war in Chad.

Maroua declaration of 1 June 1975. However, this delimitation has remained a partial one and, despite many attempts to complete it, the two parties have been unable to do so. In order to avoid further incidents between the two countries, the Republic of Cameroon requests the International Justice Court (IJC) to determine the course of the maritime boundary between the two states beyond the line fixed in 1975.

- (iv) In *Angola*, petroleum and diamonds represent the major cause of the more than 35 years of war (first against the Portuguese and, after 1975 with outside help, between themselves). Angola has the potential to be a wealthy developed African nation since it possesses large petroleum and diamond reserves, but due to nearly 4 decades of war the country remains to be seriously underdeveloped. UNITA has used its powerful position of controlling the diamond mines in the Lunda provinces to finance its guerrilla struggle against the MPLA government.
- (v) The conflict in the *Democratic Republic of Congo*, formally Zaire, is complex, complicated by the struggle for power over the country's vast resources by actors within and outside the DR of Congo. In recent years, one particular mineral, coltan[12], has been at the centre of the fight.

3 A Vagabonds In Power/Vagabonds In Rebellion (VIP/VIR) Framework for the Explanation of the Economic Dilemma and the Raw Material Games

The focus of this section is on the behaviour of the different agents involved in the raw materials games, and the interactions between them, i.e. the framework illustrates how they behave in order to exploit illegally the African raw materials. The behaviours and the interactions between the different actors are consistent with the "*dependance*" and "*domination*"

12 As already mentioned, coltan is a key element in cell phones, computer chips, nuclear reactors, and play Stations. The market for the mineral has greatly increased in recent years, exacerbating the conflict in Congo. The precious ore is mined in rebel-controlled areas at the expense of national parks and the depletion of wildlife.

development theories according to which the African countries are strategically, financially and technically weak, and are therefore not in the position to define and to implement strategies within the framework of their relations with the rest of the world. Furthermore, they are obliged to follow the rules defined and imposed by the latter.

The economic environment in which the raw materials games take place is produced by well-known historical and political facts, whose foundation is the Berlin Conference of November 15th 1884 to February 26th 1885. A main motive of the games is the scarcity of raw materials and/or the energy crisis faced by the industrial countries that are therefore obliged to use all their means to provide themselves with African raw materials at low costs. Preferences of the different actors are not defined in terms of the welfare of the African people, but in terms of the benefits that one can derive from the illegal exploitation of raw materials. In order to achieve their goals the different actors produce war and other forms of crisis.

The different sets of actors identified within the framework of this study are the following: (1) the African leaders that can be either in the government or in the opposition, (2) America, European and Asian countries, (3) multinational corporations and individuals, and (4) the civil society. There is a game between the African leaders (in the government or in the armed opposition), the multinationals, the foreign countries (neighbouring countries in Africa, America, European and Asian Countries), and the civil society. Apart from the civil society (whose goal is peace and social progress), all the other actors aim to share the benefits from strategic raw materials. Since many conflicts are taking place in the richest African areas in regard to their natural resources, one can better describe the phenomenon by focusing on the "raw materials explained conflicts". The objective of the conflicts in the African countries is not victory or gaining peace, but as already mentioned the realisation of maximum revenue that one can derive from the illegal exploitation of raw materials. It should be worth saying a word on the different sets of actors and on their relations with the other players:

- (i) *The main actors within the country*: The VIP and the VIR: The behaviour of this set of actors is the key determinant of the raw materials games, since they are those who allow the other agents to interfere in the affairs of African countries. This is the reason why the approach is called "*VIP-VIR framework*". It should be worth mentioning that there is no existing specific conceptual background or literature on this VIP – VIR feature of African leaders (even the political science has unfortunately not focused on this topic). However, it is not a caricature of their personality, since it reflects at a large extent the profile of the majority of the African leaders since the beginning of the period after independence. One characterizes them here as vagabonds because (1) of their lack of political ideology, (2) of their lack of political training and education, (3) especially of the lack of legitimacy of the power (at which they reach with no transparency and on which they do not represent their population), and finally, (4) of all the non-ethical means they use to keep the power at the detriment of their country and population. In general, there is no observable set of positive social actions that have been initiated and implemented by these leaders at a local or at a sectoral level, and that could be in the position to provide a background for their future political actions. The methodology used in this study consists to submit a questionnaire[13] to a representative sample of the population in order to have their viewpoint on the profile of their leaders. The leaders will be qualified as "vagabonds" as far as the will not fill the minimum of qualities required to overtake their political tasks.

The raw materials game is played on two symmetric fields that are different from each other, only because one field is controlled by the government while the other field is controlled by the rebellion. The leaders governing the countries (the Vagabonds In Power - VIP) and those conducting the rebellion (Vagabonds In Rebellion – VIR) are not that different from each other in regard to their ideology toward their population.[14] These two actors are almost perfectly substitutable,

---

13 The main questions and the possible answers are relative (1) to the level of political education of the leaders that may be weak, acceptable or excellent, (2) the nature of their social actions before their political engagement that may be mediocre, acceptable or excellent, (3) the way with which they acceded to the power that can be democratically or not, (4) the means used to maintain themselves on power that may be non-ethical or non-democratically, (5) the extent up to which they represent their populace that may be, partly or totally, non-existent. If the answers are weak, mediocre, non-democratically, non ethical or inexistent, the value is 0. If the answer is acceptable or at part, the value is 0.5. The value is 1 in the other cases. If the mean value of all the answers of the sample population is less than 0.5, then is the leader according to the VIR/VIP approach qualified as vagabond.

14 Corrupt leaders governing the African countries have failed to realise their commitments towards the welfare of their people. The political and dictatorial corruption is a feature of African governments/and rebellions. They are in general vagabonds, with no political ideology, and are helped by America,

since in many countries the actors alter between the government and the rebellion. One can therefore consider the two as largely the same type of actors. As weapons, protection, and personal wealth are guaranteed by America, European and Asian countries (and to some extent by multinationals and individuals), theses actors are used as "*marionettes*" in order to loot the natural resources of their countries.[15]

- (ii) *The neighbouring countries*: In the neighbouring countries, the game is played by other VIPs and VIRs that use their countries as transmission channels of weapons and raw materials between the conflicting countries, America, European and Asian countries, and foreign individuals (see for instance Reno, Williams, 1997a: 493-510, and 1997b :165-185). They behave exactly like the other VIPs and VIRs in the conflicting countries. Their goal is not the peace in Africa, but personal benefits in terms of weapons, money and raw materials.
- (iii) *America, European and Asian Countries*: America and European countries use since more than 500 years different methods in order to exploit illegally energy sources from Africa. War that is activated by these actors in many African countries today is only the modern means of exploitation after slavery, colonisation, unequal exchange, etc... The European countries and the USA still exert a remarkable influence on the economy and politics, and involve themselves either directly or indirectly in the different conflicts in Africa (see Reno, Williams, 1997a: 493-510, and 1997b: 165-185). It is very important nowadays to add the Asian countries (especially China and Japan) in this set of actors. The Asian countries use other means to interfere as shareholders in the raw materials games.[16] The goal for these actors is

---

Asian and European countries to access to the power and to be maintained there as far as they are ready to serve the interests of these foreign countries.

15 For instance, diamonds allowed the rebels in Sierra Leone to provide themselves with weapons by unscrupulous mercenaries via other African countries (Liberia and Burkina Faso). According to the UN, the value of the revenues for the rebels in Sierra Leone lies over USD 125 millions per year.

16 For this purpose, and as stressed by Servant, Jean-Christophe (2005: 14-15), China (1) offered credits facilities (2 billions of US dollars in December 2004) to the corrupt government in Luanda (Angola) in the exchange for 10,000 barrels of oil production per day, (2) uses diplomatical means in order to increase the shares in the African raw materials, (3) and is qualified by many observers as a "neocolonial power" within the framework of South – South cooperation.

not the peace, but the maximisation of the volume of raw materials they can import from Africa at low cost.[17] These countries deliver weapons to conflicting parties in Africa and interfere in many conflicts in order to establish their geopolitical ideologies and/or to protect their economic interest in the conflicting countries. Because of the energy crisis that the industrialized countries (America, Europe, and Asia) are facing, they are ready to use all means to provide themselves with African raw materials at low cost.[18] In the particular case of France and Africa, AGIR ICI et SURVIE (1995a: 3-12; 1995b: 14-31; 1996: 1-22; 1997: 7-16; 1999: 12-37) describes how the French politicians within the framework of the so – called "*Françafrique*" cooperate with the African VIRs and VIPs in order to implement their Africa politics, whose aim is the control and exploitation of the raw materials. For instance, the informal organization plays an important role – via the so–called "operation epervier" – in which a coup could allow it Idriss Déby to replace Habre as the head of state in Chad. Various reports of the UN also underline these roles played by America and Europe in the crises in Africa; for this purpose. Ukraine is cited by the United Nations as a supplier of weapons to actors in Sierra Leone. It should also be worth underlining that America and Europe represent the demand side of the market for raw materials, whether they are legally or illegally exported from Africa. They represent therefore (i.e. as the demand side of the illegal exploitation of raw materials) a decisive factor of the crises in Africa. The diamonds production is sold in such business centres as Anvers, New York, London, Tokyo, and Tel Aviv. It is well known that the final product from diamonds is sold at a proportion of 45% in the USA, at about 25% in Europe, and to a considerable extent also in Japan. The rest of the world shares less than 5% of the market (see for instance Glitter, Greed 2003: 22-45).

- (iv) *Multinationals and Individuals*: The actions of multinational corporations are parallel to those of their countries, and they work

---

17 Many industrialized countries depend strongly on the import of African raw materials.

18 They entertain conflicts with weapons, use diplomacy, and corrupt the African leaders, and manipulate the mass media in order to ensure a dominant position in the game.

very often in close collaboration with their governments.[19] These multinationals are very often used as channels to implement the Africa politics of their respective governments. Their attitude, supported by their mass media, is either active or passive and contributes a lot to the generation and to the intensification of conflicts in the African continent. The presence of multinationals and their actions in the countries in crisis are clearly pointed out by the UN and by the international opinion. It is, for instance, the role of Exxon and Shell in the Ogoni crisis in Nigeria and the role of Elf with many conflicts in French-Speaking Africa that are highlighted. These actors operate in activities related to the extraction and exportation of raw materials, as well as in those activities related to the import of illegal weapons in conflicting countries. The system is also based on illegal activities of mercenaries who take a very active part in the game as weapons and raw materials transporters. They are pilots and other military instructors from European and other countries that are sometimes recruited by private multinational corporations.

- (v) *The "naive" Civil Sociey*: The "*naive*" civil society, including some foreign NGOs, and to some extent the UN, is reduced to passive roles. Although the goal of their actions is peace and progress, their means to achieve these goals are extremely limited in comparison to those of the other actors.

4 Relevance of the VIP/VIR Approach: The Case of the DR of Congo

The Democratic Republic of Congo (formerly Zaire) is an excellent example of how the abovementioned actors operate in order to exploit illegally the raw materials.[20] This case study is important because the Congolese crisis is

---

19 For instance, the so–called "*Françafrique*" is well known as an informal institution, composed of French politicians, businessmen, and multinationals like Elf, through which the French Africa politics is defined and implemented (see especially AGIR ICI ET SURVIE (1995a: 3-12; 1995b: 14-31; 1996: 1-22; 1997: 7-16; 1999: 12-37).

20 However, other African countries like Liberia, Sierra Leone, Angola and Chad are also typical examples of raw materials games with analogous sets of actors.

the greatest inter-states war in the contemporary history of Africa, with 9 African countries that are directly involved in the conflict and with more than thirty armed groups that are fighting there. It is the first and so far greatest Pan-African war and also the most damaging one after the Second World War, with over 3,8 millions of persons that have died so far. The evidence from the DR of Congo shows that the country is characterized by the existence of VIPs and VIRs, and how they cooperate with neighbouring countries, with Europe and America, with multinationals and individuals, in order to exploit illegally the raw materials.

4.1 The VIRs and the VIPs in the DR of Congo

Using the above outlined framework for studying the profile of the leaders, the results are quite relevant in the DR of Congo. It should however be worth mentioning here that a sample of the population itself has not been used here to answer the questions summarized above. Instead, a review of books and articles[21] about Congo DR, its political facts and its leaders has helped to have an idea on the profiles of the leaders. In the DR of Congo, the leaders are characterized as VIRs and/or VIPs (1) because they have no genuine political education and therefore have no political ideology and/or social projects, and (2) because they are brutal dictators and corrupt leaders. Taking into account the political history of the last 50 years, none of the leaders in this country has been democratically elected. The leaders in this country cannot proof that they have taken part at a social project whose results can be shown and taken as an example. Mobutu, who took part in the assassination of Lumumba, is on the top of the list of the vagabonds who govern in Africa. Kabila (the father) was not known on the African political scene before reaching to the power after Mobutu. Only few months before, he was helped by the neighbouring countries in order to succeed MOBUTU as the head of the state in Kinshasa. The son Kabila who governs today in Kinshasa has no political education and also no education at all in respect of the average level needed to fulfil his responsibilities. Furthermore, his power in Kinshasa has no legitimation. He is also a vagabond like his father and MOBUTU.[22] The

21 These books and articles (about 120) cannot be cited here as references, but are just considered as moral persons. Though the review, one has tried to find the opinions of their authors about the questions summarized above.

22 Examples from other countries are quite relevant: (a) Nigeria is a country characterized by various political coups since independence, in which soldiers

leaders in the rebelion who control the important areas of raw materials are not quite different from Mobutu or from Kabila. For this purpose it is interesting to mention some of them: Jean Pierre Bemba, of the "*Mouvement de Libération du Congo*" (MLC), an old friend of Mobutu, is a rent-seeker and one of the richest persons in Congo after Mobutu; the other rebellion leaders like Kin-Kiey Mulumba, Wamba Dia Wamba, Mbusa Nyamwisi and Roger Lumbala of the "*Rassemblement Congolais pour la Démocratie*" (RCD), or Thomas Lubanga of the "*Union des Patriotes Congolais*" (UPC) are also, as it will be seen, marionettes who are used by the neigbouring countries within the framework of the raw materials games.

4.2 The Neighbouring Countries and the Conflicts in the DR of Congo

What can be observed for the last four decades is the involvement of neighbouring countries as a feature in over 70% of the conflicts in Africa.[23]

---

replace soldiers without improving the situation they met before reaching to the power; (b) In Angola, although Eduardo Dos Santos was elected in 1975 without opposition, he has remained over 20 years as the head of state and head of government without sharing the power. He has also been unable to maintain peace in the country since he led the Popular Movement for the Liberation of Angola (MPLA) to maintain the civil war against the National Union for the Total Independence of Angola (UNITA), led by Jonas Savimbi, a rebel who controlled a great part of the country with his own illegal institutions; (c) In Chad, the leaders of the conflicting parties of the civil war of about 30 years (especially Gougouni, Kamougue, Habre and Idris Déby) have never been motivated by the welfare of the populace or by peace; (d) Other examples, like Liberia with Charles Taylor and the consequences of 14 years of civil war, or like Sierra Leone with the 1991 to 2002 civil war between the government and the Revolutionary United Front (RUF) (that resulted in tens of thousands of deaths and the displacement of more than 2 million people - well over one third of the population - and many of whom now being refugees in neighbouring countries) - confirm that the leaders were vagabonds.

23 In West Africa, such countries as Ivory Coast, Burkina Faso and Liberia have played, as described by Kourouma, Ahmadou (2000: 32-53), an important role in the development of the crisis in the subregion. The UNO mentions Liberia and Burkina Faso as countries that have diamonds flows from Sierra Leone. Burkina Faso is in charge of the order and delivery of weapons to Sierra Leonean rebels via Liberia in the exchange for diamonds. In Liberia, Charles Taylor put at the disposal of the Sierra Leonean rebellion his military air bases

In the DR of Congo, nine African countries[24] are directly involved in the crisis through their relations either with the government, or with the rebellion. The "*Alliance des Forces démocratiques pour la Libération du Congo*" (AFDL) is supported by Uganda and Rwanda and helped Laurent Désiré Kabila to overturn Mobutu and to access to power in Kinshasa; the "Mouvement de Libération du Congo" (MLC) is led by Jean Pierre Bemba who operates in the province of "*Equateur*" and is supported by Uganda; the "*Rassemblement Congolais pour la Démocratie*" (RCD), led by Kin-Kiey Mulumba, Wamba Dia Wamba, Mbusa Nyamwisi and Roger Lumbala, is supported by Rwanda and Uganda; the "*Union des Patriotes Congolais*" (UPC) is led by Thomas Lubanga and is also supported by Rwanda. Testimonies abound on the role that these neighbours – especially Rwanda, Uganda, Angola, and the Central African Republic (CAR) - are playing in the illegal exportation of raw materials. The diamonds production in the Central African Republic increases although no additional investment has been made in this sector since many decades. The origin of this increase is linked to the exportation of diamonds from the DR of Congo through the river separating the two countries. Although Rwanda possesses no coltan as a mineral resource, it has been shown that this country is one of the most important African exporters of this precious metal.

4.3 America, Asia and Europe, the Multinationals and Other Actors

Only by observing the facts, everybody who has an interest I the DR of Congo or who has been there for a while can give testimony on the presence of America, European and Asian countries through their linkages with their multinationals just in the richest areas of the country, especially in the Shaba area. The mass media as well as the civil society and the non-governmental organizations underline daily the role that these countries and their multinationals are playing in the illegal exploitation of raw materials in the

---

for the delivery of weapons from Burkina Faso. In compensation, Monrovia received parts from the rebels' diamonds. According to many analysts, Liberia exports over 60 times more diamonds than the country is able to produce (see for example Gershoni, Yekutiel 1997: 55-76). The UN cites Guinea and Gambia as illegal channels of the exportation of diamonds from Liberia and Sierra Leone (see for instance UN 2003 as quoted by US Department of State 2003 : 7-15).

24 Angola, Libya, Chad, Namibia, Zimbabwe, Central African Republic, Sudan, Rwanda and Uganda.

DR of Congo.[25] According to these primary sources, the following facts are quite relevant and highlight the role played by the industrialized countries and their multinationals:

- A total of 27 Belgian and British multinationals have violated the set standards of practice by looting DRC's natural resources.
- Barclays Bank and Standard Chartered Bank are on the list of predominantly British and Belgian international conglomerates that have been exposed by the United Nations as the main culprits in the looting of mineral resources in the war-ravaged Democratic Republic of Congo (DRC).[26]
- Notable multinationals, including the British-based Barclays Bank, the Amalgamated Metal Corporation (UK), Ashanti Goldfields (Ghana), Bayer AG (Germany), De Beers (UK), Kinross Gold Corporation (Canada), Orion Mining Inc. (SA), and Standard Chartered Bank (United Arab Emirates) are involved in activities related to the illegal exploitation of raw materials from the DR of Congo;[27]
- The multinational companies are alleged to have used various unethical and unprocedural techniques to maximise profits through the exploitation of the DRC's mineral resources (see UNO 2003: 1-17, Cuvelier, Jeroen and Tim Raeymaekers (2002[28]). For instance "Approximately 25 percent of Eagle Wings coltan is shipped from Kigali to the Ulba Metallurgical Plant of Kazatomprom in Kazakhstan, and another 25 percent is sold to the parent company of Eagle wings, Trinitech International Inc. in the United States". This is in spite of the fact that the recipients of the coltan deny of having ever received any

---

25 See especially UNO (2003: 1-17), which also points out clearly the role played by this set of actors in the illegal exploitation of raw materials from the DR of Congo in his *"third and final report on the illegal exploitation of natural resources and other forms of wealth in the DRC"*.

26 Britain and Belgium are signatories to the OECD conventions and their companies have operated in violation of standing rules and regulations.

27 Oryx Natural Resources, a subsidiary of the international Oryx Group and owned by the controversial Mohammad al Shanfari of Oman, but based in the United Kingdom, and Ridgepoint International, owned by Billy Rautenbach, who is based in Zimbabwe, are also named by many observers in this context.

28 Available at www.ipisresearch.be/publication_report.php.

minerals from the DRC. The UN report also charges that Eagle Wings collaborates with the Rwandan Patriotic Army (RPA) to "receive privileged access to coltan and captive labour" in areas hitherto controlled by Rwanda (UNO, 2003: 1-17).

- Chartered planes are used in the illicit transfer of the minerals, which are said to pass through various African countries en route to foreign markets. Several countries, including the US, Germany, Belgium and Russia, have pledged to step up efforts to stem the illegal movement of minerals from the DRC.

From all this it can be seen that the VIP/VIR approach is applicable in such a case as the DRC but that it may also be used in the explanation of developments in other resource-rich countries. Indeed, the evidence with the DRC shows that the leaders will be more vulnerable and in the position to co-operate with other actors in the raw materials games as far as they have a bad profile, as outlined in the above proposed framework. Studies on conflicts based on raw materials in Africa should therefore focus on the profile and on the ethic of the leaders as key determinants of their role in the crises. A way of preventing crisis on an international level may be to identify and to help politicians with positive profiles to access to the power, as it seems to be the case in Liberia with the ascension Ellen Johnson Sirleaf. Other studies and researches should help to improve the knowledge of the national and international opinions about the potential African leaders, by sampling and publishing information that may be relevant within the framework of political ethics. A quarterly publication of a "Political Ethic Perception Index" of African leaders may be of great importance and useful for the international community in the orientation of its economic and social partnerships.

5 Conclusions and Policy Recommendations: How to Escape from the "Crisis – Poverty – Crisis" Spiral?

As it has been stressed in this study, the abundance of raw materials explains to a large extent the conflicts that characterize the recent history of Africa. This explains also, at least partly, the Dutch Disease phenomenon in Africa, i.e. why the abundance of raw materials coexists with economic decline and increasing absolute poverty. This economic dilemma is produced by a system that is well conceptualised, a so–called AORM-induced "CRISIS – POVERTY – CRISIS" spiral or raw material game. America, European and Asian countries, African leaders, the multinationals and others play the game, and the goals of their actions are not the realisation of peace, but generating the maximum revenue that can be derived from the illegal exploitation of raw materials.

In order to escape from this spiral some actions are urgent: (1) Strategies to avoid conflicts should be developed; (2) Endogenous development strategies based on raw materials should be implemented; and (3) America, Asia and Europe should really cooperate with the African countries in the prospect of a sustainable development path.

5.1 The Necessity to Develop Strategies to Avoid Conflicts: Lessons from the Cameroonian Diplomacy concerning the Crisis with Nigeria

The case of Cameroon in the border conflict with Nigeria since more than 30 years teaches us that a peaceful solution rather than an armed conflict is possible in Africa. Although Cameroon has a strategic advantage over Nigeria in case of a war (control of the Atlantic Ocean and other geographic advantages that are provided by the "*Fako*" or Cameroon mountain) the different governments that have been in place since 1960 have shown, with a great success, their ability to find peaceful solutions. The border between Cameroon and Nigeria is very rich in oil (especially the Bakassi area), and Nigeria tries since over 30 years to overtake this area by arguing that it belongs to Nigeria. Confrontations have occasionally been noticed between the Cameroonian and Nigerian troupes, and they were therefore in the position to initiate a conflict at each moment. Instead of going ahead towards an armed conflict, Cameroon has used her diplomacy channels to cushion the pressures, (1) by developing good economic relations with Nigeria based on the informal sector, and (2) by bringing the problem to the International Court of Justice at The Hague. More than 3 millions of Nigerians, who came into Cameroon as refugees during the Biafra war, are fully integrated in the Cameroonian society. Following this example, the African countries have nowadays the chance and the obligation to implement a diplomacy based on the slogan "PEACE, NEGOTIATION AND FRATERNITY RATHER THAN ARMED CONFLICTS".

5.2 An Endogenous Development Strategy Based on Raw Materials is Possible

The African countries have hitherto failed to achieve the main goals of their development policies at part because of the exogenous features of the implemented policies (top-down approach of economic development), as initially pointed out by the "dependence" and "domination" development theories. It is therefore important to define and to implement new strategies that have to be endogenous and are in the position to reduce the externalities faced by the African countries within the framework of their international economic relations. The endogenous development is an alternative that promotes a sustainable growth based on the environment as well as on the local culture, and taking into account local practices, local know how in all fields, as well as a local conception of welfare. As underlined by Vachon, Bernard (1991: 104), the endogenous development should create a favourable environment for local initiatives, in order to increase the capacity of local communities to adapt to new rules of economic growth at a macro-economic level, or to find other forms of development which will integrate (through other forms of production and organization) the main social and environmental issues. It should be worth mentioning that this type of development relies on three main postulates which are (1) the development as global process, (2) the participation of micro-initiatives to the global development, and (3) the human capital as driving force of development(see Vachon , Bernard 1991: 108). Escaping from the primary commodity dilemma means that the raw materials should be properly and efficiently used to sustain the process of economic development. Since development itself is a dynamic and quite complex process in which the raw materials are only one factor among various others, the actions to be taken at different levels can only be elements of a well-conceptualised African and global development strategy. One should not forget that many issues are to be raised here if one takes into account the related studies on this topic in the area of growth and development theories. A central question will therefore arise: is a strategy still possible? In order to answer this question, the table 1 of this work is of importance. It recapitulates the abundance of African raw materials and highlights their potential use in different industrial activities, among which many are not too complicated to understand and/or to implement. The transformation of raw materials in processing can reach in the African countries from a craft stage to an industrial stage within the framework of economic development. The African countries possess still a deep tradition and knowledge in the craft transformation of some raw materials, as it can be seen through a review of the encyclopaedia of their cultural goods. Furthermore, numerous specialized books and documents related to the techniques of transformation of the raw materials (from the craft to the industrial stages) are available, and one can learn a lot in a 2 or 3 days workshop. The technique used for dyeing is not more complicated than the technique used to prepare "foufou", "atieké" or "peper soup". However, the challenge for the African countries is to implement new education and training policies in such a way that (1) the techniques are integrated with the culture; (2) and that local transformation of raw materials becomes one of the main goals of economic policy. Botswana is a typical example of an African country that tries to exploit properly the raw materials so as to improve the welfare of the people.

5.3 For a New Africa Politics in Europe, in Asia and in the USA

In America, in Asia and in Europe one has to understand the important role played by the African continent as a "cradle of the humanity" in the world history, as well as the important role played in many other fields: over 75% of the existing plants and over 65% of the fauna of the world are in Africa (estimations made from Lancaster, Roy 2006:12 – 268 and Grundmann, Emmanuelle 2005: 4-400). The existing conflicts, in which America, Asia and Europe interfere, destroy also the environment (the fauna and the flora). This is the case not only in Africa, but the whole world is losing in the game, since the "*world heritage*" is destroyed. As well many other values are destroyed that are optional, testamental, educational and that are contributing a lot to the welfare of the world; especially for future generations.

At the actual stage, America, Asia and the European countries have to cooperate with the African countries in the following fields:

- (i) Economic sanctions against governments that are actively involved in conflicts;
- (ii) Prohibiting that multinationals that are involved in conflicts can enter the international capital markets;
- (iii) Promotion of national and international initiatives to find peaceful alternatives to war when crisis situations emerge; and
- (iv) Development of a new partnership for endogenous development that is based on the local exploitation of raw materials, in which process the African human capital should be mobilized and integrated.

References

Agir ici et Survie (1995a): "Acques Chirac et la Françafrique. Retour à la case Foccart?" Paris: Editions l'Harmattan, 3-12.

Agir ici et Survie (1995b): "L'Afrique à Biarritz. Mise en examen de la politique africaine de la France", Paris: Editions l'Harmattan, 14-31.

Agir ici et Survie (1996): "Présence militaire française en Afrique: dérives…", Paris: Editions l'Harmattan, 1-22.

Agir ici et Survie (1997): "Tchad Niger: Escroqueries à la démocratie"; Paris: Editions l'Harmattan, 7-16.

Agir ici et Survie (1999): "Trafics, barbouzes et compagnies… aventures militaires françaises en Afrique", Paris: Editions l'Harmattan, 12-37.

Artadi, Eedwards and Sala-i-Martin, Xavier (2003): "The Economic Tragedy of the XXth Century: Growth in Africa", National Bureau of Economic Research, Cambridge Working Paper (9865), 1- 22.

Auty, Richard (1997): "Natural resources, the state and development strategy". In: Journal of International Development, (9), 651-663.

CNUCED; Department of Energy Statistics (various issues);

Davis, Donald (1995): "Learning to love the Dutch disease: Evidence from the Mineral Economies", World Development (23), 1765 – 79.

Fosu, Augustin Kwasi (1996): "Primary exports and economic growth in developing countries", World Economy (20), 465 – 75.

Gershoni, Yekutiel (1997): "War without End and End to a War: The Prolonged Wars in Liberia and Sierra Leone". In: African Studies Review (3), 55-76.

Glitter, Greed (2003): "The Secret World of the Diamond Cartel", Oxford: The Disinformation Company Publishers, 22-45.

Goudie, Adams and Orme, Andrea (1999): "The Physical Geography of Africa", Oxford: Oxford University Press, 15-125.

Grundmann, Emmanuelle (2005): "Ma grande encyclopédie des animaux", Paris: Editions Milan, 4-400.

International Monetary Fund: "International Financial Statistics", Washington DC: Yearbooks 1980, 1995, 2000 and 2004.

Jeroen, Cuvelier and Tim, Raeymaekers (2002): "European Companies and the Coltan Trade: an Update". An International Peace Information Service Report. Online: www.ipisresearch.be/publication_report.ph.

Khan, Mahmood Hasan (2001): "Rural Poverty in Developing Countries: Implications for Public Policy", Washington DC: International Monetary Fund, Economic Issues (26), 15 – 42.

Kornprobst, Jacques (2002): "Metamorphic Rocks and Their Geodynamic Significance", Amsterdam: Kluwer Academic Publishers, 45-62.

Kourouma, Ahmadou (2002): Allah n'est pas obligé", Paris : Editions le seuil, 32 – 53.

Lancaster, Roy (2006): "Encyclopédie des plantes et arbres de jardin", Paris: Editions Solar, 12 – 268.

Lima, de Faria (2003): "Structural Classification of Minerals". Volumes 1, 2 and 3, Amsterdam: Kluwer Academic Publishers, 34-56.

Minns, Williams (1984): "Geography of Africa", Oxford: Macmillan Education Publishers, 5 – 67.

Ndeffo Fongue, Joseph (2004): "Conflits et matières premières en Afrique: un tour d'horizon", GREDPEM (Yaounde), unpublished manuscript, 43 – 57.

Ndikunana, Leone and Kinsangani, Emizet (2003): "The Economics of Civil War: The Case of the Democratic Republic of Congo", Harvard: University of Massachussets Press, 1-12.

Pumphrey, Carolyn and Schwartz-Barcott, Rye (2003): "Armed Conflict in Africa", Lanham: Scarecrow Press, 1- 26.

Ranis, Edwards (1991): "Towards a model of development". In: Lawrence Krause and Kim Andrea (eds): Liberalization in the Process of Economic Development, Berkeley: University of California Press (California, Berkeley), 59 – 101.

Reno, Williams (1997a): "Wars, Markets and the Reconfiguration of West Africa", in: comparative Politics (4), 493-510.

Reno, Williams (1997b): "African weak states and Commercial alliances", in: African affairs (96), 165-185

Salim, Ahmed Salim (1999): "Preventive Diplomacy", Oxford: Kevin Mc Cahill publishers, 8-29.

Servant, Jean-Christophe (2005): "Weiße Elefanten in der Grauzone: Chinas gewissenlose Geschäfte in Afrika", Le Monde diplomatique (7663), 14-15.

Schumann, Walter (1993): "Handbook of Rocks, Minerals, and Gemstones", Oxford: Houghton Mifflin Publishers, 11-19.

Schumann, Walter (1992): "Minerals of the World", Oxford: Sterling Publishers, 76-85.

Summerfield, Anderson (1985): "Tectonic background to long-term landform development in Tropical Africa"; in: Douglas, Irving & Spencer, Thomas (eds) Environmental Change and Tropical Geomorphology, Oxford University Press; New Edition (Oxford), 281 - 294.

United Nations (2003): "Third and final report on the illegal exploitation of natural resources and other forms of wealth in DRC"; United Nations Security Council, New York; 1-17. Online: http://wwww.reliefweb.int/rw/rwb.nsf/AllDocs-ByUNID/706b89b947e5993dc1256c590052b353.

US Department of State (2003): "Sierra Leone. Country Reports on human rights Practices", Washington DC: Bureau of Democracy, Human Rights and Labor, 7 - 15.

Vachon, Bernard (1991): "Le développement local: théorie et pratique. Réintroduire l'humain dans la logique de développement", Boucherville: Editions Gaétan Morin, 104-108.

Winter, Nelson (1995): "Natural resources, national income and economic growth in Africa", World Development, (22), 35-59.

WIDER (1998): “Resource Abundance and Economic Development; Improving the Performance of Resource – Rich Countries”. The United Nations University, Helsinki, Research for Action (44), 1-3.

Ziegler, Jean, 2003 : “Die neuen Herrscher der Welt und Ihre globalen Widersacher”, München: Bertelsmann Verlag, 1- 4.

Zussman, Deer, Howie (1996): “An Introduction to the Rock-Forming Minerals”, Oxford: Prentice Hall publishers, 22 – 27.

Annex: Map of conflict areas in Africa

Source: *Accessed by the author.*

Crisis Prevention in Resource-rich Countries - National, Regional and International Economic Strategies

Karl Wolfgang Menck

1 Introduction

Recent crises (economically defined as "development in reverse" in a seminal study by Collier, Elliot, Hegre, Hoeffler, Raynal-Querol, and Sambanis, 2003) in developing countries have initiated proposals to design primary commodities agreements that should be extended by a crisis-related conditionality. Specific support in cases of revenue losses should be offered to countries that are threatened by passing a crisis or by managing the post-crisis reconstruction of the economy. International rules and procedures among others were recommended to prevent the access of countries to such funds that spend the primary commodity revenues in a conflict-supporting manner. Furthermore, rules for transparency on the spending of revenues from the export of primary commodities and international regulations to combat money laundering and illegal payments transfers that may be causing conflicts should be provided.

The study is designed to focus on the economic issues as mentioned by Goudie and Neyapti: „Socio-political instability runs from minor forms to extreme conflict in the form of civil and international war. This study puts its determinants into the two main categories: direct economic ones, such as elements of economic policy or characteristics of the prevailing economic structure, and non-economic or indirect economic causes, primarily political, social or cultural in character although economic forces may drive them. The economic determinants receive the main emphasis because they often have received relatively less attention in the analysis of conflict than political, diplomatic or military factors" (Goudie/ Neyapti, 1999: 9).

The paper focuses on Angola and takes also into consideration the situation in the Democratic Republic of Congo (DR) and in Sudan. These states are resource-rich SSA countries being exposed severely to conflicts as it is demonstrated by the conflict intensity as well as by the extent of refugee movements (Heidelberger Institut, 2004: 4). The respective states are so-called LICUS (Low Income Countries Under Stress) states (DFID, 2005, Annex; Cabinet Office Prime Minister's Strategy Unit, 2005: V; World Bank, Evaluation: 2).

The procedure of the paper is as follows: The second section describes the crisis in the respective countries and the roots of the conflicts. The following third section analyses the evolution of the conflict from the traditional economic perception and from the most recent institutional-economics based approach. The fourth section assesses recent deliberations to install an international commodity-based policy approach and other measures that may be suitable to prevent a diversion of resources to conflicts. Also concomitant internal measures in the resource-rich countries and crisis-related technical assistance measures by donors are recommended. Policy conclusions are elaborated in a final section.

The findings read as follows: Resource-rich economies are exposed to a crisis when export earnings are spent in a manner that discriminates parts of the population and supports initiatives by violent actors to reverse the situation by military means (Auty, 1998). The impact of transnational companies is ambiguous: they provide technology and marketing skills to explore the resource stocks, and the companies are also part of the mechanism that generates the conflict:. A strong co-operation between the companies and the elites is perceived by the public to divert income in a manner that strengthens the violation of human rights in the respective countries. The companies however do not serve as substitutes for "failed states" by providing services. The availability of incomes from natural resources is also a means to destabilise neighbouring countries or to invite them to start border-crossing operations being determined to gain access to the commodities. Actions on the international level are recommended to interrupt the access of potentially violent actors to funds, equipment and staff by "cutting of the market", by enhancing transparency on the spending of earnings from commodity exports, and by creating an adequate frame for the co-operation with transnational companies. Furthermore, regional collaboration may provide joint activities to stop smuggling and illegal trafficking of primary commodities. Developed countries are recommended to grant inputs mainly to strengthen sectors such as education, health, sanitation, housing, water and sanitation. Good governance, ownership, and the strengthening of the civil society are furthermore proposed to remove internal sources of conflicts. It has to be acknowledged that those groups that benefit from the control over resources and traded primary commodities will not contribute to any activities that may help to make international regulations more effective. The supervision of illegal transactions through international regulations requires an additional administrative capacity that extends far beyond the available current staffing and funding opportunities.

Finally, it is recommended to perceive safety and stability in commodity-exporting SSA as a common good in terms of supply and demand of commodities on a national, regional and a global scale.

2 The Roots of the Crises in SSA Resource-rich Countries: Case Studies

2.1 Mismanagement of Revenues from Primary Commodities

Although it is widely accepted that the roots of the conflict are complex, it is also acknowledged that the availability of raw materials and the economic issues such as the utilisation of the earnings from natural resources are prominent factors that have caused crises and have prolonged their "lifetime". Additionally, it has to be considered that the evolution and the profile of the crises differ according to the history and the actual state of society, politics and economics. However, there are some common elements.

In *Angola* the MPLA domain was the oilfields and the UNITA had the privileged access to the diamond trade. The respective income was spent for military equipment and warfare business to strengthen the informal networks (Futungo) to the benefit of the clients and to secure areas of concern and exploitation by a civil war. With the support of the respective governments the oil fields in Angola were accessed by many transnational oil exploration companies. The foreign investors perceived the Futungo system as a channel to set up a close collaboration with the local decision-makers (UNITA and MPLA respectively) so as to secure property rights and accountability that were needed to start and to extend investment for the oil business. The diamonds trade was an opportunity to seize an autonomous selling system by UNITA that was nurtured by actors up to the end of the East-West-Conflict as a counterbalance against the pro-Communist MPLA. In the nineties the UNITA was strong enough to continue diamond trade without considering any government rules and obligations. UNITA staff and government soldiers regularly traded stones, and sanctions failed because there was no effective control. In 2002 the Kimberley agreement was enacted which enforced the supervision of the diamonds trade. The contract provided means against smuggling and the requirement to certify all the deliveries, including the transit trade (Smillie, 2002: 1; International Crisis Group, 2003: 1; World Bank, 2003a: 4; Stuvoy, 2002: 41 and 89).

With regard of *Congo (DR)* there is a widespread conviction that the conflict is also the outcome of the mismanagement when spending the revenues from the natural resources (Lanotte, 2003: 81). A study argues that in the Congo (DR) a "grotesquely political culture" is being related to the income from primary commodities (Koyame/Clark, 2002: 202; Young, 2002: 16 and 24). A political opposition and a civil society could not be installed, among others, due to ethnical rivalries (Afoaku, 2002: 111). It is argued: "The exploitation of resources (such as rubber, copper, zinc, uranium, gold, tantalite, timber etc.) has, directly or indirectly, shaped the historical experience of the country..." (Grignon, 2004: 43). Studies have described the commodities case in the country as a "geological scandal" to express the fact that since the colonial times "national wealth is monopolised by the country's rulers and their foreign business partners to the detriment of the mass of the people" (Nzongola-Ntalaja, 2002: 2 and 235; similarly McCalpin, 2002:42). Lanotte mentions an "Eldorado congolais" (Lanotte, 2003: 169).

Muchai mentions that at least 100 million US were spent annually in the eighties by the Congolese government and related groups to buy weapons, and it is supposed that this amount originated mainly from the sale of primary commodities (Muchai, 2002: 188). In 2001, among 60 per cent of the oil export earnings were spent for military equipment purchases, and in the course of the recent oil boom the annual military expenses are estimated to have almost doubled (Human Rights Watch, 2003: 456; Energy Information Agency (EIA) of the United States Government, 2004).

The *Sudan* case is determined by a long-lasting internal conflict between the North and South along ethnical lines as well as religious disputes that covered in economic terms the exploitation of the resources in the South (Human Rights Watch, 2003: 120; Hashim, 2004; Johnson, 2003: 145; O'Ballance, 2000: 123). The oil income was spent in a manner that escalated the conflict between the northern and the southern part of the country (World Bank, 2003b: 18). An overwhelming part of the income was spent to buy military equipment that was felt as being necessary to protect themselves against other groups fighting to gain a larger share in the minerals' revenue.

2.2 Transnational Companies

Another feature of the evolution of the crisis in the respective resource-rich countries is it that transnational companies were urged to invest in mining and in oil exploration. Up to 1990 it was legitimised by the political intention to avoid that the Eastern Bloc may have gained direct access to the stocks and thereby might strengthen its economic, political and military position. Later on the companies mainly from the Western industrialised countries competed so as to gain exploration rights to enhance their supply basis and to curb the number of suppliers in the international market. The actors of the "failed states" enabled the companies to get access by the way of bilateral and hidden contracts, and the lack of local capabilities to run the exploration and the sales by well-endowed local private companies contributed to this development. Government apprehension is ambiguous: on the one hand the transnational corporations supported the mismanagement of resource earnings by close collaboration with the local elites and the government, and there was no real contribution of the companies to the local people nor to the overall economic and social development; on the other hand cases indicate that the transnational companies provided services to the people and the country that otherwise would not have been available.

The *Angolan* example runs as follows: "...the popular attitude among the oil communities is that by virtue of their over-bearing presence, the amount of physical and material resources at their disposal, oil companies are the only government they know. Incidentally, because they are more visible than government, oil companies personnel and facilities have become easy targets during communal protests and violence. Oil companies are in fact seen as an alternative government. And as if in response to this unusual situation, some oil companies have now departments of agriculture, health, education, and so on, much like governments, have ministries. Some of the companies in the oil industry have annual budgets for community development and corporate contributions bigger than what some State governments allocate to development there is a popular opinion that multinational oil companies sometimes behave like States, especially through their ability to maintain a security outfit, using firearms and ammunition" (Fitzgerald, 2001: 208; similarly Ukeje/Odebiyi/ Sesai/Olabisi, 2002: 39).

In the 1980s, foreign investors were requested by the *Sudanese* government to exploit resources in the South (UNCTAD, 2004a: 39 and 388). However, the Sudanese government indicated that the scope of activities of European or US-Based companies and of Saudi-Arabian investors should not be extended (O'Ballance, 2000: 147). Later on, US-based and Canadian companies, and recently Indian and Chinese companies were appreciated as partners (Dunn, 2002: 59).

Economic stability in the *Congo (DR)* was felt by the ruling elites as being more convenient than having unrest in the country. The trade of commodities in a region of Africa traditionally being characterised by internal and regional conflicts should be strengthened and enhanced (Nzongola-Ntalaja, 2002: 225 and 233). The recent collaboration with Indian and Chinese companies indicates that the Congolese decision-makers were very adaptive to make friends who did not care very much about the human rights case as long as primary commodity deliveries could be secured to the benefit of the foreign investors that had established "transnational networks of pillage and corruption" (Nzongola-Ntalaja, 2002: 235; similarly Human Rights Watch, 2003: 48, 233, 510 and 633; O'Ballance, 2000: 205; Koyame/ Clark, 2002: 209; Young, 2002: 26).

2.3 The Regional Dimension

The location of the mineral deposits in the remote eastern part of the *Congo (DR)* has activated in a failed and divided state ethnic groups and tribes to collaborate with relevant groups in the neighbouring countries and to exploit the commodities in the Congolese territory (Nzongola-Ntalaja, 2002: 237; Lanotte, 2003: 174). There was a strong economic pressure from eastern neighbouring countries to enhance the resource basis as long as a dense population and the lack of commodities had caused internal poverty in the adjacent states (Longman, 2002: 136). When internal economic tensions in Rwanda and Burundi escalated, fugitives turned to the *Congo (DR)* region. Fractions and groups that were eager to strengthen their conflict capabilities by utilising Congolese economic resources inferred military and power-related actions from *Congo (DR)* temporarily to Rwanda and Burundi.

Case studies referring to *Congo (DR)* and *Sudan* underline additionally that regional co-operation supported illegal transactions such as smuggling, and there were no joint efforts to suppress illegal imports from third states such as arms trade or the delivery of mercenaries' services as long as it was expected that such transactions were shifted to other countries.

3 The Economic Determinants of the Crises in SSA Resource-rich Countries

3.1 Crisis Patterns from a Traditional Point of View

When dealing with conflicts in resource-rich SSA countries one has to acknowledge that conflicts are an indispensable part of development: Development is change. Turning the attention to the respective countries it may be assumed that a resource-rich country can provide an economic basis to mitigate the tensions that otherwise arise from the lack of exports earnings. The (foreign exchange) income from resources exploitation and commodity sales may allow it to realise the best-case scenario with regard of private and public investment. The state and the private sector are then assumed to dispose of earnings that are distributed in a manner so that social, regional or ethnic tensions can be avoided. Public funds (being collected from taxes and customs duties on the resources exports) should be allocated in such a way as to create property rights, to enforce education, health, housing, water and sanitation, and to build a civil society. Crises – as in the case of *Angola*, *Congo (DR)* and *Sudan* – indicate that resources have not been spent as it is outlined in this scenario: the conflicts are the outcome of inadequate government management and due to the lack of a genuine public ownership of the natural resources, and it is envisaged that changes in the economic governance system may help to eliminate the causes for losses in development (see also Table 1).

The volatility of the commodity prices may be another or an additional reason why crises are generated in resource-rich countries (Goudie/Neyapti, 1999: 9). Collier, Elliot, Hegre, Hoeffler, Raynal-Querol and Sambanis (2003) argue as follows:"A distinct reason why countries dependent on natural resources and other primary commodities for their exports tend to have a record of conflict and poverty is that they are exposed to shocks. The prices of primary commodities are highly volatile, and periodically such countries face a crash in export prices. Such large declines in export income in turn tend to produce a contraction in aggregate output and severe pressure on the budget. Episodes of rapid economic decline increase the risk of conflict, and some evidences indicate that the output losses are persistent" (Collier et al., 2003: 180). Regarding the foreign exchange income of the respective countries, the evolution of the commodity markets in the past does not explain the generation of economic tensions in these resource-rich countries.

3.2 An Alternative Economic Version to Explain Crisis Evolution in Resource-rich SSA Countries: Failed States

The crisis in the respective states supports the assumption – based on findings of institutional economics - that especially mineral-resource rich countries can be classified as failed states(see table 1). Although there are different types of such states as has been recently elaborated, the term encloses nations being described by some common elements (Hauck, 2004: 411). Among others, due to colonial heritage the government's potential to regulate and to allocate resources to the needs of overall economic and social development has not been installed. The respective governments – often called "semi-democracies" - do not provide public goods as much as being supplied by strong states, and examples are the lack of security, the inadequate provision of basic services, and the absence of essential civil freedoms (Eizenstat, Porter, Weinstein, 2005: 136; DFID, 2005: 8; Cabinet Office, Prime Minister's Strategy Unit, 2005). It is also argued that the "state failure need not necessarily result from the incapacity of public institutions". Instead, while „state failure can harm a great number of people, it can also benefit others", especially governing elites and their allies. These "elites" prefer extensive unproductive, profit-seeking activities in a political system they control and do not build a well-functioning state in which economic progress and democratic institutions flourish" (Nafziger, 2003: 298).

Commodity-rich countries are often described by the term "Pfründenkapitalismus" (Hauck, 2004: 421). This term expresses that potentially violent actors and their supporters use the income of the primary commodity sector for the sake of private activities to strengthen "the use of resources to exploit others for an economic gain", and to spend the export earnings to buy weapons and related goods as well as mercenaries' services (Anderson, 1999: 26; similarly Craft/Smaldone, 2002: 693; Collier, Elliott, Hegre, Hoeffler, Raynal-Querol, Sambanis, 2003: 63; Junkert, 2003: 36; Moran/ Pitcher, 2000: 501; UNCTAD, 2004a: 166, Böge, 2004: 46; Mair, 2004: 3; Eavis, 2003; OECD, 2004: 39; African Development Bank, 2004: 197; Garfinkel/ Skaperdas/Syropolos, 2004; Schneckener, 2004a: 7; Schneckener, 2004b: 178; Wohlmuth, 2004: 21; Cabinet Office, Prime Minister's Strategy Unit, 2005: 18).

Table 1: The Origins of the Conflicts – a Survey

Country Crisis-related Main commodities	Origins
Angola Oil, diamonds	Informal networks to the benefits of the clients ("Futungo") Strive of UNITA and MPLA Collaboration with foreign investors and mismanagement of spending the income from the commodities exports.
Congo (DR) Mineral commodities	Mismanagement of spending the revenues, monopolisation of national wealth to the benefit of the country's rulers and their business partners: - "Eldorado congolais", "grotesquely political culture" - Lack of political opposition and civil society
Sudan Oil	Conflict between the North and the South along ethnical and religious lines. Northern Sudan military commitment in the South to enable foreign investors to exploit oil reserves and to allocate the revenues in the North. Southern Sudan struggle for independence and to share

Most important trends emerge: "Commodity rents have tended to become a focal point for distributional struggles that have undermined policy and institutional performance" (Kremer/O'Connel, 2004: 227); and "..in oil-dependent societies, State policies create and mould new classes and social groups, and in turn the State becomes susceptible to their pressures and political action... for the ruling elite, the State is both a source of benefit as much as a means for defence against domestic discontent and undue external penetration" (Ukeje/Odebiyi, Sesay, Olabisi, 2002: 5; similarly Global Witness, 2004: 4). Illegal activities are initiated by the preference of looters to trade easily accessible and portable high-value items such as diamonds (Ginty, 2004: 862).

4 Commodity-related Policies to Remove Causes of Crises

4.1 Trade policy, Diversification, and a Crisis-related "Renaissance" of International Commodity Agreements

Policy options to remove the origin of unrest and crises in the resource-rich SSA countries should be perceive as an outstanding public good in terms of commodity supply and demand, as a contribution to economic growth and social welfare in the exporting economies, and as beneficial for the commodity purchasing companies the traditional concepts of international economics and politics as well as of international security have to be reformulated. Governments in developing countries have to acknowledge that the origins of the conflicts in the respective African states cannot be put aside with the traditional economic and foreign policy. Governments in African countries are not capable to improve the framework and thereby to mitigate or eradicate crises in a sustainable manner. As an alternative, Naim recommended to "develop more flexible notions of sovereignty, to strengthen existing multilateral institutions" and "to move from repression to regulation" (Naim 2003, p. 34). It is necessary to underline the needs of a more comprehensive commodity policy in the respective areas of policy formulation, and to contribute to a new order by additional instruments for a commodity policy. Policy instruments that have been applied in the past successfully and efficiently will still be available, and add are new instruments that may have a stabilising impact in developing countries and will safeguard the regular supply of commodities in a long-term perspective. Recommendations refer also to new forms of development co-operation, to specific forms of humanitarian assistance, to innovative measures of trade policy and investment promotion as well as to related policies for the regional collaboration. Interventions into the flow of goods, services and resources should be minimised by strengthening actions within the business community and by sharing the co-operation of NGOs. The subsequent considerations describe proposals which have been raised in the discussion and actions being decided upon.

4.1.1 Trade Liberalisation and Diversification

Although there are economic, political and social roots in the evolution of crises it can be argued that the resource-endowment in the respective countries may also be considered as an indispensable "crank" to be applied productively when averting the origins of the crises. Options as being recently discussed draw the attention to trade liberalisation, to the establishment of new commodity agreements, and to an enlarged transparency related to the behaviour of transnational corporations. It is furthermore supposed that there should be concomitant actions by the developing countries as well as by the business community.

Trade liberalisation in the industrialised countries is assumed to strengthen the competition between the stakeholders in the raw materials sector (Implementation Report, 2003; UNCTAD, 2004a: 293; Economic Commission for Africa, 2004: 178; Aktionsplan, 2004: 50). It is argued that shocks due to rapid changes in the commodity markets may be better overcome and that the foreign currency incomes may so be stabilised. Selling to developed countries in open markets enables the business sector to abstain from close collaboration with national stakeholders in developing countries. This implies that the opportunities of government and related agencies decrease to receive illegal payments and to earn income outside of the legal framework. Although the rationale of the argument is plausible, it has to be acknowledged that such a policy might at least in the short run not be efficient as an instrument to reduce the incidence of crises. The reason is that so far Africa has not been successful to penetrate the OECD markets. African economies, and mainly the commodity exporting states, did not succeed as large-scale suppliers of manufactured goods in developed countries. It is argued that other suppliers, mainly those in Asia and Latin America, are more competitive than African producers. As NEPAD states "...Africa has been integrated into the world economy mainly as a supplier of cheap labour and raw materials. Of necessity, this has meant the draining of Africa's resources rather than their use for the continent's development. The drive in that period to use the minerals and raw materials to develop manufacturing industries and a hilly skilled labour force to sustain growth and development was lost. Thus, Africa remains the poorest continent despite being one of the most richly endowed regions of the world" (NEPAD, 2001: para 19; similarly Economic Commission for Africa, 2004: 6).

Many studies have argued that bad governance – exemplified by weak governments and poor public administration, lack of services that are needed to set up manufacturing plants, and interventions into the market allocation mechanism by quickly changing regulations and rules – creates a climate being hostile to the enlargement of investment for the diversification of the productive sector. Taking this for granted, investment in the commodity sector is more profitable as the returns are assumed to be calculable and governments would abstain from regulation, as this would curb the income from raw materials' exports. Furthermore, the developed countries are still hesitant to enable market access to developing countries' suppliers as long as there is a need to protect internal job opportunities, especially in economically weak regions.

Theoretical and empirical analysis concludes that internal adaptation to trade liberalisation is the complementary policy for the African countries to react, and a broad range of exportables implies the chances to compensate losses due to price decreases and fluctuations of commodities. Commodity exporting countries as those in SSA are to be advised to participate in the worldwide division of labour through specialisation, and the reasoning about the Washington Consensus has laid out the route that diversification is preceded by investment and human capital accumulation in developing countries. Such efforts of the private sector however require an adequate frame such as good governance that will strengthen the internal adaptation process through liberalisation of markets and enabling access to resources such as capital and skills as well as to the markets.

However, there is a lack of diversification because of poor macroeconomic governance and the lack of entrepreneurial spirit due to many government regulations in a "failed state". Change implies a continuous long-term adaptation approach, and this would destroy in transitory phases more job opportunities and capital. Revised versions of the Washington Consensus propose that the interim adjustment processes and overcoming the related social tensions should by mitigated by development co-operation efforts. Such efforts should be geared to provide the resources to sectors that might best support the structural change, such as education, health as well as housing, water and environment, and business development. However, such proposals are not easy to be implemented due to weak governments and the limited willingness of stakeholders to invest in diversification.

4.1.2 Shutting Rebel Organisations out of Markets

Regarding resource-rich countries, extended and revised international commodity agreements may be a means – as Paul Collier and his co-authors argue – to contribute to the "shutting rebel organisations out of markets" by sanctions and thereby to remove causes of conflicts (Collier, Elliott, Hegre, Hoeffler, Raynard-Querol, Sambanis, 2003: 178; Muchai, 2002: 195). Such agreements are expected to provide that potentially violent actors do not receive funds that are deployed to conflict generation. Joint commodity agreements may be enriched by regulations that enable states to trace back illegally traded goods whose export income is spent by potentially violent actors to fuel conflicts.

The Kimberley agreement was initiated in the year 2000 by NGOs (ActionAid, Amnesty International, Global Witness, Oxfam International, Partnership Africa Canada and World Vision) and launched officially in

November 2002. The deliberations were an input to the negotiations on an Angolan peace accord, and it was felt being urgent to utilise commodity agreements in a conflict-averting manner. The consensus provided that shipments of diamonds have to be accompanied by a certificate that is validated, and that the importing countries transmit confirmation of receipts to the authorities in the exporting countries. The certificates have to be filed for three years. Transfers of diamonds from member countries to purchasers in non-member countries are not permitted. In case of transit the rules have to be applied adequately by the respective countries. The implementation of internal controls is a duty of the member states; they have to install certification and to set up authorities being enacted to supervise the import and export of diamonds. The contracting states have committed themselves to crosscheck data on diamond production and trade as well as to communicate control protocols to responsible authorities in other countries (Smillie, 2002: 14). Additionally, there are self-regulations of the business sector to apply the rules of the Kimberley agreement.

Further joint actions in the commodity sector have not been implemented yet. In the past international commodity agreements did not succeed; they failed either in terms of price or earnings stabilisation or in stabilising the supply of quantities. Obviously, commodity markets cannot be manipulated either by suppliers or by purchasers. Traditionally, the suppliers do not stick to the joint rules especially in periods of declining prices, and purchasers hesitate to apply to the agreed procedure especially in a period when commodities are scarce and when there is a rising demand and price. Weak trade controls lead to circumvention and enable illegal trade, especially under the umbrella of regional collaboration. Recent research on the impact of sanctions in Africa reveals the limited efficiency to enforce global rules (Hefeker/Menck, 2002).

The technical procedure to identify the source of commodities requires a large input in terms of supervision and control at borders, as well as documentation and assessment. These tasks will be implemented efficiently if there are only very few trading places and licensed traders as in the case of diamonds. There should be no physical restraints that abrogate the intention of the supervision. The identification of gems regarding the source is not applicable in cases when stones from different sources are mixed. There are yet no provisions to check each of the 800 million diamonds being delivered annually to the world market. A tight control of certificates' distribution and the supervision of the trade flows requires an administrative structure that will not be available unless bilateral and multilateral donors have provided resources to install the offices, to define the rules, to implement the certification, and to control the border-crossing trade.

4.1.3 Extractive Industries Transparency Initiative

Furthermore it is recommended to increase the transparency of spending the natural resources revenues by supervision and monitoring what should be provided under the auspices of an international organisation. The Extractive Industries Transparency Initiative (EITI) was launched in 2002 at the Johannesburg Summit and recommends: "Mining, gas, and oil companies cannot control how governments spend taxes, royalties and fees. But they do have a responsibility to disclose the payments they make to citizens so that they can hold their government accountable... We are not calling on companies to disclose commercially confidential information, but rather to publish the same basic data on net payments made to government and other public authorities which they are required to disclose to many developed countries". It is concluded by the supporters of the initiative: "we propose that publicly traded resource companies be required by regulators to disclose net payments, including taxes, royalties, fees and other transactions with governments and/or public sector entities, for the products of every country in which they operate" ("A call for mandatory disclosure"; similarly Aktionsplan 2004: 61). Companies and international financial organisations are invited to join and to release contracts that do not fit to the criteria of the transparency initiative.

The *Republic of Congo (DR)* has now undertaken initiatives to enhance transparency in the spending of the oil revenues, while other resource-rich countries have not done the same yet (International Monetary Fund, 2005: 7; Financial Times, 17/03/2005).

When negotiating the agreements the business sector hesitated to join because companies argue that their competence is not strong enough to interfere into government actions in the resource-rich countries nor is the business sector qualified to assess the conflict potential of partners being involved in co-operation projects. The transparency about company payments and the recipients may not coincide with business-based considerations to keep competitive edges. Persons and institutions benefiting from payments will obstruct transparency to protect their private sources of income. Additionally, sanctions may be circumvented either by competing companies and/ or partners in developing countries who are substitutes for violent actors. Money laundering activities by local partners are another means to thwart transparency initiatives. There are so many ways to hide transactions that do not fit to the standards of payments to the transparency initiative rules.

A supervision as envisaged by the transparency initiative may be unnecessary if the business sector acts in a conflict-avoiding manner. The conditions to control the behaviour are improved especially in the developing countries if the enterprises adhere to crisis-preventing standards.

The OECD has elaborated not yet obligatory proposals addressing the business sector as well as the developing countries' state authorities. Enterprises are invited to

1. "Contribute to economic, social and environmental progress with a view to achieving sustainable development.
2. Respect the human rights of those affected by their activities consistent with the host government's international obligations and commitments.
3. Encourage local capacity building through close co-operation with the local community, including business interests, as well as developing the enterprise's activities in domestic and foreign markets, consistent with the need for sound commercial practice.
4. Encourage human capital formation, in particular by creating employment opportunities and facilitating training opportunities for employees.
5. Refraining from seeking or accepting exemptions not contemplated in the statutory or regulatory framework related to environmental, health, safety, labour, taxation, financial incentives, or other issues.
6. Supporting and upholding good corporate governance principles and develop and apply good corporate governance practices.
7. Developing and applying effective self-regulatory practices and management systems that foster a relationship of confidence and mutual trust between enterprises and the societies in which they operate..." (OECD, 2000: 19).

An OECD analysis recommends further measures by foreign investors such as:

- "Support government capacities to define or enforce national legal frameworks and corporate governance regimes in line with international laws/ norms, in order to ensure accountability...
- Support efforts to find solutions for special claims of indigenous peoples such as those for ancestral land rights, and formalisation of control over investment projects, employment preferences, etc.
- Provide for the effective enforcement of national legislation on labour and environmental standards.
- Promote the use of peace and conflict impact assessments by local, national, international/ big business...

- Encourage Diasporas to become engaged in positive development roles in their countries of origin."
- Furthermore it is recommended to create an enabling environment and space for dialogue.(OECD, 2001: 69).

As The World Development Report 2005 has recommended, a government that is really accountable should provide a frame that makes it possible that companies abstain from rent seeking, corruption and similar actions. The investment climate should be designed in the frame of a long-lasting process whose contents and whose schedules are determined by the interaction between the transnational investors, the local stakeholders, and the people (World Bank, 2005: 6).

4.2 Internal Crisis Management in Resource-rich Economies: Ownership and Good Governance

International actions – provided that they are agreed upon and ultimately implemented – need to be supported by national efforts of the developing countries. International agreements are necessary, but are not sufficient to dry out the supply of resources being available for conflict-generation and being absorbed for crisis generation. Potentially violent actors and supporters are not induced to change their attitudes and to abstain from power. The failed states/ the shadow states will persist and deploy the income generated by the commodity sector to mobilise internal means to nurture conflicts. "Ownership" as a development strategy has therefore to become an inherent element of crisis-prevention in resource-rich countries, as for instance in the resource-rich SSA economies (UNCTAD, 2004b: 271).

The case studies underline that priority should be given to strengthen the capabilities of the state and to strengthen NGOs and the civil society in order to provide that export earnings from the commodity sector and the commodities trade are really allocated according to the preferences of the society and so as to avert crises. Internal efforts have to be directed to include forms of promotion and compensation in kind to those who do not really participate in the overall economic development of countries with a commodity sector, with the purpose to strengthen the profitability of investment and labour in the whole economy. There is an understanding that measures at eradicating poverty through education and training, health services, microfinance projects, small industries support, and the promotion of the agricultural sector may be perceived as means to strengthen the capabilities of those who do not share in the economic gains from the commodity sector. This new behaviour of governments and actors in commodity-producing countries could be a message to those who in the past argued that conflicts for income shares are the only means to overcome discrimination (NEPAD, 2001: para 16; Wohlmuth, 2004: 32).

A conflict-avoiding form of collaboration of resource-rich SSA countries with transnational corporations in the mining sector should be in the focus of the internal policy processes in developing countries. An unholy alliance against minorities or dissenting parties may be put aside through strengthening the local ownership of the commodities that are produced, by strengthening local enterprises, skills, financial resources, and management. Additionally, a strong bias of the commodity sector in the overall economic structure and in the exports has to be altered gradually by diversification. Short-term economic tensions due to the loss of job opportunities and because of the destruction of physical capital in outworn industries can be mitigated by governmental support that provides assistance to sectors and incentives to adjust the economy (NEPAD, 2001: para. 39; Economic Commission for Africa, 2004:158). Compensations in kind as public services as education, health, housing, water and sanitation may invite potentially viable actors to decide on peaceful ways to gain instead of power.

Summarising, proposals such as these presented in this section did in the past not work as it is shown in the three case studies (see Table 2). The above-mentioned recommendations are based on the concept of "ownership" that had been installed in the context of the official technical and financial development co-operation so as to remove inefficiencies due to the lack of support from the local stakeholders. The development collaboration is intended to support and to strengthen primarily the local actors to create overall economic growth and social welfare in the commodity-exporting countries. However, it is one of the central elements of the debacle of the resource-rich countries when they have weak governments that there are not enough stakeholders working for the public welfare and the general interest.

Another argument underlines that an "ownership"-based conditionality cannot be successfully concluded, realised and implemented in resource-rich developing countries. Developed countries argue that there is no urgent need to grant financial and technical assistance to the raw materials' producing and exporting economies as there is no economic incentive by the governments in the resource-rich countries to submit national economic policies to the rules of the donors and the international financial institutions. Developed countries are ambiguous when approaching resource-rich countries: in order to eradicate unrest and in order to stabilise the internal processes so as to secure a continuous supply of commodities at reasonable prices the government and the business sector in the purchasing countries are keen to request that appropriately formulated conditions tied to aid are then accepted by the relevant stakeholders in the exporting economies. The same actors want to keep good economic and political relations and thereby are reluctant to press strongly for reforms and appropriate policies, especially if commodities are badly needed.

Table 2: Survey of Crises-related Policies' Proposals

Policies	Actions	Stakeholders
Trade and commodities revenues	Trade liberalisation and strengthening the manufacturing sector in commodities exporting countries (embedded in trade agreements)	Developed countries, African countries, WTO, EU
	Shutting rebel organisations off the markets under the umbrella of commodity agreements: - by governmental law enforced actions - by voluntarily committed initiatives of the business community (proposed)	Developed countries, African countries, WTO, UNCTAD, business community
Foreign investment and collaboration with the national political and business authorities	Extractive Industries Transparency Initiative: - governmental and internationally binding agreements - voluntary actions by the business community and the governments (Decided, open to access, DR of Congo has joined) OECD recommendations (proposed)	Developed countries, African countries, Group of Eight, OECD, business community
Crisis management by African countries	Development efforts and their support by development co-operation focussing on - ownership, - good governance, - civil society, and - enabling a favourable environment for local and foreign investment. Humanitarian assistance and support of after-crises reconstruction (embedded in the DAC Guidelines for Development Assistance)	African countries, multilateral financing institutions, bilateral donors, NGO's, NEPAD

Source: Author's compilation.

5 Policy Conclusions

Concluding from the observation that resource-rich SSA states are exposed in a very specific manner to problems of crisis generation and crisis persistence it is necessary that policy proposals are identified that remove the causes of crisis generation and duration. Considering the observation and taking notice of the increasing demand for primary commodities from rapidly advancing developing countries as well as from industrialised countries a shift in the crisis management approach and in the perception of commodity policy is recommended. Conflicts and crises originating from the commodity sectors will have an immediately negative impact on the exporting and on the purchasing countries. Taking notice of the increasing demand for commodities mainly by developing countries in Asia there should be provisions that enhance the long-term supply and the continuous and regular availability of commodities. Therefore it is important that the trade in primary commodities is closely interrelated with mechanisms to ensure the global economic, social and political stability. These mechanisms are in the interest of the business community but also in the interest of the governments in developed and in developing countries. There should be more systematic links between the commodity supplying countries with regard of commodity trade, commodity-related crises and conflict management and the commodity purchasing countries with regard of related instruments of development co-operation. However, the proposed policy is a challenge to all stakeholders, and there are many risks inherent in the process that may be removed by continuous assessments as well as by adapting the mechanisms of commodity market governance to the specific needs and to the prevailing conditions: "This strategy does not promise a silver-bullet" (Eizenstat, Porter, Weinstein, 2005: 146).

Trade policy of the commodity purchasing countries should imply voluntary self-regulations to prevent corruption and mismanagement of commodity revenues in developing countries by sticking to strict rules of transparency. Foreign investors and international trading companies are called upon to pursue social and other standards and to select partners according to their ethical behaviour. The business community should negotiate international codes of conduct, and they should be implemented. Global rules and standards agreed upon voluntarily have to be installed to avoid illegal actions that nurture unrest emanating from the commodity sector (Cabinet Office, Prime Minister's Strategy Unit, 2005: 57).

International investment should be initiated by the economic policy in the supplying countries as well as in the purchasing economies to enhance the competition in the commodities sector, and to strengthen the private sector in exploration and trade. The developing countries are requested to create the adequate economic and political frame for investment, mainly by establishing good governance, by strengthening the market access, and by better protecting the property rights. Countries that are purchasing commodities are called upon to foster foreign direct investment by avoiding double taxation and by establishing commercially viable regulations with regard of the calculation of transfer prices within joint companies. Recently specific tax incentives in the field of oil exploration have been raised as an issue by the G8 in preparation of the Gleneagles Economic Summit 2005 (Financial Times, 07/06/2005).

Development co-operation should focus on internal stability by strengthening democracy, participation of the people in decision-making, supporting a civil society as well as enhancing measures at poverty eradication. Development co-operation is advised to help to diversify the economic structure. Also investment in the commodity sector has to be promoted, to enlarge competition and to reduce the concentration of political and economic power of the business community in the respective sector. Private investment in the supplying countries to produce and to sell commodities by small- and medium-sized companies should be strengthened. Economic reforms strengthening the market in the commodity sector have to be supported. Privatisation efforts to reduce the role of the state in the commodity sector - by state-owned companies - should be enhanced.

Humanitarian assistance is required, as well as actions that enhance the capabilities of the state, of the NGOs and of the business sector. There should be decisive global actions as decided upon by the G8 in the commitments towards Africa and the Millennium decade. (DFID, 2005: 22, World Bank, 2005: 4; Cabinet Office,. Prime Minister's Strategy Unit, 2005: 40).

At the regional level activities as being recently decided upon in the NEPAD should be enriched to remove causes of conflicts in commodity-exporting countries. Actions as the Peer Review Mechanisms are supposed to identify causes of conflict and unrest. Regional trade and economic reforms and voluntary actions at the regional level to stop illegal trade and related activities such as financial flows are badly needed (Cabinet Office, Prime Minister's Strategy Unit, 2005: 78).

References and Bibliography

A Call for Mandatory Disclosure: "A Call for Mandatory Disclosure of Payments and Transactions with Governments by Multinational Natural Resource Companies", their Subsidiaries and Business Partners, online: http://www.etan.org/lh/misc/PetRegSub/04pwypappeal-en.doc, accessed 27/07/2005.

Afoaku, Osita (2002): "Congo's Rebels. Their Origins, Motivations, and Strategies", in: John F. Clark (ed.), The African Stakes of the Congo War, New York and others, Palgrave Macmillan, pp. 109 – 128.

African Development Bank (2004): "African Development Report 2004", Oxford University Press.

Aktionsplan (2004): "Die Bundesregierung, Aktionsplan ‚Zivile Krisenprävention, Konfliktlösung und Friedenskonsolidierung'", Berlin, 12. Mai 2004, online: www.bmz.de/themen/dokumente/aktionsplan.pdf , accessed 27/07/2005.

Anderson, Mary B. (1999): "Do No Harm. How Aid Can Support Peace – or War", London, Boulder

Auty, Richard M. (1998): "Resource Abundance and Economic Development. Improving the Performance of Resource-Rich Countries", Research for Action 44, Helsinki, UNU/ WIDER Publications.

Böge, Volker (2004): "Muschelgeld und Blutdiamanten. Traditionale Konfliktbearbeitung in Zeitgenössischen Gewaltkonflikten", Hamburg, Deutsches Übersee-Institut, Schriften Nummer 63.

Cabinet Office, Prime Minister's Strategy Unit (2005): "Investing in Prevention, A Prime Minister's Strategy Unit Report to the Government. An International Strategy to Manage Risks of Instability and Improve Crisis Response", online: http://www.strategy.gov.uk/downloads/work_areas/countries_at_risk/cri_report.pdf, accessed 27/07/2005

Collier, Paul, Elliott, Lani, Hegre, Håvard, Hoeffler, Anke, Raynal-Querol, Marta, Sambanis, Nicholas (2003): "Breaking the Conflict Trap, Civil War and Development Policy", Washington D.C. 2003, World Bank, Oxford University Press.

Craft, Cassady and Smaldone, Joseph P. (2002): "The Arms Trade and the Incidence of Political Violence in Sub-Saharan Africa, 1967 – 97", in: Journal of Peace Research, 39 (6), pp. 693 – 710.

DFID (2005): "Why we need to work more effectively in fragile states, Department for International Development", online: http://www.dfid.gov.uk/pubs/files/-fragilestates-paper.pdf, accessed 27/07/2005.

Dunn, Kevin C. (2002): "A Survival Guide to Kinshasa, Lessons of the Father, Passed Down to the Son", in: John F. Clark (ed.), The African Stakes of the Congo War, New York and others, Palgrave Macmillan, pp. 53 – 74.

Eavis, Paul (2003): "Strengthening Global Security through Addressing the Root Causes of Conflict", in: Trócaire Development Review, Number 4, pp. 57 – 64, online: http://www.trocaire.org/policyandadvocacy/trocairedevelopmentreview/strengtheningglobalsecuritybyadressingrootcausesofconflict.pdf, accessed 27/07/2005.

Economic Commission for Africa (2004): "Economic Report on Africa 2004, Unlocking Africa's Trade Potential", New York, Addis Ababa: Economic Commission for Africa.

Eizenstat, Stuart E., Porter, John Edward and Weinstein, Jeremy M. (2005): "Rebuilding Weak States", in: Foreign Affairs, 84 (1), pp. 134 – 146.

Energy Information Administration (EIA) of the United States Government (2004): "Sudan, Country Analysis Brief", online: http://www.eia.doe.gov/emeu/cabs/-sudan.html, accessed 27/07/2005.

Fitzgerald, Valpy (2001): "The International Political Economy of Conflict in Poor Countries, in: War and Underdevelopment", Volume I, The Economic and Social Consequences of Conflict, Frances Stewart/Fitzgerald, Valpy (Eds.), Oxford, Oxford University Press, pp. 204 – 224.

Financial Times (17/03/2005):" George Soros: Transparency can alleviate poverty".

Financial Times (07/06/2005): "G8 considers tax incentives to oil companies to boost refining capacity."

Garfinkel, Michelle R., Skaperdas, Stergios, and Syropoulos, Constantinos (2004): "Globalization and Domestic Conflict", online: http://www.econpwa/-wustl.edu8089/eps/othr/papers/040/0406003.pdf, accessed: 27/07/2005.

George Soros (2005): "Transparency can alleviate poverty", in: Financial Times, 17.3.2005.

Ginty, Roger Mac (2004): "Looting in the Context of Violent Conflict: a Conceptualisation and Typology", in: Third World Quarterly, 25 (5), pp. 857 – 870.

Global Witness (2004): "Time for Transparency, Coming Clean on Oil, Mining and Gas Revenues", Washington D.C.: Global Witness Publishing Inc.

Goudie, Andrew and Neyapti, Bilin (1999): "Executive Summary, in: Goodie, Andrew", Neyapti, Bilin (Ed.), Conflict and Growth in Africa, Volume 3: Southern Africa, Paris, OECD, pp. 9 – 14.

Grignon, François (2004): "International Response to the Illegal Exploitation of Resources in the DRC", in: Mark Malan, João Gomes Porto (eds.), Challenges of Peace Implementation, The UN Mission in the Democratic Republic of the Congo (DRC), Pretoria, Institute for Security Studies, Pretoria, pp. 43 – 52.

Hauck, Gerhard (2004): "Schwache Staaten? Überlegungen zu einer fragwürdigen entwicklungspolitischen Kategorie", in: Peripherie, 24 (96), pp. 411 – 427.

Hashim, Muhammad Jalal Ahmad (2004): "To Be or Not To Be, Sudan at Crossroads, Bucks", online: http://www.sudanjem.com/english/books/TOBEORNOTOBE-/2004, accessed 31/08/04

Hefeker, Carsten and Menck, Karl Wolfgang (2002): "Wie wirkungsvoll sind Sanktionen? Das Beispiel Südafrika", HWWA-Report 220, Hamburg, Hamburgisches Welt-Wirtschafts-Archiv.

Heidelberger Institut für Internationale Konfliktforschung (2004): "Konfliktbarometer 2004, Krisen, Kriege, Putsche, Verhandlungen, Vermittlungen, Friedensschlüsse, 13. Jährliche Konfliktanalyse", überarbeitete Ausgabe, Institut für Politische Wissenschaft der Universität Heidelberg.

Human Rights Watch (2003): "Sudan, Oil and Human Rights, Brussels", London, New York, Washington D.C., Human Rights Watch.

Implementation Report (2003): "Implementation Report by Africa Personal Representatives to leaders on the G8 Africa Action Plan", online: http://www.g8.fr/evian/english/navigation/2003_g8_summit/summit_documents/implementation_report_by_africa_personal_representatives_to_leaders_on_the_G8_Africa_Action_Plan.html, accessed 27/07/2005.

International Crisis Group (2003): "Angola's Choice: Reform or Regress, Luanda, Brussels, Africa Report No. 61.

International Monetary Fund (2005): "World Economic and Financial Surveys, Advance Copy, Regional and Economic Outlook. Sub-Saharan Africa, online: http://www.imf.org/external/pubs/ft/afr/reo/2005/eng/01/pdf/ssareo.pdf, accessed 27/07/2005.

Johnson, Douglas H. (2003): "The Root Causes of Sudan's Civil War", Oxford: The International Africa Institute.

Junkert, Mathias G. (2003): "Auf den Spuren der Kriegsherren, Die Vereinten Nationen und die Privatisierung der Gewalt, Am Beispiel UNAMSIL in Sierra Leone", Marburg: Tectum Verlag.

Körner, Peter (1998): "Regionalisierung des internationalen Konfliktmanagements: Die multinationale westafrikanische Eingreiftruppe ECOMOG", in: Afrika Jahrbuch 1998, Politik, Wirtschaft und Gesellschaft in Afrika südlich der Sahara, Herausgeber: Institut für Afrika-Kunde, Rolf Hofmeier, Opladen 1999, pp. 43 – 52.

Koyame, Mungbalemwe and Clark, John F. (2002): "The Economic Impact of the Congo (DR) War", in: John F. Clark (ed.), The African Stakes of the Congo (DR) War, New York and others, Palgrave Macmillan, pp. 201 – 224.

Kremer, Michael and O' Connel, Stephen A. (2004): "Comments On Jeffrey D. Sachs", John W. Mc Arthur, Guido Schmidt-Traub, Margaret Kruk, Chandrika Bahadur, Michael Faye, Gordon McCord, Ending Africa's Poverty Trap, in: Brookings Papers on Economic Activity, Number 1, pp. 217 – 229.

Lanotte, Olivier (2003): "Rèpublique Democratique du Congo (DR)", Guerres sans Frontières, Bruxelles, GRIP

Longman, Timothy (2002): "The Complex Reasons for Randa's Engagement in Congo (DR)", in: John F. Clark (ed.), The African Stakes of the Congo (DR) War, New York and others, Palgrave Macmillan, pp. 129 – 144.

Mair, Stefan (2004): "Konfliktpotenziale in Afrika", online: http://www.reader-sipo.de/artikel/3012_AIII1.html, accessed 15/09/2004.

MBendi (2005): "Sudan: Oil and Gas Industry", online: http://www.mbendi.co.za-/indy/oilg/ogorf/af/su/p0005.html, accessed 27/07/2005

McCalpin, Jermaine O. (2002): "Historicity of a Crisis, The Origins of the Congo (DR) War", in: John F. Clark (ed.), The African Stakes of the Congo (DR) War, New York and others, Palgrave Macmillan, pp. 33 – 50.

Moran, Mary H. and Pitcher, M. Anne (2004): "The „Basket case" and the „Poster child": Explaining the End of Civil Conflicts in Liberia and Mozambique", in: Third World Quarterly, 25 (3), pp. 501 – 519.

Muchai, Augusta (2002): "Arms Proliferation and the Congo (DR) War", in: John F. Clark (ed.), The African Stakes of the Congo (DR) War, New York and others, pp. 185 – 200.

Nafziger, E. Wayne (2003): "Inequality and Conflict, in: Emmanuel Nnadozie (Ed.) African Economic Development", Amsterdam and other places, Academic Press, pp. 295 – 312.

Naím, Moisés, (2003): "Five Wars of Globalization, in: Foreign Policy (134)", pp. 28 – 38.

NEPAD (2001): "The New Partnership for Africa's Development (NEPAD)", online: http://www.uneca.org/eca_resources/Conference_Reports_and_Other_Documents/nepad/NEPAD.html, accessed 27/07/2005.

Nzongola-Ntalaja, Georges (2002): "The Congo (DR) from Leopold to Kabila", London, New York ZED Books.

O'Ballance, Edgar (2000): "Sudan, Civil War and Terrorism, 1956–99", New York, Macmillan.

OECD (2000): "The OECD Guidelines for Multinational Enterprises", Revision 2000, Paris, OECD.

OECD (2001): "The DAC Guidelines", Helping Prevent Violent Conflict, Paris, OECD

OECD (2004): "African Economic Outlook 2003/04, Paris, OECD/AfDB.

Schneckener, Ulrich (2004a): "States at Risk – Zur Analyse fragiler Staatlichkeit", in: Ulrich Schneckener (Hg.), States at Risk. Fragile Staaten als Sicherheits- und Entwicklungsproblem, Berlin, SWP Studie, 43, pp. 435 – 28.

Schneckener, Ulrich (2004b): "Der Umgang mit fragilen Staaten – Ergebnisse und Empfehlungen", in: Ulrich Schneckener (Hg.), States at Risk. Fragile Staaten als Sicherheits- und Entwicklungsproblem, Berlin, SWP Studie, 43, pp. 171 – 194.

Smillie, Ian (2002): "The Kimberley Process, The Case for Proper Monitoring", Ottawa, Partnership Africa Canada, International Peace Information Service, Network Movement for Justice and Development, Occasional Paper 5, online: http://www.diamonds.net/kp/KP%20Monitoring%20article%20Oct%202002.pdf, accessed 27/07/2005.

Stuvoy, Kirsti (2002): "War Economy and the Social Order of Insurgencies. An Analysis of the Internal Structure of UNITA's War Economy", Arbeitspapier Universität Hamburg, Research Unit of Wars, Armament and Development, Hamburg, Number 3, Forschungsstelle Kriege, Rüstung und Entwicklung, Universität Hamburg.

Ukeje, Charles, Odebiyi, Adetanwa, Sesay, Amadu and Olabisi, Aina (2002): "Oil and Violent Conflicts in the Niger Delta", Ile – Ife, Center for Development and Conflict Management Studies, Obafemi Awolowo University Press, Centre for Development and Conflict Management Studies, Monograph Series Number 1.

UNCTAD (2004a): "The Least Developed Countries", Report 2004, New York and Geneva, United Nations.

UNCTAD (2004b): "World Investment Report 2004: The Shift towards Services", New York and Geneva, United Nations.

Wohlmuth, Karl (2004): "The African Growth Tragedy: Comments and an Agenda for Action," Bremen, Institute for World Economics and International Management, Berichte aus dem Weltwirtschaftlichen Colloquium der Universität Bremen, Nr. 91, Bremen.

World Bank (2003a): "Transitional Support Strategy for the Republic of Angola", Report No. 25471-ANG, AFC02 Africa Region, online: http://www-wds.worldbank.org/servlet/WDSContentserver/WDSP/IB/2003/03/22/000094_94603031304013163/RENDERED/PDF/multi0page/pdf, accessed 27/07/2005.

World Bank (2003b): "Sudan, Stabilization and Reconstruction, Country Economic Memorandum", Volume I: Main Text, June 30, online: http://www-wds.worldbank.org/servlet/WDSContentServer/WDSP/IB/2003/08/23/000094946_03081404004140/RENDERED/PDF/multi0page/pdf, accessed 27/07/2005.

World Bank (2005): "World Development Report 2005: A Better Investment Climate for Everyone, Washington D.C., World Bank, Oxford University Press.

World Bank, Evaluation of World Bank Support to Low-Income Countries under Stress. An Approach Paper", online: http://web.worldbank.org/-WBSITE/EXTENAL/PROJECTS/STRATEGIES/EXTLICUS/O,,contentMDK:202976618~menuPK532111~PK64171351~piPK:64171507~theSITEPK:571778,00.html, accessed 27/07/2005.

Young, Crawford (2002): "Contextualising Congo (DR) Conflicts: Order and Disorder in Postcolonial Africa", in: John F. Clark (ed.), The African Stakes of the Congo (DR) War, New York and others, Palgrave Macmillan, pp. 13 – 32.

Unit 2: Commodity Dependence and Export Diversification. Towards New Strategies and Policies for Nigeria

edited by Afeikhena Jerome, Karl Wohlmuth and Mareike Meyn

Nigeria's Commodity Dependence and Options for Diversification. An Introduction

Afeikhena Jerome and Karl Wohlmuth

1 The Issues

Until recently, virtually all developing countries in Africa, Asia and Latin America were heavily dependent on exports of few primary commodities. While the other regions have made significant strides in diversifying their export base, African countries, perhaps with the exception of South Africa and Mauritius, are still dependent on a narrow range of low value-added commodities and natural resource exports.

However, contrary to the widely held perception, it is not true that Africa has made no progress towards export diversification over the last two decades. Africa has indeed made some head start, but the progress made has been rather limited and confined to few countries despite substantial engagement in trade and the decline in tariff rates over time. The heavy dependence on primary commodities as a source of export earnings has made the continent vulnerable to market vagaries and adverse weather conditions. Price volatility, arising mainly from supply shocks and the secular decline in real commodity prices, and the attendant terms-of-trade losses have exacted heavy toll on the continent in terms of incomes, indebtedness, investment, poverty and development (UNCTAD, 2003). However, the dynamic gains from trade integration might outweigh the negative static effects. Benefits from cooperation in the fields of infrastructure, technology, education, and health, as well as the option of a stronger bargaining position, higher economies of scale and increased investment due to bigger markets have also to be taken into account.

Globally, there are currently over 65 countries that still rely on primary commodities for more than 50% of export earnings (Bonaglia/Fukasaku, 2003 and Farnan 2005:1), with a majority of them in Africa. These countries are mired in poverty in spite of their systematic insertion into the global economy through export markets. With the possible exception of a few oil producers and countries that moved into skill-intensive and technology-based industries, thus incorporating value-adding processes into their primary sectors, no country relying on primary commodity exports has been able to move into the high-income bracket as indicated in Figure 1. A cursory examination of this figure reveals that several African countries perform poorly on this count with Nigeria on the lowest rung.

Figure 1: Commodity Dependency and Income Levels

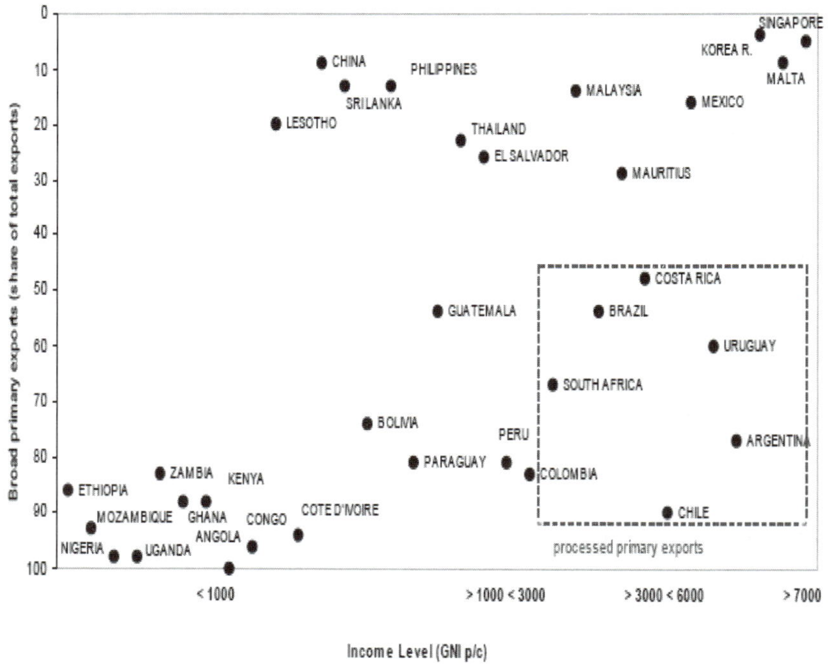

Source: Farfan 2005, p. 2.

The literature has devoted much attention to the well-known problems of primary commodity dependence, such as the secular deterioration in the commodities terms of trade and the "natural resource curse" or the "paradox of impoverishing abundance", and there is a well-documented correlation between commodity dependence and slower growth rates (Sachs/Warner, 2001).

Firstly, commodity-dependent economies are deemed to have lower growth prospects as a result of limited demand for these commodities globally due to their low income elasticity and depressed, if not outright declining terms of trade. Standard cross-section growth regressions lend support to this view. For example, Sachs and Warner (2001) find a statistically significant inverse association between resource-intensity - as measured by the share of primary commodity exports in GDP in 1970 - and growth, after controlling for other important determinants of economic performance. Isham et al. (2002) contend that different export structures create different institutional capacities to manage shocks, since all the natural resources are not the same. Countries that are abundant in "point-source" natural resources (e.g. oil or diamonds) tend to develop weaker institutions (and hence are more exposed to shocks) than those rich in "diffuse" natural resources (e.g. fertile land).

Secondly, empirical evidence abounds on the adverse consequences of primary commodity dependence on various dimensions of poor governance (Sachs and Warner, 1995; Auty, 2001 and Collier, 2002). Commodity-dependency, especially in the case of one or a reduced number of primary products has been associated with low institutional development and political instability. In settings where initial political and economic institutions are relatively weak, dependence on primary commodities, especially natural resources such as oil, appears to have encouraged predatory government behaviour and rent-seeking, deterring the development of stable, democratic institutions that are conducive to growth. It also provides poor incentives for human capital investment, and discourages learning by doing, knowledge spillovers, and an increasing use of technology, at least compared to the production of manufactured goods (Birdsall, 2006: 9 and contribution of Jerome in Unit 1 in this YB). The political science view also stresses that government finance tends to become detached from broad-based taxation. Primary commodities typically generate high location-specific rents that governments can tax heavily without recourse to taxation and the associated transparency and accountability.

Thirdly, primary commodity dependence has also been associated with a substantially higher risk of civil war. Collier and Hoeffler (2002) have ignited the scholarly debate on the issue. In their econometric work they unearthed the counter-intuitive finding of an association between dependence on primary commodity exports causing grievance and the risk of civil war. They advanced the controversial explanation that dependence on natural resources heightens a country's risk of war because it affords rebels an opportunity for extortion. The robustness of this statistical finding is increasingly being questioned and this has inspired many of the subsequent inquiries into the relationship between natural resource dependence and the onset of civil war (Ross, 2004, Fearon, 2005, Nathan, 2005 and Humphreys, 2005). So far, the most vociferous criticism is attributable to Nathan, 2005; it is argued that the study is filled with empirical, methodological and theoretical problems that lead to unreliable results and unjustified conclusions.

It is generally agreed that natural resources have powerful effects on civil war but they do so in ways that are profoundly political. More importantly, resource abundance can create low capacity states that are vulnerable to rebel challenge (Ron, 2005: 444). While these problems have multiple causes, primary commodity dependence is a credible part of the explanation.

More recent studies, however, cast aspersion on the foundation of the "resource curse". It is becoming glaring that most of these studies are deficient methodologically. Lederman/Maloney (2002:7), for example, found that the negative impact of natural resources on growth would disappear, once a longer time span is considered and the potential for omitted variables and for endogeneity is taken into account in the estimation procedure. Successful cases in several parts of the globe also point to the existence of a broad array of policy options for encouraging export diversification and reducing dependence on primary commodities (Buitelaar, 2001; Fisher, 2001; and Helleiner, 2002). Historical evidence from several natural resource-rich OECD countries further indicates that resource endowment is not necessarily a curse; rather resource-based activities can lead to growth over long periods (Davis, 1995; Wright/Czelusta, 2002; Blomström/Kokko, 2003).

While significant attention has been devoted in recent years to export diversification strategies in Africa, most of the contributions, however, acknowledge that giving factual content to this diversification strategy is far from easy. In light of the host of both external and internal barriers to diversification, the viability of this strategy and the reforms needed in the African context have been widely challenged. Empirical research rooted in the theory of comparative advantage, conducted by Owens/Wood (1997) and Wood/Mayer (2001), indicates that the factor composition of desirable sectors might run contrary to the original factor endowment of a typical SSA country. To them, the shortage of skilled labour and the constraints that this places on their ability to diversify into secondary and tertiary goods sector precludes the ability of these countries to produce anything substantial but primary commodities.

Breaking the yoke of primary commodity dependence is by no means insurmountable as demonstrated by several developing countries in Asia and Latin America that in relatively recent times have successfully diversified their exports against all odds. Without doubt, Nigeria can reduce its commodity dependence and launch itself from a "rentier economy" being overtly dependent on oil to an economy on a high and sustainable growth trajectory. This can be achieved within the context of a major overhaul of its domestic policies and complementary international policies, and in the process the country can reap the maximum benefit from the growth potential that is offered by trade globalization. Against the backdrop of persistent macroeconomic crises, there appears to be implicit recognition within the government that this is the desired path as indicated by the current frenzy and array of policy reforms being undertaken.

This Unit of the African Development Perspectives Yearbook is thus devoted to primary commodity dependence and export diversification strategies in Nigeria. It is the first systematic attempt to embark on this challenge.

2 The Contributions

The six contributions in this Unit appraise various important strategic aspects of exports diversification in Nigeria with an emphasis on policy. The first contribution by *R. Okoh* presents compelling evidence on Nigeria's limited integration with the world economy and its inability over time to diversify exports away from oil due to structural bottlenecks. Many of these constraints cut across all economic sectors and are related to Nigeria's poor overall economic performance.

Despite major efforts at reform, Nigeria has not been able to take advantage of global trading opportunities, and hence to reap the growth-inducing and poverty-reducing benefits of trade. There are many reasons for this, including the difficulty of tackling comprehensively the inter-linkages of multiple trade challenges and the increasing focus on "behind the border" measures, such as sanitary and phyto-sanitary regulations and other technical barriers to trade, in multilateral trade negotiations. Rather than simply having to lower tariffs, the new requirements have potentially far-reaching implications for domestic institutions and policy reform. The next contribution by *M. Meyn* thus examines the role that trade capacity building could play in the diversification process of Nigeria. It is necessary for Nigeria to bundle all the activities required for a better market access in a strategy on trade capacity building.

Escaping commodity dependence also requires the development of other more dynamic sectors and activities. In this regard, the next four papers are sectoral and they evaluate the export potential of different sub-sectors using different methodologies. *O. Uzor* uses the Global Value Chain (GVC) framework to discuss commodity dependency and options for upgrading in the oil palm sector of Nigeria. *O. Olutayo* and *A. Omobowale* examine the production, processing and marketing of Cocoa as it affects rural development in Nigeria and exports; *O. Ujah* evaluates the export diversification potential of Cassava in the Nigerian Economy, while *A. Uzochukwu* is preoccupied with leather and leather products as a route to diversify exports.

The first paper by *R. Okoh* discusses global integration and commodity dependence in Nigeria. It starts from the premise that commodity dependence has been a major feature of Nigeria since attaining nationhood in 1960. Agriculture was the mainstay of the economy in the 1960s but this has been replaced by crude oil exports that currently account for 96 percent of foreign exchange earnings and around 70 percent of total revenues and capital formation. Agricultural exports, once the drivers of the economy, currently constitute approximately 3 percent of total earnings from merchandise exports or 0.2 percent of the GDP.

The author posits that poor countries in Africa and elsewhere, including Nigeria, are the least integrated internationally and they have also derived the least benefits from globalisation. Simply opening up the economy to the fierce competition that has characterized the global integration process has not benefited the Nigerian economy but rather it has exacerbated its dependency problem. The result is that Nigeria has become capital input import-dependent, being reliant on a single export commodity - oil.

The major factor that has helped to entrench the commodity dependency status of the Nigerian economy is the structure of merchandise exports that is dominated by the export of crude oil, natural gas (in recent times), and a few traditional agricultural products such as cocoa, palm oil and rubber. Manufacturing contributes only a little to the commodity export value. Nigeria's non-oil and non-agricultural exports are primary commodities and natural resource based semi-manufactures. The heavy dependence on oil export and a few agricultural commodities has made the economy highly vulnerable to external shocks, which are periodically transmitted through sharp changes in the world demand for these commodities. The price volatility of Cocoa, Nigeria's most important agricultural (non – oil) export product, was very high at 44.6 percent between 1973 and 2003, while the crude oil volatility level was 36.1 percent in the same period. The volatility of palm oil and natural rubber prices were also high at 27.6 and 24 percent, respectively.

The author evaluates the constraints confronting both the agricultural and the manufacturing sectors. She contends that the agricultural sectors face a number of demand-side and supply-side constraints. The demand-side constraints are mainly at the global level, albeit there are shifts in consumption patterns over time. The supply-side constraints are legendary and include among others: an inadequate incentive framework; the absence of a price support mechanism and pervasive distortions in macroeconomic and sectoral policies, including misaligned exchange rates and a heavy taxation of agricultural exports; and the low level of indigenous capacity or of technologies which are responsive to local conditions.

The manufacturing sector also suffers from a number of demand-side and supply side-constraints. The demand-side constraints are both domestic and global. On the domestic front, the basic problem is weak effective demand arising from dwindling consumers' purchasing power, aggravated by the influx of less expensive second hand goods that compete unfairly with local manufacturers. Consequently, the accumulation of unsold inventory remains high what further constrains the industrial capacity utilization rate. On the global front, Nigeria's manufactured goods have a very low demand, and they are faced with stiff competition from highly efficient producers in Asia and in other parts of the world. The supply-side constraints in the manufacturing sector are also numerous and include: deficient infrastructure; ageing and deteriorating machinery and equipment due to a weak science and technology base; low levels of entrepreneurial capacity; weak linkages between industry, research institutes and universities; the poor enabling environment and the resultant high cost of doing business, as revealed in the weak legal framework; weak business, financial, and information management systems, and practices; and a poor payment system. Manufacturing activities in Nigeria thus involve low skilled assemblage stages of international production chains in which most of the technology and skills are embodied in imported parts and components, and the greater part of the value added accrues to producers in more advanced nations.

She contends that the reality of the inherent instability associated with the dependence on a single export commodity has informed the need for diversification of Nigeria's export sector in order to take advantage of the changing dynamics of the global market place. Nigeria has so far adopted a number of macroeconomic policies and has entered into various bilateral, regional and multilateral agreements, but these efforts are yet to produce the desired results. Notwithstanding these problems, Nigeria still has potential for improvement and expansion of non-oil exports. For instance, there is demand for Nigerian textiles, pharmaceuticals, etc. in Africa, but the scale of production is yet too small to take advantage of the demand. On options for diversification, she argues that Nigeria's commodity dependence and the subsequent poor integration into the global market have been hampered by its inability to produce and to export market-dynamic products. Nigeria thus needs to reform and to restructure its manufacturing and agricultural sectors, to strengthen regional integration, and to create an enabling environment through good governance and the provision of the necessary infrastructure.

The logical starting point for becoming more competitive in the global market would be to change its current export mix through market research and product development towards "market-dynamic products" which will enable the country to take advantage of a number of trade preferences. In reforming the agricultural sector, she suggests that agricultural production should not be left completely to the vagaries of market forces as recommended by some multilateral institutions, including the World Bank and

WTO if it must break loose of commodity dependency trap. Nigeria must become more selective in regional, bilateral and multilateral agreements. The implication of every section of such agreements must be thoroughly evaluated before the economy is committed. The adoption of modern farming practices is paramount to attaining maximization of output. The capacity of farmers must be developed in order to improve the rate of adoption of green revolution technologies.

Though the various trade schemes established by ECOWAS have not had the desired impact, Nigeria needs to increase its efforts to expand its share of trade in ECOWAS. Regional integration through ECOWAS should enable entrepreneurs and investors responding to liberalized factor and product markets within the region and stepping up their response in terms of productivity, scale and scope of marketing. This should help to build up their capacities to exploit global opportunities in a gradual step-by-step process. As complementary policies, the government needs to embrace good governance that is responsive to the need of the governed and is adhering to the rule of law. Government must also provide adequate security for both local and foreign investors by putting in place an effective legal framework, which is responsive to the needs of both the local and the foreign investors.

A major impediment to the diversification efforts of developing countries is trade capacity, and this view is emphasised also by the international community. This is given added impetus by the Doha ministerial declaration on trade-related technical assistance and capacity building. Trade capacity relates mainly to the aspect of non-price external competitiveness that directly affects trade. It is an all-embracing concept encompassing the availability of trade-oriented infrastructure, institutions and know-how necessary to export competitively to foreign markets, and the ability to gain access to those markets through bilateral and multilateral negotiations and by participation in multilateral trade organizations.

The second paper by *M. Meyn* evaluates the role that trade capacity could play in the diversification process of Nigeria. Drawing on recent literature, the author observes that the concept of trade capacity building is comparably new and only came on the agenda in the mid-1990s. Trade capacity building should enable developing countries to identify their trade policy objectives and to formulate trade policy in such a manner that all relevant stakeholders are brought on board. It should also support the countries' export expansion and diversification strategy as well as assist in strengthening trade-related institutions in order to participate effectively at bilateral and multilateral trade negotiations. It thus embodied two parts, namely 'trade policy' and 'trade development'. While trade policy addresses countries' ability to analyse, negotiate and implement trade agreements, trade development investigates how supply-side and demand-side constraints could be overcome.

The requirements for participation in regional and multilateral negotiations are constantly changing and becoming more demanding for a typical developing country. Effective participation in the WTO, for example, entails implementing agreements and obligations on a broad range of issues, including import licensing, customs valuation, intellectual property law, and sanitary and phyto-sanitary standards. Additionally, bilateral and regional agreements and regulations have to be negotiated and implemented, which also stresses the already limited capacities.

Specifically on Nigeria, the author opinions that the Federal Ministry of Commerce is the principal government organ that is responsible for Nigeria's trade policy formulation, its trade negotiations, and the implementation of trade agreements, sometimes with inputs from other government institutions. However, coordination among governmental institutions is weak, and no institutionalised consultation mechanism exists. Consultations are often ad-hoc, resulting in a rather diffuse trade policy process.

In spite of Nigeria being a founding member of the WTO when it was transformed in 1995 from GATT, it is yet to incorporate WTO provisions into national law so that businesses and investors are unable to appeal to WTO provisions in Nigerian courts. Furthermore, Nigeria's mission to WTO is small, with only eight delegates in Geneva responsible for all sub-agreements in addition to facilitating improved market access for Nigerian products, seeking technical assistance, and protecting the country's interests at the World Intellectual Property Organisation (WIPO), The United Nations Conference on Trade and Development (UNCTAD), and the International Trade Centre (ITC). Obviously, the quantity and complexity of all these obligations overstretch the efforts of Nigeria's small mission to WTO. The complexity of the WTO Agreements puts constraints on Nigeria's capacities. The country is currently not in a position to implement the manifold obligations of the WTO sub-agreements due to lack of technical, institutional and human resources.

In addition to its international and regional obligations, Nigeria is involved in multiple bilateral trade and investment agreements with industrialised and developed countries with the two most important being the US African Growth and Opportunity Act/AGOA (since 2000) and the EU Lomé/Cotonou Agreement (since 1975). To date, both trade initiatives provide non-reciprocal duty free-market access for most Nigerian products. Unfortunately, Nigeria has failed to take advantage of the AGOA initiative. Though its trade surplus vis-à-vis the USA is the highest on the continent, Nigeria exports almost exclusively crude oil and natural gas to the USA (93% of total exports in 2000). Trade preferences under the EU Lomé/Cotonou regime that are granted since 1975 have also been insufficiently used by the country, and the Free Trade Agreement negotiated by ECOWAS (Free Trade Agreement/FTA) by the year 2000 is currently not being implemented.

The author argues that it is difficult for Nigeria to overcome its resource curse and to diversify its production due to a multiplicity of problems including the Dutch disease, infrastructural deficiencies and high transaction costs, macroeconomic fragility, corruption, lack of finance, and other supply-side constraints. However, all these deficiencies can be overcome when a comprehensive strategy, a strong consultation process among actors, and a future-oriented and visionary political process are emerging in Nigeria.

Nigeria has four major umbrella organisations that should represent the private sector's interest in trade negotiations. However, the organised business organisations are very weak and diffused so that the institutionalisation of businesses in Nigeria remains in infancy. The country has established a National Council, comprising government officials, organised business, organised labour, and civil society actors, following the example of South Africa, which adopted an inclusive trade policy strategy when negotiating the EU-South Africa FTA. However, the National Focal Point on Multilateral Trade Matters (NFP), which should serve as a forum for consultation and advice and should cooperate closely with the Nigeria Trade Office in Geneva, does not work as envisaged. There is also a demonstrable lack of domestic research capacity and a missing link between government policy formulation and responding to a broad critical civil society that may provide valuable inputs to the debate. The training needs of the private sector are also huge.

The author puts forward several concrete proposals what needs to be done in Nigeria. These include: the need to formulate a coherent trade strategy that is consistent with Nigeria's development goals; measures for improved market access and the identification of niche products into new markets; building-up of human capital and expertise in trade negotiations and strengthening related institutional capacities; effective participation of the private sector, of parliamentarians and of the civil society in trade negotiations; and moving towards deeper regional integration.

The next four contributions are product-specific. Key potential sectors of the Nigerian economy are considered with regard of export potentials and import substitution possibilities.

O. Uzor is using the Global Value Chain (GVC) analysis for appraising the chances of palm-oil production in initiating a process of structural upgrading in Nigeria. GVC analysis differs from comparable approaches in that it looks at the dynamics of firms/countries within global production networks, and focuses on productive systems as opposed to sectors or industries in isolation. It allows for a distinction between external and internal barriers.

Specifically, the author evaluates the output trend, the production system, the upgrading possibilities, the problems and chances in the export market of

Palm Kernel Oil (PKO) and Palm Kernel Cake (PKC) based on the results of fieldwork undertaken in Enugu, Nigeria. He contends that palm oil production and exportation in Nigeria has a relatively long history dating back to the pre-colonial era. Nigeria was a leading world producer and exporter of palm oil products in the 1960s with an average annual output of 43 per cent of world output. However, by 1997, Nigeria accounted for only 7 per cent of world production and for an alarming 1.7 per cent in 1995-1999. Despite currently low production and an output that fails to meet local demand and export chances, palm oil is arguably still an important segment in Nigeria economy, providing rural and urban income, employment opportunities and industrial inputs. The palm oil industry is based largely on semi-wild palms; these are standing scattered in rural villages and so it is very difficult to establish its extent and size. However, about 90 per cent of the output comes from dispersed smallholders that cover an estimated area of over 2,345,000 million hectares in the southern part of Nigeria. The current estimate of palm oil production in the country is about 900,000 metric tonnes of palm oil and 400,000 metric tonnes of palm kernel annually.

The results from the fieldwork reveal among others that the supply system in the palm kernel sub-sector is an embodiment of agents or dealers and rural smallholder farmers. On average, 3 tonnes of kernel per week are processed by each of the enterprises in the PKO enterprises cluster, while in dispersed enterprises an average of 2 tonnes of kernel per week are processed. The enterprises in the cluster perform better than the dispersed ones as a result of collective efficiency due to economies of scale in the cluster. The refineries in the South Eastern region consist of 10 medium-scale and 3 large-scale enterprises located in three industrial towns, namely Aba, Nnewi and Onitsha. Furthermore, the enterprises engaged in the extraction activity in Enugu fall within the micro and small enterprises sector due to the limited number of employees. The average age of the enterprises covered is 13 years. 95 per cent of the enterprises are sole proprietorship, while only 5 per cent are of a joint-venture partnership type of business. The labour force is a mixture of skilled and unskilled labour. About 97 per cent of the equipment in use is locally fabricated while 3 per cent are imported. The locally fabricated machines however do not possess an integrated drying system. Hence the enterprises have to depend on sun intensity for drying of kernels before oil extraction.

The author identifies various constraints afflicting the sector that cut across several broad areas, including inefficiencies in micro-, meso-, and macro-economic policies as well as internal weaknesses inherent in these enterprises. Topping the list is inadequate energy. Extraction typically requires high-energy voltage. About 94 per cent of the enterprises that were sampled have indicated that they cannot afford the cost of heavy generating plants, what makes them dependent on public energy supply that is erratic. Other constraints identified are: multiplicity of taxes; the poor policy environment; stiff competition from imports; lack of inputs making them overtly dependent on locally fabricated machines; and lack of finance. Not surprisingly, entrepreneurs in PKO extraction are confronted with insufficient start-up capital; a high pressure on working capital for daily business activities; and low investment capital for business expansion.

To revamp the sub-sector and to improve its chances in the value chain, the author recommends an integrated rural and urban production system that will offer an alternative strategy for poverty reduction in Nigeria. He recommends strengthening smallholder farmers currently dominating the sub-sector; consolidating landholdings with a view to inducing private initiative in medium-sized plantation; adopting the cluster development principles for PKO extraction enterprises; technology upgrades in the sub-sector through fostering cooperation between local S&T institutions with foreign research institutions; and adhering to the principles of good governance.

Another potential production and export sector is cocoa. Bass (2006) identified cocoa production and trade as playing an inglorious role in Africa's primary commodity dilemma due to the specific characteristics of the commodity, as the structural oversupply and the technology used in production along the value chain make it difficult for West African producers to reap benefits. In spite of this gloomy picture, some leeway for diversification does exist. In this regard, the fourth paper to this Unit by *O. Olutayo and O. Omobowale* appraises cocoa production, processing and marketing in Nigeria and their impact on rural development.

The authors posit that Nigeria joined the league of cocoa-producing nations around 1874 when the crop was introduced to the country from Spain. The commodity was first exported from Nigeria in 1892 and the volume then substantially increased. Subsequently, by 1960, when Nigeria attained independence, cocoa had emerged as a major export crop, with Nigeria ranking second in the world. After independence, cocoa remained a major source of finance for the then Western Region that was one of the three regions in Nigeria. Some attempts were made at diversification with the establishment of the Cocoa Industry Limited (CIL) in 1960. However, this modest achievement was to decline about a decade later as cocoa-processing began a downward spiral from processing of 12,052 tons in 1985 to just 390 tons in 1992 and non in 1993. Coincidentally this was the period of the oil boom.

For as long as the Cocoa Marketing Board lasted, it remained the sole government agency responsible for the purchase and export of cocoa products. By 1986 however, in line with the liberalization policy of the government, embedded in the Structural Adjustment Programme (SAP), the marketing board was scrapped while cocoa production, sale and export was liberalized. For the inexperienced investor, production standards involving grading and fermentation were neglected as low quality cocoa beans were presented for sale. Nigeria's cocoa lost value in the international market and cocoa production declined. Nevertheless, Nigeria's cocoa remains a major source of foreign exchange after petroleum. After the all time low figure of 100,000 tons recorded in 1987, cocoa production picked up again and reached a peak of 345,000 tons in 1998 before plummeting again to 165,000 tons the following year.

The hope for respite came with the government's intervention through the inauguration of a thirty member National Cocoa Development Committee (NCDC) on 2nd December 1999. The membership cuts across certain cocoa stakeholders representing the 14 cocoa-producing states, cocoa farmers, processors and marketers, and the Federal Ministries of Agriculture and Rural Development and Commerce. Also represented are the Central Bank of Nigeria and the Cocoa Research Institute of Nigeria (Federal Government of Nigeria 2005:18). The committee has the goal of increasing cocoa production per annum to 320,000 metric tons in the short term and to 600,000 metric tons per annum in the long run (Federal Republic of Nigeria 2005:18).

After about seven years of operation, the NCDC prides itself in its ability to increase cocoa production from 249,782 metric tons in 2001 to 266,177.54 metric tons and 281,837.63 metric tons in 2002 and 2003 respectively. This represents only a marginal increase judged against the goal of increasing production to 320,000 and 600,000 tons in the short and long run respectively. The authors faulted NCDC's composition and strategy that utilizes a top-bottom approach in its formulation and implementation of its programmes that is highly centralized. The NCDC membership includes 30 individuals, with at least 18 of them being top government officials.

According to the authors, the challenge presently facing the Nigerian social structure is encapsulated in the fact that about 70 percent of the Nigerian population live under the poverty line of $1 per day while the economy continually concentrates on the export of primary products. Cocoa potentially stands as a major contributor to Nigeria's development. To revamp the subsector, they propose a reintroduction of cocoa marketing boards, albeit constituted by indigenous cocoa farmers in cooperatives. They should be encouraged to fabricate local machines (with linkages with colleges of technology, polytechnics and universities) and to create marketing pools for marketing on a ward basis. Furthermore, and in view of the fact that cocoa products are consumed locally, priority should be accorded to processing for domestic consumption and export while the surplus produced could be processed as raw materials for industries locally and for exports.

The fifth contribution by *O. Ujah* considers the diversification potential of Cassava. It notes that diversification of the Nigerian economy is one of the four focus areas of the policy reform programme. The strategy adopted by the government in this regard is the provision of an enabling environment that will engender private sector participation in the production of staples including cassava.

With an estimated 34 million tons produced annually, Nigeria is the world largest producer of cassava, ahead of Brazil and Thailand, but Thailand is the leading exporter of the commodity as Nigeria consumes most of its output locally. Until recently, cassava has remained on the import prohibition list. The current regime initiated a cassava initiative in 2002 geared towards boosting its production and export, leading to the recognition of the commodity as a strategic crop. As part of this initiative, plans are ongoing to establish 600 cassava-processing plants all over the 26 cassava producing states in Nigeria.

The author reviews the Nigerian agricultural sector as it impacts on cassava production and he notes that experience garnered over the years and recent trends in agricultural development worldwide have necessitated the formulation of more focused agricultural sectoral policies, including a policy on land geared towards a sustainable use of agricultural lands; a policy on national agricultural mechanization; a policy on national cooperatives development; and a national seed policy. A national agricultural plan was also launched in 2001. However, these policies do not explicitly address cassava. Even the National Economic Empowerment and Development Strategy (NEEDS) policy document formulated in 2004 only makes peripheral reference to cassava. The need for a cassava policy is thus imperative.

Nigeria nonetheless has acquired considerable experience in all facets of the cassava value chain. The activities of international organizations, such as the Food and Agricultural Organisation (FAO) and the International Institute of Tropical Agriculture (IITA), and local research institutions, including universities, have no doubt played a key role in this endeavour. The production level has been increasing in recent years from about 26 million metric tons in 1991 to 32.6 million metric tons in 2001. The author however associates the increased production to an increase in the area cultivated rather than to productivity gains. The yield per acre declined from 118,818 hg/ha in 1997 to 95,003 hg/ha in 2001. Productivity enhancement is a major challenge. Comparative yield figures for 2003 indicate that Nigeria at 95,369 hg/ha fared poorly compared to Thailand at 175,524 hg/ha and Brazil at 133,118 hg/ha. However, Nigeria's cassava production level was slightly higher than the West African average of 93, 358 hg/ha.

There has been a substantial increase in the producer price from 2,006 naira/ton to 18,329 per ton over the same period. Despite this price increase, demand has remained stable or even increasing. The author posits that the current export orientation of the commodity has implication for meeting local demand and therefore steps have to be taken so as not to jeopardize the food security intent of cassava-based livelihoods. The author notes that cassava has considerable export potentials. Nigeria has entered into accords with a number of countries, including China, South Africa and Botswana, for the exportation of cassava products to these countries.

Several hurdles still remain to contend with. These include the lack of standardized weight and measures in most markets; inadequate transportation modes; inability to attract medium and large-scale processors; absence of large scale cassava processors; and inability to diversify cassava utilization to embrace new food and export products. Others include high costs of machinery and tools; delays in forging appropriate machinery and equipment for cassava processing; low productivity; and price instability in the export market. Despite these problems, there is cause for optimism. The author adjudged the quality of cassava produced in Nigeria to be the best in the world because of the high starch content. Nigeria also made her maiden shipment of about 40 tons of cassava chips to China in 2005.

The recommendations put forward by the author include the need to fine-tune export incentives, policies and marketing channels. He suggests putting in place a cassava policy that will strive to integrate the production, processing, marketing and exportation of the commodity and to enunciate realistic standards and quality; subsidization of farmers through improved planting materials that are disease-resistant and high yielding; and modernization by attracting foreign investors. He recommends that the proceeds from the deregulated downstream sector of the oil economy should be channelled into the procurement of machinery that should be located strategically so as to aid processing and packaging.

The last paper by *A. Uzochukwu* evaluates the potential of leather and leather products as a viable non-oil export in Nigeria. In the face of the global relocation of the leather and footwear manufacturing sub-sectors from high cost industrialized countries to developing countries, the author contends that Nigeria has a high potential to emerge as a global champion. This is buttressed with the interest leather and leather products from Nigeria are currently attracting in several European and African countries, including Italy, Spain, Swaziland and Morocco, the apparent increase in leather exports in recent years, and the establishment of the FATA Tanning Leather Company, Kano in 2003, currently the largest in Africa and having started exporting a large consignment of leather and leather products. Moreover, the company has entered into partnership with one of the biggest shoes manufactures in Italy to set up a shoe-making factory in Nigeria in a bid to exploit the AGOA initiative.Nigeria is also endowed with the third largest livestock population in Africa, albeit confined to Northern Nigeria, though most of the current output of hides and skin is at the moment consumed locally.

Based on a questionnaire administered to leather firms and tanneries in Northern Nigeria, the author identifies inadequate infrastructure and the attendant high costs; corruption and red tape; bureaucratic burdens arising essentially from unpredictability of government policies; high taxes; and the difficulty in accessing credit as the main constraints affecting productivity and growth in the sub-sector. Furthermore, the leather associations identify lack of business contacts; inadequate market information; lack of trade support services; and unavailability of trade finance, in that hierarchical order as the major constraints to exporting.

The policy options proposed by the author for the development of the leather sector in Nigeria are: improvement in infrastructure in the leather zone, especially electricity, water and telecommunications; provision of credit facilities and other associated support services; stability and harmonization of government policies affecting leather and leather products; establishment of modern tanneries outside of Kano through public-private partnerships; and promoting cooperation by business associations in the leather sub-sector.

While the two first papers relate to the overall strategies and to capacity building, the other four papers highlight the chances that Nigeria has when it aims at revitalising its agriculture sector with vigour. Palm oil, cocoa, cassava, and leather are sub-sectors of importance, and the products from these sub-sectors count among the great number of potential traded goods that can be generated from a new agricultural development strategy that is considered now by the government of Nigeria.

3 The Strategy

Nigeria has made progress since 1999 in designing and implementing a new development strategy. However, the contributions to this Unit show that much more is needed to change to a new economy. A creative response to the globalisation trends is needed, as well as a coherent strategy to overcome the dependence of the country on primary commodity exports. It is necessary to address the huge imbalances between the beneficiaries of the oil economy and those living from production in the non-oil economy, but also the economic imbalances between the regions and the states have to be addressed. There are considerable gaps in Nigeria between visions and plans on the one side and the realisation and implementation of programmes on the other side.

Four strategic elements emerge from the analyses and discussions in this Unit:

1 A Creative Response to Globalisation Trends is Needed:

It is quite necessary to evaluate the prospects and chances of globalisation for Nigeria. Nigeria should assess carefully the degree and the forms of its world market integration that have been reached, and how it the world market integration can be optimised. It is necessary to evaluate as well the internal and the external bottlenecks for world market integration (of a policy-type, or institutional and structural) so as to be able to exploit the chances of globalisation. The problems "behind the border" are severe, and – as some progress was made with policy reforms - especially institutional and structural reforms matter.

Nigeria is now trying to understand the real chances of globalisation by looking beyond the oil economy towards the productive agricultural subsectors so that they can benefit from market access and globalisation. But much more is needed than just opening up markets by liberalisation and deregulation, and by trying to get market access for new agricultural products. Planning carefully for the further measures and for the right type of opening markets is necessary Globalisation is a much deeper process than opening the economy. It is necessary to have coherent policies, and to create an institutional set-up and structures so as to benefit from globalisation in terms of goods, services, technology, finance, skills and labour, and more so by integrating into global production chains.

Nigeria is affected by vulnerability, volatility and shocks, and the country has to understand better the sources of it so as to develop appropriate market development and regulatory instruments that may help to reduce the impacts on the economy. New types of marketing boards that are based on public-private-partnerships can be relevant, especially when the country is moving towards an agriculture-based export diversification policy. As the contributions to this Unit show the global production chains are becoming more and more important so that it is necessary to analyse the demand and supply constraints of the country having these chains and their relevance for Nigeria in view. Exploiting the chances of globalisation also means that an improved access to markets has to be secured by innovative bilateral, regional and international trade, technology and investment agreements. In this regard Nigeria has to improve its policies and institutions and has to change attitudes.

Obviously Nigeria can exploit lucrative trade and economic options in Africa, and not only in West Africa, and also in relation to emerging and developing countries. This refers to trade in agricultural commodities and also industry and services products. A strategy for market-dynamic products is envisaged by the government but has to be supported also by the private sector so as to make the strategy more concrete. Elements of innovative planning are considered as necessary for government and the private sector, and medium-level and large-scale enterprises can play a new role in public-private-partnerships.

An important part of the new opening strategy is an agricultural development strategy that is considering the new realities of international production chains. Investment along these chains is becoming crucial for development and for world market integration. Caring for investors' safety and investors' certainty is increasingly important so that the globalisation chances can be used. A step-by-step process is recommended so as to evaluate and implement the important elements of a strategy with a creative response to globalisation.

2 New Trade Policies have to be integrated with Trade Capacity Building Efforts:

This is a very important part of the strategy to benefit from globalisation trends. Nigeria was already in the past quite active in pursuing a new trade policy as a member of the WTO and of other important international and regional organisations. Obviously much more is needed now. A coherent trade policy being in line with appropriate macroeconomic policies and innovative structural policies is needed. But, most of all, coherence between trade policy and trade capacity building is requested. Trade Capacity Building (TCB) is a broad concept, but the general meaning implies that not only trade policy matters but as well developing trade infrastructure and trade negotiating capacities and experiences, and promoting the ability to understand and to exploit trading rules. Therefore, TCB can support considerably a new export diversification strategy, and can lead to an integration of trade policy and trade development concerns.

Nigeria can play a central role in trade negotiations for Africa - because of its economic weight, and the huge economic potentials it may have in the future. But today the ability of Nigeria to involve itself successfully in increasingly complex trade negotiations is quite limited. Staff quality, coordination, institutions, experience, and so forth show weaknesses. Consultation and decision-making are not satisfactory. The contributions to the Unit reveal that consultation is not only weak but is excluding the real producer, the private sector, the business associations, the civil society, the cooperatives, the actors in the producing regions, but especially the smallholders as the real agricultural producers. The concept of TCB is therefore not confined to a strengthening of the representation if the country in WTO and the backstopping of such activities at home. A broad concept of trade policy and trade capacity building is emphasised.

However, the contributions to the Unit also reveal that the danger and the reality of a resource curse can be overcome by new strategies and policies. The new instruments of TCB also demonstrate that African countries can learn from each other in this regard. Nigeria can learn especially from South Africa in terms of successful international negotiations and in terms of domestic support of efficient trade polices. However, a consistent TCB strategy should be developed in consultation with the various actors and partners that are involved in trade, by identifying the training needs, by integrating trade and trade development aspects of policies, by considering the industrial, trade and technology components of the new export diversification strategy, and by creating awareness about the trading options of Nigeria in the global and regional integration process.

3 Coherence of Macroeconomic, Institutional and Structural Policies has to be established:

It is obviously necessary in Nigeria to make the national policies coherent. The macroeconomic policies of the country were largely exposed to the oil price developments with insignificant attempts to control for objectives and targets. Policies were not guided by clear fiscal rules to cope with fluctuating oil revenues and transparent policies towards oil savings and stabilisation funds. As well there was not a balanced and accepted policy of fiscal federalism that could help to avert conflict between various levels of government and between the local people in the oil-producing states and the tax collecting agencies of the federal government.

The public expenditure and taxation policies were not geared towards the non-oil economy, the development of agriculture and infrastructure and towards export diversification. The taxation and the financial sector policies were neglecting the producers of agricultural products. Many accusations from agricultural producers refer to the lack of a fair taxation policy that fails to give incentives for production and production integration with forward and backward linkages. Also the lack of supportive financial instruments is mentioned in the contributions to the Unit.

The gaps in monetary policy and in exchange rate policy are still severe. This is reflected in instabilities and volatilities that affect the reputation of the institutions and the credibility of policies. Affected is the investment climate of the country. A coordination of macroeconomic policies with structural policies is needed and considered as important by government but is so far not working properly. Sector polices are now developed for agriculture - a general strategy and sub-sector strategies are outlined in some detail. These sector strategies as well as the framework strategy National Economic Empowerment and Development Strategy (NEEDS) are not coordinated sufficiently with macroeconomic and structural policies. The contributions to the Unit make it clear that infrastructure policies are too weak to support a world market integration of agricultural sector producers. As well regional development policies and the policies to speed up development of border regions in Nigeria have to be improved for the purpose of successful export diversification. The contributions to the Unit reveal that products such as cassava, cocoa, leather and palm oil need also much more support in terms of marketing, infrastructure, training, finance, quality control, and setting and enforcing market standards nation-wide. Other structural policies – such as developing the services sector, research and development, training, education and extension, health, organisation and commercialisation of land, and all forms of traffic – also matter. The contributions highlight the need to come quickly to a true "productivity revolution" so that scarce factors such as land, water and the environment can be used optimally for the purpose of development.

Institutions also matter but in this regard many problems are still there. Economic policy institutions are one area where further progress is needed and where some progress had been achieved so far. Development institutions such as marketing and sector development boards need tremendous reform activity. These institutions are highly bureaucratic, and are not including in an appropriate way the private sector and the civil society. These institutions are quite often not innovative and/or not balanced in their representation and financing modalities. New type marketing and development boards can play a role as well as new financing institutions for the rural economy and the agriculture sector. New types of oil savings and stabilisation funds can and should be linked to such new development and finance institutions.

New fiscal institutions to control expenditures and revenues at all government levels are increasingly necessary.

A new federalism for Nigeria is recommended to cope with equity and efficiency problems. This is most important for the future, and the requested and implemented changes with the derivation formulae for oil revenues to be allocated to state entities show that a dynamic development in this regard is necessary. More important than sharing oil revenues by states and local entities would be a sharing based on democratically agreed upon objectives that allow for the realisation of such tasks as agricultural and rural development. As we can see from the contributions to the Unit such an effort would pay off: revitalisation of agriculture and new incentives for agricultural and livestock products are of strategic importance for all regions in Nigeria, such as palm oil for the South, cocoa for the West, leather for the North, and cassava for not less tan 26 states in Nigeria. This leads to the fourth component of the strategy to be derived from the contributions to this Unit.

4 A New Type of Agricultural Demand-led Industrialization (ADLI) Strategy is Needed:

In order to overcome the dependence from oil exports and to address the "Nigerian oil paradox" of abundance of resources and an alarming increase of extreme poverty it is necessary to redesign the economic policies and to establish appropriate institutions. There are such important attempts in Nigeria as the formulation of a National Economic Empowerment and Development Strategy (NEEDS), the development of a new agricultural strategy and policy, and of various sub-sector strategies for specific and potentially lucrative products from agriculture and livestock sectors. Important is a revitalisation of agriculture as a mainstay of the Nigerian economy. The sector studies for cassava, cocoa, leather products, and palm oil show that there are many preconditions, such as a new land policy, a rural finance strategy, a rural industrialisation strategy, a market development strategy, a cooperatives development programme, etc. There are so many historical production experiences on agriculture in the rural areas and there is accumulated knowledge in central, state and local institutions all of which could be revitalised for new production.

To tap these chances that are available in the country, a new type Agricultural Demand-Led Industrialization (ADLI) strategy is needed to focus on all these prerequisites in a coherent way (See on the concept and the relevance for Africa's industrialization: Adelman/Vogel, 1992; Wohlmuth et al., Eds., 1992). The traditional concept of ADLI was not concerned with global production chains and the new wave of internationalisation of agricultural markets that emerged during recent times of globalisation. In order to realise the new strategy that is linking broad-based agricultural development with rural and general industrialisation and services sector development rural and agricultural interest groups play a role side by side with associations of small and medium scale industrialists, the other private sector associations and all levels of government. Mobilisation of the private sector associations is key to form the basis for appropriate policies and support for adequate institutions. New type Public Private Partnerships (PPPs) will help to sustain such a reorientation towards agriculture, agro-industrial development and agriculture-based export diversification.

However, the sector case studies of cassava, cocoa, leather, and palm oil show that agricultural development on the basis of a new ADLI strategy has to be addressed not only to domestic investors, but also to international investors as global value chains matter for finance, marketing, market access, technology. acquisition, management, etc. An involvement of Nigerian agricultural producers in global value chains is also important because of the need to upgrade continuously product standards and quality as requested by the world market. Most of the new agricultural products envisaged by the

Nigerian Agricultural Development Strategy are at the moment insignificant in terms of world market supplies and shares, but all of them are important for rural employment and income generation, and for poverty alleviation and livelihood. It is obvious that a new ADLI strategy has to consider the new trends in production and processing of agricultural produce. Processing that is based on clusters can have an advantage relative to dispersed processing units. This has implications for rural development policy, for industrial policy, for training, extension and technology absorption. Local equipment for agricultural production and for processing is demanded as we see from the sector case studies, although such items are not available in respective quantity and quality. A strategy on local equipment production is necessary at the states level, but also at the local and the federal levels. Investment incentives and technology centres can play a role in this regard. An integrated rural and urban development strategy is required in the context of the new strategies based on ADLI and the Nigerian Agricultural Development Strategy.

It is important to see that the government and the private sector in Nigeria seek to revitalise "lost sectors" such as palm oil and cocoa. The attempt to promote and to develop such products for the world market by joint development committees consisting of representatives of various interest groups should be praised, but such an endeavour will work only if it is not only done top down but also bottom up and if all private sector interests, especially the small landholders and producers and the civil society have a say. Development institutions have to be organised in such a way that they are not overcentralised, not too bureaucratic, and not confined representatives from central organisations of the private sector and the government. New types of marketing boards that are broad-based and private sector-oriented have a role. In other African countries such newly built marketing institutions are already at work (Wohlmuth, 2006).

It seems also to be an advantage to define "strategic crops" like cassava in Nigeria, but this concentration of focus, incentives and support should not be to the disadvantage of other products. A neutral economic policy type of promoting agricultural products is requested. It is therefore necessary to have a common framework for the development of the agricultural sector but the strategy must be specific enough to relate to the conditions of various crops and products. The strategy must also be related to processing and supporting industry, to services, and to the environment. The strategy and the policy should conveniently be worked out along the production chain of the products. Some progress has been made in this regard, especially in cassava but also in the other products. In the production of cassava serious gaps can be observed as expansion there is highly land using and not productivity-enhancing. A "productivity revolution" is needed. The case of cassava also reveals that agricultural development and export diversification have to be coordinated with food security policies as local demand for cassava has to be met beside of exports in a situation where more and more people are in extreme poverty.

An increasing level of exports is possible if problems on the supply and on the demand side are overcome, if a balance between exports and domestic demand can be established by appropriate incentives, and if a balance between small, medium and large producers can be realised. Getting foreign investors involved in the environment of such a new agricultural development policy is a great chance to get it implemented, and this brings back the issues of macroeconomic stability, institutional renewal, and active structural policies. Most important is it how to divert oil revenues for the agricultural sector, either by taxation or by oil stabilisation and savings funds. However, the discussion about such a funding of agricultural development has not yet started. So far, oil funds were used for import substitution industrialization, for infrastructure and for rent-seeking purposes.

Leather processing as a sector case reveals that there are other links to globalisation that may benefit the country. The global industrial relocation of leather and footwear industries provided chances to many developing countries. Also Nigeria can benefit if the necessary preconditions are met. International joint ventures and partnerships play a role. However, not only international investments and global production chains matter, but also international joint ventures and cross-border partnerships, either in design, or in production, or in marketing or in research and development.

This Unit has identified four strategic elements for a revitalisation of the Nigerian economy that is based on the development of the agricultural sector, and that leads to export diversification and an exploitation of globalisation chances. A new set of policies and institutions is necessary to make all strategy elements and policies coherent, so that local capacities can be used more widely. This is the first attempt to design a coherent strategy for Nigeria based on the abundance of resources in the rural areas.

References

Adelman, Irma and Steven J. Vogel (1992): "The Relevance of ADLI for Sub-Saharan Africa", pp. 258-279, in: Wohlmuth, Karl, et al. (Eds.): "African Development Perspectives Yearbook", Vol. 2, 1990/1991, Industrialization Based On Agricultural Development, Münster: LIT Verlag.

Auty, Richard (2001): "The political economy of resource-driven growth". In: European Economic Review 45: pp. 839-946.

Bass, Hans Heinrich (2006): "Structural Problems of West African Cocoa Exports and Options for Improvements", pp. 245-263, in: Karl Wohlmuth et al., Eds., African Development Perspectives Yearbook, Vol. XI, Africa - Escaping the Primary Commodities Dilemma, Münster: LIT Verlag.

Blomstrom, Magnus and Ari Kokko (2003): "From natural resources to high-tech production: the evolution of industrial competitiveness in Sweden and Finland," CEPR Discussion Paper No. 3804.

Bonaglia, Federico and Kiichiro Fukasaku (2003): "Export diversification in low-income countries: an international challenge after Doha", OECD Working Papers No. 209.

Buitelaar, R. (2001): "Mining, cluster and local economic development in Latin America", abridged version of R. Buitelaar, aglomeracionnes mineras y desarollo local en america latina, CEPAL/ECLAC/Alfaomega, Bogotá.

Collier, Paul (2002) "Primary commodity dependence and Africa's future", mimeo, World Bank, paper presented at the 14th ABCDE in Washington, 29-30 April 2002. (Online): http://econ.worldbank.org/files/14984_Collier-full.pdf. Accessed:, 23/05/06.

Collier, Paul and Anke Hoeffler (2002): "On the incidence of civil war in Africa." In: Journal of Conflict Resolution, 46 (1): pp. 13-28.

Davis, Graham. A. (1995): "Learning to love the Dutch disease: evidence from the mineral economies", in: World Development, 23 (10): pp. 1765-1779.

Fearon, James (2005): "Primary commodity exports and civil war", Journal of Conflict Resolution, Special Issue on Natural Resources and Armed Conflict, 49, (4): 483-507

Farfan, Oscar H. (2005): "Understanding and escaping commodity-dependency: a global value chain perspective", Prepared for the Investment Climate Unit, International Finance Corporation. The World Bank Group.

Federal Republic of Nigeria (2005): "Cocoa rebirth handbook", Abuja: Federal Republic of Nigeria.

Fisher, Ronald (2001): "Trade liberalization, development and government policy in Chile", Centro de Economía Aplicada, Universidad de Chile, Documentos de Trabajo, No. 102, (online): http://www.dii.uchile.cl/~cea/pags/publicaciones.

Hausmann, Ricardo and Roberto Rigobon (2003): "An alternative interpretation of the 'Resource Curse: Theory and policy implications", NBER Working Papers 9424, National Bureau of Economic Research, Inc.

Helleiner, Gerald. (Ed.) (2002): Non-traditional export promotion in Africa: Experience and Issues, Palgrave, New York.

Isham, Jonathan, Michael Woolcock, Lant Pritchett and Gwen Busby (2003): "The varieties of the resource experience: how natural resource export structures affect the political economy of economic growth", Middlebury College Economics Discussion Paper, No. 03-08.

Jerome, Afeikhena (2005): "Managing oil rent for sustainable development and poverty reduction in Africa", Paper Presented at the UNU-Wider Jubilee Conference, Thinking Ahead: The Future of Development Economics, Helsinki, June 2005. (Online): http://www.wider.unu.edu/conference/conference-2005-3/conference-2005-3.htm, accessed 21/02/06.

Lederman, Daniel and William F. Maloney (2002): "Open questions about the link between natural resources and economic growth:" Sachs and Warner revisited, Central Bank of Chile, Working Papers No 141, Febrero 2002.

Macartan, Humphreys (2005): "Natural resources, conflict and conflict resolution: uncovering the mechanism", in: Journal of Conflict Resolution, 49 (4): 508-37.

Nancy, Birdsall (2006): "A stormy day on an open field: asymmetry and convergence in the global economy", UNU-WIDER Research Paper No. 2006/31, UNU-WIDER, Helsinki: World Institute for Development Economics Research.

Nathan, Laurie (2005): "The frightful inadequacy of most of the statistics: a critique of Collier and Hoeffler on causes of civil war", Discussion Paper No.11, Crisis States Research Centre, September.

Owens, Trudy and Adrian Wood (1997): "Export-oriented industrialization through primary processing?", in: World Development, 25:9, pp. 1453-1470.

Ron, James (2005): "Paradigm in distress?, Primary commodities and civil war." In: Journal of Conflict Resolution, Special Issue on Natural Resources and Armed Conflict, 49(4): 443-450.

Ross, Michael (2004): "What do we know about natural resources and civil war?" In: Journal of Peace Research, 41 (3) pp 337-356.

Sachs, Jeffrey and Andrew M. Warner (1995): "Natural resource abundance and economic growth", Development Discussion Paper No. 517a, Harvard Institute for International Development, Cambridge, MA.

Sachs, Jeffrey and Andrew M. Warner (2001): "The curse of natural resources", in: European Economic Review, 45: pp. 827-838.

UNCTAD (2003): "Economic Development in Africa: Trade Performance and Commodity Dependence", United Nations, New York/Geneva.

Wohlmuth, Karl (2006): "Are successful strategies feasible? An introduction", pp. 3-25, in: Karl Wohlmuth et al., Eds., African Development Perspectives Yearbook, Vol. XI. Africa - Escaping the Primary Commodities Dilemma, Münster and Hamburg: LIT Verlag.

Wohlmuth, Karl (1992): "Towards A New Industrial Strategy For Sub-Saharan Africa – An Introduction", pp. 3-29, in: Wohlmuth et al., Eds., African Development Perspectives Yearbook", Vol. 2, 1990/1991, Industrialization Based On Agricultural Development, Münster and Hamburg: LIT Verlag.

Wood, Adrian and Jörg Mayer (2001): "Africa's export structure in a comparative perspective", in: Cambridge Journal of Economics, 25 (3): pp. 369–394.

Wright, Gavin and Jesse Czelusta (2002): "Resource-based growth: past and present", mimeo, Stanford University.

Nigeria - Global Integration and Commodity Dependence

Rosemary N. Okoh

1 Introduction

Commodity dependence has been a feature of the Nigerian economy right from the time it attained political independence from British colonial administration. In the 1960's agriculture was the engine of growth of the Nigerian economy. It contributed the largest share of the nation's gross domestic product (GDP), employed 70 percent of the labour force, the major supplier of food to Nigeria's growing population and raw materials for industries; major market for Nigeria's manufactured goods; the major source of Government revenue, capital formation and foreign exchange. The major commodities traded internationally in the 1960's included cocoa, groundnuts, cotton, palm products and rubber. This scenario was dramatically altered as crude petroleum export increased and subsequently became the new engine of growth of the Nigerian economy and has remained so till date. The Nigerian economy has become dependant on the earnings from crude petroleum exports for 96 percent of its foreign exchange earning and 70 percent of its total revenue and capital formation (Central Bank of Nigeria (CBN), 2000:198). Agricultural exports (cocoa bean, rubber and oil palm) now constitute just a little more than 3 percent of total earning from merchandise export and contributes only 0.2 percent of GDP (FAO, 2002:10). The export of crude oil is almost solely responsible for Nigeria's foreign exchange earnings, government revenue and capital formation and hence growth and development. Nigeria is indeed one of the world's commodity dependent developing countries.

The major objective of this paper is to examine the nature of commodity dependence and its implications for Nigeria's integration into the global market with a view to proffering policy recommendations, which would help the nation to move out of this dilemma. Commodity dependent countries (CDCs) concentrate on a very limited range of products derived mainly from the exploitation of natural resources and/or products with low value added, that use mainly unskilled labour (Commission of the EU 2002: 9). Accordingly, these commodities provide very limited scope for productivity growth. Commodity dependent countries are said to be finding themselves increasingly marginalized in the world trade relations and seem to be trapped in a vicious circle of (1) declining income, (2) persistent poverty and dependence (Richardson, 2003:1-4).

This paper is structured as follows: first the introduction, next we present a critical theoretical overview of Nigeria's commodity dependence problem, third, we examine the internal and external constraints Nigeria faces to diversify and to integrate into the global economy; the fourth section discusses options for diversification and exploitation of new export markets in terms of agro-based and manufactured diversification attempts, and the fifth section presents the conclusions and policy recommendations.

2 A Critical Theoretical Overview of Nigeria's Dependency Problem

Global integration relates to two main themes in international relations. The first refers to the extent to which local and international policies have subsumed and integrated into a new set of essentially global processes and transactions, and the second relates to the extent to which the processes of globalisation have eroded the capability and capacity of nation states as sovereign economic regulators (Chete, 2004:542). Global integration has been variedly defined. In general it connotes a process of growing interdependence and interconnectedness among the world's regions, nations, governments, businesses, institutions, communities, families and individuals. The process of global integration is characterised by increasing mobility in terms of investment driven by international capital; transnational companies look for of new sites of resources and markets through-out the world. Another characteristic of globalization is the information technology, which allows transnational organizations to coordinate production throughout the world according to individual consumer interests (Ohamae 1995: 2-4). The extent of global integration can be gauged by developments in trade and financial flows. In fact global integration may be summarily defined as "a loose combination of free-trade agreement, the internet and the integration of financial markets that is erasing boarders and uniting the world into a single, lucrative but brutally competitive market place" (Chete, 2004:546). The proponents of global integration argue that by removing the barriers to trade between national economies, countries can achieve significant economic benefits from specialization according to their comparative advantages, from economies of scale due to enlargement of the effective market size, from the importation of products manufactured by highly capital-intensive industries abroad, and from the stimulus to employment provided by reduced pressures to concentrate capital and high wages in a limited number of highly capital-intensive industries (Norton and Alwang, 1993:108). The major proponents of global integration agree that if an economy increases its openness to trade it will benefit from increased growth rates because it enhances its access to a variety of imported inputs that embody new technology. It is further argued that the integration of developing countries into the global market would improve the standard of living brought about by consumption of goods and services at competitive prices and access to global high-tech inputs at competitive prices (Mussa, 2000:1-2).

To reap these benefits and participate meaningfully in the global market place, national economies must have in place an appropriate supportive and competitive environment as well as an adequate institutional capacity. Economies that lack the institutional capacity for global trade and investment will find it difficult to participate meaningfully and to gain from global integration. The implication is that the poor countries in Africa and elsewhere, including Nigeria, are the least integrated internationally and that they have also derived the least benefits from globalisation. According to Obadan (2004:12) these countries have been the underdog of the global economy, heavily burdened by debt and poverty, and highly disadvantaged in participating in the global economy. They have not been able to take advantage of the opportunities offered in the spheres of wider markets for trade, an expanding array of tradables, larger private capital flows and improved access to technology. This corroborates the conclusion reached by Okoh (2004b: 27) that opening up of the economy to the fierce competition that has characterized the global integration process has not benefited the Nigerian economy but rather it has exacerbated its dependency problem. Nigeria has become dependent from capital inputs and is reliant on a single export commodity oil.

A number of theories originating from the Marxist tradition addressed the issue of dependency, exploitation and unequal exchange:

1 The dependence of the periphery on foreign capital and the exploitation of surplus by the centre;
2 The dependence of foreign technology;
3 Terms of trade deterioration;

4 Mechanisms that reduce real wages in developing countries below what they would otherwise be; and
5 Various socio-cultural aspects of neo-colonialism (Thirlwall, 1999:188).

Dos Santos (1970:235-237) for instance defined dependence as "a situation in which the economy of certain countries is conditioned by the development and expansion of another economy to which the former is subjected". Dos Santos identified three types of dependence as they have evolved historically thus:

1 Colonial dependence, based on trade and exploitation of natural resources;
2 Financial-industrial dependence, which geared the economic structure of the dependent nations to the needs of the centre; and
3 Technological-industrial dependence, which was entrenched through multinational corporations that began to invest in industries geared to the internal market of developing countries.

There is no gainsaying however, that many colonies suffered as a result of economic dependency on foreign powers, which directed production toward external rather than domestic needs. And several nations still suffer the effect of foreign and domestic monopoly powers in the production of industrial raw materials, capital, inputs-plants and machinery in what is now referred to as "neo-colonialism". Nigeria clearly exhibits these three forms of dependence. For instance, during the colonial administration, Nigeria developed its capacity to produce and export cocoa, rubber, groundnuts, etc. To this end, the necessary infrastructure was put in place to facilitate the efficient operation of exports of these commodities. With the discovery of crude oil at Oloibiri in 1956, the export of crude oil commenced almost immediately in 1958. The development of the external sector intensified to the neglect of the domestic production and necessary infrastructure. Nigeria's export and production sectors have followed the colonial pattern up to the present time.

To the proponents of the dependency theory, unequal development must be seen as an integral part of the world capitalist system. The main feature of these theories is that because the centre (industrialized countries of the world) has greater economic power than the periphery (developing countries), it is able to develop at the expense of the periphery (Norton and Alwang, 1993: 103-104). They argue that the lack of development in less developed countries is a product of the same forces that led to the development in the centre. Again, in the periphery productivity may not be high enough to support resources in the production of manufactured goods and imported inputs for export production might absorb more foreign exchange than the exports eventually yield (Thirlwall, 1999:466, Okoh, 2004a: 7-9). With imports growing faster than exports in the periphery, growth can only be attained and sustained if the periphery can finance an ever-growing balance of payments deficit on the current account by capital flows. This however is unlikely. In view of the foregoing the proponents of the "dependency theory", hold that poverty becomes imminent as long as the periphery remains in the global market. The only solution would be recourse to protectionism, which could help to reduce the import dependency of the periphery (Prebisch, 1950:30). This is however not a recommendation for developing countries to operate in autarchy but to regulate their import pattern.

Critics of the dependency theory argue that its is too simplistic and lack rigor and formality in analysis. It is argued that the theory cannot easily be tested empirically; rather it is designed to provide a framework of ideas to accommodate the many aspects and features of the functioning of the world capitalist economy and the many types of dominance and dependence (Thirlwall, 1999:189).

It is clear that the solution of the dependency problem cannot be the withdrawal from the global economic system. With the success stories of Asian countries there is no doubt that greater integration into the world economy provides the surest path to greater global security, world peace and a more hopeful future. Nigeria and other African countries need however to discover how best to manage the process of global integration so that they can share the benefits and minimize the cost of global integration.

3 Internal and External Constraints Nigeria Faces to Diversify and to Integrate into the Global Economy

3.1 Internal Constraints

The major factor, which has helped to entrench the commodity dependency status of the Nigerian economy, is the structure of merchandize exports that is closely tied to the structure of output, which in turn is heavily dependent on imported technology. The structure of merchandize exports in Nigeria is dominated by the export of crude oil, natural gas (in recent times) and a few traditional agricultural products such as cocoa, palm oil and rubber. Manufactures, which are mainly natural resource based semi-manufactures, such as cocoa butter, cocoa powder or processed skin, contribute only little to the export value. Nigeria's major trading partners are USA, Brazil, India, Spain, and France. Others are Korea, ECOWAS countries and Japan (UNSTATS, 2005:1). Table 1 shows the structure of Nigerian exports, while other details are available in appendix 1.

Table 1: Structure of Nigeria's Merchandize Exports

Year	Total Exports US$ Million	Value of Oil Export US $ Million	% Oil Exports to total Export	Value of Non-Oil Export US $ Million	% Non-Oil to total Export	Value of Agricultural Export US $ Million	% Agriculture to total Export	Value of Manufactured Export US $ Million	% Manufactures to total Export
1980	25939.9	24928.2	96.1	1011.6	3.9	1011.6	3.9	0	0
1985	13134.0	12582.3	95.8	5516	4.2	5516	4.2	0	0
1988	6932	6319.3	91.1	612.7	8.9	440.7	6.4	172	2.5
1989	7871	7469.9	94.9	401.1	5.0	255.7	3.2	145.4	1.8
1990	13671.1	13265.5	97.0	405.5	3.0	228.2	1.7	177.3	1.3
1991	12264	11792	96.1	472.0	3.8	213.6	1.7	258.4	2.1
1992	11886	11641.6	97.9	244.4	2.1	189.3	1.6	55.1	0.5
1993	9924	9696.2	97.7	227.8	2.3	227.8	2.3	0	0
1994	9425	9180.6	97.4	244.4	2.6	244.4	2.6	0	0
1995	11734.4	11452.7	97.6	281.6	2.4	281.6	2.4	0	0
1996	16117.0	15826.8	98.2	290.1	1.8	290.1	1.8	0	0
1997	15207.3	14857.5	97.7	349.7	2.3	349.7	2.3	0	0
1998	8971.2	8971.2	95.5	403.7	4.5	403.7	4.5	0	0
1999	16123.5	15865.5	98.4	257.9	1.6	257.9	1.6	0	0
2000	27079.3	26727.2	98.7	352.0	1.3	347.7	1.27	8.3	0.03
2001	18046.1	17739.3	98.3	306.7	1.7	306.7	1.7	0	0
2002	18607.1	18272.1	98.2	334.9	1.8	334.9	1.8	0	0
2003	24078.3	23211.4	96.2	866.8	3.6	611.8	2.5	255.0	1.1

Sources: Central Bank of Nigeria (1990: 160, 1997: 175, 2000: 170), UNSTATS (2005), FAO (2005).

The Agricultural Sector

The agricultural sector faces a number of demand-side and supply-side constraints. The demand-side constraints are mainly at the global level. The changing nature of demand in the world commodity market is a major cause for the fall of prices for developing countries' agricultural products. Also the technology change which has led to the development of synthetic substitutes for raw materials and the pursuance of protectionist policies by the developed countries have contributed to the retardation of Nigeria's agricultural exports. Like the manufacturing sector, the agricultural export products have a low income elasticity and a high price elasticity of demand. Moreover, Nigeria has experienced a change in the domestic consumption pattern from locally produced to imported food items since the latter are often better in price and quality.

In addition to these demand-side constraints, Nigeria faces manifold supply-side constraints to expand its agricultural production. These are:

1 The country's high dependence on crude oil has reduced the incentive to focus on agricultural production. Additionally, incentive frameworks for agricultural production have been often inadequate;
2 Absence of a price support mechanism and pervasive distortions in macroeconomic and sectoral policies, including misaligned exchange rates and heavy taxation of agricultural exports;
3 Inadequate working capital and policies that reduce the role of state institutions in innovations and investment in the sector.
4 Land tenure system, which encourages land fragmentation and small scale production. Inhibiting acquisition of land for large scale farming.
5 The rapid shift of the labour force from rural to urban areas.
6 Dependence on rain-fed agriculture. Operations are at small-scale, often at subsistence level;
7 Low level of indigenous capacity and technology responsive to local conditions;
8 The rate of adoption of green revolution technologies is high but access to accompanying inputs such as fertilizers is low.

The Manufacturing Sector:

The manufacturing sector in Nigeria also suffers from a number of demand-side and supply side-constraints. The demand-side constraints are both domestic and global. On the domestic front, the basic problem is the weak effective demand arising from dwindling consumers' demand due to less expensive second hand goods. These goods come into the country through both official and unofficial routes and compete with local manufacturers. Consequently, the accumulations of unsold inventory remain high, which further constrain the industrial capacity utilization rate.

On the global front, Nigeria's manufactured goods show a very low demand and are faced with stiff competition from more efficient producers in Asia and other parts of the world (Okoh, 2004a: 26).

The supply-side constraints for Nigeria's manufactured products are numerous, including deficient infrastructure facilities due to inadequate funding and aging, deteriorating machinery and equipment, energy shortages and high costs for energy and water. All this increases the cost of production and makes Nigerian products uncompetitive in the global market. The second set of constraints relate to a weak science and technology base. These include a low engineering capacity to translate and commercialise scientific research findings, the inability to maintain existing machinery, a low level of entrepreneurial capacity, a lack of institutional mentoring and technological support, and paucity of trained and skilled artisans, all resulting from weak educational structure which de-emphasise the development of science and technology. Thus, there are only weak linkages between industry, research institutes and universities.

Other supply-side constraints for Nigeria's manufacturing sector include poor macroeconomic policies and high cost of doing business. The countries legal and institutional framework is weak, information management systems and practices are poor, and the access to credit is insufficient due to a low asset base of numerous sole proprietors operating in small scale. Moreover, there are weak backward- and forward linkages in the manufacturing sector and systematic and operational constraints that impede the competitive capacities of large manufacturing companies. Further constraints are frequent changes in government policies, mass labour actions, and frequent power outages that necessitate the additional cost of acquiring an electricity generating set (NPC, 2004: 79).

3.2 External Constraints

The heavy dependence on oil exports, however, has made the economy highly vulnerable to external shocks which are periodically transmitted through sharp changes in the world demand for - and prices of - petroleum products. The crude petroleum sector is generally not amenable to the manipulation of trade policy instruments because its value depends more crucially on movements in world prices regulated by the Organization of Petroleum Exporting Countries (OPEC) (Oyejide, 2003:188-189). The value of crude oil export increased from approximately US$ 3.3 billion in 1970 to US$ 24.9 billion in 1980 and declined thereafter to US$ 23.2 billion in 2003 (UNSTATS, 2005:1-2; CBN, 2000:82-84). Table 1 shows the lopsided distribution of exports towards crude oil constituting an average of 96 percent of total export, while non-oil export constituted an average of 4 percent in 2003.

Of the non-oil exports, three major commodities, namely cocoa beans, natural rubber and oil palm contribute to about 75 percent of total agricultural exports, while few manufactured exports and solid minerals make up the remaining 25 percent of non-oil exports (CBN, 2000:82, UNSTATS, 2005:1, AGOA.info, 2005:1).

The non-oil export sector has exhibited high level of vulnerability to external shocks. The dependence on the production and export of few primary commodities is highly correlated with the dependence on the importation of foreign materials, technology, equipment, and transportation facilities. As the Commission of the EU, (2002:9) rightly observed, manufacturing activities in Nigeria focus on low skilled assembly where most of the technology and skills are embodied in imported parts and components and the greater part of the value added accrues to producers in more advanced nations. This explains the persistent balance of trade deficits recorded by the non-oil export sector.

Export revenue is a major determinant of Nigeria's balance of payments position, its external indebtedness, its fiscal situation, the levels of savings and investments and hence its aggregate supply and demand schedules. An important feature of global commodity markets in the past three decades has been the high level of price volatility accompanied with a general decline in the trends of real prices. Nigeria's crude oil and major agricultural export commodities have experienced wide variations prices as Table 2 shows.

Table 2: Prices of Nigeria's Major Commodity Exports (US$)

Years	Cocoa m/ton	Palm Oil m/ton	Rubber m/ton	Crude Oil Per barrels
1973-1975	1437	501	808	10.95
1976-1980	2780	483	1200	22.16
1981-1985	2278	548	1016	29.04
1986-1990	1455	336	991	16.58
1991-1998	1366	496	1081	17.09
1999 - 2003	1443.20	641	1443.2	23.55
1973 - 2003	1742.5	500.45	1107.16	20.20
Standard Deviation 1973 – 2003	777.53	137.94	272.12	7.29
Coefficient of Variation 1973 - 2003	44.6%	27.6%	24%	36.1%

Sources: CBN, (2000: 59), UNSTATS (2005); FAO (2005); authors computations.

The price volatility of cocoa, Nigeria's most important agricultural export products, was with 44.6 percent between 1973 and 2003 very high. The volatility of palm oil and natural rubber prices were also high with 27.6 and 24 percent, respectively.

Thus, with low demand conditions, countries specializing in production of primary commodities can be expected to have a declining share in the world trade unless they have a major cost or quality advantage over competitors. Nigeria, however, has even lost its competitiveness for non-oil merchandise as a result of the depreciation of the Naira vis-à-vis major currencies of the world and the subsequent increase in prices of imported inputs. The exchange rate depreciated from US$ 1 = NGN 2.02 in 1986 to US$ 1 = NGN 140.00 in 2005, representing a depreciation of 6830.67 percent in the past 20 years. The removal of subsidies on inputs also led to increased cost of production (CBN, 2001:182, The Guardian, 2005: 17).

For a single commodity dependent economy, large fluctuations of the amplitude of between 30 and 200 percent in export revenue from one year to the other make planning a Herculean task as they have adverse short-term effects on income, investment, employment, and the domestic price level with consequent negative effects on growth. The fluctuations in commodity prices exhibit peaks (or booms) that are interspersed by long troughs (or slumps) which have had large impact on the Nigerian economy. For instance, the collapse of the international primary commodity markets in the early 1980s with the associated deterioration in terms of trade reversed dramatically the economic fortune of the Nigerian economy. The economy went into crisis as crude oil production and prices fell, the value of non-oil exports fell, the foreign exchange reserves depleted, the balance of payments showed a high deficit, and industrial production almost came to a halt as producers could not import foreign capital inputs.

4 Options for Diversification and Exploitation of New Export Markets

4.1 Agro-Based Diversification Attempts and Manufactured Diversification

The inherent instability associated with the dependence on a single commodity has informed the need for diversification of Nigeria's export sector in order to take advantage of the changing dynamics of the global market place. Nigeria adopted a number of macroeconomic policies to promote agro-based and manufacturing diversification.

The macroeconomic policies adopted in attempt to diversify the agricultural sector are outlined succinctly in Table 3.

Table 3: Summary of Macroeconomic Policies in the Agricultural Sector in Nigeria, 1960 to Date

Period 1960-1985	
Exchange rate	Fixed exchange rate regime. Appreciation of the real exchange rate by ca. 61% between 1970 and 1980.
Trade policy	1. Abolition of export duties on export crops in 1973. 2. Reduction/abolition of import duties on food, agricultural inputs, raw materials and agricultural machinery and equipment
Monetary policy	1. Restructuring of marketing boards and establishment of the Nigerian agricultural cooperative banking 1973; introduction of an agricultural credit guarantee scheme in 1977. 2. 6 and 12 % of merchant and commercial bank loans were reserved for the agricultural sector. 3. Introduction of a rural banking scheme in 1977.
Fiscal policy	Reduction of capital expenditure on agriculture from 6.2% to 4% of total capital expenditure
Sector policy	Accelerated capital allowance on agricultural capital from 10% to 20%.

Continuation on the next page.

Continuation of table 3 from previous page.

Period 1986 to 1988	
Exchange rate	Market determined exchange rate through the establishment of a Second Tier Foreign Exchange Market (SFEM). The operational framework for SFEM is the closed auction system. 1st and 2nd tier rates merged in 1987 to form an enlarged foreign exchange market (FEM).
Trade policy	1. Removal of controls on imports and exports quotas and tariffs. 2. Abolition of commodity marketing boards. 3. Price liberalization, removal of price controls for most commodities (petroleum and fertilizer prices were however not liberalized as attempts to do so led to riots).
Monetary policy	1. Regulation of the financial sector 2. Market determination of interest rates and credits 3. Deregulation of external trade and payments arrangements. 4. The adoption of a market determined exchange rate for the Naira. 5. Substantial reduction in complex price and administrative controls and more reliance on market forces.
Fiscal policy	Reduction of federal government expenditures resulted in budget deficits. Reduction of subsidies albeit resisted by Nigerians.
Sector policy	Introduction of a variety of tax incentives. Large scale irrigation projects, public grain storage facilities etc.

Continuation on the next page.

Continuation of table 3 from previous page.

Period **1989 to 1993**	
Exchange rate	Operation of a dual exchange rate
Trade policy	Further deregulation of trade and measures for increased access to both internal and external markets.
Monetary policy	1. Removal of controls on interest rate. 2. Introduction of open market operations (OMO) in treasury securities with banks through discount houses. 3. Restrictive monetary policy.
Fiscal policy	3-year rolling plan for public investment (1990 – 1992). The plan prioritised “core” projects and identified a set of “non-core” investment projects. Restructuring of public expenditures towards infrastructure development health, and education, which were neglected during the SAP era
Sector policy	Fertilizer project and irrigation projects.

Continuation on the next page.

Continuation of table 3 from previous page.

Period 1994-date	
Exchange rate	Introduction of Interbank Foreign Exchange Market (IFEM) in 1989. Introduction of Autonomous Foreign Exchange Market (AFEM) in 1995. Reintroduction of Naira exchange rate controls in 1994 and "guided deregulation" in 1995. Further deregulation from 1997 e.g. removal of the limit on personal house remittances by foreign nationals as well as personal and business travel allowances.
Trade policy	Deregulation and privatization of public enterprises. Founding member at World Trade Organization (WTO) conditions. Removal of a number of foodstuffs from export prohibition list, such as rice, yams and beans. Tariff reduction for 18 agricultural items in 2003.Reintroduction of import controls and prohibition of importation of some agricultural products to avoid dumping in 2005.
Monetary policy	Reintroduction of interest rate controls in 1994.Deregulation in 1996. Ceiling on lending rate to 22 percent in 2002.
Fiscal policy	Special budgetary allocation for research, extension and innovation in cultivation practices and agro-processing in 2004.
Sector policy	Reintroduction of import prohibition for some foodstuffs in 2003. Presidential agricultural initiatives for the development of cassava, rice, maize, vegetable oil, cotton, oil palm, livestock and aquaculture in 2004.

Sources: CBN (1996-2002), Husain and Faruqee (1994), CBN (2003, 2004, 2005), UNSTATS (2006).

It becomes obvious that the policies adopted over the past decades have changed over the time and are not coherent. From the mid-1980s on, Nigeria's macroeconomic policies were increasingly influenced by the Bretton Woods organisations and have become more and more restrictive. Consequently, agricultural support policies declined and remained poor until today.

4.2 Macroeconomic Policies to Diversify the Manufacturing Sector

Various policy measures were undertaken to enhance manufactured non-oil export earnings. In the 1960s and 1970s, a highly protective import regime was imposed. The policy of import substitution was continued until the early 1980s in order to expand non-oil manufactured exports and to reduce the economy's dependence on capital-intensive imports.

However, increasing debts and macroeconomic instabilities forced the government to implement the Structural Adjustment Programmes (SAPs) of the Bretton Woods institutions (1986-1994). The major elements include:

1. Removal of the overvaluation of the exchange rate and subsequent determination by market forces;
2. Tariff reforms and trade liberalization;
3. Removal of price controls; and
4. Public sector and public enterprise reforms, including privatization, commercialization, deregulation and fiscal prudence.

The basic objectives of the SAPs were to achieve macroeconomic stability, to restructure the economy's productive base, to diversify the economy, and to improve the allocation of resources and improve the effectiveness of the public sector.

In addition to the SAPs, the government introduced Export Incentive Schemes in 1986 that are in force until today. Two institutions were established to facilitate the administration of the incentives, namely the Export Promotion Council and the Nigerian Export Bank. The Export Promotion Council is responsible to administer the export incentives through funds and duty drawback schemes and the Nigerian Export Bank provides financial facilities to banks, such as rediscounting and refinancing facilities. Like this, exporters should be supported and encouraged. Table 4 provides an overview of incentive schemes adopted to boost non-oil exports in Nigeria.

Table 4: Incentive Schemes Adopted to Boost Non-oil Exports in Nigeria

Incentive Scheme	Operation Agent	Objective and Remark
Refinancing and rediscounting facility and foreign input facility	Central Bank of Nigeria (CBN)	To provide liquidity to banks by supporting their export finance business.
Current retention scheme	CBN and commercial banks	To enable exporters to hold export proceeds in foreign currency in their banks.
Tax relief on export credits provided by commercial banks.	Commercial banks and the Federal Board of Inland Revenue	To encourage banks to finance exports by reducing their tax burden.
Export credit guarantee and insurance scheme.	CBN	Assists banks to bear the risks of export credits; increase the volumes of export financing.
Duty drawback scheme	Customs Department; Standard Organization of Nigeria, Nigeria Export Promotion Council, (NEPC), commercial and merchant banks, CBN.	To reimburse customs duties paid by exporters on imported input used for export production. This has not been widely used by exporters due to the cumbersome procedural requirements involved.
Export expansion grand	Nigeria Export Promotion Council (NEPC)	To encourage companies to engage in export business rather than domestic business: especially exporters who have exported semi-manufactured or manufactured products of > NGN 50,000
Export price adjustment	NEPC	A form of export subsidy designed to compensate exporters of products whose foreign prices have become relatively unattractive due to price declines and price fluctuations.

Continuation on the next page.

Continuation of table 4 from previous page.

Incentive Scheme	Operation Agent	Objective and Remark
Subsidy scheme for the use of local raw materials in export production	NEPC	To encourage exporters to use local raw materials in export production.
Export development fund	NEPC	To assist exporters to participate in trade fairs, foreign market research etc. by partly overtaking the costs.
Abolition of export licensing	Federal Ministry of Commerce and Tourism	To reduce administrative obstacles for exporters.
Supplementary allowance in favour of pioneer companies	Federal Ministry of Commerce and Tourism	To extend incentives to pioneer companies in order to promote exports.
Accelerated depreciation and capital allowance.	Federal Ministry of Commerce and Tourism.	To extend export incentives to industrial organizations.
Manufacturing bond scheme	Federal Ministry of Commerce and Tourism.	To assist potential exporters of manufactured products to import raw materials for production duty free.
Export liberalization measures, buy-back arrangements	Federal Ministry of Commerce and Tourism.	To liberalize and promote exports
Export processing zone	Federal Ministry of Commerce and Tourism.	Opened in mid-1996 in Calabar to facilitate and enhance exports.
National credit guarantee scheme	Federal Government of Nigeria (FGN) / CBN	Introduced in 2004, to mitigate the risk associated with lending to the real sector. The beneficiaries include SMEs enterprises for manufacturing activities.

Sources: CBN (1960 -2003), Ogunkola and Oyejide (2001).

Prior to 1986, there was no clear export promotion policy in Nigeria. The emphasis was not on foreign exchange generation, but on foreign exchange conservation which was used in the framework of the import substitution strategy. However, the import substitution strategy, which was vigorously pursued in the 1960s and 1970s, further entrenched the dependency of the Nigerian economy on the external sector. The strategy involved the replacement of imported merchandize with those produced locally through the procurement of assembly plants and other inputs. The import substitution strategy as practiced in Nigeria negated the objective of reducing the country's dependence on imports and foreign exchange as backward and forward linkages were missing so that almost all inputs required had to be imported. The strategy failed to expand Nigeria's non-oil exports and ended up in the mere assemblage of goods rather than manufacturing. Other reasons for the failure of the import substitution strategy were its inward looking policies and the overbearing involvement of the government which promoted inefficiencies.

A more focused export promotion programme with a greater involvement of the private sector commenced with the introduction of the structural adjustment programme (SAP). Some of the major provisions of the SAP led to a drastic devaluation of the (overvalued) Naira, which helped non-oil exporters to produce more competitive. Privatization of companies helped to harness the profit-driven potential of entrepreneurs and to improve the allocation and use of resources. The performance of non-oil exports improved in the post SAP era and foreign exchange receipts from non-oil exports rose from US$ 551.6 million in 1985 to US$ 612.7 million in 1988. However, this positive trend was not sustainable. Foreign exchange receipts from non-oil exports declined to US$ 244.4 million in 1992 and further to US$ 227.8 million in 1993. The value of the non-oil export earnings remained below the 1988 value until 2003 when it rose to US $866.8 million (CBN, 2000:38; FAOSTAT 2006:1; UNSTATS, 2004:1).

The boost of non-oil exports in the early days of the SAP was a result of the aggressive pursuance of SAP objectives in its first two years, which improved the efficiency of resource allocation and attracted investment of profit-motivated private sector operators. However, the increase in non-oil exports was short lived due to several factors (Dalil, 1996:229-231):

1. General decline in the level of production as exchange rate depreciated and cost of production became very high making marketing of imported products more profitable than production;
2. Overall decline in international prices for most commodities exported from Nigeria resulted in a downward trend of the terms of trade;

3. Emergence of a set of export disincentives whose impacts may outweighed the effects of the export incentives put in place, such as bottlenecks at ports, numerous taxes and levies, cumbersome administration etc.;
4. An increase in the volume of unrecorded trade, particularly through the west-coast;
5. Decreased domestic purchasing power and increased poverty as an effect of the SAP resulted in decreased economic activities.

Despite these problems, some limited successes to increase non-oil exports were achieved. According to a report presented by the Nigerian Export Import Bank (NEXIM) Nigeria exported 14 non-oil items in 1990 (mainly cocoa and cocoa products which accounted for 54.3% of total non-oil exports) and 29 non-oil items in 1993 (where cocoa and cocoa products constituted to 25.1% of total non-oil exports financed by NEXIM (NEXIM, 1995:12). In the period 1999-2003 Nigeria was also able to increase its export values for pharmaceutical products, chemical products and cargo vessels (UNSTATS, 2006:1-4).

In terms of market diversification, the export promotion efforts have yielded some success. Between 1980 and 1989 the data on Nigeria's export destinations showed that 49.5% of exports went to the EU, 33.3% to USA, 4.3% to ECOWAS and 12.9% to the rest of the world (CBN, 1995:3). In 2005, Nigeria's export destinations have somehow changed with 38.3% of total exports to USA, 11.8% to the EU, 9.9% to India, 6.8% to Brazil and 33.2 % to the Africa and the rest of the world (Heritage Foundation, 2006:2).

In summary, the performance of Nigeria's non-oil exports has remained below expectation as oil still amounts for 96.4% of the value of total exports. Non-oil exports only contributed to 3.6% of total exports in 2003 with agricultural products accounting for 70% of non-oil exports.

Notwithstanding these problems, Nigeria has the potential to expand its of non-oil export. For instance there is demand for Nigerian textiles, pharmaceuticals, etc. in Africa but the scale of production is yet too small to take advantage of the demand. Also Nigerian art and the tourism industry have potentials which are not yet being exploited.

5 Conclusions and Policy Recommendations

Nigeria's integration into the global market has been hampered by high dependence on a single commodity and its inability to produce and export market dynamic products. It would however, not be in Nigeria's best interest to opt out of the global market. For Nigeria, to fully benefit from the global integration, its dependent output structure must be altered and the capacity of the manufacturing and agricultural sectors must be built-up to take advantage of international trade. How then can Nigeria increase its share of the global market? Adeolu, (2004:425) opined that for countries to gain from trade, they must strive to become more competitive in the global market. To achieve this Nigeria needs to reform and restructure its manufacturing and agricultural sectors, strengthen regional integration, and create an enabling environment through good governance and the provision of necessary infrastructure. The following sections examine options for reform.

Reform of the Manufacturing Sector

The logical starting point for becoming more competitive in the global market would be to change the current export structure through market research and product development. Expanding production in the current product mix alone will not bring the required breakthrough since the products are not "market-dynamic". In the long run, there is the need to develop the capacity of the manufacturing sector to produce capital goods, such as plants, machinery, and transport equipment as well as market-dynamic niche products that enjoy preferences in industrialised countries. For instance, Nigeria's integration into the global market has been hampered by its inability to produce and export market-dynamic products and to take advantage of a number of EU preferences under the Lomé and Cotonou Agreement. Thus, Nigeria was not able to develop significant production and export capacity in the sectors where preference margins in the EU have been significant, such as chemicals, foot wear and textiles (Oyejide, 2003:201).

In the short to medium term, market studies should be commissioned by NEXIM and other related government agencies to identify new market for existing products and to identify and develop new products for exiting and new markets. Manufacturers should embark on aggressive marketing strategies and product improvements in order to increase their sales and to improve their consumer acceptability. The importation of finished goods should be curtailed to expand the option for local manufactures as it is the case with the imposition of quotas on Chinese textiles by the EU to safeguard European producers (BBC, 2005).

Secondly, Nigeria needs to enter into the knowledge society, which is the fastest growing wealth-generating sector in the global market. The importance of entering the knowledge society is that it underlies the attainment and development of new and modern ways of working and organizing manufacturing and services. In the long run, investment in the knowledge sector will help to reduce poverty, strengthen the competitiveness of firms and enhance the possibility of sustainable development in manufacturing activities. The success of these efforts will depend much on the reform of the educational structure, placing more emphasis on building capacities in engineering, information technology and science disciplines. Furthermore, there is the need to strengthen the weak linkages between the industry and research institutes and universities. The recent launch of the Nigerian satellite is a step in the right direction as it provides necessary infrastructure for the needed breakthrough in the information and communication technology.

Thirdly, the creation of an enabling environment for efficient production should be government's top policy priority. This includes the provision of an efficiently operating social and economic infrastructure, such as reliable electricity supply, a proper road network, improved water supply, an efficient communication system, and an efficient payment system by strengthening the Bank of Industry and other specialized financial institutions (e.g. the Nigerian Agricultural, Rural and Cooperative Bank). The provision of concessional loans and credit guarantee schemes should be enhanced and enlarged to large manufacturing companies.

Fourthly, efforts must be made to increase the production capacities of private sector operators by expanding their asset base through mergers and joint ventures and by easy access to credits. Like this, the vertical and horizontal integration to forge viable links between and among different segments of operations in the manufacturing sector could be encouraged. Also, the implementation of the privatisation programme should be hastened up.

Fifthly, the government should ensure macroeconomic stability because it shapes the overall investment climate and determines the degree of confidence investors have in an economy. It also facilitates planning and enables the business community to forecast future returns on current investment. According to CBN (2000:95-96), the attainment of sustainable macroeconomic stability requires low inflation rate, price stability, and a stable foreign exchange policy and the adoption of a market-determined interest rate through the application of indirect tools of monetary policy, fiscal prudence, transparency and accountability.

Finally, in the short and medium term, the clearance procedures for importers and exporters in Nigerian ports should be reformed and made more business friendly. Other bottlenecks that act as disincentives to exporters and importers, such as high berthing and loading/unloading costs, an erratic application of custom regulations and corruption should be critically reviewed and appropriate adjustments should be made.

Reform of the Agricultural Sector

Agricultural production in Nigeria cannot be left completely to the vagaries of market forces as recommended by the World Bank, WTO, etc. if successful diversification should be achieved.

Nigeria has to become more selective in regional, bilateral and multilateral agreements. The implication of every section of such agreements must be thoroughly evaluated before the economy is committed. For instance the implementation of the agreements of the WTO has led to the dumping of cheap poultry products, rice, etc and the subsequent abandonment of local production (Oyejide, 2003: 201-204). Nigeria must be selective in signing trade agreements to ensure that the economic benefits to the country far outweigh the costs. The services of non-governmental organisations (NGOs) and consultants with vast experience in economic and trade policy management can be employed to carry out such evaluations. It is recommended that every policy measure, particularly those originating from bilateral or regional agreements, is evaluated and that the selection for implementation is made on the bases of its contribution to national income, output and subsequently to export growth.

Secondly, the adoption of modern farming practices is of paramount importance to maximize the output. The capacity of farmers must be enhanced and the rate of adoption of green revolution technologies must be increased. Any intervention to enhance the capacity in agriculture must be broad based and holistic in nature. It must involve a "bottom-up" approach of development, which covers rural communities and agricultural policy making institutions. At the community level, agricultural policy makers must harness the capacity building power inherent in the "social capital" to foster social networks and information exchange networks. With such a collective action, a social and institutional environment could be achieved that is ready to adapt and change. Policy decisions, particularly involving rural development, must incorporate consultations with the recipients to ensure the sustainability of programmes and projects. Moreover, the rural population is in a better position to articulate and analyze their deficiencies, problems and needs, as well as their capacities and assets.

On a more specific note, the following measures could be adopted to strengthen the capacity of individual farmers, their communities, policy-makers and governmental institutions.

1. At the community level, farmers' capacity could be built up through increased access to public infrastructure and services and training on improved farming and business practices. Moreover, improved access to fertilizers, insecticides etc. should be improved by eliminating policy distortions and monopolies.

2 There is the need to develop and disseminate new technologies according to the needs of the farmers, thereby focusing on the local situation. Farmers need to be trained to adopt modern cultivation methods in order to expand their agricultural output and to improve the quality of products. Such an approach would also improve the pace of technology diffusion and adoption.

3 Most farming communities lack access to appropriate infrastructures, such as an irrigation system that would allow cultivation activities all year. The availability of irrigation can increase agricultural productivity by up to 100%. It is highly recommended that government, donor agencies and private sector investors assist farmers to develop small scale irrigation facilities.

4 At the institutional level, the capacity of research institutes needs to be enhanced since the technological breakthrough in order to enhance capacity in agriculture requires a dynamic, creative and strong Nigerian research system. Research institutes should be provided with adequate resources to enable them to conduct necessary research in the areas of crop, livestock, fishery and forestry development, and to encourage a proper liaison between agricultural research institutions, agricultural extension agents, policy makers and farmers. Human resource development may also be supported by workshops and training for farmers, agricultural agents and policy makers.

5 Efforts should be made to enhance the effectiveness and efficiency of institutions and organizations which support the agricultural support systems (land tenure, agricultural marketing, etc).

6 Enable farmers to increase their scale of operation in order to benefit from economies of scale by encouraging partnerships, cooperatives or communal farming. Increase their access to credits by empowering specialized financial institutions, such as the Nigerian Agricultural and Cooperative Bank, to provide according assistance. Also, the government needs to encourage more private entrepreneurs to invest in the sector.

7 Ensure adequate and timely supply of farm inputs. Farmers' cooperatives, community based organizations and private entrepreneurs should be given easy access to inputs. This will remove bottlenecks that are often encountered by farmers when they try to access these inputs from public officers.

Strengthening Regional Integration

Though the various trade schemes established within ECOWAS have not had the desired impact, Nigeria needs to increase its efforts to expand its share of intra-regional trade. There is no doubt that the regionalization of economic activities will give room for an economy to build up capacities in all critical areas. Regional integration through ECOWAS should enable Nigerian entrepreneurs and investors to respond to liberalization and to improve their productivity, production scale and marketing abilities. This would help them to build up their capacities to exploit global opportunities in a gradual step-by-step process.

Create an Enabling Environment through Good Governance

The Nigerian government should practise good governance, which is a participatory, consensus-oriented, accountable, transparent, effective and efficient, equitable and inclusive policy approach that is responsive to the need of the population. Good governance follows the rule of law, includes different society actors and institutions in decision making processes, and applies effective auditing, monitoring and evaluation procedures to ensure the optimal delivery of government policies according to the national development targets. The government should provide security for both local and foreign investors by putting in place an effective legal framework, which does not permit multiple interpretations used for rent-seeking activities. Government action must be responsive to the needs of manufacturers, farmers, service providers and foreign investors. By eliminating bottlenecks that act as disincentives for production and exports, the government can stimulate private sector activities to enhance both agro-based and manufacturing activities.

References

Adeolu, Adewuyi (2004): "Can Nigeria Benefit from Globalisation? Constraints, Opportunities and Challenges". In: Nigerian Economic Society (NES) (eds.) 2003, Globalisation and Africa's Economic Development. NES, Ibadan, pp. 425.

AGOA (2005): "Bilateral Trade Profile: US-Nigeria". Online: www.agoa.info/?view=country_info&country=ng&story=trade, accessed: 22/06/2005.

British Broadcasting Corporation (BBC) (2005): "Business News", 24/08/2005. Online: www.bbcworld.org.

Central Bank of Nigeria (CBN) (2003): "Budget Statement 2003". In: Bullion, 27(1):2-7.

Central Bank of Nigeria (CBN) (2004): "Budget Statement 2004". In: Bullion, 28(1):1-9.

Central Bank of Nigeria (CBN) (2000): "The Structure of the Nigerian Economy and Implications of Development". Ream Communication Ltd., Lagos, Nigeria.

Central Bank of Nigeria (CBN) (1990, 1997, 2000, 2001): "Statistical Bulletin", Lagos, Nigeria.

CBN (1995): "Nigerian Trade Summary", Lagos, Nigeria.

CBN (1960-2003, 2005): "Annual Reports and Statement of Accounts for the years 1960-2003", 2005, Lagos, Nigeria.

Chete, Louis (2004): "Globalisation and the Nation-State Autonomy versus Global Hegemony: A Critical Review of Contending Positions". In: NES (eds.) Globalisation and Africa's Economic Development. NES, Ibadan, Nigeria, pp. 542-546.

Commission of the European Union (2002): "Trade and Development Assisting Developing Countries to Benefit from Trade. A Communication from the Commission to the Council and the European Parliament", Brussels.

Dalil, Abu (1996): "Nigeria: Non-oil Export Performance". In: Proceedings of CBN/WORLD Bank Collaborative study on Nigeria: Prospects for Development Vision 2020, Held at the Sheraton Hotel and Towers, Abuja, April 15-17, 1996

Dos Santos, Thioniel (1970): "Structure of Dependence". In: American Economic Review, vol. 2, Papers and Proceedings, May, pp. 234-237.

Food and Agriculture Organisation (FAO) (2002), Dependence on Single Agricultural Commodity Exports in Developing Countries: Magnitude and Trends (online): http://www.fao.org/documents/show_cdr.asp?url_file=/DOCREP/005/Y3733E/y3733e0d.htm, accessed 01/06/2004.

FAO (2005): "Key statistic of food and agriculture external trade". Online: http://www.fao/esless/toptrade.asp, accessed 15/04/2005.

Food and Agriculture Organization (FAO) (2004): FAOSTAT. Online: http://www.fao.org, accessed 10/11/ 2004.

FAOSTAT, (2006): "Agricultural Export Values and Volumes. Online: http://faostat/fao.org, accessed 15/04/2006.

Heritage Foundation, (2006): "Index of Economic Freedom". Online: www.heritage.org, accessed 01/04/2006.

Rashid, Faruqee (1994): "Nigeria: Ownership Abandoned". In: Husain, Ishrat and Faruqee, Rashid (eds.), Adjustment in Africa: Lessons from Country Case Studies, World Bank Regional and Sectoral Studies. The World Bank, Washington DC, USA. Pp. 238 – 285.

Mussa, Mohamad, (2000): "Meeting Challenges of Globalisation". A paper presented at the Plenary session of African Economic Research Consortium, Bi-annual Workshop Plenary, May 2000, at Nairobi, Kenya.

National Planning Commission Nigeria (NPC) (2004): "National Economic Empowerment and Development Strategy (NEEDS)", Government Printer: Abuja.

Nigerian Export Import Bank (NEXIM) (1995): "Annual Report", Government Printer: Lagos.

Norton, George and Alwang, Jeffery (1993): "Introduction to Economics of Agricultural Development". Mc Graw-Hill, INC, New York.

Obadan, Mike (2004): "Globalisation and Economic Management in Africa". In: NES (ed.) Globalisation and Africa's Economic Development. NES, Ibadan, Nigeria, pp. 12.

Ogunkola, Olawale and Oyejide, Ademola (2001): "Market Access for Nigeria's Exports in the European Union: An assessment of impact of the Lome Convention and Uruguay Round". The Nigerian Journal of Economic and Social Studies. 43(1): 15-46.

Ohamae, Kenichi (1995): "The End of Nation-State: The Rise of Regional Economics". Harper Collins, London.

Okoh, Rosemary (2004a): "The Global Market Place: How far can Nigeria go with the present Non-Oil product Mix. Conference Paper, TIPS/DPRU: African Development and Poverty Reduction: The Micro-Macro Link", Cape Town, 13th to 15th October 2004. Online: http://www.tips.org.za/events/forum2004/-Papers/The_global_market_place_Okoh.pdf, accessed 01/06/06.

Okoh, Rosemary (2004b): "Global Integration and the Growth of Nigeria's Non-oil Exports". A paper presented at the African Conference on Growth, Poverty and Human Development in Africa Organized by the Centre for Study of African Economies (CSAE), Department of Economics, University of Oxford, Oxford, March 2004. Online: http://www.csae.ox.ac.uk/conferences/2004-GPRaHDiA/papers/3f-okoh-CSAE2004.pdf, accessed: 26/06/2006.

Oyejide, Ademola (2003): "Nigerian Trade Policy in the Context of Regional and Multilateral Trade Agreements". In: Aiyede, Remi / Alayande, Babatunde / Mabawonku, Azees (eds.) Readings in Development Policy and Capacity Building in Nigeria. Development Policy Centre, Ibadan, pp. 201-204.

Prebisch, Raúl (1950): "The Economic Development of Latin America and its Principle Problems", UN Department of Economic Affairs, New York, USA.

Richardson, John (2003): "Coments", Ministerial Roundtable on "Commodities, Markets and Rural Development". ECOSOC meeting on "The role of rural development in the achievement and implementation of internationally agreed development goals including those contained in the UN Millenium Delaration". Held at the UN headquarter, ECOSOC Chamber, New York, USA on the 30th April, 2003.

The Guardian, (2005): "N.N.: Exchange Rate for Leading Currencies", 31/03/2005, page 17, Lagos.

Thirlwall, Philip (1999): "Growth and Development". 6th Edition, Macmillan Press Ltd., London.

United Nations Statistics (UNSTATS) (2004): "Trade Developments". Online: http://unstats.un.org/unsd/dpbasicquerryresult.aspx?px=hi&cc=2709,270900,2710&r=566&rg=2&rg=2&y=2003,2002,2001,2000,1999,&so=8, accessed 10/11/2004.

UNSTATS (2005): "Trade Developments". Online: http://unstats.un.org/unsd/dpbasicquerryresult.aspx?px=hi&cc=2709,270900,2710&r=566&rg=2&rg=2&y=2003,2002,2001,2000,1999,&so=8, accessed 15/04/2005.

UNSTATS (2006): "Agricultural and Manufactured Exports for Nigeria". Online: http://unstats.un.org/unsd/comtrade, accessed 15/04/2006.

The Relevance of Trade Capacity Building in Nigeria for Effective Participation in International Trade

Mareike Meyn

1 Introduction

The concept of trade capacity building is comparably new and only came on the agenda in the mid-1990s. Prior to this development, donors' trade support concentrated on export promotion (1960s and 1970s) and trade liberalisation (since the 1980s). With trade capacity, the focus has been broadened, following the realisation that functioning institutions and human and institutional capacities are crucial to effective participation in international trade (Jensen, 2005:2). The OECD Development Assistance Committee defines trade capacity building in a very broad manner. In other words, trade capacity building should not only a) enable developing countries to identify trade objectives and to formulate their trade policy by integrating all relevant stakeholders, but also b) support countries' export expansion and diversification strategy, and c) assist to strengthen national and regional trade-related institutions in order to participate best at regional and international trade negotiations (OECD 2003:2 and 2001:22). Jensen (2005:2) emphasises that this broad definition comprises two components of trade capacity building, namely trade policy and trade development. Trade policy addresses countries' ability to analyse, negotiate and implement trade agreement while trade development investigates how supply-side constraints could be overcome.

The discussion in this paper focuses on Nigeria's capacity to trade (trade policy). In this context, the relevance for Nigeria to formulate a national trade strategy and to build national and regional capacities in order to work towards a regional trade strategy within ECOWAS is discussed. Furthermore, the involvement of businesses, private sector support institutions and research institutions in trade negotiations is evaluated. As the discussion shows, an inclusive approach, involving all stakeholders, is crucial for successful trade negotiations.

2 The Concept of Trade Capacity Building in Nigeria

Given the widespread acceptance and adoption of world-wide policy towards trade liberalisation world-wide – on a bilateral, regional and multinational level, and the increasing pressure on developing countries to participate accordingly, the strengthening of trade-related capacities is regarded as crucial for enabling developing countries to benefit from the opportunities arising from trade liberalisation and for defending their interests (Bonaglia and Fukasaku, 2002). To use international trade as successful development strategy, a county needs to identify its trade interests clearly and translate these interests into policies and negotiation strategies. Furthermore, resources have to be set free to implement trade policies and the role of the single actors needs to be defined. Critical elements for such a successful trade policy are a) government leadership, i.e. government's commitment to the official trade strategy, b) institutional capacity at all levels from trade analysis to the implementation of existing agreements, and c) the inclusion of all state and non-state actors involved (Solignac Lecomte, 2001:6).

As can be obtained from Figure 1, an effective trade policy framework needs to be in place, including:

1) A consistent trade strategy that fits into the country's overall development strategy and Nigeria's regional development strategy;
2) An effective consultation mechanism, including all relevant stakeholder (private sector, research institutions, trade unions, parliament, other civil society members);
3) An effective communication among the relevant Ministries and public authorities (e.g. Ministry of Commerce with the Ministry of Agriculture and Customs and Excise Departments);
4) A trade supportive network, providing decision makers with relevant inputs (e.g. in-puts from indigenous research institutions and private sector support institutions) (OECD 2001:14).

To allow the creation of an effective trade policy, Nigeria needs capacities

a) *At the policy-making level*: Analytical capacities for trade analyses, the formulation of a coherent strategy and the negotiation capacity to set through identified interests;
b) *At the institutional level:* The effective implementation of a trade agreement requires the knowledge, capacity and equipment of according institutions, such as customs and excise services, standard agencies or anti-dumping proceedings.

Figure 1: The Process of Trade Policy

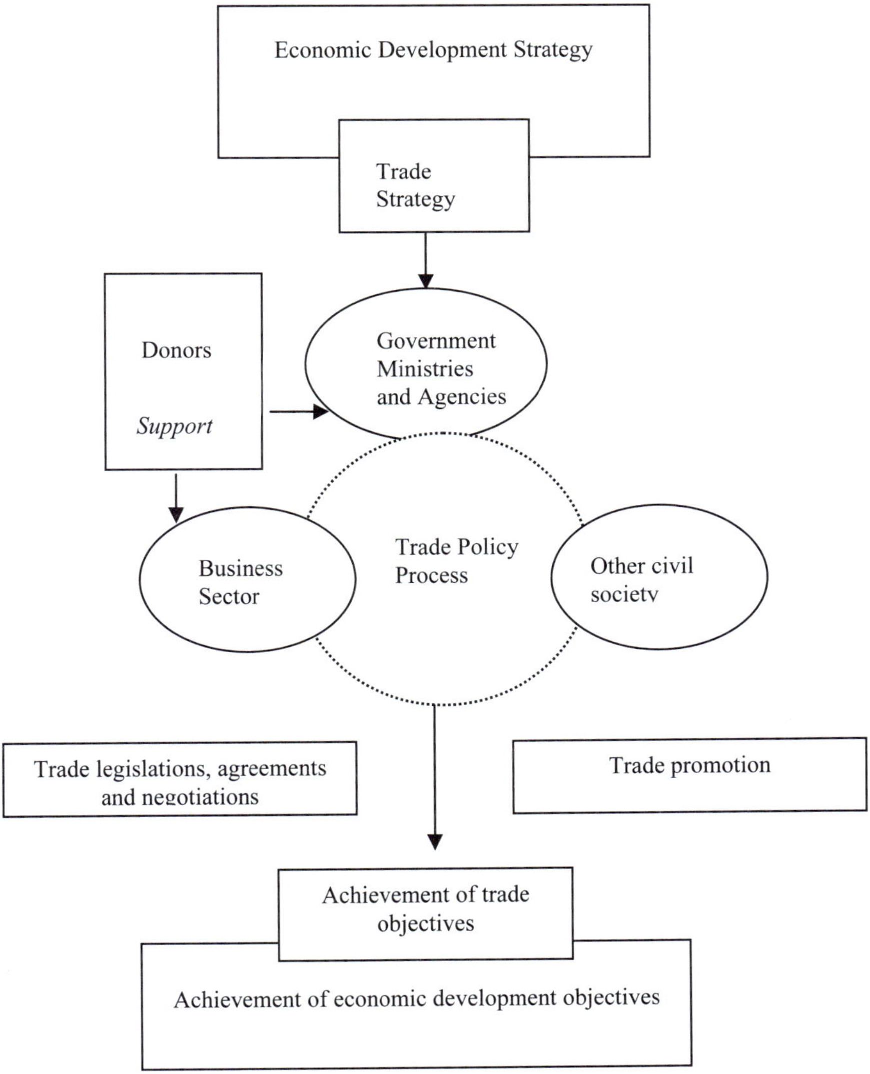

Source: Solignac-Lecomte (2001): 7.

c) *At the marketing and management level:* It is important to build a platform where all relevant actors (private sector, trade unions, research institutions, other civil society actors) can articulate their interests, which are translated in a national trade policy. The implications of trade agreements must in turn be made public towards the different national interest groups. This policy approach of "inclusiveness" ensures that the trade policy is in accordance to the overall national development strategy and "owned" by the country (UN, 2005; Bilal and Laporte, 2004).

Donor countries' ability to support this trade policy process is generally judged as limited since the ownership of trade reforms is regarded as crucial. Donors can however assist developing countries to define their trade strategy in accordance to national development goals and in cooperation with the business sector and other civil society actors. Technical and financial support should focus on institutions rather than on individuals so that structures can be improved and the process of trade policy can be smoothened (Solignac Lecomte, 2001:13-8). Moreover, donors can help developing countries to implement policy and legislation changes that are necessary for trade policy reform (UN, 2005).

3 Nigeria's Capacity to Participate in Regional and International Trade Negotiations

The requirements for active participation in regional and international forums are constantly increasing. Developing countries like Nigeria are supposed to participate in the multilateral trading system through the WTO, which means that they have to implement agreements and obligations with respect to import licensing, customs valuation, intellectual property law, sanitary and phytosanitary standards, etc. Additionally, bilateral agreements and regulations have to be negotiated and implemented, which also stresses Nigeria's limited capacities. An-other problem arising from different regulations with different trading partners under different trade agreements is that it adds to the complexity of Nigeria's trade regime, bearing the risk of making it unmanageable for the private sector and to contribute to the inconsistency the country's trade policy.

Nigeria comprises 36 federating states and a federal capital territory. The Federal Ministry of Commerce is the principle government organ that is responsible for Nigeria's trade policy formulation, trade negotiations and the implementation of trade agreements. Inputs also come from the Ministry of Foreign Affairs, the Federal Ministry of Finance, the Central Bank, Customs Services and the executive organs Federal Executive Council, National Council of State and the Senate.[1] The Federal Ministry of Commerce is responsible for the coordination of trade policy inputs made by the different actors. However, the coordination among governmental institutions is weak and no institutionalised consultation mechanism exists. Consultations are often made on an ad-hoc basis, resulting in a rather diffuse trade policy process (Jerome, 2005:4, 2002:16). In 2000, the government established the Economic Policy Coordinating Committee (EPCC) in order to strengthen a coordinated approach of economic policies, including trade policy formulation. The staff of the EPCC works in close cooperation with senior officials from various Ministries, the Central Bank, and the Revenue Service, and is supposed to monitor macroeconomic policies, including trade policy and to give policy directions (Jerome, 2002:20-1).

3.1 International Trade Obligations

Nigeria is a founding member of the WTO in 1995. However, it has not incorporated WTO provisions into national law so that businesses and investors are unable to appeal to WTO provisions at Nigerian courts (WTO, 2005:19). Nigeria's mission to WTO is small, with eight delegates being responsible for all sub-agreements, including trade in goods, services, trade facilitation, rules of origin, anti-dumping, technical barriers, import licensing, competition, intellectual property, standards, environment, dispute settlement etc. The Nigeria Trade Office in Geneva is also supposed to assist with improved market access for Nigerian products in bilateral and multilateral negotiations, to seek technical assistance that should help Nigerian businesses to tackle export markets and to cooperate closely with the responsible authorities in Nigeria (Intracen, 2005). Additionally, the staff of the Nigeria Trade Office is responsible to perceive the country's interests at the World Intellectual Property Organisation (WIPO), The United Nations Conference on Trade and Development (UNCTAD) and the International

[1] See Jerome, 2002 and 2005 for detailed information on the responsibilities of the single institutions in the process of trade policy.

Trade Centre (ITC).[2] Obviously, the quantity and complexity of all these obligations overextend Nigeria's small mission to WTO.

Furthermore, the complexity of the WTO Agreements puts constraints on Nigeria's capacities. The country is not in a position to implement the manifold obligations of the WTO sub-Agreements due to lack of technical, institutional and human resources (WTO, 2005). The effective participation at WTO also has financial implications which Nigeria can ill afford at this stage. For example, the implementation of the 1993 WTO obligations in the fields of customs valuation, SPS and the TRIPS Agreement costs a country around US$ 150 million (Finger, 2001).[3] Jerome (2005:6) also criticises that many of the WTO obligations do not sufficiently reflect Nigeria's interests, e.g. in the fields of intellectual property rights and standardisation. Like most African countries Nigeria entered with the signature of the WTO Agreement into obligations it was not entirely aware of.

3.2 Regional Trade Agreements

Nigeria is a founding member of the Economic Community of West African States (ECOWAS), which exists since 1975, today comprising 15 West African states of which 12 are classified as Least Developed Countries (LDCs).[4] In 1990, member countries agreed to establish a Free Trade Agreement (FTA) by 2000. The Customs Union (CU), originally scheduled for 2004, has been postponed to 2007. Moreover, ECOWAS announced to create a common agricultural policy (ECOWAP) in 2005, which is sup-posed to improve the region's food security and to assist with targeting the Millennium Development Goals. The ECOWAP foresees to fully integrate West African agricultural products into regional and international markets

---

2 See Nigeria Trade Office to WTO: http://www.nigeria-wto.ch/activities.htm, accessed 08/02/2006.

3 The SDT provision of the WTO Agreement provides for technical assistance to help developing countries to implement sanitary and phytosanitary standards, the agreement on technical barriers to trade, customs valuation, and the provisions of GATS and TRIPS. See the Doha Development Agenda Database at http://tcbdb.wto.org/index.asp?lang=ENG.

4 The ECOWAS member states are Benin, Burkina Faso, Cap Verde, Côte D'Ivoire, The Gambia, Ghana, Guinea, Guinea Bissau, Liberia, Mali, Niger, Nigeria, Senegal, Sierra Leone and Togo.

and to take control of trade in agricultural products (AllAfrica.com, 2005). At the time of writing, no progress regarding the implementation of the ECOWAP has been reported.

Information about the level of registered intra-regional trade differs between less than 5% (World Bank, 2002:133) and around 11% (ECOWAS Secretariat, 2006). The level of in-formal trade is however expected to be much greater comprising around 20% of total trade flows of West African countries (Hashim and Meagher, 1999 as quoted in Brüntrup, 2006:67). Nigeria's trade with the region is hardly connected to its ECOWAS membership. According to the World Bank (2002) Nigeria's exports to the African region concentrate on Côte D'Ivoire, Cameroon, Ghana, DR Congo, Chad and Senegal (around 30% of all exports), while its imports from Sub-Saharan Africa are with around 5% of total imports neglectable.

To date, only seven members have implemented the FTA, excluding Nigeria. Though Nigeria committed to implement the ECOWAS Protocol on Free Movement of Goods and People it has not yet lifted its tariff barriers on processed goods for ECOWAS imports (ECOWAS, no date; WTO, 2005:21-2). It is criticised that Nigeria's trade regime is becoming more protective and incoherent with an increasing number of ad hoc decisions in the areas of import restrictions and import bans. Moreover, Nigeria's political will for deeper regional integration as well as government's ability to transpose regional decisions into practise and to ensure an according administrative application are considered to be rather low (Mair, 2001:189).

So far, ECOWAS has not established a supra-national body and is hardly sharing sovereignty. ECOWAS policies depend therefore on intergovernmental relations and are dominated by those governments that are actively involved. Since ECOWAS is politically divided by the Francophone (WAEMU) members and the Anglophone members it is moreover difficult to find a common regional position and coordination costs are very high (Mair, 2001).

3.3 Bilateral Trade Agreements and EPA Negotiations

In addition to its international and regional obligations Nigeria is involved in multiple bilateral trade and investment agreements with industrialised and developed countries.[5] The two most important to name are the US African

5 Currently Nigeria has preferential trade agreements and/or bilateral investment agreements with the USA, Tunisia, Egypt, Cuba Vietnam, Niger, Canada, Indonesia, South Africa, Iran, Algeria, China, The Gambia and Benin. Further-

Growth and Opportunity Act (since 2000) and the EU Lomé/Cotonou Agreement (since 1975). To date, both trade initiatives provide non-reciprocal duty free-market access for most Nigerian products.[6]

Different from many other African countries, Nigeria failed to take advantage of the AGOA initiative. Though its trade surplus vis-à-vis the USA is the highest on the continent, exceeding by far the one of South Africa,[7] Nigeria exports almost exclusively crude oil and natural gas to the USA (93% of total exports in 2003) (WTO, 2005:25). While other African countries, such as Lesotho, Mozambique or Kenya experienced increased exports of clothes or apparels due to AGOA, this has not been the case for Nigeria. This shows that it is very difficult for Nigeria to overcome its resource curse and to diversify its production. While other low-income African countries were able to overcome their manifold supply-side constraints and to expand and diversify their exports to the USA, Nigeria continued to export its traditional oil-related products under a new trading regime. The main reasons are seen in the Dutch Disease problematic, infrastructural deficiencies and high transaction costs, macroeconomic fragility, corruption, lack of finance and other supply-side constraints. (WTO, 2005:viii).[8] Due to these reasons, trade preference under the EU Lomé/Cotonou regime granted since 1975 have also only insufficiently used by the country. In 2004, 86,5% of Nigeria's total exports to the EU were petroleum-based while the share of agricultural products declined from 10% in 1999 to 7% in 2004 (EU DG Trade, 2005).

---

more, Nigeria intends to enter into bilateral FTAs with Egypt and South Africa (WTO, 2005:17).

6 AGOA is an expanded GSP initiative and can be withdrawn unilaterally at any time.

7 Nigeria's exports to the USA increased from US$ 3.7 billion in 1999 to 14,6 billion in 2004 (AGOA.info, 2006).

8 The countries of the ECOWAS region are considered to belong to the bottom line regarding their institutional set-up, their regulatory quality and governments' effectiveness. Due to these fundamental institutional weaknesses trade liberalisation with the EU is expected to be detrimental for them (Busse et al. 2005).

3.4 Participation of the Private Sector, Parliamentarians and Civil Society in Trade Negotiations

Nigeria has four major umbrella organisations which should represent private sector's interest in trade negotiations: 1) the Manufacturer's Association of Nigeria; 2) the National Association of Chambers of Commerce, Industry and Agriculture; 3) the Association of Small Scale Industries; and 4) the Association of Nigerian Exporters. However, the organised business organisations are very weak and diffused so that the institutionalisation of businesses in Nigeria remains in infancy. Core competences like the promotion of SMEs and trade and business facilitation are also insufficiently developed and the services provided are often of limited use for the private sector. It is mainly large companies that lobby for their interests vis-à-vis the government on an ad-hoc basis while the voice of most private sector representatives is heard and considered when formulating trade policies (Jerome, 2005:4, Agbaje, 2005).

Nigeria established a national council, comprising government officials, organised business, organised labour and civil society actors, following the example of South Africa, which adopted an inclusive trade policy strategy when negotiating the EU-South Africa FTA.[9] However, the National Focal Point on Multilateral Trade Matters (NFP), which should bring the different actors together, serve as forum for consultation and advice and is supposed to cooperate closely with the Nigeria Trade Office in Geneva, does not work as envisaged and needs to be strengthened on the institutional level and with respect to human capital (Intracen, 2005). Still, private sector representatives and civil society actors are not sufficiently aware or included into trade negotiations, the communication and cooperation of government institutions on federal levels and on the national level remains on an informal basis, and the communication between the trade hub offices in Nigeria and Geneva is insufficient (Jerome, 2005:4-5; Agbaje, 2005).

Another problem is Nigeria's lack of trade-related domestic research capacities and the missing linkage of government policy with a broad critical civil society providing valuable inputs to the debate. Though there are many

---

9 South Africa established the "National Economic and Development and Labour Council" (NEDLAC) during TDCA negotiations, comprising government officials, mainly from the Department of Labour, organised business (represented by two business representative organisations), organised labour (represented by three trade unions) and civil society actors (represented by different councils) (Bilal and Laporte, 2004:16-7).

research institutions and Universities in the country, they have other research priorities and not the capacities to compile comprehensive trade analyses.[10] Thus, there is hardly domestic input to provide trade negotiators with relevant background information.[11] Moreover, Nigeria does not have enough qualified trade negotiators and trade analysts with technical, in-depth knowledge – a problem it shares with many African countries. In fact, a person who represents Nigeria in trade negotiation needs to perform in law and trade issues and link this knowledge to the social dimensions of these issues, which are ideally discussed with the civil society. In Nigeria, trade negotiations are mainly drawn by government officials, who do not necessarily have sufficient skills and knowledge to negotiate effectively. Furthermore, these officials are often inadequately linked to the private sector and other civil society interest groups (Agbaje, 2005). However, it would not sufficient to enhance the capacities of individuals in trade negotiations and trade-related areas. Thus, the improved training for individuals in a given environment is likely to result in the leave of civil servants who are looking for better paid jobs as consultants in the private sector or at donor agencies. It is therefore important that institutional capacities are simultaneously improved (Solignac Lecomte, 2001:19, 37).

3.5 Training Needs of the Private Sector to Support Trade Development

It is indispensable that compliance with international standards is crucial to serve the markets in industrialised countries. Nigeria has had and continues to have problems in meeting industrialised countries' Sanitary and Phytosanitary Standards (SPS). One reason is that Nigeria's most important ex-port markets, the EU and the USA, have adopted standards that go beyond those internationally codified by the International Standards Organisation

---

10 Another problem seems to be duplication of research activities due to the federal system. Thus, there are 11 different institutes in Nigeria working on agricultural diversification and rural development (FMST, no date).

11 See the list of the research establishments in Nigeria and their mandates (http://www.fmst.gov.ng/docs/Man-datesResearchInstFedEstab2004.pdf, accessed 09/02/06). However, two institutes, namely the Trade policy Research and Policy Centre in Ibadan and the Institute for Public Analysis in Lagos, are said to have the potential to provide trade-related background information for policy making (Jerome, 2002:36).

(ISO).[12] These technical barriers to trade replace in view of global trade liberalisation more and more conventional trade barriers like tariffs and quotas (WTO, 2005). Nigeria needs technical and financial support to build-up laboratories and to build-up accreditation and certification systems in order to conform to these standards (Oguntona, 2006). However, though the need to enhance production capacities and product quality of agricultural and manufacturing goods is indisputable relevant for Nigeria's export success, it has to be emphasised that Nigeria's lack of non-oil exports is not solely supply-side related. To improve the effective market access for agro-based and simple manufactured products it would also be necessary that industrialised countries grant more generous rules of origin and require standards that do not only serve consumer interests but also developing countries interests.[13]

Currently, diverse TCB projects are ongoing in Nigeria, supposed to help the country to overcome its supply-side constraints. The TCB projects are funded by national and international donors, such as GTZ, USAID, DFID, EU, UNIDO, WTO/OECD, ITC and World Bank Group are running in Nigeria.[14] However, to date these programmes have had hardly helped to overcome Nigeria's supply-side constraints. The reasons are competing agendas and insufficient coordination of donor projects. Moreover, not all projects adopt a broad understanding of trade capacity building that reflects Nigeria's institutional weaknesses and supply-side constraints. Another problem is that TCB and the formulation of a development-oriented trade strategy do not seem to be a political priority of the government so that the ownership of donors' activities is not guaranteed.

---

12 The EU and UNIDO are running together with the Federal Institute of Industrial Research in Oshodi and the Standards Organisation of Nigeria programmes to improve the standardisation and certification process (Loesener, 2006).

13 Nigeria focuses on improved market access for agricultural products at negotiations of the WTO Doha Round (WTO, 2005:19).

14 See Development Gateway (http://aida.developmentgateway.org/CountryIndex.do?view=Aida&cnt=NGA , accessed 09/02/06) for an overview of donors' activities in Nigeria.

4 What Needs to be Done to Improve Nigeria's Capabilities to Participate Effectively in Trade Negotiations?

When entering into international trade negotiations, Nigeria is supposed to formulate and set through its trade interests and, in many cases, its interests in trade related aspects, such as competition policy and government procurement. As discussed earlier, Nigeria is heavily overextended with all aspects of negotiating effectively, starting from the deficient analysis of trade flows, the formulation of trade interests, and the negotiation and lobbying power to set through its interests.

Nigeria's strained trade capacities at various levels hamper the country to take active part in regional trade (as the most powerful nation within ECOWAS) and in international trade (to optimise the exploitation of trade preferences under the Cotonou Agreement and AGOA). It is therefore necessary for Nigeria to evaluate the chances and risks of the single trade regimes it is involved in, to determine its interests and to formulate a coherent trade strategy that is consistent with its development goals. To achieve this, the NFP should be strengthened so as to allow an inclusive trade strategy that links the public sector to relevant interests groups, such as private sector representatives, trade unions, researchers, and other civil society organisations. A consultation mechanism should be established between the government and the single interest groups, which would allow the government to take the interests of organised employers and organised labour better into consideration while the different lobby groups would be able to get a better idea of compromises that need to be made in regional and international trade negotiations. In this context it would be important that the national interest parties have agreed on a comprehensive development strategy for Nigeria guiding any trade negotiation. The involvement of academics in providing relevant research and analysis could also help the parties to get a better idea of the implications of the respective trade agreement and whether it is compatible with Nigeria's overall development strategy.

However, to improve Nigeria's trade capacities and to create an inclusive trade strategy in order to allow the country's effective participation in trade negotiations cannot be achieved in the short run but requires increased human and institutional capacities as high-lighted in the following discussion.

Cost-benefit analysis

An analysis of potential costs and benefits of an FTA as well as the identification of interests are indispensable to formulate a coherent national negotiation strategy. Nigeria has not been able to diversify its exports to the EU and the USA though both markets have provided free market access. Due to its low production capacities within the agricultural and the manufacturing sector, Nigeria could not benefit from improved market access. It is therefore essential that Nigeria investigate the options for expanded capacities in the single sub-sectors and that it identifies niche products into new markets.[15] In this respect, it is also important to analyse whether non-tariff barriers, such as sanitary and phytosanitary standards, minimum volumes or labelling requirements exist, and how these NTBs can be overcome to improve Nigeria's effective market access. Additionally, the country also needs to investigate the fiscal impacts of trade agreements (e.g. in the forthcoming FTA with the EU and within ECOWAS) and formulate adjustment strategies. Since Nigeria is comparably protected within ECOWAS, where WAEMU[16] determines the highest level of protection that is lower than bound tariffs at WTO, high adjustment costs are expected for Nigeria when entering into an ECOWAS CU (Brüntrup, 2006:59).[17]

Build-up human capital and expertise in trade negotiations and strengthen institutional capacities

The scarcity of resources regarding trade analyses, the lack of capacity of trade negotiators and the lack institutional settings prohibit the effective implementation of trade agreements, for instance in the fields of customs administration and trade facilitation. Considering that Nigeria lacks capacity at almost every level, this implies that its national and regional trade policy formulation is to a considerable extent dependent on international research and technical support of donors, which bears the risk that the country resorts its trade policy to foreigners. To develop national capacities to identify

---

15 To what extent the recently established One Stop Investment Center (OSIC) that comprises 14 government agencies and is supposed to streamline and simply conditions for investors, will be able to provide sector and industry specific information as envisaged (Oguntona, 2006) remains to be seen.

16 The Francophone countries Benin, Burkina Faso, Côte D'Ivoire, Guinea Bissau, Mali, Niger, Senegal and Togo form the West African Economic and Monetary Union (WAEMU). The WAEMU has a common currency, the CFA Franc, linked to the € and a common external tariff.

17 Though there are considerations to increase the WAEMU CET for agricultural products and to form a common agricultural policy in an ECOWAS framework (Brüntrup, 2006:59).

Nigeria's interests in trade negotiations and to formulate a strategy which mirrors the awareness of all aspects and challenges of a trade agreement as well as its coherence with national and regional trade policy and the overall development strategy, Nigeria needs technical assistance. Thus, national administration and analytical capacities need to be improved and all stakeholders, from Ministries over standard agencies to private sector representatives, need to be included. However, the consultancy process can only be successful is strong political commitment towards an inclusive trade strategy is given (Dunlop et al., 2004:11). The relevance of well-prepared trade flow analyses and a coherent negotiation strategy cannot be overestimated as a South African negotiator of the EU-South Africa FTA emphasises: "*There is no substitute during tough negotiations for a good argument and proper preparation.*" (Smalberger, 2000:49).

In this context it is also the communication, coordination and cooperation among national Ministries that needs to be improved. Formal information mechanisms between Minis-tries need to be developed and responsibilities must be clearly defined. Furthermore, effective linkages to the national business sector and to the single Federal Ministries need to be expanded to allow the finding of a sort of national consensus. As the experience of South Africa during the EU-South Africa FTA negotiations showed, the leading roles of the Department of Trade and Industry (DTI), high political commitment and government leadership, and a strong involvement of all relevant stakeholders into negotiation processes was key for success (Bilal and Laporte, 2004:10-3).[18]

Effective participation of the private sector, parliamentarians and civil society in trade negotiations

For Nigeria, it is crucial to establish an international trade forum when negotiating trade agreements. Through this forum, the private sector would be (indirectly) involved in discussions, influence the agenda, and formulate requirements for technical assistance without biasing negotiations towards

---

18 The DTI lead negotiations but worked closely with the Ministry of Agriculture and the Department of Foreign Affairs. The Ministry of Agriculture established the Agricultural Trade Forum, where the private sector made his voice heard – from large exporters to small farmers. Like this, close consultation not only with key industries but also the agricultural sector was guaranteed. The Department of Foreign Affairs coordinated the inter-national negotiations, e.g. by linking with the Embassy in Brussels (Bilal and Laporte, 2004:13-7).

the protectionist demands of few large companies.[19] A joint approach, including all (formal) businesses and all other relevant actors, such as trade unions, research institutions and government officials would also offer the chance to channel information on trade negotiations to the public and avoid a "closed-shop". Moreover, it helps to save time and to bundle different interests in one forum (Bilal and Laporte, 2004:17).

To get involved, a strong commitment of the according interest groups is crucial, which is deemed to be difficult considering the weak organisation of Nigeria's private sector representatives. However, demand-driven private sector support institutions that are capable to manage themselves and are not completely depend on funding and input from donors are a prerequisite for effective partnering. Otherwise it is only few big businesses that lobby for their interests, which are not necessarily in the interest of other stakeholders, such as consumers and the manufacturing industry.

In addition to the private sector, it is also important that Nigeria includes parliamentarians and other parts of the civil society, such as research institutions, trade unions and NGOs into its trade policy. Though participants in trade policy formulation within Nigeria countries are only few compared with developed countries, where well-organised private sector support, research institutions and parliaments exists, an inclusive approach is nonetheless relevant. Otherwise, governments' trade policy bears the risk that it does not fit into the country's overall development strategy and is not carried by the population. As discussed, South Africa applied an inclusive approach when negotiating the EU-South Africa FTA, including all Ministries concerned, private sector representatives, federal parliaments, social and economic stakeholders (such as trade unions and research national and institutions), and foreign expatriates.[20] According to Lewis et al. (2004: 163):

> "Indeed it appears that the South African government has been unique in the space that it has given to civil society, notably business and labour, in the preparation and conduct of trade negotiations. This effective extension of tri-partism to the international arena has undoubtedly contributed

---

19 In this respect, Bilal and Laporte (2004:20) point out the relevance that the private sector presents the expected impact of an FTA well-founded and in written form so as to provide trade negotiators with relevant insights to be used during negotiation process.

20 For a further discussion of how trade policy can be mainstreamed into development processes in Least Developed Countries see UN, 2005.

to the consistency of South Africa's trade policy and is a ringing endorsement of the benefits of participatory governance of trade policy formulation."

Obtain knowledge about international negotiation mechanisms

To obtain knowledge about the negotiation strategy of international trading partners, to lobby for Nigeria's interests, i.e. in the area of improved market access, and to gain public sympathy in the respective countries as well to understand the complex decision-making processes are regarded as crucial factors for the successful outcome of trade negotiations. This is most of all the case in the current negotiations of Economic Partnership Agreements (EPAs) with the EU, which Nigeria negotiates in the ECOWAS framework.[21] Again, Nigeria could learn from South Africa, which created a comprehensive network of formal and informal contacts in the EU and experienced the complexity of the EU's decision-making process when negotiating the EU-South Africa FTA (Bilal and Laporte, 2004:23-4). Moreover, expertise from NGOs based in the EU and the USA could assist Nigeria and other ECOWAS countries in gaining important insights into negotiation mechanisms. Thus, it would be important

Moving towards deeper regional integration

Considering the limited resources of all ECOWAS countries, a regional approach could help to pool capacities and resources in the most effective way and improve the representation of the region's interests. The example of the CARICOM regional negotiation mechanism shows that it is also possible for poor, developing countries to pool resources together and tackle trade-related complementary problems on a regional basis. However, such an approach requires a clear mandate and defined responsibilities in order to negotiate effectively in behalf of the region. Another factor that is important to note is that a regional approach is no substitute for national preparations (Dunlop et al., 2004). Indeed, the creation of a regional negotiation mechanism requires strong commitment towards deeper regional integration of all member countries since "In the end, a regional process can only be as strong and as fast as the national member countries want to go." (Dunlop et al., 2004:22). For Nigeria this implies that it has to define its economic and strategic interests in ECOWAS and to engage accordingly. Nigeria's (failed) Fast-Track approach with Ghana

---

21 Comprising all ECOWAS countries plus Mauritania. EPAs enter into force in January, 2008 and include a WTO compatible reciprocal trade agreement between regional blocks of ACP countries and the EU.

is an example of a potentially successful strategy where two (or more) member countries decide to implement an FTA and CU faster than the other members of the regional integration body. Again, government's strong commitment for regional integration and the overcoming of protective national interests are a pre-requisite for the success of such an approach.

5 Conclusions and Policy Recommendations

In summarising Nigeria's experiences and deficiencies of trade capacities, it can be stated that the creation of an effective trade policy framework is a long-term goal, which requires major investments in institutional and human capacities and a strong private sector – these are prerequisites which so far have not be given due priority in Nigeria. Donor agencies can support the process of trade capacity building. It is however important that the recipient's national sovereignty with respect to its trade policy formulation is accepted and that the trade and development interests of a do-nor country do not infringe. Thus, it is mainly the developing country's ability to make independent decisions regarding its trade policy that should be strengthened. Such an approach has been lacking since most trade reforms in African countries are donor-driven and lack "ownership".[22] Prowse (2002:1244-5) defines the prerequisites for successful trade capacity building as follows:

> "The success of … [trade capacity building] can only be determined over the medium-term taking into account the extent to which the trade agenda including the policy recommendations are meaningfully included into the country's development process, and the extent to which bilateral and multilateral agencies continue to respond to the capacity building needs … Ultimately, success can only be defined on the basis that realised trade improvements will promote growth and contribute to welfare gains."

At the end of the day, the lack of trade capacity is only part of the overall problem of economic underdevelopment and the exclusion of African countries

---

22 See Solignac Lecomte (2001:21-44 and 2003) and Prowse (2002) for an evaluation of successive and limitative factors of effective trade capacity building and the problems of donor activities' coordination. In 2002/02 donor countries' trade-related technical assistances accounted for 4.8% of total development aid (OECD 2003:4).

from international trade. Trade capacity cannot be tackled in isolation and African countries like Nigeria that have limited resources to confront numerous problems, such as widespread poverty and high income inequality, low production capacities and high dependency on few export products, corruption and poor public services, have to focus on the most urgent needs (Rodrik, 2001). Nevertheless, in the light of a changing and more complex international trading environment, the building of trade capacity is an important policy field. Nigeria does not only need to identify and articulate its interests but must also formulate a coherent trade strategy that is in accordance with its overall development strategy. This requires that the Nigerian government is fully committed to establish an inclusive, development-oriented trade strategy. Only then can external support to expand institutional and human capacities and to improve the inclusion of non-state actors and the coordination among federal and national Ministries be successful. Thus, the success of building up trade capacity depends to a large extend on policy makers and their approach towards trade policy and the role trade policy plays in economic development.

References

Agbaje, Adigun (2005): "Institutional Framework and the Process of Trade Policy Making in African Countries", unpublished Powerpoint presentation.

AGOA.Info (2005): "Information and resource webpage on the African Growth and Opportunity Act". Online: http://www.agoa.info/, accessed 22/01/2006.

AllAfrica.com (2005): "ECOWAS Heads Of Govt Adopt Common Agricultural Policy Today". Online: http://www.unmillenniumproject.org/documents/ThisDay01-18-05.pdf, accessed 03/05/06.

Bilal, San and Laporte, Geert (2004): "How did David prepare to talk to Goliath? South Africa's experience of trade negotiating with the EU". ECDPM Discussion Paper No. 53, September.

Bonaglia, Federico and Fukasaku, K. (2002): "Trade Competitively: Trade Capacity Building in Sub-Saharan Africa". Paris: OECD.

Brüntrup, Michael (2006): "Rethinking Protection for Agricultural Markets in Sub-Sahara Africa". In: Brüntrup, M. / Melber, H. / Taylor, I. (Eds.): Africa, Regional Cooperation and the World Market. Uppsala: Nordiska Afrikainstitutet.

Busse, Matthias, Borrmann, Axel and Neuhaus, Silke (2005): "Trade, Institutions and Growth: An Empirical Analysis of the Proposed ACP/EU Economic Partnership Agreements for ECOWAS Countries". Hamburg: HWWA.

Dunlop, Adam, Szepesi, Stefan and van Hove, Kathleen (2004): "Organising trade negotiating capacity at regional level. A Caribbean case study". ECDPM Discussion Paper No. 54, September.

ECOWAS (Economic Community Of West African States) (no date): "Status of the ECOWAS Priority Programme in Nigeria". Online: http://www.sec.ecowas.int/sitecedeao/pays/web/nigeria-m.htm, accessed 08/02/06.

ECOWAS Secretariat (2006): Official website: http://www.sec.ecowas.int/sitecedeao/english/achievements.htm , accessed 02/05/06.

EU, DG Trade (2005): "Bilateral Trade Relations. African, Caribbean, Pacific. Statistic Analysis 2004", online: http://europa.eu.int/comm/trade/issues/bilateral/re-gions/acp/stats.htm , accessed 23/02/06.

Finger, J.M. (2001): "Implementing the Uruguay Round Agreements: Problems for Developing Countries". In: The World Economy vol. 24:9, pp. 1097-1108.

FMST (Federal Ministry of Science and Technology) (no date): "Research Establishments in Nigeria and their Mandates." Online: http://www.fmst.gov.ng/docs/MandatesResearchInstFedEstab2004.pdf., accessed 09/02/2006.

Hashim, Yahaya and Meagher, Kate (1999): "Cross Border Trade and the Parallel Currency Market – Trade and Finance in the Context of Structural Adjustment". Nordiska Afrikainstitutet Research Report 113.

Intracen (2005): "The World Trade Net Nigeria Network." Online: http://www.intracen.org/worldtradenet/docs/networking/country_reports/country_report_nigeria.pdf, accessed 08/02/2006.

Jensen, Michael Friis (2005): "Capacity Building for Pro-Poor Trade: Learning from the Limitations in Current Models". Human Development Report Office. Occasional Paper, online: http://hdr.undp.org/docs/publications/background_papers/2005/HDR2005_Jensen_Michael_Friis_15.pdf, accessed 27/09/05.

Jerome, Afeikhena (2005): "Institutional Framework and the Process of Trade Policy Making in Africa: The Case of Nigeria." Paper presented at the International Conference: "African Economic Research Institutions and Policy Development: Opportunities and Challenges" by the Secretariat for Institutional Support Economic Research in Africa (SISERA), Dakar 28-29 January, 2005.

Jerome, Afeikhena (2002): "Institutional Framework and the Process of Trade Policy Making in African Countries: The Case of Nigeria." Interim Report submitted to the African Economic Research Consortium (AERC), Nairobi.

Lewis, David, Reed, Kabelo and Teljeur, Ethel (2004): "South Africa: Economic Policy-Making and Implementation in Africa: A Study of Strategic Trade and Selective Industrial Policies". In: Soludo, C., Ogbu, O. and Chang, H.-J. (Eds.):

The Politics of Trade and Industrial Policy in Africa. Forced Consensus?, pp. 151-78, New Jersey: Africa World Press.

Loesener, Otto (2006): "Industrial Development and Market Entry: The Role of Technical Support Services in Nigeria". In: Wohlmuth, Karl et al. (Eds.): African Development Perspectives Yearbook vol. 11/2006: Africa – Escaping the Primary Commodities Dilemma, pp. 497-507, Lit-Verlag: Hamburg and Münster.

Mair, Stefan (2001): "Fallstudie ECOWAS". In: Mair, Stefan and Peters-Berries, Christian (Eds.): Regionale Integration und Kooperation in Afrika südlich der Sahara. EAC, ECOWAS und SADC im Vergleich, pp. 183-293, Weltforum Verlag: Bonn.

OECD (Organisation for Economic Co-operation and Development) (2003): "Trade Capacity Building: Critical for Development". OECD Policy Brief August.

OECD (2001): "The DAC Guidelines. Strengthening Trade Capacity for Development". OECD: Paris.

Oguntona, Timothy (2006): "The Development Dimension of Economic Partnership Agreements (EPAs) – Are We Still On Track?" Main Points of Contribution, Working Group C on Liberalisation Process, InWent International Policy Dialogue, 27-28 April, 2006, Berlin

Prowse, Susan (2002): "The Role of International and National Agencies in Trade-related Capacity Building". In: The World Economy vol. 25:9, pp. 1235-61.

Rodrik, Dani (2001): "Trading in Illusions". Foreign Policy, March/April. Online: http://www.foreinpolicy.com/issue/marapr_2001/rodrick.html, accessed 12/04/03.

Smalberger, Wilhelm (2000): "Lessons Learnt by South Africa during Negotiations". In: Bertelsmann-Scott, T. / Mills, G. / Sidiropoulos, E. (Eds.): The EU-SA Agreement. South Africa, Southern Africa and the European Union, pp. 47-52, Johannesburg: SAIIA.

Solignac Lecomte, Henri-Bernard (2003): "Building Capacity to Trade: What are the Priorities?" OECD Development Centre Working Paper No. 223, November.

Solignac Lecomte, Henri-Bernard (2001): "Building Capacity to Trade: A Road Map for Development Partners. Insights from Africa and the Caribbean". Overseas Development Institute (ODI) Working Paper, July.

UN (United Nations) (2005): "Integrated Framework (IF) for Trade-Related Technical Assistance for Least Developed Countries. United Nations: New York and Geneva.

World Bank (2002): "African Development Indicators 2002. Drawn from the World Bank Africa Database". World Bank: Washington D.C.

WTO (World Trade Organization) (2005): "Trade Policy Review Nigeria". TPRB/247, WTO: Geneva.

Oil Palm Production in Nigeria and Improved Export Chances: The Need for Upgrading

Osmund Osinachi Uzor

1 Introduction

Recent studies on Africa have shown that most countries still depend on limited number of unprocessed raw materials as major source of their export earnings (Collier, 2002, Bond, 2003). This tends to expose them to the risks of instability as a result of price volatility in the world market. With few exceptions, notably South Africa and Mauritius, the region has not been able to transform the quality or increase the values of their primary commodities in order to generate higher export revenue. Also Nigeria depends on primary commodities as the principal source of external revenue generation.

Global value chain analysts have underscored the need for primary commodity upgrading in African economies.[1] Upgrading the quantity and quality values can have implicit effects on economic development in terms of employment creation, economic linkages etc. (UNCTAD, 1995; Cramer, 1999). In this respect, upgrading involves not only the strategies that will enhance increase in the volume of exports, but also transform the nature of the commodity into a higher quality value and output (i.e. horizontal vs. vertical upgrading). Upgrading in terms of quality and quantity provides an incentive for possible integration of the commodity into the global value chain (Gibbon, 2001).

Nigeria has failed to diversify the economy away from its over-dependence on the capital-intensive oil sector, which provides 20 per cent of GDP, 95 per cent of foreign earnings, and about 65 per cent of budgetary revenue. The share of non-oil sector to total export has never been stable and currently lies below 6 per cent. It declined from 3 per cent in 1990 to 1.8 per cent in 1996 and

---

1 For details on global chain and primary commodity upgrading analyses see Gereffi 1999; Cramer (1999); Gibbon (2001).

increased again to 4.5 per cent in 1998. However, it fell to 1.3 in 2000 but peaked to 5 per cent in 2002, and precipitously later fall to 3.3 in 2003 (CBN, 2004). The consequences of over dependence on oil in this context, ranges from risks of economic instability as a result of oil price volatility in world market, vulnerability to local conflicts on the basis of agitation for increased control of oil resources by inhabitants of the Niger Delta where oil is found, to the neglect of other important sectors like agricultural cash crops and mining.[2]

This article evaluates the importance of oil palm products to the Nigerian economy and appraises the chances for upgrading the sub-sector. Specifically, the article is centred on Palm Kernel Oil (PKO) and Palm Kernel Cake (PKC) production in Nigeria and evaluates output trend, production system, the upgrading possibilities, problems and chances of the sub-sector in the export market. The economic effect of clustering in terms of increased output and reduction of production constraints in PKO extraction is investigated. The article is based on field studies undertaken in the oil palm industry in the Enugu region of Nigeria. The article will also try to identify challenges the sector faces in the local economy thereby putting forward some policy objectives on how to revitalise the sector. The article is organised into seven sections. Following the introduction, section 2 provides the conceptual framework of the article. The scope and methodology of the study is outlined in section 3 and the production structure of the palm kernel industry is discussed in section 4 on the example of the Enugu region. The development constraints in PKO extraction enterprises and pro-active policy measures on private sector investment in PKO are discussed in sections 5 and 6 respectively while section 7 concludes the article.

2 Conceptual Framework

2.1 Definition

Value chain analysis has assumed prime importance in recent years. It has succinctly been described as the process that is required to bring a product or service from the conception, through the intermediary stages of production,

---

[2] For detailed understanding of problems and implications of dependence on primary commodity see Collier, 2002

then delivery and finally disposed off after use (Kaplinsky, 2000: 28). In other words, the value chain is the classified set of units (designing, production, marketing and recycling) in which a particular upgrading activity can take place. In the context of PKO and vegetable oil production, the value chain entails planting and harvesting the palm fruit, the crushing of kernel shell, the extraction of oil and the refining the oil.[3] Upgrading can be done in each unit and in different forms, namely functional upgrading, process upgrading and product upgrading.[4]

2.2 Upgrading the Nigerian Oil Palm Industry

Oil palm production and exportation in Nigeria has a relatively long history dating back to the pre- colonial era. In 1834, about 14,000 tonnes of palm oil, valued about £ 33 to £ 34 per ton, were exported from the Niger Delta to England (Helleiner, 1966: 97). The export of palm kernel and palm oil together increased from 200,000 tonnes in 1900 to 450,000 tonnes in 1954, accounting for about 25 per cent of Nigeria's exports value then (Helleiner, 1966: 98). Correspondingly, the share of Nigeria's palm kernels exports increased from 45.5 per cent of world exports in 1938 to 58.1 in 1961. The share of Nigeria's oil palm export increased from 29.4 per cent of world exports in 1937 to 32.6 per cent in 1959 (Kilby, 1969: 141). Nigeria continued to be the world leading producer and exporter of oil palm products between 1961 and 1965 with an average annual output of 43 per cent of global production. However, by 1997, Nigeria accounted for only 7 per cent of world production (Kajisa et al, 1997). The average share of palm produce to total non-oil exports has been on a downward spiral from 9.8 per cent in 1970-1974 to 3.8 per cent in 1975-1979 and an alarming 1.7 per cent in 1995-1999 (Aigbokhan, 2001). The trend dwindled from the 1970s onwards as indicated in Figure 1 due to a combination of factors including the civil war; oil boom effect, and unfavourable agricultural policies (Forrest, 1993, Kajisa et al, 1997). Despite current low production output that fail to meet local demand and export chances, oil palm is arguably still an important segment in Nigeria economy, providing rural and urban income, employment

---

3 Crushing and extraction units can be internalised by a vegetable oil refinery firm depending on the size and technology capability of the firm.

4 For more details on relationship between value chain and upgrading see Kaplinsky, 2000; Humphrey and Schmitz, 2002; Kaplinsky and Readman, 2001.

opportunities and industrial inputs. Figure 1 shows that between 1970 and 2002, there was a progressive but low marginal annual increase in oil palm production.

Figure 1: Annual Output of Palm Oil and Palm Kernel (1970-2002), in thousand tonnes

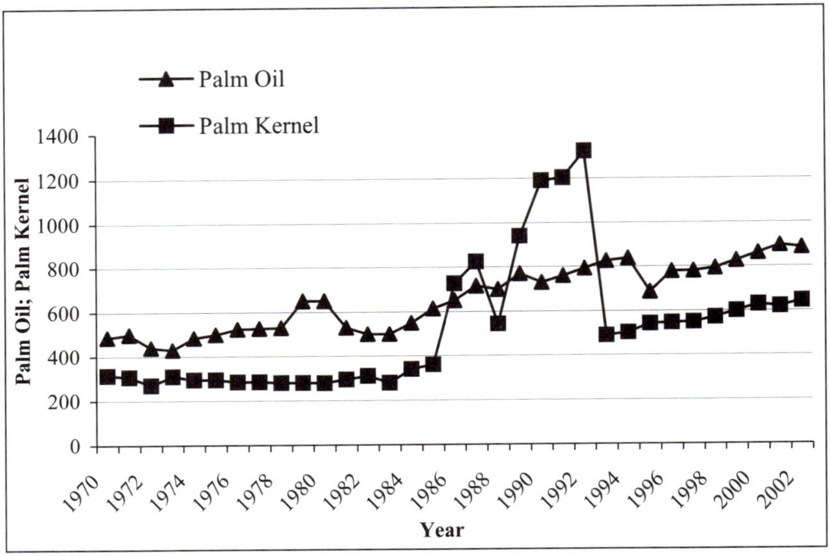

Source: Central Bank of Nigeria, 2003, pp (120).

The output has a mean annual capacity of 654.91 and standard deviation of 145.04 within the period. Palm kernel production on the other hand, experienced a negative trend between 1970 and 1985; with the turning points in 1986 showing very high marginal annual increase of 102 per cent and in 1992 with the highest production output of 1321 tonnes. This was the period of Structural Adjustment Programmes (SAP) that favoured agricultural production and rural economy in Nigeria (Adubi and Okunmadewa, 1999). The trend changed drastically in 1993 with annual marginal decreases of 62.9 per cent and a relatively low output level.[5] Figure 2 presents the world leading

5 The palm kernel industry has a mean annual output of 522.24 with standard deviation of 290.93 in the period 1970-2002.

producers and exporters of PKO. As shown in the Figure, Malaysia and Indonesia that were at the same level with Nigeria in the 1960s have forged ahead with Nigeria's share of export being zero.

Figure 2: Palm Kernel Oil: World Production and Export (in metric tonnes)

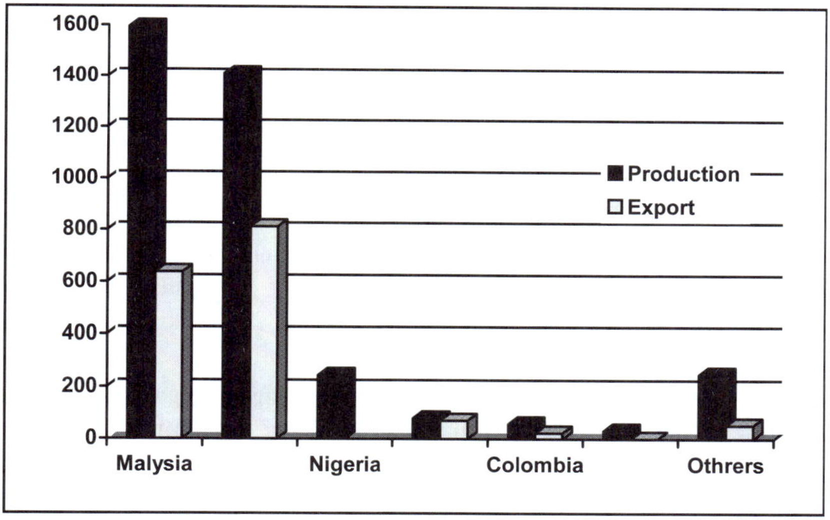

Note: World total production = 3,667 metric tones
World total export = 1,601 metric tones

Source: FAS (2004)

Table 1 below shows the form of upgrading applicable to Nigeria oil palm industry. Horizontal upgrading implies to increase the present output in order to meet local demand and to encourage producers to export their products. This can be done in three forms: (a) The gradual replacement of low yielding wild Durra species to high yielding Tenera in the rural smallholder farming system; (b) An increase in private sector investment in medium-scale plantation farming; and (c) An improvement in extraction technique of red oil palm, PKO and PKC.

Table 1: Forms of Upgrading in Oil Palm

Forms of Upgrading	Specific forms	Example	Determinants
Horizontal	Quantity and quality upgrading	(a) High yield specie: from low yield Durra to high yielding Tenera (b) Increase private investment (c) Technology improvement in oil extraction mechanism	Land reform and improved investment climate
Vertical or Functional	Functions and product quality	Standardisation in oil processing and improved coordination	Human capital development and improved investment climate

Source: Author's compilation.

The non-volume related upgrading (vertical upgrading) involves the ability to stimulate product differentiation and standardisation that form the basis for possible sectoral and inter-firm linkages as well as innovation. Both upgrading processes require an enabling environment since private investment is key for upgrading processes (Gibbon, 2001).

2.3 The Value Chain of the Nigerian Palm Kernel Sub-Sector

PKO belongs to the so-called lauric oils family. Lauric oils contain about 50 per cent of lauric acid while other fats contain 1 to 3 per cent (Pantzaris and Ahmad, 2001). In South-Eastern Nigeria, the rural peasants perform the bulk of palm kernel shell crushing. Mechanised shell separations systems have been developed but not fully commercialised. The kernel shells are removed manually with little hammers. The palm kernel dealers or agents operating in the region assemble the nuts in large quantity by buying directly from the peasants in rural markets and supply to extraction enterprises in urban areas. Each rural market operates on different specified market days (once in every fourth days). This helps the agents to plan their logistic works in terms of collection and supply to the extraction enterprises. Since the palm kernel hard-shells provide no further economic value, only few small-scale enterprises are engaged in this stage of production. The extraction of kernels is mostly undertaken by small-scale enterprises located in urban areas since extraction is energy intensive. Locating the extraction activities to rural areas would involve high production cost for extraction and vegetable oil refinery enterprises because the rural infrastructure is in poor condition. Supply of PKO to the vegetable oil refineries also requires logistic planning and prompt delivery. Large firms tend to internalise their extraction units in order to reduce transaction costs and maintain efficient production. Figure 3 provides an overview of the PKO and PKC production in South Eastern Nigeria.

Figure 3: Value Chain Structure in PKO and PKC Production in South Eastern Nigeria

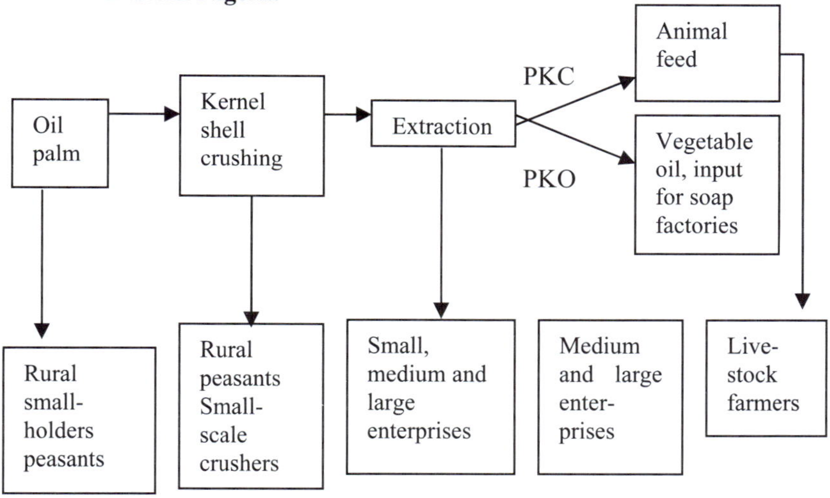

Source: Author's compilation.

During refinery, the PKO undergo several hydrogenation stages to produce refined vegetable oil and other food products as well as cocoa butter substitutes (Pantzaris and Ahmad, 2001).

3 Scope and Methodology

The aim of this study is to show the importance of oil palm production in Nigeria economy with reference to palm kernel production. In this context, the linkages, the production system, and the constraints are identified. The analysis shows why quantitative and qualitative upgrading is necessary in Nigeria's oil palm industry. Upgrading the oil palm sector can contribute to poverty alleviation with respect to income and employment generation and is important for Nigeria's diversification efforts in order to overcome its oil dependency. Due to limited resources the field study was restricted to palm kernel and PKO production in Enugu city. In Enugu city, there are three zones of PKO extraction enterprises: Abakpa/Emene zone (13 micro-scale and 2 small-scale enterprises), Agbani/Uwani zone (15 micro-scale and 10 small-scale enterprises), and Ogbete-/Railway zone (25 micro-scale and 5 small-scale enterprises). This gives a total population of 70 micro and small-scale PKO extraction enterprises in Enugu city with 25 of them clustered behind Enugu railway station and at Uwani Industrial Estate.[6] With 30 per cent sample ratio, 20 enterprises were selected from the population size of 70 PKO extraction micro- and small scale enterprises. The distribution of the enterprises by location was as follows: Abakpa/Emene (4 enterprises), Agbani/Uwani (7 enterprises), and Ogbete/Railway (9 enterprises). A vocational training centre for PKO production in Enugu was visited. It is important to investigate the nature of technology, the kind of training and services offered by the centre. Information related on features of the enterprises and the production systems in terms of input/output structure of the PKO and PKC were generated and analysed. All enterprises interviewed are registered members of the Enugu Palm Kernel Extraction Association (EPKEA). Most of the businesses were owned by men, only six women entrepreneurs were engaged in the palm kernel extraction business.

The study was conducted in two phases. The first phase was between November 2003 and April 2004, while the second part was conducted between January and June 2005. It was not possible to generate data with a pre-set standardized questionnaire since micro level data collection is very difficult in Nigeria due to poor business and institutional records as well as due to the nature of the interviewees. Face-to-face interviews were applied because some of the entrepreneurs do not keep records and are sceptical in responding to questionnaires. This method gave the author the opportunity to observe the production processes and systems; the nature of technology in use and how the enterprises cope with them. Based on Levy and Lemeshow

6 Micro-enterprises are enterprises with one to nine employees; small enterprises are enterprises with ten to forty employees while medium-scale enterprises are enterprise with 50 to 99 employees (World Bank, 1999:16).

(1999) analogue, a simple cluster sampling method was used to select the investigated sample.[7]

4 The Economy of the Oil Palm Sector in Nigeria

4.1 Output Trends in Nigeria's Oil Palm Industry

The three principal products of oil palm products are red palm oil, palm kernel oil, and palm kernel cake. The red palm oil is derived from the processed pulp of the oil palm Elaeis guineensis fruit and serves as source of calories and vitamin A in developing countries, while palm kernel oil is derived from the kernel of the fruits (Hyman, 1990). The palm kernel cake (PKC) is the dried chaff from compressed palm kernels, which are used for the production of animal feeds and manure for the farmland.

Table 2: Oil Palm Production Systems in Nigeria as at 2003

Production system	Estimated Area (in hectare)	Percentage
Semi-wild groves	2,100,000	89.55 %
Estates	95,000	4.05%
Small-holders	150,000	6.40%
Total estimate	2,345,000	100%

Source: NIFOR, 2003 (as quoted in Omoti, 2003).

7 "If one city block contains ten households and another contains six households, it would not be possible to take a 30 per cent sample of households from each of these two blocks. However, if a general strategy is to have second stage sampling fractions as nearly equal as possible among the two blocks, then we would select three from the block having ten households, and two households from the block having six households, and we would include a scenario such as this under the general rubric of simple two-stage cluster sampling" (Levy and Lemeshow, 1999: 275-6). In other words, unequal probabilities of selection in one stage can be compensated for in the succeeding stage to produce an equal probability of selection overall (Henry, 1990: 30).

It is very difficult to establish the extent and size of the Nigeria's oil palm industry because it is largely dominated by semi-wild palm stands scattered in rural villages. Table 2 shows the estimated land area covered by oil palm in Nigeria. About 80 per cent of the production output comes from dispersed smallholders that cover an over estimated area of 2,345,000 million hectares in the southern part of Nigeria. The current estimate of oil palm production in the country is about 900,000 metric tonnes of oil palm and 400,000 metric tonnes of palm kernel annually (Omoti, 2003: 43).

4.2 The Input-Output Structure in the Palm Kernel Enterprises Sub-Sector in South-Eastern Nigeria

4.2.1 The Palm Kernel Supply Zone

Figure 4 below illustrates the territorial input and output structure of various production activities involved in palm kernel sub-sector. The production activities are divided into three zones namely, the palm kernels supply zone; the PKO and PKC extraction zone, and the refinery zone.

Figure 4: Territorial Input-Output Structure in Palm Kernel Economy in South Eastern Nigeria

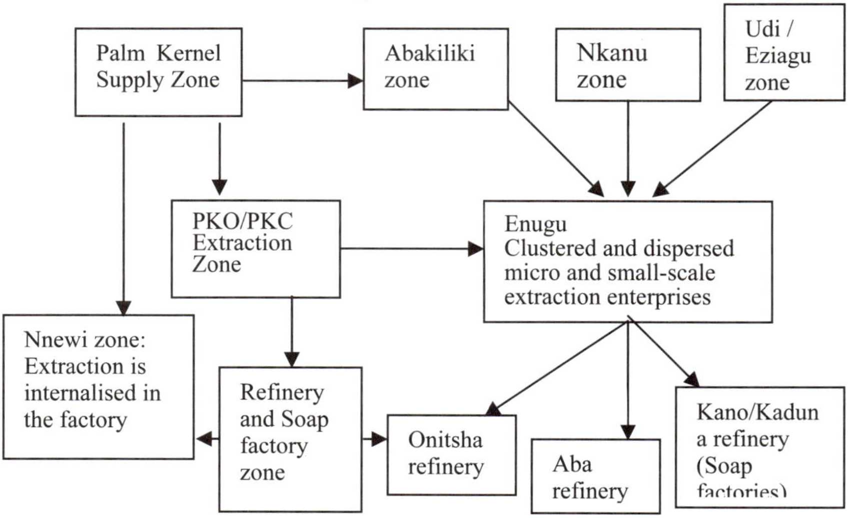

Source: Author's compilation.

The supply system in the palm kernel sub-sector is an embodiment of agents, dealers and rural smallholder farmers. The palm kernel supply zones comprise Abakaliki, Nkanu and Udi/Eziagu. The Abakaliki and Nkanu zones supply 85 per cent of the kernels processed for PKO and PKC in Enugu, while the rest comes from the Udi/Eziagu areas. On average, 3 tonnes of kernels per week are processed by each enterprise in the PKO enterprises cluster, while in dispersed enterprises an average of 2 tonnes of kernels per week is processed. The refineries in the South-Eastern region consist of 10 medium scale and 3 large- scale enterprises located in three industrial towns namely Aba, Nnewi and Onitsha.

4.2.2 The PKO and PKC Extraction Zone

The enterprises engaged in extraction can be classified as micro and small enterprises according to their number of employees. The average age of the enterprises covered by the sample is 13 years. 95 per cent of enterprises are sole proprietorship, while only 5 per cent are joint-ventures. The labour force is a mixture of skilled and unskilled labour. The classification of skilled workers is not based on educational qualification but on training and experience in PKO extraction methods. Skilled workers are those workers that received vocational training on PKO extraction system either through the Volunteers Service Agency (VSA) or by in-house-training processes.[8]

97 per cent of the entrepreneurs interviewed have higher education with about 57 per cent of them with engineering background (see Table 3). The entrepreneurs have varied experience in technical and managerial knowledge but deficient experience in production organisation. Therefore, raw- and production materials are left in a disorganised manner, which undermines the division of labour in the production system. Among the male entrepreneurs, there is mixture of mechanical and agricultural engineers competing alongside with those that have business and economic background. The female entrepreneurs are ex-school teachers with National Certification of Education (NCE) qualification. Others are trained agricultural extension officers who have experience in oil industry.

---

8 In 1987, the regional government in Enugu established VSA for training of prospective entrepreneurs and workers in PKO extracting business as youth unemployment reduction strategy. An average of six volunteers is trained annually. The one-year training course covers a range of activities such as cost management, machine operating, techniques and processes involved in the palm kernel drying before extraction.

Table 3: Educational Background of Entrepreneurs in Mirco- and Small Scale PKO Extraction Enterprises

Qualification / Entrepreneur	Agricultural Engineering	Mechanical Engineering	Economics /Business Studies	NCE	Others
Male	5	4	5	1	2
Female	---	---	---	2	1

4.2.3 Production Output in the Palm Kernel Extraction Enterprises

Table 4 shows the mean monthly production output of the enterprises interviewed. The enterprises in the cluster and the dispersed enterprises have a similar production system and production networks. However, the volume of output differs.

Table 4: The Aggregate Mean Monthly Output in Clustered and Dispersed Small-Scale Enterprises in Enugu

Cluster	Projected Output (in tonnes)	Real Output (in tonnes)	Output Shortfall (in %)	Dispersed	Projected Output (in tonnes)	Real Output (in tonnes)	Output Shortfall (in %)
PKO	72	48	33.3	PKO	60	36	40.00
PKC	120	96	20.00	PKC	96	60	37.5

Note: *Output shortfall is the difference between the monthly projected output and monthly real output (in tonnes).*

Source: *Author's compilation.*

The projected and real outputs explain the extent of productivity in the sub-sector based on market-demand. The projected output represents the estimated monthly output of the enterprises under constant energy and raw material supply with prevailing labour force and machine capacity. The real output is the actual monthly output realised under prevailing irregular energy supply, frequent machine break downs and uncertain weather conditions.

The table further reveals that PKO production records higher output shortfall than PKC production. The shortfall indicates producers' inability to meet the local demand resulting to induced importation. In order to exploit export chances and to improve the position of Nigeria's PKO production in the global value chain, the production capability has to be upgraded. Exports are possible once the local market is saturated with good quality products (Cawthorne, 1995).

The table further shows that the enterprises in the cluster perform better than the dispersed ones in terms of production output. This is as a result of increased efficiency of production. The cluster offers small producers the chance to benefit from economies of scale and joint action, by meeting the requirement of the processors. For example, two or more small enterprises in the cluster often undertake joint supply of PKO in order to meet the requirements of the refineries. In the event of a machine break down, one can move the kernels to another firm's production unit and continue with the production. The engineers in the cluster provide free machine maintenance services for non-engineers. Also, the enterprises in the cluster try to reduce energy consumption and cost by adopting a rotational production system.[9] Moreover, the enterprises in the cluster enjoy constant supply of palm kernels because they buy in large quantity at reduced cost. The palm kernel dealers tend to concentrate on the enterprises in the cluster because the probability of getting supply contracts is higher than from dispersed enterprises.

5 Development Constraints in PKO Extraction Enterprises

Several publications on small-scale enterprises (SSE) development in developing countries have revealed various constraints the sector faces due to inefficiencies in micro- macro- and meso-economic policies as well as internal weaknesses of small enterprises (Smith, 1982; Levy, 1991; Hansohm, 1992; Osoba, 1992; Boehm, 1997; Oladeji, 1998; etc.). Five major constraints were identified in the PKO extraction industry in Nigeria, namely, 1) energy problems, 2) the multiplicity of taxes, 3) distortions of the socio-economic and policy environment, 4) a poor state of technology, and human capital development, and 5) finance.

---

9 The rotational production system implies that a group of enterprises produces according to a particular time schedule as result of limited energy supply.

5.1 Energy Supply Problem in Extraction Enterprises

Energy problems are considered to top the list of the constraints according to the interviewees. 94 per cent of the enterprises investigated cannot afford the energy costs of heavy generating plants and depend on public energy supply for production. The average power failure ranges from 4 to 5 hours per day and 1 to 3 days per week. This means that production stops within these periods, consequently delaying supplies to refineries and resulting in unmet demand for vegetable oil. Table 5 shows the average monthly cost of energy paid to the Power Holding Company of Nigeria. An average of N9,500.00 is paid by the micro- and small enterprises in the extraction industry monthly. Two companies that have generating plants spend an average of N35,500 monthly.[10]

Table 5: Average monthly energy cost of interviewees (2003-2005)

Energy supply	No. of enterprises in the Sample	Average Monthly costs
Public energy supply	18	N 9,500.00
Public and private energy supply	2	N 35,500.00*

Key: N = Naira

Source: Author's compilation.

Most entrepreneurs interviewed argued that there is a connection between high fix costs for electricity and the inefficiency of power supply. Thus, consumers have to pay in any event – with or without power supply.

5.2 Multiplicity of Taxes

The growth of a small enterprise also depends on an efficient regulatory system. The business environment such as political stability, a stable and non-corrupt government, an efficient legal system, competitive taxation and efficient administration processes play an important role in small enterprises development. An uneven enforcement of regulatory obligations can create

---

10 The costs were derived from daily purchase of diesel, monthly expenses on plant maintenance and the monthly energy bill.

discontinuities. For instance, high tax obligations such as tax duplications can induce a disproportionate burden on business operation (Levy, 1991: 20).

Table 6: Forms of Taxation in PKO Extraction Enterprises

Forms of Taxes	Average amount paid annually	In percentage of total taxation
Income Tax	N 5, 966.70	35%
Produce Tax	N 1,700.00	10%
Environment Tax	N 3,000.00	17%
Local Govt Permit	N 1,750.00	10%
Business Premises	N 4,800.00	28%
Total	N 1,7216.70	1.00

Key: N = Naira

Source: Author's compilation.

Table 6 shows different types of taxes and levies the small enterprises in PKO extraction industry have to pay annually. For example, the produce tax and the local government business permit levy are a tax duplication that tends to discourage investors. There is an indirect subsidy for entrepreneurs operating in government-established industrial estates since they enjoy exemptions from business premises tax and subsidised monthly workshop rents. A business environment that promotes tax discrimination discourages competition among the enterprises. Competition is, however, considered to be an important element that fosters growth in small enterprises.

5.3 Distortions of the Socio-Economic and Policy Environment

Recent government polices, such as the tree planting programme and the rural development programme have tried to expand the oil palm sector in order to meet domestic demand for food and industrial uses, to generate employment and to improve rural quality of life and income. In contrast, the neglect of the rural areas in terms of a poor road network, poor rural market development and a lack of financial incentives works against this avowed goal. Consequently, the oil palm sector is not responding to government policies. Moreover, market orientated economic reforms always induce uncertainty at the beginning. Such reforms provide however the opportunity for economic improvement through learning and competition. The PKO extraction enterprises are subjected to stiff competition as a result of trade liberalisation in Nigeria. This has posed challenges to local entrepreneurs to adapt and improve their entrepreneurship skills as well as to the government to provide an enabling environment for competition. Many entrepreneurs lack technical skills and machinery to act competitively. Capability and capacity building in terms of technology and human skill development are fundamental instruments for small enterprises competitiveness and development strategy (Romijn, 1999: 13). Unfortunately, these policies have been neglected in Nigeria.

5.4 Poor State of Technology and Human Capital Development

Small enterprises in PKO extraction operate mostly with local fabricated machines produced from scraps with low resistance capacity. In the production process, there is a frequent machine breakdown and considerable time is spent in assembling, adjusting and re-coupling of the entire machine system. The machines work in a single calibrated system of compressing and separating. Production depends on the sun intensity for drying of the kernels; hence there must be a constant study of the weather condition. The sub-sector is labour intensive with high educational gaps between the entrepreneurs and the workers. Entry to business requires only the knowledge of the simple machine operation and initial capital. 55 per cent of the respondents would opt for foreign machines with integrated dryer system in order to increase oil extraction rate. They argued that since the technical know-how is already at hand, adaptation of foreign machines in their production system would be easier. The remaining 45 per cent argued that foreign machines are too expensive and cannot be financed by the average small enterprise in Enugu. Therefore local fabricated machines would need to be improved.

5.5 Lack of Finance

Lack of finance is one of major factor that affects the development of small enterprises in the sub-sector adversely. Like other small-scale enterprises, this problem is accentuated by the inherent constraints associated with smallness. Small enterprises are confronted with poor capitalisation. One reason is entrepreneurs' unwillingness to allow external participation since they fear to loose control over their businesses. On the other hand, the smallness of the sector discourages investors' interests and banks' motivation to grant loans (Inang and Ukpong, 1994). Despite various special credit schemes adopted for small enterprises development by the previous Nigerian government, the World Bank and the African Development Bank, small enterprises in PKO extraction still lack reasonable access to credit facilities.[11] The entrepreneurs in PKO extraction are confronted with insufficient start-up capital, high pressure on working capital for daily business activities, and low investment capital for business expansion. The ownership structure contributes to their smallness and low capitalisation degree. Thus, only 0.05 per cent of the enterprises interviewed were joint ventures, suggesting that the pool of resources is small. The sub-sector continues to rely on informal sources for finance. The Small- and Medium-Scale Industries Equity Investments Scheme (SMIEIS) introduced by the Central Bank of Nigeria has remained an ineffective instrument in addressing small enterprises' financial constraints. This is because the conditionality and modalities of the scheme are beyond the premise of small enterprises.[12]

6 The Need for Pro-Active Investment Policies in the PKO Extraction Sub-Sector in Nigeria

Small-scale farmers continue to dominate the production structure in the Nigerian oil palm industry. To upgrade the production output of PKO in Nigeria requires the collaboration of the private and the public sector. The first step is to identify how landholdings can be consolidated in order to induce private initiative to invest in medium-scale palm plantation. Smallholder farming in the oil palm sector is necessary and should be strengthened through medium-scale palm plantation in order to meet the local demand as well as to

---

11 The successive loan schemes include the Small-Scale Industrial Scheme (1971), the Agricultural Credit Guarantee Scheme (1973), Nigeria Agricultural and Co-operative Bank (1973), Nigerian Bank for Commerce and Industry (1973), Small and Medium scale Enterprises Loan Scheme (1992), National Economic Reconstruction Fund (1994), Family Economic Advancement Program (1997), World Bank SME Loan Scheme I (1973-1989) and World Bank Loan Scheme II (1989).

12 For the eligibility of the fund, a prospective small enterprise must be registered as a limited liability company with the Corporate Affairs Commission and must comply with all relevant regulations of the Companies and Allied Matters Act (1990) such as filing of annual returns, including audited financial statement. The scheme promotes exclusion since small enterprises that cannot afford the cost of incorporation will not have access to the fund.

exploit export chances. Increased participation of private firms in medium-scale plantation would also be desirable since development efforts of large-scale plantation failed in the past. Large-scale plantations are usually owned by the government and are poorly managed. These large-scale projects involve huge capital outlays and can also result in conflicts for agrarian land. To this end, the Nigerian Land Use Decree of 1978 has to be reformed in order to be attractive for private sector investment in rural areas.

The second step is to identify how local and national technology policy can positively influence private sector investment in small-scale PKO extraction enterprises. Nigerian technology policy has not been able to address the basic technologies that are fundamental for small-scale enterprise developments (Oladeji; 1998: 128). Despite the importance of the PKO industry for Nigeria's socio-economic development, the Science and Technology (S&T) policy has not identified the sub-sector as policy priority. Government intervention would however be important in order to improve production efficiency and technology application in the sub-sector. This could be done by encouraging private investment in new technology on PKO extraction and by fostering cooperation between local S&T institutions such as RMRDC (Raw Materials Research Development Council, Industrial Development Council (IDC), Project Development Agency (PRODA) and Scientific Equipment Development Institute (SEDI) with foreign research institutions in order to identify ways to support product upgrading in the sub-sector. Capacity building has to be intensified in these institutions in order to promote research works.

The third step is to identify the relationship between good governance and increased private sector investment in PKO extraction enterprises.[13] The there is correlation between good governance and economic development. If the governance structure and the political system are poor, sustainable growth cannot be achieved. Good governance implies the effective management and equitable distribution of the country's resources and the adherence to a public code of conduct by being transparent and accountable for policies. Good governance also signifies the ability of the government to recognise the importance of a social pact with its citizens thereby protecting the vulnerable.

---

13 Wohlmuth (1999) defines governance as the manner and method in which the government exercises its political power, how institutions and structures are created and used in exercising the political power; how the decision-making processes and the method of implementing actions are being organised, and how government and the general public are related. Governance is legitimate when it adopts democratic principles and respect for human right and adopts the values and principles of the international community.

In economic terms, good governance implies the ability of the government to protect property rights and maintaining the rule of law (Gradstein, 2004).

Poor governance signifies the selective distribution of resources in a manner of political patronage, poor management of the resources, ineffective public institutions, the neglect of the rule of law, and corruption. Corruption and the poor economic policies have contributed to the low level of investment.[14] For example, the multiplicity of taxes, extortion and harassments of small entrepreneurs by local authorities and unguided procedures in business registration increase the cost of production in Nigeria. In fact, foreign investors can only be integrated in the production process of oil palm sector, especially in PKO refinery, if the investment climate will improve.

The fourth step is to identify the relationship between poverty reduction and private sector investment in the oil palm industry. In this context, the domestic investment climate and investment policies are key factors for economic growth and poverty reduction. Policy measures that tend to encourage private sector investment, such as structural reforms including the privatisation of state enterprises, the development of small-scale enterprises (especially those in informal sectors), foreign exchange stabilisation, institutional development and macroeconomic stability should be pursued intensively.

7 Summary and Policy Recommendations

The article has articulated some options for Nigeria's policymakers to contend with in diversifying the economy away from over dependence on crude oil by upgrading the oil palm industry. Gains from diversification will be reflected in increased household income generation, employment creation and a diversified export base. Upgrading the oil palm sector in terms of quantity and quality would not only strengthen local production, but would also increase the share of Nigeria's non-oil exports. The linkages in the sector suggest that an integrated rural and urban production system will offer an alternative possible strategy for poverty reduction. Harmonising the taxation system and providing efficient energy supply as well as improving the rural infrastructure would

---

14 In analysing the relationship between corruption and private investment, Everhart and Sumlinski (2001) describe corruption as a form of taxation on investment called "Corruption tax". It increases the cost investment and reduces the motivation of business incentives.

improve the investment environment in the oil palm sector significantly. Land reform that guarantees property rights and institutional reforms that strengthen the enforcement of contracts are fundamental for smallholder farmers in rural areas and local/foreign investors in order to increase production. Furthermore, the analysis has shown the positive impact of enterprises cluster on production activities of the small enterprises in the sub-sector. The collective efficiency existing in the cluster helped to reduce the production constraints thereby leading to higher production output compared to the dispersed enterprises. Therefore, adopting the cluster development principles for PKO extraction enterprises will help to increase output and to increase the effectiveness of small enterprises development intervention strategies. Finally, based on the findings, it is recommended that focusing on financial support alone is not the optimal path for small enterprises development; rather investment in technology learning and skill development should be the fundamental policy objectives.

References

Adubi, A. A. and Okunmadewa, F. (1999): "Price, exchange rate volatility and Nigeria's agricultural trade flows: A dynamic analysis." In: AERC Research Paper 87. Nairobi.

Aigbokhan, B. (2001): "Resuscitating Agricultural Production (Cocoa, Cotton, Groundnuts, Palm oil, Rubber, etc.) For Export". Paper Presented at the 10th Annual Conference of Zonal Research Units of the Central Bank of Nigeria. On the theme Resource Endowment, Growth and Macroeconomic Management in Nigeria, held in Owerri, June 4-8, 2001.

Boehm, U. (1997): "Human Resources Developemnt in African Small and Medium enterprises: the role of Apprenticeship". In: Wohlmuth, K./ Bass, H. H. /Kappel, R. Wauschkuln, M., Regional Perspectives on Labour and Employment, African Development Perspectives Yearbook, vol. 5, Münster/Hamburg: Lit, pp 319-333.

Bond, P. (2003): "African and Globalisation: Can the new Partnership for Africa's Development Work?" In: Karl Wohlmuth, Achim Gutowski, Tobias Knedlik, Mareike Meyn and Sunita Pitamber, African Entrepreneurship and Private Sector Development. Lit Münster Vol. 9, pp. 187-201.

Cawthorne, P. (1995): "Of Networks and Markets: The Rise and Rise of a South Indian Town: Tirrupur's Cotton Knitwear Industry". In: World Development. vol. 23, No.1, pp 43-56.

CBN (Central Bank of Nigeria) (2003): "Statistical Bulletin-Price Statistics: In: Statbull". Vol. 13 part C. The Central Bank of Nigeria.

Collier, Paul and Gunning, Jan W. (2000): "The Potential for Restraint through International Trade Agreements". In: Collier, Paul and Pattillo, Catherine (Eds.): Investment and Risk in Africa. Macmillan Press, Basingstoke et al., pp. 338-351.

Cramer, C. (1999): "Can Africa Industrialise by Processing Primary Commodities? The Case of Mozambican Cashew Nuts". In: World Development Vol. 27, No. 7, pp 1247-1266.

Everhart, S. S. and Sumlinski, M. A. (2001): "Trends in Private Investment in Developing Countries (Statistics for 1970-2000) and the Impact on Private Investment of Corruption and the Quality of Public Investment. International Finance Corporation (IFC)". Discussion Paper No. 44 The World Bank, Washington D.C.

FAS, (2004): "Palm Kernel Oil: World Supply and Distribution. Foreign Agricultural Service", Official USDA estimates for April 2006. Online: http://www.fas.usda.gov/psd/complete_tables/OIL-table2-164.htm, accessed 02/05/2006.

Forrest, T. (1993): "Politics and Economic Development in Nigeria". Boulder: Westview Press Inc.

Gereffi, G. (1999): "International trade and industrial upgrading in the apparel commodity chain". In: Journal of International Economics 48, pp 37-70.

Gibbon, P. (2001): "Upgrading Primary Production: A Global Commodity Chain Approach". In: World Development vol.29. No.2, pp 345-363.

Gradstein, M. (2004): "Governance and Growth". In: Journal of Development Economic 73pp 505-518.

Hansohm, D. (1992): "Small Industry Development in Africa Lessons from Sudan". Münster/Hamburg: Lit.

Helleiner, G. K. (1966): "Peasant Agriculture, Government, and Economic Growth in Nigeria. Homewood, Illinois: Richard Irwin, INC.

Henry, G .T. (1990): "Practical Sampling". In: Applied Social Research Methods Series, Vol. 21. Sage Publications, New Park, London, New Delhi.

Humphrey, J. and Schmitz, H. (2002): "How does inserting in global value chains affect upgrading in industrial clusters?" IDS, University of Sussex, Brighton BNI 9Re, UK.

Hyman, E. L. (1990): "An Economic Analysis of small-scale Technologies for Palm Oil Extraction in Central, and West Africa". In: World Development, Vol. 18, No. 3, pp 455-476.

Inang, E. E. and Ukpong, G. E. (1994): A Review of Small-Scale Enterprises Credit Delivery Strategies in Nigeria". In: CBN Economic & Financial Review, vol. 30, No.4, pp 249-27.

Kajisa, K., Maredia, M. and Boughton, D. (1997): "Transformation Versus Stagnation in the Oil Palm Industry: A Comparison Between Malaysia and Nigeria". Staff

Paper 97-5 Department of Agricultural Economics Michigan State University East Lansing; Michigan 48824.

Kaplinsky, R. (2000): "Globalisation and Unequalisation: What can be learned from value chain analysis". In: The Journal of Development Studies, vol. 37. No. 2, pp. 117-14.

Kaplinsky, R. and Readman, J. (2001): "Integrating SMEs in global value chains, Towards Partnership for Development. UNIDO ,Vienna.

Kilby, P. (1966): "Industrialization in an open Economy: Nigeria 1945-1966". The Syndics of the Cambridge University Press, London, New York

Levy, B. (1991): "Obstacles to Developing Small and Medium Sized Enterprises: An Empirical Assessment". Working paper 558, The World Bank; Washington D.C.

Levy, P. S. and Lemeshow, S.(1999): "Sampling of Populations, Method and Applications". Third Edition. John Wiley & Sons, INC, New York.

Oladeji S. I. (1998): "Technology policy and the development of small and medium scale enterprises in contemporary Nigeria". In: Technovation, 18 (2). 125-132.

Omoti, U. (2003): "Oil Palm Research at NIFOR". In: BUROTROP Bulletin, NO. 19 Feb., pp 43-46.

Osoba, A. M. (1992): "The Missing Middle - New Chances and Programmes of Developing the small-scale Industries in Nigeria". In: Wohlmuth et. al (eds) Industrialisation based on Agricultural Development, African Development Perspectives Yearbook, vol. 2, Münster/Hamburg, Lit, pp 529-546.

Pantzaris, T. P. and Ahmad, M. J. (2001): "Properties and Utilisation of Palm Kernel Oil". Malaysia Palm Oil Board (Europe) Brickendonbury: Hertford.

Romijn, H. (1999): "Technology Support for Small Industries in Developing Countries: From 'Supply Push' to 'Eightfold-C'". Development Studies Working Papers No. 128, University of Oxford Queen Elizabeth House.

Smith. H. (1982): "Growth Constraints on Small-Scale Manufacturing in Developing Countries: A critical review". In: World Development, Vol. 10: 6, pp. 429-450.

UNCTAD (1995): "Recent Development in the Diversification of the Developing countries' commodity exports". Report by The United Nations Conference on Trade and Development. UNCTAD/COM62, New York, and Geneva.

UNCTAD (1996): "Trade and Development Report". The United Nations Conference on Trade and Development. New York, and Geneva.

Wohlmuth, K. (1999): "Good Governance and Economic Development in Africa: An introduction". In: Wohlmuth, K., Bass, H. and Messner, F. (eds.), Good Governance and Economic Development, African Development Perspectives Yearbook, Münster: Lit Verlag, Vol. 6, pp 3-64.

Production, Processing and Marketing of Export Crops for Rural Development: The Case of Cocoa in Nigeria

Akinpelu O. Olutayo and Ayokunle O. Omobowale

1 Introduction

In spite of the campaigns and attempts at diversification, African nations have remained entrapped in the primary products web. Primary products, which at a time served as 'blessing' necessary for development, have become impediments for the same development in contemporary times. They have largely remained so due to the inability to adequately process for domestic consumption and exports, and to secure the profits available both domestically and at international markets. Of all export crops, cocoa is of particular importance to Nigeria's economy. And so it has been since the colonial period

Nigeria joined the league of cocoa producing nations around 1874 when the crop was introduced to the country from the then Spanish Island of Fernando Po (Olayemi 1974:47). The first cocoa export from Nigeria was in 1892 (Ajayi and Oyejide 1974:225). The volume of exports subsequently substantially increased from 21 tons in 1895 to 159,503 tons in 1960; the year of independence (Nigeria Cocoa Board 1982). Cocoa emerged as a major export crop under British rule due to the policy of the government, which favoured the export of cash crops as source of foreign exchange for development. Thus, of all the export crops, cocoa came out as a major source of foreign earning for Nigeria at independence in 1960, contributing up to 21.6 percent of export revenues (Daramola and Okunola 1999: 1081). Besides, in the same year, Nigeria ranked second out of the five largest exporters of cocoa, contributing to about 17 percent of total world cocoa beans export of 896,900 metric tons (FAO, 1964:7).

After independence, cocoa remained a major source of government finance as the Western Regional Government of Nigeria depended on its proceeds to finance its development projects. Apparently realizing the need to diversify into processing in order to improve cocoa value for higher returns, the Western Region Government established the Cocoa Industry Limited (CIL) in 1960 (Daramola and Okunola 1999: 1081). The establishment of CIL was intended to encourage diversification through processing for domestic consumption and export. And indeed, available data show that Nigeria increased its cocoa processing from 20,000 tons in 1968 to 28,000 tons in 1974 (FAO 1975:5). However this modest achievement was to decline just about a decade after when cocoa processing began a downward slide from 12,052 tons in 1985 to just 390 tons in 1992 and to zero in 1993 (Daramola and Okunola 1999:1081). Attempts to increase the volume of cocoa processing were made by the government with the introduction of the Structural Adjustment Programme (SAP) and the scrapping of the Cocoa Marketing Board in 1986. The goal was to discourage importation and thereby propel local processing and increased income for local producers. Indeed, the income of local producers substantially increased (despite the precipitous decline in volume). The average producer price for cocoa increased from mere N 7,500 (US$ 5.35) per ton in 1988 to N 85,766 (US$ 91.80) per ton in 1999 (Aigbokhan 2001:11-12). However, the high rate of inflation which averaged 32.06 percent during this period (Central Bank of Nigeria 2002:308), limited the purchasing power of local producers and proved to be detrimental for improvements. Thus, the diversification objective of SAP failed as rural producers groaned under harsh economic conditions, which made whatever increased income they earned of little value in actual terms. And hence, the chances of increased processing for local consumption and export were hampered. As a result, Nigeria has remained largely an exporter of raw cocoa beans with little chances of gaining market for products, which may be extracted from processed cocoa. And so the hope of diversification for greater profit has remained a mirage, more than four decades after the first attempt was made.

This paper examines the possibilities of production, processing and marketing of cocoa for rural development in Nigeria. It discusses the socio-economic setting of Nigeria in section 2, the situation of rural producers in the urban marketing framework and Nigeria's agricultural policy in section 3, and the marketing of cocoa products in Nigeria in section 4. Section 5 concentrates on the Cocoa Rebirth Initiative and finally, section 6 centres on policy recommendation and suggestions.

2 The Socio-Economic Setting of Nigeria

According to the 1991 population census, Nigeria's population was 88,992,220 (with a projection of 131,702,942 for 2005), with the rural population taking up 63.72 percent of the number (Ekong 2003:36). Nigerians are engaged in a wide spectrum of socio-economic activities cutting across both agricultural and non-agricultural sectors. In spite of the fact that the contribution of agriculture to national income has declined over the years (Buren 2001:831), it remains a major employer of labour, especially in rural areas where 80 percent of the population is engaged in agricultural production (see table 1 below).

Table 1: Major Employers of Labour in Rural and Urban Nigeria (2003)

	Urban (%)	Rural (%)
Agriculture	**25.7**	**80.0**
Employers and Self-Employed	20.3	46.4
Employees	0.6	0.8
Unpaid Apprentices and Household workers	4.8	32.8
Non-Agriculture	**74.3**	**20.0**
Employers and Self-Employed	47.9	17.1
Employees	21.0	1.5
Unpaid Apprentices and Household workers; of which	5.4	1.4
- Manufacturing	17.1	8.5
- Construction	2.2	0.3
- Commerce	33.0	0.4
- Transport and Communication	3.7	9.3
- Services	17.6	1.4
- Others	0.6	0.1

Source: Ekong (2003): 212.

Among those practicing agriculture, 46.4 are employers/self-employed, while 0.8 percent are employees. The remaining 32.8 percent are unpaid apprentices and household workers who apparently engage in farming as part of their training processes. As for those practicing non-agricultural professions in rural areas, 17.1 percent are employers or self-employed, 1.5 are employees while 1.4 percent are unpaid apprentices and household workers.

The data above simply confirms the prime position of agriculture in Nigeria's economy. However, from its initial contribution of about 75 percent of the Gross Domestic Product (GDP) at independence in 1960 (Buren 2001:831), the contribution of agriculture to GDP has considerably declined over the years to 34.6 percent in 2003 (Central Bank of Nigeria 2003:63). Idachaba (2000:3) attributed the decline of agriculture to factors such as oil boom and inappropriate tax policies of the government on agricultural products, which substantially reduced the income of the local producers. This is further aggravated by the urban biased development policy, which is financed by excess revenue extracted from rural resources, thus limiting the purchasing power of rural producers. Despite the gloomy state of Nigeria's agriculture, it remains a veritable source of income for the majority of rural producers who are mainly engaged in subsistence farming. In as much as rural producers practice agriculture for subsistence, their profit margin and therefore economic power to compete for goods and services in the larger market is largely reduced due to their inability to gain direct access to the market and the corruptible nature of their goods that are quickly rotten. Hence, they are at the mercy of local cocoa dealers who offer only low prices that have to be accepted by primary producers who have hardly any negotiation power (Oxfam, 2004: 4-5).

As shown in Figure 1, the value chain of Nigeria's cocoa starts from local producers who grow, harvest, ferment and dry cocoa. The local dealers provide funds and purchase cocoa beans from the local producers and thereafter sell them to urban and international companies, such as Cocoa Industries Limited (Nigeria) and the global player Nestlé (Bass 2005: 248, Kaplinsky 2004: 16, Daramola and Okunola 1999: 1081). The Nigerian and international companies further add value by processing cocoa beans to cocoa liquor, cocoa powder, chocolate, confectionaries etc. Thereafter, they brand the finished products and market them to consumers. The consumers finally purchase the finished product and also provide feedback on its quality, thus allowing improved value addition.

Figure 1: The Value Chain of Nigeria's Cocoa

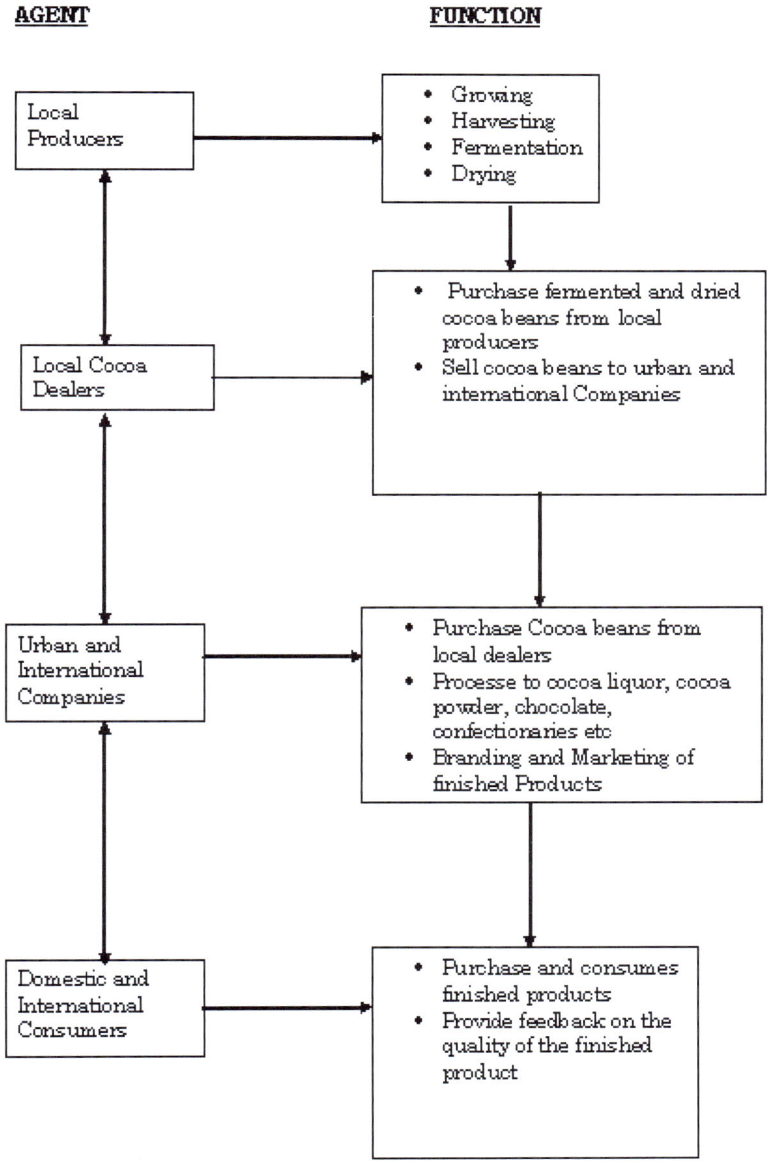

Source: Authors' presentation.

Since the contribution of rural producers stops at the primary level for cocoa production, the power-exchange relations further tilts in favor of local dealers and processing companies. This also implies power-biased exchange relations between urban and rural areas, which result in the out-pricing of rural dwellers from goods (including basic needs) while urban dwellers pay lower prices for products. This is even the case for goods sourced from rural areas such as food items (see table 2). The reasons that account for this are a better infrastructure and a higher competition level in urban areas, resulting in lower prices. In the process, rural producers are entrapped in poverty strain, which in the long-run creates normative bars around their deplorable state. Thus, attention is not directed at the unbalanced exchange relations, while their state of being, though man-made, is taken as an unavoidable reality of the modern economy.

Table 2: Consumer Price Index (Rural and Urban)

	1999		2000		2001		2002		2003	
	R	U	R	U	R	U	R	U	R	U
Food	65.5	62.6	66.9	65.5	85.2	86.1	96.3	97.3	102.0	104.8
Clothing & Footwear	90.6	79.7	92.6	86.8	91.1	92.8	90.5	96.6	105.8	116.6
Housing Water Electricity & other Fuel	59.5	67.8	75.3	74.3	74.8	73.8	88.7	80.6	115.4	116.8
Health	99.3	78.7	103.8	88.7	98.5	85.7	104.1	88.5	121.3	112.8
Transport	70.4	61.1	74.4	65.3	76.7	72.7	70.6	83.4	99.8	99.5
Communication	-	-	-	-	-	-	105.2	95.8	102.1	98.3
Recreation & Culture	58.3	61.7	66.5	65.7	76.6	72.8	83.9	80.5	121.4	97.0
Education	-	-	-	-	-	-	101.5	87.1	126.4	109.2

Notes: *R = Rural; U = Urban.*
Source: *Central Bank of Nigeria (2003):151-152.*

Table 2 reveals that rural dwellers have to pay more than urban dwellers for selected basic goods. Specifically, they had to pay more for health services, communication, recreation, culture and education. And since they have to pay highly for these services in spite of their meagre income, they are invariably unable to afford those things, which may enhance social mobility. Thus, rural Nigeria continually experiences a re-production of poverty notwithstanding the potential wealth coming from the primary goods they produce. And so, the possibility of diversification at the most basic productive level becomes a mirage, as local producers concentrate on primary production, which brings immediate earnings germane for subsistence.

3 Rural Producers in the Urban Marketing Framework

The pivotal position of rural producers in the survival of urban areas cannot be over emphasized. This has been the situation even in pre-colonial Nigeria when rural areas served as the 'economic back-bone' of societies. The socio-economic arrangement was such that while the urban served as both, home and administrative headquarters, the rural served as centre of production (especially agricultural) and supplied the urban out of its surpluses (Olutayo, forthcoming).

The colonial economic structure however brought about some degree of social change as production was modified from subsistence to cash cropping, essentially, in line with the colonial development policy. As this signalled a new beginning in rural production for urban demand, taxation also served as a catalyst for the integration of the rural population into the money economy. The taxes imposed could only be paid by producing and exchanging what was required by the colonial entrepreneur. And since a lot of the rural production had little commercial value in the new urban market, production had to change to what was required in the urban market and in international markets. This explains the massive production of cocoa and other export crops during the colonial period. Cocoa in particular became so entrenched in the socio-economic structure that south-western Nigeria became a predominant producer and was referred to as Nigeria's cocoa belt (see figure 2). At this stage, the cocoa beans produced were not meant to be processed for local consumption but destined primarily for industries abroad. Thus, the nation was constrained to an international division of labour which limited expertise only to primary production.

Figure 2: Map of Nigeria Showing South-Western Region (Old Cocoa Belt)

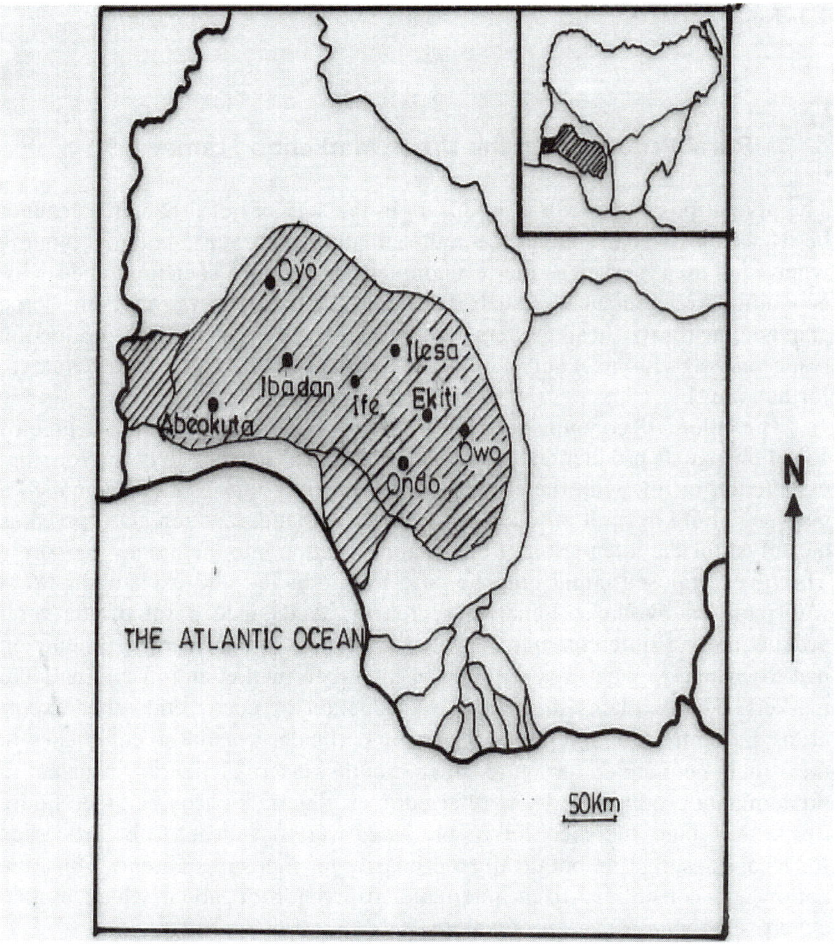

Source: Authors presentation.

After independence, the urban biased marketing framework persisted wherein rural farmers were 'forced' to sell their products to survive in the money economy. And with the oil boom, farmers were further relegated, even when their 'cash crops' formed the basis of 'development' before and during the earlier parts of the inflow of oil revenue. When government's focus of attention shifted to oil, cocoa production declined substantially while local producers suffered under fluctuating international pricing. Figure 3, shows that Nigeria's cocoa production plummeted from the 1970s on, apparently due to what has been termed the 'oil curse', to an all-time low in the mid-1980s. It subsequently increased after the implementation of the SAP in 1986, reaching its peak in the 1990s before plummeting again.

Figure 3: Nigeria's Cocoa Production in Tons 1960-2002

Source: Central Bank of Nigeria (2002): 257.

However, in view of the potential positive contribution increased cocoa production could make to Nigeria's economy, the Federal Government of Nigeria, in conjunction with 14 cocoa producing states in the country, launched the Cocoa Rebirth Initiative in February, 2005 (Federal Republic of Nigeria 2005:3). The Cocoa Rebirth Initiative, which is discussed in section 5, is expected to enhance cocoa production, not only in the old western cocoa belt but in all 14 cocoa producing states (see figure 4). This attests to the prime place of cocoa in the Nigerian economy.

Figure 4: Map of Nigeria Showing Fourteen Cocoa Producing States

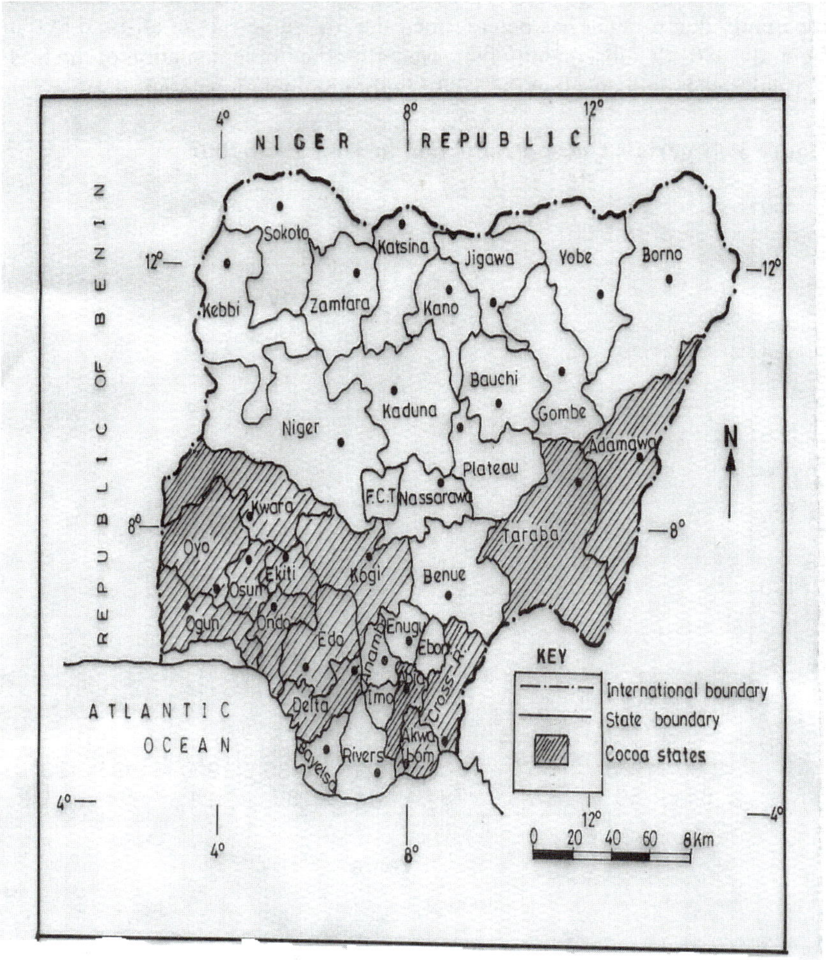

Source: Authors presentation using the information contained in the Federal Republic of Nigeria (2005): 18.

4 Agricultural Policy, Cocoa Production and Marketing in Nigeria

In as much as Nigeria strives to enhance development for the betterment of its citizens, its development policy cannot be isolated from its colonial and post-colonial relations. Principally, the colonial policy was based on agricultural exports to the developed world. It was expected that the revenue extracted from the sale of agricultural products would be invested in the development of the country. It was expected that the development of the country will empower the people, increase trade with Great Britain and prepare Nigeria for self-government. To achieve this, infrastructural development such as the constructions of roads, hospitals, water supply and schools among others were implemented. Therefore, development boards such as the Nigeria Local Development Board (NLDB), the Western Region Development Board (WRDB) and Western Region Production Development Board (WRPDB) were put into place by the middle of the 20th century in order to assist the colonial development policy. Expectedly, the policy emphasis of these boards was to enhance local production of export crops through loans and incentives, for onward transportation to international market (Olutayo 1991:311-319).

Of all export crops, cocoa became vital, both for Nigeria's economy and for international markets. Hence, the production and marketing of cocoa in colonial Nigeria became an issue of primary importance when its supply was threatened by the 2nd World War. This led to the establishment of the Cocoa Marketing Board in 1947 with the main purpose of securing cocoa exports in order to secure revenue for the general administration and development of Nigeria and to meet the demands of British industries and consumers. The cocoa board was responsible for the marketing of Nigerian cocoa and was also empowered to fix local purchasing prices. Since the board fixed a low purchasing price, it made surplus profit while local producers suffered under harsh economic condition. Whereas the guiding principle for extracting surplus revenue from cocoa, through low pricing was to invest the surplus in development, the urban biased development policy effectively bypassed the rural inhabitants (who were the direct producers of the 'wealth') from development. The situation was further compounded with the absence of a conducive environment for domestic processing. Thus, domestic value addition did not take place and local producers had to accept what they were offered since they were at the risk of losing all due to the nature of their crops.

This situation continued during the post independence period since government development programs still depended on finance extracted from rural farmers. Particularly, the bulk of revenue of the South-Western Region came from agricultural products. According to Olatunbosun (1975: 22), about 96 percent of export duties paid to the Nigerian government between 1964 and 1971 came from products under the auspices of the Marketing Board which was in charge of the sales of cocoa and some other export crops (see table 3).

Table 3: The Contribution of the Marketing Board to National Revenues 1964-1971 (Million Naira)

Year	Total Customs & Excise Duties	Total Export Duties	Total Export Duties arising from Marketing Board products	Total Excise Duty	Total Federal & State Revenue
1964/65	116.8	29.6	26.4	27.2	330.4
1965/66	121.6	30.2	25.0	43.2	358.0
1966/67	217.4	28.0	26.6	72.0	325.2
1967/68	172.4	30.0	28.8	32.6	304.8
1968/69	202.4	29.6	28.4	66.4	427.0
1969/70	254.0	39.4	38.4	76.0	441.0
1970/71	292.6	44.0	42.4	108.4	493.0
TOTAL	**1,377.2**	**230.8**	**220.0**	**425.8**	**2,679.4**

Source: Olatunbosun (1975): 23.

As stated earlier, in spite of the successes made in agricultural production and its contribution to government finance, agricultural production massively declined from 1970 on as a result of the oil boom. As table 4 below shows, the contribution of non-oil production to national revenue declined from 73.7 percent in 1970 to as low as 17.9 percent just four years later. Since then, the contribution of non-oil products to national revenue has remained largely below 30 percent with the most recent available data showing just 19.4 percent in 2003.

Table 4: Government Revenue from 1970-2003 (in Million Naira)

Government Revenue1970-2003 in Million Naira					
Year	**Total Federally Collected Revenue**	**Oil Revenue**	**% of Total**	**Non-Oil Revenue**	**% of Total**
1970	634	166.6	26.3	467.4	73.7
1971	1168.8	510.1	43.6	658.7	56.4
1972	1405.1	764.3	54.4	640.8	45.6
1973	1695.3	1016	59.9	679.3	40.1
1974	4537.4	3724	82.1	813.4	17.9
1975	5514.7	4271.5	77.5	1243.2	22.5
1976	6765.9	5365.2	79.3	1400.7	20.7
1977	8042.4	6080.6	75.6	1961.8	24.4
1978	7371	4555.8	61.8	2815.2	38.2
1979	10912.4	8880.8	81.4	2031.6	18.6
1980	15233.5	12353.3	81.1	2880.2	18.9
1981	13290.5	8564.4	64.4	4726.1	35.6
1982	11433.7	7814.9	68.3	3618.8	31.7
1983	10508.7	7253	69.0	3255.7	31.0
1984	11253.3	8269.2	73.5	2984.1	26.5
1985	15050.4	10923.7	72.6	4126.7	27.4
1986	12595.8	8107.3	64.4	4488.5	35.6
1987	25380.6	19027	75.0	6353.6	25.0
1988	27596.7	19831.7	71.9	7765	28.1
1989	53870.4	39130.5	72.6	14739.9	27.4
1990	98102.4	71887.1	73.3	26215.3	26.7
1991	100991.6	82666.4	81.9	18325.2	18.1
1992	190453.2	164078.1	86.2	26375.1	13.8
1993	192769.4	162102.4	84.1	30667	15.9
1994	201910.8	160192.4	79.3	41718.4	20.7
1995	459987.3	324547.6	70.6	135439.7	29.4
1996	520190	408783	78.6	111407	21.4
1997	582811.1	416811.1	71.5	166000	28.5
1998	463608.8	324311.2	70.0	139297.6	30.0

Continuation on next page.

Continuation of Table 4 from previous page.

Year	Total Federally Collected Revenue	Oil Revenue	% of Total	Non-Oil Revenue	% of Total
1999	949187.9	724422.5	76.3	224765.4	23.7
2000	1906160	1591676	83.5	314483.9	16.5
2001	2231533	1707563	76.5	523970.1	23.5
2002	1731838	1230851	71.1	500986.3	28.9
2003	2575096	2074281	80.6	500815.3	19.4

Sources: Central Bank of Nigeria (2002: 203-209 and 2003:13).

Notwithstanding the declining contribution of agriculture to Nigeria's revenue structure, it is on record that successive governments at the federal level have implemented programs targeted at enhancing agricultural production and rural development. The regime of General Gowon came up with the National Accelerated Food Production Programme (NAFPP) in 1975 (Idachaba 2000:13-19). It entailed government's direct involvement in food production so as to arrest the escalating prices of food crops. Initially, it seemed a policy with high prospects of success but General Gowon was toppled before the NAFPP could be successfully implemented. Thus, the NAFPP suffered from the unwillingness of the succeeding military regime of General Murtala Mohammed to support the program of the regime it had condemned. General Mohammed did not implement another regulative agricultural development policy before he was assassinated in 1976. His successor, General Obasanjo, subsequently introduced the Operation Feed the Nation (OFN).

Like the NAFPP, the OFN was intended to increase the volume of agricultural products. It sought to achieve this through incentives such as providing subsidies on fertilizers and other farm implements and facilities. However, the success of the OFN ended with the transition to civil rule in 1979. The government of President Sheu Shagari simply discontinued it in favour of another program, named the Green Revolution Programme (GRP) in 1980. Just like the programs earlier, its prime target was increased agricultural production. But once again, it had to start afresh because the reigning regime would rather have its own program and not the sustenance of the one implemented by a previous regime. This lasted until 1983 when the civilian government was overthrown. By 1986, with the implementation of the Structural Adjustment Programme (SAP), due to economic decline and international pressure, development policy was on economic deregulation and the withdrawal of government from direct agricultural production and marketing. This implicated the closure of the Cocoa Marketing Board alongside other national agricultural marketing boards and thenceforth, the non-controlled involvement of the private sector in agricultural production, processing and marketing (Federal Republic of Nigeria 2005: 12).

Indeed, the implementation of the SAP reforms and the closure of the Cocoa Marketing Board were supposed to enhance the income of local producers and to increase production, processing and marketing in Nigeria The reverse was however the case. Rather, the reform that set free market forces and eliminated state control created a class of indigenous entrepreneurs who were interested in maximizing their profits without necessarily giving adequate consideration to standards. These entrepreneurs emerged as dealers who purchased cocoa from local farmers for onward sale to national and multinational corporations.

Since emphasis has been on the profit that accrues to cocoa dealers, little or nothing has been done to possibly process for local consumption. And thus, attention has been taken away from the potential market and profit, which may be gained by processing cocoa in Nigeria, towards profit that accrues to the dealers instantly. Furthermore, since the primary concern of the inexperienced dealers was to secure as much cocoa as possible for sale, the need for high quality and well fermented cocoa was de-emphasized. As a result, a large quantity of cocoa could not be exported due to poor quality (Federal Government of Nigeria 2005: 12, International Cocoa Organization 2001).

Cocoa production decreased from 306,000 tons in 1993 to 165,000 tons in 1999 as a result of international price declines (Central Bank of Nigeria 2002: 257). This contributed to the need to make the revitalisation of Nigeria's cocoa industry a state policy, with the inauguration of the National Cocoa Development Committee (NCDC).

5 The Cocoa Rebirth Initiative

The 30 members National Cocoa Development Committee (NCDC) was inaugurated on 2nd December 1999. The membership cuts across certain cocoa stakeholders representing the 14 cocoa producing states, cocoa farmers, processors and marketers as well as the Federal Ministries of Agriculture and the Federal Ministries of Rural Development and Commerce. Also represented are the Central Bank of Nigeria and the Cocoa Research Institute of Nigeria (Federal Government of Nigeria 2005:18). The Committee has the goal of increasing cocoa production per annum to 320,000 metric tons in the short term and 600,000 metric tons per annum in the long run (Federal Republic of Nigeria 2005:18). Though the NCDC did not clearly state what it means by 'short term' and 'long run', it however, intends achieving its aims through the implementation of the *Cocoa Rebirth Blueprint*[1] which states:

- "Increased local consumption would reduce the quantity going into the international market and bring about a concomitant increase in price.
- Value addition which involves alternative utilization of cocoa beans and of cocoa by-products and the general cocoa economy.
- Sensitization and training of cocoa farmers to bring out the best in varieties planted, tree management, good quality formulation, drying, soil management and others.
- Rehabilitation and regeneration of old moribund cocoa tree/plantations will arrest dwindling harvest outputs.
- Soil rejuvenation research will help to bring exhausted/marginal cocoa soils back to life.
- Youth attraction into cocoa farming is needed for replacement of the current ageing generation of farmers.
- National cocoa survey would give state of plantations, production figures, variety grown, fermentation system, etc on state by state basis.
- An aggressive cocoa breeding program is needed for clones which are disease resistant."

In order to ensure the successful implementation of its blueprint, NCDC is divided into seven sub-committees including:

(a) Inputs Procurement;
(b) Inputs distribution;
(c) Sensitization and Training;
(d) Monitoring and Evaluation;
(e) Regeneration and Rehabilitation of Cocoa;
(f) Alternative uses of Cocoa and Alternative Sources of Funding NCDC;
(g) Organization and Mobilization of Cocoa Farmers.

Out of these seven sub-committees, the Cocoa Rebirth Handbook discusses the activities of only four sub-committees (see Federal Government of

---

1 Federal Government of Nigeria (2005): 28.

Nigeria 2005: 22-23). These include the Regeneration and Rehabilitation Subcommittee, which intends to put in place 7,000 ha of cocoa comprising of both new planting and replanting schemes. The Subcommittee on the Alternative Uses of Cocoa has identified 20 cocoa products developed by the Cocoa Research Institute of Nigeria (CRIN). These products include cocoa bread, cocoa juice, cocoa cola, coca toffee, cocoa custard, cocoa cake, cocoa biscuit, cocoa wine, milk cocoa and coffee chocolate. Others include cola chocolate, cashew chocolate, CRIN vita (a beverage formulation), liquid detergent, body cream, hair shampoo, soichoco and choco-gari (a formulation of cocoa and cassava chips), black soap and cocoa husk-based livestock feeds (Federal Republic of Nigeria 2005: 24-27).

Indeed, this is a welcome development. Expectedly these products should be embraced by Nigerian manufacturers provided they are certified fit for consumption by the National Agency for Food and Drug Control (NAFDAC). It can be expected that the products would enjoy large patronage as they are modified variants of commodities which are highly consumed in Nigeria. However, it is unfortunate that nothing tangible seems to have been achieved so far. The products are not yet on the market, nor is there any proof that they have been certified by NAFDAC. In order to possibly diversify cocoa production and to achieve the availability of these products there is the need for public-private partnerships so that funds could be secured from the private sector for the commercialization of the products engineered by the Cocoa Research Institute of Nigeria (CRIN). Since the products potentially stand the chance of wide patronage, domestic entrepreneurs should be interested in undertaking investments in the venture.

The Subcommittee on Organization and Mobilization intends to mobilise cocoa farmers to establish small scale industries and to set-up cooperative societies and the Subcommittee on Sensitization and Trading focuses its attention on the training of farmers. Between June and August 2004, it trained 2,795 farmers in 13 out of the 14 cocoa producing states on improved techniques of cocoa planting and management.

The activities of the NCDC have resulted in increased cocoa production , raising from 249,782 metric tons in 2001 to 266,177.54 metric tons in 2002 and 281,837.63 metric tons in 2003 (Federal Government of Nigeria 2005: 21). However, this represents only a marginal increment if one considers the set goal of increasing cocoa production to 320,000 and 600,000 metric tons in the short run and long run respectively. The NCDC has laudable goals but its composition and strategy seem faulty. It utilizes a top-bottom approach in the composition, formulation and implementation of its programs taking a highly centralized nomenclature and nature. The National Cocoa Development Committee (NCDC) membership includes 30 individuals, with at least

18 of them being top government officials while the remaining 12 are representatives of cocoa associations. These 12 individuals actually represent a collection of elite cocoa dealers and few rich farmers while the majority of local farmers, who produce about 90 percent of the total cocoa output and whose interest ought to be protected in order to achieve the goals of NCDC and to ensure value addition through processing, are not represented by the NCDC (International Cocoa Association 2000). Thus more needs to be done in order to enhance commercial production, marketability (both domestic and foreign, especially in this age of globalisation) and fair pricing for local producers to be well compensated for their efforts while at the same time erasing the view of farming as a wretched profession reserved for illiterates in Nigeria's rural social structure. It is then, that the target population of youths that needs to replace ageing farmers will be attracted to the profession. This may be achieved using the recommended below.

6 Policy Recommendations: A Bottom-Up Approach

The call and quest for modernization may be instrumental for the development of Nigeria after all. This may be true provided modernization is allowed its real meaning. It is good to modernize. It pays to make things suitable for present day use by coming up to date. However, 'modernization' may not be in terms of breaking down the family system and concentration in the export of primary products. Modernization is only effective if it evolves in response to the challenges posed by the environment. This is because societies actually develop when they interact with their social and physical environments. When doing this, they identify impediments that stand against their survival and devise means of overcoming these impediments by developing relevant ideas, schemes, technology, etc.

The challenge presently facing the Nigerian social structure is encapsulated in the fact that about 70 percent of the Nigerian population live in absolute poverty (that is, under US$ 1 per day) while the economy continually concentrates on the export of one primary product namely crude oil. This paper calls for the domestication of the modernization idea. Hence, 'modernization' would only be beneficial if it prioritizes the welfare of the generality of the people and not the concentration of capital in few hands and the specialization of primary goods production. It is therefore proper to devise means of processing raw materials for domestic consumption and for exports in order to be freed from the trap of specialization in primary products.

In relation to cocoa, which potentially stands as a major contributor to Nigeria's development, modernization should be seen as a way of improving the situation by actively involving local producers in the production, processing and marketing of cocoa. This may be achieved by creating local cocoa marketing boards on a ward/community basis. Such boards are to constitute indigenous farmers in cooperatives (using the indigenous networks) around cocoa production. They should also be encouraged to liaise with colleges of technology, polytechnics and universities in order to enhance cocoa production and processing. Furthermore, and in view of the fact that cocoa products are consumed locally, priority should be given to domestic processing. Each local marketing board should be responsible for the grading of cocoa on the basis of international standards. In order to achieve this, the Standards Organization of Nigeria (SON) should assist local marketing boards to meet international standards. It is expected that, as cocoa quality improves, local producers will attract more income from their products as demand for increases. Linkages with domestic research institutes could further enhance this diversification drive.

Though these ideas are not in themselves novel, they involve a reengineering of the existing social structure. This would involve the adaptation of imported technological knowledge, acquired from formal educational institutions, to the indigenous social structure through an understanding of indigenous ways of life. As such, existing rural social networks and the knowledge deriving there-from become of utmost importance for improvement. The history of industrial Europe bears witness to the fact that an understanding of the internal dynamics of social relations and a conscious effort to critically assess and improve upon them constituted an important framework for the development of the welfare system in the 1950s. Fortunately, the rural social structures in Nigeria still thrive on indigenous knowledge structures, which have proved indispensable even for those in urban areas. A very relevant example in this instance is the Esusu network around which economic survival hinges. Through this Esusu network, for instance, cooperatives may be established around production, processing and marketing. Students and pupils should learn about these indigenous knowledge structures, including indigenous production, processing and marketing. Indeed, this indigenous knowledge should be part of their curriculum as it would entail being able to solve environmental survival techniques and developing relevant instruments. Of utmost significance is the need for government policy instrument in this educational endeavour. Perhaps of equal importance is the development of a proper infrastructure such as good road networks and easy access to credits. Moreover, it is important to protect farmers in the market place by involving them in processing activities and the marketing of cocoa.

The realization of this bottom-up approach for development will be feasible only when major stakeholders are effectively brought together as equal partners. The government has to see itself as a representative of the common interests of all, but, most importantly, of the local farmers. Hence, the government should create an enabling environment for the rural farmers to form the cooperatives and to protect them against the exploitative tendencies of local dealers in the market place. Therefore, the practice in which some non-farmers constitute themselves as "shop-owners" and fix prices should be discouraged. Cooperating farmers should be purposely allocated shops by the local governments in charge. To ensure this, civil society organizations need to be empowered to sensitize the farmers to form cooperatives and create linkages, along with the government and with relevant academic institutions in order to improve on the existing indigenous technologies. Improved indigenous technologies can evolve when fairs are organized among the different institutions of learning in association with the wards within which they are located. In fact, this is also where private sector participation is very apt. Entrepreneurs should be the harbingers of technology development and their participation in this venture is to their ultimate advantage since it improves product technology and quality, thus raising the product price. Entrepreneurs should be encouraged to invest into cocoa diversification through tax incentives and through low interest rates on loans. It is expected that via these measures Nigeria will gradually develop its technological base, not only for cocoa but also for other sectors. Nonetheless, it may be preferable that such entrepreneurs should be direct stakeholders in the areas where these technologies are needed, so that entrepreneurs who are interested in the welfare of local producers and the development of rural area emerge.

References

Aigbokan, Ben (2001): "Resuscitating agricultural production (cocoa, cotton, groundnuts, palm oil, rubber, etc) for exports", online: http://216.239.59.104/search?q=cache:_TvWIydq7eIJ:www.cenbank.org/OUT/PUBLICATIONS/OCCASIONALPAPERS/RD/2001/OWE-01-6.PDF+Cocoa+exports+in+nigeria&hl=en, date accessed 21 July 2005.

Ajayi, S.I. and Oyejide A.A. (1974): "The role of cocoa in Nigeria's economic development", in: Kotey, R.A., Okali, C.O. and Rourke, B.E. (eds): The economics of cocoa production and marketing, Proceedings of Cocoa Economics Research Conference Legon, April 1973, Legon: Institute of Statistical, Social and Economic Research, University of Legon, pp. 225-235.

Bass, Hans (2005): "Structural problems of West African exports and options for Improvements". In: Wohlmuth, Karl et al. (Eds.): Africa - Escaping the Primary Commodities Dilemma, African Development Perspectives Yearbook, vol. 11, 2005/2006. Lit-Verlag: Münster and Hamburg, pp. 245-263.

Buren, Linda (2001): "Economy: Africa South of the Sahara", London: Europa Publications, pp. 876-904.

Central Bank of Nigeria (2002): "Statistical bulletin", Volume 13, Abuja: Central Bank of Nigeria.

Central Bank of Nigeria (2003): "Annual report and statement of account for the year ended 31st December", 2003, Abuja: Central Bank of Nigeria.

Daramola, A. G. and Okunola J.O. (1999): "Government policy on cocoa processing in Nigeria: Implication for Production and Trade in Proceedings of the International Cocoa Research Conference", Salvador, Bahia Basil, 17-23 Nov 1999, pp. 1079-1085.

Ekong, Ekong (2003): "An introduction to rural sociology", Uyo: Dove Educational Publishers.

FAO (Food and Agriculture Organization) (1964): "Cocoa statistics", Rome: Food and Agriculture Organisation of the United Nations, April 7.

FAO (Food and Agriculture Organization) (1975): "Cocoa statistics", Rome: Food and Agriculture Organization of the United Nations, January 18.

Federal Republic of Nigeria (2005): "Cocoa Rebirth Handbook", Abuja: Federal Republic of Nigeria.

Idachaba, Francis (2000): "Topical issues in Nigerian agriculture: Desirable and workable agricultural policies for Nigeria in the first decade of the 21st century", Department of Agricultural Economics, Ibadan: University of Ibadan.

International Cocoa Association (2000): "How many smallholders are there worldwide producing cocoa? What proportion of cocoa is produced by smallholders?" Online: http://www.icco.org/questions/smallholders.htm, date accessed March 9 2006.

International Cocoa Organization (2001): "What are the consequences of liberalization on the quality of cocoa?" Online: http://www.icco.org/questions/liberalisation.htm, date accessed March 9 2006.

Kaplinsky, Raphael (2004): "Competition policy and the global coffee and cocoa value chains", online: http://www.ids.ac.uk/ids/global/pdfs/Rkaplinskycocoa-coffee05.pdf, date accessed April 30 2006.

Nigeria Cocoa Board (1982): "Annual bulletin of statistics on cocoa, coffee and tea", Ibadan: Nigeria Cocoa Board.

Olatunbosun, Dupe (1975): "Nigeria's neglected rural majority", Ibadan: Oxford University Press.

Olayemi, J.K. (1974): "Cost and returns to cocoa and alternative crops in western Nigeria", in: Kotey, R.A., Okali, C.O. and Rourke, B.E. (eds): The economics of cocoa production and marketing, Proceedings of Cocoa Economics Research Conference Legon, April 1973, Legon: Institute of Statistical, Social and Economic Research, University of Legon, pp. 47-58.

Olutayo, Olanrewaju Akinpelu (1991): "The development of underdevelopment: Rural economy of colonial South Western Nigeria", a Ph.D. thesis submitted to the Department of Sociology, Faculty of the Social Sciences, University of Ibadan, Ibadan, Nigeria.

Olutayo, Olanrewaju Akinpelu (forthcoming): "Rural social relations and Africa's development". Manuscript to be published in: Ilorin Journal of Sociology.

Oxfam (2004): "Research on government involvement and support to agriculture in the Middle-Belt of Nigeria", Abuja: Oxfam GB (unpublished).

The Diversification Potential of Cassava in the Nigerian Economy

Oliver Chinedu Ujah

1 Introduction

Despite the dismal economic growth throughout much of the 1990s, Nigeria's return to democracy in 1999 has begun to boost economic recovery and growth. The real gross domestic product (real GDP) has increased faster than ever since 1991 when it was 4.7 per cent. The real GDP increased from 3.83 percent in 2000 to 4.21 percent in 2001 and to about 10 percent in 2003, as against the population growth of about 2.8 per cent (CBN, 2003: 31; FGN, 2004: 2). Much of Nigeria's economic growth, in the last four decades, has been driven by crude oil. Indeed, the boom-burst economic cycle experienced over these years is directly related to Nigeria's over-dependence on crude oil exports.

Generating a stronger and stable economic growth requires that the oil-dominated economy (in terms of revenues) of Nigeria has to be diversified in order to minimize the impact of changes (shocks) in the crude oil industry. Nigeria hopes to achieve this by promoting increased production in the non-oil sector of the economy. In 2002-2003, agriculture contributed about 50 per cent to the country's GDP (Eboh, et al. 2004: 7), and the crop's sub-sector contributed about 22.68 per cent to the Agricultural GDP (30.80 per cent) in 2003 (CBN, 2003: 136). In 2004 , the share of the agricultural sector stood at 31.20 per cent with the crops sub-sector contributing about 26.08 per cent (CBN, 2004: 147).

Nigeria's quest for achieving a growth rate of about 7 per cent by 2007 hinges on the increased economic activity in the non-oil sector. Diversification of the economy while emphasizing poverty reduction is one of the four main foci of Nigeria's policy reforms. Agriculture has been identified as the priority non-oil sector, but the current budgetary allocation of only 2% (out of the 1.6 trillion naira) to the sector, as proposed in the 2005 budget presented to the National Assembly on 12th of October 2004 by President

Olusegun Obasanjo, negates this notion. The main strategy adopted by the government is the provision of an enabling environment that will include private sector initiatives in the production of staples such as cassava, rice, maize, etc. Cassava (Manihot esculenta crantz) is the staple food for many tropical countries, especially Nigeria. Cassava thrives well in Nigeria; it is widely consumed, and it has potentials for export. Cassava starch, chips and pellets are products of interest in the international market. Nigeria is the largest producer of cassava in the world followed by Brazil, but Thailand is the leading exporter of the commodity as Nigeria consumes most of the cassava locally. Nigeria's cassava has remained on the export prohibition list until 2004 when it was removed from this list.

Nigeria's total production of cassava, if processed into "garri" (a fermented, toasted, dried and granular product, and a major staple food in Nigeria), is capable of generating about US$ 5 billion (in export) annually according to government sources. The current level of production of cassava per annum in Nigeria is estimated at 34 million tons. This achievement is attributable to the adoption of high-yielding varieties and better processing techniques. Following President Obasanjo's cassava initiative (Initiative on Cassava Improvement, Utilization and Commercialization, especially Export in 2002) on cassava production and export (Olori, 2002: 1; and Bamiyo, 2003: B29), which has led to the recognition of the crop as a strategic crop that can become a panacea for the nation's economic recovery, Nigeria hopes to export about US$ 5 billion worth of cassava by 2007 (Waziri, 2004: 58). Nigeria hopes to achieve this through a short-term approach, involving the establishment of 600 cassava processing centers in the 26 cassava-producing states where it can turn raw cassava into flakes, chips and other value adding products.

The National Economic Empowerment and Development Strategy (NEEDS), recently launched by the Federal Government of Nigeria in May 2004, targets a minimum annual growth rate of 6 per cent per annum in agriculture and a value of about US$ 3 billion in agricultural exports, a major component of which will be cassava by 2007 (NPC, 2004: 69). Within the context of NEEDS and given the dominant role of agriculture in the Nigerian economy (in terms of its contribution to GDP), there is need for analyses of the incentives (prices, subsidies, etc); trends of production, yield, as well as cultivated and harvested areas; export values; technologies; constraints and/or leakages in the "cassava pipeline" (including lack of information on informal trade and market exchanges, especially across the borders); and opportunities in the cassava sub-sector. This is critical given cassava's prospects for food security and poverty alleviation, supply of industrial raw materials, and overall economic growth. This is the gap this paper hopes to fill.

The remaining part of this paper is structured into three major sections. Section 2 x-rays Nigeria's agricultural policy landscape; importance of cassava to Nigeria; Nigeria's cassava experience and trends; gender and research issues in cassava; and Nigeria's local cassava marketing channels and prospects. Section 3 examines Nigeria's export potentials in cassava, while Section 4 draws some policy conclusions and makes some recommendations.

2 Nigeria's Agricultural Sector Policies and an Outlook on Cassava

2.1 Agricultural Sector Policy

The first Nigerian Agricultural Policy (NAP) came into effect in 1988 and was targeted at improving the sector so as to obtain the growth rate required to propel general growth in the entire economy. The main features of that policy included the evolution of strategies that should ensure sufficiency and improvement of the level of technical and economic efficiency in food production; reduction in risks and uncertainties; a unified and all-inclusive extension delivery system; promotion of agro-allied industries; provision of rural infrastructure, rural banking, primary healthcare, cottage industries; etc.

In the past five years, however, the experience gained in the implementation of the agricultural policy over the years and the recent trends in agricultural development worldwide have necessitated the formulation of more focused sub-sector policies. The sub-sector policies include the Land Resources Policy that guides a sustainable use of agricultural lands; the National Agricultural Mechanization Policy; the National Cooperative Development Policy; and the National Seed Policy that assigns primary responsibility for commercial seed supply to the private sector. These sub-sector policies are enshrined in the new policy thrust on agriculture laid down in the document of the Obasanjo administration that was introduced in 2001. After a close review of strategies and instruments previously adopted in the period of the first NAP, the Obasanjo administration evolved new strategies for laying a solid foundation for a sustained increase in agricultural productivity and for enhancing output that was necessary for growth.

The key objectives and strategies of the New Nigerian Agricultural Plan - 2001 can be seen in table 1 (the table shows the policy areas, the objectives, and the action plans for the implementation of the new agricultural plan) below. The details of this new plan reveal that elements of state-led development continue in Nigeria. The public sector will dominate research and extension services, and will produce some inputs such as animal vaccine and agro-chemicals in collaboration with the private sector. There is also reference to re-establishing, in cooperation with the private sector, marketing companies for agricultural commodities.

Table 1: New Nigeria Agricultural Plan

Policy areas	Objectives	Action plans
Commodity pricing policy	Remunerative prices and incomes for farmers	Market information and markets; making operational Multi-Commodity Development and Marketing Companies
Agricultural trade policy	Promotion of agricultural exports and import substitution	Continuation of existing policies as modified by WTO accession; Exploitation of green box opportunities
Exchange rate	Realignment of exchange rate	Full implementation of exchange regulations
Agricultural land	Nationally acceptable land tenure system optimizing use of land	Implementation of the New Land Policy to promote sustainable use of land
Food production increase	Food self-sufficiency; technical and economic efficiency in food production	A wide range of subsidy schemes, and public sector investments
Industrial raw material crops	Increase the supply of raw materials to agro-processors	Strengthening the National Agricultural Industrial Crop Production Program
Extension service	Creation of an effective national extension service	Integration of the national extension service with the Agricultural Development Projects (ADPs) extension system
Agricultural credit	Achieve availability and accessibility of credit at affordable rates for profitable agriculture	Merger of the NACB and PBN Regulation and supervision of NBFIs
Agricultural insurance	Protection of farmers against natural hazards	Insurance coverage to be extended to 50% of the farmers

Continuation on next page.

Continuation of table 1 from previous page.

Policy areas	Objectives	Action plans
Agricultural produce marketing	Effective distribution of produce to stabilize supply and price	Promotion of an organized marketing system through a functional commodity exchange and the operation of a buyer of last resort mechanism through Commodity Development Companies that are approved by the Government
Agricultural commodity storage	Reduction of intra- and inter-seasonal price variability for food security	Establishment of a national strategic food reserve through the encouragement of a State Buffer Stock Storage Program
Agricultural commodity processing	Accelerated development of processing to increase value added and to reduce losses of perishables	Promotion of Small and Medium Enterprises (SMEs)
Agricultural research	Development of high yielding production materials and of appropriate technologies	Upgrading of laboratories and other facilities of research institutes, and closer collaboration with universities
Agricultural mechanization	Increased use of mechanical power in farming	A zero tariff on agricultural machinery; expansion of NCAM as a leasing center for machinery
Rural infrastructure	Improvement of quality of life and tapping resources of the rural areas	Public investment in rural water supply, markets, electrification, communications, and transport

Source: DFID, 2003.

Given the high priority placed on agriculture (both for poverty reduction in the rural areas, and for the improvement of the economy generally) in the

Nigerian economic policy (1999 – 2003), the government has concentrated on sectors where the country has a comparative advantage and by which strategy it hopes to change the nature of Nigeria's exports from primary to processed and manufactured goods. This priority placed on agriculture is understandable, given the leading role of the sector in the nation's economy in terms of its contribution to national output, GDP, and the employment of labour. The government has also encouraged, through some of its agencies, the establishment of cooperatives groups that would help to organize the activities of cassava producers and processors. Some of the notable groups are the Cassava Growers Association (CGA) and the Cassava Processors Association of Nigeria (CAPAN); they are located in different states of the country.

Currently, only the NEEDS document (NPC, 2004), as a policy document, gives emphasis on cassava, unlike the previous agricultural policy documents that are quite general and not specific to individual crops. However, the NEEDS document is silent on the roadmap towards achieving its cassava objectives. This highlights the need for a comprehensive cassava policy, not just outlining an ordinary initiative.

2.2 Why Cassava?

Cassava is one of the most important crops in Nigeria, playing a dominant role in the rural economy, especially in the Southern agro-ecological zones, and it is increasingly gaining importance in other parts of the country (FMANR, 2004: 4). Cassava is also an input in the production processes of over twenty different products that are widely consumed by over 70 per cent of the Nigerian population (Bamiyo, 2004: B 29). Small-scale farmers produce cassava largely by using rudimentary implements; these farmers have an average land holding of less than two hectares and produce with an abundant family labour. Almost all the cassava produced in Nigeria is used for human consumption, and less than 5 per cent is used in industries. In the year 2000, 90 per cent of the total cassava production was used as food, and the balance was used as livestock feed (Nweke, 2004a: 82). Cassava is also the most important staple in terms of calories consumed.

Cassava is important, not just as food crop (a powerful poverty fighter in Nigeria), but even more so as a major source of income for producing households. As a cash crop, cassava generates cash income for the largest number of households (in comparison with other staples), contributing positively to poverty alleviation. For example, in 2002, cassava cash income accrued, as follows, to more households than that of alternative staples such as yam and maize: 40 per cent of COSCA (Collaborative Study of Cassava in Africa) households earned cash income from cassava; maize, 35 per cent; and yam, 24 per cent. As a food crop, cassava fits well into the farming systems of smallholder farmers in Nigeria because it is available all the year round, therefore, providing household food security. Compared to grains, cassava in more tolerant to low soil fertility, and more resistant to drought, pests, and diseases. Moreover, cassava roots store well in the ground for months after maturity, reducing storage problems.

Cassava has many uses. It is an important source of ethanol, industrial starch (modified and unmodified) and glucoses, glue, etc. Cassava starch and its derivatives have over 58 uses (Agu, 2004a: 16), and are used extensively in food and non-food industries. In food and pharmaceutical industries, starch is a thickener in gravies, baby foods, soups, sausages; filler in tablets, capsules, food and other pharmaceutical products; concentrate in soft drinks production, bakery and confectionery (as a partial replacement, up to 20 percent, of wheat flour); sweetener in commercial production of fructose, maltose caramel, glucose and monosodium glutamate (MSG); and dextrin for adhesive manufacture for use in footwear, wood paper, packaging and other industries. In fact, the use of cassava and cassava derivatives is spread over food, beverage, animal, plastic, building, laundry and pharmaceutical industries, as well as animal feeds.

The main cassava belts of Nigeria are the south-eastern (Abia, Anambra, Ebonyi, Enugu and Imo States), south-south (Akwa Ibom, Bayelsa, Cross River, Delta, Edo and Rivers States), south-western (Ekiti, Lagos, Ogun, Ondo, Osun and Oyo States) and the central zones (Benue, Kogi, Kwara, Nassarawa, Niger and Plateau States, plus the Federal Capital Territory, Abuja) (see figure 1 showing the map of Nigeria with all the component states), even though over four-fifth of the cultivable land area of Nigeria is suitable for cassava growing. According to the International Institute of Tropical Agriculture (IITA), Benue and Kogi States in the central zone are the largest producers of Cassava (IFAD and FAO, 2004: 4). Cassava is typically inter-cropped (mix-cropped) as the main crop, while rotation and fallow systems are the traditional systems used by the farmers to maintain soil fertility. However, population pressure has resulted in reduced fallow, continuous cropping, and reduced soil fertility.

Figure 1: Map of Nigeria

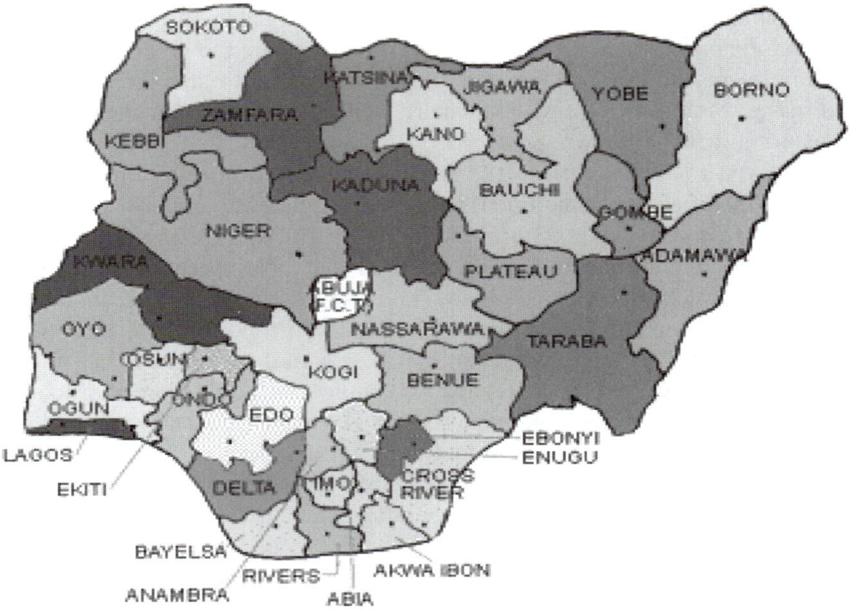

Source: *http:*www.motherlandnigeria.com/geography.htm.

2.3 Nigeria's Cassava Experience and Trends

Nigeria has acquired a considerable level of experience in the development (research), multiplication, and processing of cassava into various food, feed and raw material forms; and the continued dominance in cassava production is of great interest. Between 1991 and 2001, Nigeria's cassava production has continued to increase (from 26 million metric tons in 1991 to 38 million metric tons in 2005, see table 2 and figure 2) (FAOSTAT, 2004). This increased production can be associated with an increase in the cassava area harvested within the same period (see table 2 and figure 2). This is surely not a sustainable path for cassava development. The cassava area harvested increased from 2.5 million hectares in 1991 to about 4.1 million hectares in 2005. Regrettably, the trend in cassava yield per hectare shows a decline from 1998 to 2005. The cassava yield per hectare decreased from 118, 818 hg/ha in 1997 to 92,712 hg/ha in 2005 (see table 2 and figure 2). Moreover, the cassava producer price in Nigeria, within the period of (1991 - 2002) witnessed a tremendous increase from 2,066 Naira/ton in 1991 to 33,960 Naira/ton in 2002 (figure 3).

Table 2: Cassava Data of Nigeria (1991-2001)

Year	Cassava area harvested (ha)	Cassava yield (hg/ha)	Cassava production (mt)	Cassava producer price (Naira/ton)
1991	2,551,000	101,936	26,004,000	2,066
1992	2,755,000	105,931	29,184,000	2,340
1993	2,844,000	105,935	30,128,000	4,640
1994	2,927,000	105,928	31,005,000	4,450
1995	2,944,000	106,671	31,404,000	6,610
1996	2,946,000	106,646	31,418,000	10,570
1997	2,697,400	118,818	32,050,000	11,860
1998	3,042,500	107,461	32,695,000	11,510
1999	3,072,000	106,436	32,697,000	13,620
2000	3,030,000	105,644	32,010,000	14,317
2001	3,430,000	95,003	32,586,000	22,100
2002	3,455,000	94,787	32,749,000	33,960
2003	3,490,000	94,307	32,913,000	_
2004	4,118,000	92,712	38,179,000	_
2005	4,118,000	92,712	38,179,000	_

Source: FAOSTAT (2004).

This analysis shows that despite the increase in cost of production of cassava, there is greater demand for the commodity due to population increases and the vital role of the commodity in the food security of the nation and the people. With the current emphasis on giving cassava an export orientation, there is no doubt that meeting local demand will be a "Herculean task" if positive steps are not taken to ensure that the food security of cassava-based livelihoods is not jeopardized.

Figure 2: Cassava Profile of Nigeria from 1991 – 2005

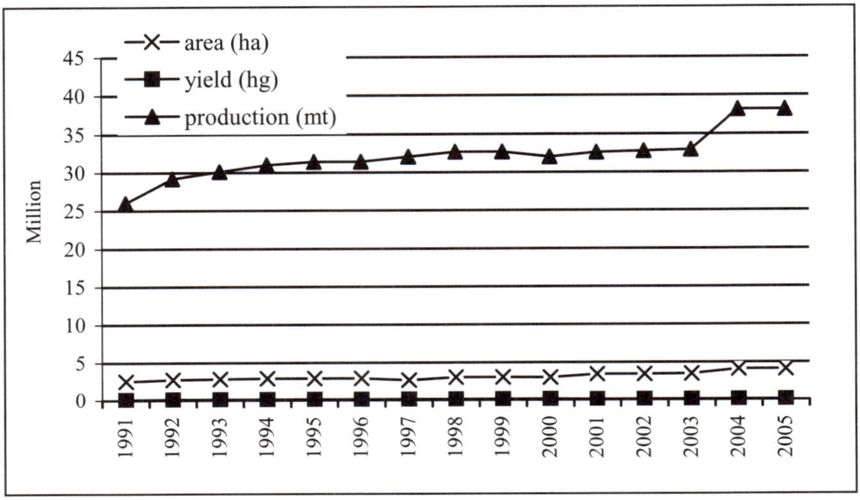

Source: FAOSTAT (2005).

Figure 3: Cassava Producer Price in Nigeria from 1991 – 2002

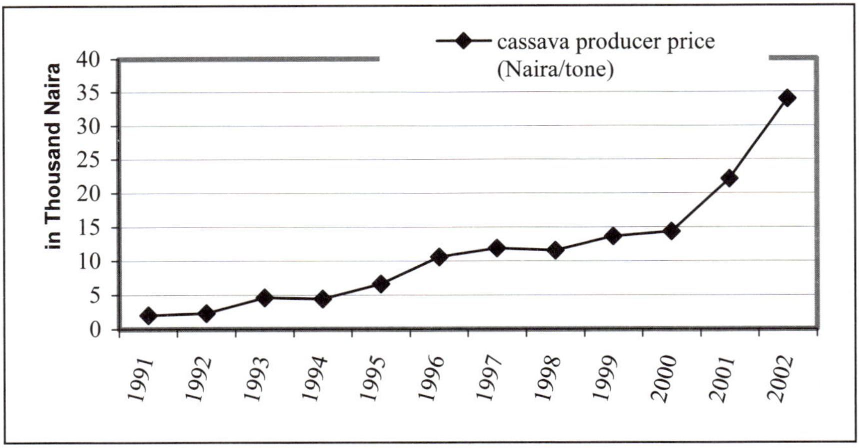

Source: FAOSTAT (2005).

Developments in the Nigeria's cassava sector certainly have impact in the West Africa region since the country produces more than half of the regions' cassava output. In 2005 alone, Nigeria produced about 38,179,000 tons out of the 56,048,960 tons produced in the region, and is leading other major producers like Brazil and Thailand (see table 3, which shows cassava production, harvest area and yield in West Africa, Brazil, Nigeria and Thailand).

Table 3: Cassava Production, Area Harvested and Yield in West Africa, Brazil, Nigeria and Thailand

Cassava Production (metric tons)				
Year	Western Africa	Brazil	Nigeria	Thailand
1963	11,227,824	22,248,640	7,783,000	2,111,100
1973	14,122,422	26,527,008	9,600,000	5,668,000
1983	14,754,292	21,847,888	9,950,000	18,988,528
1993	40,231,950	21,855,690	30,128,000	20,203,000
2003	50,410,923	22,235,900	33,379,000	18,430,000
2005	56,048,960	26,644,700	38,179,000	16,938,000
Area Harvested (hectares)				
Year	Western Africa	Brazil	Nigeria	Thailand
1963	1,462,198	1,617,810	801,000	139,200
1973	1,708,064	2,103,751	970,000	432,000
1983	1,896,087	2,061,203	1,100,000	1,017,857
1993	4,037,759	1,811,830	2,844,000	1,438,080
2003	5,399,689	1,670,390	3,500,000	1,050,000
2005	6,054,845	1,933,110	4,118,000	985,920
Yield (Hectogram per hectare)				
Year	Western Africa	Brazil	Nigeria	Thailand
1963	76,787	137,523	97,166	151,659
1973	82,681	126,094	98,969	131,204
1983	77,814	105,996	90,455	186,554
1993	99,639	120,628	105,935	140,486
2003	93,359	133,118	95,369	175,524
2005	92,569	137,833	92,712	171,799

Source: FAOSTAT (2005)

In 2005 also, Nigeria has harvested more than half of West Africa's cassava area (about 4,118,000 hectares) out of the region's 6,054,845 hectares. Brazil and Thailand harvested comparatively smaller cassava areas (see table 3).

However, the trend of cassava yield in West Africa, Nigeria, Brazil and in Thailand shows that Thailand has virtually dominated the cassava world in terms of productivity from 1963 to 2005 (see table 3). In 2005, cassava yield (hg/ha) was 171,799 in Thailand, 137,833 in Brazil, 92,712 in Nigeria, and 92,569 in West Africa. Even though Nigeria's productivity level has been surpassing that of the West Africa region, its lower productivity level compared to Thailand and Brazil (table 3) is a critical challenge that the country needs to address through further research and extension.

2.4 Role of Gender and Cassava in Nigeria

In most parts of the rural areas of the country, division of labour within the household is gender-specific and age-specific. Women normally do the weeding, planting and harvesting but the increased involvement of women in land clearing and preparation (traditionally done by men) has been necessitated by the migration of men from home for off-farm employment. Also, the reduction of the fallow period has made land clearing and preparation easier and has increased women's involvement in such activities.

Women play a central role in cassava production and processing, contributing about 58 per cent of the total agricultural labour in the southwest, 67 per cent in the south east, and 58 per cent in the central zones, with involvement in virtually all activities including hoeing, weeding, harvesting, transporting, storing, processing, marketing, etc (IFAD, 2004: 20). They are almost entirely responsible for the processing of agricultural products. They assist their husbands in marketing cassava and other crops, and they also market their own crops. In some cases, women buy agricultural produce from their husbands and from other farmers and market this at a profit. At times, they buy cassava in the soil, harvest, process, and market. Small-scale cassava processing is the domain of women, although most of the mechanized equipment (graters and grinders) are owned and operated by men. Post-harvest technologies, particularly those that are labour saving and that serve as a stable source of income, are hijacked by men (RUSEP, 2004: 1). This means that increased cassava utilization and exportation may have a lot of positive impact on women if gender sensitivity is taken into consideration.

2.5 The Role of Agricultural Research and Capacity Building

The activities of international organizations such as the Food and Agriculture Organization (FAO), the International Institute of Tropical Agriculture (IITA), the International Fund for Agricultural Development (IFAD), the International Center for Tropical Agriculture (CIAT), and the International Development Research Center (IDRC), through the Global Cassava Strategy, have brought to the fore the emphasis that cassava is an essential part of the diet of more than half a billion people worldwide and will spur rural development, raise income for producers, processors and traders as well as will contribute to the food security status of the producing and consuming households. The attainment of food security requires that a nation should produce those food crops from which it will enjoy some natural and economic advantages. Cassava, for a developing economy like Nigeria, offers considerable benefits and potentials.

National research organizations, which include universities, research institutes, and the national agricultural research centres, have made tremendous achievements in cassava research and added substantially to some of the successes that have contributed to increased and more diversified cassava production. Notable in this direction is the IITA, in collaboration with the National Root Crops Research Institute (NRCRI), Umudike, the IFAD-supported Root and Tuber Expansion Programme (RTEP), and all the other state Agricultural Development Projects (ADPs), including national research institutes who have developed and continue to multiply improved cassava varieties that are resistant to cassava mosaic disease (CMD) in order to avert a national food crisis (Babaleye and Sanni, 2004: 18). This effort is encapsulated in the IITA's Integrated Cassava Project (ICP) with the primary objective of promoting the cassava industry in Nigeria. The IITA's ICP responds to an urgent and increasing need of resource-poor farmers, processors and consumers to increase and to sustain cassava-based agricultural production, food systems, commercialisation and trade, thereby spurring rural and agro-industrial development in Nigeria. The Federal Government (FG) is making a determined effort to boost the export of cassava as part of its plan to diversify the economy and to earn more foreign exchange from exports other than petroleum products. To this end, the Federal Government recently gave IITA one hundred million Naira to support their cassava research endeavours.

The IITA (International Institute for Tropical Agriculture), Ibadan, has developed cassava crossbreeds that are capable of yielding over 50 metric tons of cassava roots per hectare, as opposed to the conventional 20 metric tones per hectare. In addition, the Cassava Enterprise Development (CED) project, which is a public-private partnership (PPP) involving the United States Agency for International Development (USAID), the Shell Petroleum Development Company of Nigeria, the International Institute for Tropical Agriculture (IITA), the Cassava Producers and Processors Association, the Rural Women Foundation, and other partners in support of the Presidential Initiative (Olori, 2002: 1; Bamiyo, 2003: B29) on Cassava, will provide income for cassava farmers in 11 states of Nigeria (around the Niger Delta) and will also improve the technology transfer to address the cassava mosaic disease (CMD) as well as to develop cassava processing. It will also help to identify further commercial markets for cassava, such as ethanol production, livestock feed, and use in baking. Furthermore, the UNIDO has initiated cassava-based programmes in Oyo, Abia and Benue States (Tsokar, 2004: 58). The main objective of this initiative is the promotion of the product in the international market.

In the area of processing, various agro-engineering centres or institutions such as the Rural Agro-Industrial Development Scheme (RAIDS), the Projects Development Institute (PRODA), the Federal Institute of Industrial Research (FIIRO), the National Root Crop Research Institute (NRCRI), the Techo Quip Limited, as well as the agricultural engineering departments in several universities in the country, have developed many mechanized units designed to remove constraints that processors face at the household level (FMANR, 2004: 5; TELL, 2004: 35). Even though not much success has been recorded towards mechanizing cassava peeling (labour-intensive), industrial "garri" fryers have been developed by institutions such as RAIDS, PRODA, FIIRO and IITA but these products are more suitable for use in large-scale commercial enterprises or cooperative organizations than at the household level. Attempts at mechanizing the peeling step have achieved very limited success due to the non-uniformity in root geometry. Moreover, FIIRO has done extensive work on partial replacement with cassava flour of wheat in bread making. With even as little as 20 per cent replacement, quite a lot of foreign exchange will be saved for the country, plus achieving employment generation and value adding.

On the other hand, the Standard Organization of Nigeria (SON) and the National Agency for Food and Drugs Administration and Control (NAFDAC) are currently collaborating with the IITA and with other stakeholders to ensure that the necessary standards and the regulatory practices for the development of cassava industry in Nigeria are met (Babaleye and Sanni, 2004: 21). The underlying objective of this collaboration is to ensure that Nigeria's cassava products meet international standards. A publication (expected soon) titled "Standards for Cassava Products and Guidelines for Export" is expected to be a major output of this collaboration.

2.6 Nigeria's Cassava Market and the Market Access

Marketing is a problem to most farmers who may not have resources to transport unprocessed cassava tubers to the market, especially those living in villages with poor feeder roads (FMANR, 2004:17). Poor farmers, who are the major producers of cassava in Nigeria, transport their cassava tubers and products to the rural markets and nearby urban markets on heads (head loads), bicycles, motorbikes, and lorries given the bulky nature of the product. Nigeria's cassava market is characterized by fluctuations in supply, with the law of supply and demand determining the product prices. In other words, cassava and cassava products are devoid of government intervention or distortion.

Private individuals do the marketing activities in cassava and they operate in both the urban and the rural markets. Trade in fresh cassava roots is limited because it is perishable and bulky. To avoid this, farmers normally sell tubers either as roots that are un-harvested in the ground or in heaps at the farm gate or at rural markets. Cassava is also generally traded in processed form – 'garri', chips, or flour/paste in order to forestall deterioration. The marketing channel of most cassava products in Nigeria is depicted in the flow chart below (figure 4). Cassava products both in processed and unprocessed forms can move directly to the rural and urban consumers (i.e. households or industrial consumers) or through intermediaries, including processors, rural/urban wholesalers or assemblers, and rural/urban retailers.

In Nigeria, there is a potential market for cassava products in animal feed, flour, and starch industries, but the size of the industrial market is small because of an inadequate supply of cassava products, a weak link between industrial processors and producers for cassava products, and a preference for imported starch (FMNAR, 2004: 7). Industrial utilization of cassava products is expanding in many textiles, pharmaceutical, meat processing, and laundry sub-sectors of the economy but this accounts for less than 5 per cent of the total production. There is strong demand for cheap food, especially cassava products, within Nigeria. Currently, on the local scene, cassava chips are being industrially converted to alcohol in one of Nigeria's foremost alcohol manufacturing companies, the Nigerian Yeast and Alcohol Manufacturing Company (NIYAMCO), consuming about 24 metric tones of cassava chips daily. In the year 2000, only 10 per cent of Nigeria's cassava production was used for livestock feed (Nweke, 2004a: 82).

Figure 4: Marketing Channels of Cassava and Cassava-based Products in Nigeria

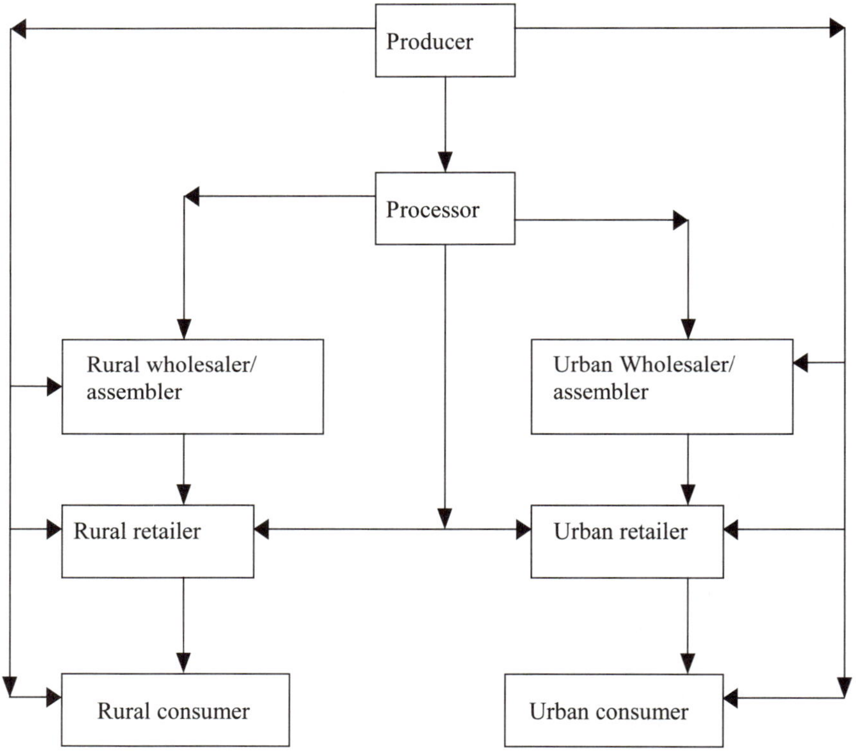

Source: Author's presentation.

The petroleum drilling industry needs over 240, 000 metric tons of cassava starch per annum for use as a dispersant in oil drilling; the soft drinks industry needs about 174,000 metric tons per annum of syrup concentrate from cassava; Nigeria also imports about 60,000 metric tons of dextrin per annum; and ethanol production industries need about 1,000,000 metric tons of cassava per annum for making cassava chips which is a major raw material input in the industry (Agu, 2004b: 18). If the current 88 million litres of alcohol imported each year for the liquor industry is produced from cassava roots, it would open up a market for about 600,000 tons of cassava roots (Nweke, 2004a: 81).

3 Nigeria's Export Potentials in Cassava

The production and distribution of goods and services for domestic and international markets has been recognized as an engine of economic growth and development (ITC, 2004: 7). Nigeria has a substantial economic potential in its agricultural sector, especially in agro-processing for the large domestic, regional and global markets (RUSEP, 2001: 12). In 2001, the IITA had established the RUSEP (Rural Sector Enhancement Programme) to promote market development especially for cassava (Nweke, 2004b: 4).

Nigeria, like other African countries, has been negotiating a lot of international and regional trade agreements including ECOWAS – CAP, EU – ACP Cotonou Agreement, AGOA, and NEPAD within the WTO framework (ITC, 2004: 13). Unfortunately, none of these agreements has been specific on cassava. But participants at two recent conferences organized by NEPAD, IDEAA and IFPRI in 2003 and held in South Africa strongly recommended that cassava be promoted as a "poverty fighter" across Africa and should be facilitated by a continental action or a Pan-African Cassava Initiative (PACI).

Formal regional trade within the ECOWAS is small because Nigeria seems to have the same agricultural commodities as other members of the sub-region. However, Nigeria has recently entered into accord with China, South Africa, and Botswana for the exportation of cassava products to these countries. Nigeria's current annual production of close to 40 million metric tons of cassava is expected to generate roughly $38 million (about 5 billion Naira) on annual basis in foreign exchange. This offers a great opportunity to diversify the nation's income, thereby creating employment and alleviating poverty.

The 2002 Trade Policy of Nigeria (TPN) emphasizes that investment is still needed to modernize the agricultural sub-sector, with the promotion and diversification of exports in both traditional and non-traditional markets as one of the key objectives (ITC, 2004: 11). The export diversification strategy of Nigeria is multi-dimensional in terms of promoting the traditional non-oil exports of cocoa, rubber, cassava, etc with emphasis on value-added addition to export production. Existing export incentives include measures such as the duty drawback scheme, the export expansion grant, and the manufacture in-bond scheme. However, in real terms little government assistance has been provided to agricultural exports. The lifting of ban on cassava export in 1996 led to a substantial increase in production (TCC, 1998: 1). The lack of standardized weights and measures in most markets (including the cassava market) makes it difficult to assess the efficiency of the marketing systems; the lack of an adequate transportation system is another hindrance since reliance on highway transportation means that roads are heavily travelled and in need of regular maintenance and upgrading – and rail transportation is virtually non-existent. Moreover, large-scale cassava processing is virtually non-existent in Nigeria. Cottage (household), micro, small and medium processors dominate the cassava sector.

These problems are inimical to the ability of the nation to maximize the benefits of her multilateral and global trade agreements. Some of these agreements include the Lomé IV Convention with an interim agreement signed in 2000 in Cotonou, Benin, and extended to 2008, providing the continuation of favourable terms for access to the EU market; ECOWAS Trade Liberalization Scheme (ETLS) with about 50% of close to 1,000 industrial products admitted under the trade scheme manufactured in Nigeria; and the African Growth and Opportunity Act (AGOA) of 2000 which provides for manufactured goods with predominantly local content and value added to be exported to the US at concessionary or zero duty rates. These agreements and other bilateral and multilateral agreements including NEPAD offer a large scope for maximizing Nigeria's cassava potentials. Nigeria should, therefore, look for opportunities within these agreements to pursue her cassava agenda.

One of the greatest challenges that may hinder the unprecedented development of the cassava productivity in Nigeria could be the inability to diversify cassava utilization so as to embrace new food and industrial products for export. Tackling this problem will ensure that glut, which can discourage production and will increase poverty, is nipped in the bud.

Another important concern is the sourcing of appropriate technologies (machinery and equipment) to produce quality products that will be able to penetrate the international market. The planned fabrication of prototype machines and proven technologies are yet to come on stream despite several overseas trips made by the members of the Cassava Initiative Committee/CIC (Bamiyo, 2003: B 29). However, a Chinese group working with various local research teams has come up with appropriate machinery, which can process cassava into garri, fufu, chips, as well as starch and pellets, for small, medium and large scale industrialists. Some of this machinery includes a washing machine, a chipping machine, a grater (different sizes and shapes), a roaster, a mixer, a dryer or fryer, and a weighing and sewing machine (for product weight and product bagging/packaging), including other accessories, which has a capacity of producing up to 35 tons/day. There are also capacities for small, medium and large-scale operators, ranging from 50 mt to 500 mt intake of cassava tubers per day of three shifts (Agu, 2004a: 16). But, the cost of the existing machinery and equipment is a major obstacle to this drive towards a cassava-diversified economy for Nigeria. For example, the costs assumed in the establishment of small-scale processing plants include: 2.5 million naira for garri processing; 3 million naira for cassava flour; 3 million naira for cassava chips/pellets; 8 million naira for starch; 45 million naira for cassava ethanol; 2.5 million naira for powdered fufu; 12.5 million naira for glucose syrup; and 7.5 million naira for cassava noodles (Bamiyo, 2004: B 28). Very few Nigerians can afford this kind of high-cost investments without financial assistance. Also, the production cost of cassava in Nigeria is a glaring inhibition against the competitiveness in the global cassava products market.

Furthermore, the development of high-yielding TMS (Tropical Manioc Selection) varieties has increased labour requirements for harvesting. The implication of this is the need for the development of labour-saving technologies for cassava harvesting in Nigeria. This is the most critical challenge facing the cassava transformation in Nigeria. This challenge is more urgent than reaching further increases in cassava yield (Nweke, 2004a: ii). But despite the development of high yielding and disease-resistant varieties, the productivity level of cassava in the country has been on a downward trend between 1997 and 2003.

This notwithstanding, the global outlook for Nigerian cassava exports is dim due to the high cassava production cost and the declining world market price of cassava products at the international market. The cost of doing business in Nigeria is very high and this is a major impediment for the competitiveness of cassava-based businesses in Nigeria. As an example, the average producer price of a ton of cassava pellets in Nigeria in 2003 in dollar terms was US$ 202.90; this is certainly much higher than the Thai market price (US$ 65.84) of cassava pellets in 2002 (IFAD and FAO, 2004: 22)

Given this scenario, the pertinent question remains: Can Nigeria realise such huge cassava exports as they are assumed in NEEDS? I believe this is realizable given the specific measures and targets embarked upon by the Federal Government of Nigeria and by international agencies like FAO and IFAD. The specific measures include the production of cassava breeder stock (cassava germplasm), foundation stock (cassava starting stock), and certified stock (cassava ministakes or stock cultures) with the expected impact of increasing cassava production from 40 to 150 million metric tons in 2007 (FMF, 2005: 4). This gives an annual increase of about 30 million metric tons, with subsequent processing it is expected to save about 50.5 billion Naira in the import of ethanol, starch, adhesives, glucose, etc. President Obasanjo's Initiative on Cassava estimates that, by 2007, a total of 23, 992, 000 tons of cassava will be demanded in Nigeria, while about 83, 346, 248 tons will be export-led demand (IFAD and FAO, 2004: 13). According to Nigeria's Minister of Commerce, Alhaji Idris Waziri, Nigeria's cassava has been adjudged to be the best in the world because of its starch content of about 85 per cent compared to that of the closest rival, Thailand, which has about 65 per cent as starch content.

Furthermore, it is gladdening to note that Nigeria recently, in the last weekend of April 2005, exported her maiden shipment of cassava chips of about 40 metric tons to China. This is a very landmark achievement despite all the policy, infrastructure, and marketing constraints. What then remains to be done is the fine-tuning of export incentives, policies (subsidies, price stabilization, government roles at various levels, etc), and marketing channels to ensure that Nigeria truly becomes a giant, not just in cassava production, but also in cassava exportation. This needs to be captured in a "Cassava Policy" which must ensure that the cassava farmer, no matter where his/her location is in the country, must be integrated into the production, processing, marketing, exportation and other aspects of the expected policy.

While acknowledging that all the constraints may not be tackled at the same time given resource constraints, some practical and quick steps can be taken. For instance, the export incentives (subsidies) administered by the Nigerian Export Promotion Council (NEPC) and which were designed to encourage the meaningful diversification of the economy, are limited to a few privileged beneficiaries (Balogun, 2001: 12). Government should, through NEPC, make these incentives rural farmer-friendly by ensuring that these facilities (incentives) are available and accessible to the rural farmers. Also, there is the need for coordinated efforts at all government levels (federal, state and local) to ensure the full realization of this "cassava dream". While all the levels of government should jointly establish modern processing and marketing structures in all the cassava-producing local governments of the country, the local and state governments should ensure the establishment and sustainability of viable cooperatives that can help rural farmers to achieve the quality and the standards that are necessary for export. Such an arrangement has the potential of creating better domestic trading and marketing networks, and better avenues for targeting other important government policies. The federal government on her part should, through the Nigerian Export Processing Zones Authority (NEPZA), establish cassava processing zones in all the Senatorial Zones (State-level political entities; there are 3 senatorial zones in each State of Nigeria) of the country for easy assemblage, marketing and export of cassava products, and equally should ensure that financial benefits accruing from this get to the rural farmers who actually generate such production. Furthermore, there seems to be the need for the proposed cassava policy to ensure an efficient and integrated private sector participation in the processing and marketing of cassava products in Nigeria. The private sector should be encouraged to set up private processing facilities and to complement government efforts by developing marketing networks.

On the production cost side, what is needed primarily is the increase in the per hectare productivity of cassava to offset the current cost of production. In this regard, Nigeria's Special Programme for Food Security (SPFS) offers a good opportunity. Nigeria's Special Programme for Food Security, assisted by the Food and Agriculture Organization (FAO) of the United Nations, is an intervention on the activities of farmers in Nigeria. It is being implemented currently in 109 farming communities across Nigeria with each Senatorial Zone having a site. Two important objectives of the programme are: to assist farmers in achieving their potential for increasing output and productivity and consequently their incomes on sustainable basis; and to strengthen the effectiveness of research and extension services in bringing technology and new farming practices developed by research institutes to farmers and ensuring greater relevance of research to the practical problems faced by small farmers (FMARD and FAO, 2004: 3). Nigeria;s SPFS should, therefore, be leveraged to specifically target cassava revolution in the country.

Moreover, the SPFS of Nigeria offers a unique opportunity to address soil-related productivity problems through its soil fertility initiative (SFI). The specific objectives of this initiative are to: promote soil fertility awareness amongst stakeholders; expand availability of low cost and high quality sources of plant nutrients and promote their efficient use by farmers; and reduce land degradation as well as promote sustainable land use for soil fertility improvement. Nigerian soils are generally known to be of low quality, lacking in important nutrients and easily prone to erosion. Soil constraints and problems that militate against high crop yields are soil erosion, salinization, flooding, declining fertility, desert encroachment, mismanagement and misuse, etc (Akamigbo, 2000: 62). Low soil fertility affects many cassava-growing areas because the periods are shorter as the pressure on arable land homesteads is increasing (FMANR, 2004: 15). Since the direct use of soil amendments in cassava cultivation is low, the yield potentials of the various varieties of the planted cassava crop are not often attained. Therefore, leveraging the SFI for the cassava transformation strategy will ensure that fertility is maintained and productivity enhanced at small to medium scale farming.

4 Policy Conclusions and Recommendations

4.1 Conclusion

The current economic hardships as experienced by a vast majority of Nigerians, occasioned by the deregulation of the downstream oil sector, could be very much less severe if the economy were more diversified. The job of turning around the Nigerian economy could be daunting, but the prospects are good, given the fact that there is the consciousness among all stakeholders of the need to create a national economy that is highly competitive, responsive to incentives, private sector-led, broad-based, diversified, market-oriented and open, but based on internal momentum for its projected economic growth. From the South-South of Nigeria to the south-east, from the south-west to the middle-belt up to the north-central, both state and local governments are encouraging farmers to clear more lands and to focus on cassava planting. This is a sign of an imminent cassava revolution in Nigeria. In September of 2004, the Nigerian Economic Summit Group (NESG) launched the Nucleus Estate Initiative (NEI) under the umbrella of the Agriculture and Food Security Policy Commission (AFSPC) of the NESG, Lagos. This initiative is a private sector response to the government's call for private sector participation in the economic development of Nigeria. According to NESG (2004: 1), the NEI is an implementation strategy of developing larger-scale farmers, using a network of several rural-based or low income farming groups that are linked to a major farmer, processor or marketer as a central pool. It is hoped that this initiative will benefit cassava farmers immensely.

With the development of improved cassava varieties with higher productivity and resistance to the virulent CMD (Cassava Mosaic Disease) by the IITA, and given the greater level of emphasis by various tiers of government that is laid now on agriculture with cassava as the arrow-head, Nigeria will experience an "explosion" of cassava production in the country in the next couple of years. This, we hope, will put a check to the large importation of cassava products, especially starch and its derivatives. With a 20 per cent substitute with cassava flour in confectioneries industry alone, about US $40 million (about 5.5 billion Naira) can be saved for the country on an annual basis.

The most important cassava products for export are cassava chips and pellets that are targeted at the animal husbandry sector of Europe, Asia and the USA and over 10 million metric tons of cassava chips/pellet was consumed as animal feed in Europe in the year 2000 (Bamiyo, 2003: B29).

According the Minister of Commerce, Ambassador A. D. Idris Wasziri, Nigeria is expected to begin the export of cassava chips to the rest of the world by September 2005, all things being equal (Tsokar, 2004: 58). Nigeria, he said, has already received orders of about 500, 000 tons of cassava from China. This is an indication that Nigeria's cassava could be competitive. So, given a good cassava policy, Nigeria is most likely to attract other foreign countries with her cassava resources.

4.2 Recommendations

Nigeria cannot afford to continue ignoring the potentials of cassava as a foreign exchange generator and as an import substitute. All cassava products have export potentials ranging from the simplest, which is garri, to the most complex (modified starch). If well planned, cassava exports alone can generate greater annual foreign exchange than petroleum resources. Nigeria's dream of exporting at least US $5 billion worth of cassava and cassava products will be realized if the following recommendations are taken into consideration:

- The proceeds from the deregulated downstream sector of the oil economy should be channelled into the procurement and strategic location of quality machinery to aid processing and packaging of cassava products.
- The fourth-year practical sessions of some federal universities, including the universities of agriculture, should be leveraged to provide the practical experiences in the field for students that are needed for reducing the production cost of Nigeria's cassava. They should be provided with the improved machinery and equipment needed for the product-market chain. This will be beneficial to such universities and the nation at large, since they possess the large and contiguous land necessary for the scale of production required for meeting the demand of cassava for both food and industry. Such university farms can be used as a model or standard farm.
- Cassava-based products should be fortified with essential micronutrients so as to curb the menace of nutrient-related illnesses among starch-dependent households in Nigeria. This may require further research and development (R&D) and has the potential of introducing new cassava products, as well as substituting for other products, that

can capture the international market. R&D should be supported by both the government and the private sector, and should also be targeted towards addressing the declining productivity level of the cassava sector.

- There is the need for a cassava policy that will enunciate realistic standards and quality, in terms of production (higher productivity and lower production costs), processing (more efficient processing), packaging and marketing of cassava and cassava-based products, so that value can be added for local and foreign markets. This policy should embody a clear cassava trading process on how cassava will move from the farm to the local and export market and stressing the value-adding points along the process; and the policy should be developed in collaboration with the producers of the products in the cassava industry, and should embody issues about monitoring and the enforcement of quality.
- Given the fact that investment is still needed to modernize the Nigerian agricultural sector, foreign farmers, who have been negotiating for new a base in Nigeria, should be encouraged to invest in the cassava sector through appropriate incentives that can encourage easy land acquisition.
- Nigeria should subsidize cassava farmers at all levels by offering free and improved (disease-resistant and high-yielding) planting materials throughout the year. The Nigeria Special Programme for Food Security offers a bright opportunity for developing a holistic traditional cassava transformation strategy for the country.
- Cassava Export Processing Zones should be set up in all the cassava producing states of the country to maximize the benefits of the law establishing the NEPZ (Nigerian Export Processing Zone) including exemption from taxes, duties, foreign-exchange restrictions and import/export license requirements, etc.

References

Akamigbo Francis, O. R. (2000): "Nigerian Agriculture and the Challenges of the 21st Century: Nigerian Soils." In: Agro-Science, vol. 1. No. 1, pp. 62 – 67.

Agu, Chuma (2004a): "Cassava Starch: Plays Dominant Role in Food, Non-food Industries", in: Business Day Newspapers, Tuesday, June 1, 2004.

Agu, Chuma (2004b): "Investing in Protein-Enriched Garri", in: Agribusiness, Business Day Newspapers, September 21, 2004.

Babaleye, Taye and Lateef, Sanni (2004): SON, NAFDAC Collaborate with IITA on Cassava Processing, in: Business Day Newspapers, Tuesday, September 7, 2004.

Balogun, E. D. (2001): "Resuscitating Agricultural Production for Exports", online: www.cenbank.org/OUT/PUBLICATIONS/OCCASIONALPAPERS/RD/2001/OWE-01-9.PDF, accessed 26/04/06.

Bamiyo, Festus (2003): "Solution to Cassava Production and Export Problems", in: The Guardian, Saturday, November 8, p. B 29.

Bamiyo, Festus (2004): "Cassava: The Vision of A Nation", in: The Guardian, Saturday, September 18, p. B 28.

CBN (Central Bank of Nigeria) (2003): "Annual Report and Statement of Accounts – 2003", CBN, Abuja.

CBN (2004): "Annual Report and Statement of Accounts – 2004", Central Bank of Nigeria, Abuja.

DFID (Department for International Development) (2003): "Promoting Pro-Poor Opportunities through Commodity and Service Markets", Programme Report (Draft), Chemonics International Inc., Emerging Market Economics (EME), RBS Consulting and DA Associates.

Eboh, Eric, Oji, Kalu, Oji, Okey, Amakom, Uzochukwu and Ujah, Oliver Chinedu, (2004): "Towards the ECOWAS Common Agricultural Policy Framework: Nigeria Case Study and Regional Analysis", Under subcontract from the Economic Community of West African States (ECOWAS).

FGN (Federal Government of Nigeria) (2004): "Framework for Nigeria's Economic Growth and Development (2003 – 2007)", Federal Government home grown Economic Blueprint unveiled at the Ninth Nigerian Economic Summit in Abuja, online: http://www.nigeriavillagesquare.com, accessed 20/09/04.

FMANR (Federal Ministry of Agriculture and Natural Resources) (2004): "Cassava Development in Nigeria: A Country Case Study Towards a Global Strategy for Cassava Development", online: www.globalcassavastrategy.net/Africa/nigeria/n0000e00.htm, accessed 20/09/04.

FMARD (Federal Ministry of Agriculture and Rural Development) and FAO (Food and Agriculture Organization) (2004): "National Special Programme for Food Security (NSPFS) – The Journey So Far", FMARD and FAO, Abuja.

FMF (Federal Ministry of Finance) (2005): "Federal Ministry of Agriculture: Performance Matrix and Indicators", online: www.fmf.gov.ng/, accessed 01/04/05.

IFAD (International Fund for Agricultural Development) and FAO (Food and Agriculture Organization) (2004): "A Cassava Industrial Revolution in Nigeria: The Potential for a new Industrial Crop.", online: ftp://ftp.fao.org/docrep/-fao/007/y5548e/y5548e00.pdf, accessed 20/03/05.

ITC (International Trade Centre) (2004): "Nigeria: An Overview of the Business Challenges of the Evolving International Trading System", International Trade Centre – UNCTAD/WTO. Online: http://www.intracen.org/worldtradenet/-docs/networking/country_papers/nigeria_overview.pdf., accessed 21/03/05.

NPC (National Planning Commission) (2004): "Nigeria: National Economic Empowerment and Development Strategy (NEEDS)", NPC, Federal Secretariat, Abuja.

NESG (Nigeria Economic Summit Group) (2004): "Launching of the Nucleus Estate Initiative". Online: www.nesgroup.org, accessed 21/10/04.

Nweke, Felix (2004a): "New Challenges in the Cassava Transformation in Nigeria and Ghana", EPTD Discussion Paper No. 118, Environment and Production Technology Division, International Food Policy Research Institute (IFPRI), Washington, D. C.

Nweke, Felix (2004b): "Mechanization for Cassava Commercialisation as a Livestock Feed and Industrial Raw Material in Africa", Paper presented at the NEPAD/IGAD regional conference "Agricultural Successes in the Greater Horn of Africa", Nairobi, November 22 – 25, 2004, Conference Paper No. 11c.

Olori Toye (2002): "Development – Africa: Promoting Cassava as a Source of Food Security", Inter Press Services – Terraviva Europe, Belgium, Nov. 14, 2002.

RUSEP (Rural Sector Enhancement Programme) (2001): "Needs Assessment Study for Market-driven Agricultural Technology Transfer and Commercialisation in Abia State", Nigeria, IITA, Ibadan, Funded by USAID, online: www.rusep.org, accessed 23/09/04.

RUSEP (Rural Sector Enhancement Programme) (2004): "Empowering Women Groups for Industrial Cassava Processing", Reports and News, online: www.rusep.org, accessed January 2005.

TELL (2004): "Techo Quip shines at Cassava Exhibition", TELL Weekly Magazine, No. 27, 05/07/ 2004.

TCC (Trade and Compliance Centre) (1998): "Nigeria: Trade Policy Review Summaries – 1998", Trade and Compliance Centre, USA, online: www.mac.doc.gov/tcc/data/commerce_html/countries/Countries4/Nigeria/Trade Policy/1998/, accessed 29/03/2004.

Tsokar, Karls (2004): "Cassava Chips to be Exported Soon, says Minister", The Guardian Newspapers, Sunday, October 10.

Waziri, Idris (2004): "Cassava Chips to be Exported Soon", The Guardian Newspapers, Sunday, October 10, 2004.

Leather and Leather Products: A Viable Non-Oil Export Potential for Nigeria

Amakom Uzochukwu

1 Introduction

With a GDP of about $41.7923 billion in 2004 (CBN, 2004:140), Nigeria is the second largest economy in Sub-Saharan Africa after South Africa and the tenth largest producer of crude oil in the world at 2.1 million barrels per day and a fast growing agro-industrial sector.

One of these sub-sectors in the agro-industrial sector is leather and leather products that are presently attracting high interest from the international business community in Italy, Swaziland, Spain and Morocco among others. Presently the world footwear and leather products sector is moving from high-cost industrialized countries to developing countries, and many developing countries (Nigeria inclusive) have strong potentials in this sector regarding raw material and human resources, but have mainly remained suppliers of raw and semi-finished products. According to "Meet in Africa: Intra-African Trade Promotion Programme (IATPP) of 1998", held in Cape Town, South Africa, this has been attributed to a limited number of African companies having developed the capacity to produce finished products what then implies that if efforts are geared to get this issue tackled, Nigeria will favorably compete with some other countries in the exports of leather and leather products.

Effort towards achieving this will provide partly a solution to the call for the diversification of the Nigerian non-oil sector[1] and consequently will increase the country's revenue-generating capacity, thereby reducing unemployment. According to Markham (2004: 13), in the current export strategy paper, within the context of the national development policy as contained in the development agenda of the National Economic Empowerment

[1] The leather industry presently constitutes over 34 percent of the Nigerian non-oil export.

and Development Strategy (NEEDS), the development objective of the export policy, known as the export strategy for the next five years (2005-2010), is among other things to provide a strategic framework and to guide for national consensus building; to mobilize core export-stakeholder public institutions and policy-making bodies, trade support service providers, organizations, institutions and associations that represent non-oil private sector exporters, and export companies for needed substantial support services; and to promote export-oriented cross-sectoral development of Nigeria's human and non-oil natural resources. Also the new export policy aims at production capacity building to realize the non-oil export potential of Nigeria in key agro- and agro-allied products like leather, cassava, etc and to stimulate on a broad front export-led balanced development of the economy managed in a manner that permits mass participation in the activities and consequent economic rewards of export by the great majority of the Nigerian population nationwide.

The list of exportable products recommended by stakeholders for regular promotional support in the new export policy includes a range of manufactured products and services. The shortlist of products includes manufactured products like Leather and leather products, Textiles and garments, Engineering goods, Plastic products and paints, Electric cables, Handicrafts, Pharmaceuticals, Ceramics, Solid minerals, and other Manufactured products with a minimum of 35- 40% local value addition.

The second line of priority products that is identified comprises Services, Leather goods, Leather, Hides and Skins, Building materials, Agricultural commodities (pulses, spices, gum arabic, cashew, oil seeds, coffee, cotton, etc. with emphasis on local value addition), and Manufactured products. The implication of this classification is that for the products on the "shortlist" and according to the second line of priorities, the Nigerian Export Promotion Council (NEPC) will endeavor to provide, inter alia: product specialists; links for sourcing experts; appropriate reference books and documents; a database on identified potential buyers; and assistance in marketing and technology for value-added processing. As a general approach, NEPC will explore with potential exporters the possibility of maximizing local value addition to the products prior to exportation. Therefore the development and promotion of the export of products in the shortlist will benefit from preferential access to special resources, comprising finance, suppliers' credit, technical experts and advisory services, training, new technology, research support, and marketing to pave the way for successful ventures. This has led to one of the main strategies in the Nigerian Export Policy (NEP) which is the promotion of high value leather and leather goods export, providing facilities including bonded warehouses for the import of raw materials such as raw hides, pickled wet blue, crust and finished leather, components and chemicals, etc. to the 100 percent export-oriented industries.

The investment and export drive of the present administration to transform the nation's economy, to generate employment and to reduce poverty has received a boost as Nigeria now exports finished leather to some parts of the world, especially to African countries. This feat was achieved through the successful takeoff of a multi-million dollar 'FATA Tanning Leather Company', the largest in Africa and located in Kano that has commenced production of all types of leather shoes and other leather works. The company commenced operations in 2003 with a target of over 100 million Euros in 2004 (Sakaba 2004:10). This target was nearly realized as the company's export value in 2004 was over 65 million Euro (CBN 2004: 166). The company presently has entered into a joint partnership with one of the biggest shoe manufacturing companies in Italy-FILANTO to set up a shoe-making factory in Nigeria all in the bid to exploit the bountiful opportunities in the Nigerian leather sector under the AGOA. The Export Processing Zone concept may be considered a composite export incentive under which artificial enabling conditions are created within geographical enclaves to attract companies to establish export-oriented factories and other industrial facilities. The approved activities are warehousing, freight forwarding and customs clearance; handling of duty-free goods (trans-shipment, sorting, marketing, packaging, etc.); banking, stock exchange and other financial services; and insurance and re-insurance. Manufacturing activities include assembling or processing of goods for export, provided exports total at least 75% of turnover during the assessment year. Under the 1992 domestic laws on taxes, levies, and duties new industrial undertakings, including foreign companies and operations inside or outside an EPZ in Nigeria, are allowed full income tax holidays for three consecutive assessment years under certain provisions. Up to 25% of production may be sold in the Nigerian territory against a valid permit, and on payment of the duties in force. Enterprises operating in a zone and supplying or purchasing goods and services to or from customers within the customs territory may pay in foreign currency under the rules and regulations applicable to external trade.

Foreign investment, including capital gains, in the zones may be repatriated at any time. Profits and dividends earned by foreign investors in the zones may also be remitted at any time. No import or export licenses are required. Land is provided rent-free at the construction stage. Foreign exchange regulations do not apply within the zones, and approved enterprises operating within them are exempted from all government taxes and levies. Imports may include any capital goods, consumer goods, raw materials, components or articles intended to be used for the purposes of and in connection with an approved activity, including any article for the construction, alteration, reconstruction, extension or repair of premises in a zone or for equipping such premises. Presently, EPZs are located in Kano in Kano state, in Calabar in Cross River state, and in Onne in River state.

This drive also has led to the establishment of a EPZ in Nigeria, and Kano which has the highest concentration of tanneries and a bee hive of leather materials collection is the location. In other words, it is an industrial cluster where investors will enjoy tax holiday relief, unrestricted repatriation of foreign capital investments along with capital appreciation of such investments, rent-free land during the construction of factory premises. More than this, made-in-Nigeria goods are entitled to preferential tariffs in the EU and in the US (as a result of the US-initiated AGOA), and there are also other benefits.

Under the EPZ the provision of the Industrial Development (Income Tax relief) Act with respect to a Pioneer Status qualifies for a tax holiday of 3-5 years to any manufacturing exporter who exports at least 50% of his annual production, while additional concessions are also available in the local raw materials development, in local value-added generation, and in labour-intensive or export-oriented activities that involve significant training (FMIN 1999:9).

In a nutshell, the scheme is targeted to promote the diversification of the export base of the nation through the acceleration of export business with attendant loaded incentives, that include areas such as industrial production, offshore banking, insurance and re-insurance, international stock, commodities and mercantile exchanges, commercial industrial research, agriculture and agro-allied industry, mineral processing, as well as international tourist resort development and operations. Kano happens to be one of the centres primarily selected to tackle the issue of wastages and under-utilization of abundant hides and skins that are produced in the other states of the north like Sokoto, Katsina, Kaduna, Bauchi and Maiduguri. These free trade zones serve as industrial clusters for products that are processed for exports, and most of the problems encountered by small and medium enterprises (SMEs) are taken care of at these centres collectively.

The establishment of such industrial clusters have been applauded by Schmitz (2004: 3) when he was analysing the benefits that such movements had for the Brazilian leather sector. He observed and recorded a series of events and developments that could explain the success of the clusters with leather and footwear industry in the local and external markets (they account for a very high share of the Brazilian shoe exports and cover also a large share of the local market). In the history of the cluster development, the observed characteristics were all the same that the specialized literature had identified as requirements for the success in the development and operation of industrial clusters: division of labour and specialization among firms; the provision of specialized products and services at short notice; the emergence of suppliers to provide raw materials and components; the growth of suppliers of second hand machinery and spare parts; the emergence of agents who sell to distant national and international markets; the growth of specialized producer services in technical, financial and accounting matters; and the formation of associations providing services and lobbying for its members.

Nigeria's trade policy is governed by three main trade agreements to which it is a signatory. They are the Uruguay Round Agreements which established the Multilateral Trading System; the ACP-EU Cotonou Partnership Agreement; and the ECOWAS Trade Treaty and Protocols which established the ECOWAS Trade Liberalization Scheme. Nigeria also participates in the UNCTAD Generalized System of Preferences (GSP) and the Global System of Trade Preferences (GSTP). In the end, all these trade agreements only provide opportunities. Taking advantage of the opportunities represents the crux of the matter. To enable a signatory country to take advantage of the opportunities, that country has to be competitive because all the Agreements are based on trade liberalization.

Under the trade policy as it relates to the leather and other agro-allied sectors, the management dimension of the infrastructure and the utility services is being addressed in order to establish and nurture a conducive business environment through, inter alia, improved and pro-development management of the trade and exchange liberalization policies, and to build upon successes achieved and eliminate the failings. Also trade policy targets to implement a series of coordinated trade-related micro-level actions that are likely to impact favourably on the exporting community and on backward linkage groups as well as to ensure that those officials charged with the responsibility of trade policy negotiations maintain close consultation with the trade constituencies and socio-economic groups on whom the outcome of trade negotiations impact and to coordinate trade policy measures and eliminate any contradictions or overlapping. The trade policy is also to determine export sector and product and target market priorities and to set appropriate support measures. Apart from close consultation with trade and export constituencies, participation in trade negotiations should be preceded by product and product sector selection and prioritization with full involvement of the stakeholders.

At present, the EU is the largest trade partner of Nigeria. The policy consideration is to maintain Nigeria's market share and to increase it. The EU market has a great absorptive capacity. There is also the old traditional trade link with UK that should continue to be nurtured. Recently, there were calls for Nigeria to pull out of the WTO Agreement. The calls were based on certain aspects of the results of trade liberalization represented by the influx of low-priced imports that caused many local industries to close down. However, a close examination of the situation reveals that the trade negotiations leading to the signature of the Agreements were not flawless and that the liberalization process was not properly managed. In particular, there were no efforts to make use of the Safeguard Clauses. Moreover, the systemic problem of the "high cost of operating business" has not ceased to continue to erode Nigeria's competitiveness. The best option is for the government to address the cost problem.

This paper is an attempt to showcase the export potentials that abound in the Nigerian leather sector, and hence the choice of this industry for analysis of a thrust sector in the country's export policy. Also the study intends to find those bottlenecks that could render the export policy targets unattainable, and to make recommendations on how to improve the situation in the sector. The paper is divided into four sections: Section 1 is the introduction; Section 2 showcases Nigeria as a leather producer and exporter by Nigerian national states and cities; Section 3 deals with the determinants of Nigeria's leather export capacity, applying some descriptive statistics as well as analytical techniques; and Section 4 presents policy recommendations for leather export development in Nigeria.

2 Nigeria as a Leather Producer and Export

The raw materials for leather and its products are mainly from livestock, and Nigeria is endowed with the third largest livestock population in Africa with the dominant breeds as: great humpless, small humpless, West African dwarf cattle, short horned red zebu, short horned zebu, Adamawa zebu, and long horned zebu for cattle; Balami, Uda, Yankasa, West African dwarf sheep for sheep; Red Sokoto, Gahel goat, and dwarf goats for goats (Felsner & Schmel, 2002: 6). The country's cattle territory is essentially in the Sudan Savannah where the limiting factors are the amount of water supply available as one moves north from the Middle Belt or Guinea Savannah towards the Sahara, and the existence of tsetse fly infested forests to the south (Ogujiuba, Amakom & Uka 2004: 4). Only about 10% of the country's cattle population live in the tse-tse fly infested forest of the south.

In the cattle territory there is found also about 70% of the country's population of sheep and goats that have adapted to the ecological constraints.

In the Guinea Savannah and the Southern forest zones is found the remaining 30% made up of the indigenous dwarf breeds of sheep and goats while various exotic breeds of pigs are found in different areas of the country. The sector is different from other agricultural-based sectors because unlike other agricultural based sectors, there is no need for cultivation but for improvement in the already available raw materials. A telling indicator is evident from fresh hides and skins production which are 100 percent locally sourced from livestock such as cattle, sheep, goats, camels, etc. Table 1 below shows the production of hides and skins, slaughter statistics and wastage of hides and skins in Nigeria.

Table 1: Production/Slaughter and Waste of Hides and Skins and the Stock of Livestock in Nigeria

Item	Cattle Hides	Goat Skins	Sheep Skins	Hides & Skins	Hides & Skins	Hides & Skins	Cattle Hides, Fresh	Cattle Hides, Fresh	Goat Skins, Fresh
Element	Prod.	Prod.	Prod.	Prod.	Domestic Supply	Waste	Slaughtered/ Prod. Animals	Prod.	Slaughtered/ Prod. Animals
Unit	Mt	Mt	Mt	Mt	Mt	Mt	Head	Mt	Head
1982	33760	11200	5700	47287	47287	9457	1644364	32887	4650000
1983	37242	12100	5900	45901	45841	9180	1510051	30201	5050000
1984	38896	13000	6300	50660	50522	10132	1687997	33760	5600000
1985	40385	13800	6600	55242	54997	11048	1862079	37242	6050000
1986	39628	15600	6800	58196	57584	11639	1944820	38896	6500000
1987	38395	16400	7000	60785	60118	12157	2019237	40385	6900000
1988	40156	17400	7200	62028	57340	12406	1981418	39628	7800000
1989	27916	19000	7600	61795	58045	12359	1919737	38395	8200000
1990	28880	19000	8000	64756	59438	12951	2007783	40156	8700000
1991	30063	19400	8600	54516	44206	10903	1395794	27916	9500000
1992	24292	19800	8800	55880	51970	11176	1443987	28880	9500000
1993	29498	20000	9200	58063	52856	11613	1503142	30063	9700000
1994	36000	20400	9200	52892	46644	10578	1214599	24292	9900000
1995	36600	20400	9200	58698	57518	11740	1474888	29498	10000000
1996	42720	20000	11350	65600	62800	13120	1800000	36000	10200000
1997	42770	21000	15820	66200	58915	13240	1830000	36600	10200000

Continuation on next page.

Continuation of table 1 from previous page:

Item	Cattle Hides	Goat Skins	Sheep Skins	Hides & Skins	Hides & Skins	Hides & Skins	Cattle Hides, Fresh	Cattle Hides, Fresh	Goat Skins, Fresh
Element	Prod.	Prod.	Prod.	Prod.	Domestic Supply	Waste	Slaughtered/ Prod. Animals	Prod.	Slaughtered/ Prod. Animals
Unit	Mt	Mt	Mt	Mt	Mt	Mt	Head	Mt	Head
1998	42800	21000	16220	74070	72725	14814	2136000	42720	10000000
1999	42840	21600	16620	79590	78245	15918	2138500	42770	10500000
2000	42880	21960	17200	80020	78675	16004	2140000	42800	10500000
2001	42920	22000	17140	81060	79715	16212	2142000	42840	10800000
2002	42960	22400	17600	82040	82361	16408	2144000	42880	10980000
2003	43000	22400	18000	82060	81525	16412	2146000	42920	11000000
2004	43080	23160	18300	82960	82626	16592	2148000	42960	11200000

Notes: *Prod. represents Production, Mt represents metric tones.*
Source: *http://Faostat.fao.org.*

The above table 1 shows the total production/waste and the slaughter statistics of hides and skins from Nigeria according to the FAO[2] showcasing Nigeria's great potentials in the production of hides and skins. From the above table 1 one can see that the production of cattle hides, goatskins and sheepskins has been on the increase what indicates the availability of raw materials and the prospects of not running into short supply. Raw materials availability has been acknowledged as a basic comparative advantage towards the export of leather and leather products (Vila Lobos, 1999).

Though there is dearth of data on local consumption of hides and skins in Nigeria, evidence has shown that due to low rate of exports in the sector local merchants trade most hides and skins produced in Nigeria as Pomo[3] (or Kanda) for consumption. Chemonics International Incorporated (2002: 5)

---

2 The figure may have been underestimated when compared from data of real production that is taken to Kano for processing. The discrepancy has been attributed to the activities of the local merchants who sometimes hide information.

3 Pomo or Kanda is a local name given to dry hides and skins mainly for consumption.

takes the opinion that, though there are no reliable data on hides and skins consumption in Nigeria, it is evident that consumption is competing with industrial applications, especially cattle, sheep and goatskins. Such activities led to the introduction of Small and Medium Industries Equity Investment (SMIEIS) by the Bankers Committee (BC) of the CBN so as to streamline the activities of both the producers and the merchants by strategizing and making stronger the existing trading associations[4] towards being a vehicle for rapid industrialization, sustainable economic development, poverty alleviation, and employment generation through harmonized marketing and export activities. The significance of SMIEIS derives from the critical economic role of the real sector i.e. the sector that engages in actual production. The scheme requires that all the banks in Nigeria should set aside 10 percent of their profit before tax annually for equity investments in small and medium industries. This arrangement is to eliminate the burden of interest and other charges associated with normal bank lending. The scheme is therefore an innovative way of financing the real sector and it has a considerable development potential. The incidence of these otherwise uncoordinated activities has been borne by poor marketing and financing due to the poor linkage to the overall macroeconomic and trade policies.

For the past decade livestock accounts for more than 5% of the nation's GDP and is playing a vital role in the country's external trade through the export of hides, skins and leather, though only about ten percent of the production is exported as depicted in figure 1 below.

From figure 1 below, one can see that the export of hides and skins in Nigeria is increasing after a decline in the mid-nineties. The figure 1 also shows a consistent increase in exports of the products since 1999. The export policy from this period onwards recognizes the leather and leather goods alongside the readymade garments, computer software and agro-processing as the most viable or as thrust sectors, hence the setting of some targets for these sectors and the provision of 80% export-oriented leather industries to be declared as 100% export-oriented and the provision of incentives similar to that of 100% export-oriented sectors to them too.

A telling indicator has been noticed from reported slaughter statistics for cattle, sheep, goats and camel which has increased from 1,824,822, 4,253,598, 7,205,63, 18,123 (Mt) in 1996 to 3,028,320, 6,008,474, 11,563,199 and 102,585 (Mt) in 2003 for cattle, sheep, goats and camels respectively (Federal Department of Livestock and Pest Control Ser-

4 Traders Associations are an umbrella that coordinates the activities related to each commodities' marketing-acting activities.

vices/FDLPCS, 2004, Abuja). A substantial number of cattle slaughtered are imported on hooves over the borders into Nigeria, mostly unrecorded, and as such no reliable data is available but believed to be in the region of 30-40 percent of the total slaughter (Felsner and Schmel, 2002: 6).

Figure 1: Nigeria Export of Hides and Leather (Millions of Naira)

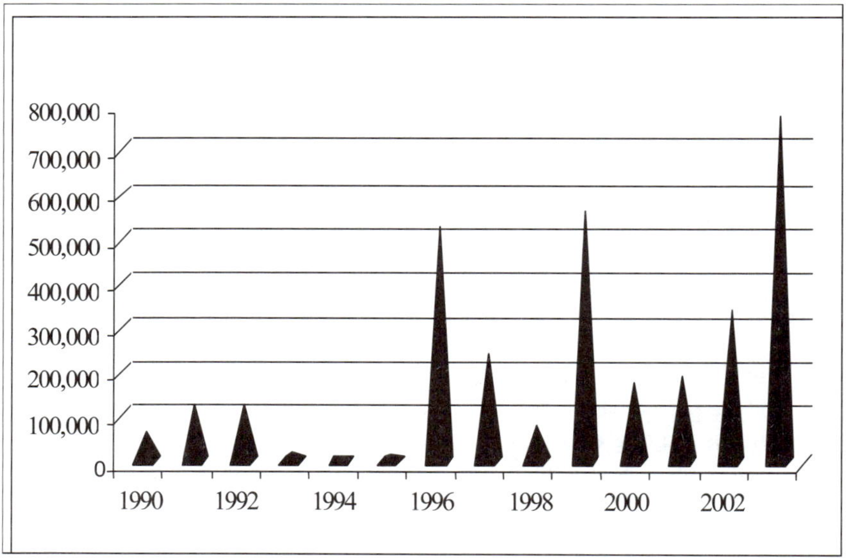

Source: *FOS Annual abstract of Statistics 1999: pp. 464; and The Nigerian Statistical Fact Sheets on Economic & Social Development 2004: pp. 398 & 42.*

Table 2 below and figure 1 above are telling indicators of Nigeria's potentials in hides and skins and in leather exports. From table 2 and from table 5 one can see that leather exports were seen to be very vibrant next to petroleum and its products (1st, 2nd and 3rd) and cocoa beans which happen to be the fourth in 2003 with a total of $156 million in proceeds what is still much lower than the $420 million that was targeted for the year 2003 according to the export policy. The proceeds from leather products exports according to the CBN increased to more than $316 million in 2004 (more than 100 percent increase) what is about 36.8 percent of the total non-oil exports.

Table 2: Nigerian Export Mirror 1999-2003

Rank	HS code and product label	Exports 2003 (US $m)	Export growth 1999-2003 % p. a	World trade growth 1999-2003 % p. a		Share in the world (%)	Leading markets	
				Value	Quantity		1st %	2nd %
	All Goods	22,676		8				
	All Goods (WTO)	20,255						
8	0306 Crustaceans	65.5	5	1	5	0.5	FRA 38*	NLD 37
22	0801 Brazil nuts, cashew nuts & coconuts	11.6	-6	0	10	0.8	IND 98	USA 1
14	1207 Oil seeds	20.7		3	3	1.7	JPN 49	SYR 30
4	1801 Cocoa beans, whole or broken, raw or roasted	491.9	29	13	1	9.9	NLD 37	FRA 14
9	1804 Cocoa Butter, fat and oil	28.2	0	5	3	1.5	FRA 44	GBR 16
21	2302 Bran, sharps and other residues	12.4	86	6	1	2.4	USA 34	MEX 33
10	2609 Tin ores and concentrates	27.0	39	-10	-6	24.4	THA 99	MYS 1
16	2615 Niobium, tantalum, vanadium or zirconium ores	19.7	12	7	1	3.2	CHN 33	EST 30
1	2709 Crude Petroleum Oils	19,432.5	7	12	1	4.7	USA 52	BRA 7

Continuation on next page.

Continuation of table 2 from previous page:

Rank	HS code and product label	Exports 2003 (US $m)	Export growth 1999-2003 % p. a	World trade growth 1999-2003 % p. a		Share in the world (%)	Leading markets	
				Value	Quantity		1st %	2nd %
3	2710 Petroleum Oils, not crude	508.3	-2	11		0.3	USA 93	SGP 2
2	2711 Petroleum Gasses	1,325.0	43	19	5	1.2	ESP 51	USA 25
19	2716 Electrical Energy	12.9	15	21		0.1	NER 100	
18	4001 Natural Rubber, Balata, gutta-percha, etc	16.6	-4	11	3	0.3	FRA 34	GBR 24
6	4105 Sheep/Lamb skin leather	74.2	18	4	17	5.8	ITA 46	ESP 45
5	4106 Goat/Kid skin leather	81.9	22	17	23	10.1	ITA 76	ESP 19
13	4403 Wood in the rough	23.9	-18	2	7	0.2	IND 93	BGD 3
17	5201 Cotton, not carded or combed	17.5		-1	3	0.2	PAK 64	BGD 18
15	7204 Ferrous waste and scrap	20.3	196	18	7	0.1	IND 97	NLD 2
12	8431 Machinery parts	24.4	165	6	11	0.1	GBR 93	NLD 4

Notes: *(1). ITA=Italy,, ESP = Spain, FRA=France, NLD=Netherlands, THA= Thailand, MEX=Mexico, GBR=Great Britain, SGP=Singapore, IND=India, PAK=Pakistan, etc.*

(2). Numbers attached to countries are the percentage of the particular commodity in question that is exported to the country. FRA 38 for Crustaceans therefore indicates that 38 percent of Nigerian Crustaceans is exported to France.*

Source: *UNCTAD.*

The inability of the leather sector to have taken the rightful position in meeting the target has been attributed to low efficiency caused by low technical know how[5] cum high cost of doing business hence low capacity utilization of only 48 percent (CBN 2004: 105). Nigeria's exports of leather from sheep/lamb and goats between 1999 and 2003 grew at the rate of 18% and 22% per annum that was almost the same as the world growth rate of 17% and 23% respectively, to be seen from table 2 above. This is a clear indication of the high export potential of leather products whose exports constitute of 10.1% for sheep/lamb skin and 5.8% for goat skin of the shares in the world with Italy and Spain being the leading markets. Among the main export commodities, brazil nuts, cashew nuts & coconuts, cocoa beans (whole or broken, raw or roasted), cocoa butter, fat and oil, oil seeds, natural rubber, balata, gutta-percha, wood in the rough, crude petroleum oils, and petroleum gasses are all from the southern region of the country, while sheep/lamb skin leather, goat/kid skin leather, cotton (not carded or combed) are from the northern region of the country.

Priority status of these exported products have raw hides and skin, leather and leather products, crusts, hand bags, belts and purses that meet international quality standards. The Nigerian red goatskin has become so popular in Europe, and is currently known as "Morocco leather" (NIPC 2004, www.nipc.org). In Nigeria, municipal abattoirs[6] and large packing stations remained reliable sources of good quality hides, and total production is currently about 40,000 tones annually of which only about 3,000 tons or less than 10% is exported (NIPC, 2004). The remaining quantity is under-utilized within the country irrespective of its sound quality.

According to Chemonics International Incorporated (2002:5), there is high demand for Nigerian hides and skins for food and industrial applications, and Nigeria's export of sheep and goatskins to Europe alone are valued at US$ 87 million. During the period January 1999 to February 2000 out of a total of 64,033 cattle hides that were produced, only 2,378 (3.7%) were made available to the tanneries. With regard to skins 73,764 sheep and goat skins which were produced during the same period, about 26,748 (36.2%) skins were consumed as roasted delicacies (Federal Department of Livestock and Pest Control Services/FDLPCS, Abuja, 2001). In terms of finished leather

---

5 There is still low foreign direct investment in the leather sector. Most of their activities that ought to be automated are still carried out through the traditional methods which have led to some loss in quality and productivity

6 Though some proportion of the slaughtering still takes place outside abattoirs.

production for the year 2001, it is estimated that approximately 40,000 – 60,000 square feet of bovine leather destined for the local market was produced, while the production of crust and finished leather from sheep and goat skins was in the region of 30-35 million square feet for the year million square feet being taken up by the domestic market (Felsner & Schmel, 2002). Production of hides and skins is increasing also in other parts of northern Nigeria such as Sokoto, Katsina, Bauchi and Borno states (see the Nigerian map in figure 2 below for the location of hides/skins and leather production states, and Aba in Abia State as the primary user of the raw materials).

Figure 2: Map of Nigeria showing Hides and Skins and Leather Towns

Source: Accessed by the author

How is the export activity in Nigeria organized regionally and by merchants? Some areas are most important in this context:

Maiduguri: Maiduguri is the capital of Borno state and serves as the collection point for hides and skins produced in Borno and Yobe states. Leading hides and skins merchants in Maiduguri estimated the weekly exports of raw hides and skins to neighboring countries in the region of 2,000 cattle hides, made up of 90% dried and 10% dry salted, and about 10,000 skins usually representing 30% sheep skins and 70% goat skins, but during the wet season (July-September) the percentage of sheep skins is reduced substantially (Borno State Ministry of Agriculture/Veterinary Services Maiduguri, 2004). Other details are presented in table 3. Sheepskin measures around 7 sq. ft. up while goatskins have a unit area of 4.0 - 4.5 sq. ft. The table 3 below is the break down of exports of five large merchants in Maiduguri and reveals their monthly trading/throughputs as supplied by the State Ministry of Agriculture/Veterinary services. Only one mechanized tannery (NEITAL NIGERIA LTD) which is located near to the central abattoir exists in the state, and presently the Bank of Industry (BOI) is interested in the firm. The table 3 below shows the export volume of the main five largest exporters in Maiduguri, indicating also the types of hide.

Table 3: Exports of Hides and Skins of Five Large Merchants in Maiduguri

Names of Merchant	Exports capacity (Mt)
Alhaji Dalori & Sons	40,000-60,000 salted skins (70% goat, 30% sheep) 4, 000-6,000 salted cattle hides
Abatcha Umar & Sons	40,000-70,000 salted skins (70% goat, 30% sheep) 4,000-6,000 salted cattle hides
Satom Saleh & Sons	80,000-150,000 salted skins (70% goat, 30% sheep) 6,000-10,000 salted cattle hides
A.A Naif & Sons	20,000-50,000 salted skins (70% goat, 30% sheep) 1,000-2,000 salted cattle hides
Alhaji Ali & Sons	30,000-40,000 salted skins (70% goat, 30% sheep); no trading in hides

Source: Chairman of Borno State Hides and Skins Dealers Association Maiduguri, Nigeria, (Association's Record).

Bauchi: According to the department of Veterinary Service/Hides and Skin Extension of the State Ministry of Agriculture/Veterinary Services, due to low export patronage the only mechanized tannery there - "BASIC

TANNERY AND LEATHER WORKS LTD", which has the capacity of processing goatskins into wet blue - is eager to find an investor or a joint venture partner to revive the factory. The state has about 242 registered slaughter slabs and 66 registered markets where hides and skins are traded (Bauchi State Ministry of Agriculture/Veterinary Services, 2004).

Sokoto: Sokoto is the capital of Sokoto state and serves as a collection point for Kebbi, Zamfara and Sokoto states. There exist about 12 prominent hides and skins merchants amongst whom is Alhaji Yusuf Karaye who trades on 35,000-40,000 skins/month, consisting of about 70 percent goatskins and up to 1,500 cattle hides (Felsner & Schmel, 2002: 15). The two major tanneries in the town are DANGE Leather Processing Industries and Sokoto Leather & Tanning Industries. The table 4 below shows that from Sokoto there have been inconsistent movements in the purchases of hides/skins made by registered traders/merchants. This may be attributed to low export patronage due to the low quality of their hides and skins when compared with that of Kano and other cities.

Table 4: Recorded Purchases of Hides and Skins by Registered Traders

Year	Cattle Hides	Sheepskins	Goatskins
1999	791,181	5,700,150	6,156,843
2000	381, 308	3,415,966	3,086,070
2001	89,652	836,600	745,400
2002	533,120	6,003,416	4,879,969
2003	202,669	4,071,256	3,347,252

Source: Sokoto State Ministry of Agriculture/Veterinary Services (2004).

Katsina: In Katsina the tanning sector comprises rural tanneries producing leather made from sheep and goatskins. The state is the home of the proposed DAURO TANNERY LTD Company with a planned processing of 1,500 sheepskins per day into crust leather for export. The planned raw material intake according to Felsner & Schmel (2002) will only account for an estimated volume of less than 40 percent of the total yearly skin production of the state. Therefore, there will be a problem with the skin supply unless efforts are made to shift the raw materials to tanneries in Kano that is about 250 km south of the state which will then increase the unit production costs. There are about 11 major registered hides and skin merchants in the city with numerous unregistered merchants (Felsner & Schmel 2002).

Kano: Kano is today the central collection point for hides and skins in Nigeria, especially those that could not be processed in tanneries at other northern cities (Kaduna, Sokoto, Bauchi, and Maiduguri). The Export Processing Zone (EPZ) has promoted hides/skins and leather processing and related export activities. A number of registered tanneries and leather processing centers abound in EPZ area of Kano. Table 5 below shows the names and the value in dollars of the top 14 finished leather exporters in Nigeria for the year 2004, with more than 90 percent of these firms being concentrated around EPZ area of Kano.

Table 5: Top 14 Finished Leather Exporters in Nigeria for the Year 2004

S/No	Name of Exporter	Products Exported	Value ($US)
1.	Fata Tanning	Finished Leather	104,071,573.94
2.	Unique leather finishing	Finished leather	58,140,423.83
3.	Mario Jose Enterprises Ltd.	Finished leather	30,198,737.39
4.	Hafuwa Enterprises Ltd	Finished leather	28,212,777.31
5.	Mamuda Industries Ltd.	Finished leather	25,612,601.47
6.	Mahaza company Ltd	Finished leather	14,281,880.00
7.	Tanorth Tannery Ltd	Finished leather	11,873,159.22
8.	Cadina Company Nigeria Ltd	Finished leather	8,874,114.98
9.	Nasmier Enterprises Limited	Finished leather	7,900,765.67
10.	Multitan Limited	Finished leather	7,550,381.56
11.	Montbrizon Industries	Finished leather	7,215,466.33
12.	International Tanneries Limited	Finished leather	5,659,932.17
13.	Trends Venerate Limited	Finished leather	2,315,310.04
14.	Gashash Tanneries Limited	Finished leather	1,813,099.05
	Total		**313,720,222.96**

Source: CBN (2004): 166.

This is a clear harbinger to the leather export potential in Nigeria and a sign of a positive struggle towards achieving the leather export targets that are set in the national export policy considering that more than $150 million in exports is added in just a year. The issue then rotates on the need to minimize the under-utilization or wastage of hides/skins and of leather produced in Nigeria when studies have revealed that export markets exist for over 40 percent of the firms in the industry (Sakaba 2004: 10). This study intends to identify - through the analysis of findings from actors in the sector - the main constraints militating the sector's efficiency, marketing capacity and productivity that are responsible for the low export capacity. These factors, if marshaled out and tackled, will then no longer be responsible for the under-utilization and the wastages in the sector, thereby helping policymakers to achieve their objectives of export diversification, investment and employment generation, and consequently in poverty reduction. This analysis of determining factors will be achieved through the combination of secondary and primary data[7] from sampled leather enterprises, from leather industrial unions, and from state agencies dealing in hides/skins and leather production activities.

3 Determinants of Nigeria's Leather Export Capacity

According to Schmitz (2004: 4), the availability of raw materials to the traditional leather manufacturing industries of the developed countries is influenced by the import restrictions imposed by developing countries. The above issue is evident from table 6 below which presents the restrictions to imports of hides and skins in selected countries of which Nigeria is among the top countries affected.

Table 6: Restrictions to Hides and Skins in Selected Countries

Bovine	Restriction	Small Skin	Restriction
France	None	Nigeria	From crust
Germany	None	Ethiopia	From wet blue
Great Britain	None	New Zealand	From wet blue
USA	None	India	From finished crust
Russia	From wet blue	Indonesia	From finished crust
Australia	From wet blue	China	From crust (pigskins & goat skins)
Argentina	From wet blue		
Brazil	From wet blue		

Source: Schmitz (2004) as adapted from Vila (2000).

7 The primary data is generated through direct interviews and the administering of questionnaires to different actors and agents to ascertain their opinions.

Another issue according to UNIDO (2000) is the high share of material costs in the total costs of leather and footwear manufacturing in developing countries and in economies in transition that is one reason for their preference for job subcontracting in the production of shoes. Materials costs according to UNIDO (2000) have a large influence on the total production cost; they represent 54% of the total cost in Hungary, 76% in Zimbabwe and 45% in Italy. It is argued that the high production costs have a negative effect on the exports in developing and transition economies.

In another study by UNIDO (2002:64) on the Nigerian manufacturing sector it was found that indirect costs are working against capacity utilization, efficiency and productivity, just as Collier (2000) has argued that transaction costs faced by African manufacturers are typically high, because manufacturing firms are intensive users of services that are particularly expensive in Africa. UNIDO (2002) also has argued that some of these costs are induced by inappropriate government policies while some are inherent in the production process. The theoretical and empirical evidence concerning some factors like costs (raw materials and indirect costs) and other variables that hamper high productivity and exports of hides/skins and of leather products have been summarised in Box 1[8] below.

Box 1: Competitiveness in the Production and Export of Leather and Footwear

At the beginning of the 1990s, the two most fundamental determinants of competitiveness in footwear production were considered to be, production costs and the differential impact of trade barriers. At that time, other less quantifiable factors that influence competitiveness were considered to be the following: technological developments; proximity to major markets and the role of quick response; requirements for high quality production; access to technology and management, design and marketing skills; the increasing importance of offshore, joint venture, and contract production; and some more country–specific factors such as political and infrastructure constraints and the availability of raw materials and components (Landell-Mills 1990).

The significance of several of the above-mentioned factors for the next five years has been subject to revisions. At a recent conference, it was predicted that factors - different from shoe-making technology - to make

8 SATRA conference as used as a source in the box is explained thus: SATRA is the world's leading research and technology organisation for consumer goods.

shoes better, quicker or more productively than before will be driving the footwear industry in the new millennium (SATRA Conference, Hong Kong, April 2000).

The importance of trade barriers and quotas may also diminish with China's admission to the WTO. Trade barriers and existing quotas in the EU and the United States would fall and the possibility for China to negotiate worldwide reductions on import duties would be open (World Footwear, September/October 2000).

The global supply chain of footwear, which developed in the last decade and which is replacing the traditional pattern of integrated shoe-making (leather processing, tanning, finishing, and shoe manufacturing in many developed countries), has been an agent for the transfer of designs, the introduction of modern management practices, quick response, and technology and quality improvement to the producing developing countries that are participating in outsourcing, and has provided the producer countries with indirect access to major markets.

Competitiveness in the production stages of the chain has been addressed, in many instances, through the promotion of collective efficiency by enterprises operating within clusters and industrial districts. The design and managing of different types of marketing and distribution global chains represent the challenge of the present decade to stay competitive in a fast changing world.

Labour costs continue to be a dominant factor of competitiveness. The slow technical development in footwear operations, particularly in the production of uppers, makes footwear manufacturing such a labour-intensive operation that entrepreneurs are induced to search for countries and regions with lower wages. More efficient use of labour is required even in regions/countries usually considered sources of unlimited cheap wages, as is the case of Southern China. The differences in labour costs in 1998 provide a partial explanation for South Korea, Taiwan and Hong Kong having been displaced from the group of the ten top footwear producers in the course of the last decade.

Source: Schmitz, H. (2004), "The Leather Global Value Chain and the World Leather Footwear Market", Interviews with US and European Buyers, IDS Working Paper 100, Brighton, Sussex: IDS

The brief theoretical and empirical evidence as summarized in Box 1 and the earlier part of the section has elucidated some problems and determinants of the leather industry exporting activity globally.

Nigeria is a country aspiring to become one of the world leather exporters through the current drive to harmonize and to improve the industry performance. Are in the country some similar bottlenecks militating this drive as shown from other countries' experiences? What are the possible factors that determine the export propensity of the industry especially at the firm level?

Data[9] used for the analysis were derived from questionnaires that were administered to 68 leather firms/tanneries scattered around the northern part of the country, and 52 of these questionnaires were appropriately completed and returned.

The questionnaires gathered data about the economic and social conditions of the leather firm and its development potential, and focused on three main activities: (a) the firm's performance, where an attempt was made to determine the profitability and productivity of the enterprise; (b) administration – business inspection, tax administration, and the manner in which legal conflicts are resolved; and (c) infrastructure, where the costs of providing electricity, water, telecommunications, transportation and security are addressed. In general, the instrument provided quantitative measures of major regulatory and administrative costs and costs imposed by poor infrastructure. Figure 3 below presents the results from the enterprises/tanneries responses on major bottlenecks to leather productivity, efficiency, marketing, and export capacity.

The results from figure 3 show that inadequate supply of infrastructure or lack of it thereof, high utility prices, official corruption, bureaucratic burdens (including red tape and rent seeking), and difficult access to credit and financing were the major perceived constraints to the growth in productivity, efficiency, marketing, and export activity of the Nigerian leather sector across locations.[10]

---

9 Data for the study were obtained through a survey of some tanneries and leather firms in Nigeria. The data were collected between July and September 2004, by Paul Onwude (Kaduna, Sokoto, Katsina and Maiduguri) and by Daikem (Kano and Bauchi) of the Nigerian Tanners Council (NTC).

10 In a related 2002 World Bank Enterprise Survey/WBES study, financing, corruption, infrastructure and inflation were evaluated by over 60 percent of the firms sampled from Africa as major or moderate constraints to enterprise operations and growth. However, in the Ukraine, taxation was the most troubling of all the issues with over 70 percent of the firms citing it as a major or significant barrier to business development, followed by insufficient local purchasing power and inflation (see Nemickas, A. et. al., 2002).

Figure 3: Major Bottlenecks to Leather Export Productivity, Marketing and Efficiency in Nigeria (%)

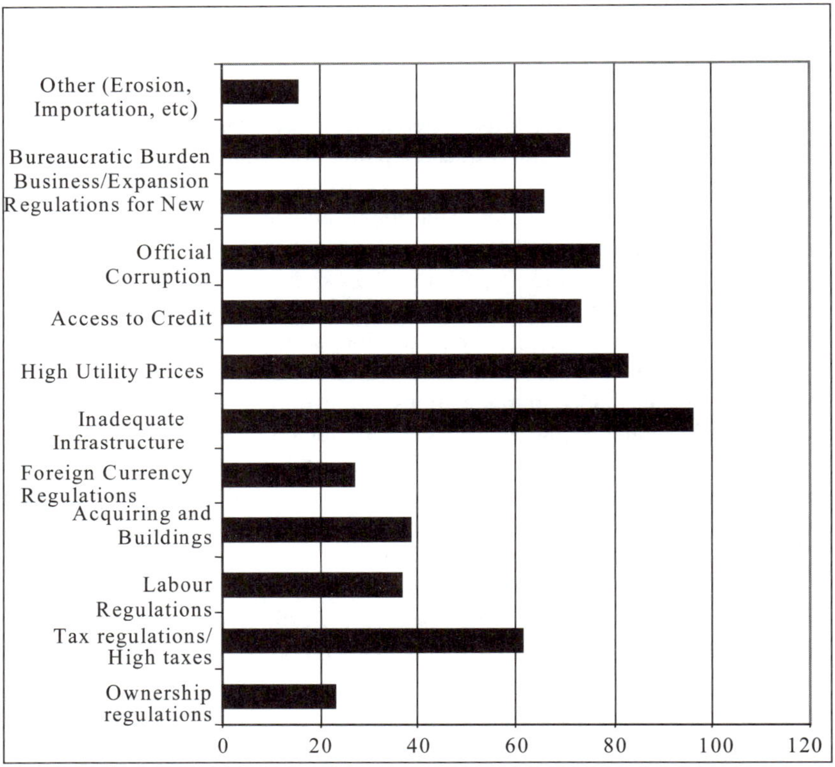

Source: Authors' computation.

Detailed analysis of the supply and the reliability of infrastructure confirmed the inadequacy of main electricity supply with attendant high costs of other basic utilities such as communication, transportation, security, and water. A telling indicator to this is the alarm recently raised by the Bureau for Public Enterprises (BPE) indicating that Nigeria loses N140bn yearly to power outages and it is observed that the greater part of the incidence is borne by the manufacturing sector (The Guardian, May 5, 2005:17 & 63).

Further enquiry shows that bureaucratic burden was perceived more from the instability and unpredictability of changes in the laws, regulations and policies what has made both planning and execution difficult. 80 percent of the respondents thought that the laws and regulations were highly or completely unpredictable, and materially affected the operation and the growth of their business. Also official corruption has been linked to the increase in bureaucratic burden. Corruption in the economy has heightened the cost of registration, while regulations for business expansion have taken longer time and processes due to the same factor.

There is lack of information about how and where to access funds outside the traditional banking environment hence compelling firms to raise funds internally because bank financing is both expensive and difficult for small and medium firms to qualify for, due to their excessive collateral requirements and high interest rates.

The next major constraints to doing business in the Nigerian leather sector are regulations to new business and to business expansion and tax regulations/high taxes. The high taxes were blamed on multiple taxation through the different arms of the government due to the lack of harmonization between the federal, state and local governments.

However, these problems notwithstanding, some leather firms in the northern Nigeria, especially the EPZ area of Kano, have succeeded over time in innovating, growing and even exporting to other countries as can be seen in table 5 above. A high share of this success is attributed to the acquisition of skills by the workers, done mainly through learning-by-doing, through inter-firm linkages with foreign technology suppliers, notably those from Europe and East Asia. However, it is obvious that vulnerabilities emerge in the production strategy of the sector due to low capital goods capability. This is in line with Oyelaran-Oyeyinka's (1997:14) opinion that, "a weak local capital goods capability continues to slow down a full acquisition of major innovation capability… ".

Nigerian producers of hides/skins and leather products have an association that is being harmonized and empowered under the Small and Medium Industries Equity Investment (SMIEIS) programme. The tanneries have an association office that is situated in Kano, Kano state of Nigeria. Apart from the tanneries association, the main domestic user of the primary product (hides and skin) is located in Aba, Abia state of South Eastern Nigeria (Skoup and Company and the World Bank 2003). By the late 1980s, Aba in the South Eastern part of Nigeria was recognized as the "shoe center of West Africa". Presently, the leather and allied products manufacturers' cluster in Aba has over 11,000 enterprises located in 6 main sub-clusters and providing employment to more than 27,000 people (plus temporary seasonal labor force of almost 20,000), and has an annual turnover of over US$100 million (Skoup and Company and the World Bank 2003). Each sub-cluster has an independent association with a duly elected officer. Each line is usually made up of 90-100 enterprises. On the average, the associations have between 16-28 lines.[11] Five of these main sub-clusters produce footwear, 85 percent of which are ladies' footwear. The 6th sub-cluster is made up of two associations – mainly producers of traveling bags, school bags, ladies' bags, wallets, belts, and other leather related products.

Efforts were made to get the associations[12] perceptions on business and policy constraints as well as on other constraints that inhibit their collective export capability. From a long list of constraints[13] that the leather associations identified the lack of business contacts and the lack of information (market information exchange) seem to be major obstacles against speeding up collective exports of both hides and skins and semi-finished and finished leather products in the industry. These constraints are followed by factors such as lack of training and advice, lack of trade support services, and finally the unavailability of trade finance. Other constraints identified by these associations include the high cost of chemicals and machinery, and the relative costs of production and poor infrastructure that limit productivity. The result is presented in figure 4 below. It was interesting to notice that exchange rate and trade policy were not perceived as major constraints to the association in the leather sector. According to the leather associations, the country's exchange rate has been fairly stable while the trade policy effect is felt mostly by the textile sector though there is complaint about the pressure of the new global competition that they are yet to handle. The result is similar to the result found in India, Mexico and Brazil by Nadvi (2005: 5).

---

11 The lines as used here comprise at some times up to fifteen to twenty shops under the same roof.

12 About 60 members from the Nigerian leather associations selected from both the northern part of the country, where there is a concentration of tanneries, and the southern part, especially from Aba, constituting the main domestic users of such services, completed the questionnaires on the associations' perception of collective export, efficiency and marketing constraints.

13 The constraints listed are: regulatory framework and legal norms, taxes, skilled labour, investment incentives, exchange rates, trade policy, industrial policy, trade support services, information asymmetry, business contacts, insufficient demand, inflation, competition from imports, trade finance (access to credit), cost of raw materials, training and advice, price controls, etc.

Figure 4: Constraints of leather Exports (Leather Associations)

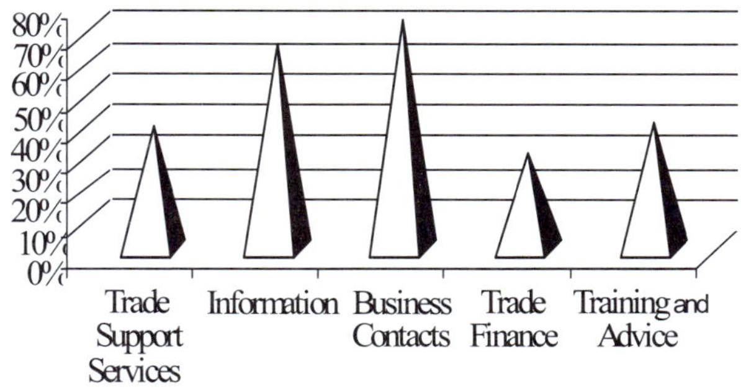

Source: Authors computation.

4 Policy Recommendations for Leather Exports Development

The study identified some bottlenecks responsible for the low export propensity of hides/skins and leather products in Nigeria and the attendant low capacity utilization. These constraints if tackled will speed off the realization of the Nigerian export targets on hides/skins and leather products and this also will position the economy towards escaping from over-dependence on oil and primary commodities. In view of the findings, the study recommends the following for the development of the Nigerian leather sector:

- Improvement of infrastructure (electricity, water, communication, etc) in the leather zones of the country, especially the EPZs of Kano, Calabar, Onne and Aba leather clusters where there is a concentration of tanneries, leather and manufacturing firms. This is necessary to reduce the cost of doing business that was found to be a factor hindering a higher export propensity in the sector. Power should be given priority if the leather sector and the entire manufacturing are expected to take up their rightful place in the economy.

- New policies and new support structures, notably credit facilities, are critically needed to boost the full acquisition of a major innovation capability in the sector. Re-focusing the Nigerian Bank of Industry, the Nigerian Agricultural and Cooperative Bank and the Rural Development Bank, and also the Nigerian Export and Import Bank will go a long way in providing the required credit facilities for the sector.
- High bureaucratic burden was observed as a major constraint to the leather sector's export propensity. Further inquiries among leather exporters linked this to inconsistencies in government policies, hence an appeal for harmonization of all the policies. There is also the need for the state and the local governments to inform businesses about or to get them involved in the process of developing new rules, regulations or policies that affect them, and the need to harmonize all these policies to cut across the three tiers of the government. Just as the National Economic Empowerment and Development Strategy (NEEDS) has outlined some policy issues, these issues should also be extended to the State Economic Empowerment and Development Strategy (SEEDS) and to the Local Economic Empowerment and Development Strategy (LEEDS) in order to have a smooth operation of such policies. This will also take care of multiple taxes as found in the study that has increased the overall tax amount.
- Establishment of modern operational tanneries in Sokoto, Maiduguri and Bauchi to reduce the cost of traveling to Kano for processing. This can be achieved through public-private partnership or by a Build and Operate process if the potentials are well made known to interested investors.
- Business associations in Nigeria's leather sector still have a function in promoting local cooperation and with it in promoting industrial upgrading in the industrial clusters. This could be achieved by increased cooperation through the business associations and a greater use of some of the services that are provided by them. Evidence from Nadvi (2005: 5) has shown that there is a positive relationship between the performance of firms and their relationships with business associations; particularly evident was the case of Guadalajara, Mexico for which case regression analysis has shown that cooperation through the business associations was the most significant factor associated with firms' performance.

Beyond the findings from the study there is also need to:

- Reviving the Institute for Leather Research in Zaria, Kaduna state to take up its rightful position of finding problems militating leather production and export is a must. If the Institute is brought up and is doing the work properly the extension service workers and the veterinary departments from the agricultural ministries of the affected states will benefit immensely from their activities.
- Exploring bilateral trade agreements within the Africa region and beyond is important to complement the already existing multilateral agreements. Bilateral agreements with countries, investors and interested partners outside of Nigeria are vital because of the small size of the internal market. Africa has less than half the population of China or India. Bilateral links with outside Africa will channel the transfer of skills and technology. Technological improvements in the sector are still very low and will be improved if this is achieved.
- Strengths and opportunities of hides/skins and leather products in Nigeria should be made known to the world at large through posting them on the websites of different agencies such as the Nigerian Investment Promotion Commission (NIPC), the Nigerian Exports Promotion Council [(NEPC]), the Nigerian Export Processing Zones Authority (NEPZA), the National Planning Commission (NPC), the Federal Ministry of Information (FMI), the Federal Ministry of Finance (FMF), etc. so as to attract foreign investors into the sector by informing them that all the opportunities needed for its growth and sustenance is in place.
- Liaising with UNIDO, an international organization stepping into leather development in Nigeria, is also important. UNIDO has the capability of stepping into capacity building provisions necessary for the development of the sector. This will close the gap in training, consulting and advisory services as identified by the firms through exchange programs with regard of leather experts from other successful leather-producing and -exporting countries.

In the view of new policies at the Federal, State and the Local government levels in Nigeria to promote export of agro-allied products like leather and leather products and manufactured products, when viewed in relation to other countries of the world that are competing for opportunities in world trade, Nigeria still faces inflation and interest rates higher than those of most of its competitors. Government borrowing, emanating from budget deficits both at the Federal, State and the Local government levels, still crowd out the private sector. The private sector's inadequate access to credit is worsened by lack of publicity and information on the existence of numerous - regrettably uncoordinated - facilities and assistance that the government has made available to exporters. There is need for harmony among the three tiers of government so as to achieve these goals.

It is also true that some of the facilities, especially infrastructures, are not working well or have lapsed into abeyance. The unsatisfactory rural road network constitutes disincentive to agricultural and agro-allied exporters like leather and leather product dealers who have to transport goods from the hinterland to the ports at costs much higher than competitors incur for similar purposes in other parts of the world. The railway system is in a dire need of modernization. To join the race of high international trade performers, Nigeria, as a matter of priority, must have low-priced, reliable and efficient utility services that are an essential pre-condition for attracting export-related foreign and local investment and for establishing a positive business climate. Land transportation and delivery is cumbersome and overburdened (in several cases understandably for security and other reasons) by the existence of several different and overlapping authorities whose missions do not seem consistent with one another.

Documentation requirements and procedures as complained by practitioners are time wasting, costly and inconsistent with officially declared policies while cross-border travel and businesses face similar hassles and delays that exercise a critical constraint to expansion and development of regional trade and to Nigeria's participation in it. These are basic issues that should be seriously be addressed to enable the new export strategy to stay on course hence being beneficial to all the sectors including leather and leather products.

The benefits of exporting are insatiable, and it is an accepted dictum that rapid income growth is always associated with the expansion of manufactured goods exports. There is need for policymakers to provide incentives as enumerated in the recommendations above for export growth. These measures when taken should increase firm-level efficiency what will provide and sustain enough ground for competing at the international level, hence helping in the realization of the export drive. Measures that will reduce the transaction costs associated with exporting (handling cost and cost of infrastructure) should not only be provided but made effective.

References

Bauchi State Ministry of Agriculture/Veterinary Services (2004): Unpublished Records.

Borno State Hides and Skins Dealers Association Maiduguri, Nigeria (2004): "Association's Records" (Unpublished).

Borno State Ministry of Agriculture/Veterinary Services Maiduguri, Nigeria (2004): Unpublished Records.

CBN (Central Bank of Nigeria) (2004): "Annual Reports and Statement of Accounts", pp. 140-166, CBN, Abuja.

CCI (Chemonics International Incorporated) (2002): "Agribusiness Development Assistance Projects in Nigeria - Export Opportunities for Hides and Skins in Nigeria" CHEMONICS/USAID RAISE PCE-1-00-99-00003-00, pp. 4-8.

Collier, Paul (2000): "Africa's Comparative Advantage", Chapter 2 in: Jalilian, H., Tribe, M. & Weiss, J. (eds): Industrial Development and Policy in Africa, Edward Elgar, Cheltenham, UK.

FAOSTAT (2004): FAOSTAT data, last updated February 2004, online: www.fao.org, accessed 16/09/2004.

FAOSTAT (2005): FAOSTAT data, last updated February 2005, online: www.fao.org, accessed 01/05/2005.

FDLPCS (Federal Department of Livestock and Pest Control Services) (2004): Abuja.

Felsner, Gerhard and Schmel, Ferenc (2002): "Agro-Industries and Sectoral Branch, Leather Unit Programme Development and Technical Cooperation Division" US/NIR/01/11-52, Technical Report Prepared for United Nations Industrial Development Organisation (UNIDO).

FMIN (The Federal Ministry of Industry of Nigeria) (1999): Nigeria Export Policy (1997-2003), Abuja, 1999.

FOS (Federal Office of Statistics) (1999): "Nigeria Exports of Major Commodities", Federal Office of Statistics Annual Abstract of Statistics 1999 Edition, Abuja, ISSN 00776-0626.

FOS (Federal Office of Statistics) (2004): "Nigerian Statistical Fact Sheets on Economic & Social Development, Nigeria Exports by Products 1999-2003", Nigeria Foreign Trade Summary and Statistical News Merchandise Trade.

ITC (International Trade Centre): Country or Product Approach – Leather, 1998-2002, International Trade Statistics, UNCTAD, online: www.unctad.org,

Landell-Mills (1990), In the Leather Global Value Chain and the World Leather Footwear Market, http://www.factbook.net/leather-patterns.php

Markham, Theodore (2004): "A Framework of Export Strategy for the Federal Republic of Nigeria 2005-2010", produced by Nigeria Export Promotion Council Abuja and the Commonwealth Secretariat London.

Nadvi, Khalid (2005): "Dynamic Transformations for Base-of-the-Pyramid Market Clusters", in: Journal of the Academy of Marketing Science; Vol. 33, No. 4.

Nemickas, A., Senchuk, B. and Babanin, O. (2002): "Ukraine: An Assessment of the Business Enabling Environment", IFC Survey and Sectoral Analysis Project in Ukraine, October 2002.

Nigerian Tanners Council, Information, 2004

NIPC (Nigerian Investment Promotion Commission) (2005): "Local Sourcing of Raw Materials: Role of Raw Materials Research and Development Council (RMRDC)". Online: www.nipc-nigeria.org/sup_role.htm, assessed 21/02/ 2005.

Ogujiuba, Kanayo, Amakom, Uzochukwu and Uka, Eke (2004): "A Review of Value Added in the Agricultural Sector: Background and Issues", Position Paper for Committee on Agriculture of National Assembly, (unpublished), Abuja.

Oyelaran-Oyeyinka, Banji (1997): "Nnewi: An Emergent Industrial Cluster in Nigeria", Ibadan, Technopol Publishers.

Sakaba, Amos (2004): "Leather and leather products: Nigeria Is Among World Best", in: The Investment Facilitator, A Publication of the Nigerian Investment Promotion Commission (NIPC), Volume 1, Number 1, October, 2004, pp. 10-11.

SATRA (2000): The Leather Global Value Chain & the World Leather footwear market - Evolution of the Leather Value Chain Global Value Chains, SATRA Conference Hong Kong, April 2000, online http://www.factbook.net/leather_evolution.php, accessed 20/11/2004.

SATRA Conference, Hong Kong, April 2000, Analysis of the World Leather Value and Footwear Market, http://www.factbook.net/leather_evolution.php accessed November 20, 2004F

Schmitz, Hubert, (2004, pp. 1-5) "The Leather Global Value Chain & the World Leather Footwear Market", Interviews with US and European Buyers, IDS working paper 100, Brighton, Sussex: IDS

SKOUP & Company and the World Bank, (2003, pp. 20-26) "Nigeria Cluster Development in Eastern Nigeria: Administrative and Infrastructure Costs' Survey of the Manufacturing Sector (Abia and Anambra States)", Report Prepared for the International Finance Corporation (IFC) and the World Bank (IBRD)

Soderbom, Mans and Teal Francis (2002): "The Performance of Nigerian Manufacturing Firms: Report on the Nigerian Manufacturing Enterprise Survey 2001" Oxford: UNIDO and Centre for the Study of African Economies (CSAE).

Sokoto State Ministry of Agriculture/Veterinary Services (2004): Unpublished Records.

The Guardian (2005): "Nigeria loses N140bn yearly to power outages especially in the manufacturing sector", The Guardian, Thursday, May 5, 2005, pp. 17 and 63.

UNCED (United Nations Conference on Environment and Development) (2002): "Agenda 21 adopted in Rio de Janeiro in 1992", Johannesburg Summit 2002, Country Profiles.

UNCTAD, homepage, www.unctad.org assessed March 20, 2005

UNIDO (2000): "Structure and Production Costs in the Footwear Manufacture", prepared by Ferenc Schmel for the 14 Session of the Leather Products Industry Panel, December 11, 2000, online: http://www.unido.org/userfiles/timminsk/-LeatherPanel14SchmelCosts.pdf, accessed 08/05/2006.

UNIDO (2002): "Industrial Development Report 2002/2003", online: http://www.unido.org/doc/24397, accessed: 08/05/2006.

Vila, Lobos (1998): "Meet in Africa: Intra-African Trade Promotion Programme" Report on the Meet in Africa for Leather Products, Cape Town, ITC/DTCC/98/2416. online: http://www.intracen.org/sstp/doc/report/-leather.htm, accessed 08/05/2006

Vila, Lobos (1999): "Report of the Sixth Session of the Sub-Group on Hides and Skins, Intergovernmental Group on Meat, online: http://www.fao.org/unfao/bodies/ccp/ccp62/x0508e.htm, accessed 08/05/2006.

Vila, Lobos (2000): "Labour Department and BASF Internal", in: Status and Outlook of the Leather Industry in the New Millennium, presented at the Round Table of the Leather Industry, pp. 1-6, Bologna, 06/05/2000.

World Footwear, September/October 2000

Unit 3: Escaping the Primary Commodities Dilemma by Pro-Active Policies: The Case of Cameroon

edited by Chicot Eboué, Touna Mama, Karl Wohlmuth and Tobias Knedlik

Escaping the Primary Commodities Dilemma by Pro-Active Policy Reforms in Cameroon - An Introduction

Touna Mama, Ernest Bamou, and Chicot Eboué

1 The Issues: The Primary Commodities Dilemma

Commodity prices had plunged dramatically in the ten years preceding the Rio Summit in 1992 and have almost consistently continued to spiral downwards since then. In 2001, real commodity prices for agricultural raw materials and minerals, ores and metals have fallen to 60 percent of their price levels in 1980 (UNCTAD, 2001). Falling prices have meant that large increases in export volume by the commodity producers have not translated into greater export revenues, leading to severely declining terms of trade for many commodity-producing countries. When the purchasing power of an exporting country declines, it is unable to purchase imported goods and services necessary for its sustenance, as well as generating income for the implementation of sustainable development programs.

A vast majority of developing countries (DCs) depend on commodities as a main source of revenue. Primary commodities account for about half of the export revenues of DCs and many of them continue to rely heavily on one or two primary commodities for the bulk of their export earnings. For many countries, the declining terms of trade associated with a fall in commodity prices have also led to a build-up of unsustainable debt.

Depressed commodity prices also meant that many countries dependent on primary exports have been forced to increase production in attempts to compensate for falling prices. This has led to a situation of more land resources being used for export crop production, reducing land available for domestic food cultivation, and increasing deforestation of non-agricultural land. Declining prices for primary commodities also prevent primary commodity producers from investing in safe and environmentally sound methods of production. The lack of transfer of technology prevents commodity producers from developing and least developed countries, particularly those involved in the production of agricultural commodities and resource extraction, such as mining and minerals, to invest in ecologically sustainable modes of production.

The history of commodity price stabilization efforts and the collapse of commodity agreements are indicative of the vested interest of Northern industrialized countries (under pressure from domestic corporate lobbies) to keep commodity prices at a consistently low level of prices. It is also illustrative of the legacy of colonial economic relations between the North and the South that continues today under the guise of Structural Adjustment Programs (SAPs) and multilateral trade rules favouring developed countries. The marginalization of commodity-dependent countries, particularly the Least Developing Countries (LDCs), from international trade and financial systems have weakened their control over their terms of trade and severely undermined their capacity to set remunerative incomes for their commodity producers, particularly the small farmers.

The linkages between the declining prices for primary commodities and the issues of sustainable growth and development are clear. Depressed commodity prices lead to declining terms if trade for commodity-dependent countries, leading to balance-of-payments problems and resulting in debt. The lack of financial resources available within the country as a consequence of debt servicing and the decline in the purchasing power vis-à-vis imports leads to diminished funds for development. This will, of course, lead to impoverishment, social conflict, a decline in social welfare provisions, and to environmental degradation. Lack of funds and pressure to generate more revenue from finite resources will severely hamper efforts to implement a sustainable management of natural resources and good governance.

Unless international action is taken to stabilize commodity prices and to ensure a remunerative income for commodity producers and commodity-producing countries, many DCs will not emerge from the poverty trap, exacerbating their dependence on foreign aid and blocking efforts to invest in social and economic capital for sustainable growth and development.

Despite more than a decade of policy reform and structural adjustment, the supply response has been weak in many of today's DCs. Then, the most relevant proposal for escaping from this primary commodity dilemma is export diversification. It is considered in the literature as one of the main solutions to the instability of export earnings of DCs. The first and oldest argument, based on the conclusion of MacBean et al. (1980) on the instability of export earnings, shows that the instability index of export earnings is higher for DCs who have a narrow export base than for developed countries with a wider base of exports. For them, commodity and geographical concentration were not the cause of export earnings instability as was previously believed, but depended on the type of commodity (i.e., export earnings from coffee, rubber and cocoa are more unstable than those from oil, banana, sugar and tobacco). The second, and more current, group of arguments is partly a rebuttal of the development literature against the Ricardian static concept of comparative advantage which, when carried to its logical conclusion, advocates complete specialisation to maximise gains from trade. Comparative dynamic advantage is thus used to justify exports diversification.

The reasons for basing export diversification on comparative dynamic advantage are two-fold:

- As a reaction to autonomous factors (taste, technology, industrial capacity, producer competitiveness, etc.) the comparative advantage of a country changes with time;
- Changes caused by the economic policy in place (e.g. tariff barriers) affect the comparative advantage. These changes render the dynamic comparative advantage more significant than the static one.

With the dynamic theory, this means that 'a nation's pattern of development is not determined once and for all, but must be recomputed as underlying conditions change or are expected to change over time. Therefore DCs are not necessarily or always relegated by traditional trade theory to export mostly primary commodities and import mostly manufactured products' (Salvatore, 1990: 313).

In addition to these two main groups of arguments in favour of export diversification, others taken from the supply and demand side approaches, from debt and industrialisation analysis, and those having to do with the country's economic performance, environment, tariff barriers, risk aversion, etc., are well developed by Luvanga and Musando (1993) and Ssemogerere and Kasekende (1994). In fact, it has been shown in the literature that growth in the demand for raw materials is less than it used to be. Among the reasons most cited for this are, inelastic income demand, discovery of substitutes, and trade barriers. Salvatore (1990) shows that since 1980 the prices of raw materials are decreasing and that the income demand elasticity of developed countries is lower than 1 (one). Also, the discovery in developed countries of raw material substitutes as well as the setting up of trade barriers, in reaction to the global competition pressure, has reduced their demand. All of this suggests that export diversification is the only way of increasing the exports of DCs who are mainly raw material exporters.

It is shown in the supply approach to development that changes in a country's resource endowment are the main supply factors that argue in favour of diversification. Marketing information that makes it possible to identify what is available in the market and what is in demand is also necessary in orienting supply with a view to world market penetration.

Comparative dynamic advantage suggests, as a reaction to changes in local resource endowment (improvement in human capital, changes in production technology, and availability of imported inputs due to a reduction of trade barriers, etc.), the development of new products as a result of adjustments in the productive structure and therefore the emergence of new exports.

It appears in the debt accumulation approach that just as it is true that debt can make it possible for a country to increase its future production capacity, it is also true that creditors are primarily interested in a country's capacity to repay its debts. This capacity is generally appreciated from the ratio of debt servicing, which is a proportion of export earnings. The weakness or reduction of a country's export earnings shows its incapacity or low capacity to repay its debt and therefore compromises the capacity for indebtedness or results in an increase in the country's debt.

In DCs this can imply a reduction in social services (transport, health, education, etc.) that are generally financed through debt. These implications can have disastrous economic and social consequences. It is therefore dangerous for a country to specialise in raw materials for which income demand elasticities in developed countries (the main buyers) are low, and thus cannot facilitate increases in export earnings. Under these conditions, diversification is the only solution.

It has also been shown that countries whose export earnings have grown are those whose total exports show a high proportion of manufactured products. In this connection, a positive relation has been established in economic literature between export diversity and the degree of industrialisation. This also implies that countries graduate to higher and sophisticated products thereby creating opportunities for the less developed.

On the supply side, it has been shown that industrialisation gives a country several opportunities for innovation (creation of new products or differentiation of existing products) that make it possible to introduce 'new products' into the market. On the demand side, product differentiation favours the effect of substitution within the same group of products (Ssemogerere and Kasekende, 1994). Easy control of the industrial production environment and gains from competitiveness that are resulting from the possibility of cost reduction also justify industrialisation as a factor of diversification.

In general, the main arguments for diversification include: a long-term tendency towards declining terms of trade for primary products; the variability in export earnings and their implications for growth; and the poor correlation between real per capita incomes and natural resource dependence.

However, any serious 'business plan' for trade promotion and export diversification must be based on a realistic assessment of a country's position in the international division of labour, complemented by an analysis of how to develop new areas of competitive advantage. Bonaglia and Fukasaku (2003: 21-22) think that this cannot be done without an assessment of:

- External opportunities and constraints in view to answer the following questions: How is world demand evolving? What are the most dynamic products? What are the entry conditions for these products in international markets? How are these products to be placed into global commodity chains? What is the governance structure of the commodity chain?
- Internal opportunities and constraints aiming at answering the following questions: What are the strengths and the weaknesses of the private sector? How are government policies affecting the private sector's ability to trade? How is the country placed in terms of producing the most dynamic export products and meeting the market entry conditions? Which interest groups are likely to consider themselves as affected by a specific policy?

2 The Contributions: Preconditions for and Chances of Export Diversification

This Unit aims at answering some of the up-cited questions in the case of Cameroon. The key findings of the four contributions can be outlined as follows: *Chicot Eboué*, *Touna Mama* and *Ernest Bamou* analyse how the country could organize to go beyond the SAPs and to cope with the new and tremendous challenges of the Millennium Development Goals (MDGs), especially to achieve sustainable economic growth and development. After accessing the past SAPs process and concluding on their failure in terms of boosting growth and development in Cameroon, they provide a new route to achieve that objective which is mainly based on: the improvement of the governance and the combat of corruption; the reduction of the legal and judicial insecurity of investment; the compensation of the absence of a fiscal system adapted to certain sectors of activity; the upgrading of the local enterprises hampered by outdated equipment and underutilization of their capacities; the improvement of the quantity and quality of road, port, airport, railway, energy, telecommunications and storage infrastructure; the decentralisation of governance; and, moreover, the diversification of exports and of the entire economy towards products with comparative advantage. Rationalization of resource utilization, reaching the achievement point of the Highly Indebted Poor Countries (HIPC) initiative, and financial deepening are proposed as the main financing sources of such activities.

Touna Mama and *Valérie Ongolo Zogo* analyse the ways to promote exports and regional trade in the Economic and Monetary Community in Central Africa (CEMAC) through transport infrastructures. After outlining various barriers to trade, among which transport costs are the main, the authors derive from a partial equilibrium model the direct and indirect benefits of a new road linking Yaoundé to Libreville. They show that the direct benefits for Cameroon are fiscal and trade-related, since the country is a net exporter within CEMAC. Indirect benefits are also accruing to Gabon, given the 'inter-closing' of markets at the border with Cameroon. In view to finance the new road in a period of budget limitations in the two countries they give preference to a public financing mode, thanks to the total net positive effect in the economies interlinked, and especially the positive impact on inter-regional trade. The possibility to couple public finance with private finance, through the Built-Operate-Transfer (BOT) system, is also envisaged.

Celestin N'Donga analyses the challenges and prospects of investments and of industrialization in Cameroon. After giving a detailed history of the industrialization policy reforms in Cameroon since 1960 and their impact on the sequencing of development of the country, he thinks that priority has to be given to industry for the country to meet the MDGs. Competitive products and industries are then envisioned. It then appears that bauxite-aluminium, forest-timber, cotton-textile, energyand food industry are interesting sub-sectors despite the adversity of other competitors in the world market. However, to boost the related industries, an appropriate institutional frame and an enabling economic environment for supply have to be put in place as well as a new shape of the public-private sector partnership.

Alexandre Magloire Schouamé and *Mireille Etogo Messomo* analyse the way for an efficient diversification of export-led agriculture in Cameroon with reference to food production and non-food agriculture supply. Using the Hecksher-Ohlin-Samuelson scheme they show that there is much room looking at the world demand to promote the local supply of Natural Rubber, Palm Oil and Arabic Gum. Looking at the sub-regional market (CEMAC) a diversification through food products, vegetables, fruits and biological products can enable the country's exports to oil suppliers' countries like Chad, Congo, Gabon and Equatorial Guinea. The success of such diversification requires a multi-dimensional action, including the reform of the agricultural development strategy so as to increase the yields and to adapt the structure of the production to the bio-ecological diversity of the country, and improving the sub-regional trade policy frame to allow the private sector to respond favourably to non-price incentives.

3 The Strategy: How to Escape from the Primary Commodity Dilemma

From this unit, one can rightly conclude that it is time for the Cameroonian government to engage more firmly into the promotion of economic development and especially export diversification so as to allow Cameroon to escape from the primary commodities dilemma in view to achieve the MDGs. The success of this new development policy requires a broad strategy to exploit the existing comparative advantages, what implies a more efficient nexus between the public, private financial and non-financial sectors and the other economic stakeholders including businessmen, trade unions, people's organizations, religious hierarchy, academic and research community, and other components of the civil society as well as the international resource providers and regional and sub-regional institutions. Such an approach depends mainly on the:

- Improvement of the governance and the combat of corruption;
- Reduction of the legal and judicial insecurity of investment;
- Compensation of the absence of a fiscal system adapted to sectors of activity with potential comparative advantage;
- Upgrading of the local enterprises hampered by outdated equipment and underutilization of their capacities;
- Improvement of the quantity and quality of road, port, airport, railway, energy, telecommunications and storage infrastructure; and
- Decentralisation of governance.

Indeed, everybody or anybody who is affected by or benefits from any diversification endeavour must take active part in its planning, decision-making, and implementation. Everybody must take responsibility and get involved in the pursuit of sustainability, as it is the people's right to have a sustainable life. Individual actions, however, are best coordinated and taken together to attain synergy and optimum results. Operationally, therefore, diversification must be pursued in a way that involves and benefits from the complementary actions of the three key stakeholder groups, namely, public institutions (the Head of State and the remaining government, the Parliament, the Social and Economic Council), civil society, referring to society at large outside of government, and international donors and regional and sub-regional institutions.

Due to Cameroon's 'strong' presidential system, the Head of State is expected to constitute the driving force and to demonstrate a firm determination to promote a new form of social contract that transcends ethnic or religious particularities so as to embrace excellency and efficiency meritocratic values which favor functional solidarities. He must therefore stimulate an internal dynamism of change and turn international support into an accompanying factor and not a vector of organization of the society. Thus, he must create in minds the need and urgency for change, show to the people that it deserves a better life and create psychological disruption points within the population (Nyambal, 2006).

The government provides the legal and regulatory framework that sets order and the direction of economic diversification. Actions by civil society and international, regional and sub-regional institutions in the country are governed and influenced by the policies and regulations imposed by the government. The government then has to take the lead in crafting the future, setting directions, providing facilities and incentives of all kinds for the achievement of the so said goals. The government of Cameroon adopted the market oriented economic system with the first Structural Adjustment Program (SAP) in 1988. It must, therefore, strengthen the four major functions of a government attached to a free enterprise economy, notably the functions of:

- *Strategist*, which consists in creating a credible, attractive, stable and predictable legal and regulatory frame to govern markets;
- *Regulator*, which aims to guarantee the rules of competition and consumer security;
- *Stabilizer*, which helps to reduce macroeconomic instabilities; and
- *Solidarity*, which aims to seek for equity and social justice.

Parliament is expected to ratify international and bilateral agreements and initiate draft bills geared to improve the business environment. Its role of controlling government activity must be reinforced at the same time as the functions of its Committees like the Finance and Economic Committee in particular.

Despite its nature as a consultative body, the Economic and Social Council must effectively fulfil its mission of favouring collaboration among the various regions and professional categories of the countries. It must therefore play a key role in the tripartite dialogue Government-Civil Society-International Donors in favour of economic diversification. Meanwhile, it needs to be staffed with experts, and its organization chart should be reviewed and implemented.

The private sector dominates the production sector where jobs, goods and incomes are generated. Thus, the sector directly determines the sustainability of production activities, and influences the sustainability of the consumption behaviour of the public through the goods and services they produce, and the manner by which they promote and package them. The participation of the sector in all sustainable diversification initiatives is thus critical. As part of the problem, they must be part of the solutions, including the planning and execution of such solutions (Sevaly, 2001).

The civil society [including Consular Chambers, Chambers of Commerce, Industry, Mines and Handicraft (CCIMA), Chamber of Agriculture, associations and employers' unions like GICAM (Cameroon Employers' Union), MECAM (Association of Cameroon Enterprises), SYNDUSTRICAM (Union of Cameroon Industries), Road Transporters' Union (STR), the Inter-Professional Cocoa and Coffee Board (CIPCC), Unions of foresters, academicians and researchers, Non-Government Organizations, etc.] should also be involved in the diversification of the economy. It has to serve as the voice of its beneficiaries and bridge between government and beneficiaries and among stakeholders. Through these linkages, it is quite effective in awareness raising and advocacy. However, it has to be organized in view to fully participate in the improvement of the business environment through the dialogue with the government, namely in the Inter-ministerial Committee extended to the private sector, which is a forum of discussions between the government and the private sector.

The international donors (World Bank, International Monetary Fund (IMF), African Development bank, etc.) and regional and sub-regional cooperation institutions [African Union (AU), Economic Commission for Africa (ECA), Central African Economic and Monetary Community (CEMAC), etc.] could also play an important role in the economic diversification not only by their advices but also by financing it. The lack of resources has been a critical restrictive factor in the pursuit of sustainable development policies in most developing countries. Government and civil society in these countries rely so much on external resources. These resources come in the form of funds, expertise or technical know-how, and equipment and technology. This makes the third group of stakeholders a major actor that plays a critical role in sustainable economic diversification. In view of this, it is imperative that they be actively involved in tripartite discussions for an economic diversification strategy.

References

Bonaglia, F. and Fukasaku, K. (2003): "Export Diversification in Low-Income Countries: An International Challenge After Doha." OECD Development Centre, Working Paper No. 209, Paris: OECD.

Luvanga, N. and Musonda, F. (1993): "Export Promotion Through Diversification: Prospects for Non-traditional Exports", in: (Eds.), M. S. D. Bagachwa and A. V. Y. Mbelle, Economic Policy Under a Multi-party System in Tanzania, Dar es Salaam.

MacBean, A. I., Alasdair, I. and Nguyena, D. I. (1980): "Commodity Concentration and Export Instability: A Mathematical Analysis", in: The Economic Journal. Vol. 90. pp. 354-362.

Nyambal, E. (2006): "Créer la Prospérité en Afrique: Dix Clés pour Sortir de la Pauvreté." Série Le Monde en questions, Collection L'Esprit économique, Harmattan, Innoval, Paris, France.

Salvatore, D. (1990): "International Economics". Third Edition, Macmillan Publishing Company, New York, USA.

Sevaly, S. (2001): "Involving Stakeholders in Aquaculture Policy-making, Planning and Management". In: R.P. Subasinghe, P. Bueno, M.J. Phillips, C. Hough, S. E. McGladdery and J.R. Arthur (eds.), Aquaculture in the Third Millennium, Technical Proceedings of the Conference on Aquaculture in the Third Millennium, Bangkok, Thailand, 20-25 February 2000, NACA, Bangkok and FAO, Rome, pp. 83-93.

Ssemogerere, G. N. and Kasekende, L. A. (1994): "Constraints to the Development and Diversification of Non-traditional Exports in Uganda: 1981-90", AERC Research Paper, No. 28, Nairobi, Kenya

UNCTAD (United Nations Conference on Trade and Development) (2001): "Export Diversification Index", UNCTAD Handbook of Statistics, Online: Geneva.

Beyond the Structural Adjustment Programs: The Roadmap to a Sustainable Growth Path for Cameroon

Touna Mama, Ernest Bamou and Chicot Eboué

1 Introduction

Cameroon plunged into economic crisis in 1987 and the latter half of the 1980s was marked by the implementation of significant macroeconomic and structural reforms within the framework of Structural Adjustment Programs (SAPs). These SAPs were aimed at streamlining public finance, improving the business environment, achieving global economic competitiveness, as well as growth and development in general. Thanks to the commitments of the Millennium Development Goals (MDGs) Agenda, the fight against poverty became the focal point of the economic policy of the country. The government initiated, in the early 2000s, a poverty reduction strategy based on a sustained growth, which is expected to play a key role in the social and economic development of the country.

After almost 20 years of these reforms, the country is yet to achieve the high growth rate and low poverty rate of the early 1980s. Gross Domestic Product (GDP) growth has stabilized at an average rate of 4.5% per year in the past 10 years and only a slight decrease of 13 percentage points is recorded in the poverty rate which evolved from 53% in 1996 to 40.2% in 2001 (World Bank, 2004 and 2005). With a steady growing population of about 2.1% per year and numerous requirements for development, this profile of expansion remains poor compared to the real potentials of the country and the MDGs, which expect an average growth rate of 7 to 8% to shift the poverty and unemployment curves and hope for a significant increase in the national per capita income.

Given the expectation that the population will reach 22 to 25 millions people in ten years time, one can rightly pose the question of how should the country organize itself to cope with the new and tremendous challenges: health and education constraints, environment and sustainable development constraints, public services and goods delivery, fighting against poverty, economic and financial deepening, etc?

Our paper aims at answering this question by showing that diversifying the economy to escape from the primary commodities dilemma is the road toward sustainable growth in Cameroon. It proceeds as follows: The past SAPs, including the ongoing Poverty Reduction Strategy Programs (PRSP), are accessed in the next section. Section 3 summarizes the recent performances and retains the lessons from the growth prospects derived from model simulations. Section 4 suggests new paths to sustainable growth and development in Cameroon. Section 5 simulates the impact of the suggested new paths. Section 6 concludes the paper.

2 Structural Adjustments Programs in Cameroon: More Hell than Heaven

One of the fundamental themes of SAPs is the reform of the economic incentive system, which aims at reorienting the latter towards tradable rather than non-tradable goods (Serageldin, 1989). These SAPs are accompanied by measures aimed at progressively liberalising economic activities with a view to increasing their competitiveness on the local and foreign markets. Actually, this entails evolving from a controlled economy to a more liberal and highly performing economy. All these programmes generally comprise stabilisation and adjustment measures, as well as efforts to mobilise foreign aid in favour of a growth-oriented strategy. Since 1988, 8 SAPs have been implemented.[1] The SAPs were triggered by the economic crisis at the end of the 1980s. The main features of this crisis were: declining world prices for the country's main exports; drastic deterioration in the balance of payments; an overvalued exchange rate; a large fiscal budget deficit; negative economic

1 The four first were financed by a Stand-By Facility of 18 months (1988-1990), 9 months (1991-1992), 18 months (1994-1995) and 12 months (1995-1996) respectively. The fifth (1996-1997) was financed by an interim program of 12 months. The sixth (1997-1999) was a three years medium term program financed by an enhanced structural adjustment facility. The seventh (2000-2003) was a facility for growth and fight against poverty (Touna Mama and Tsafack, 2000). The ongoing program (since 2004) is based on the Highly Indebted Poor Countries (HIPC) initiative, which will led to the cancellation of a significant portion of the country's external debt.

growth and negative agricultural growth and increasing poverty (Bamou et al. 2006).

Various reforms have been implemented as part of the SAPs. These have included: fiscal and monetary policy reforms; exchange rate devaluation; banking and financial sector reform; trade liberalization and agricultural policy reform. The aims were to: reduce inflation through tight fiscal and monetary policy; rationalize public sector spending through cuts and better budget management; progressively liberalize interest rates; stimulate private initiative and reduce production costs through market deregulation and improved price incentives; shift the bias in production incentives away from non-tradable goods and services towards tradables; revive agricultural productivity through market liberalization and the reform of public sector enterprises; revitalize international trade by consolidating the process of sub-regional integration and diversifying trade and foreign trading partners [Blandford et al. (1995) and World Bank (2004)].

Reform of the public sector focused on reforming public finances, restructuring public services, and redefining the role of the state in order to free resources for the provision of public goods and essential infrastructure and services. Measures were taken to control state expenditure, increase state revenue and reduce public sector debt. Efforts to control public sector spending included: a freeze and cuts in public sector salaries and allowances; early retirement programs for state personnel; cuts in the student population in government vocational schools; a reduction of embassy staff as well as 'costly' and 'non-profitable' economic missions; restrictions on the mobility of public sector personnel to reduce travel costs. Following these reforms, the state wage bill fell by 12 percent in 1992. Further salary cuts in January and November 1993 led to a sharp fall of almost 35 percent in the payroll during the 1993/94 fiscal year (MINEFI/DP, 2000). Many public and parastatal enterprises were privatized or liquidated and the remaining ones were restructured.

Cameroon is a member of the Economic and Monetary Community for Central Africa (CEMAC). The most significant initiative of the community has been the Regional Fiscal Reform Programme (RFRP), which was adopted by Cameroon in 1994, and aimed at simplifying and harmonizing the setting and collection of indirect taxes and international tariffs.

Financial and banking sector reforms involved a number of measures including reform of the banking system by liquidating non-profitable establishments; emergency measures to relieve the liquidity crisis by discharging arrears and rescheduling credits at the Central Bank; restructuring agricultural credit; and better control over banks by supranational authorities. As a result, most small and medium size enterprises are unable to access credit from formal financial institutions and rely on relatives and informal moneylenders. Some donor-funded microfinance programs also supply credit to them, but these are not widespread, or well developed, and they lack coordination with the formal banking sector (Ongolo Zogo et al., 2005).

Through monetary policy agreements with France, the local currency (CFAF), like that of all the other countries of the CFA zone, has since 1948, been freely convertible into French Francs (FF) at a fixed parity of CFA 50 per FF 1. After 1985, the economic and financial situation of the zone worsened following the deterioration in the terms of trade due to the collapse in the international prices of major exports, a decline in competitiveness due to the appreciation of the FF against the currencies of the zone's major trading partners and other constraints including, the very high cost of labour (Clément et al., 1996). From the early 1990s, persistent poor macroeconomic performance showed that internal adjustments alone could not sufficiently revitalize the economy and that monetary adjustment should also be considered. Countries of the CFA agreed on the virtues of a stable common currency compared to national currencies and in January 1994, therefore, decided to devalue the CFA.

3 Growth Prospects for Cameroon: The Implications of the Millennium Agenda

Growth has been moderate and volatile since 1980, with an average annual growth of 3.7% between 1980 and 2003. The low contribution of the manufacturing industry to GDP (an annual average GDP 12.1% between 1993 and 2003) indicates among others, a low processing of raw materials. Similarly, growth stagnation reflects limited diversification. This global long term growth trend tends to hide important variations in economic performances throughout the period. Between 1980 and 1982, real GDP recorded a sustained average annual growth of 6.3% boosted by agricultural and oil exports (World Bank, 2004).

As from 1983, the combined negative effects of unsuitable domestic policy options and poor international market conditions gradually dragged the country into the economic crisis that lasted from 1987 to 1994, despite the five SAPs signed with international donors. As can be observed in Table 1 on the next page, this crisis was characterized by a drastic fall in oil export earnings and deterioration of the terms of trade.

Table 1 Cameroon's Macroeconomic Performances: 1979-2004

Indicators	1979-85	1986-93	1994-99	2000	2001	2002	2003	2004
	Annual growth rate (in percentage)							
GDP	7.3	-2.7	3.4	4.5	4.5	4.0	4.1	3.5
Non-oil-GDP	5.4	-1.9	3.7	7.3	5.5	4.9	4.9	4.7
Agriculture	6.0	0.4	6.7	3.6	3.73	3.7	3.7	4.2
Manufacturing	12.8	-0.8	3.0	4.3	1.0	0.8	0.8	0.5
Inflation (CPI)	10.9	2.3	8.8	4.3	1.0	0.8	0.8	2.6
Terms of trade	-1.8	-8.8	1.2	-2.4	-9.9	-4.4	6.6	1.5
	Percentage of GDP							
Export	30.2	19.0	23.8	23.3	21.9	19.9	20.2	19.7
Oil export	22.2	14.0	9.4	4.0	3.0	2.6	2.3	6.5
Non-oil export	8.0	5.0	14.4	19.3	18.9	17.6	17.9	13.2
Import	30.7	17.5	21.4	19.7	23.2	20.7	19.9	18.6
Trade balance	-0.5	1.4	2.3	-1.3	-0.8	0.3	1.1	-1.3
Investment	25.5	19.2	15.8	16.0	20.3	19.8	18.1	18.3
Government	5.8	6.0	2.3	2.1	2.2	2.3	2.3	2.4
Private	19.7	11.5	10.3	13.9	18.1	17.5	15.8	15.9
Government revenue	21.2	16.4	13.6	19.9	17.7	17.9	16.8	15.6
Oil		3.7	3.7	6.6	4.8	4.9	4.2	4.0
Non-oil		12.7	10.0	13.2	12.9	13.0	12.6	11.6
Government spending	20.7	23.0	16.9	15.6	16.9	16.0	15.5	13.8
Current	12.1	15.6	14.7	12.1	13.6	13.3	13.3	11.6
Capital	8.5	7.4	2.2	3.3	3.3	2.5	2.1	2.2
Budget balance	0.5	-6.6	-3.4	2.3	-0.6	-2.9	1.4	-0.1
Total external debt	131.3	102.5	72.5	67.2	60.0	52.2	49.0	43.9

Sources: World Bank (2001 and 2004), INS (2005a, b and c) and MINEFI/DAE (2005)

Between 1986 and 1993, real GDP decreased by an annual average 5% and per capita income dropped in 1993 to half of its 1986 level. Meanwhile, current public spending evolved from 11% to 19% of GDP, while investment decreased drastically from GDP 12.4% in 1986 to 3.5% in 1993. This decrease was worsened by the boom in the external debt service. The decline in public investment accompanied by that of private savings, following the drop in revenue, and the debt service, that continued to increase, led global investment to collapse by more than GDP 25% in average between 1980 and 1994 to less than GDP 14% between 1990 and 1993.

The economic recovery started in 1994 and continued till 2004, thanks to the combined efforts of authorities to implement more prudent economic policies aimed at restoring economic stability. However, the structural constraints of domestic demand and supply did not allow the country to take long term advantage of the opportunities offered by the previous reforms. The real annual average real GDP growth of about 4% between 1995 and 2003 is spurred by the invigorated non-oil private sector despite the continuous decline in oil production and energy problems that inhibit growth in general and that of the manufacturing industry in particular. The sustained inflation that followed the CFAF devaluation gradually reduced during the same period. Public finances improved over the period 1995-2000, due to prudent budgetary policy and changes in the tax administration, and declining since 2001 mostly because of oil revenue declining, which will not allow the government to sustain the budget surplus of year 2000.

Despite the observed slight recovery, the country has lost a great part of its potential GDP. Its ability to halve the poverty rate following the MDGs in the next ten years is still uncertain. One can then guess what has been lost in terms of activity and to what extent the loss can be partially captured statistically. In other terms, what should have been the GDP of the country if the crisis did not appear?

Departing from a growth theory equation, we try to measure the Potential GDP, from the direct measure of the private potential output, in addition to the public structural value added and structural direct and indirect taxes.[2] Potential Output is issued from the combination of quantities of potential factors of production. Hence, structural employment, combined to structural private capital stock, net of the effects of public employment or capital stock, and in addition to other global long term productivity factors, creates the net structural private GDP. Thus potential GDP is the sum of private GDP, public value added and structural indirect taxation. The output from the private sector in the economy is derived from a Cobb-Douglas function as follow:

---

2 The Potential GDP is the maximum net value added a country can supply, given the maximum use of its quantities of factors, and given the best prospects of technical progress or/and maximum efficiency in the global productivity of factors.

$$Y_t = A_t \cdot (L_t \cdot N_t)^a \cdot K_t^{(1-a)} \quad (1)$$

Where Y_t is private real Value Added, L_t employment, and N_t the number of actual hours spent per worker, Kt the capital stock, and A_t any scale factor representing technical progress or any shock affecting output.

The natural logarithm of equation (1) gives potential private output (y_t):

$$y_t = a \times (l + n) + (1 - a) \times k + gfp \quad (2)$$

Where (l + n) represent the potential labour and the trend number of hours used per worker (those two variables are substitutes when the potential is attained), k the trend of the capital stock and gfp the global factor productivity.

Private potential output (Y_t) is thus the exponential of equation (2). The potential GDP is thus the sum of the public sector value added (PSVA) and the amount of indirect taxes on local products (T).

$$\text{Potential GDP}_t = Y_t + PSVA_t + T_t \quad (3)$$

The potential labour is estimated as follow:

$$L_t = N . (Prop\_15/64 . Pop\_tot) . (1 - NAIRU) - Lpub \quad (4)$$

$$NAIRU = a_0 - a_1 . \left[(w - p_t) / L_t \right] + a_2 . RER_t - a_3 . (i_t - p_t) \quad (5)$$

Where (Prop_15_64) is the percentage of people able to work in the whole population (Pop_tot), given the number of hours used, Lpub the public labour obtained from the number of people employed by the government plus the number of people employed in public local firms, NAIRU the non-accelerating rate of unemployment, RER the real exchange rate, w-pt the real expected wages, p the local inflation rate, i the nominal interest rate. The determinants of NAIRU in the open-economy case are trend factors. They are obtained by using moving averages of the original series.

To construct real expected wages, we use public wages and salaries which are available since 1987, unit real wages being the ratio of real wages to official labour, ignoring –by simplification– the informal labour market. Then we depict its trend, after that we extrapolate backwards to 1965. Real interest rate is calculated using the nominal bank deposit rate which is available since 1965. We determine expected inflation using a moving average of order 2 of the observed inflation (CPI change, base 1995). The RER is obtained from the ratio of the product of the official $/FCFA exchange rate with the unit value of imports, over the unit value of exports, base 100=1995. From the regression of NAIRU, we then write down equation (4), for a trend rate of activity (number of hours used per worker) equal to (0.5), what means that in this economy, people work half of the maximum period. We can therefore estimate equation (2). Moreover, we use a partial adjustment equation of investment, as a proxy of the capital stock. Hence we can write:

$$K_t - K_{t-1} = I_t \quad \text{then} \quad K_t = I_t + K_{t-1}$$

$$K_t = \left(I_t + I_{t-1} + I_{t-2} + I_{t-3} + I_{t-4} + \ldots + I_{t-n-1}\right) + K_{t-n} = \left[\sum_{n=1}^{t-n-1} I_t\right] + K_{t-n} \qquad (6)$$

The powers of K_t are diminishing all along the past values. It is why we proxy K_t by gross domestic investment only. For this reason, we apply the rate of investment to the GDP at factor costs to get private investment, fix capital investment helps to measure the initial capital stock, and the rate of depreciation is 10%. Finally, we estimate equation (2), using natural logarithms of the private labour from equation (4) given the estimation of NAIRU, and the stock of capital proxies by equation (6). This helps to determine the trend value added of the private sector, considering the residuals of the production function as a sufficient measure of global factor productivity.

The value added of the public sector is supposed to be measured by public consumption. This is a rather crude measure of public value added, which includes policy and perhaps counter-cyclical actions. Now, we just consider the trend component (moving average of order 2) of this policy instrument, which normally weakens the impact of counter-cyclical effects on activity.

Further, we take into account taxes on local products, since gross domestic product at factor cost in constant $ prices of 1995, does exclude indirect taxes. Now, in developing countries, especially in Sub-Saharan African countries, taxes on international transactions count for more than 30% of the government total revenue. While indirect taxes only represent 11.5% on average of the gross domestic product at factor costs in constant 1995 prices, we think this is an underestimation of the tax burden in the economy. In Sub-Saharan African countries, general government consumption does represent an average of 12.5% of GDP during the seventies (1975-1979), 13.1% during the first half of the eighties (1980-1985) and18.6% in the second half of the eighties (World Bank, 1992). As such, a mean average in the whole period of

15% of GDP is not unrealistic, what induces a tax burden of international transactions amounting to (30% of 15% = 4.5%) of gross domestic product. This figure is to add to 11.5% of the indirect taxes levied on home goods. The whole tax burden in the economy is therefore equal to 15% on average in the whole period 1965-1999, featuring the third component of the right hand side of equation (3).

Figure 1 gives the resultant output gap. It can be seen that the output loss is always growing from 1965 to 1988, culminating this last year at 1.6 billions US$. But the crisis does impact not only on the rate of use of the quantities of factors, but also on the level of the supply possibilities frontier.

Figure 1: Output Gap (Potential GDP - GDP at Market Prices) US$ 1995, Cameroon 1965-2000

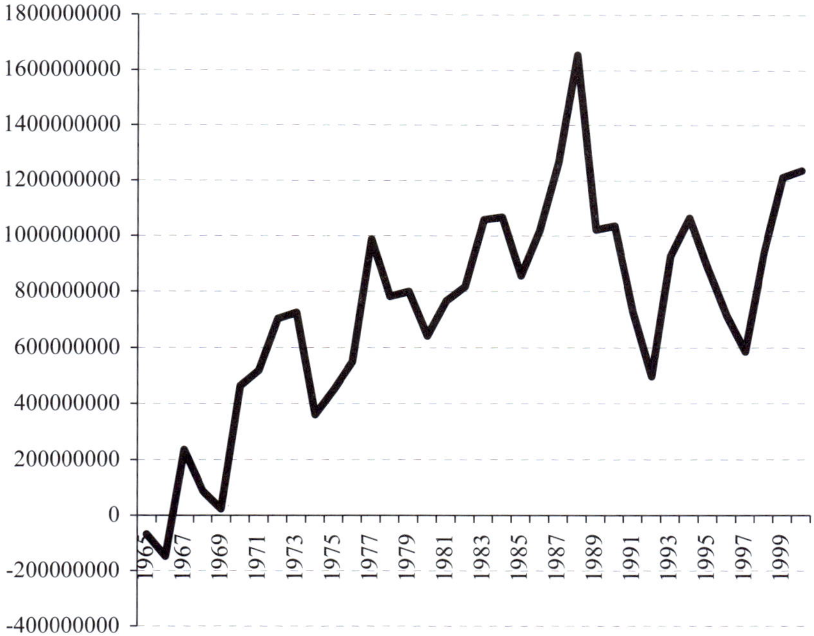

Source: Authors' construction

The potential is reduced because of the loss in the efficiency of the global factor productivity. Nevertheless, this reduction is somehow volatile, because it will amount to 0.5 billion US$ in 1992, and increase to more than 1 billion

US$ in 1994, and be reduced to 0.6 billion US$ in 1997. Since then, the output loss is once more steady, and will culminate to 1.2 billion US$ in 2000, despite the return to growth.

We can concluded that even the increase in potential output loss is stopped in the years of implementing the first SAP, the losses, significantly reduced as compared to pre-SAP, are still important. The growing of the losses since 1997 is marking the stopping of the mechanical effect of the 1994 devaluation.

From the economic performances described above, it can be observed that the implemented SAPs in Cameroon are limited in terms of boosting growth. The limits lay on the public management side, as well as on the supply side.

On the public management side, the priority given to restoring the budget balance and the current account balance while insuring satisfactorily the external debt service, has put a negative bias towards the internal debt payment, thus reducing tremendously the main sources of finance of domestic agents. Meanwhile, the rate of investment has been adversely affected, and the various initiatives of the private sector blurred. Moreover, the short term step by step approach on reducing the public deficits, introduced a new rigidity in the way to shape the economic policy, increasing the variance of policy decisions, which rendered highly incoherent, the process of these decisions and random nature of their long term impact effects. Hence, because of a dominant stabilization component, the SAPs have not envisioned a clear path of development, which involves a durable growth strategy. The various cuts in public spending, regarding public consumption as well as salaries to civil servants or public investment including the reduction of the Public Enterprises investment, have notably decreased the purchasing power of the population.

On the supply side, despite the privatisation of public enterprises, the SAPs have not been able to improve on the supply constraints, in terms of quantity and quality of growth. The traditional sources of growth, relaying on the primary commodities are still valid today (MINEFI/DAE, 2005), and have not been substituted by industry and services sectors, new '*niches or paths of growth*'. Of course, the too long policy and administrative lags in the privatisation process are also in question here. In addition to a weak growth-oriented policy, SAPs have failed to increase the total capital stock able to renew the country's mode of development, in favour of an innovation and services-led growth path. Meanwhile, SAPs have yielded some benefits. Among others are (World Bank, 2004):

- the better profile of public spending and more rationale public budget choices;
- the strengthening of the banking system given the new and more active role of the surveillance institutions;
- the lessening of the state budget burden with the privatization of public and parastatal enterprises;
- the reduction of the level of the trade and current account deficits, which softens somehow, the external position of the country;
- the increase in the quality of governance, despite the corruption-rooted environment;
- the improvement in macroeconomic stability, which helps the state to gain more credibility vis-à-vis the population, donors and foreign partners.

However, regarding the limits of SAPs, we can conclude that it is not the appropriate instrument of development in Cameroon especially. The country should now engage in a new economic policy aiming at a sustainable development process.

4 New Route to Sustainable Growth and Development in Cameroon

The content of the new route to sustainable growth and development in Cameroon requires envisioning a process of take-off, implying whatsoever some persistent current account deficits, which will be resolved on a longer period than the one adopted in the SAPs framework. Moreover, such a program should give an answer to the following five questions (Eboué, 2003):

- How to build a supply-determined economy, and insure an equal opportunity system to all citizens, as well as an efficient approach for their access to a globalized world?
- How to enhance more complementarities between the official side and the informal side of the economy;
- How to give medium to long term grounds to the economic policy orientation?
- What are the different aspects as well as the tools for the reform of the institutions adequate to an emerging economy?

- What can be the new culture of development in Cameroon, in particular and in African countries in general?

Answering these five questions appears as a pre-requisite to a re-definition of a long term development approach in Cameroon (Bekolo-Ebé et al., 2004). Such a development approach depends mainly on the:

- improvement of the governance and the combat of corruption;
- reduction of the legal and judicial insecurity of investment;
- setting-up of a fiscal system flexible for certain sensitive sectors of activity;
- upgrading of the local enterprises hampered by outdated equipment and underutilization of their capacities;
- improvement of the quantity and quality of road, port, airport, railway, energy, telecommunications and storage infrastructure;
- diversification of exports and the entire economy;
- decentralisation of governance [Bamou et al. (2005) and Ondo Maña (2005)].

In 1998 and 1999, Cameroon topped the chart of the most corrupt countries in the world, according to Transparency International. The country has done a bit better in the recent years. However, it still holds a dishonorable place in this shameful hit parade so much so that one can consider corruption as being endemic in country. This situation has tarnished the country's brand image. The government, in its efforts to fight against corruption, formed an ad hoc committee to coordinate the work of observers and groups carrying out this work in every ministry and public services. These structures have not so far succeeded in the challenge to reduce corruption. On the contrary, the situation seems stable or more or less deteriorating because of various obstacles including the definition of the areas of responsibility, no power to call upon for public intervention, a scandalous level of accountability by the hierarchy. In general, the members of these commissions are public employees looking for promotion and prominent members of civil society hungry for positions. They have to do everything possible to stay on the right side of those who have appointed them. Although corruption has not been eradicated, it can be pushed back. As one local barrister said 'we have to create a law against corruption, and protect the magistrates'. The country judicial system is badly equipped and the magistrates have poor physical protection in their task, exposing them to corruption as well (Banque Mondiale, 2005).

Intensification of the training of magistrates in OHADA business law mechanisms to which Cameroon adheres is required. Actually, legal business insecurity constitutes a major constraint to the growth of investment in Cameroon, notably foreign investment. This insecurity can be explained by the outdated existing regulations, as well as the difficulty in determining, in a given case, the legal standard enforceable. It notably stems from the lack of competence in legal practitioners, either in terms of law or ethics.[3] To resolve delays in judicial procedures, generalized controls of all jurisdictions must be organized and the number of hearings on business disputes increased.

Energy supply must be improved. Energy plays an important role in the quest for new boosters for the sustainable economic growth. As a matter of fact, the country recorded a substantial deficit in energy supply which explains the ceding to AES-SONEL (a private company) of the only electricity production and distribution company (SONEL). Since this privatization actions have been undertaken to offset this deficit, notably, the construction of thermal plants, studies on the construction of the Lom Pangar water storage dam to supply the Edéa hydro-electric power plant during periods when River Sanaga is low, the liberalization of the production sub-sector and provision at the level of the National Investment Corporation (SNI) of a financing mechanism in favor of those Small and Medium Enterprises (SMEs)/Small and Medium Industries (SMIs) wishing to invest in the domain of mini/micro hydro-electric plants and biomass. However, in the opinion of private operators and considering the industrial development ambitions of the country, thermal energy solutions can only be short term in nature, due to their high cost. The State must therefore, provide the necessary impetus and incentives to the development of hydro-electric energy, which is the medium and long term solution (MINEE, 2005).

As shown by Ongolo Zogo and Touna Mama in the chapter relating on Transport Infrastructures and Cameroon Exports Promotion in Central Africa, the development of basic infrastructure, notably, road infrastructure is crucial. This constitutes a competitiveness issue for Cameroon as well as for

---

3 OHADA is a supra-national organization for the harmonization of business law in Africa. It was created on October 17, 1993 in Port-Louis, Mauritius and comprised 16 countries in 2004 including Cameroon. It aims at setting up of a harmonized, simple, modern and adapted business law to enable an easier access to economic activities as a pre-requisite for the economic integration of these countries, guarantee a safe legal environment for economic activities, and enhance investment and promote arbitration as an instrument to settle contract-related disputes.

the two landlocked countries of CEMAC (Chad and Central African Republic). Meanwhile, emphasis must be laid on the liaison between the major cities on the one hand and the major cities and the rural world on the other. The latter is expected to determine the competitiveness of subsistence agriculture, an important source of input for the ago-industrial sector. Accelerating the institution of the Special Telecommunications Fund (STF) which is supposed to finance the development of the country's telecommunication system, complete liberalization of the telecommunications sector, involvement of decentralized territorial authorities in strategies for financing infrastructure and acceleration of studies of the possibilities to render operational the Build-Operate-Transfer (BOT) system, which will involve private sector in the supply of infrastructures, must also be considered.

The formulation of a program for updating local enterprises, an internal competitiveness challenge for the latter, on which depends the improvement of their productivity. Most of the existing local enterprises were created during the protectionist period (1960 to 1970) and are no longer adapted to the present liberal environment. The process must be promoted by the government given the magnitude of the financial resources required. Since all aspects of the enterprise are concerned and considering the country's commitments to the multilateral trade organizations, the government could intervene at the level of quality standards, technical training, access to New Information and Communication Technologies (NICTs) and databanks, control and analysis of products, audit/consultancy, research/development, etc.

Then, diversification of the economy is a pre-requisite to go forward in the agenda of development for Cameroon. The main problem lays on the secular failure context of the country, as well as of many Sub-Saharan countries, to gather savings from agriculture, which could be invested into manufactures, so as to sustain the development of a more modernized agriculture, while an intermediary-goods industry could emerge progressively, before turning to final goods industry. This transition has been postponed because peasants have been for a very long time state price takers, home prices being largely inferior to world prices, without benefiting from appropriate incentives to modernize their plants. Since this sub-optimal indexation prices mechanism has been broken for ten years now, it seems crucial to help agriculture play the historical role it played elsewhere throughout the world, in inducing food security and diversity, but in the meantime, the increase of the saving rate and the funding of an emerging manufacturing sector.

Moreover, the challenge for the country is to define a strategy of medium-level technology-based but high-level value added industries. This imposes a tremendous revision in its industrial policy pursued for the last four decades, and also the evolution of some important GDP contributors but low competitive industries (aluminium and beverages industries), given the widely admitted constraints to competitiveness in the globalized market, which will surely in a couple of years otherwise disappear from the market. A new industrial policy has to be coupled with a new services policy. Tourism, therefore, appears as a sector to strengthen, given the small size of costs of transaction at the entry (Ongolo Zogo et al., 2005).

The human capital stock is a clue in this process of development. The country has a well endowed and educated population. Hence, the lower labour productivity indicates the inadequate education system. The re-orientation of the later is, therefore, crucial to increase productivity.

As apparent from the Export Diversification Index (EDI) derived from the UNCTAD (2001) and the Primary Commodities' Share (PCS) in the total of exports indicator derived from Bonaglia and Fukasaku (2003), Cameroonian exports are highly concentrated on few primary commodities, despite the efforts to get away from primary products dependency.[4] Diversifying exports is therefore a pre-requisite to go forward with the agenda of development for Cameroon. One could ask which products are adequate to help the country increase its world market share, and hence enable the country to capture a greater part of its potential? In other words, towards which products should the necessary active export promoting strategy be directed? Bamou (2001) gives a insight to such a question by identifying 19 non-oil non- traditional competitive and profitable exports, of which 4 are primary agriculture and 15 industrial.[5] This paper indicates that there is scope for exports diversification in Cameroon. Among other conditions to promote this diversification are:

---

4 A higher value of the EDI and PCS indicates a greater degree of export concentration. UNCTAD (2001) shows that in 2001 Cameroon is the most concentrated country in its trade with EDI = 0.90, even compared to some poorer countries like Senegal (EDI = 0.77) or Mozambique (EDI = 0.83). In like manner, Bonaglia and Fukasaku (2003) show that in 2000, despite the slight decrease of the PCS of Cameroon (from 0.99 between 1966 and 1970 to 0.97 between 1996 and 2000), it was still higher as compared to that of other middle income countries (0.86 for Botswana and 0.88 for Ghana and Kenya between 1996 and 2000).

5 Domestic Resource Cost (DRC), which is the ratio of local input costs to the value added issued from exports, and Financial Capital Profitability (FCP), which sets the value added per unit of installed (or used) capital stock, are respectively used as competitiveness and profitability indicators.

- reducing the scope and level of exports taxes;
- setting up financial institutions specialized in export promotion;
- increasing the rate of involvement of government departments and stakeholders in the exports promotion strategy, along the lines defined by the World Trade Organization (WTO) Commission for the country.

An appropriate decentralisation policy should also enable the identification of a social utility function, envisioning clearly the future, and promoting a participatory process where all Cameroonians could contribute, so as to foster growth and development.

5 Projected Impact of the New Route

The endogenous elasticity growth determinant forecast model is used to estimate the impact of the suggested new route. This model, adapted from that used by MINEFI/DAE (Ministry of the Economy and Finance/Direction of economic Affairs) to project short and medium term macroeconomic aggregates of the country, is similar to the quasi-models often structured around Input-Output Tables and financial programming models constructed around flux of funds developed by the International Monetary Funds (IMF). Meanwhile, it comprises a higher endogenous degree in determining GDP per sector of production. The projections rely on:

- Exogenous data (internal and external economic situation (prices), statistics on the real sector and foreign trade as well as the government program);
- A system of econometric equations that ensures coherence between the real variables (real interrelations);
- A set of accounting relationships that ensures the equilibrium of flux of funds, and thence financial interrelations.

Growth determinants comprise the fundamentals of the medium and long term production capacity (private physical capital drawn by private investment, public capital (infrastructure and others), human capital drawn by performances in education, health and the job market) and short term fluctuation elements of demand (budgetary and monetary policies) or supply (natural and cyclical shocks) that are included in equations used to determine sectoral growth rates. The other components of the macroeconomic frame are determined according to accounting equations and standard financial programming principles. The growth module comprises GDP in resources and employment, prices, and finance sectors (household, enterprise, the State, finance firms and the rest of the world flux of funds). Our presentation shall only focus on the supply side of the real GDP projection module. The real GDP components are projected according to the methods of tendencies, elasticity, ratios and weighting (see Bamou et al. (2005) and N'Cho-Oguie et al. (2004) for more detailed information on these methods).

In general, the elasticities (elsi) are estimated from the log-linear functions specified as follows:

$$Q_{it} = f(Pr_{it}, Q_{i(t-1)}, Cip, Rev, Kp_t, Kg_t, H_t, S_t, Dum_i) \quad (7)$$

Where Q_{it}, $Q_{i(t-1)}$, Pr_{it}, Cip, Rev, Kp_t, Kg_t, H_t, S_t and Dum_i are quantity of product i at the period t and t-1, prices of product i at the period t, import capacity, revenue, stock of private physical capital at the period t, stock of public physical capital at the period t, stock of human capital at the period t, stock of social capital at the period t, and related product i dummy variable, respectively. The estimated elasticities are given in Table 3 on the next page.

The growth rate of each sub-sector at period t (grQit), is calculated as the weighted sum by the elasticities of the contributions of the determining factors of growth in the sub-sector, to which is often added, the growth cyclical objectives of the sub-sector of the period t (Plcit). This growth rate can be expressed as follows:

$$grQ_{it} = \sum_i els_i.(Pr_{it}, Q_{i(t-1)}, Cip, Rev, Kp_t, Kg_t, H_t, S_t) + Plc_{it} \quad (8)$$

The growth rates of the sectors are, on their part, calculated after the summation of the production levels of the sub-sectors of period t. The level of production of the sub-sectors of period t is obtained by adding the production growth of period t to the previous level, in the following manner:

$$Q_{it} = (1 + grQ_{it}).Q_{i(t-1)} \quad (9)$$

Considering the fact that attracting more investment is the main indicator of the improvement of the economic environment involved by the proposed new route, three investment hypotheses (pessimist, base line and optimist) are added to the adjusted official sectoral and cyclical effects hypotheses and simulated with the model. In those scenarios, the official 2005 related hypotheses are maintained constant to consider the fact that nothing can be changed again in that year which is already at the end.

Table 3: Estimated Elasticities of the Model

	Short term effects				Long term determinants					
	Lag	Px-r	Cip	Rev	Kpv	Kgv	Khu	Elt	Tel	Rd
Subsistence agriculture	0.267	0.25					0.239			
Perennial agriculture	0.251	0.139			0.161		0.054			
Agro-industries	0.157	-0.09			0.561	0.326	0.2	0.051		
Other manufacturing	0.402	-0.05			0.113		0.012	0.6		0.014
Building and public works	0.8		0.014	0.24	0.5216 1/					
All tradable services	0.305		0.061	0.71					0.22	

Notes : *Lag : Lag variable; Px-r : Relative price; Cip : Import capacity; Rev : Revenu ; Kpv : Private capital ; Kgv : Public capital ; Khu : Human capital; Elt: Electricy supply; Tel: Telecommunication supply; Rd: Road infrastructure; 1/: Ratio Kpv/Kgy;*

Source: *N'Cho-Oguie et al. (2004)*

As it can be seen in Table 3, summarizing the scenarios hypotheses that in the pessimist scenario, the nominal GDP share of private and public investment are respectively increased from 16.9% and 2.9% to 20% and 5%, carrying the nominal GDP share of total investment from 19.8% to 25%. All sectoral and cyclical effects are neglected (equal to zero). Only average and long term effects are considered in this scenario. As in the case of the other two scenarios, the official growth hypotheses of the sub-sectors exogenously projected are maintained constant. As compared to the pessimist scenario, only the nominal GDP shares of private and public investment are changed. They are respectively increased from 16.9% and 2.9% to 25% and 7.5%, carrying the nominal GDP share of total investment from 19.8% to 32.5%.

The optimist scenario coupled with the increased of nominal GDP share of total investment to 40% (30% for private investment and 10% for public investment) with official positive sectoral and cyclical effects. Either called optimist, the GDP share of total investment is still low compared to that of some countries of the region (Central Africa) with higher growth rate. In some of those countries, only the stock of inward FDI is higher than 50% of GDP in 2004 (Angola: 88.8%, Chad: 72.9, Congo Republic: 66.7%, Equatorial Guinea: 123.7%, São Tomé and Principe: 123.4%) and the region accounts for 51.8% (UNCTAD, 2005).

The 'optimist' investment scenario can be not only achieved, but exceed the levels when accounting for the revenue windfall from completing point of the Highly Indebted Poor Countries (HIPC) initiative of may 2006, and the government wiliness to enhance private investment[6] and rationalize resource utilization. Knowing that some, and at least most NICTs, goods and services are purchased by the government at more than twice their local market prices (see Table 4), reallocation to investment of saved revenue from rationalization of resource utilization can even contribute alone to achieve the optimist scenario.

Table 4: Prices of some NICT Products purchased by the Government (in CFAF)

Product code	Specification	Official Price + 12% profit margin offered	Market Price	Comment
15.002.010009	Tuner TV and Capture video card	85,904	25,000	-
15.010.010221	USB Flash memory 2.0 64 Mo	231,436	30,000	For 512 Mo
15.010.010222	USB Flash memory 2.0 64 Mo	418,790	30,000	For 512 Mo
15.012.010025	CDR 74 Fuji	1,680	500	-

Continuation on the next page.

6 The Prime Minister, Head of Government, presided a two-day meeting at Yaoundé (2-3 November 2006) of the inter-ministerial committee extended to private sector. Participants worked under three sub themes: conditions for a strong and sustainable economic growth, financing the economy, and enterprise governance. The Prime Minister says finance law of 2007 will take into consideration resolutions of the forum. From 7 to 9 November 2006, the government co-organized at Yaoundé, with the Commonwealth Business Council (CBC), the 'Cameroon Investment Forum' under the theme: "New business opportunities: International trade and investment perspectives".

Continuation of Table 4 from the previous page.

Product code	Specification	Official Price + 12% profit margin offered	Market Price	Comment
15.019.010117	Laptop Sony VAISO Pentium 4	4,463,200	1,800,000	Local market prices are already more than twice international prices
15.019.010063	Compaq Presario 2818, Pentium 4, M17, Memory 256Mo, 40 Go HD, Combo DVD/CDRW, USB 2.0, ATI Mobility Radon 64Mo, 15 TFT, Monitor 15"	3,494,165	1,400,000	-

Source: MINCOMMERCE (2006) for official prices

The scenario results are summarized in the annex (Table A1). These results shows that an enabling economic environment, which attracts more private and allows more public investment, is indispensable to growth, consumption and international trade in Cameroon and consequently, the fight against poverty in particular and reaching the millennium goals in general.

As shown by the curves in Figure 2, the millennium economic growth goal (7% per annum) is reached the year following the increase in global investment by 26% only (scenario 1). The country even obtained the sought two-digit growth as global investment increased by 64% to reach 32.5% of the GDP. The millennium economic growth goal would double in the next two years if global investment reaches 40% of the GDP.

Growth, timid in the primary sector, depicted here part of the primary commodities dilemma. The poor performance of the subsistence agricultural sector, at least in the first two scenarios, is mostly due to the non-consideration of cyclical effects, which have greater impact on trends of this sub-sector.

It stands out from the results in Table A2 in the annex that the tertiary and secondary sectors are those who drive the observed growth. This is a clear sign that effort shall be done to diversify the economy from the primary sector to these two sectors and that further investment in primary commodities sector will not yield the globally observed results. The good performance of the agro-industry sector and building and public works is constrained by the fall in performance of the oil sector, mostly due to the depletion of wells.

Even if, in conformity with the theory, public and private consumption declines with increased public and private investment, this decline is more than compensated the following years, thanks to the income effects attributable to production growth. Similarly, trade is clearly boosted in the year of the increase in investment as well as thereafter. The increase in investment automatically leads to an additionally demand for imported capital, semi-manufactured and even finished goods. Export growth is only felt in the years following the rise in investment, due to the adjustment period necessary for investment to yield profits.

Figure 2: Projected Annual Real GDP Growth: 2005-2008 (in Percentage)

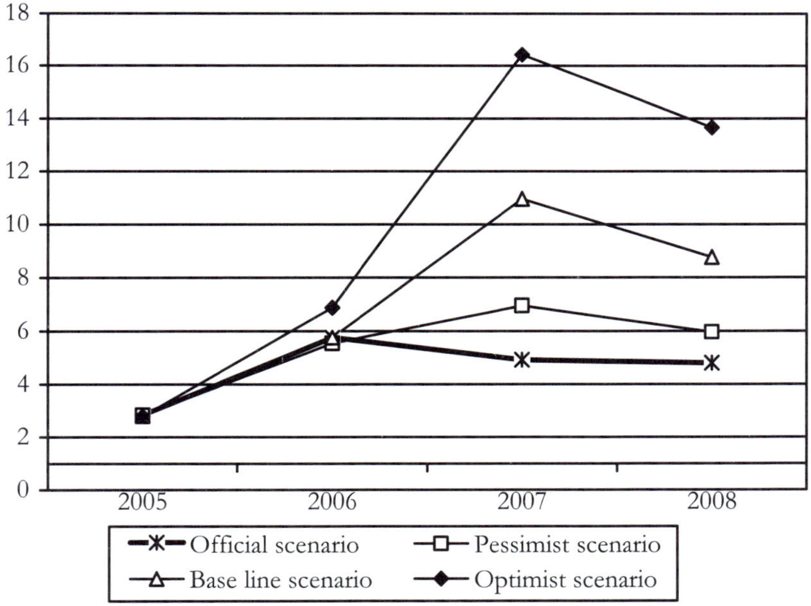

Sources: Authors' estimations and MINEFI/DAE (2005) for 2005

These effects do not take into consideration the behavioral changes and constraints faced by the economy, incorporated in the elasticities, that the abovementioned reforms can induce.

Taking these changes into consideration and orienting investments in more pro-growth non-traditional sectors dominated by primary commodities would obviously improve the results observed. Similarly, the status quo of the prevailing conditions could not only prevent the above-mentioned reforms from becoming effective, but also constrain their expected effects.

6 Conclusions and Policy Recommendations

Cameroon is a small but growing population country that can envision a brighter future for its economy and citizens. Its growth has been more resource-intensive than quality-based in the last thirty years. Unfortunately, much has been spent on rent-seeking activities, and the supply has not been maximized. Important GDP losses have been encountered during the crisis years, and the booming oil years in the first half of the 1980's have not enabled wisdom in macroeconomic management, and Structural Adjustment Programs (SAPs) have failed to serve as the country's engine of growth and development.

Yet, there is still room to capture part of the growth lost and accelerate the country's development. This will imply, in particular, a very sustainable programming of activities to diversify the supply to capture opportunities offered by the improvement in market access due to multilateral trade negotiations. Export diversification and export promotion is therefore the great route to escape from the primary commodity dilemma. For this to happen, the supply capacity of the various sectors, especially the secondary non-oil sectors, have to be upgraded. Growth-impeding externalities such as income inequalities, food-insecurity, damages on environment, and the low level of education for the whole population, but especially for the rural youth and women, etc., have also to be mitigated.

Financial resources will certainly be a great constraint to meet this challenge. Rationalization of resource utilization, reaching the achievement point of the Highly Indebted Poor Countries (HIPC) initiative, and financial deepening are some solutions. These require a resolved and determined government willingness to mobilize these resources in view to promote export diversification and export promotion. Policies have in the past suffered too much from administrative, human management and political lags. Many decrees supposed to improve the macroeconomic or policy management are still waiting for implementation. It is then absolutely imperative for the government to speed up reforms and create a more efficient nexus between the state, the private sector, and the other stakeholders like Non-governmental organizations (NGOs).

Table A1. Projection Simulation Hypotheses: 2005-2008 (in percentage)

	Official scenario				Pessimist scenario				Base line scenario				Optimist scenario			
	2005	2006	2007	2008	2005	2006	2007	2008	2005	2006	2007	2008	2005	2006	2007	2008
Nominal GDP share of total investment	19.8	21.5	22.8	24.2	19.8	25.0	25.0	25.0	19.8	32.5	32.5	32.5	19.8	40.0	40.0	40.0
Nominal GDP share of private investment	16.9	17.4	18.9	20.0	16.9	20.0	20.0	20.0	16.9	25.0	25.0	25.0	16.9	30.0	30.0	30.0
Nominal GDP share of public investment	2.9	4.0	4.0	4.2	2.9	5.0	5.0	5.0	2.9	7.5	7.5	7.5	2.9	10.0	10.0	10.0
							Sectoral and cyclical policy effects									
Primary sector																
Subsistence agriculture	2.5	2.5	2.5	2.5	2.5	0.0	0.0	0.0	2.5	0.0	0.0	0.0	2.5	2.5	2.5	2.5
Perennial and industrial agriculture	3.0	2.0	2.0	2.0	3.0	0.0	0.0	0.0	3.0	0.0	0.0	0.0	3.0	3.0	3.0	3.0
Breeding and hunting	3.0	3.0	3.0	3.0	3.0	0.0	0.0	0.0	3.0	0.0	0.0	0.0	3.0	3.0	3.0	3.0
Fishing	2.0	2.0	2.0	2.5	2.0	0.0	0.0	0.0	2.0	0.0	0.0	0.0	2.0	2.0	2.0	2.0
Forestry	5.0	-2.2	2.3	2.2	5.0	0.0	0.0	0.0	5.0	0.0	0.0	0.0	5.0	5.0	5.0	5.0
Secondary sector																
Mining industries	0.0	0.0	0.0	0.0	0.0	0.0	0.0	0.0	0.0	0.0	0.0	0.0	0.0	0.0	0.0	0.0
Oil	0.0	0.0	0.0	0.0	0.0	0.0	0.0	0.0	0.0	0.0	0.0	0.0	0.0	0.0	0.0	0.0
Agro-industries	0.0	-4.0	-3.0	-3.0	0.0	0.0	0.0	0.0	0.0	0.0	0.0	0.0	0.0	0.0	0.0	0.0
Other manufacturing industries	0.0	0.6	0.6	-3.0	0.0	0.0	0.0	0.0	0.0	0.0	0.0	0.0	0.0	0.0	0.0	0.0
Electricity, gas and water	2.5	3.0	3.0	8.0	2.5	0.0	0.0	0.0	2.5	0.0	0.0	0.0	2.5	2.5	2.5	2.5
Building and public works (BTP)	0.0	0.0	1.0	0.0	0.0	0.0	0.0	0.0	0.0	0.0	0.0	0.0	0.0	0.0	0.0	0.0
Tertiary sector																
Trade, restaurants and hotels	-1.1	-1.0	-1.0	-1.0	-1.1	0.0	0.0	0.0	-1.1	0.0	0.0	0.0	-1.1	0.0	0.0	0.0
Transports, warehouses and communications	0.0	-1.0	-1.0	1.5	0.0	0.0	0.0	0.0	0.0	0.0	0.0	0.0	0.0	0.0	0.0	0.0
Bank and financial organizations	1.0	-1.5	-1.0	0.0	1.0	0.0	0.0	0.0	1.0	0.0	0.0	0.0	1.0	1.0	1.0	1.0
Others tradable services	0.0	-1.0	-1.0	0.0	0.0	0.0	0.0	0.0	0.0	0.0	0.0	0.0	0.0	0.0	0.0	0.0
Intermediary financial services indirectly measured (SIFIM)	1.5	1.5	1.5	1.5	1.5	0.0	0.0	0.0	1.5	0.0	0.0	0.0	1.5	1.5	1.5	1.5
Public administration non-tradable services	2.0	0.0	0.0	0.0	2.0	0.0	0.0	0.0	2.0	0.0	0.0	0.0	2.0	2.0	2.0	2.0
Other non-tradable services	7.2	7.2	7.2	7.2	7.2	0.0	0.0	0.0	7.2	0.0	0.0	0.0	7.2	7.2	7.2	7.2

Sources: Authors and MINEFI/DAE (2005) for 2005

Table A2: Projected real GDP and Sectoral Growth Rates: Supply and Demand for 2005-2008 (in percentage)

	Official scenario				Pessimist scenario				Base line scenario				Optimist scenario			
	2005	2006	2007	2008	2005	2006	2007	2008	2005	2006	2007	2008	2005	2006	2007	2008
Supply																
Primary sector	***3.9***	***4.1***	***4.1***	***3.7***	***3.9***	***2.9***	***2.5***	***1.8***	***3.9***	***2.9***	***2.6***	***1.7***	***3.9***	***4.8***	***5.0***	***4.2***
Subsistence agriculture	4.3	3.7	4.2	4.3	4.3	2.0	1.3	1.1	4.3	2.0	1.3	1.0	4.3	4.5	4.5	4.1
Perennial and industrial agriculture	5.1	2.8	-0.2	0.6	5.1	2.5	4.2	2.6	5.1	2.5	4.9	3.4	5.1	5.5	9.4	8.3
Breeding and hunting	3.0	4.8	4.7	4.7	3.0	4.8	4.7	4.7	3.0	4.8	4.7	4.7	3.0	4.8	4.7	4.7
Fishing	2.0	4.0	4.0	4.3	2.0	4.0	4.0	4.3	2.0	4.0	4.0	4.3	2.0	4.0	4.0	4.3
Forestry	2.1	7.5	6.3	0.0	2.1	7.5	6.3	0.0	2.1	7.5	6.3	0.0	2.1	7.5	6.3	0.0
Secondary sector	***-0.7***	***8.8***	***3.8***	***5.1***	***-0.7***	***5.3***	***2.7***	***5.3***	***-0.7***	***6.0***	***4.9***	***7.7***	***-0.8***	***7.7***	***8.5***	***13.2***
Mining industries	-9.0	6.0	-10.1	0.4	-9.0	6.0	-10.1	0.4	-9.0	6.0	-10.1	0.4	-9.0	6.0	-10.1	0.4
Oil	-9.0	6.0	-10.1	-3.2	-9.0	6.0	-10.1	-3.3	-9.0	6.0	-10.1	-3.3	-9.0	6.0	-10.1	-3.3
Agro-industries	-4.7	1.3	4.7	5.8	-4.7	9.4	13.3	11.8	-4.7	12.7	18.8	17.0	-4.7	16.3	25.1	23.3
Other manufacturing industries	4.9	14.9	9.4	6.2	4.9	3.0	2.7	2.5	4.6	3.0	3.8	3.9	4.6	4.8	7.6	11.1
Electricity, gas and water	2.5	3.0	3.0	8.0	2.5	0.0	0.0	0.0	2.5	0.0	0.0	0.0	2.5	3.0	3.0	8.0
Building and public works (BTP)	6.2	6.4	7.7	7.4	6.2	6.4	9.6	11.1	6.2	6.4	13.1	14.6	6.2	6.4	17.0	18.8
Tertiary sector	***4.7***	***4.6***	***6.1***	***5.1***	***4.7***	***6.9***	***11.6***	***8.1***	***4.7***	***6.9***	***18.5***	***12.1***	***4.7***	***7.3***	***26.6***	***17.5***
Trade, restaurants and hotels	4.8	5.0	6.3	5.0	4.8	6.4	12.9	8.9	4.8	6.4	21.3	13.6	4.8	6.5	31.0	19.7
Transports, warehouses and communications	5.8	4.0	6.0	5.3	5.8	12.8	14.9	9.5	5.8	12.8	23.3	14.2	5.8	15.5	33.7	20.5
Bank and financial organizations	4.7	3.9	6.1	5.0	4.7	6.1	12.8	8.9	3.9	6.1	21.2	13.5	3.9	7.2	32.2	21.0
Others tradable services	5.4	5.4	7.9	6.9	5.4	6.6	13.0	8.9	5.4	6.6	21.4	13.6	5.4	6.6	31.0	19.7
Intermediary financial services indirectly measured (SIFIM)	2.5	2.3	2.3	1.8	2.5	0.8	0.4	-0.2	2.5	0.8	0.4	-0.2	2.5	2.3	2.4	2.1
Public administration non-tradable services	2.8	3.0	3.0	2.6	2.8	3.0	3.2	2.6	2.8	3.0	3.2	2.6	2.8	3.0	3.2	2.6
Other non-tradable services	5.2	6.0	6.4	6.2	5.2	6.0	6.4	6.2	5.2	6.0	6.4	6.2	5.2	6.0	6.4	6.2
Real GDP at factor cost	**2.9**	**5.8**	**4.9**	**4.8**	**2.9**	**5.5**	**7.0**	**6.0**	**2.8**	**5.8**	**10.9**	**8.8**	**2.8**	**6.9**	**16.4**	**13.7**
Demand																
Final consumption	0.5	0.8	3.3	2.8	0.5	-3.3	7.7	5.7	0.5	-11.8	12.9	8.5	0.5	-20.1	19.0	13.3
Private	-0.5	0.3	2.8	2.4	-0.5	-4.4	7.8	5.8	-0.5	-14.1	13.9	9.1	-0.5	-23.9	21.1	14.4
Public	7.8	4.0	7.0	5.3	7.8	4.0	7.0	5.3	7.8	4.0	7.0	5.3	7.8	6.0	9.0	7.3
Total exports of goods and services	5.6	8.3	5.2	5.6	5.6	5.3	4.3	5.9	5.6	5.5	5.2	8.1	5.6	6.9	7.9	13.2
Total imports of goods and services	2.7	-2.2	4.2	3.8	2.7	0.2	4.9	3.6	2.7	4.4	8.1	5.8	2.7	9.3	12.3	9.1

Sources: Authors' estimations and MINEFI/DAE (2005) for 2005

References

Blandford, D., D. Friedman, S. Lynch, N. Mukherjee, and D. E. Sahn (1995): "Oil Boom and Bust: The Harsh Realities of Adjustment in Cameroon". In David E. Sahn (ed.), Adjusting to Policy Failure in African Economies. Ithica, New York: Cornell University Press.

Banque Mondiale (2005): "République du Cameroun: Acquis et Défis dans la Lutte Contre la Pauvreté". Report No. 32820-CM. Washington D. C. USA.

Bamou, E., Tchanou, J. P., and Mkouonga, F. H. (2006): "Trade Related Reforms and Food Security: The Case of Cameroon". In Harmon, T. (ed.) Trade Reforms and Food Security: Country Case Studies. FAO, Rome, Italy. Mimeo. pp. 97-118.

Bamou, E., Bamou, T. L., and Tchanou, J. P. (2005): "Evaluation of Trade and Investment Policy Reforms in Cameroon". Contribution to the African Economic Research Consortium (AERC)/United Nations Development Program (UNDP) project: Trade Negotiations, Trade and Investment Policies, Growth and Poverty Reduction in Selected African Countries: A Study Framework. Presented at the 11th GTAP Conference at Addis-Ababa, Ethiopia. Online: https://www.gtap.agecon.purdue.edu/resources/res_display.asp?RecordID=1944

Bamou, T. L. (2001): "Promotion of Exports Diversification: Towards Which Products?" AERC Research Paper. No. RP116. Nairobi, Kenya.

Bekolo-Ebé, B., Eboué, C., and Touna Mama (2004): "Basic Concepts of Post-Adjustment and Sustainable Growth Sources in Cameroon. Report by Commission No.2 of the Workshop on the Ways and Strategies to a Durable and High Growth in Cameroon." Yaoundé, General Secretariat of the Presidency of the Republic, Cameroon, 16-18 February.

Bonaglia, F. and Fukasaku, K. (2003): "Export Diversification in Low Income Countries: An International Challenge after Doha." OECD Technical Paper. No. 29.

Clément. A. P. Mueller. J. and Le Dem. J. (1996): "Aftermath of the CFAF Countries Devaluation". IMF Occasional Paper, No. 138. Washington D.C., USA.

Eboué, C., 2003: 'La Nouvelle Economie du Développement : Les Enjeux Africains'. In Bekolo-Ebé, B, Touna Mama, and Fouda, S. (eds.). Dynamiques de Développement : Débats Théoriques et Enjeux Politiques à l'Aube du 21 Siècle. Paris : Montchrestien (Mélanges en l'honneur de Georges NGANGO). pp. 67-106.

INS (Institut national de la statistique) (2005a): "Les Comptes Nationaux du Cameroun 1993-2003: Selon le SCN 93". Yaoundé, Cameroun.

INS (2005b): "Annuaire Statistique du Cameroun : 2003". Yaoundé, Cameroun.

INS (2005c): "Bilan du commerce extérieur : 2004". Yaoundé, Cameroun.

MINEFI/Direction des Affaires Economiques (DEA) (2005): "Loi des Finances 2006: Rapport Economique et Financier Exercice 2005". Yaoundé, Cameroun.

MINCOMMERCE (Ministère du Commerce) (2006): "Mercuriale des Prix et Tarifs de référence pour l'Exercice 2006: Tome I. Suite à l'Arrêté" No. 000010/MICOMMERCE/CAB/ du 03 Avril 2006, Fixant les prix et tarifs de référence des équipements, fournitures de bureau, travaux et services divers destinés aux administrations publiques et parapubliques. Direction de la Protection du Consommateur, Yaoundé, Cameroun.

Ministère de l'Economie et des Finances (MINEFI)/Direction de la Prévision (DP). (2000): "Rapport Economique et Financier: Exercice 1999/2000". Yaoundé, Cameroun.

Ministère de l'Energie et de l'Eau –MINEE- (2005): "Plan Energétique". Yaoundé, Cameroun.

N'Cho-Oguie, C., et Charlier, F. M. avec la collaboration de Bela, L., Tchatchouang, L. R., Bamou, E., Eyeffa Ekomo, S. M. L., Mengue Mengue, J., Mezama Mbidan, G. K, Nkou, J. P. and Tchana Tchana, F. (2004): "Description du Modèle SIPAE: Un Système Intégré de Cadrage Macroéconomique pour le Cameroun." MINEFI/DP. Yaoundé, Cameroun.

Ondo Mañe, D. (2005): "Emergence of the Gulf of Guinea in the Global Economy: Prospects and Challenges". IMF Working Paper. No. WP/05/235. IMF, Washington D.C., USA.

Ongolo Zogo, V., Abena Nguema, C. et Sabate, V. A. assistés par Lessie Doré, L. et Djiofac, C. (2005): "Les Pays Africains Dans Les Négociations De L'OMC Sur Le Commerce des Services: Le Cas Du Cameroun." Online: www.ileapinitiative.com/index.php.

Serageldin, I. (1989): "Pauvreté. Ajustement et Croissance en Afrique." Banque Mondiale. Washington. D.C.

Touna Mama et Tsafack-Nanfosso, R. A. (2000): "L'Economie Camerounaise: De la Crise à la Reprise". Dans Cameroun 2001: Politique, Langues, Economie et Santé. (eds.) Etudes Africaines, L'Harmattan, Paris, France, pp. 137-164.

United Nations Conference on Trade and Development (UNCTAD) (2001): "Export Diversification Index". UNCTAD Handbook of Statistics. On-line: Geneva, Swiss.

UNCTAD (2005): "World Investment Report 2005: Transnational Corporations and the Internationalization of R&D". United Nations (UN), New York and Geneva.

World Bank (2001): "World Bank Africa Database: 2001". The World Bank, Washington D.C. USA.

World Bank (2004): "Republic of Cameroon Development Review: A New Resolve to Sustain Reforms for Inclusive Growth." The World Bank Report No. 29268-CM. Washington D. C. USA.

World Bank (2005): "World Development Indicators 2005". The World Bank, Washington D.C. Online: http://devdata.worldbank.org/data-query/, accessed on: 13/12/2005.

Transport Infrastructures and Cameroon Exports Promotion in Central Africa

Valérie Ongolo Zogo and Touna Mama

1 Introduction

For several decades, divergent, complementary and/or contradictory initiatives have been taken to launch the economic take-off in Sub-Saharan Africa (SSA) countries. The Structural Adjustment Programs (SAPs), the Heavily Indebted Poor Countries (HIPC) initiative, the New Partnership for African Development (NEPAD), all are in keeping with the general pattern, together with a particular emphasis on measures aiming at favouring trade and regional integration. The construction of these regional economic spaces leads to a greater competitiveness and diversification in the economies concerned with the main objective to reduce their dependence to primary commodities. Recent research studies have pointed out the weakness of African transport infrastructures as one of the major explanatory factors of the poor competitiveness of African products in the world market, and for the marginalization of Africa from world trade. Amjadi and Yeats (1995, p. 4) have in fact shown that transport costs in African countries can be assigned to trade barriers, which may even be considered as more significant than custom duties. Limâo and Venables (2001, p. 460) explained the low volumes of inter African trade as being due to the lack of transport infrastructures.

Indeed, a deterioration of transport infrastructures raises transport costs and reduces trade volumes by 28 percent. These observations, which were made at the African level are even more relevant in the case of Central Africa as shown by Ongolo Zogo and Touna Mama (2003, p. 91). There exist no effective trans-national roads, and inter-states road network is essentially made up of dirt roads. In the context of SAPs, a particular attention was given to the transport sector in most of SSA countries through the Transport Sectoral Project (TSP). Part of this program targeted the rehabilitation of inter-state roads and the financing of road infrastructures in the CEMAC countries in order to materialize the existing trade potential between these different markets. The underlying objective of this initiative, which was sponsored by the World Bank, was to develop intra-zone trade, and promote export and regional integration with the purpose to reduce the dependence of those countries vis-à-vis developed countries. Those capital-intensive projects were often confronted with financial problems due mainly to the budget constraints faced by the States concerned and the lack of reliable information on their net benefit. The importance of this issue justifies the effort that public authorities should devote on acquiring the ways and means to boost the financing of road infrastructures in Central Africa.

The purpose of this study is to carry out an effect analysis of the benefits of road infrastructure investment by taking the specific case of the road linking the Gabonese capital and Southern Cameroon; since Gabon and Cameroon are the two dominant economies in the region. The paper will then present a conceptual framework of export development in developing countries as in Cameroon with a link with transport infrastructures. The empirical framework of Cameroon-Gabon road will then be conducted through an evaluation analysis of benefit effects. Finally, some recommendations and policy implications will be made concerning the institutional framework, financing road infrastructures reforms, and the way to use infrastructure for promoting sub regional exports and to reduce dependence of Central African countries.

2 Transport and Export Development in Cameroon

2.1 Conceptual Framework

For a long time, trade liberalization has been considered as the main foundation on which the design of economic development strategies is based. For a few years however, several studies have questioned the relationship between trade liberalization and growth as concerned developing countries. Greenaway, Morgan and Wright (2002, p. 235) show that liberalization indices should first be specified in a better way before concluding in favour of the efficiency of such measures. Export promotion is another path to stimulate growth in SSA. Onafowora and Owoye (1998, p. 502) confirm the significant impact of trade liberalization on growth in SSA countries but also stress that export promotion is an outward-looking strategy. These concepts are in line with the export-led growth models approach. Recent models of trade set up the role of supply capacity for export performance (Redding and Venables 2004, p. 53). In this approach, market access, which includes both the quantity and the quality of physical infrastructures, is one of the most important components of export performance for a few years also; economists have shown renewed interest in transport infrastructure development as a growth vector in facilitating trade.

In the context of World Bank Structural Adjustment loans in SSA, many countries implemented trade policy reform measures. Meier and Steel (1989, p. 27) have listed export promotion as one of the main objectives to achieve. The reform measures aimed at creating export promotion units, simplifying export procedure, reducing export taxes, and introducing export insurance. Furthermore, Balassa (1990, p. 385), showed that exports are responsive to price incentives in SSA countries and that among the latter, market-oriented countries achieve better performances than interventionist ones. Furthermore, the Hamilton and Thompson's analysis (1994, p. 1389) main finding was that in a regional context, the export-led growth model is efficient if the promotion of non-traditional exports is addressed within broader development strategies and regional cooperation. For industrial goods, the creation of Regional trading agreements (RTAs) is the main public policy, which aims at promoting intra regional trade. They lead on the theory of Customs Unions and, Free Trade Area for trade promotion. Robson (1998, p. 37) recognizes the trade creation effect of RTAs and breaks it down into two parts as assumed by the traditional trade theory hypothesis, namely, a substitution of foreign goods effects, and a consumption effect.

In Central Africa, Bakoup and Tarr (2000, p. 166), have presented three main issues of the RTA to promote trade in CEMAC zone, which are: improved access to market, preferential tariff reduction, and implementation of the common external tariff. They argue that given Cameroon's regional market power, the country will gain from the agreement. However, these trade opportunities are strongly affected by transaction costs. For the World Bank (1996, p. 67), high transport cost is the main barrier to regional trade integration. To develop trade opportunities in market-oriented economies, African governments and regional institutions should focus interconnecting road building. This objective is at the heart of NEPAD's strategies for support infrastructure development.

Several theoretical developments highlight the importance of road infrastructures for the economy in general. Keeler and Ying (1988, p. 72) focused on the benefits of investment in highway infrastructure in U.S. since 1950. The authors have shown that the benefits are large enough to justify between one third and one half of the Federal-aid highway system costs. Martin, (1999, p. 14) established the role of public infrastructures for regional inequalities and growth. The paper highlights the positive effect of infrastructure improvement reducing transaction costs between regions and increasing the growth rate.

Gravity models directly establish the link between transport costs and regional trade flow. In fact, they use transport and transaction costs to explain trade volumes between economic spaces. Larue and Mutunga (1993, p. 155) and Foroutan and Pritchett (1993, p. 79) applied these models to African trade. In these models, macroeconomic and monetary variables, transport costs or distance are used to explain export demand and inter-State trade. In these studies, emphasis is particularly put on monetary variables, since transport costs do not have a significant explanatory effect.

In his conclusions on trade policy in Africa, Lyakurwa (1991, p. 21) underscores the importance of transport conditions and recommends infrastructure improvement to accelerate regional integration. In the same way, Martins and Rogers (1996, p. 26) hypothesize that direct integration gains from industrial de-localization are conditioned by the existence of a critical mass of infrastructures.

Transport economists have established a link between transport costs and regional trade volumes. According to Bauchet (1988, p. 112), for a country A to sell a product in country B, the freight rate must be such that its price in country B is rendered lower than the price of the product made in B and Cost Insurance Fret (CIF) price lower than factory gate price. Transport costs represent a gross protection for products made in B. They limit the tradable nature of products from A. The low level of transport infrastructures therefore, strongly explains the low level of trade, and the low level of market integration.

2.2 Transport Costs and Trade in Central Africa

The transport sector in general, and road infrastructures in particular, constitute a significant share of public capital expenditures since their direct returns could not be realized. This observation can be justified in Public Economics by the concept of non pure public goods or services, which can be defined as non-rival or non-excludable goods or services but not absolutely; that means consumption by one does not reduce the availability for consumption by others. Those characteristics cause problems for the production of such goods as it is set up by Buchanan (2006) and justifie the intervention of public sector for instance. Given the essential nature of road infrastructures, its importance in the functioning of other sectors, and for the competitiveness of export products;

transport conditions are considered as the main physical barrier to trade and public policy in transport can be used to promote trade.

The following diagram (Figure 1) drawn from Mwase (2001, p. 3) summarizes the linkages between road infrastructures and export promotion. This diagram shows the direct and indirect outcomes that can be expected from investments in road infrastructures as far as trade policy is concerned.

Figure 1: Road Infrastructures and Export Promotion

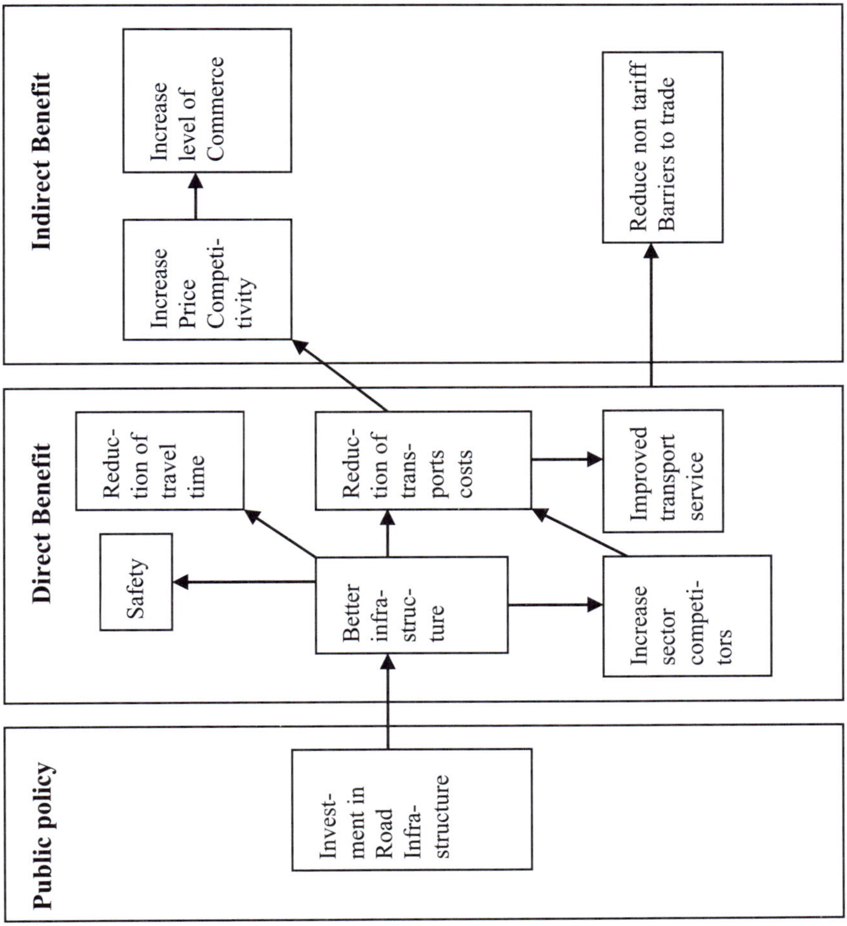

Source: *Authors presentation based on Mwase (2001).*

The general background of CEMAC trade relationship is characterized by the importance of traditional products (crude oil). Another distinctive feature of trade in this zone is a limited intra regional linkage that handles only close to 5 percent of total trade[1] and 1.3 percent of total exports. The situation is due mainly to the dominance of France and other EU countries in trade relation with CEMAC countries, and the lack of diversification as far as industrial structure is concerned. Cameroon tends to consolidate its position as a leader in the sub region; its exports increase while its imports decrease as percentage of total trade within the CEMAC zone. Gabon's total exports to CEMAC amount to 0.8 percent and its imports from CEMAC, 2.3 percent in 2002. The trade relation is more important at a bilateral level. Cameroon is the 11th supplier of Gabon in term of volume with instability of the export trend from Cameroon to Gabon. Those trends are resumed in the Table 1 below.

Table 1: Cameroon and Gabon Intra regional Trade Flows as Percentage of Total Trade and Cameroon Trade with Gabon as Percentage of Total Trade in CEMAC

Year	1998	1999	2000	2001	2002	2003
Gabon						
Exports to CEMAC	0.2	2	1	1.2	0.8	--
Imports from CEMAC	1	2	3	3.10	2.3	--
Cameroon						
Exports to CEMAC	6.62	5.70	4.80	3.12	4.25	--
Imports from CEMAC	0.02	0.02	0.01	0.01	0.01	--
Cameroon						
Exports to Gabon	30.76	31.65	26.15	25.54	18.15	27.45
Imports from Gabon	09.78	08.21	06.31	07.09	10.11	05.20

Source: Compiled by the authors from DSCN, and INS 1998, 2002, 2005.

External trade policy in CEMAC has been harmonised since the introduction of Common External Tariff (CET) by all the CEMAC countries and it can explain the changes in the pattern at the end of the 1990s.

Between Cameroon and Gabon, export flows essentially involve non traditional commodities, and more specifically current consumption of food crops, which are sensitive to seasonnal changes and transactions costs. The competitiveness of manufactures is weak, either because the percentage of goods produced by both Cameroon and Gabon are high or because the margin

---

1 See Zafar and Kubota, World Bank Working Paper Series n. 52, 2003.

rates due to transport costs are lower at the international level than at the regional level. This diagnosis is still pertinent.[2] Gabonese merchants would therefore benefit more from supplying EU import products to consumers.

Even for those consumption food crops, non tariff barriers are significant. As shown by Bamou (2002, p. 12), those barriers are related to the transaction costs incurred while transporting these goods from one State to another (police checkpoints, poor quality of roads, and insufficiency of storage infrastructures).

This trade relationship in CEMAC is characterized by a high level of qualitative restrictions. With the harmonization of customs and fiscal policies in the sub-region, those results may basically be explained by the existence of significant non tariff barriers, namely, high transport costs. In effect, institutions in charge of regional integration in CEMAC are deeply concerned by the problem of weakness of transport infrastructures, which drawback regional integration. Their main objective is therefore to adopt a sub-regional master plan on transport infrastructures which must serve as a formal framework for mobilizing funds for financing transport infrastructures in the sub-region.[3] A study by Sylte (1999, p. 8), shows that regional road transport may add up to 70 percent to the price of cheap goods, versus 30 percent for customs duties and 17 percent for international transport up to the Douala port. This is the reason why the Transport Sectoral Project was implemented by the World Bank in SSA countries since.

Transport conditions in CEMAC are largely determined by road conditions. Roads have the largest modal share of regional transport in Central Africa. The World Bank study by Sylte (1999, p. 9) estimated that road network in CEMAC countries carries between 80 to 90 percent of the traffic and 95 percent of the total freight.

At the level of each state these roads are usually in poor condition due to insufficient investments. Transit road infrastructures have been identified by the CEMAC secretariat as a priority with the assistance of "Agence Française pour le Développement (AFD)", European Union (EU) and African Development Bank (ADB). From Cameroon to Gabon, the integrative priority itinerary is: Yaoundé – Ebolowa – Ambam – Abang Minko – Eboro – Bitam – Oyem – Njole – Bifoun – Libreville; that is 450 kilometers.

---

2 See Bela, 1995, p. 8.

3 See UNECA, 2004.

Road infrastructures

Most of roads in the sub-region are unpaved and in poor conditions as shown by Sylte (1999, pp. 12, 13). Since 1996, some CEMAC countries, namely Gabon and Cameroon have started to develop a priority road network.

In the context of TSP, a road building program for regional integration has been initiated as well as the rehabilitation of transit itineraries financed by AFD, ADB and FED. This program included paving the Ebolowa-Ambam axis (AFD financing), building the bridge over the Ntem river (FED financing), and paving the Ambam-Eking axis in progress (ADB financing). The statement of those construction works in progress on the integration road between Cameroon and Gabon and their costs are presented in the Table 2 below.

Table 2: Road Rehabilitation Works for Regional Integration between Cameroon and Gabon

Name of the Project	Nature of the Work	Length (in Km)	Total Cost (in million CFA Francs)
Yaoundé – Nsimalen	Rehabilitation	12	5 000
Nsimalen– Mbalmayo – Ebolowa	Rehabilitation	130	25 000
Ebolowa – Ambam	Construction	100	30 000
Ambam – Eking	Construction	27	8 000
Ntem Bridge	Construction	--	3 740
Total		**269**	**71 740**

Source: Ministry of Public Work Cameroon, 2003.

Chains of procedures applied to merchandises exports concern both the transportation of goods from the origin to the destination, and various formalities related to this movement. For intra-community imports, two provisions are to be considered as concerns custom duties. National products in principle were exempted from custom duties after the abolition of the TPG in 1998. For example, a Cameroonian industrialist exporting his output to Chad is exempted from paying domestic taxes provided that he can prove that the goods have been exported by showing the D_6[4] document. To be re-exported to another country, goods imported from third countries and nationalized after the payment of customs duties must be taxed again at the rate of the common external tariff (CET).

4 The D_6 Document is a Transit document to be stamped at the frontier.

The freight market has been liberalized following the implementation of TSP. The only particular provisions are those concerned with the transport of merchandise in transit to landlocked countries: Chad and Central Africa Republic (CAR). The freight is distributed according to a key provided by the convention regulating surface transport, and organized by the national private offices of freight management located in Douala. In the other cases, the market is not organized. Most of the goods transported are for one's own account. Freight rates are negotiated by mutual agreement, and are a function of the quality of the road (dry season or raining season).

The SITRASS Report (1989, p. 43) on truckage costs reduction policy in Sub-Saharan Africa and in Cameroon, has analyzed the freight rate structure, and has shown the contrast in terms of transport costs and prices between the local, national and international links. The price of a ton kilometre in Cameroon, as in the other countries, was an increasing function of distance and of total cargo. But with the improvement in the quality of the infrastructure, the trend has been reversed because of cut-through competition between small carriers.

3 Empirical Impact Analysis of the Effects of Cameroon-Gabon Road Infrastructure

3.1 Description of the Project

The transnational road Cameroon-Gabon project is within the framework of priorities decided by the CEMAC countries since 1993 in the way of putting in place a regional road network. This is concerned with the reduction of transaction costs and charge rupture costs relative to the road quality and the use of ferry and represent the available means for the movement of goods and persons between the two countries.

The chosen option was composed of two aspects:

- Allow the registration in every national program, the project concerned with the paving of roads towards boundaries;
- Realise the Ntem project aiming at improving traffic at the three boundaries (Gabon, Cameroon and Equatorial Guinea).

The first aspect was to be realized by the Cameroon government through the public investment budget and with traditional financial assistance from AFD and ADB. This first phase has already been completed.

The second aspect dealing with the Ntem project is made up of two works: the Ngoazik and Eboro bridges. The works are realized by the European Development Fund (FED) and the AfDB. The supervisors and deputy supervisors are respectively the ministers in charge of Public Works and the chief of mission of Italian consortium C. LOTTI ASSOCIATI.

This regional project aiming at linking Yaoundé to Libreville was partly finished in August 2005. Improvements brought to the quality of the road infrastructure can already allow a measurement of achieved benefits.

3.2 Model and Data

For transport infrastructures, the approach to project evaluation corresponds to an application of the general model of Public Economic Calculus. This approach permits to measure the aggregate surplus following the realization of public investments projects. Usually, the State is the decision maker and finances the road infrastructure project.

Among several issues that can serve this purpose, Cost-Benefit analysis should generally be used for road infrastructures to establish whether the projects are worth undertaking. By computing the main impacts of a public decision to their monetary value, Cost-Benefit analysis is a powerful tool. The key technique is to identify all the options and quantify in monetary terms link to the project. Prest and Turvey (1965, p. 702) identified four major steps to implementing this method.

In the first step, the different options of the project with their main economic characteristics are identified. Then costs and benefits (direct and indirect) should be listed. Those costs and benefits are evaluated in the third phase. For non-market benefits, the use of market substitutes will be the estimating method in this study.

The last step of the method consists in determining the economic profitability of the project through a discounted balance sheet of costs and benefits; that is:

$$Max \frac{\sum A_t / (1+a)^t}{\sum C_t / (1+a)^t} \qquad (1)$$

Where a is the annual discount rate, t the time of the project, At is annual benefits of the project, and Ct is the cost of the project. The relevant decision criterion for the Cost-Benefit method is the positive sign of net benefits or that of benefit-cost ratio.

The different elements of benefits and costs are a function of the economic and social context in which the investment must be realized, and of the issue of the project. As far as road infrastructures are concerned, the effects deal with both transport function and the level of economic activities.

A transportation Cost-Benefit analysis is complex because it involves many factors which must not be ignored or double-counted. Another way of assessing economic and social effects of transportation project is to measure the consequences of the infrastructure construction project on the competitiveness and businesses opportunities through case study analysis according to a specific aim (see Bruinsma et al., 1997).

Our approach will be to list the different direct and indirect benefits and costs of the road infrastructure project between Cameroon and Gabon and to assess the effects of this project on trade opportunities between the two countries.

The benefit here can be evaluated in terms of time, trade opportunities and public taxes. Before the improvement of road infrastructures a trip between Yaoundé and Libreville had duration of two and a half days with many police harassments. After the building of the road, the duration fell to 24 hours. The following table 3 summarises the road investment effect categories

Table 3: Road Investment Effect Categories in Cameroon

	Market/ Non Market	Reference Unit	Value per unit
Vehicle maintenance	Market	Cost per km	1.6 CFA per km on paved road 2.4 CFA per km on unpaved road
Fuel taxes	Market	Cost per liter	92.5 CFA per liter
Road tolls	Market	Cost per vehicle	500 CFA per vehicle
Transport time	Non market	Trip time	50 Hours before the road and 24 after the investment
Traffic	Non market	Vehicles per day	250 on unpaved road to 400 on paved road
Body accidents Killed	Non market	Cost of body accidents killed	2 millions CFA per killed
Trade effects	Non market	Evolution of exports in value	millions of CFA Francs to be estimated

Source: By the authors from the data collected in Transport Ministry and Road Safety Department and our own survey.

The expression of aggregate benefits provided by a road investment is given by:

$$A = N_0\left(c_0 - c_1\right) + \left(N_1 - N_0\right)\left(\frac{c_0 - c_1}{2}\right) + \Delta p + \Delta x - \Delta s + \Delta e \qquad (2)$$

where the different parts of the equation are defined as:
$(c_0 - c_1)$: valuation of the average satisfaction of users of the investment project, this variable is included in vehicle maintenance cost and reduction of travel time for private users; but for the State, this satisfaction is assumed to be the maintenance cost differential. We will consider here the private user gains.

N_0: number of users before the investment

N1: number of users after the investment

D_p: Valuation of the amount of tolls payable

D_x: variation in the amount of taxes on fuel

D_s: variation of the cost of accidents.

D_e: algebraic valuation of net export benefits

Particular attention should be paid to this last variable, which represents the indirect benefits of the Cameroon road users. It is a question of making a monetary valuation of the reduction in transaction costs as the new road infrastructure is used, and to make a projection of the net export receipts flowing to public authorities. Quantitative assumptions will be made to determine the monetary equivalents of gains in term of gain in time, comfort and security.

The economic cost of the investment in the road infrastructure Ct is the present value of the various expenditures allowed to this operation, namely studies, land acquisition, construction, maintenance and exploitation (i.e. operating costs). Estimation of these costs has been carried out by the Ministry of Public Works in accordance with the data given in Table 3 above.

The model will use the average benefits instead of marginal ones. The data used in this model to evaluate the net profit of the paved road from Yaoundé to Libreville are compiled by the authors from many sources (from qualitative surveys conducted by Public Works and Transport Ministries during the elaboration of the Transport Sectoral Project, questionnaire directed at carriers, and offices of Fund for the Stabilization of Hydrocarbon Prices).

Transaction cost savings represent the valuation of the average satisfaction of users:

We find here the value of time, the benefits linked to safety.

The data on the variables N0, N1, Dp, Dx, Ds are obtained from feasibility studies on the construction of the infrastructure commissioned by the Ministry of Public Works. The scale here is the year.

To estimate De, we used the components of export growth in a trade model where distance is considered as a barrier to trade model (Fugazza, 2004, p. 17). The approach is that of a gravity model equation where the dependent variable was export from Cameroon to Gabon and the explanatory variables are: supply capacity, bilateral trade costs and Gabon population. Regression estimation procedure was used. The equation to be estimated using Eviews Software was:

$$\ln\left(X_{CG}\right) = \alpha + \lambda_0 \ln GMc + \beta \ln CSc + \gamma_1 \left(dist_{CG}\right) + \gamma_2\, road_{CG} + \eta\, Gpop + \mu_{CG} \quad (3)$$

The variables in the equation were specified as follows:

X_{CG}: exports in millions of CFA francs from Cameroon to Gabon

GM_C: Gabon market capacity represented by country domestic demand for consumption at market price series in billions of CFA francs from IMF statistical appendix.

CS_C: Cameroon supply capacity represented by country GDP at market price series in billions of CFA francs from IMF statistical appendix

$dist_{CG}$: border dummy. It will be represented by trip time which changes with changes in road condition.

$road_{CG}$: road condition dummy; 0 before the paving road and 1 after.

Gpop: Gabon population.

μ_{CG}: stochastic error.

$dist_{CG}$ and $road_{CG}$ are assumed to capture bilateral trade costs.

α, β, λ_0, γ_1, and γ_2, η were parameters to be estimated. The data used to estimate this equation are presented in the following table 4.

Table 4: Model Data

Year	Xcg	GMc	CSc	$dist_{CG}$	$road_{CG}$	POPG
1991	8644	936.2	3340	50	0	983820
1992	9072	966.6	3195	50	0	1014900
1993	7342	970.0	3155	50	0	1046100
1994	6954	1272.9	3416	50	0	1077500
1995	10147	1355.9	4130	50	0	1109000
1996	16504	1502.1	4571	50	0	1140100
1997	25835	1557.2	4932	50	0	1170600
1998	23236	1641.8	5331	50	0	1200500
1999	19572	1566.6	6388	50	0	1229600
2000	9003	1516.0	7049	50	0	1258000
2001	11477	1662.4	7374	50	0	1286600
2002	12994	1945.7	7583	24	1	1315400
2003	24867	1826.4	7976	24	1	1344400
2004	26735	1930.9	8350	24	1	1373400

Source: Author's Calculation

The results of the estimation did not allowed interpreting the impact of road conditions on export. The sample is too short to draw any serious conclusions; the coefficient of the road conditions variable is not significant on any acceptable error probability level. R square is too low, F statistics indicate that the whole estimation has not a great advantage. We will stay away from including the estimation in the model and just elaborate on expected/potential effects of road conditions on exports.

3.3 Results of Assessing the Economic Effects of Cameroon-Gabon Road Infrastructure

The benefit analysis of the Cameroon-Gabon road will be done by calculating the direct and indirect benefits). Table 5 below gives the results of this benefit analysis and shows the effects of road infrastructure on Cameroon state revenues (toll and special taxes), cost of accidents.

Variation of export in value per year due to the new road could not be estimated by regression equation but the general trend from the last two years shows and important increase of Cameroon exportations to Gabon since 2002; from 12994 to 24867, and 26735. Due to the fact that there are only few observations after the construction of Cameroon-Gabon road, it was not possible to get significant results as far as export differential was concerned. The net benefit of the new infrastructure is without export effect is positive.

Table 5: Nets Benefits of the Gabon-Cameroon Paved Road

	Reference Unit	Value per year
$(c_0 - c_1)$	FCFA per kilometre	8 755 950
N_0	Vehicles per year	146 000
$(N_1 - N_0)$	Difference in Vehicles per year	54 750
Δp	F CFA	82 125 000
Δx	F CFA	531 759 375
Δs	F CFA	- 176 000 000

Source: *Estimated by the authors*

- Due to the improvement of road infrastructure, the State expenses for road maintenance will be reduced from 35 000 CFA Francs per kilometre per year for the unpaved road, to 2450 CFA Francs for the new paved road. The maintenance cost differential per year is: 8 755 950 Francs which are gained by the State.
- The Valuation of the amount of tolls payable, Dp is equal to the traffic differential times the number of toll stations between Yaoundé and Gabon border which is 3, that is 82.125 Millions CFA Francs.
- The number of vehicles per day, raised from less than 250 on unpaved roads to 400 with the paved road. (N1 - N0) per year is 54 750.
- The variation in the amount of special taxes on petroleum products; Dx is deduced from the generated traffic. The fuel tax average is 92.5 per litre making the hypothesis that tourism cars and trucks have the same repartition rate in the fleet. For the 300 kilometres in Cameroon

zone, the estimation of the fuel consumption is 105 litres per vehicle. On this amount, petroleum taxes paid by this road user are estimated at 9712.5 CFA Francs. Then Dx is 531 759 375 CFA Francs.

- For the variation of the cost of accidents, the number of killed before the road was 35 per 10000 vehicles per year. After the road investment the rate falls to 28 per 10000 vehicles per year. The cost of one killed in Cameroon is estimated at 2 millions CFA Francs according to the Road Safety Division of Transport Ministry. The number of killed before the road investment was 320. After the road, the number killed is supposed to rise to 408 due to the increase in traffic. The variation of cost of accident Δs is then – 176 000000 CFA Francs.

4 Conclusions and Policy Implications

The purpose of this study was to carry out impact analysis of the effects of road infrastructure investment on the road linking the Gabonese capital and the south of Cameroon in term of export promotion. Cameroon and Gabon have many trade opportunities essentially for agricultural non traditional products. Those opportunities have for a long time been limited by barriers to trade, and transport costs are the most important non tariff barrier to trade in Central Africa. The results of the study show that annual direct benefits for the community are important for state budget through toll payments and taxes on petroleum products. In a social approach, the new road infrastructure reduces enclosure but also increases the number of victims of accidents on the road. It is also an important way for reducing transaction costs linked to trade.

The indirect benefits are related to export promotion due to diminishing transaction costs and exporter margins. Since the new road contributes to reduce vehicle maintenance costs, the transport cost and cost prices will be cut down. Beyond the commercial reforms that strengthen regional trade, physical infrastructures have a great importance for trade. Market capacity is the most important variable for export promotion between Cameroon and Gabon and to justify instability of export trend. But the potential industrial exports in the region resulting to a new industrial strategy promoting supply capacity could not have chance to boost more income elasticity-good in the region if transport costs and condition are not improved and this conclusion is more pertinent for agricultural goods. But the budgetary constraints often oblige public authorities to restraint road investments. National infrastructure enhancement has also to be coordinated at a regional level to intensify the benefits of such projects.

The above conclusions suggest the following policy implications for international transport in Central Africa concerning essentially the institutional framework and the financial reforms.

In general, measures to promote trade in Sub Saharan African countries deal with transport in transit towards landlocked countries in order to facilitate imports and exports in those countries. Those measures did not aim at promoting intra regional trade. By implementing them, they enforced the market price competitiveness of European goods on local markets. By enhancing road quality, market prices of Cameroon's goods in Gabon may be reduced and this will typically induce trade between the two countries. Since the opening of the partially built road between Gabon and Cameroon, the first observations show an increase of Cameroon food crops supply in the Libreville principal market.

In countries like Cameroon, where the roads are perceived by population as a pure public good, a mixed policy with public financing and private management of roads infrastructures seems to be more appropriate to enforce road conditions. But with high budgetary pressures that the country has to face, this option is not feasible in a short to medium term.

Instead of considering roads as social services, the roads should be brought into the market place by charging for their use on a fee-for-service basis and manage them like private enterprises[5]. Road funds must be established and the funds collected from toll payable and fuel taxes must be used for building new infrastructures or for maintaining the existing ones since high freight costs are the main barriers for inter-regional imports and exports. Road investments and especially new infrastructures are mainly funded by external resources (80 to 90 percent from 1997 to 1999[6]).

The debate may be oriented towards the different ways in privatising road management to promote foreign investment in this sub-sector. The key issues here are enforcing the institutional framework in the transport sector and the legal framework for foreign direct investments.

---

5 That is the main issue stressed out by UNECA and World Bank in the frame of SSATP program.

6 See Sylte 1999, SSATP Working Paper, 43.

References

Amjadi, A. Rienke and Yeats, Alexander J. (1995): "Have Transport Costs Contributed to the Relative Decline of African Exports?", World Bank Working Paper, 1559.

Bakoup, Ferdinand and Tarr, David (2000): "The Economic Effects of Integration in Central African Economic and Monetary Community: Some General Equilibrium estimates for Cameroon", African Development Review, 12 (2), 161- 190.

Balassa, Bela (1990): "Incentive Policies and Export Performance in sub-Saharan Africa." World Development, 18 (3), 383-391.

Bamou, Lydie (2002): "Promoting Export Diversification in Cameroon: Toward which Products", African Research Consortium Research Paper, 114.

Bauchet, Pierre (1988): "Le transport international dans l'économie mondiale", Paris: Economica.

Bela, Lazare (1995): "Régime de la taxe unique et la coopération économique au sein de l'Union Douanière et Economique de l'Afrique Centrale (UDEAC)", CODESRIA, Document de travail, 2.

Bruinsma, Frank R., Sytze A. Rienstra, and Piet Rietveld (1997): "Economic Impacts of the Construction of a Transport Corridor: A Multi-level and Multi-approach Case Study for the Construction of the A1 Highway in the Netherlands." Regional Studies, Vol. 31, No. 4, pp. 91–402.

Buchanan, James M. (2006): "The demand and supply of public goods." Online: Econlib.org/library/Buchanan/buchCv5c4.html, accessed: 02/11/2006.

CEMAC (2003): "General Statistics Yearbook", Bangui.

DSCN (1998, 2002, 2004): "Statistics Yearbooks", Yaounde.

Foroutan, Faezeh and Pritchett, Lant (1993): "Intra-Sub-Saharan Africa: Is it too little?" Journal of African Economies, 3 (1), 74-105.

Fugazza, Marco (2004): "Export performance and its determinants: supply and demand constraints", UNCTAD Policy Issues in International Trade and Commodities Study Series, 26.

Greenaway, David, Morgan, Wyn and Wright, Peter (2002): "Trade liberalisation and growth in developing countries", Journal of development economics, 67(1), 221-244.

Hamilton, Nora and Thompson, Carol (1994): "Export promotion in a regional context: Central America and Southern Africa". World Development, 22 (9), 1379-1392.

IMF (1996): "Cameroon – Selected Issues and Statistical Appendix", Staff Country Report, N°96/125.

IMF (1997): "Gabon – Selected Issues and Statistical Appendix", Staff Country Report, N°97/54.

IMF (2005): "Cameroon Statistical Appendix", online: http://www.imf.org/external/-pubs/cat/longres.cfm?sk=18267.0, accessed: 12/05/2006.

IMF (2005): "Gabon – Selected Issues and Statistical Appendix", online: http://www.imf.org/external/pubs/cat/longres.cfm?sk=18228.0, 12/05/2006.

INS (2005): "Annuaire Statistique du Cameroun", online: http://www.statistics-cameroon.org/stats/datastruct/comext/balcom/echangecamcemac.htm, accessed: 02/05/2006.

Keeler, Theodore, E. Ying and John, S. (1988): "Measuring the benefit of a large public investment, the case of the U.S. Federal-aid highway system", Journal of public economics, 36 (1), 69-85.

Larue, Bruno and Mutunga, James (1993): "The gravity equation, market size and black market exchange rates". International Economic Journal, 7 (2), 134-161.

Lyakurwa, William (1991): "Trade policy and promotion in Sub-Saharan Africa", African Research Consortium, Special Paper, 12.

Limaô, Nuno and Venables, J. Anthony (2001): "Infrastructure, Geographical Disadvantage, Transport costs, and Trade", The World Bank Economic Review, 15 (3), 451- 479.

Martin, Philippe (1999): "Public policies, regional inequalities and growth", Journal of Public Economics, 73 (1), 85-105.

Martin, Philippe and Rogers, Carol Ann (1996): "Localisation industrielle, intégration régionale et infrastructures publiques théorie et implications pour l'Afrique", RPI, Document spécial 2.

Meier, Gerald M. and Steel, William F. (1989): "Industrial Adjustment in Sub-Saharan Africa", Oxford University Press.

Ministry of Public Work Cameroon (2003): "Road rehabilitation program."

Mwase, Ngila (2001): "Liberalization and Deregulation of the Transport Sector in Sub-Saharan Africa: Experiences, Challenges and Opportunities", Paper presented at the African Economic Research Consortium.

Onafowora, Olugbenga A. and Owoye, Oluwole (1998): "Can Trade Liberalisation Stimulate Economic Growth in Africa?", World Development, 26 (3), 497-506.

Ongolo Zogo Valérie and Touna Mama (2003): "Intégration physique à travers le développement des infrastructures en Afrique Centrale", in Ben Hammouda, Bekolo-Ebe et Touna Mama, 2003, L'intégration régionale en Afrique Centrale. Bilan et perspectives, Karthala.

Prest, Alan Richman and Turvey, Ralph (1965): "Cost-benefit analysis", a survey, Economic Journal, 75 (5), 683-735.

Redding, Steve and Venables, Anthony (2004): "Economic Geography and International Inequality," Journal of International Economics, 62 (1), 53- 82.

Robson, Peter (1998): "The Economics of International Integration", London, Routledge.

SITRASS (1989): "Politiques de réduction du coût de camionnage en Afrique sub-saharienne". Cas du Cameroun, Rapport.

Sylte, Ole K. (1999): "Review of the Road Sector in Customs and Economic Union of Central Africa States (UDEAC)", SSATP Working Paper, 43.

Touna Mama, 2002, "Infrastructure et Développement dans le nouveau partenariat pour le développement de l'Afrique" in: Ben Hammouda (H.) et Kasse (M.) (2002): Le NEPAD et les enjeux du développement en Afrique, Maisonneuve et Larose, Paris.

UNECA (2004): "Trade and Regional Integration, Forum on Transport Infrastructures and Regional Integration", Uneca.

UNCTAD (1999, 2002, 2005): "Statistic Yearbooks."

World Bank (1996): "World Development Report", Washington DC, World Bank.

World Bank Africa Data base (2005): CD-Rom

Zafar, Ali and Kubota, Keito (2003): "Regional Integration in Central Africa: Key Issues", Africa Region World Bank Working Paper Series, 52.

Investments and Industrialization in Cameroon: Challenges and Prospects

Celestin N'Donga

1 Introduction

The economy of most African countries is increasingly being marginalized. This is because their focus is on primary production structures and industrial activities of technologically low natural resources.

Although this paper deals with the case of Cameroon, it falls within the systemic approach of the change in the fundamental tendencies to design optimal and critical conditions of a real restructuring of a national industrial policy whose aim is to stimulate a strong and constant growth which will a sustainable fight against poverty and social exclusion, thereby improving the national economy, taking into account the new world dynamics of the globalization of production and exchanges.

For nearly three decades, Cameroon's economic policy had been shaped by economic programs negotiated with the international financial community under the Bretton Woods institutions (signing of the first agreement with the World Bank in 1989). Under the appellation of structural adjustment and public stabilization of finances, the management method of the national economic policy set aside the five year development plan used by Cameroon from 1960 (year of independence of the country) to 1986 (end of the 6th FYP) within which the industrial policy was carried out (RC/DSDRE, 1989).

The results of this change in orientation have affected the macro-economic aggregates: the stabilization of public finances and the restoration of budgetary and balance of payment equilibriums, the better follow-up of monetary policies, the return to the path of positive growth, with an average GDP of 5% since 1994/95 (Hakim B. H., 2002).

But it has been observed that the return to a positive growth was strongly stimulated by the devaluation of the CFA franc in 1994, principally supported by demands due to the absence of a consequent supply. Investment is the essential factor for a strong and sustainable growth but unfortunately it has not followed.

This characterized fragile situation of Cameroon's industrial activity, which is more of a structural problem rather than a problem of economic crisis, was exposed by the wave of the liberalization of the country's economy in the structural adjustment process. It was evident that neither the many fiscal or custom advantages granted to enterprises within the framework of preferential systems of the Investment Code, nor the enormous subsidies given to public and semi-public companies have achieved the main objective expected, namely the establishment of a consistent and coherent industrial sector (WB/RC, 1996).

In fact, as soon as the first tariff and non-tariff barriers were uplifted, Cameroon's secondary sector (with the exception of oil industries) quickly went out of breath in the face of competition from foreign products. It was to meet up with this situation that at the beginning of the 1990s, the Government of Cameroon adopted the policy of promoting industrial exports in the place of the industrial policy of import substitution practiced since independence in 1960. The results obtained after the adoption of this new strategy show a very low contribution of the industrial sector to growth (WB/RC, 1985).

Thus, the experience of the two conventional industrial policy methods – importation substitution industry on the one hand, and industrial exportation promotion on the other hand, has not enabled Cameroon to make a real take-off likely to lay a solid base for its economic growth.

This is enough evidence to call for a remodelling of the national industrial policy with a view to escaping the primary commodities dilemma through pro-active growth policies, which is the subject of this analysis and which is articulated in five main sections.

The first section deals with (i) some important aspects of the problem of Cameroon's industrial policy since its genesis in the 1960s. The second section looks at the (ii) justification of IIS and EPIP and their shortcomings. The third section examines the unavoidable stake of (iii) remodelling the institutional context for the promotion of investments in Cameroon. The fourth section concerns the complex issue of (iv) reconfiguration of the national industrial sector. The last section deals with (v) two typical cases of the execution of the operational program of the national industrial policy.

With regard to the first point, the recent evolutions of the Cameroonian economy show a very low contribution of the secondary sector to the growth of the GDP. Surprisingly, the confinement of the national productive apparatus in one subset limited to eight industrial poles of activities based on primary and technologically low intensive resources postpones to a more uncertain future the attainment of the industrial objective which is the prime mover of development. This situation is a setback for Cameroon's economy in an environment marked by the globalization of production and within which exchange and production trends of goods and services are largely dominated by the commercialization of highly and intermediary technological intensive products. Consequently, the resolution of the industrialization equation in Cameroon in the wake of the third millennium lies in the double plans of competitive optimum capacities and technological complexity.

In this regard, attracting investment appears to be the important element of the process of remodelling the institutional environment so as to put in place a conducive framework for business. The Investment Charter of the Republic of Cameroon constitutes an answer to this preoccupation. Its aim is to make a qualitative and quantitative progress, that is to say, a considerable change in the Cameroonian economic environment. This requires the conception of a new structure for the management of the national industrial framework within the context of market economy on the one hand, the elaboration and/or the adaptation of legal and regulatory texts appropriate for a pertinent and efficient regulation of economic activities on the other hand. The final objective is to ensure a solid base for a strong and sustainable growth; hence, the need to set up competitive enterprises capable of generating wealth as well as stable employments.

Practically, it is necessary to carry out a consequent remodelling of the national industrial sector so as to define a strategic national industrial perimeter within which the current major issues of Cameroon's industrialization can be handled, notably those relative to diversification, optimum capacities of competition and technological complexity. For the remodelling to be effective, it must depend on an operational program which relies on three main pillars namely: the key industrial channels, the physical infrastructure which accompany the industrial remodelling, and the attractive and competitive institutional framework of investments.

This strategy falls within the international context of the globalization of exchanges and of production within which, apart from the enterprises, there exist an unrestrained competition between States in capital markets in search of profitable investments. Also, the establishment of a Public/Private Sector partnership becomes indispensable with a strong State on the one hand, and a trustworthy Private Sector, creator of wealth and endowed with unquestionable managerial skills on the other hand.

The ultimate objective of this approach is to try to mobilize the human and natural potential resources (surface and underground) on which Cameroon has to build an indigenous, diversified and coherent industrial sector capable of adapting itself to the exigencies of globalization and whose strong constraints (challenges) confronting Cameroon's industry today is its positioning in the production segments of manufactured goods and services which technologically are intermediaries meant for exportation.

2 Genesis and Development of the Industrial Sector

When Cameroon became independent in 1960, it was a country endowed with basic economic assets which enabled it to carry out a coherent industrial process: good agricultural production and breeding potential, important export-based resources, a relatively well developed communication infrastructure and a solid finance system. The characteristics of the principal features as well as the initial conditions of its first industrialization program can be summarized as follows (FYP, 1961):

- The agricultural and breeding production potential was favourable but it was not sufficiently put into value, the level of domestic consumption was limited, the agro-industrial integration was slow and its economy was highly dependent on foreign supplies;
- The production of important export-based resources (cocoa, coffee, cotton, timber, tea, banana, rubber and palm oil), suffered under an extensive system dominated by manual labour which minimized the possibilities of needs;
- Apart from the aluminium factory created in Edea in 1955, there were no manufacturing industries;
- The communication infrastructure was relatively good compared to that of many developed countries, but the secondary interconnections were not used rationally, thereby limiting the development of domestic trading channels. This situation unfortunately favoured subsistence farming;
- The public finance and balance of payment were positive thanks to external assistance which sponsored most of the investments for more than one decade, but the domestic saving did not represent the actual effort made in economic development.

Cameroon inherited an industrial sector with an annual growth rate of 1.5%, employed 3% of the working population, which accounted for approximately 7% of the GDP (FYP, 1966). Between 1960 and 1975, the contribution of manufacturing industries increased from 7% to 13.5%. This increase was stimulated mainly by a keen domestic demand that was satisfied by the products of emerging import industries of substitution (IIS) although export industries slightly contributed to the evolution (FYP, 1971).

This industrial sector was built in a five year planning process through which productive and development investments were elaborated and programmed. The State was then the main stakeholder assisted by public institutions dedicated to the mobilization of financial resources and to the promotion of private initiatives (SNI, BCD, FOGAPE, CAPME, CNCE, MAGZI,).

To attract foreign capital, the State put in place a system of incentives - the Investment Code - whose various preferential fiscal and custom systems offered great advantages through tax exemptions especially for the importation of raw materials and production equipment, revenue exportations, benefits and dividends. This was done for long periods, ten years on average (Loi, 60/64).

This situation was a real booster for the first phase of industrialization in two main categories of activities, namely exporting agro-industry products and import substitution manufacturing industry products.

Concerning agro-industries (cocoa, coffee, cotton, palm oil, rubber, timber), they were essentially industries which exported primary products, and to a certain extend, goods which have undergone the first transformation: roasted coffee, cocoa butter, raw palm oil, rubber, timber sawing and threaded cotton (FYP, 1971).

As for import substitution manufacturing industries destined for the satisfaction of the local demand, their activities were limited to packaging operations, simple assembling and mixing, which did not need any technological input. Among these industries are food and brewery, chemical products and construction material industries (FYP, 1971).

It should be noted that in both categories of industries, the enormous fiscal and custom advantages granted to enterprises authorized under the different systems of the Investment Code did not spur them either to embark on a wider transformation so as to export more elaborate export products, nor to revalorize raw natural resources to satisfy the local demand. Consequently, it is not surprising to realize that four decades after independence, more than 80% of Cameroon's exports are made up of raw or semi-manufactured basic products. In the same light, the iron, bauxite, limestone, syenite and natural gas sites are known but are not exploited, whereas the country imports a large quantity of these minerals (aluminium oxide, clinker, butane, propane and various colorants) or their substitute for their running (FYP, 1966).

At this stage, it can be noted that Cameroon did not lack the political will to promote exports or to valorise the natural resources of our soil and subsoil, but rather the permeability and the less discriminating incentive framework, which opened the way where some less reliable investments had failed because of the search for high profitability. Generally, these operations did not last for long, thereby resulting in financial, economic and social stagnations.

Generally, the negative effects of this first wave of industries called import substitution industries are visible at many levels. Firstly, at the level of the allocation of resources, the importance given by the State to these industries and the high protection they enjoyed in the face of competition of imported products have rendered local enterprises inefficient from the economic point of view and made them to be less inclined to export developments because of the de facto monopoly which they enjoyed on the local market by being exempted from competition through licenses, tax concessions (sometimes stabilized for up to 25 years) and other administrative mechanisms.

This policy not only imposed an unbearable burden on the State in the case of public and semi-public enterprises, but also stifled the development of a real entrepreneurial spirit. Finally, it imposed additional charges on customers. During this time, the importation of industrial equipment goods and finished products of enterprises increased, not satisfied by the local supply (FYP, 1976).

It is also important to note the negative incidence of the policy of import substitution industries on the exportation of basic products. Without minimizing the negative effect of the permanent reduction of the terms of exchange on the performance of export agro-industries, it must be noted that the industry needs for human resources have played a role in the reduction of agricultural production by accelerating rural exodus among the male active population, a phenomenon which is not compensated for with productivity because of the lack of, or low mechanism of agricultural activities.

Considering this situation compared with the will for industrialization characterized by a variety of management laws and those of investment incentive mechanisms, we must admit that neither the availability of natural resources nor the generosity of the incentive framework are the only explanations for an industrialization process. We need to reflect deeply on the pertinence of these arguments, which have quickly been brandished whenever the issue of Cameroon's industrialization is evoked.

This remark can be verified if it is applied to the second phase of Cameroon's industrialization marked by the policy of industrial exportation promotion. It is even more explicit since it concerns private investment per say, the disengagement of the State from the productive sector, which along the way occurred under the structural adjustment programs, and the stabilization of public finances (Kamgnia, 1997).

Indeed, the reform of the institutional arsenal of incentives for investments in favour of private initiative is geared primarily towards the promotion of export industries. It is in this context that Ordinance N° 90/001 of 29 January 1990 to set up the Free Trade Zone within the framework of an open market economy based on exportation was signed. On the contrary, at the end of the chain, there are two important events in the wake of the third millennium.

- *Firstly*, Cameroon's exports are still dominated by basic agricultural products: cocoa, coffee, cotton, timber, rubber, basic aluminium, to which has been added petroleum since the end of the 1970s (FL, 2003).
- *Secondly*, the growth of industrial exports became negative since the beginning of the 1990s. This reduction was accelerated with the relaxation of extractive industries (petroleum) and was recently worsened by the severe crisis in the supply of electricity, which Cameroon is going through since 2001 after the privatization of the National Electricity Corporation /SONEL (FL, 2003).

Thus, the failure of the export promotion industrial policy, which took over from that of the import substitution industries, has brought about a real change of direction. In addition, this double failure in Cameroon's industrialization process is even more significant because it is a country which is particularly blessed with a great development potential on the one hand, and formerly well equipped with investment promotion and incentive laws on the other hand. However, and this is probably the pertinent lesson to be learned from this analysis, the soil and subsoil natural assets can be an added advantage compared to other geographical competitive sectors. Nevertheless, this advantage is determinant only if the country shows an intrinsic attractive capacity that will help in the optimal revalorization of internal factorial appropriation (national human and natural resources). In the specific case of Cameroon, this issue is so acute today because of the constraints of the stabilization of public finances negotiated with financial donors, especially IBRD and the IMF, as well as the negative effects of an abrupt liberalization of the national economy on the young industrial sector of Cameroon (Dymond and Hart, 2000).

For these reasons, the remodelling of the institutional environment for the promotion of investments is an exercise which depends on a specific technology adapted to the principles and exigencies of the market economy that is fully ensured by the two principal stakeholders, namely: the State as a strategic agent, regulator and facilitator on the one hand, and the Private Sector, creator of wealth on the other hand.

This vision questions the theoretical principles and the methodological approaches which were used as basis and justification for the conception and elaboration of the first two industrialization strategies of Cameroon.

3 Justification of IIS and EPIP and Their Shortcomings

3.1 Industries Import Substitution (IIS)

Import substitution policy was advocated in the 1950s and 1960s, first of all for political reasons. Newly independent countries expressed a strong will for political and economic self-determination. It was therefore necessary to produce, locally, as many products as possible so as to reduce dependency vis-à-vis their colonizers, hence the general rule was the protection of the economy. African countries in general followed the same trend after their political independence and this had to be completed by their economic independence. Cameroon was not an exception to this rule.

Import substitution policy was also justified by the economic trend of the structural school of thoughts which was essentially contrary to the neo-classical theory. Economists of this (Singer, 1950) and (Prebish, 1959) schools of thoughts felt that developing countries had many distorted structures whose growth and development could not be efficiently regulated by a laisser-faire attitude. They all defended the thesis of "export pessi-misms" of the post- war period and this constituted a reaction against the prescriptions by which developing countries with a comparative advantage in the production of primary products must specialize in and export them to Western European countries, in exchange for the importation of finished products.

Six groups of reasons for import substitution policy (Greenway, 1987) can easily be identified: the instability of the exportation of primary products, the deterioration of terms of exchange of producing countries of these primary products, the growth impoverishment, the strategy of multi-national firms, the protectionism of developed countries, and the theory of new industries. The analysis of these reasons was made by some authors (Njinkeu, 1991).

The instruments for the implementation of the IIS are double-fold: on the one hand, there is the commercial policy which uses instruments such as direct and indirect customs duties, import licenses and other quantitative restrictions, coupling and the "drawback" principle, and on the other hand, arguments of the industrial policy like the authorization procedure, the subvention of factors of production and the regulation of prices. Countries that practice the import substitution policy generally accept multiple exchange rates and the control of exchange.

3.2 Export Promotion Industrial Policy (EPIP)

As mentioned earlier, the export valorisation policy can be justified by the neo-classical theory as well as the virtue of price mechanisms. Supporters of this theory use five groups of reasons: international trade benefits, the advantage of economies of scale, the success of countries that have applied this industrialization strategy, the absence of situation revenue.

The theory of international trade shows that trade is profitable when a country uses its resources in activities where it has a comparative advantage and where it realizes the maximum economy of currency. This means that the production of goods that are not profitable should be limited or suppressed and imported from other countries. "Under certain conditions, this form of specialization improves the social welfare. If it is a small economy and if there is no exogenic or endogenic distortion in the market of products or factors, then the expansion of the export sector, the contraction of the substitution sector to importation combined with a liberal commercial policy is optimal" (Greenway, 1987)

The above arguments remain valid and are stronger when one considers the dynamic aspect of the process of growth. One can establish a causality relationship between the importance of international trade and economic growth rates. The intuition here is that to face competition, the entrepreneur is bound to acquire the best technology, thereby ensuring a sustainable growth.

The size of the market is an important element when selling out of the national territory. This argument is even more valid for countries like Cameroon which had a population of 11.6 million inhabitants with a per capital revenue of 1000 dollars in 1989, compared to countries like Nigeria with 113.6 million inhabitants or Thailand with a per capital revenue like that of Cameroon (1229 dollars), but with a population evaluated at 55.4 million. In order to set up factories large enough to be profitable, it is necessary to sell to foreign markets. This cannot be possible if at the same time the country closes its borders; the answer of foreign partners in such a case would be to also close their borders. The expansion of the market favours not only the activity directly concerned, but also those upstream, thereby leading to the establishment of a coherent industrial fabric.

The argument emanating from all the analysis favourable for the valorisation of exports is the success of economies which have opted for liberalization. The performances of the Western countries compared to those of the Eastern countries are generally used. For developing countries, the comparison uses as example newly industrialized countries of Asia, but also some African countries like Botswana whereas the countries which had opted for planned economy like Tanzania, Ghana and Ethiopia had a negative growth rate for the period 1965 – 89.

The EPIP instruments neither discriminate production for the local market from other markets, nor do they constitute a stimulant for exportation production. At the level of commercial policy, subvention estimates for exports, for the exoneration of charges and drawback systems are generally preferable. Talking about industrialization policy, there exist credit facilities for exportation, institutional mediums and facilities such as Industrial Free Zones. The reality of prices at the macro-economic level constitutes the rule, the exchange rate being that of equilibrium.

3.3 Shortcomings of IIS and EPIP

In the above-mentioned analysis, it appears that IISs and EPIPs are reaction (IIS) or adaptation (EPIP) policies to liberal economic principles. In both cases, there is more or less the weight of public authorities, contrary to the standard theory which pretends to systematically reject the intervention of the State, whereas the facts show the contrary, considering the place of industrial organization in public policies of groups in the market economy where governments have a dynamic approach in the stimulation of research and innovation for the benefit of enterprises, especially small and medium size enterprises or industries (OCDE, 2004). These new approaches increasingly portray the necessity for public authorities to be deeply implicated in the catalytic diagnosis and action of the industrial fabric.

The critical exigency of this approach is related to the fact that industrial organization is the result of a triangle made up of the competitive policy, the commercial policy and the technological policy: this is the competitive triangle. But be it the IIS or the EPIP, none of these two strategies covers entirely its three fields which allow three types of public intervention: strategic State, regulatory State (passive/active regulation) and developing State. It is on these principles that a new coherent and strong industrial policy which needs a remodelling of the institutional environment and a reconfiguration of the national industrial landscape can be conceived.

4 Remodelling the Institutional Environment of the Industrial Sector

The question of remodelling the institutional environment is principally in terms of attracting investments and competitions among enterprises. Since the industrial policy generally occurs in a domain that is already endowed with economic activities, the assessment of the performances sometimes and logically shapes the strategies to be used to create or to reinforce a more competitive arsenal meant to attract new investments.

In addition, in conformity with this methodology, a succinct appreciation of the performances of Cameroon's industrial sector will be studied, after which the ways and means to improve the institutional framework for the promotion of investment in Cameroon will be examined.

4.1 Performance of Industrial Sector

Considering the preceding analysis, it is easy to understand the low performances of Cameroon's industrial sector during the above mentioned historical periods in terms of production, technical effectiveness, investment or the ability to access foreign markets. We realize first of all that the boom in petroleum activities in the context of protectionism can explain the high growth rate in the secondary industrial sector witnessed at the beginning of the 1980s.

The continuation of the liberalization of the national economy, coupled with the decline in oil production, resulted in severe production consequences because of the unpreparedness of national industrial companies to face competition with foreign products. The value-added pre and post liberalization tendencies are similar to those of production. The disparities, which exist between the different sub-sectors, do not discredit this situation. As it has frequently been mentioned before, these disparities are often the results of secured incomes emanated from the many tax and custom advantages laid down in the different systems of the Investment Code. It is under this context that we should interpret the good performance of enterprises in the timber sub-sector because they belong to most of the Free

Zone Regime. In fact, and contrary to the expectation of the Government and development partners, the liberalization of the economy did not have a mechanical effect to foster capital investments. On the contrary, the return to the annual average growth rate of 5% in 1994 was brought about by an increase in domestic demand compared to supply and particularly in household consumption (+3.7%). This low level of domestic supply also explains the domestic demand brought forward and which shows a negative contribution in the GDP (- 4.7%), (FL, 1998/99).

In a prospective manner, by referring to the performances of the FDI registered during the last ten years, there is a high concentration in resource-based industries, the forest/timber sub-sector owning most of the capital. For example, more than 90% of the companies authorized under the Free Zone Regime belonged to this sub-sector before the publication of the 1998/99 financial law which cancelled the advantages of this system. As mentioned in a study on foreign investments in Africa carried out by UNIDO in 2003, the FDI during the last ten years were mostly interested in service, transportation, distribution and construction activities, either through privatization operations (energy, railway, telecommunications), or through a punctual important project like the Chad – Cameroon Pipe-line project. There were few, if not no manufacturing activities for industrial transformation. Consequently, it is difficult to expect an improvement in export products from the manufacturing industries using medium or high intensity technology. All in all, the sectors whose share of export activities is particularly important are the resource-based agro-industry, the oil sector and the aluminium industry. In this domain, the extension of the Cameroon Shipyard and Industrial Engineering Ltd. (CNIC) constitutes a real sign of hope, given its location on a highly technological activity sector, with more than 95% of whose products and services are exported (CNIC, 2004).

Given the administrative bottlenecks, which hold back the finalization of the incentive framework appropriate for the CNIC and requested for by Financial Donors, it is clear that the environment is not yet ready or adapted to carry out such investments. But it is in this direction that Cameroon must imperatively turn if it has to fit into the new global industrial dynamics dictated by the manufacturing of goods and services which conforms to average and high technological profiles. In any case, the problem related to the take-off of the CNIC also applies to the future of ALUCAM in the aluminium sector, as well as to CICAM in the cotton industry, or in a radical way to the National Refining Company (SONARA) in the petrochemical sector. This is so because due to their advanced level of obsolescence, all these companies are faced with the necessary resolution of their double handicap of optimal productive capacity and technological complexity for their survival in the medium term (about 5 years).

In its 2002/2003 Report on Industrial Development, UNIDO came out with a composite index, which helps to measure the Competitive Industrial Performance (CIP) Index of the industrial sector. This index is a barometer to judge a country's capacity to produce and export manufactured articles in a competitive manner. In a list of 87 countries, Cameroon occupied the 75th position in 1998, three places behind the position it occupied in 1985 (72nd). On the other hand, Cameroon's CIP index (0.08) has not changed between the two periods. In the same vain, we note that the greater majority of Cameroon's exports are found among the 125 less dynamic categories of exports worldwide, that is to say those whose growth rate is lower than the average rate of all the world exports. Even within these low growth rate categories, Cameroon has nearly half of the total number of articles with close to zero or even negative growth (UNIDO, 2002/03).

4.2 Prerequisite for a Remodelling of the Industrial Sector

The history of the two industrialization phases of Cameroon (IIS and EPIP) shows that it is neither the lack of the industrialization will, nor the advantages granted to enterprises.

Because of the broad tax and custom facilities of the preferential system of the Investment Code, coupled with the incorporated and inland production tax and because of the introduction of a strong mechanism for the protection of national industries, the local companies hung to their initial sectors with little or no effort either to integrate the sectors upstream or downstream, or to improve their industrial technologies brought about by the evolution of large industries for the transformation of raw material (cocoa, coffee, cotton, timber, palm oil, etc…). Such a situation only increased the dependence of Cameroon's industry on imported know-how thereby widening the gap in the national industrial sector. In addition, the tariff barriers put in place to protect the emergent industry had a negative incidence on industrial exports. Although industrial exports represented close to 20% of the industrial production in 1965/66, it fell to less than 17% in 1975/76. This contrast between the rise in imported output and the fall in industrial exports had a negative effect on the balance of trade, which dropped to an alarming level at the end of the 1970s, almost a deficit of 25 billion CFA F in 1978/79 (MINEFI, 1999-2002).

A further look at these considerations shows that one of the major objectives of the economic policy of post independence, namely the creation of stable jobs and the multiplication of incomes in the next ten years, were far from being reached. The situation worsened with the fall in the purchasing power of households because of the expensive nature of unprotected local products. This resulted in a considerable loss of State revenue due to the tax and custom incentives granted to enterprises.

It was realized that various reforms carried out did not bring any solution to the industrial policy of Cameroon, which hampered the harmonious growth of its industrial sector. This was characterized by judicial instability due to disparities between the different legal documents on the same subject, the constitution of economically unjustified revenues which was prejudicial to common right systems, the absence of incentives compared to structural variables (training, research and development, innovation, technological development), thereby limiting labour and capital productivity. Added to this were the external constraints of the export promotion policy and of access to foreign markets: the absence of the notion of comparative advantages due to the unrestrained international competition, difficulties in transferring technologies, the international trading regulations (WTO/TRIPS) and standards (ISO/SPS) which made access to markets of developed countries hypothetical. Here, it should be mentioned that access to markets is an essential component of competition in the new global economy. The Marrakech Agreement/End of the Uruguay Round (UR) 1994, brought in some significant changes in the conditions of access to markets thanks to the limitation of non tariff laws put in place to protect the industrial sector. However, the difficulties of the new round of negotiations (after the Seattle Round) launched in Doha (2001) and referred to as "the Development Round" for certain domains such as the agricultural and textile domains revealed that Cameroon must be prepared to face an international exchange environment that is less and less favourable to its industrial production (Dymond and Hart, 2000).

At this juncture, we can rightly say that the redeployment of Cameroon's industry is going on without a real remodelling of the national industrial policy. This remodelling requires two main prerequisites: fostering an attractive institutional framework with clear public and private principles of good governance on the one hand, and the laying of the bases for industrial competition on the other hand.

a) The Quality of Institutions

Economic operators strongly criticise on the institutional framework of affairs in Cameroon. They consider particularly that eighteen years of Structural Adjustment Programmes have weakened the socio-economic context of the nation. They remain sceptical about the recovery of the economic growth in the absence of adequate infrastructure, without a consequent purchasing power, without a medium term economic vision and in a non transparent financial context on the part of the State whose way of life is alarming (GICAM, 2005). This situation can partly be explained by the consequences of the conditions related to the different structural adjustment programmes and the stabilization of public finances.

In fact, the problem today is the near absence of follow-up institutions for development and growth. In this effect, it is important to remember that at the dawn of independence, industrialization was seen as the principal means of ensuring real national autonomy. To achieve these goals, in addition to the very favourable incentives, Cameroon had institutions which supported investments with important funds and which were anxious to promote Cameroonian private companies. These institutions can be listed in two groups namely: financial institutions: Cameroon Development Bank (BCD), and the National Investment Corporation (SNI)), and facilitation institutions: (Cameroon Chamber of Commerce, Industry, Mines and Crafts, the Industrial Park Management Mission (MAGZI), the National Centre for External Trade (CNCE). An active marketing policy called the Exchange General Program was followed by the IIS policy, which, through a strict classification of import products, set up a de facto oil mechanism for tariff and non-tariff protection.

There exist a narrow relationship between the quality of institutions and development. The unfruitful experiences of the two previous industrialization attempts (import substitution and export promotion) clearly demonstrated that the tax and custom advantages, the accumulation of capital (physical as well as human), are no determinant of themselves. Very recently, under the banner of the structural adjustment program, it was realized that comfortable macroeconomic and structural policies could lead to development deadlocks thereby leaving the issue of poverty untouched (IMF, 2003).

In this perspective, the remodelling of the industrial environment must lead to the setting up of organized public or mixed institutions for their direct positive impact on the development of the private sector. They can be in the form of establishments and/or management set-ups for the regulation of the market or for, to borrow a definition, which is often quoted, the informal and formal constraints to economic, political and social interactions. Taken from this angle, pertinent and viable institutions enable the setting up of an attractive and incentive framework, which sets aside uncertainty, encourages efficiency and contributes to the reinforcement of the industrial sector in particular and an economic development in general.

These institutions can equally take the form of legal/regulatory entities, mechanisms or frameworks which act directly on the economy by adopting appropriate and well advised structural policies in a voluntarist approach translating the role of the State: solid and regulatory strategy at the operational level and beyond the provisions of the Investment Charter which create a group of promotion, facilitation and regulatory institutions, the ongoing deep restructuring project of the National Investment Corporation contributes to this logic. The same thing applies to the rehabilitation of MAGZI that is underway.

b) Basic Physical Infrastructure

Today, Cameroon has a serious handicap in the domain of infrastructure: seaports, railways, roads, air facilities and digital energy. This handicap will surely have a repercussion on the other CEMAC sub-regional countries (CAR, Chad) for which Cameroon is the main opening on to the sea. It is not important to go into the details of this issue whose negative effects are visible on the daily life of enterprises, be it the shortage of electricity, the shallow nature of the Wouri canal, the low performance of the railway network, the difficulties to access a high debit smooth communication system, just to mention only these few cases. Generally, the putting in place of this basic infrastructure is the preserve of the State, which today can hardly commit itself before the attainment of the HIPC initiative completion point. This is where the State must show its strong will in the search for solutions to these constraints with a full implication of the private sector (for example BOT).

These two points are the criteria to break the main bottlenecks which today make Cameroon's industry fragile and discourage new productive investments, be they national or foreign. We observe how these two criteria are at work in the re-dynamisation program of some key sectors, notably in the restructuring of the forest/timber sector, the redeployment of the bauxite – aluminium oxide – aluminium at the centre of which is the extension project of the ALUCAM factory (from 85 000 t to 260 000 tons in the year 2010), the re-dynamisation of the textile – cotton sector with SODECOTON upstream, CICAM (weaving, spinning) in the middle and the sewing development downstream.

This approach is part of a search for new prospects of an industrial policy in Cameroon that is coherent, capable of adapting to the stakes of globalization with competitive industries on the domestic, regional and international markets.

5 Towards a New Industrial Policy in Cameroon

By this we mean the principal and axiomatic management, which consists in stating that the present state of Cameroon's industrial sector does not conform to the norms of modernity. Because, being weakened by more than one decade of structural adjustment, the State has somehow lost the strategic reflex needed to carry out a real industrial development which constitutes the basis of the strength of modern nations. As mentioned earlier (section 3.3), the State should indeed take up its rule of regulator, facilitator and developer of basic infrastructure, be it at the level of the motivations characterising it or its organisation mode.

The main objective of this industrial policy is to build a coherent and harmonious industrialisation of Cameroon within the framework of a ten-year program with three phases:

- *1st phase*: building a competitive and attractive economy through the implementation of the Investment Charter in the Republic of Cameroon
- *2nd phase*: rethinking the national industrial sector by defining a national strategic industrial perimeter.
- *3rd phase*: Implementing structuring and/or takeoff programs which either have a strong impact on the national socio-economic, infrastructural and environmental landscape, or an experienced know-how likely to march Cameroon's industry with technologically high technology intensity manufacturing activities. For practical reasons, this phase is examined under the 2nd phase.

5.1 Implementation of Investment Charter

The Investment Charter in the Republic of Cameroon was drafted in 1999 and ultimately included in the country's industrial arsenal on the 19th of April 2002 (law N 2002/004). Because this law has never been implemented two years (legal deadline) after its adoption and promulgation, another law N 2004/20 of 22 July 2004 extended the deadline by five years.

In spite of the high level of national expertise, the Charter was specially conceived as a strategic instrument aimed at assisting the national economy to carry out a significant change of its productive system. Its efficient implementation would help to conveniently solve the crucial problem of the institutions as mentioned above, by bringing concrete solutions to the attractive and competitive structural deficit of Cameroon's economy.

The Investment Charter is based on the use of market technology to build an industrial organisation, which can start off a dynamic to catch up with the technology. Its structure is based on four main pillars:

- *Firstly*, a regulatory mechanism of markets and competition articulated around a Regulatory and Competitive Council.
- *Secondly*, a system of assistance and management of private initiative carried out by specific organs like Industrial Partnership Councils, the Entrepreneurship Institute, the Trade and Industry Observatory, the Standardization and Quality Board and the Intellectual Property Centre.
- *Thirdly*, an institutional mechanism for the promotion and facilitation of investments and exportation revolving around the Investment and Export Promotion Agencies.
- *Fourthly*, an arsenal of general and specific incentives whose preferential tools are sector codes.

This means consecrating the respective roles of the State - facilitator and regulator on the one hand, and of the private sector - initiator of growth and creator of wealth on the other hand.

It is strongly wished that the State pays the highest attention to the implementation of the Investment Charter because by doing so, Cameroon will in fact give priority to the industrial policy as the main tool to boost the economic growth. That is why the Charter (Article 28) dwells on the composition of the management organs of the institutions in place, pursuant to this law shall be joint, equal and tripartite (public sector, private sector and the civil society) (Article 43) “All sectoral laws and regulations repugnant to this law shall be harmonised”.

5.2 Definition of a National Industrial Strategic Perimeter

The definition of a strategic industrial perimeter is as a result of the unavoidable exigency for reshaping the Cameroonian productive system in order to take up the current challenge with a view to setting up a real industrial reform.

The main objective targeted in this reshaping is notably attached to the following stakes:

- Optimal and efficient exploitation and valorisation of the soil and subsoil resources of Cameroon, which is against the tendency for the primarisation of the national production system. This can be done through the adoption of the maximisation principle of the manufacturing value-added chain.

- Efficient insertion of Cameroon's economy in the global international division of productive processes which have become complex and amplified by the globalisation phenomenon of markets within enterprises and the State in carrying out frantic competition.
- The uplifting of major infrastructural constraints by systematically integrating their resolution in the principal structuring industrial programs.

The strategic positioning of Cameroon in the sector of high technological industrial activities which either form the structure of the traditional sectors (mechanical construction, electro-mechanics, chemical engineering, high power electricity, surface treatment of material), or set the pace for current and future technologies (electronic engineering, computer engineering, bio-technology and composite material).

This strategic perimeter today relies on six key sub-sectors namely:

- The bauxite – aluminium sub-sector
- The forest - timber sub-sector
- The cotton – textile sub-sector
- The energy sub-sector
- The technological development sub-sector
- The food industry sub-sector

Each of these key sub-sectors revolves around a few targeted industrial nucleuses, which must act as takeoff elements during restructuring, re-conversion, re-dimensioning operations. This is the case for example of the bauxite – aluminium sub-sector with the ALUCAM group as the central nucleus (with its international partners, the Canadian ALCAN group). In the same way, the textile – cotton sub-sector is attached to two pillars: SODECOTON upstream for the production of cotton (basic raw material) and at the centre CICAM in the weaving, spinning and improving domain for the production of raw and finished cloth for the local market as well as for exportation.

The internal analysis of the sub-sectors with a view to stimulating them constitutes a step in this industrial organisation process (Tirole, 1988). It results in naturally the issue of connection and coherence between the sub-sectors due either to necessary complementarities (the bauxite – aluminium and energy sub-sectors), or to conflicts in strategy (the textile – cotton sub sector-and the agro-industry sector on the allocation of human resources in the northern part of Cameroon where the rural population today depends essentially on their cotton revenues).

Thus presented, it is difficult to dissociate the implementation action from the Investment Charter of the restructuring program of the national industry sector and it is this double work, which justifies and explains the remodelling principle of the national industrial policy.

6 Case of Industrial Development Policy

Here, we can mention two application cases of industrial remodelling which are about to be implemented, these are: The electrolysis of ALUCAM extension project on the one hand, and the project to delocalise the Douala and Limbe Cameroon Naval and Industrial project.

6.1 The Case of ALUCAM (Cameroon Aluminium Smelting Company)

Created in 1955 with a capacity of 55 000 tons, ALUCAM, in which the State owns 48% of the shares, has not undergone the changes taking in place within the international aluminium industry. Today, for existing factories which have a competitive energy (between 18 and 20 USD/MWh) the minimum capacity level is 240 000 tons. But for a new factory located near the ocean, the optimal standard capacity is 500 000 tons.

On the one hand, the extension of ALUCAM has been done in a context of severe crisis in electricity supply in Cameroon, notwithstanding the fact that this sector was liberalised and the main supplier of electricity (the former SONEL) privatised. Today, ALUCAM demand is 145 megawatts (MW) of electricity, which correspond to a little more than one third of the total available energy at the national level. Increasing ALUCAM's capacity to 260 000 tons will require 450 MW to make the foundry function. It is therefore imperative to resolve the interface with the energy sub-sector, hence the need for a follow-up with a program of hydroelectricity production which at the same time puts in place a system to regulate the debits (the Lom Pangar Reservoir) and hydroelectricity production equipment (The Nachtigal Central). The Lom Pangar Nachtigal Complex is located on the same river Sanaga (ALCAN, 2005).

On the other hand, ALUCAM's extension poses a problem of the re-dimensioning of port facilities in Douala (the depth of the channel and the length of the quay), of the reinforcement of the Douala - Edea railway, of the maintenance of the road to Douala. This is so because in order to produce 260 000 tons of aluminium, more than 500 000 tons of aluminium oxide must be conveyed to Edea from Equatorial Guinea (Friguia), hence the intensification of the traffic which greatly influences transportation infrastructure.

We can equally note that the realisation of ALUCAM's extension to 260 000 tons is an indicator of a new factory of 1 000 000 tons in Kribi by the year 2015, thereby increasing the national capacity to more than 1 250 000 tons of aluminium by this date. But at this stage, the consumption of the equivalent aluminium oxide being about 2 500 000 tons, corresponding to the mining of 5 500 000 tons of bauxite, the opening of a mine (Minim – Martap/Ngaoundal in the Adamawa Province and/or Fongo Tongo in the West Province of Cameroon) becomes an interesting issue to be tackled naturally with all the train of accompanying actions in the energy (close to 1800MW necessary) infrastructural domain, (the Edea – Kribi railway and a deep seaport in Kribi, the reinforcement of the Ngaoundere – Edea railway, the Douala – Nkongsamba – Mbo Plain railways, etc.).

On the contrary, by setting aside a minimum of 30% of the initial investment (900 million US dollars) to local sub-contracting agents, such a project will reinforce local industrial integration thereby maximising the fallouts on the industrial fabric as well as the national socio-economic landscape.

It is the operational mastery of this type of industrial organisation, here simplified for this purpose, which will help to qualify the ALUCAM project as a restructuring and takeoff project.

6.2 The Case of CNIC (Cameroon Shipyard and Industrial Engineering Ltd.)

Contrary to ALUCAM, which is a resource-based industry (bauxite – aluminium oxide – aluminium) with a strong impact on infrastructure, the CNIC, in which the State owns 95% of the shares, is in the domain of technologically high intensive complex industrial activities. Its major implications will therefore be technological in the port, maritime, naval construction and oil technologies (submersive and semi-submersive platforms).

The CNIC is a conglomerate, which was created in February 1988. Since then, its capital resources have increased from 800 million CFA F from February 1988 to 15 billion CFA F today. Given its present location constraints within the Douala Autonomous Port which reduces its productivity by 25%, and considering the perspective and opportunities of the contract for the naval repair of the offshore oil platforms in the Golf of Guinea whose optimum and profitable exploitation requires appropriate industrial and technological infrastructure, the extension of the SNIC in Limbe which opens to the Atlantic Ocean, was set up and adopted for the sustainable redeployment and development of the company.

The Limbe CNIC is located east of the facilities of the National Refinery Company on the site of the Limboh Cap and it constitutes a reference industrial support partner for the industrial services of petroleum activities. The global design of the company has made provisions for the following developments on about 900 meters between the seashore and the land:

Towards the Sea:

- the development of a harbour and infrastructure to host a floating dock (Bamousso) of 10.000 tons for the dry repair of 30.000 Tdw ships and a rig floating dock of 25 000 tons (rig dock) for the dry repair of semi-submersive platforms and check-ups;
- the construction of quays for the repair of ships and floating rigs;
- the development of infrastructure for a floating dock of 40 000T of the Suez Max type, for the dry repair of tankers of up to 106 000 Tdw;
- the construction of two moles to check sea swell;

Towards the Land:

- the development of a surface area of about 45 hectares with 10 hectares retrieved from the sea for industrial building facilities;
- the complete development of 25 hectares for the construction of 3500 modern housings for the staff of the CNIC which will increase from 1500 workers today to 3600 in 2009.

The project for the construction of industrial infrastructure for the repair of ships and oil platforms has been designed on the basis of a twenty-year exploitation life cycle whereas the economic life span of industrial infrastructure is estimated at fifty years, a situation which justifies the structuring character of this investment which amounts to 200 million US dollars allocated in two phases. Particularly the construction in Limbe of a South mole of 1200m long and at least 14m deep will give a significant impulse to the creation of the Limbe Autonomous Port.

7 Policy, Conclusions and Perspectives

At the end of this presentation which outlines an important path (among a variety of paths) for a remodelling of the national industrial policy, it is clear that the task is immense, the stakes full of interpretation and the constraints many and varied. At the wake of independence, the industrialization which was carried out in the first five year development plans was geared towards increasing the revenues of the people in the next ten years. The strategy adopted was that of import substitution industries so as to reduce the strong foreign dependence emanating from the then essentially primary economy. This policy brought about the creation in Cameroon of an industrial embryo, one of the most diversified in sub-Saharan Africa.

However, it is regrettable to note that Cameroon's industrial sector has been highly destabilized by the structural adjustment process and the resulting liberalization of the national economic environment. All these events exposed the structural shortcomings of Cameroon's economy. The change of orientation, which took place at the end of the 1980s, and the choice of the strategy for the promotion of industrial exports, did not help to improve the structural deficiencies of the country's economy. On the contrary, the constraining and brutal disengagement of the State from the productive sector and the vast operation to privatize public and semi-public enterprises instead contributed to worsen the situation by undermining at the lower rang of society those who survived the severe economic crisis witnessed in the mid 1980s (Hakim B. H., 2002).

The structural adjustment and liberalization programs implemented by the State during the last two decades have certainly helped to stabilize public finances and put the country back on the path of positive growth (average GDP growth rate of 5%) between 1994 and 2001. However, Cameroon's economy today is stifled with a GDP growth rate oscillating around 3% since 2004. This negative evolution at least shows that the positive results registered after the great depression of the mid 1980s does not mean that Cameroon's economy is faring better. We should instead look for the underlying reasons of the failure of this neo-liberalization policy applied to Cameroon's economy. Formulas have in fact been applied by plagiarism without considering the great changes witnessed in the world economy since the early 1990s (Krugman, 2000), the era of the wave of the liberalization of Cameroon's economy. Attempts have always been made to throw out the baby with the bathing water by trying to accuse globalization, but it is an abuse of reasoning. While acknowledging that globalization has some negative effects on the political systems of developing countries in general (Hochraich, 2002), it is also true that even though its nature has been intensified and accelerated by the information and communication technologies (ICT), the phenomenon is not new. Such idea of the end of the 20th century and of the beginning of the 21st century like the paroxysm of free trade and the main and primordial cause of the destructuring of an economy like that of Cameroon should simply be classified in the category of the myths which have stood out as landmarks in the history of the economic though (Bairoch, 1999). This is because examples of projects like the redeployment of the integrated bauxite-aluminium sector and the ALUCAM extension project on the one hand, and the Limbe Shipyard project on the other hand, prove that the implementation of important structural industrial programs is not incompatible with a structural adjustment process. On the contrary, by repressing the productive machinery, the growth registered from the macroeconomic and financial stabilizations can only be low and without a promising future, given that it depends essentially on an inflation-based demand in the absence of a consequent internal supply. Surprisingly, the dependence on external supply can only destabilize the balance of trade in the long run, hence a perpetuation of the cycle of indebtedness.

In this regard, it is instructive to note that the case of ALUCAM and CNIC are good examples that contradict the neo-liberal principles, which led to the destabilization of the young industrial sector of Cameroon in the last three decades. (Section VI). On the other hand, the HIPC context in Cameroon did not prevent ALUCAM and CNIC in which the participation of the State is preponderant, from being attractive on the international market of capital where they had received important investment funds. Nevertheless, be it for CNIC or for ALUCAM, the facilitating role of the State (in addition to its position as shareholder), has always appeared as a critical and decisive element in their realization and it can boost durably their competitiveness.

At this stage, the important conclusion to be made is the necessity and emergency for the State of Cameroon, as a political power, to completely and unequivocally ensure its function of strategic State and facilitator of a Public/ Private sector partnership in the re-dynamisation process of the national industry through the strategic reconfiguration of key sectors: Bauxite-aluminium, Hydrocarbons, Forest-Timber, Textile-Cotton, Building materials, Food industry (Plantain, Cassava and Maize), just to mention only the most immediate and in view.

In this perspective, the principal signs expected by business milieu concern three main themes: an attractive environment, basic physical infrastructure (power, communication and telecommunications), and safe judicial and legal framework. The handling of these issues cannot operate validly in a logical economic policy supported by the problem of indebtedness, because the prospective perspective and approach required by the process proposed is not the natural vision of the national economy, but its reconstruction. This can be considered as a strong need and also as an opportunity to boost the national economy after the recent attainment of the HIPC initiative completion point in April 2006, given the cancellation of the debt, for a post-adjustment policy (Eboué, 2004).

This granted, the problem which is still to be solved is that of the deflection of the technological, economic and environmental impacts of the reconfiguration programs of the above-mentioned key sectors in the entire national productive sector through the implication of the network of local small and medium size enterprises in the sub-contracting of industrial services and others services. In fact, there is the risk of being in a situation similar to that of the Chad/Cameroon Pipe-line Project where the essential of the industrial activities and services of this important project (the biggest project South of the Sahara in the last two decades) has been entrusted to foreign firms.

To solve this problem, there must be an organization strategy of industrial clusters around different key sectors by the deployment of a program for the updating of local small and medium size enterprises through a companionship with foreign firms which are interested in Cameroon's industrial programs. The objective of such an exercise is the optimization of the local content in the realization of the said programs so as to strengthen and intensify local inter-industrial exchanges.

As Public Authority, and in its role of regulator, the State is once more called upon to correct the imperfections of the market.

In this context, the issue of the industrialization of Cameroon in the wake of the third millennium is so important that it can only be through a real remodelling of its industrial policy. Hence, the need for a real consensus which should be translated by a solid Public /Private Sector partnership that is a manifestation of a strategic State, regulator and facilitator on the one hand, and a Private Sector that is trustworthy and creator of wealth on the other hand. Such is the crucial mission attached to the stakes of the new industrial policy in the train of the great ambitions of the new seven-year term of office of the President of the Republic.

Bibliography

ALCAN (2005): Press Release. Online: http://www.alcan.com, accessed on: 26/10/2005.

Bairoch, Paul (1999): "Mythes et Paradoxes de l'Histoire économique", Paris : La Découverte.

Ben Hammouda, Hakim (2002): "Crise globale, un regard du Sud". Maisonneuve & Larose.

Ben Hammouda, Hakim (2003): "Les économies de l'Afrique Centrale", Commission économique des Nations – Unies pour l'Afrique, Maisonneuve & Larose.

CNIC (2004): "Projet de construction d'infrastructures de Réparation des Plates-formes Pétrolières à Limbe (Yard Pétrolier de Limbe)", Rapport Technique.

Dymond, W, A. and Hart, M, M. (2000): "Post-Modem Trade Policy: Reflections on the Challenges Multilateral Trade Negotiations after Seattle", Journal of World Trade, 34(3), 21-38.

Eboué, Chicot (2004): "Contribution au Séminaire organisé par la Présidence de la République du Cameroun et le PNUD sur la Croissance Forte et Durable à Yaoundé", Document de travail.

FMI (2003): "Perspective de l'Économie Mondiale - Croissance et Institution"s.

GICAM (2005): "Le Bulletin Industriel d'Information du Patronat".

Greenway, D. (1987): "Characteristics of Industrialisation and Economic Performance under Alternative Development Strategies", Banque Mondiale, Document de Travail.

Hochraich, D. (2002) : "Mondialisation contre Développement – Le cas des pays asiatiques, Syllepse.

Kamgnia, D. B. (1997): "Impact de la Réforme de la Politique Commerciale au Cameroun: Recettes Publiques et Performance Économique", RPI, Document de Travail 13.

Krugman, Paul R.. (2000): "La mondialisation n'est pas coupable - Vertus et Limites du libre-échange", La Découverte.

MINEFI/DSCN & INS (1999/2002): "Annuaire Statistique du Cameroun et Comptes Nationaux.

Ministry of Economy and Finance (2003): "Finance Law 2003 – Chapter 2: Production Sector", Economic and Financial Report, 17.

Ministry of Economy and Finance (2003): "Finance Law 2003 - Chapter 5: Foreign Sector", Economic and Financial Report, 34.

Ministry of Finance Cameroon (1961): "Five year Economic and Social Development Plan", Presentation Report, 1.

Ministry of Finance (1998): "Finance Law 1998/1999", Economic and Financial Report.

Ministry of Finance Cameroon (1966): "Five year Economic and Social Development Plan, Section I: Take-off point and Orientations for the second five year plan", 1 – 7.

Ministry of Economy and Planning Cameroon (1971): "Five year Economic and Social Development Plan, Chapter II: Economic Growth since 1964/65", 7 – 9.

Ministry of Economy and Planning Cameroon (1976): "Five year Economic, Social, and cultural Development Plan: Chapter II: Realisation of the third plan", 27 – 44.

Njinkeu, D. (1991): "Incidence de la Protection Douanière sur les exportations camerounaises", Université de Yaoundé, Faculté des Sciences Économiques.

OCDE (2004): "2ème Conférence de l'OCDE des Ministres en charge des Petites et Moyennes Entreprises: Partenariats, Grappes, Réseaux et Droits de Propriété Intellectuelle: Perspectives et Enjeux des PME Innovantes dans une Économie Mondialisée", Rapport.

Prebisch (1959): "Commercial Policy in the Underdeveloped Countries", American Economic Review, Vol. 49, pp. 251 – 256.

RC(République de Cameron) (1960) : "Loi n° 60/64 du 22 juin 1960 portant Code des investissements du Cameroun."

RC (1964) : "Loi n° 64/LF/6 du 06 avril 1964 adaptant la loi n° 60/64 aux institutions fédérales. "

RC (2002): "Loi n° 2002/004 du 19 avril 2002 portant Charte des Investissements en République du Cameroun."

RC (2004): "Loi n° 2004/020 du 22 juillet 2004 modifiant et complétant la loi n°2002/004."

RC/DSDRE (1989): "République du Cameroun: Déclaration de Stratégie de Développement et de Relance Économique", Rapport.

Singer, H. W. (1950): "The Distribution of Gains between Investing and Borrowing Countries", American Economic Review, Vol. 40, pp. 473 – 475.

Tirole, J. (1988): "The Theory of Industrial Organization", MIT Press.

UNIDO (2003): "Industrial Development Report 2002/2003: Competing through innovation and learning."

World Bank (1985): "Cameroun - Politique et Planification industrielles", Rapport sectoriel N° 5150-CM.

World Bank (1996): "Cameroun - Evaluation du Secteur Privé", Rapport N° 13955-CM.

World Bank (1987): "Cameroun - Country Economic Memorandum", Report N° 6395-CM.

Food Production and Non-Food Agricultural Supply: Towards an Efficient Diversification of Export-led Agriculture in Cameroon

Alexandre Magloire Schouamé and Mireille Etogo Messomo

1 Introduction

Cameroon has traditionally relied on raw materials exports to generate foreign currency. Oil constitutes about a half of the total exports; its second largest merchandise export is logs, which make up about 13.5% of the total exports. As main cash crops, cocoa, coffee and cotton constituted altogether about 20.5% and 18.6% of the total exports, respectively in 2002 and 2003.[1] This concentration leaves the country highly vulnerable to unfavourable market or climatic conditions. A drought or a drop in prices on the international markets can quickly drain its foreign exchange reserves, stifle its ability to pay for essential imports and plunge the country into debt. Furthermore, changes in the international prices of these products can lead to a great volatility in the terms of trade. Table 1 shows the trends in the prices for major exports of Cameroon between 1980 and 2000, and reveals that the variation coefficients, i.e., the ratios of standard variation to average prices, are particularly high, reflecting the extremely volatile nature of world prices for these products.[2]

Graph 1 below leads to the same conclusion, i.e. the extreme instability in commodities prices.

---

1 In accordance with the data taken from the 2003 Annual Report of the Bank of Central African States, page 261.

2 Over the past 40 years, real prices of agricultural commodities relative to prices of all manufactured goods have declined significantly, even as nominal prices have risen. They declined by about 2 percent per year over the past four decades (FAO, 2004).

Table 1: Changes of Export Shares and in the Prices of the Major Export Goods of Cameroon, 1980-2000

	Share of Total Exports of Goods					World Prices (U.S. Dollar)			
Products	1980	1990	2000/ 2001	2002	2003	Average	Standard Deviation	Coefficient Of Variation %	Increase in Prices %
Oil	28.6	49.7	49.5	44.0	39.8	21	6	28.6	-1.4
Cocoa	15.0	6.5	7.9	12.6	10.7	1539	436	28.3	-2.3
Robusta coffee	15.2	6.7	4.6	2.8	3.1	87	36	41.4	-6.8
Cotton seed	3.0	3.3	5	5.1	4.8	8	14	175.0	2.3
Export bananas	1.7	1.3	3	2.5	3.1	70	1	1.4	-2
Rubber	0.5	1.2	1.1	1.2	1.5	43	11	25.6	-1.8
Timber, unbarked logs	7.8	6.4	19.5	13.5	14.7	184	77	41.8	2.3
Other products	28.2	24.9	9.4	18.3	22.3	-	-	-	-

Note: *Through 2000/2001, reporting is based on fiscal year July-June.*

Source: *Authors' compilation is based on the data from MINPAT(1993a), MINPAT (1993b), BEAC (2003) and Republic of Cameroon (2003).*

Of course, the growth path in the country has suffered and still suffers from this instability in commodity prices and revenues (Touna Mama and Schouamé, 2004).

A decline in the agricultural terms of trade can be counteracted by increases in the quantity produced and exported so as to maintain or increase the real value of export earnings, but export quantities have not grown sufficiently to cover the loss.

Unfortunately, the prospects are not very good for primary commodities and for the raw materials dependent-countries, which, if nothing is done, will continue to experience serious negative trade effects, including (Ng and Yeats, 2002): declining or relatively low growth in global demand for these goods[3]; falling real prices for traditional products[4]; very unstable prices and

3 According to Stern et al. (1976), income elasticities of demand for these goods are generally well below unity. Moreover, Ng and Yeats (2002) found that a vast majority of thirty-five traditional and non-traditional primary products had

export earnings; a continued marginalization in world trade; and diminished growth and industrialisation prospects.

Graph 1: Indices of Prices of Selected Primary Commodities and Raw Materials: 1993-2006 (1993: base 100)

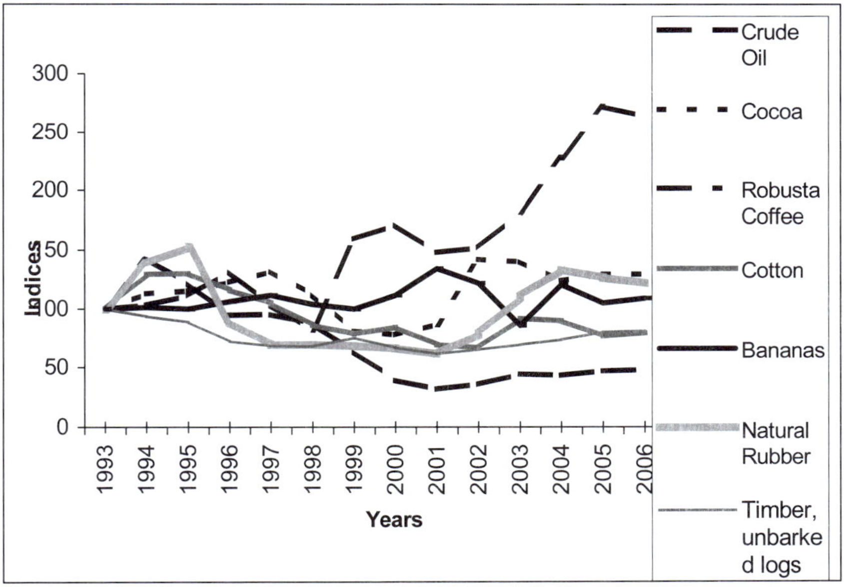

Source: The prices used in the calculation by the authors of the indices shown in this graph are extracted from BEAC site (www.beac.int)

---

either static or negative demand growth prospects. In particular, assuming a 2.5 per cent world GDP annual growth rate, they estimated that global trade in traditional products should grow by under one per cent a year. From the same viewpoint, Mayer et al. (2002), by using a comprehensive measure of export dynamism, which controls for long-term and short-term growth, found that no primary commodity ranked among the most dynamic products.

4 The UNCTAD LDC Report 2002 estimated that the real commodity prices of LDC non-fuel exports declined by over per 30 per cent between 1986 and 1999. Between 1997 and 2001, copper prices fell by 27 per cent, cotton prices by 39 percent, and coffee prices by 66 per cent (UNCTAD, 2002, chap. IV).

The long-term decline in real prices reflects the tendency for productivity and production to grow at a faster rate than demand. Volatility reflects the impact of exogenous factors such as the weather. These problems are exacerbated by market distortions, arising from tariffs and subsidies in developed countries, tariffs in developing countries and the market power in some commodity supply chains of large transnational corporations. These distortions also limit access to lucrative markets and hinder attempts to secure a greater share of the final product price on the part of producers and exporting countries (FAO, 2004). All these various effects cost both farmers and governments in the developing world dearly.

It is therefore essential for these countries to seek to diversify their economy in order to stabilise export earnings and to foster income growth.[5] Diversification strategies enable farmers to produce different crops (horizontal diversification), or to engage in different value added activities (vertical diversification). Thus, many different routes to diversification exist, including resource-based manufacturing and processing of primary products.

However, Wood and Mayer (2001) argue that Africa cannot really follow a development path based on manufactured exports and should rather improve the volume and quality of primary exports, processed and unprocessed. Based on the Heckscher-Ohlin model, Wood and Mayer (2001) and Wood (2002) analyse the role of natural resources in Africa's future development. Based on comparative analyses of how land-abundant resource endowments impact upon the sectoral structure of output and exports, they outline two main trajectories for Africa's development.[6]

- Africa's comparative advantage lies in primary sectors: the share of primary products in Africa's exports over the next few decades would come from natural-resource-based products. Due to the presently low level of manufacturing output, there is a scope for dramatic increase in a variety of different manufacturing industries over the next few decades. Manufacturing is likely to be concentrated in a small number of countries and areas with better links to world markets.

---

5 Indeed, the main arguments for diversification include: long-term tendency toward declining terms of trade for primary products; variability in export earnings and their implications for growth; and the poor correlation between real per capita incomes and natural resource dependence.

6 For an intensive review of relevant bibliography on natural-resource-based, export-led growth, see OCDE, 2003 and UNIDO, 2004.

- Most of the increase in Africa's exports over the next few decades would come from natural-resource-based products: this is because they still account for an overwhelming share of total output. This would comprise non-traditional resource-based products; processed as well as unprocessed products, such as fish and horticultural expansion, partly due to environmental considerations. Primary processing, including small-scale agriculture, will spread the benefits of development and be just as demanding in terms of skills and technology as core manufacturing activities.

Additionally, Parrott and Kalibwani (2004: 54) believe that "organic agriculture is a viable and sustainable development option for Africa and that adopting organic agriculture does not mean a return to some form of low technology, backward or traditional agriculture – but that, instead, it pursues a blend of innovations originating from both scientists and farmers".[7] According to them, for most of the Sub-Saharan African countries, the best potential for organic exports undoubtedly lies in low volume-high value crops (such as coffee, herbs, spices, medicinal), non-perishable items, those which offer opportunities for adding value locally and tropical fruits.

Considering the above facts and prospects, this study seeks to identify ways in which Cameroon can improve its export performance by diversifying agricultural production. In other words, how to develop non-traditional agricultural exports and the local capabilities to respond to national, regional, and international market opportunities? Which sub-sectors with comparative and competitive advantages could benefit from the implementation of supporting measures to increase production and to achieve an efficient and diversified export-led agriculture in Cameroon? Indeed, diversification toward high-value crops can help to reduce the vulnerability of the economy or the high dependence of its export earnings on a limited number of products. Agricultural diversification can also help to reverse the lack of profitability, detracted investment, and dampened growth in the agricultural sector. This strategy can be realised by making the sector more profitable as it becomes flexible in meeting the local and international demands and enables poor people to do something new and remunerative yet within their sphere of competences and resources (Barghouti et al., 2004).[8]

---

7 Parrott and Kalibwani (2004) draw on a 2003 IFOAM publication "Organic and Like Minded Movements in Africa" by Nicolas Parrott and Bo Van Elzakker.

8 Diversification appears therefore as a great step forward in agricultural development and as a spur to sustainable growth in the rural sector.

The specific objectives of the study are:

- To identify new markets to target within the context of Cameroon's export-led agricultural diversification policy;
- To identify agricultural products for which Cameroon has a comparative advantage in exporting and assessing their market prospects; and
- To make some inferences for policy consideration based on the findings of the study.

The main policy issue of this paper is that such an approach will require fine-tuning the supply policy in the country, at the official level but also at the private sector level. The promotion of an exports-led agriculture, thanks to a general economic liberalization policy, pre-supposes not only diversification towards non-traditional exports but also an increase in the exportation of the traditional products that constitute the basis, albeit a narrow one, of Cameroon's exports.

The impact of expanding the commodity exports of developing countries has received considerable attention in the literature. The "export pessimism" hypothesis (Prebisch, 1950) was based on the fact that developing countries concentrated on exporting primary commodities while industrialised countries were the main producers of manufactures. Primary goods demand tends to be inelastic with respect to income, and therefore, if supply grows faster than demand, this leads to lower prices and deteriorating net barter terms of trade vis-à-vis manufactures. Also, primary commodities tend to be inelastic with respect to price, so that in the short-term higher production and productivity lead to relatively greater price declines, such that marginal revenues from additional output are negative, reducing the welfare of the country that is increasing production as well as of other producing countries. The policy implication of this logical sequence is that developing countries ought to constrain production and diversify out of primary commodities.

Godfrey (1984) argues in the Berg Report (World Bank, 1981) that "Africa's share of world trade in most commodities could be increased with relatively small effects on prices" (p.23). According to him, those calling for an expansion of commodity exports by SSA countries should modify their prescriptions considerably, and greater emphasis should therefore be place on diversification from commodities with a low income-elasticity to high income-elasticity products.

Related to the issue of markets is the matter of products that are likely to penetrate the markets. Potentials for trade may exist but trade may not materialise, especially if Cameroon lacks comparative advantage in products that could be exported to such countries. The need to identify products that could further enhance the overall market diversification effort is therefore obvious. The importance of this issue to export promoting agencies in a country like Cameroon derives from the fact that it may enable them to identify special financial products and other services that may facilitate the generation of such exports.

The rest of the paper reviews and discusses major policy issues related to export-led agriculture in Cameroon. It consists with the introduction of five sections. Section 2 provides a general overview of the comparative advantages of Cameroon's agriculture products. Section 3 identifies constraints and opportunities in some of those sub-sectors that need to be promoted. Section 4 gives an account of the government's integrated rural development strategy aiming also for export diversification. Section 5 concludes and discusses policy implications.

2 Assessing the Comparative Advantages in the Agricultural Sector in Cameroon

According to the standard Heckscher-Ohlin trade theory[9], a country's trade structure reflects its comparative advantage, which in turn is determined by the relative endowment of production factors (land, labour, skill and capital).

In Cameroon, agriculture is the main support of the economy. Until 1978, agriculture was the main source of growth and of foreign exchange earnings, when oil production started and became the cornerstone of economic growth. But, oil has now been declining for several years owing to the depletion of reserves, so that an increased diversification of the non-oil sector is as of now essential. This underscores, if necessary, the importance of agriculture in the economy.

Anyway, nearly 75% of the population live in rural areas, and 95% of those are agricultural smallholders. For instance, tree crops are an important source of employment and revenues for smallholders, and tree crops are also some of the most important cash crops may it be for export earnings or from a national market development point of view. Coffee and cocoa have contributed to the development of the economy and remain the two main cash crops in terms of export earnings. Rubber and palm oil have also been key sectors that have, at times, benefited from support of the government (by

9 See Krugman and Obstfeld (2003).

the way of subsidies, marketing boards, etc.), from multi- and bilateral donors, and from the private sector (large agro-industries). However, the share of Cameroon in these commodities has been decreasing constantly, especially to the benefit of South East Asian Competitors (Thailand and Malaysia having become the world leaders for, respectively, rubber and palm oil).

Otherwise, food crops ensure both the self-sufficiency of the rural population and the food supply to the towns.

Agricultural competitiveness and the agricultural growth potential are central issues in an export-led agriculture strategy. Which sub-sectors with comparative advantages should be promoted? How is the country placed in terms of producing the most dynamic agricultural export products and in meeting the market entry conditions?

The World Bank (1991) stands up for the existence of a potential comparative advantage in the Cameroonian agricultural sector. Indeed, Cameroon presents a comparative advantage in a growing number of crops due to contextual opportunities such as: agro-climatic conditions characterized by a combination of dry and tropical areas[10]; techniques, and experience in these traditional crops; the quality of the final product; the availability of land[11] and labour[12]; the dynamic village production; and competitive agro-industries. Moreover, factors like a strategic geographic position in the Gulf of Guinea, and a potential market of 200 million consumers from the Central African Sub-region and from Nigeria can help to support economic diversification in Cameroon. However, building a strong competitive

---

10 Cameroon has on its territory all types of inter-tropical climates. Also, Cameroon has good soils (e.g. volcanic, ferralitic) in regions of high, medium and low altitude.

11 According to the data from FAO, in 2001 Cameroon's agricultural area amounted to 9,160 thousand hectares, 61.1% of which were arable land and 13.1% were for permanent crops. Permanent pasture represented 21.8% of the agricultural area while the irrigated area was 0.5% of the arable and permanent crops area.

12 Concerning the human potential, the agricultural sector-related active population of Cameroon accounts for more than 40 per cent of the total population. To this population, mainly rural, must be added professional agricultural farmers searching for new opportunities and being endowed with sufficient financial resources (e.g., businessmen, and retired high-ranking officials in conversion to agriculture).

advantage will be crucial in order to respond to the market demand and to face the regional and international markets.[13]

Bamou Tankoua (2002) provides an indication of the order of priority of Cameroonian non-traditional exports by classifying them according to their world market access prospects. Based on the calculations of competitiveness and financial capital profitability indexes[14], findings include:

- Some 33 new export products are identified and can be considered as non-traditional[15];
- The majority of these are competitive and profitable and can thus be promoted in priority within the export diversification framework that the government intends to put in place;
- Nearly three-fourths are industrial goods;
- Cameroonian exports in general and non-traditional ones in particular are constrained by tariff and non-tariff barriers, as well as by an inadequate national and international socioeconomic environment.

One of the important questions in the Cameroonian non-traditional export diversification process that the research did not address so far is the identification of the potential destinations of those exports.

Gergely (2002) has carried out another microeconomic study on the agricultural sub-sector's competitiveness. The study focused on Cameroon's key marketed products, including basic food crops: plantain, cassava, corn, and potatoes; poultry from the animals' sub-sectors; and cocoa and coffee.

---

13 For a full discussion of this topic see Fèvre (2002).

14 Domestic Resource Costs (DRC) has been chosen as an indicator of competitiveness in order to answer whether the country can gain by producing or importing, or whether the local production can use the resources better than the rest of the world. The DRC is derived from the microeconomic profit function-based prices. The financial profitability, which seems to be important to private exporters, has been measured with the financial capital profitability ratio (FCP).

15 Namely, nine primary products: Prawn, barks, wheat, beans, corn, orange, rice, saps and vegetable extracts; and twenty four industrial products: matches, beer, soft drinks, paper boxes, glass bottles, chocolates, hydraulic cements, wood sheets, insecticides, aluminium household articles, perfumes, food pastries, paints and varnishes, cereal preparations, preparations for soups and potages, beauty/make up products, plastic bags, soaps, powder soaps, bran and wheat residuals, sugars, cotton cloth, and aluminium sheets.

The study calculated the economic return of the production in each sub-sector. The economic return is seen as a comparative advantage indicator, the domestic resource cost coefficient (or "DRC" coefficient). Assuming all national production is either exportable or can replace imports to generate or to save foreign exchange, the DRC coefficient measures the cost of gaining or saving foreign exchange through domestic production. When the cost is less than the international prices, the DRC is less than one and the national economy enjoys a comparative advantage. The figures in table 2 show encouraging results for most of Cameroon's agricultural sub-sectors.

Table 2: Comparative Advantage of Agricultural Sub-sectors

Competitiveness of selected basic food crops						
Product	Plantain			Corn		
Domestic resource cost coefficient	0.58			0.50		
Marketing cost in % of total cost	39			51		
Competitiveness of selected export crops						
Products	Cocoa			Coffee		
				Robusta	Arabica	
	Ebolo-wa	Southwest	Mbam-Lékié		Grade 1	Grade 2
DRC coeff.	0.2	0.2	0.2	0.9	0.6	0.4
Producer price at equilibrium/kg	202	227	296	199	423	331

Source: Nicolas Gergely (2002), pp 14, 35, 77, 78, 79 and 80.

In general, regarding food crops, activities are economically profitable. DRC coefficients have been calculated for two or three geographical areas, but because of lack of data, it has not been estimated for cassava and potatoes. With respect to cocoa, three representative models have been brought out. The first model is the extensive one characterized by a very low level of input use, as it is the case in most production areas (Ebolowa, for instance). Here, yields are supposed to reach 264 kg per ha. The second model denotes a semi-intensive farming with application of pesticides and where yields are reaching 576 kg per ha. Such is the case in the Southwest geographical area of the country. The third model is the relatively intensive one, representative of the Mbam and Lékié administrative divisions and characterized by the spraying of crops. Yields are valued at about 624kg/ha.[16]

Concerning Arabica coffee, an extensive model is used whereby coffee (150 kg/ha) is intercropped with food crop cultivation, and a semi-intensive model (550kg/ha) has been used to evaluate sub-sector performance. The cultivation model for Robusta is typically semi-intensive (400 kg/ha). Available data have made it possible to calculate the DRC coefficients for each sub-sector as well as the equilibrium producer price. The results show that, while cocoa/coffee sub-sector activities are economically profitable given that all the DRC coefficients are less than one, in contrast the financial return calculations show a tremendous variation in international prices.

Finally, Douya (1998) has analysed the competitiveness of the cotton sector and has deduced the competitiveness of the agricultural chains and the non-competitiveness of the industrial chain (cloth manufacturing).[17]

Cameroon has a natural propensity for the development of new, promising growth sub-sectors, such as pepper, horticulture, watermelon, and organic farming. As a resource-rich country, it can develop and foster new areas of competitive advantage by designing and implementing a sound strategy for export diversification. Today, the introduction of new biotechnologies, as well as the use of information and communication technologies and geographical information systems, holds great promise for increasing agricultural output. Opportunity analysis lays stress on changes in demand patterns in OECD countries that reflect changing dietary habits but also increased awareness in food quality, health and environmental protection. For all that, world trade is rapidly growing for high value

---

16 For detailed studies of the relative profitability of various land use systems that are integrating tree crops in Cameroon refer to Gockowski, Temich and Vosti, (2001); and Gockowski and Dury((1999),pp. 239-241.

17 Cotton is the main cash crop in the North province in Cameroon. SODECOTON takes care of 350,000 cotton production to whom CFA 40 to 45 billion are paid each year, thousands of litres of insecticides shared and fertilisers distributed. SODECOTON also pays CFA 7 billion in taxes to the State each year. It represents 5,000 temporary and permanent workers, for a total annual salary of CFA 8 billion. Cotton is the only cash crop produced by farmers of the North. It is for this reason that a whole unit has been created at SODECOTON to carter farmers by supplying them inputs. The company spends at least CFA 1.7 billion every year on road maintenance. In 2004, 306,000 tons of cotton were bought from local farmers. The figures dropped to 250,000 tons in 2005 due to bad weather and high cost of raw materials.

commodities, including in particular foodstuffs that could easily be supplied by commodity-dependent developing countries, and processed forms of many products currently exported by them in an unprocessed stage could be supplied. Industrialised countries and a small number of developing countries have generally been successful in exploiting these dynamic and lucrative markets, while others, particularly African countries, have been left behind. In the same viewpoint, the demand from oil-exporting neighbouring countries (Chad, Gabon, Equatorial Guinea, Nigeria, Angola)[18] and the strong growth of the urban population (4.8 to 5 per cent a year) ensure that there is an important market for food products as it appears in table 3 below.

Table 3: Food Balance – Cereals Excluding Beer (2000-2002)

	QUANTITY (1000 tonnes)					RATIO TO CONSUMPTION			
Countries	Production (+)	Exports (-)	Imports (+)	Seed feed and other uses (-)	Consumption (=)	Production	Exports	Imports	Seed Feed and other Uses
Cameroon	1 342	3	521	310	1 550	0.87	0.00	0.34	0.24
Central African Rep.	184	-	52	32	204	0.90	-	0.25	0.16
Chad	1 117	-	64	121	1 060	1.05	-	0.60	0.11
Congo	7	-	248	5	250	0.03	-	1.0	-
Gabon	30	-	160	65	125	0.24	-	1.28	0.52
Equatorial Guinea	-	-	-	-	-	-	-	-	-
Angola	555	-	627	220	962	0.58	-	0.65	0.23
Nigeria	20 165	66	3 657	6519	17 237	1.17	0.00	0.21	0.38
Democratic Rep. of Congo	1490	13	435	58	1854	0.80	0.01	0.23	0.03

Source: FAO Statistical Yearbook 2004, Vol. 1/1. Table D.3

---

18 For instance, in the case of Gabon, agriculture's contribution to GDP is 4 per cent in 2002. The country does not have a strong agricultural tradition, and 59 per cent of food is imported (AfDB/OECD, 2004, p. 152).

3 Opportunities for an Export-led Agriculture

Three groups of products are reviewed below according to the ultimate objective of the integration of the Cameroonian agricultural production and processing into international markets, namely: traditional export crops; food crops; and fruits and vegetables (see table 4 below).

3.1 Opportunities for Selected Traditional Export Crops

Production diversification does not exclude the possibility of diversifying within the traditional commodities. Traditional export crops still have a major role to play in the economy. They not only are vital contributors to foreign exchange earnings but also account for a significant proportion of tax income and gross domestic product. This can be demonstrated through some traditional export crops like rubber, palm oil, Arabic gum, and cocoa.

a) Natural rubber

In 2001, Cameroon produced 53,000 tons of natural rubber, i.e. 0.9% of the world production, thus ranking the country as 13th within world producers and as 4th of the African producers (World Bank, 2002a). This production amounted to 54,600 tons in 2003 and is projected to 60,700 tons in 2006.[19] Within the 40 leading items of merchandise exports and exports of services of Cameroon in 2003, natural rubber is the 8th.[20] The average annual percentage growth of natural rubber's export was 10 % in 2003, while the percentage share of exports in total world exports based on 2003 export values was 1.0%. The two largest markets for Cameroon's natural rubber exports in 2003 was France and Italy with respectively a 27% and 18% share in Cameroon's exports. Smallholders represent only 10% of the plantation acreage, and 5.7% of the national production, which is dominated by two large agro-industries (Cameroon Development Corporation and Hevecam).[21]

---

19 Refer to BEAC site: http://www.beac.int/stateco/dedsbcam.pdf visited on May 2006.

20 At the HS 4-digit level; refer to Table 3.

21 The Cameroon Development Corporation is a state corporation that is the second largest employer in the country after the State. The estates, a small part of its assets, were sold in October 2002. The three other crops units (palm oil, rubber, and bananas) received no bids. The banana plantations have been under

The natural rubber sector in Cameroon has been suffering from a total lack of investment, due to the absence of a real national strategy to invest in the sector, which led to the gradual loss of interest, especially for the smallholders. The sector now lacks dynamism and incentives but holds the potential of high returns.[22]

b) Palm-oil

Cameroon produced, in 2001, 159,000 tons, thus being the 3rd largest African producer (World Bank, 2002a). The sector has been growing dramatically over the past 8 years, as 28,900 ha were planted between 1996 and 2001 (4,800 ha/year). As opposed to the case of rubber, smallholders represent 40% of the plantation acreage, and up to 26% of the national production. The sector is characterized by a strong duality between the industrial and the artisan production, but both sectors enjoy considerable growth. Some agro-industrial units, such as the Cameroon Oil-Palm Company (Socapalm), were privatised, what has led to an increase in planted surface and production. The sector is extremely dynamic, given that it is supplying for the domestic demand of the food market. However, like rubber, it suffers from a lack of investment that led to the ageing of the plantations (30% are now of more than 25 years of age).

---

private management since 1987. Concerning Hevecam, the largest rubber company in Cameroon, it went private to an Indonesian conglomerate in 1996, the Panwell Group.

22 Although there are no processing industries in Cameroon (tyres production, re-treading, mattress production), rubber is doing very well on the export market, because of destination purchase (Michelin, Good Year, Firestone). In addition, there are no significant trade restrictions on rubber.

Table 4: Agricultural Exports of Cameroon between 1999 and 2003

Rank[1]	HS Code	Product label	Exports 2003 (US$ m.)	Net Exports 2003 (US$ m.)	Export growth 1999-2003 % p.a. value	World trade growth 1999-2003 [2]		Share in World (%) [3]	Leading markets[4]	
						Value	Quantity		1st %	2nd %
26	0603	Cut flowers and flower buds for bouquets, fresh or dried	1,6	1,5	23	4	6	0.0	FRA 83	NLD 7
34	0709	Vegetables fresh or chilled	1,0	1,0	-2	8	6	0.0	FRA 50	BEL 28
3	0803	Bananas and plantains, fresh or dried	245,3	245,3	5	2	0	3.5	GBR 46	FRA 26
18	0804	Dates, figs, pineapples, mangoes, avocadoes, guavas	3,8	3,8	-4	11	8	0.1	FRA 73	BEL 11
10	0901	Coffee	39,5	39,0	-24	-11	2	0.5	ITA 38	FRA 21
25	1211	Medicinal plants	2,0	2,0	12	0	2	0.2	ESP 56	FRA 24
4	1801	Cocoa beans, whole or broken, raw or roasted	227,1	227,1	20	13	1	4.6	NLD 69	GBR 10
9	1803	Cocoa paste, whether or not defatted	46,5	46,5	14	23	7	3.8	FRA 59	USA 41
22	1804	Cocoa butter, fat and oil	2,3	2,3	-33	5	3	0.1	FRA 100	NLD 0
15	1805	Cocoa powder, without added sugar	8,7	8,7	112	33	5	0.7	NLD 100	USA 0
40	1901	Malt extract, food preparations of flour, meal, starch or malt extract	0,8	-6,6	23	9	8	0.0	FRA 72	BEL 28
17	2005	Prepared or preserved vegetables (excl. frozen)	4,2	3,4	11	5	5	0.1	FRA 99	CHE 1
31	2104	Soups, broths & preparations thereof	1,2	-2,5	61	7	10	0.1	CAF 63	STP 26
30	2401	Tobacco un-manufactured; tobacco refuse	1,3	0,4	-24	0	1	0.0	USA 71	NIC 25
8	4001	Natural rubber, balata, gutta-percha etc	64,3	64,3	10	11	3	1.0	FRA 27	ITA 18
24	4002	Synthetic rubber & factice from oil	2,1	1,9	114	5	4	0.0	FRA 100	BEL 0
6	5201	Cotton, not carded or combed	96,4	96,4	1	-1	3	1.2	CHN 19	THA 13
27	5208	Woven cotton fabrics, 85% or more cotton, weight less than 200g/m2	1,5	-5,4	-30	2	5	0.0	FRA 79	ITA 8

Notes: *The indicators are based on the partner countries' export statistics (mirror).*

1. *A ranking of the 40 leading items of merchandise exports and exports of services (transportation services, travel, and other) under review at the HS4-digit level in 2003.*
2. *World trade growth 1999-2003, % p.a value: The average annual percentage growth of world imports of the product under review, 1997-2001, based on the least-squares fit. World trade growth 1999-2003, % p.a quantity: The average annual percentage growth of world imports of the product under review, 1997-2001, based on the least-squares fit. Data at the 6-digit level of the HS has been used for these calculations. The world trade growth of unit values can be calculated as the difference between the growth rate in value and quantity.*
3. *Percentage share of exports of Cameroon in total world exports based on 2003 export values.*
4. *The two largest markets for Cameroon's exports in 2003 and their share in the country's export.*

Source: *International Trade Centre's Market Analysis Services: UNCTAD*

This already very dynamic sector has been expanding dramatically in a very spontaneous manner. It is the tree crop product with the strongest domestic demand in Africa. As a food crop it is part of the basic local consumption, and so the market will closely follow the demography. As a matter of fact, Cameroon already faces a strong supply deficit that is leading, despite the country's production capacity, to the importation of important volumes of palm oil from neighbouring countries.

c) Arabic gum

Arabic gum could be an interesting investment opportunity because of the product's strong market power and concentration. Protectionist barriers by the industrial countries to the import of gum Arabic do not represent a limit on the development of trade in this commodity. In all of the important importing countries of Europe, North America or Japan, there are no specific quotas or import duties raised on gum Arabic imports. The demand has been steadily on the increase, and projections forecast an annual growth rate of 5% a year (from 50,000 tons in 2001 to 90,000 tons in 2010).[23] Arabic gum enjoys a competitive position due to its low prices, its competitiveness vis-à-vis major substitutes, and numerous industrial applications (food and pharmaceutical in particular). Africa is the world's major supplier of Arabic gum, the production being concentrated in what is commonly called "the gum belt", with 15 countries involved officially in either the production or the export.

The main producers are Chad, Sudan, Nigeria, Mali, and Niger. Although Cameroon is involved in the trade of this commodity, it is believed that much of it is, in fact, re-export from other producing countries. However, it is interesting to note that Cameroon presents the right geo-climatic conditions for growing acacia. The North of the country is very similar to the zones of production of Sudan or Chad.

d) Cocoa

The demand for cocoa is predicted to grow steadily following the demand for chocolate, although the demand for cocoa butter has been down. New markets for chocolate are opening up worldwide (Eastern Europe, Russia,

---

23 Refer to World Bank, 2002c: The Prospects and Constraints of Development of Gum Arabic in Sub-Saharan Africa. (Online): http://www.worldbank.org/af/rd_meeting/2002/arab_rpt.chniml.pdf, accessed 29/05/2005.

China). Africa, and especially the Western African countries (Cote d'Ivoire, Nigeria, Ghana) and Cameroon are the world's biggest producers of cocoa (60% of world production).[24] World exports grew yearly by 2.3 percent over the 30 years reaching 2.2 million tonnes in 2000 (FAO, 2002). Average annual percentage growth rates of export quantities represented 7% (cocoa paste) and 3% (cocoa butter) over the 1999-2003 period. The European Union, the United States and the Russian Federation are the largest importers.[25] The two largest markets for Cameroon's exports are France and the United States (see table 4).

World imports grew by 28.8 percent annually to reach 2.5 million tonnes in 2000 (FAO, 2002). The relative rigidity of short-term supply coupled with low price elasticity of demand in consuming countries[26], and the long gestation period of the crop[27], cause alternating short periods of booms and long periods of oversupply with depressed market prices.

Cocoa is Cameroon's main cash crop. In 2001, Cameroon produced 130,000 tonnes of cocoa beans, accounting for about 4% of the world production (5th rank in world producers). In fact, Cameroon produces 125,000 - 130,000 tonnes of cocoa a year, a quantity that has not changed much over the last 30 years. The current area in cocoa production is

---

24 In 2003, the eight largest cocoa-producing countries were Cote d'Ivoire, Ghana, Indonesia, Nigeria, Brazil, Cameroon, Ecuador and Malaysia. These countries represented 90% of the world production.

25 Although cocoa is largely produced in developing countries, it is mostly consumed in industrialized countries. The buyers in the consuming countries are the processors and the chocolate manufacturers.

26 Cocoa is inelastic in both price and income in the short term. Changes of income have a larger effect on consumption than changes in price. For example, a 10% decrease in the price of cocoa in the USA in the short term will result in a 1.99% rise in consumption; while a 10% increase of income would double the effect, giving a 4.26% increase in consumption. For a selection of countries being for most of them major consumers, in global terms a 10% change in price moves consumption in the opposite direction by 0.91%. Similarly, when taken on a global scale, the effect of a 10% rise in income will increase consumption by 6.47%. For more details see: International Cocoa Organization (ICCO) (1993), The World Cocoa Market: An Analysis of RecentTrends and of Prospects to the Year 2000; and R. Dand, (1999), International Cocoa Trade. 2nd edition. Woodhead Publishing.

27 Between 3 and 4 years.

estimated at 416,000 hectares, mainly in small production units (1.5 to 3 hectares with 1 to 3 workers).[28]

Major problems preventing better performance of the cocoa production sub-sector are, firstly, of an economic and social character; and secondly, they are of a technical and technological nature. In more detail, the main problem areas include: (a) aging of plantations, with around 50% being over 30 years old, especially in the Central and Southern Province; (b) the rural exodus of the population; (c) the difficulty in passing on the real estate; (d) poor yields (an average yield estimated at 300 kg/ha); (e) the small proportion of selected varieties of cocoa trees; (f) plant health problems[29]; and (g) management of production systems (low standard of maintenance and equipment).

Moreover, throughout Cameroon, there exists no real cocoa farmer extension service although it might prove useful.[30] Planting is good, but the farmers do not have the resources, and in some cases, the expertise to successfully produce high quality cocoa.

However, Cameroon has some important points in its favour for revitalising production: abundant reserves of land; low-cost production systems; experienced producers and good organization; relatively cheap labour; and marketing and primary processing networks.[31] For a cocoa sector displaying highly differing regional characteristics, a strong smallholder dynamics in cocoa growing areas, and limited interventions by public bodies, CIRAD propose a project in two phases[32]: (a) setting up a regionalized technical information and agro-economic decision support system that is accessible to

---

28 International Cocoa Organization, PC/21/3, May 10, 1999: Members' Report on the situation and prospects for cocoa production in their countries.

29 The main problem is Phytophthroa pod rod and capsids. Pod rod is an even more significant problem in the Western provinces of the country where rainfall is exceptionally heavy and humidity is high. Due to this, many of the smallholdings have been abandoned despite the high fertility of volcanic soils.

30 These are some of the reasons why cocoa farming is getting less and less profitable for smallholders.

31 However, it should be noted that, contrary to Cameroon, main producers like Brazil and Malaysia are not necessarily large exporters, especially due to the size of their processing industry, which absorbs local production.

32 Refer to the CIRAD proposal in support of Perennial Tree Crop Development on Family Farms in Sub-Saharan Africa, available at http://www.worldbank.org/afr/rd_meeting/2003/session_3_cr_2.pdf.

producers (individually or in their organizations), and (b) developing a programme for contract-based relations between producers (individually or in their organizations) and the public and private support sector.

3.2 Opportunities for Selected Food Crops

In the face of declining prices for traditional cash crops, recent years have witnessed a remarkable performance by food crops – such as corn, cassava, plantains, potatoes, yams, beans, millet, sorghum, etc.

a) Cassava

In Cameroon, cassava is one of the primary plant products making the largest contribution to feeding the population. Production was estimated at 2,114,000 tonnes in 2005. Cassava cultivation is a task performed primarily by women, and the same goes for the associated small-scale processing operations. Farms are mainly on a small scale, and frequently combine cassava with other crops. The high yields are of the order of 14.5 tonnes per hectare. Cassava production predominated in the Southern zone, with the main producing regions being the Centre, the Coast, the East, and Adamaoua; all these regions account for over 70 percent of national output. Per capita consumption is estimated at 120 kilograms per year; and consumption is largest in the producing areas.

Efforts to expand cassava production are hampered by the high costs of marketing, intrusive road and highway checks, difficulties in harvesting, the lack of producer information on the prices at final markets, the dearth of suitable equipment for processing, and the inaccessibility of a number of production areas, especially in the rainy season.

b) Potatoes

Potato production is estimated at 160,000 tonnes at present; this figure has virtually doubled since 1995. Yield per hectare is 20 tonnes, falling short of the agronomic potential, which is approximately 30 tonnes/hectare. Production is concentrated in the provinces of the West, the North West, and more recently the province of the Far North. The flows of exports intended for Gabon and Equatorial Guinea are estimated at 25,000 tonnes. Per capita consumption is estimated at 11kg/year, with an upward trend in the regions of the Great West and the Coast.

The principal constraints standing in the way of successful potato production are the problems with seeds, the administrative constraints (plant-health controls that are ineffective but mandatory and burdensome; intrusive road and highway checks), the poor condition of the rural roads, the unreliability of statistical data, and the failure to promote export.

c) Plantains

Plantains are produced throughout the Southern part of Cameroon, particularly in the provinces of the South West, the West, the Centre, the South, and the East. Plantain production employs about 600,000 farmers who each year produce 1.2 to 1.5 million tonnes, i.e., an average production of 2.3 tonnes per agricultural holding/farm.[33] Yields are estimated at about 4 to 7 tonnes per hectare, well below the agronomic potential that is of the order of 30 tonnes per hectare. Exports, primarily headed for Equatorial Guinea and Gabon, are in the range of 10,000 and 20,000 tonnes. Per capita consumption is estimated at approximately 66 kg in Yaoundé, 108 kg in Douala. Consumption in the rural areas is in the rage of 70 to 125 kg in the provinces of the South; it is practically nil in the Northern part.

The constraints on plantain production are primarily attributable to the costs of marketing (transport, intermediation, profit margins) which are high and liable to increase further; they are also due to the shortage of good-quality suckers, as well as the absence of processing development and information systems.

d) Cereals

Cameroon has continued to import cereals to meet the needs of its population. Between 1971 and 1998, imports increased by a factor of 10 from 32,100 metric tons to 348,148 metric tons. Imports per capita increased from 7.2 kg to 24 kg during the same period, while cereal production per capita declined from 157 kg to 85 kg. The deterioration of the productive environment (changes in ecosystems, declining soil fertility, etc.) has threatened the relevance of the current production system. Similarly, the sector is facing constraints, particularly a lack of rural infrastructure, inadequate dissemination of economic information, as well as reduced productive capacity. During the last decade, the supply response in agriculture has generally been unable to respond to market signals or to meet the needs of rural households. Hence, the national cereal policy aims, among other things, to consolidate cereal production in current production system so

---

33 This comparison highlights the leading role played by smallholdings, i.e., farms with less than one hectare planted with plantains.

as to increase food security and raise farmers' incomes; and to promote production, particularly in areas where competitiveness in domestic and sub-regional markets is good.

e) Corn

Corn production is found in all provinces of Cameroon. Production is estimated at 1 million tonnes in 2005 with a yield of 2 tonnes per hectare, falling short of the agronomic potential that is of the order of 5 tonnes per hectare. Nine percent of this output is used in agro-industry to manufacture grits and feeding stuffs, 4 percent is exported to Gabon, Congo, and Chad, with the remainder divided up among own-consumption and marketing. Per capita consumption of corn is estimated at 8 kg in Yaoundé, somewhat less in Douala; it is in the range of 80-100 kg in the North, and 30-50 kg in the West and North West.

Efforts to expand corn production are essentially hampered by breakdowns in the marketing system, the high costs of product collection, and the lack of storage facilities or high-quality seeds.

However, in spite of this performance, the sector is still failing to achieve its full potential on account of a multitude of constraints associated with the small scale of rural farm (0.5-1 hectare), deficient human resources, difficulties in obtaining inputs, nonexistent or problematic transport infrastructure, the dearth of financing and organization for the sector, and lastly, the lack of an appropriate institutional environment and of support services.

Wilhelm (1997) analyses these constraints in terms of risks. Food supply and distribution tends to involve very high levels of risk and uncertainty. There are upstream collection risks caused by unstable produce supply from numerous spatially dispersed producers, lack of information on product availability, and insufficient, irregular and expensive transport services. Downstream risks encountered by traders involve price and demand fluctuations caused by various unpredictable factors as well as disabling institutional factors such as inappropriate regulations and excessive and often arbitrary taxes. Furthermore, most traders lack sufficient capital and have virtually no access to credit. These constraints influence the behaviour of traders and affect their choices and trading strategies, which are similar regardless of the product or type of organization. This leads to very low productivity, as reflected in current yields that represent about one third of potential capacity, depending on market behaviour and the regions involved.

Nevertheless, the rural development strategy initiated by the Cameroonian authorities aims to increase food output by 10 percent per year, thereby raising both supply and the share of food agriculture in the growth of GDP and of exports. Demand from oil-exporting neighbouring countries (Chad, Equatorial Guinea, Nigeria, Angola) combined with strong growth of the urban population (4.8 to 5 percent a year) will ensure that there is a market for food products. On the supply side, policies designed to enhance factor productivity and specific programs for increasing yields and expanding land used for farming will make it possible to meet that increased demand.

3.3 Opportunities for Selected Fruits and Vegetables

Over the last two decades, significant technological advances in packaging and transportation and dramatic changes in the patterns of food consumption in OECD countries have opened up new opportunities for agricultural trade, with fresh food products becoming a significant part of global agro-food and fibre trade.[34] As demand for organic fresh produce is expected to continue to exceed production in developed countries, imports will be needed to meet consumers' demand. Developing countries with low labour costs and appropriate agro-ecological conditions like Cameroon may be able to fill this gap by improving production of new types of commodities, such as "off-season" and "speciality fresh vegetables" or cut flowers. Indeed, Cameroon enjoys a number of advantages, including: agro-ecological diversity; sizable production, albeit with post-harvest losses reflecting a shortage of storage facilities; farmers' experience in fruit cultivation; and sizable demand for processing of fruits and vegetables.

Farmers in most of the Southern provinces produce substantial quantities of mango, citrus, pineapple, avocado, papaya, and guava. Except for pineapple and papaya, all the other crops come from orchards distributed over areas reserved for food crops and cash crops, unless they are used as hedges encircling huts. Fruits are dominating domestic production, with about 531,000 tonnes, followed by vegetables representing about 315,000 tonnes.

Development prospects for organic farming exist in the forest areas of the Littoral and South West provinces, and in the Highland area of the West and Northern provinces. Additionally, these areas are close to Douala, the main entry and exit port of Cameroon, what is an important asset for export opportunities. Nevertheless, in some provinces (Coast, Centre, South West)

---

34 For instance, due to growing concerns with dietary health, the market for non-traditional fruits and vegetables has rapidly expanded over recent years, which will contribute to the improvement of the nutritionally balanced.

where human pressure on land does not allow the soils to recover and to clean themselves of agro-chemicals, organic farming cannot be practised.

However, there are significant constraints on the potential of export-oriented organic agriculture in Cameroon. These are internal as well as external, and have to do with the lack of appropriate equipment, a failure to ensure strict compliance with the production standards applicable to agri-business and the organic sub-sector, limited storage and warehousing capacity, costs of certification, problems of infrastructure, maintaining links with distant markets, and vagaries of world markets. Therefore, the challenges to face in order to increase production are: (a) the development of support measures for organic farming; (b) the establishment of a technical support service; (c) the integration of organic farming into the agricultural policy of Cameroon; and (d) a decrease of certification costs.

The sub-sector holds promise in terms of production and export diversification. It is therefore critical to make better use of domestic and sub-regional urban markets; and design, initiate, and implement specific development support programs for priority crops, such as pineapple, plantain, potatoes, gum Arabic, and onion. Emphasis should also be placed on facilitating trade in and exports of fresh products by opening up land-locked production areas; supporting the organization of wholesale marketing in primary harvesting areas, major trade centres, and border markets; and improving packaging structures.

3.4 Prospects of Export Diversification of Cameroon

Facing the global context and the opportunities, Cameroonian authorities have envisaged the prospects for exports. The first is export diversification that aims to improve the trade balance. Two types of products were targeted by this policy:

On one hand, the traditional export crop cocoa was selected, and a cocoa/coffee program was conceived. Over the period 2006-2010, this program based on the Rural Sector Development Strategy (RSDS) aims to double the production between now and 2015. The diversification here concerns, among other things, the production of many selected varieties of cocoa trees, which would be used to intensify and renew plantations, to increase cocoa production, and to extend plantations on new regions like Littoral, Western, and South West. This program tries to resolve the problems that limit the opportunities underlined before.

On the other hand, plantains and fruits have been chosen as food crops and fruits. The government has adopted two approaches. In the first type, these crops are taken as diversification products, with a specific double objective: (i) to serve as shade crops for cocoa (plantains) and coffee (fruit tree) in the new plantations; (ii) to ensure the productivity of cocoa and coffee, and the profitability of the investments made. In this way, the program has projected that 557,040 plantain sackers and 350 fruit trees should be planted in the regenerated areas.

In the second type of diversification, plantains are replaced into the global context of the food security reinforcement strategy and providing for foreign trade equilibrium in which the Programme de Reconversion Economique de la Filière Banane Plantain (PREBAP)[35] is taking place. Launched on December 24th, 2004, this program has four main objectives:

(i) Intensification of agricultural production; (ii) diversification and deepening industrial paths; (iii) promotion of food imports substitution on sensitive products; (iv) providing for competitive local industrial transformations. Over a three years experimental period before the implementing phase, Cameroonian authorities hope that through this program, peasants and industrialists will start to invest in plantain crops instead of farming only for consumption purposes.

Working with the Centre Africain de Recherches sur Bananiers et Plantains (CARBAP)[36] of Njombé, the PREBAP will use technologies of an industrial nature, so that the diversification will concern the transformation of plantains into several agro-industrial products like chips, dried plantains, and plantain flour. All these products will open new perspectives for their conservation and commercialisation.

On January 18th, 2006 authorities of Cameroon have projected that through this program, the plantain production must increase from 1.5 millions of tonnes to 3 millions very quickly (Actualités CEEAC, 2006).

Many stakeholders are implicated in the export diversification process within the Global Rural Sector Development Strategy (GRSDS). Representing a part of the public sector, the Ministry of Agriculture and Rural Development (MINADER) has specific objectives on the horizon 2010 and 2015 in terms of exports for many products as presented in Table 5.

---

35 Further information can be obtained at: http://www.spm.gov.cm/showtexte.php?idtexte=367&lang=fr.

36 “Centre Africain de Recherches sur Bananiers et Plantains”.

Table 5: Export Prospects (in tons) for Several Agricultural Products on the Horizon 2015

	Situation in 2005	Estimations 2005	Prospects for 2010	Prospects for 2015
Cocoa	123 000	140 000	188 000	280 000
Arabica Coffee	10 000	10 000	13 000	15 000
Robusta Coffee	50 000	50 000	72 000	93 000
Bananas	240 000	300 000	400 000	500 000
Pineapple	1000	4 000	12 000	20 000
Cotton	220 000	270 000	330 000	400 000
Palm Oil	9 000	10 000	30 000	60 000
Cereals	3 000	5 000	15 000	30 000
Legumes	3 000	4 000	8 000	12 000
Oilseeds	10 000	12 000	24 000	36 000
Vegetables	5 000	6 000	12 000	24 000
Fruits	243 000	300 000	410 000	520 000

Source: MINADER, 2006.

4 Assessing the Government Policies

As an indication of its commitment, the government designed an agricultural development strategy[37] to identify and to promote those branches of the agricultural sector offering the greatest potential based on the five major agro-ecological subdivisions of Cameroon as indicated in map 1 below:

37 In fact, the agricultural development strategy is a component of the global government's strategy for economic growth and poverty reduction, as described in the Poverty Reduction Strategy Paper (PRSP) communicated to the World Bank and the IMF in April 2003.

Map 1: Agro-ecological Zones

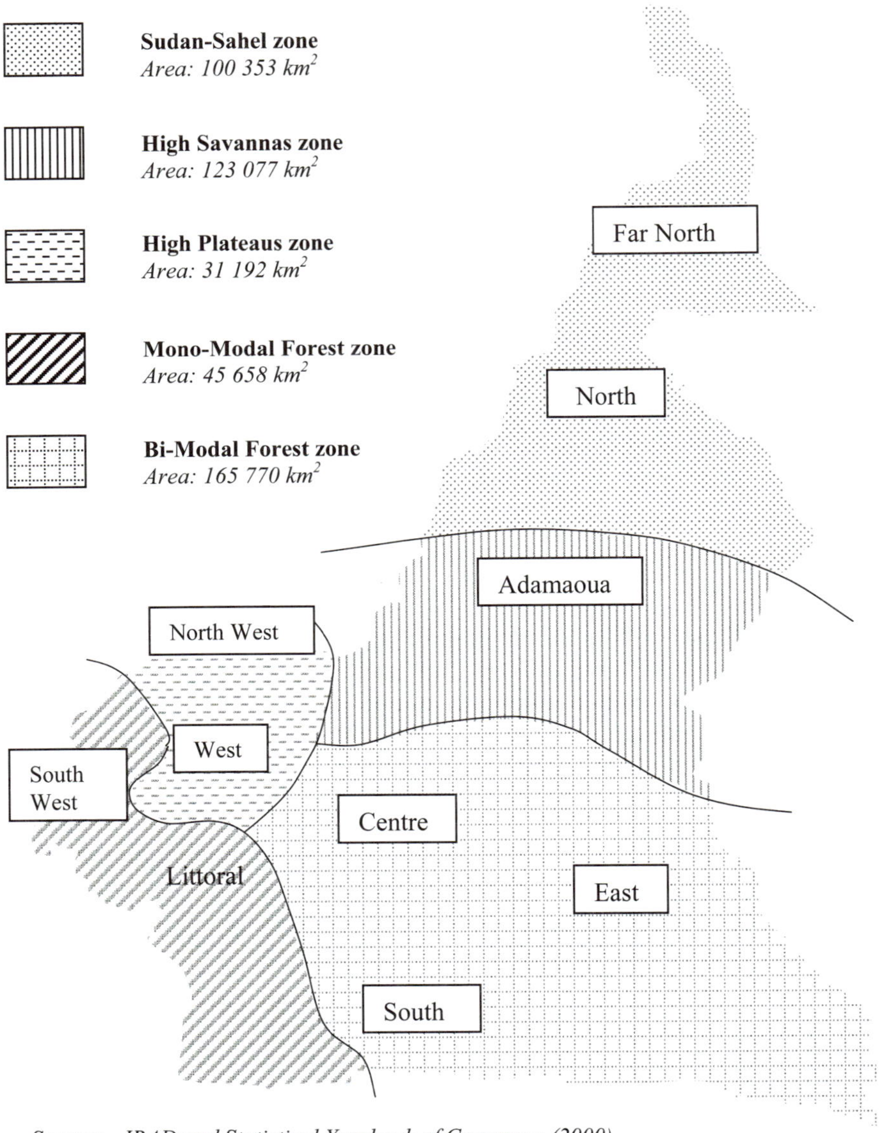

Source: IRAD and Statistical Yearbook of Cameroon (2000).

- For the *mono-modal forest zone*, i.e., the provinces of the Coast and the South-West: bananas, plantains, palm oil, ginger, and pepper;
- For the *bi-modal forest zone*, i.e., the provinces of the Centre, South, and East: cassava, corn, palm oil, and pineapple;
- For the *high plateaus* in the West and North West: corn, dry beans, potatoes, organic farming of vegetables (including watermelon);
- For the *Sudan-Sahel region*: millet/sorghum, cowpeas, onion, sesame;
- For the region of the *high savannas* in the province of Adamaoua: millet/sorghum, corn, yams, and potatoes.

This strategy focuses on two main objectives, namely boosting yields and enlarging surface areas under cultivation. Firstly, yields could be boosted by measures to facilitate farmers' access to inputs (plant material, fertilizers, plant-health products), crop cultivation techniques, equipment and material, harvesting, storage, and processing facilities, as well as marketing arrangements (information, infrastructure, etc.). Secondly, depending upon the regions and market patterns, cultivated surface areas could be increased, either by scaling back unprofitable and lower-yielding crops that would be effectively abandoned by producers, or putting new land to work.

Besides, the government aims at promoting a strong, sustainable, and equitable agricultural sector growth. It has drafted an integrated rural development strategy with four main priorities:

The *first* priority concerns the modernization of production facilities. This involves: improving access to, and the availability of, production factors such as land, water, and farm inputs for the neediest of the rural population; promoting access to innovative technology with a stronger link between agricultural research and extension; and enhancing the competitiveness of the productive sub-sectors. The government expects to place emphasis on smallholders and to give attention to developing small- and medium-scale agricultural enterprises. The authorities consider encouraging the establishment of consultation mechanisms and the development of contractual relationships between input supply companies and agricultural professional and inter-professional organizations. Similarly, they contemplate facilitating the emergence of a more effective private sector and of NGOs and rural community organizations that could effectively take over outreach and education activities, input supplies, veterinary services, seed and plant production, support for trade activities, etc.

The *second* priority deals with the restructuring of the institutional framework in order to promote greater professionalism in the rural sector, including farmers, ranchers, and fishermen, through capacity building.

Measures will be carried out to improve the quality of public service delivery and to redirect policies and institutions toward the needs of the rural poor.

The *third* priority is concerned with the enhancement of incentives by which the government hopes to establish, in partnership with the private sector, conditions for more efficient market mechanisms so as to improve access by rural producers to new technology and other requirements, including from the financial sector; and to put into effect and to enforce the existing sector regulations.

The *fourth* priority involves the sustainable management of natural resources. This management will help the government organize and encourage private and community initiatives favouring environmentally friendly development by coordinating the management of renewable natural resources, involving all the administrations and key users; restoring and safeguarding the production potential; and ensuring a reliable local management of rural community infrastructures. All measures will be designed to sustain natural resources, focusing particularly on protecting soil fertility, the conservation of water resources, the conservation of land pasture, the conservation of biodiversity, etc.

The strategy adopted for the rural sector is a "pro-active" growth promotion strategy built on smallholder agriculture; semi- and intensive farming; processing and marketing units of products and sub-products; and the specific regional agro-ecological features.

However, it is necessary to pass from declarations and exhortations on developing the potential of commodities and on diversifying to concrete policies and actions.[38] For instance, regarding research results, there has been a significant expansion in research with the birth of several research programmes. But this seems to be changing little in the sector. Research results such as the development of new high yield and resistant seeds and seedlings are not yet sufficiently taken to the peasant farmers who constitute the greater majority in production. New techniques in the production chain remain with agro-industries. Stakeholders want to make maximum use of acquired technology and only hand it over to the peasant when it is outdated. Once this happens, the results are mitigated and rural farmers go back to archaic methods. As if that were not enough, peasant farmers hardly find opportunities for capacity building. Agriculture extension workers are rare to come back.

---

[38] It is now fairly well known that "bureaucratic inertia" is a fundamental constraint that acts as a break and prevents Cameroon from exploiting the considerable potential latent in its economy.

Also farm inputs such as pesticides and fertilisers are mostly imported and taxed, thereby making them expensive. The challenge here is to endeavour to produce these inputs locally, and those that can be manufactured indigenously should be exonerated from being taxed so as to make them affordable.

Another impediment to the development of agriculture in Cameroon has to do with the factor of transformation. Companies need to be set up to transform agricultural products like mango into jams, cocoa to chocolate, or banana to wine, milk to cheese or yoghurt, and so on. This will multiply the means of consumption of these products as well as improve on sales. A vibrant transformation sector will equally solve the problem of conservation that usually discourages farmers to produce in large quantities. Besides focusing on agriculture proper, the government should provide social amenities such as electricity, potable water, and telephone so as to encourage the youths to stay in the rural areas.

Taking into account all these factors, in the global context of the Rural Sector Development Strategy, MINADER aims to help agriculture contribute to economic growth acceleration, to food-stuff security and to rural poverty reduction by half on the horizon 2015. In order to realize it, a framework was set up which contains 7 strategic objectives, 16 programs and 102 projects, requiring 540 billions FCFA for their financing between 2006 and 2011.

Priorities have been put on six types of programmes and projects: (i) projects which are jointly financed; (ii) projects financed by HIPC resources (concerning maize, plantains, palm trees, cocoa, coffee, agricultural research, fight against scourges…); (iii) projects intended to take responsibility over HIPC projects (for example support projects for plantations); (iv) projects with a great impact on the poverty reduction; (v) projects with internal financing (for instance, support projects for the young farmers installation, restart programs for cocoa and coffee); (vi) the national program of agricultural statistics restart.

Table 6 on the next page shows these strategic objectives and the corresponding programs.

The relationship between government and the private sector is put on a new foundation. The main particularities of the governmental strategy on the agricultural sector are the new partnerships public/private that would take place and the use of participative approach.

Table 6: Strategic Objectives and Programs of the MINADER

Strategic objectives	Programs
1. To make a strong development of agricultural production and supply (doubling main production between now and 2015)	1.1. Program of farms development; 1.2. Program of input supply development; 1.3. Program of competitiveness reinforcement of agricultural and horticultural products; 1.4. Program of agricultural professional organizations development; 1.5. Program of national agricultural vulgarisation and advice;
2. To make a sustainable management of natural resources (60,000 irrigated hectares between now and 2015)	2.1. Program of soil management in agriculture; 2.2. Program of water control in agriculture;
3. To promote local and community development	3.1. Program of community development and life standing improvement
4. To develop adapted financing mechanisms	4.1. Support program for the agricultural sector farming
5. To develop agricultural employment and training (15,000 supported installations of young farmers/year, 30,000 trained farmers/year)	5.1. Program of agricultural professional training development and renovation; 5.2. Support program of young farmers installations;
6. To manage food insecurity risks	6.1. National program of management of food insecurity risks;
7. To develop the institutional framework	7.1. Program of capacity building; 7.2. National program of food and agricultural statistics; 7.3. Program for the promoting of an enabling legislative environment; 7.4. Ministry working

Source: MINADER, 2006.

In the first case, all the programs, actions and measures that are set up include this partnership. Looking at the global agricultural strategy presented, it appears that at each level of priority, the private sector, through inter-professional organizations, private programs, NGOs, small-scale farmers and ranchers, is implicated. As it has been said before, until then, not only was there no real rural development strategy, but also the private sector was not taken into account, nor did it play any significant role. With the new approach adopted, the great majority of programs that are initiated emphasize the partnership public/private, as the CARBAP has done.[39] The government is also determined to support and use the private sector as the prime instrument for wealth creation by strengthening the business climate. Public enterprise reform has been a cornerstone of Cameroon's strategy to improve economic efficiency. In the agro-industrial sector, the objectives were to lift barriers to entry and, to attract new operators with capital, production, and marketing know-how. This reform was to be completed through the sale of the four largest remaining public enterprises: Cameroon Development Corporation (CDC), Cameroon Oil Company (SOCAPALM), Cotton Development Company (SODECOTON), and Cameroon Sugar Company (CAMSUCO). The latter were successfully privatized; attempts to privatize SODECOTON and CDC failed. The government is now revisiting its strategy to re-launch their privatization.

In the second case, the role of each stakeholder is clearly defined in the global strategy and in the different programs to be implemented, and this allows us to assert that there is now a real participative approach. For example, in the restart of the *cocoa/coffee program* initiated on 2005, each partner has a precise role:

- MINADER, representing the public sector, will provide technical services and some farm inputs and will ensure training and supervising for the beneficiaries of the Program (smallholder farmers, ranchers, public societies, private units of production…);
- The *Plantain Program* will provide suckers which would serve as shade trees during the first three years;
- PSCC (Public Service Company for Cocoa and Coffee farmers) will produce and divulgate performed raw materials as high level varieties of cocoa;
- Beneficiaries will participate by preparing areas for plantations.

---

39 For more details, see: http://www.lepotentiel.com/afficher_article.php?id_edition=&id_article=21049.

5 Conclusions

This paper intended to identify potential sources of growth outside the oil sector, but related to the primary sector, which has greatly contributed to growth and public finance, but has been declining for several years owing to the depletion of oil reserves. Findings indicate that Cameroon has the potential to increase food production so as to insure food self-sufficiency, but also to enable food security attainment in the neighbouring countries that lack sufficient capacity. Then, in respect with an export-led growth strategy, directed at the regional level but also at the world market level, it appears that, as a country richly endowed with natural resources, Cameroon has to develop and to foster new areas of competitive advantage by designing and implementing a sound strategy for export diversification. Of course, the promotion of exports through diversification towards non-traditional products does not turn down the increase in exportation of the traditional commodities. This process of diversification out of traditional commodities is generally triggered by factors such as rapid technological change in agricultural production, by a wide variety of commodities including cereals, pulses and high-value crops; improved rural infrastructure; policy changes; and diversification in food-demand patterns. Moreover, as underlined by Barghouti et al. (2004), successful diversification will often result in a more varied mix of activities – at the regional level of farm enterprises, and at the vertical level of economic sectors, including new input markets and emerging processing industries. This will reduce community dependency on a narrow range of outputs and, as a result, will reduce vulnerability to shocks from climatic variability and volatility of commodity prices.[40]

Then, a critical mass of mutually reinforcing measures clearly needs to be put in place: public investment in agricultural research; promotion of micro- and small-scale enterprises in rural areas; planting material improvement and access; technical and management training; facilitation of access to finance;

---

[40] While diversification may reduce risk by spreading production activities to various enterprises, additional risks are involved in the adoption of new skills and technologies to produce unfamiliar products for foreign markets. The greater part of this risk comes from having no experience or knowledge on which to base judgement as to its risks involved. Suitability of natural resources and adequacy of infrastructure for the production and processing of the new product, crop yields and product quality, market prices and competitiveness are all much more uncertain than those relating to the production and marketing of traditional products.

development of basic infrastructures to support the production sectors; improvement of market and price information; increase in productivity rates and competitiveness; boosting yields and enlarge surface areas under cultivation; reduction of high marketing costs, etc.

The government is well aware that without increased diversification, economic growth will continue to fluctuate considerably with frequent terms of trade shocks. It also seems to understand that macroeconomic reforms alone will not suffice to diversify the economy and to significantly reduce its dependence on the primary sector, which is vulnerable to changes in natural conditions and to the world market prices of its exports. For instance, without the provision of adequate credit, public investments, and an improvement in infrastructure[41], the aggregate response of agriculture to price incentives would be minimal. In fact, more stress has to be put on the improvement of non-price factors. This would encourage farmers to improve their production techniques in order to generate a supply response that is needed for the world market integration.

The success of the strategy adopted by the government, after studies conducted by a group of Cameroon's experts consisting of academic and private sector consultants, will depend on how effective the government's actions are, and how well Cameroon's private sector rises to the challenge of competitiveness and export diversification. Success also rests on sustained and stronger support by all development partners. Indeed, it should not be kept out of sight that many external constraints still prevent producers from fully exploiting existing opportunities. These constraints include tariff escalation, strict sanitary and phyto-sanitary regulations, technical barriers to trade, etc.

Because of the above-mentioned challenges, emphasis should continually be laid over the short- to medium-term on a set of complementary actions for an efficient diversification of export-led agriculture in Cameroon.

With other African governments, Cameroonian authorities should endeavour to adopt a common stance at a regional level with regard to trade negotiations in the WTO, and to take advantage of international funding

---

41 These include: irrigation and water supply systems, post-harvest handling facilities, decentralized cold storage, energy supply, transportation networks, telecommunication networks, provision of appropriate landing rights, etc. Trade infrastructure and trade facilitating measures are also necessary for export competitiveness and for reducing transaction costs on trade. There is a need to invest into improving infrastructure facilities and networks to reduce the cost of driving business and to enhance trade-facilitating services.

initiatives in favour of developing countries. They should increase pressure to advocate for issues of interest to the agriculture sector in the WTO negotiations.

With regard to the international market, the authorities in accordance with other African governments should generate consensus with other African governments on trade negotiations on agriculture. As far as the international community is concerned, the donor community should assist in funding the transition process of agriculture sector diversification. International organizations, including UNCTAD, are urged to facilitate access to market information on agriculture products. Capacity building covering financing mechanisms and practices as well as business skills in agriculture should be organized for farmers, exporters and bankers. This will enable all players to understand the requirements of trade finance instruments (receivables financing, forfeiting, factoring, warehouse receipts, etc). In this regard UNCTAD could help countries learn from the expertise available in other developing countries, which are more advanced in the area of trade finance, and so contributing to implement financing mechanisms.

In fact, despite the government's sustained efforts to diversify production and trade, to add value to commodities, and to move into dynamic, new and technology-intensive sectors of international trade, commodities will still remain an important part of the export revenues in Cameroon, and an important component of income for the poor. Thus, fluctuations in price, yield and in weather variations will continue to affect and to generate fluctuations in output, and together will create uncertainties and difficulties in managing large variations in earnings for rural households, enterprises and governments. The best method for protecting the exposure of stakeholders to commodity-related risks therefore remains an important challenge. So, price risk management instruments, such as forward contracts, futures and options, provide farmers with an opportunity to protect their short-term commodity revenues from declines in world commodity prices. These instruments, if they cannot stop the overall downward trend in prices however, can protect the farmers against the negative effects of world price volatility within a crop year. Using risk management instruments, farmers have more time to adjust to long-term downward price falls. In addition, farmers can use price risk management instruments to improve the timing of sales and potentially to achieve a better price.[42]

---

42 For more details, refer to http://lnweb18.worldbank.org/ESSD/ardext.nsf/11ByDocName/UsingMarketstoUseCom-

References / Bibliography

Bamou Tankoua, Lydie (2002): "Promoting Export Diversification in Cameroon: Toward Which Products?" AERC Research Paper 114, Nairobi: African Economic Research Consortium.

Barghouti Shawki, Kane Samuel, and Ali Mubarik (2004): "Agricultural Diversification for the Poor. Guidelines for practitioners: Guidelines for Practitioners, Agriculture and Rural Development". Discussion Papers 1, Washington, D.C.: World Bank (Online): http://lnweb18.worldbank.org/ESSD/ardext.nsf/-11ByDocName/AgriculturalDiversificationforthePoorGuidelinesforPractitioners/$FILE/Diversification_Web.pdf#search='Agricultural%20diversification%20for%20the%20poor.

Bonaglia, Frederico, and Kiichiro Fukasaku (2003): "Export Diversification in Low-Income Countries: An International Challenge After Doha". OECD Development Centre, Technical Paper No. 209, June.

CIRAD (2003): "Proposal in support of Perennial Tree Crop Development on Family Farms in Sub-Saharan Africa." French Speaking Africa Rural Development Workshops of the World Bank, Online: http://www.worldbank.org/afr/rd_meeting/2003/session_3_cr_2.pdf.

Dand, Robin (1999): "The International Cocoa Trade", 2nd edition, Abington Cambridge: Woodhead Publishing Ltd and N.W. Boca Raton: CRC Press LLC.

Douya, Emmanuel (1998): "Analyse de la compétitivité de la filière coton au Cameroun, papier présenté au symposium international sur les filières agricoles de l'Afrique subsaharienne face à la mondialisation – enjeux et perspectives pour le développement économique", Workshop 19-21 October 1998, Dschang, Cameroon.

Food and Agriculture Organization (FAO) (2002): "Agricultural Commodities: Profiles and Relevant WTO Negotiating Issues", Prepared by the Commodities and Trade Division as a background document for the consultation on Agricultural Commodity Price Problems, 25-26 March Rome: FAO Corporate Document Repository. Online: http://www.fao.org/documents/show_cdr.asp?url_file=/DOCREP/006/Y4343E00.HTM, accessed on 24/03/2005.

FAO: "FAO Statistical Databases", Agricultural Data. Online: http://apps.fao.org/page/collections?subset=agriculture, accessed on 02/10/2004.

FAO (2004): "FAO Statistical Yearbook", Issue 2- Country Profiles, Rome: Food and Agriculture Organization of the United Nations.

---

modityRisks/$FILE/crm.pdf#search='Using%20Markets%20to%20Manage%20Commodity%20Risk'.

FAO/International Trade Centre (ITC) (2001): "World Markets for Organic Fruit and Vegetables – Opportunities for Developing Countries in the Production and Export of Organic Horticultural Products", Rome: FAO.

Fèvre, Evelyne (2002): "Etude sur la relance des filières hévéa et palmier à huile. Analyse de la viabilité socio-économique des systèmes d'exploitation de l'hévéa et palmier à huile, revue du secteur rural". Food and Agricultural Organization and World Bank. Online: http://www.worldbank.org/afr/rd_meeting/2002/Rapport_etude.pdf#search='Etude%20sur%20la%20relance%20des%20filiÃ¨res%20hÃ©vÃ©a%20et%20palmier%20Ã %20huile.

Gergely, Nicolas (2002): "Study on Improving the Marketing and Competitiveness of Cameroon's Agricultural Products", unpublished.

Gockowski Jim, Temich Thomas P. and Vosti Steve (2001): "Small Holder Tree-based Systems in the Moist Tropics – An Evaluation of their Potential for Generating Sustainable Development". Paper presented at the Workshop on Complex Agroforests: Farmer Knowledge, Management, Profitability and Conservation". Muara Bungo, Jambi, Sumatra, Indonesia, 3-6 September 2001. Final Workshop Report, online: www.frp.uk.com/dissemination_documents/R7264_-_jambi-final_workshop_report.pdf.

Gockowski, Jim and Dury, Sandrine (1999): "The Economics of Cocoa-Fruit Agro-forests in Southern Cameroon". In: Multi-strata Agro-forestry Systems with Perennial Crops, Eds. F. Jimènez & J. Beer, pp. 239-241, CATIE, Turrialba, Costa Rica.

Godfrey, M. (1984): "Trade and Exchange Rate Policy: A Further Contribution to the Debate", in: Crisis and Recovery in Sub-Saharan Africa by Rose T. (Eds.): Development Centre of the Organization for Economic Co-operation and Development, Paris.

Government of Cameroon (2005): Décision n°001/MINIMIDT/CAB du 10 janvier 2005 portant création d'une cellule technique d'appui au PREBAP, Le Portail du gouvernement-Les textes législatifs et réglementaires, online: http://www.spm.gov.cm/showtexte.php?idtexte=367&lang=fr, accessed on 05/07/06.

Heckscher, Eli (1919): "The Effect of Foreign Trade on the Distribution of Income", Ekonomisk Tidskrift: pp. 497-512.

ICCO (International Cocoa Organization) (1993): "The World Cocoa Market: An Analysis of Recent Trends and of Prospects to the Year 2000: A Study", London: ICCO.

Jaffee, Steven, Ron Kopicki, Patrick Labaste and Iain Christie, (2003): "Modernizing Africa's Agro-Food Systems: Analytical Framework and Implications for Operations", Africa Region Working Paper Series No. 44, Washington D.C.: World Bank.

Johnston, Bruce F. and John W. Wellor (1961): "The Role of Agriculture in Economic Development", in: American Economic Review, 51 (September), pp. 566-593.

Krugman, Paul, Maurice Obstfeld (2003): "Economie internationale", 4ème édition, Bruxelles: DeBoeck, Collection Ouvertures économiques - Prémisses.

Kuznets, Simon (1965): "Economic Growth and Structure – Selected Essays", New York: W. W. Norton.

Le Potentiel (2006): "Banane-plantain: Les fruits de la recherche", (Online): http://www.lepotentiel.com/afficher_article.php ?id_edition=&id_article=21049, accessed: 05/07/06.

Mayer Jörg, Arunas Butkevicius and Ali Kadri (2002): "Dynamic Products in World Exports", UNCTAD Discussion Papers No. 159, Geneva, Switzerland: UNCTAD.

MINADER (Ministère de l'Agriculture et du Développement Rural) (2006): "Stratégie de Développement du Secteur Rural: Synthèse du volet Agriculture et Développement Rural". Document de travail, Yaoundé : MINADER.

Ng, Francis, and Alexander Yeats (2002): "What Can Africa Expect From Its Traditional Exports?" Africa Region Working Paper Series No. 26, Washington D.C.: World Bank. Online: http://wdsbeta.worldbank.org/external/default/WDSContentServer/IW3P/IB/2002/03/01/000094946_02021604090636/Rendered/PDF/multi0page.pdf, accessed: 20/08/2004.

OECD/AfDB (2004): "African Economic Outlook Report 2003/04", Paris: OECD.

Parrott, Nicolas and Bo Van Elzakker (2003): "Organic and Like-Minded Movements in Africa", Bonn: International Federation of Organic Agriculture Movements (IFOAM), Tholey-Theley. Online: http://www.ifoam.org/igo_survey.pdf.

Parrott, Nicolas and Fred Kalibwani (2004): "Organic Agriculture in the Continents: Africa", in: Willer, H. and Yussefi, M. (Eds.): The World of Organic Agriculture: Statistics and Emerging Trends, Bonn: IFOAM.

Prebisch, Raoul (1950): "The Economic Development of Latin America and its Principal Problems", New York: United Nations.

Republic of Cameroon (2003): "Poverty Reduction Strategy Paper", Yaoundé.

Stern, Robert M., Francis, Jonathan and Schumacher, Brace (1976): "Price Elasticities in International Trade", London: MacMillan Press.

Touna Mama and Schouamé A.M. (2004): "Deregulation Policy in Cameroon." In: Wohlmuth et al. (Eds.), The African Development Perspectives Yearbook, Volume 10 (2003/04) : Private and Public Sectors: Towards a Balance, pp. 465-504, Lit Verlag: Münster.

UNCTAD (2002): "The Least Developed Countries Report: Escaping the Poverty Trap", Geneva: UNCTAD.

UNCTAD: Info Commodities: Market Information in the Commodities Area. (Online): http://r0.unctad.org/infocomm/.

Wilhelm, Laurence (1997): "Food Supply and Distribution Networks and How Markets Work in Africa", Food Supply and Distribution to Cities in French-Speaking Africa, FOOD INTO CITIES COLLECTION – AC/03-97 bulletin 132, Project ACP/RAF/309, Food and Agricultural Organization: Rome.

Willer Helga and Yussefi, Minou (Eds.) (2004): "The World of Organic Agriculture Statistics and Emerging Trends", Bonn: International Federation of Organic Agriculture Movements (CIFOAM).

Wood, Adrian (2002): "Could Africa Be Like America?", in: Annual Bank Conference on Development Economics, Washington D.C.: World Bank.

Wood, Adrian, and Jörg Mayer (2001): "Africa's Export Structure in a Comparative Perspective", in: Cambridge Journal of Economics, 25(3), pp. 369-394.

World Bank (1981): "Accelerated Development in Sub-Saharan Africa: An Agenda for Action." Report No. 14030. Online: http://www-wds.worldbank.org/servlet/WDSP/IB/2000/04/13/000178830_98101911444774/Rendered/PDF/multi_page.pdf, accessed: 20/08/2004.

World Bank (1991): "Coopération régionale et ajustement structurel: programme de réforme de la politique fiscalo-douanière pour les Etats membres de l'UDEAC", Policy Research Department, Washington, D.C.: The World Bank.

World Bank (2002a), "Re-Investing in Smallholder Agriculture in Cameroon: Tree Crops and Sustainable Diversification Opportunities", Briefing Note WB 244196. Online: http://www.worldbank.org/afr/rd_meeting/2002/reinvest_sh_ag_cm.pdf, accessed: 12/09/2004

World Bank (2002b): "Towards More Sustainable Coffee"; Agriculture Technology Note of the Agriculture and Rural Development Department", No. 30, June. Online: http://Inweb18.worldbank.org/ESSD/essdext.nsf/26ByDocName/Crops, accessed on 23/03/2005.

World Bank (2002c): "The Prospects and Constraints of Development of Gum Arabic in Sub-Saharan Africa".

Online: http://www.worldbank.org/af/rd_meeting/2002/arab_rpt.chniml.pdf, accessed: 07/05/2005.

Unit 4: Book Reviews and Book Notes

edited by Achim Gutowski and Mareike Meyn

Book Reviews and Book Notes

Edited by Achim Gutowski and Mareike Meyn

Book Reviews

Augustin Kwasi Fosu, Paul Collier (eds.); ***Post Conflict Economies in Africa*****, Palgrave Macmillan in association with the International Economic Association, Houndmills, Basingstoke, Hampshire/New York, N. Y.: Palgrave Macmillan, 2005, ISBN: 1-4039-4346-X, pages: 272.**

Jean A. P. Clement (ed.) ; ***Postconflict Economics in Sub-Saharan Africa. Lessons from the Democratic Republic of the Congo*****, Washington D. C.: International Monetary Fund, 2004, ISBN: 1-58906-252-3, pages: 327.**

Stefaan Marysse, Filip Reyntjens (eds.); ***The Political Economy of the Great Lakes Region in Africa. The Pitfalls of Enforced Democracy and Globalization*****, New York: Palgrave Macmillan, 2005, ISBN: 1-4039-4950-6, pages: 243.**

These three books are important for a better understanding of issues of post-conflict reconstruction and economic policy in post-conflict countries. Insofar the books are important for policymakers, for donor organisations and for all those working as researchers on conflict, civil war and post-conflict reconstruction. The books give important analyses of the causes of civil war and violence and the economic and political determinants of civil war and violence in Sub-Saharan African countries. The three books together give an impression about country-specific and context-specific factors that lead to civil war and violence in Africa. These factors have to be considered when the task of peace consolidation is on the table.

The *first* book, edited by Fosu and Collier, is the most important one of this collection and contains some contributions of a more general orientation. We find an analytical model on post-conflict reconstruction issue, elaborating on utility functions for governments and rebel movements with the aim to show how these functions and the outcome can be shaped by action at various levels and how the agreements between the partners can be made more stable. The purpose is to show what the possibilities are to give incentive for a lasting peace in negotiations between governments and rebel groups, even in case of international sanctions, trade restrictions and embargoes. Most important, the steps towards a broad-based reconstruction strategy for realising lasting peace are outlined. We also find a survey on the political and economic consequences of conflict and the implications for post-conflict recovery. Moreover, an essay on the economic policy in post-conflict societies that elaborates on a strategy at various levels taking into account all the risks of civil war is presented. This essay formulates policy lessons that have to do with the risks that lead to conflict - prior, during and after a civil war – and gives recommendations for a broad-based reconstruction strategy.

There are important country cases of conflict and civil war in the book for West Africa (Sierra Leone, Nigeria, Chad), the Horn of Africa, East and Central Africa (Ethiopia, Sudan, Uganda, Burundi), and for Southern Africa (Mozambique, Angola). The contributions to the book are then summarised in form of a synthesis covering 10 important lessons for post-conflict reconstruction and appropriate policy change. Although the theoretical and methodological approaches are quite different and the coverage and presentation of the studies are heterogeneous, there is some consensus with respect to general policy lessons. This is particularly the case for the causing factors of conflicts like greed and grievance, predation and stagnation. The book gives therefore important insights into the determinants of conflict and into the issues that have to be considered when the task of reconstruction is taken up seriously.

The *second* book, edited by Clement, is more limited in scope and not so deep in analysis and coverage, although we find also some useful contributions and more general assessments on the economics of civil war and the economic reconstruction of post-conflict countries. Three overviews analyse the economics of civil war and of post-conflict reconstruction. Moreover, the economic performance during the conflict cycle is discussed. Regrettably, the analysis not sufficiently connected with the theoretical and empirical introductory chapters.

The Democratic Republic of Congo (DRC) is considered in various contributions discussing the sources of growth, the problem of hyperinflation, the challenges of financial intermediation, how to rebuild financial institutions, structural and sector-specific policies, and the long road to demilitarisation. Unfortunately, the contributions are hardly related to each other and the lessons of the single articles are not coordinated towards a new growth and poverty alleviation policy for DRC. However, the main theme of the book and the main thrust of the International Monetary Fund (IMF) – rebuilding financial and fiscal institutions for sustainable peace and reconstruction – are covered in the various contributions. It is however not always easy to identify a clear message for policy change and international donor activity. Also, it does not become clear why – when discussing the role of neighbouring countries in conflicts – the case of the Central African Republic as a neighbour of DRC is considered. The book is presented like a working report to show that the IMF takes up seriously the challenge of reforms in post-conflict economies. Lessons and policy implications are only loosely and incompletely drawn, and the main messages for other countries are over-generalised. The proposals for a future-oriented strategy for DRC and the central African region are not related to the main insights from the theories of civil war and post-conflict reconstruction. There is a list what the governments of such countries should do but the problems of weak institutions and of bad governance are not really discussed. Also the role of donors and of international organisations towards broad-based reconstruction is not sufficiently covered.

The book is of interest for those who want to see what the international community has done after the end of civil war in DRC to restructure economic policy institutions, and what the international community should do and can do to achieve sustainable economic reforms.

The *third* book, edited by Marysse/Reyntjens, is more narrow in regional scope but deeper in analytical content. The book concentrates on Rwanda and the Democratic Republic of Congo (DRC) but presents a political economy of The Great Lakes Region. It is assumed that "enforced democracy" has limits, especially in times of globalisation. Globalisation sets limits for peace consolidation and for democratisation in weak states and in countries with weak institutions. This is particular the case since international controls of trade in minerals and weapons are limited.

The book has two parts. The first part is on Rwanda as the dramatic events in this country have set the whole region "in a blaze" (p. 7). The second part analyses the contemporary evolution in DRC, and tries to "explain war and regression in the context of globalization and democratic reform" (p. 7). The part on the case of Rwanda is important not only for elaborating on country-specific peace consolidation strategies but also to get insights into other highly polarised and deeply divided societies. The roots of the Rwandan problems, economic issues like increasing poverty and inequality as well as the form and the causes of the genocide are presented, but also political opportunities to change and to reform segmented societies such as Rwanda. The type of post-conflict reconstruction in the country is critically assessed and the role of the international community to assist political and economic changes is analysed deeply and unconventionally. Although the situation is unfavourable, some elements of a new strategy are outlined and it is shown that pro-active policies are feasible. It is outlined that a more critical attitude of external actors is needed and that internal forces have to form a new platform for broad-based change towards peace consolidation and economic reconstruction.

Part 2 of the book is on DRC. State and governance failures, the problems resulting from weak institutions, and the systematic replacement of institutional structures by criminal networks are seen as central factors responsible for crises and conflicts. Such factors have – according to the authors – much more relevance than conspiracy theories related to the negative effects of globalisation and the plundering of mineral resources. On the basis of the book one learns to understand how "plunder economies" emerge and how plundering is based on activities of economic and military operators in the country and worldwide. The contributions are rich in information and in analysis of the economics of regress and fragility, the plundering of the mining sector, the role of local, national, regional and international actors, and the roots of civil war and conflict. The analysis on the situation in East Congo shows how multidimensional the causes of conflict in the region are. The analysis of the specific role of the capital Kinshasa shows the mutual impacts between the capital and rural areas with considerable impact on urban-rural inequality. Although all these contributions are not directly related to each other, they give a valid picture abut the real situation in the country. However, throughout the book no real strategy comes up to the minds of the readers. Only some general views on a future of The Great Lakes Region come up with elements such as federalism, democracy, rule of law, balancing interests of national and regional ethnic groups, and national, regional and continent- wide control of natural resources. Furthermore, the book lacks a synthesis of recommendations and does not make clear what the editors and authors have in mind when mentioning a "political economy approach" since the contributions have quite different accesses to the problems investigated.

The three books have quite different methodological approaches and cover different regions and countries. However, they allow some new insights on the multidimensional determinants of civil war and conflict in Africa, on the various approaches to effective reconstruction policies, and on the complexities of international, regional, national and local action towards peace-building. The three books are of relevance for policymakers, donor organisations and academics and can be recommended though there are wide overlaps, differences and discrepancies in methodology, policy prescriptions and in country coverage.

Karl Wohlmuth, Bremen

Daviron Benoit, Stefano Ponte; *The Coffee Paradox. Global Markets, Commodity Trade and the Elusive Promise of Development,* London & New York: Zed Books, 2005. In association with the CTA (ACP-EU Technical Centre for Agricultural and Rural Cooperation, Wageningen, The Netherlands), ISBN: 184277 456 5 hb and ISBN 184277 457 3 pb, pages 295.

This study is of relevance not only for the academic world but also for policy makers in coffee-producing developing countries and for institutions working in the field of development cooperation. The study is especially important for actors that aim to assist coffee producers to improve their position in the coffee value chain as it helps to understand the market, the actors, and feasible upgrading strategies. The association of the authors and the publishers with the Technical Centre for Agricultural and Rural Cooperation gives the study further relevance for policy advice to coffee producers in Third World countries.

The book is very rich in information and in knowledge about the sector, and also gives an analytical frame and perspective because of its Global Value Chain (GVC) approach used for the analysis of the coffee sector. The book is titled "The Coffee Paradox", arguing that the "booming" coffee business in OECD countries stands in stark contrast to the coffee sector "crisis" in producing developing countries. In fact, the "boom" and the "crisis" are related to the main attributes of the products and services supplied. Thus, the coffee sector sells not only material values, but also largely symbolic values and in-service values. The study analyses the whole value chain of productive and consumer services associated with coffee, showing that the producers are more and more limited in their share of benefits because they can claim only low returns for the material value of coffee, but are excluded from the rest of the value chain. The producers have obviously no access to higher shares from brand marks and to shares from in-service activities in developed countries.

Chapter 1 starts with an analysis on commodity trade, development of commodity producing-countries, and the role of global value chains for development. This is a good introduction showing that theories on the role of commodities in trade and development have changed over time, and that the role of primary commodities has been continuously reassessed depending on the underlying doctrine of development. Also the quality issue is brought in, by highlighting that coffee drinkers do not only consume the material value, but more so symbolic and in-service values.

In the next Chapter 2, the organisation of production in producing regions and countries is analysed deeply, including the usage of historical material. It is highlighted that for long time, land and labour were the key production factors, but that recently a trend towards a more capital-intensive "production revolution" has occurred. Also producer markets and consumer preferences have shown tremendous changes. It is obvious that after the end of the International Coffee Agreement (ICA) and after vigorous steps in producing countries towards liberalisation, deregulation and privatisation, the market structures of the coffee sector have changed fundamentally. Consumer preferences have also changed and have been "developed" by new forms of presenting the coffee, with high symbolic and in-service values which are attached to the material value. At the consumer end, the coffee market is highly interrelated with exploiting brand marks and in-service activities for generating higher value added shares.

Chapter 3 discusses in-depth the dramatic changes in input-output structures, in the geographies of production and consumption, and in the governance structures and institutional frameworks of the coffee sector. When comparing the times of the International Coffee Agreement (ICA) in the period 1957-1989 and thereafter, we observe the radical changes that have taken place with respect to structures, networks and policies. In fact, we see that the end of market regulation and political influence on the coffee market by negotiated and arranged production and export quotas has contributed to the globalisation of the coffee sector. This globalisation trend is characterised by new forms of market power and governance, by less influence of producing regions and an increasing influence of international buyers, by quick changes of the market structure, by more upgrading chances for innovative producers and traders, and by fewer options for small producers. The tables 3.6 and 3.7 highlight and summarise all these changes in a good manner. The "governance revolution" in the sector –from politically negotiated forums to a regime of few roaster companies that control the market - is presented in great detail.

Chapter 4 focuses on the quality issue by relating the debate on new quality measurement and new quality assessments to the debate on values attached to coffee (material, symbolic and in-service attributes).The changing quality assessment in the value chain at the level of producers and consumer countries is analysed. It is also carefully analysed how the recent changes in markets and in governance regimes have contributed to quality changes, and what the impact of market liberalisation, of changing consumer preferences, and of the structural change in the corporate and production sectors imply. It can be observed that also "sustainable coffee" production initiatives have been incorporated into global companies so that small players can hardly survive and expand in market niches. On the positive side, there is an increasing demand for information from the side of the consumers so that increasing transparency of global producers is required. Though mainstream producers absorb most of the share of specialty coffee supply and of most other relevant niche products, innovations in the market have a high speed and also offer potential for "out of mainstream" producers and smaller players.

Chapter 5 compares various "sustainability initiatives" and the role of "sustainability" for consumers. The authors identify an increasing number of sustainable initiatives. Though the "generations" of such initiatives show quite different patterns, they are quickly incorporated into the corporate strategies of mainstream producers, traders and corporate actors. However, some options for small-scale coffee producers might be left by such initiatives, for instance by a new form of cooperation between global corporations, governments of producer countries, and NGOs as caretakers for the interests of the small producers. This may lead to some innovative forms of social contracts between these three partners. However, the danger is great that a low level of standards is set in the industry, so that changes in the value chain are only minor. Summarising table 5.12 then shows the limited impacts of coffee certification systems on sustainability. The incorporation of such innovative certification schemes by large players often implements low standards and prevents a more sustainable production.

In Chapter 6 some case studies for the distribution of benefits in the coffee value chain are presented. The benefits share (as measured in terms of the final market price) accruing to the farmer in the producing regions has dramatically worsened since the end of the ICA for all coffee value chains except the fair trade chain. The authors intend to analyse how the situation can be changed and how the "commodity problem" of such countries can be overcome. It is argued that there are some "theoretical" possibilities to overcome the commodity problem under the new environment of liberalisation and globalisation, by a) changing quality conventions; b) promoting transparency and connectivity between producers and consumers; c) exploiting the territoriality of products (involving more local symbolic quality attributes); d) involving real agents of change (increasing the symbolic product value for small producers thereby justifying a higher share of value added). How can these theoretical approaches and possibilities be translated into the reality of market transactions – this is the final question left to be answered by the authors.

Chapter 7 discusses the ways forward and drafts an agenda for action. Only few feasible possibilities out of the menu of theoretical possibilities remain. The authors argue that there is a need for a new international order of the coffee market that is based on certain re-regulation, and anti-trust activities. Furthermore, there are possibilities to call for an enforced transparency on the geographical origin of products and to enhance diversification in production and exports. Box 7.1 summarises possible "alternatives" and the agenda for action. Though the list is quite impressive, most of the actions that are proposed have to do with IGO (Indication of Geographical Origin). For international organisations, for governments in producing regions, for NGOs, and for donors this list means that some potential for action exists, but the basic lessons learnt from this book lead to the conclusion that global corporations dominate the business and even exploit the inherent dynamics of the markets such as sustainability initiatives. International regulations and national forms of protection are needed to control the corporate market power, to enforce competition at the global level, to reduce the exploitation of local producers and to increase their share in the global value chain.

Overall, the book gives the reader a good idea of the value chain in the coffee sector and offers policy recommendations how to change the modalities and the rules in the sector. All of this is also largely relevant for assessing other agro-based value chains. The book is based on an extensive use of literature and international market reports and gives evidence of the accumulated expertise of the two authors in the area of coffee. It is valuable to read.

Karl Wohlmuth, Bremen

Siphamandla Zondi; *Regional Integration for Food Security in Southern Africa: An Appraisal*, 2004, Pretoria: Africa Institute of South Africa, Research Paper no. 73, no ISBN, pages: vi + 46.

With the exception of major famines, such as the recent ones in Zimbabwe (2002 to date) and Niger (since 2005), food shortages and under-nutrition in Africa generally escape public attention. Therefore, Siphamandla Zondi can be given credit for dealing with a much-neglected issue in a non-technical paper addressing the general public and pointing to the fact that famines in Africa are often simply the last phase of a longer period of structural under-nutrition.

The author starts by providing an assessment of the continuing impact of colonial policies on food production in Africa. Using land and labour to meet the demands of industrialised countries is seen as the root cause of producing the "wrong" crops, i.e. crops suitable for export rather than for local consumption. Post-independence governments are accused of having acted in the interest of international capital, especially by continuing to foster export crop production and commercial agriculture to the detriment of food crops produced by smallholders.

In various African countries food production has declined during the 1990s. Due to shortages in input, poor infrastructure and marketing systems, a considerable part of African farmers has returned to subsistence production, and economically active adults left rural areas. The loss of agricultural labour through HIV/AIDS, which is estimated to be around one fifth of the labour force in Zambia and a quarter in Zimbabwe, also has to be taken into account. Offsetting the negative effect of a decreasing rural labour force on production would have required a rise in labour productivity, but it was in fact mainly counterbalanced by commercially financed food imports and international food aid. Countries which were able to increase their own food production in the 1990s generally did so by increasing the land under cultivation rather than by intensifying land use which can be explained by a lack of fertiliser, irrigation systems and mechanisation. A further reason for reduced national food self-sufficiency is internal conflict and war.

A different aspect of agricultural development tackled in this paper is the change from a mainly state-coordinated economic system to a market-coordinated system following the structural adjustment in the 1990s. The author points out that the intended price incentives for farmers to produce food have been offset by the impact of currency devaluation (resulting in lower purchasing power for inputs such as fertiliser from the international market) and a bias in public funding towards the production of cash crops for export to earn foreign exchange.

As agriculture is still the most important sector, the author suggests developing its links to other sectors of the economy as the key factor for overall economic growth (see *African Development Perspectives Yearbook*, vol. II, for a comprehensive discussion of this strategy). Food security should be achieved by regional co-operation, following ideas first proposed in the Lagos Plan of Action of 1980 and subsequently in other major African initiatives. The author argues that export earnings should be re-invested into agriculture, especially smallholder agriculture, to raise productivity and to improve infrastructure, to increase funding for agricultural research, to promote environmentally-sound production methods and to enhance living conditions of rural populations. Proposed coping strategies for acute food shortages are early warning systems that are more effective and the re-introduction of a diversity of species as an insurance strategy.

As far as world trade is concerned, the author argues that the behaviour of High Income Countries, which protect their own markets against agricultural imports and dump subsidised food in Africa, is anything but favourable for the balanced development of Africa's agriculture. Along with the shift in local demand away from domestically produced foodstuffs, which are considered by urban consumers to be inferior, it reduces in particular the diversity of locally produced crops. Food aid is said to have been ambivalent in its effects. Zondi argues that on the one hand it was vital during past famines; on the other hand, it tended to open the economy to commercial imports and thus moved attention away from long-term food security policies. The same line of argument lies behind the recent decisions in Zimbabwe (and to a certain extent also in Niger) not to ask for international food aid. The problem is exacerbated by the fact that the import of genetically modified maize from the US would, in the medium-term, destroy any chance of exporting processed food to the EU, a non-GM trading region. However, the ethical implications of rejecting food aid in an acute food crisis for the sake of long-term economic development should not be overlooked.

With regard to the present food crisis in Eastern and Southern Africa (Zimbabwe, Zambia, Malawi, Swaziland, Lesotho and Mozambique), the author argues that the crisis is primarily a problem of food shortage, rather than one of access or distribution (p. 29). Against the background of the structural underproduction of food, the main factors for the present above-normal food deficits are seen in the adverse climatic conditions (drought) and in subsidised imported food, which is cheaper than locally produced food, which in turn has discouraged local producers. Emergency imports (commercial imports and food aid) did not reach the most needy in the remote villages, but mainly the urban areas – an experience which seems to be ubiquitous during famines. In this situation, the availability of food ceased to be the main problem and distribution and accessibility, including transport bottlenecks, became the relevant issues.

Although the paper puts forward many plausible ideas, there are three critical points to be raised.

Firstly, there is a considerable lack of empirical in-depth investigation in the part dealing with the historical and structural components of underproduction of food in Africa, particularly with regard to the specific situations in different African economies. Another weakness of this paper is that it "personalises" economic developments and structures (in a somehow Marxian fashion): whether the "elites", the "capitalist class", the "petty bourgeoisie", the World Bank or the IMF as social groups or international institutions consciously shaped the economic processes, is an assertion still to be proved.

The third critical issue is of a more significant nature: it might be questioned whether smallholder agriculture in Africa really has the potential to feed the African population. On a global scale, most of the increase in caloric output over recent decades has not resulted from an increase in the self-sufficient production of peasant societies in highly-diversified, ecologically sustainable agro-systems, but rather from industrialised farming, economies of scale resulting from the concentration of production, bio-engineering and the use of industrial fertiliser. Certainly, a "green revolution" in a low-income country will not necessarily solve the problem of malnutrition or occasional famines. Widespread poverty may prevent the increase in productivity from being kept within the producer region due to a lack of entitlements by a large portion of the population, i.e. famines may well occur amidst regions which very efficiently produce food for the world market.

However, an eco-adapted agricultural system in Africa today is also no insurance against malnutrition. In this respect, it is interesting to learn from Zondi that in Africa growth of per capita food output is inversely related to per capita income, which means that even the better-off countries (such as Nigeria and Zimbabwe) still absorb any increase in food production through population growth rather than by feeding individuals better. This "pre-modern" demographic behaviour puts the population at great risk in times of occasional crop shortfalls. In my opinion, progress in Africa's agricultural sector has to be complemented by industrialisation and the stronger participation in the international division of labour. This again is based on specialisation along comparative advantages (such as labour-intensive production in Africa) and a more or less industrialised agricultural system in those parts of the world that provide (with due consideration of ecological costs of modern agriculture as external effects) the best conditions for growing food staples.

Hans H. Bass, Bremen

Dani Venter, Ernst Neuland; *NEPAD and the African Renaissance*, 2005, Johannesburg: Richard Havenga & Associates, ISBN: 0-620-32510-0, pages: xxx + 532.

In 2001, the "New Economic Partnership for Africa's Development" (NEPAD), initiated by South Africa's president Thabo Mbeki, was announced by 15 African leaders. NEPAD was publicized as first African socio-economic strategy document that emphasised the personal responsibility of African stakeholders for Africa's development as well as the relevance of conflict resolution, human rights, transparency and the rule of law for sustainable socio-economic development. This book on "NEPAD and the African Renaissance" discusses extensively the relevance of Africa's renewal as well as the concept of NEPAD and its implementation.

The book is divided into five parts. *Part One* discusses the concept of renaissance for Africa. The first chapter highlights among others history, ethnicity, languages and religion in Africa to give the reader a rough understanding of the continent's heterogeneity and the complexity of its people. The second chapter discusses the concept of renaissance and its relevance in an African context. The political, socioeconomic and cultural meaning of the term "renaissance" in different historic periods is discussed as well as periods of renaissance in Africa, defined as *"important periods of political, socio-economic, cultural and technological renewal in the history of humankind..."*

(p. 27). The authors argue that all periods of renaissance have certain components in common such as a) developed political structures providing for social stability and good governance; b) economic wealth; c) social stability; d) valid legal systems; and e) science, technology and art. In today's Africa however, economic decline, increasing poverty and political repression would be dominating. The third chapter demonstrates the need for economic recovery and socio-economic renewal on the continent by discussing briefly the period of slavery, the exploitation of the continent's resource by colonial powers, the postcolonial era and the current political economy.

Part Two discusses the political and socio-economic development of African countries. First, political currents since the movements towards independence are roughly described. Facing the complexity of political currents in Africa alone, the legitimation of their discussion on few pages is questionable. This is even more the case since the authors hardly back-up disputable statements, such as *"...many African countries have taken decisive steps towards good governance and conflict resolution. There is also a pan-African trend towards democracy and respect for human rights."* (p. 89). In contrast, one could also state that six of the first 10 states around the world that are classified as "failed" according to movement of refugees, uneven economic development, severe economic decline, widespread violation of human rights, deterioration of public services and rise of factionalised elites, are African states.[1] In fact, the analysis of *Part Two* of the book is weak. Thus, it would have been interesting to know where the authors see NEPAD's potential in an African conflict country like Sudan and how NEPAD could work in a prospering economy like Botswana. Also, when discussing African economic structures, the generalisation of arguments is unpleasant. The need for "economic regeneration" in Africa is indisputable but how increased investment should be attracted and how the economies should overcome their commodity dependence is not even rudimentary analysed. The further four Chapters of Part 2 discuss (a) the different legal systems in Africa and how they (theoretically) impact on human rights; (b) the role of donors; (c) Africa's trade and aid relationship with the rest of the world; and (d) the impact of globalisation on Africa. Again, the very broad focus avoids a critical analysis. When discussing "Globalisation and Africa", the authors plead for macroeconomic stability, trade liberalisation, increased investment and product diversification without analysing what has already been done in single African countries, what are the actual difficulties and where are the socio-economic and political limits of an outward-oriented strategy. The authors' investigation of Africa's economic integration attempts

---

1 see http://www.fundforpeace.org/programs/fsi/fsindex2006.php, accessed 14/08/2006.

and its integration into the world economy remains cursory. Thus, the authors describe economic integration and trade blocks in Africa (p. 175-180) but do neither broach the issue of problems of economic integration, such as overlapping memberships or the non-complementary trade structure, nor link the topic to North-South integration. The problems the EU's Economic Partnership Agreements pose for regional integration in Africa are discussed at a later stage (Chapter 23), without however raising the implications for pan-African integration.

Part three discusses perceptions of Africa by the African media and by the Western media. It is argued that the African media is still largely dominated by a Western-style and faces manifold problems such as poor quality of journalists and anti-free press activities in many countries. The Western media again would be generally not interested in African affairs and would predominantly view the continent by the means of stereotypical images. The authors argue further that this negative view of the West on Africa as well as the generalisation of African countries as underdeveloped, chaotic and corrupt would contribute to the meagre foreign direct investment inflows to the African continent. Though this analysis has certainly its merits, it still needs to be proofed that the NEPAD plan of action can change this picture convincing the Western media that *"...there is indeed a message of hope to be found in Africa"* (p. 240).

Part four deals with the objectives of NEPAD, particularly with the issues of conflict resolution and good governance. The chapter starts with arguments for an African Renaissance by summarising socio-economic and legal obstacles for development and the concept of renaissance. The authors present NEPAD as a new, genuine African initiative on Africa's development which is however disputed. Other authors do not see NEPAD as a complete novelty but as a follower of other ambitious African plans, such as the Lagos Plan of Action (1980) or the Abuja Treaty (1991). The Abuja Treaty for instance included like NEPAD sanctions against states that persistently violate the protection of human rights and pledged for policy accountability. However, none of the various plans for Africa's development was realised so that one might even agree with the critical analysis of Taylor stating that *"NEPAD "...can be seen as recycled elements from previous plans and statements that have marked out Africa's post-independence experience at regular intervals."*[2] Since the authors of the reviewed book do discuss previous African action programmes, their statement that NEPAD is different to

---

2 Taylor, Ian (2006:31): "Partnership through Accommodation? African Development Initiatives and Universal Policy Prescriptions", in: Brüntrup, M.; Melber, H.; Taylor, I. (eds.): Africa, Regional Cooperation and the World Market. Uppsala: Nordiska Afrikainstitutet, pp. 9-39.

other African action plans since it is "*a comprehensive strategic development and action programme, which is originated in Africa as an African initiative , rather than one that is foreign driven"* (p. 271-2) cannot be reconstructed. NEPAD's goals largely address the problems that have already been identified by the international community, African intellectuals and foreign expatriates and that fit into the agenda of donor countries and international organisation: conflict prevention and resolution, human development and poverty alleviation, as well as increased investment, diversified business activities and sustainable economic growth.

Part five discusses the implementation of NEPAD. It is stated that determined effort of African leaders, the proper implementation of the African Peer Review Mechanism (a self-monitoring mechanism which offers the chance to increase good governance on the continent by internal supervision), economic growth, improved educational structures and an active role of civil society actors are necessary to make NEPAD successful. However, the problems to meet these challenges are numerous, such as the resistance of African leaders to commit themselves to good governance, manifold capacity problems, lack of financial resources, a weak civil society and powerless parliaments, poor economic performance, and open or smouldering conflicts in many African countries. *Part Five* discusses the building blocks and problems of implementing the NEPAD strategy by analysing the role of single stakeholders such as governments and bureaucrats, big businesses and entrepreneurs and human capital institutions. The problem of brain drain is discussed, the political and economic influence of the Diaspora as well as the need for African intellectuals to return to Africa. However, practical policies to reverse the ongoing brain drain, such as allowing dual citizenships, are hardly successful when living and working conditions in Africa are not significantly improving.

The last Chapter discusses the future of NEPAD by summarising the previous Chapters and by highlighting the challenges for implementing such an extensive political and socio-economic renewal strategy for the continent. The UK Plan of Action (2003) and the UK-sponsored Commission for Africa (2004) support the ideals and proposals of NEPAD and plead for increased development aid, debt release and increased investment in infrastructure and basic civil services. Also the new EU-Africa Strategy (2005), which is committed to the UN Millennium Development Goals, supports NEPAD and its focus towards regional bodies and sub-regional bodies such as the African Union. In fact, there are manifold plans of action to restore economic growth and socio-economic development in Africa – however the problem remains that not enough is done.

It is a major weakness of the book that it does not discuss how the lofty ideas of NEPAD have been realised yet and what needs to be done to improve the protection of human rights, to cut the power of the elites, and to promote a more equal development. The questions which African stakeholders have the potential and interest to renew the continent as well as the issue of socio-economic interests, dependencies and frictions between African countries are also not sufficiently addressed. The problem of the "African Renaissance" in the context of NEPAD is that, different to the renaissances of the history, it is not a wave of progress and prosperity induced by African powers but largely an intellectual construct. The fact that most of the 15 authors of the book are South Africans might be another indication that NEPAD and the African Renaissance are still largely South African elite projects.

Mareike Meyn, Bremen

OECD, African Development Bank; *African Economic Outlook 2005/2006*, 2006, Paris: OECD/African Development Bank, ISBN: 92-64-02243-0/41 2006 01 1 P, pages: 588.

The collaborative work of the OECD Development Centre and the African Development Bank resulted in the fifth edition of the *African Economic Outlook*. The African Economic Outlooks aim to provide on an annual basis an objective analysis of economic and social developments and prospects to policy makers, private sector operators, experts in donor organisations. Major conclusions of these reports are that Africa's economic performance, while showing considerable variation among countries, continues to follow the positive trend observed in recent years. This has to do with favourable growth conditions, the settlement of some civil conflicts, with the continuation of reforms, and with the improvement of some external conditions. However, in some countries human security is severely affected by weak governance, ongoing conflicts, and extreme poverty. The new edition looks carefully at the recent economic situation of African countries, examines progress that has been made with reforms, identifies problems hindering a more rapid development and the realisation of the Millennium Development Goals (MDGs), and gives a short-term forecast.

"Part One: Overview" provides a general overview regarding the international environment, the macroeconomic performance in Africa, a progress report on the MDGs, information on governance and political issues, and a summarising analysis of the state of transport infrastructure with particular reference to financing aspects.

In the *African Economic Outlook 2003/2004* an important key policy issue for Africa – energy sector policies, and the interaction of energy and poverty issues – was discussed. In the *African Economic Outlook 2004/2005* the key issue discussed was the finance of small and medium-sized enterprises. In this annual report for 2005/2006, the crucial issues of transport infrastructure development in Africa are analysed and referred to by country cases.

"Part Two: Country Studies" examines 30 countries covering 86 per cent of Africa's population and 90 per cent of the continent's economic output. The recent economic developments, the macroeconomic policies, and the structural issues are reviewed with respect to transport infrastructure but also with respect to political and social developments.

The country developments with regards to transport infrastructure are useful, allowing for comparisons of policies and approaches. In the *African Economic Outlook 2003/2004* only 22 country reports were included, and in the *African Economic Outlook 2004/2005* an enlarged sample of 29 countries was considered. We find comprehensive studies of the situation and the prospects of these countries that aim to promote a deeper understanding of the challenges and the opportunities facing these selected African economies.

This enlargement of the countries reviewed is an important improvement to the *African Economic Outlook*. However, it can be criticised that Zimbabwe is again excluded from the coverage. Though the current political and economic crisis in Zimbabwe complicates an analysis, the inclusion of the country into the report would have been important for the international community, other African countries, and also for Zimbabwe. Still, the country cases covered are more or less representative for the five African regions, and it is good that the number of countries evaluated increases. However, it would have been better to keep the chosen selection of countries from the first three issues also in subsequent reports, and not to delete any country that was already considered in a previous *African Economic Outlook*.

"Part Three: Statistical Annex" is valuable as it does not only cover basic indicators but also demographic and poverty indicators, social indicators, and political indicators. The political indicators, such as the Corruption Perception Index, the Political Troubles Index, the Softening of the Regime Index, and the Hardening of the Regime Index, are especially important for assessing the real foundation of and the support for reforms. The methodology for all indicators is carefully explained.

The editors consider their publication as a joint project by the African Development Bank and the OECD Development Centre. The idea is to combine the expertise and experience of the OECD when working on the OECD Economic Outlook and in the OECD Development Assistance Committee (DAC) with the expertise and insight of the African Development Bank when working on policies, projects and programmes in African countries. An explicit aim is the analysis of trends and short-term evolution for selected African countries by using a unique analytical model. The common framework includes a forecasting exercise for the current and the following two years by using a simple macroeconomic model, together with an analysis of the social and political situation in Africa. Mainly policymakers, donor agents, academic experts, and business people should benefit from these analyses.

A problem with the *African Economic Outlook* is the fact that the background to the modelling work is not explained more deeply. Reference is made to a standard macroeconomic model called "Africalook" (see the short description of the prediction models in the *African Economic Outlook* 2001/2002, p. 19). It is argued that the specific structural peculiarities of countries are also considered in this framework. The modelling used by the OECD Economic Outlook to forecast world demand and price developments for non-traditional imports and exports that are particularly relevant for African countries are included in the form of case studies.

It must be considered as problematic that there are two competing reports coming from Africa, the *African Development Report* from the African Development Bank (AfDB) and the *Economic Report on Africa* from the United Nations Economic Commission for Africa (UNECA). Therefore, it is not yet clear what the comparative advantage of a joint project of the OECD and the AfDB is since the other reports also present analyses, forecasts, regional economic profiles, and country studies. Both the *African Development Report* of the AfDB and the *Economic Report on Africa* of the UNECA are very rich in analysis, in forecasts, in policy recommendations, and in informative regional economic profiles and country cases. However, compared with earlier reports of the *African Economic Outlook*, the messages have become much clearer: the focus on international assistance for Africa is stronger, the comparability of country cases has been strengthened, and the relevance of the presented data and of the forecasts has improved. The specific policy field covered – in this report transport infrastructure - is important, and the information presented are useful for analysis and projections. It may however be important to work on a clear division of labour between these three institutions in order to improve the reports as instruments for policy assessment and reform.

The *African Economic Outlook* can play a great role if the new trends in global development cooperation are reflected in the context of the annual theme and specific country cases. The *African Economic Outlook* 2005/2006 highlights the development cooperation issues in general and with regards to transport infrastructure development. The country cases highlight now, more than in the past, the development assistance aspects of important policies and sectors, but also the aid dependency and debt problems of African countries, and the objectives, means and strategies for improving aid assistance. This is where the core competence of the OECD policy departments, the OECD/DAC forums, and of the OECD Development Centre really lies; and this vast knowledge should be utilised properly. With respect to the image and the logo of *the African Economic Outlook* it should be made clearer that the *African Economic Outlook* is a joint OECD-African project, with considerable African input.

Karl Wohlmuth, Bremen

Tony Addison et al (eds.); *Debt Relief for Poor Countries*, 2004, New York: Palgrave Macmillan, in association with UNU/WIDER, ISBN: 1-4039-3495-9, pages: xix + 318.

The book under review is divided into three parts. Part one is about debt relief evaluation, part two deals with growth effects of debt relief and part three is concerned with poverty effects of debt relief.

The introductory chapter, written by Addison, Hansen and Trap, gives a summary of the three parts of the volume. In chapter 2, the article written by Nissanke and Ferrarini investigates debt dynamics of Heavily Indebted Poor Countries (HIPCs) and shows one of the essential external conditions responsible for the prolonged debt crisis facing HIPCs. After discussing the fundamental features of the intertemporal borrowing model, together with other models, the authors of this chapter examined the conditions of debt sustainability and assessed other vital ideas of debt dynamics. On the basis of these concepts, the conditions that make debt burden unsustainable and debt forgiveness a rational choice for creditors and debtors are analysed. Considering the above-mentioned theoretical expositions, empirical proof of the evolvement of debt dynamics since the 1980s in selected HIPCs are analysed, the effectiveness of ex-post debt relief is presented and the HIPC facilities and their weaknesses have are explored. Finally, a proposal for using a state contingent debt contract as an ex-ante debt relief system as opposed to the existing ex-post facilities is suggested.

In chapter 3, the focus of the article written by Birdsall, Claessens and Diwan is on grasping the dynamics responsible for the findings that aid and debt relief have not been particularly aimed at countries with suitable policies and institutions. To do so, the authors empirically analysed donor and creditor behaviour. They found out that more indebted countries have received more net transfers.

Raising questions of the effect of HIPC programmes on governance and as to whether these programmes improve incentives towards better adjustment and reform policies, Berthelemy, in chapter 4, put forward the argument that HIPC programmes include many components that may improve governance and policy-making.

Based on Easterly's framework, Addison and Rahman present in chapter 5 a description of how time horizons shorten and how this causes debt problems. The authors asserted that the core cause of debt problems is a continuous decrease in institutions, both formal and informal.

In order to evaluate the potential effects of debt reduction on the economic performance of HIPCs, Pattillo, Poirson and Ricci in chapter 6 have used empirical findings that show the relation between debt and growth. The results indicate that the HIPC debt relief initiative may contribute to enhancements in per capita growth for countries that are assigned to get assistance.

In chapter 7, Hansen assessed the joint effect of debt service payments and aid flows on growth and investment using a sample of 50 countries that contains both HIPCs and non-HIPCs. The findings of the analysis indicate a small positive effect of the decrease in debt service payments on growth and investment.

In order to see if the effect of foreign indebtedness on economic growth differs across two separate groups of countries (while one group contains countries that are eligible to participate in the HIPC Initiative, the other group consists of countries that have not yet qualified for the HIPC programme), Chowdhury, in chapter 8, took a sample of 60 countries. The result shows that the economic problem affecting the HIPC group due to foreign indebtedness does not only exist within this group.

The article written by Birgsten, Levin and Persson in chapter 9 estimates the effect of the HIPC debt relief on Least Developed Countries like Zambia and Tanzania. In Zambia, the GDP growth rate increased by around 0.2 percentage units when debt relief was combined with increased public spending and lower taxation. In the case of Tanzania, it was observed that real GDP increased by 0.2 percentage units when debt relief, increased public spending and the accumulation of human capital were combined.

With the aim of reviewing how much public expenditure on social sectors considers to be effective instrument for poverty reduction and human development, Heltberg, Simler and Tarp, in chapter 10, found (in the case of Mozambique) the extent to which public services are fairly progressive. Further, it is found that easing fiscal barriers through debt relief leads to major poverty-reducing effects and makes it easier for poor people to get access to public services.

To study the possible effects of increased narrow and broad targeting of education expenditures funded by debt relief savings, Dabla-Norris, Matovu and Wade, in chapter 11, developed a dynamic general equilibrium model. They found that a considerable advantage can be gained by countries with less than a universal basic education by increased subsidies for primary and secondary education. Further, the authors found that the growth effects of transfers to poor households are meaningful. Therefore, targeting transfers towards education can be used as a relevant policy instrument for obtaining growth and equity.

In chapter 12, Morrissey assessed the ways in which aid, in the form of debt relief, can have an effect on policy reform. The core argument in this chapter is that the goal of poverty reduction can be effectively developed by pro-poor expenditures.

Containing important information on debt relief evaluation and growth and poverty effects of debt relief under HIPCs, the book is informative in the sense that it makes readers clear why HIPC debt relief alone cannot be an answer to the development questions of most poor countries.

Temesgen Kifle, Brisbane

Mennachem Katz et al.; *Lifting the Oil Curse: Improving Petroleum Revenue Management in Sub-Saharan Africa*, 2004, IMF (International Monetary Fund), ISBN: 1-58906-317-1, pages: vii + 65.

This book is based on the outcome of a workshop on macroeconomic policies and good governance in sub-Saharan African oil exporting countries. The conference was sponsored by the Africa Department of the IMF and the Oil and Gas Unit of the World Bank.

The book is made up of nine chapters and starts with a brief introduction by outlining the problems associated with the dependence on natural resources and the peculiar nature of oil economy. This is followed by recommendations aimed at improving the general development indicators in the region. Chapter two focuses on the development performance of oil producing countries in the region. The analysis reveals that non-oil producing countries, in terms of per capita GDP, life expectancy, literacy rate and human capital development perform better than oil producing states in the subregion. Chapter three focuses on the relationship between macroeconomic volatility and oil price trends. The authors further analyse empirically, the dependency of governments' budgets on oil price volatility.

In chapter four, two operational rules for fiscal policies management are deliberated. The first rule is the "Rule-based fiscal policy", which is a stabilisation instrument aimed at insulating the economy from the short-term volatility of oil price and revenue. The second rule is the "Possible fiscal rule" representing three different budget designing instruments required in the face of prevailing oil price changes. These rules are deemed to guide policy makers in the formulation of fiscal policy in order to reduce the negative impact of oil revenue volatility as well as ensuring transparency and credibility of the system.

In chapter five, the authors raise the importance of advancing policies that centre on persistence surpluses and the accumulation of assets. They further analyse how to build and use accumulated savings. Chapter six considers the variety of exchange rate arrangements in oil-exporting countries. The authors argue that the exchange rate policy must take into consideration the monetary policy and institutional framework under which it operates. Changes in international prices tend to destabilise the macroeconomic conditions of any oil producing country.

The structure of the institutions that may oversee the oil sector as well as the role of oil companies are discussed in chapter seven. The importance of stable legal structures towards the oil sector is stressed. In this context, defining the ownership of the natural resources is deemed to be very important. According to the authors, a successful institutional arrangement always tries to distinguish between strategic and tactical issues in the oil sector management. The national oil companies on the other hand, should be given the commercial freedom to concentrate on efficiency.

In chapter eight, the issue of transparency and accountability in the oil sector is extensively discussed. The authors provide an explicit explanation of the three major channels through which government revenues flow in oil producing countries. How each channel can be controlled and account for to the public is further analysed.

Transparency is not only necessary to avoid corruption and the waste of public resources but also to allow the authorities to plan for the future as well as to strengthen the political culture that allows a democratic debate on fiscal policy and spending priorities.

Chapter nine concludes with recommendations and action plans for further work.

Osmund Osinachi Uzor, Bremen

Sanjeev Gupta et al (eds.) ; *Helping Countries Develop – The Role of Fiscal Policy*, 2004, Washington: International Monetary Fund, ISBN: 1-58906-381-X, pages: xi + 528.

The book is an impressive ensemble of articles that translate the current stand of research on fiscal policy impacts in developed countries into the impacts fiscal policy may have in developing countries. Most of the authors are employees of the IMF's Fiscal Affairs Department. The book is a collection of already published articles and working papers and comprises 19 papers in five sections.

The first section discusses macroeconomic policy in developing countries and in particular its impact on economic growth. The section consists of six papers that discuss (1) the role of the fiscal stance; (2) the expenditure composition and budget financing on economic growth; (3) the relationship between the duration of fiscal adjustment processes and expenditure composition in developing countries; (4) the channels through which fiscal consolidation effects growth; (5) the relationship between debt, growth and public investment and a framework for debt sustainability; and (6) fiscal stability in the West African Economic and Monetary Union (UEMOA).

The sixth paper studies the experience of UEMOA with a fiscal rule introduced in 1999 on the belief that it would contribute to higher economic growth by leaving more room for private investment. The authors find that terms of trade problems had negative effects on growth and budget deficits in most of the countries. Moreover, a poor economic policy contributed to high budget deficits and slow growth. The paper suggests to monitoring public wages and other expenditure more closely and focusing on the quality of fiscal adjustment with special attention on poverty alleviation.

The second section on public spending and the Millennium Development Goals consists of four papers that discuss the effectiveness of public spending on education, health care and poverty alleviation as well as user payments for basic education and the efficiency of government expenditure in Africa. The last issue is addressed by a paper that investigates the efficiency of spending on education and health in 37 African countries. The results show that the spending efficiency is low compared to other regions. The inefficiency is manifested in high government wages and intra-sectoral allocations within the social sector. These misallocations include low expenditures for primary education, high expenditures for curative health care, and allocations that mainly benefit higher income groups. The authors conclude that development goals can only be reached by allocating exciting recourses more efficiently.

The third section includes three papers that discuss issues of tax revenues and economic growth. The papers consider the development of revenues in the light of trade liberalisation and reforms of tax systems in developing countries, and the aid dependency in aid-receiving countries. One paper takes the case of Ethiopia to discuss the social impact of tax reforms. Ethiopia introduced a value added tax (VAT) to replace its sales tax. The authors conclude that the VAT is less progressive than the sales tax. Therefore, the tax reform had an adverse impact on the poorest. However, since tax revenues were used for health and primary education expenditures, the poorest enjoyed a net benefit.

The fourth section discusses issues of international aid and fiscal policy. The authors deal with the macro- and microeconomic effects of increased aid as a result of the Millennium Development Goals, the volatility of aid flows and the resulting volatility of spending in aid-dependent countries, and food aid.

The final section addresses two special topics: the fiscal consequences of armed conflicts and terrorism, and a comparison of public expenditure management systems in different African countries. The paper on African expenditure management systems compares management systems in Anglophone and Francophone African countries. The authors find that the Francophone countries have some advantages in expenditure management systems, which did however not result in a better aggregate expenditure control. It is concluded that not the management systems in place but the proper operation of these systems is the problematic. Thus, budget discipline and accountability are essential.

The book comprises theoretically and empirically high quality papers on fiscal policy problems. It is written in a consistent and concentrated style. A special highlight is the statistical data on fiscal policy that cannot easily be found.

Tobias Knedlik, Halle (Saale)

Natalia Dinello (Principal Political Scientist), Lyn Squire (President of the Global Development Network) (eds.); *Globalization and Equity, Perspectives from the Developing World*, Washington DC: Edward Elgar 2005, ISBN 1 84376 884 4, pages: 253.

The basic motivation behind publishing the book is obviously the attempt to let researchers from developing and transition economies speak about globalisation and the effects it has on equity. Seven regions are covered in the book - the Commonwealth of Independent States, Central and Eastern Europe, East Asia, Latin America, The Middle East and North Africa, South Asia, and Sub-Saharan Africa. It is therefore part of the exercise that broad regions rather than country cases are covered. However, this is a problem from an analytical and strategic point of view as these broad areas cover quite diverse economies with quite diverging developments within and between countries. The selection of these regions has also to do with the network activities and partners of the Global Development Network (GDN) of the editors. The GDN aims to promote research capacity in the regions of developing and transition economies and to bridge research and policy areas. The view is that local knowledge and local research capacity matter in order to increase the benefits from globalisation in these countries. World Bank research on globalisation seems to be the basis of the used methodology, especially the view that we are in the third wave of globalisation since 1980 (with increasing direct investment to non-OECD countries and increasing immigration to OECD countries). Since studies on the effects of globalisation show quite different results (in theory and in empirical testing), the book aims to "cut through the confusion" in the literature. Three arguments on the beneficial aspects of globalisation are considered as central reference points to all studies in the book. First, trade and global economic integration have positive effects on poverty alleviation; second, globalisation reduces poverty without increasing inequality; and third, globalisation contributes to economic and political stability. As there are also critical studies on the impacts of globalisation that find out exactly the opposite effects on the equity implications of globalisation, the study sets out to "cut through the confusion" between the two "schools of thought".

When some studies show a positive influence of globalisation on poverty, inequality and stability and other studies come to the conclusion that globalisation has had adverse effects on these issues, the types and methodologies of theoretical approaches and empirical measurement are at stake. To make progress in clearing this controversy, it is often argued that these different outcomes are caused by the different definitions of the term globalisation and by different "faces" of the concept of globalisation (a positive and a normative one).

The authors are motivated by the huge task to "cut through this confusion", and to show what specific result of globalisation is due to the definition and due the type of measurement undertaken.

After the introduction, the editors present a preview, a big picture of trends, including definitions, conceptualisation, evidence, and consensus on globalisation. Globalisation is defined as a process covering economic integration, economic liberalisation and political openness. Equity is defined as the scope of opportunities for disadvantaged members of the society and as the capacities of a society to reduce inequalities and to improve the chances for its least advantaged members. However, for operational reasons, rather narrow definitions are used when comparing the effects of globalisation on countries. In fact, neither the preview nor the case studies use definitions and interpretations of "globalisation" consistently. The distinction between "globalisers" and "non-globalisers" (as based on arbitrary criteria of trade and direct investment integration) among the seven regions leads to rather absurd results (pp. 5-7). Thus, the Commonwealth of Independent States (CIS) appears to be a "globalised region", although the case study presented later in the book shows that the region has hardly liberalised its economies and lacks the institutional capacities to benefit from the globalisation trend.

This confusion continues: for all the regions covered we find no relation between the three globalisation indexes economic integration, economic liberalisation and political openness. The editors go on to investigate the assumptions that globalisation is associated with increasing inequity among regions and countries and within regions and countries. Some tests of this relationship are done and it is observed that globalisation can be associated with convergence of incomes among regions and countries. However, the type of link of growth with economic integration and political openness is important. Thus, the political, social and economic frame condition matter for establishing links that generate a positive globalisation-growth link. Concerning globalisation and increasing inequity within regions and countries, the editors come up with an interesting result: transition processes as causes of increasing inequity dominate globalisation as a factor on inequity. However, all these results are very sensitive to the used methodology. Confirmed is again the relevance of the "between-countries part of inequality" relative to the "within-countries part of inequality" in explaining the negative trend of worldwide inequality in times of globalisation. Combining the results on growth, globalisation and inequality, it can then be assumed that poverty is declining fastest in the "globalising economies". However, domestic policy matters so that observed differences between countries - with the same levels of integration and liberalisation and similar rates of growth - may occur in terms of poverty measures.

The book continues – methodologically quite differently – with case studies of the seven regions. It is not attempted by the authors to bring together the knowledge and the research results of the individual authors, and to synthesise the results for the purpose of presenting policy conclusions. It would have however been good to come up with an attempt to solve the puzzle, and to cut through the confusion. In a "Cairo Consensus" (referring to the conference site), reflecting on the research results that were presented, a consensus on two points seems to have emerged. First, globalisation as a form of a deeper integration into the world economy has the potential to overcome the fate of marginalisation. Second, the countries and regions have to address the policy issues arising from globalisation on the basis of effective strategies, taking into account the context-specific domestic circumstances. Consensus 1, saying that globalisation is an opportunity that needs to be actively captured, is according to the editors based on the results of the various contributions. The same applies to consensus 2, stating that globalisation benefits can be captured by strong institutions, good economic policies, innovation and competitiveness, and by appropriate social safety nets. However, such a consensus can easily be achieved considering its general formulation but is lost when it comes to concrete terms of assessing opportunities and policies, when presenting concrete definitions and measures, when making clear the trade-offs between policy alternatives, and when trying to balance economic and social policy issues.

Moreover, the analyses by regions do not address all the issues mentioned in the introduction and in the preview chapter. For the *Arab region* we find an elaborate measurement of the link between globalisation and inequality based on the World Bank distinction of three waves of globalisation. However, it is questionable that these indicators for the third wave of globalisation are suitable for the Arab region and an analysis of the necessary public action to come to home grown, country-specific responses to the globalisation trend are missing. Still, the methodology is interesting, combing direct and indirect methods to determine the effect of globalisation on equity. The interesting result is that the (positive) effects are smaller than for other regions.

The analysis on *Sub-Saharan Africa* is different. Some general observations on the situation and some recommendations for policy changes are given, and an assessment of the extent of Africa's global economic integration is presented. The way the issues are presented shows the tendency of over-generalisation. Sub-Saharan Africa is quite diverse, and at the aggregate "regional level" it is not possible to get much insight into required economic policy reforms and feasible public policy choices to react to globalisation. Neither the link between globalisation and equity nor the necessary policy packages are presented more deeply.

For *East Asia* we find a review of regional developments, a presentation of volatility and vulnerability arising from globalisation and also an analysis of the social effects of globalisation. It is argued that balanced policy packages are necessary for sustaining growth and global integration and to provide a social safety net for the weakest groups of the society (based on a clear definition of socially tolerable levels of inequality). The analysis, which is however also at a highly aggregated level, shows that rather deep policy changes are needed to maintain the momentum of growth and to reap future benefits of global integration.

For *South Asia*, the link between growth, poverty and inequality is explored, but not the link of globalisation with equity. It is argued that some economic liberalisation took place in the region but that much more has to be done to liberalise the markets. Public action is required at a large scale to avoid that worst case-scenarios occur, like popular revolts against liberalisation and globalisation (despite its limited extent so far). The case study shows that in South Asia a high degree of political openness and a rather low level of economic integration are associated with a more balanced policy approach towards economic and social development in times of globalisation.

The study on *The Commonwealth of Independent States (CIS)* is interesting as it distinguishes between an active and a passive form of globalisation.

"Active globalisation" is built on strong institutions and governments and on a public policy that allows the population to benefit from liberalisation (as it is the case in East and Central Europe and in China). The "passive globalisation" liberalises and integrates markets without giving public leadership and guidance and without public policy action. Additionally, the problem of natural resource abundance in the region aggravates the problems, weakening governance and public institutions. However, also some resource-poor economies in the region show weak institutions and cannot benefit from globalisation but suffer from corruption and rent seeking, which lead to negative effects on equity. Crucial for strengthening the link between globalisation and equity is therefore "institutional quality" as poor contract enforcement in such countries prevents the development of more sophisticated/more complex export goods. The balance between export and import-substitution sectors is seriously distorted. It is also emphasised that minimal social safety institutions and labour market reforms are necessary to reap the benefits from globalisation. Again, because of the lack of data no systematic analysis of the link between globalisation and equity can be done. The authors refer to the need to do more research in order to get deeper insights into the various forms of globalisation and their impacts on equity. The argument that in countries with weak institutions the form of "passive globalisation" (understood as simply liberalising markets) is not bad for the people because the new freedom can be exploited cannot be accepted as a serious argument since it has been proven that such a narrow liberalisation has negative effects on the weakest segments of population. Only the well-off people can benefit from capital and trade liberalisation.

The analysis on *Eastern and Central Europe* has - according to the author - to distinguish between periods of transitional contraction and periods of subsequent growth. Handling the problems of growing inequality and poverty after a transitional recession is a challenge for policymakers. Policymakers can be supported by globalisation because the trend requires clear policy decisions and the need to make clear tradeoffs between efficiency and equity. The study on this region is however much more concerned with transformation than with globalisation. The link between globalisation and equity is only loosely considered.

The analysis on *Latin America* is directly concerned with the effects of globalisation on Latin American economies, by reviewing the empirical results on the mobility of goods, the factor mobility, and movements of technology. Moreover, the macroeconomic dimensions of globalisation are analysed. The problem is that the results do not give clear answers and policy prescriptions. One needs to look carefully at context-specific factors that limit policy choices in times of globalisation. There is a great demand for additional researches on the links between globalisation and equity.

Regrettably, the book does not come up with conclusions and policy implications. The readers are left with quite different approaches and results but the authors are not able to realise the ambitious objectives of the study. Nonetheless, the publication is informative and shows that much more work is needed on the issues of "globalisation" and "equity".

Karl Wohlmuth, Bremen

William G. Moseley, Ikubolajeh B. Logan (eds.); *African Environment and Development: Rhetoric, Programs, Realities*, 2004, Hants: Ashgate, ISBN: 0-7546-3904-5, pages: xii + 244.

This book explores, in three parts, the relationship between ecology and development in Sub-Saharan African nations with particular reference to Western and Southern African states.

Part I, consisting of the chapters 2-4, is a discussion on the mainstream environmental discourse, environmental policies and poverty alleviation in Africa. In chapter 2, Ikubolajeh Logan criticizes Sustainable Development (SD), as being more about promoting Western hegemony over African resource management than being about community participation. According to Logan, SD enforces neo-liberal policies on African nations based on a set of perceived 'truisms', which are derived from the misconceived mainstream thought that poverty results in environmental degradation. Logan argues that the root causes for environmental degradation is not poverty but rather a discriminatory international trade system which has marginalized the Third World and especially African nations. As an alternative to SD, Logan proposes Environmental Security (ES), a model essentially concerned with empowering local communities (introducing local governance) and strengthening national and local institutional capacity. Logan argues that ES seeks to incorporate local value systems and, unlike SD, local political and social institutions are given prominence in environmental and resource management. At this juncture, Logan identifies some drawbacks of the ES model and attempts to find solutions which generally fall short of his objective to redeem ES as a more viable approach than SD. Although Logan identifies strong and independent political institutions, willingness of African governments to devolve power, and independent financial resources for local environment development as cornerstones for the success of the ES model, he fails to draw a scenario upon which these factors can be satisfied.

In chapter 3 William G. Moseley follows Logan's argument: The vicious cycle between poverty and environmental degradation paradigm is a mechanism through which the West, in the name of poverty alleviation, maintains its policy domination over Africa. As a case in point Moseley takes the case of the Southern Mali cotton industry, an industry catering to the ever increasing demands of the international markets. Moseley argues that poverty and environmental degradation has been internalized by the Government of Mali through the support of the Mali cotton industry, international institutions, and the French-owned cotton companies in Mali. The result has been the expansion of the cotton industry which, with its current unsustainable production techniques, is causing an irreversible damage to the environment (mainly soil degradation). From these conclusions, Moseley takes a giant leap and makes the conclusion that international capitalism is to be blamed for local land degradation as it creates a chain of domination that assures increasing production at the cost of the environment.

Chapter 4, by Paul Laris, broadly outlines the negative impact of fire fighting policy and misguided environmental policies on Mali's ecology during the past century (1900-1991). Laris argues that indigenous burning practices in Mali, although not perceived as beneficial by the international community and the government, was an effective mechanism of environmental management based on experience developed over centuries. However, the fact that indigenous experiences were ignored resulted in environmental degradation.

Part II, composed of Chapters 5-8, is a discussion of the impacts of state and supra-state policies and actions on local environments and living conditions. Chapter 5, by Emmanuel Kreike, deals with the environmental impacts of Apartheid Wars in the southern African region. This chapter focuses on adverse effects of forced human movement and disruption of daily human activities (such as production) on the environment. Chapter 6, by Jim Bingen, details pest management practices in Francophone Africa with special reference to cotton production. Bingen argues that pesticide and inorganic fertilizer used in Francophone Africa has caused environmental degradation. Bingen proposes a set of measures to overcome these problems: (i) adopting non-chemical pest management practices and introduce scientific pesticide spraying techniques, which limit pest pressure while at the same time increase the number of beneficial insects; (ii) enforcing regulation on import and export of harmful pesticides and chemical agents; and (iii) opening a channel of communication with farmers to initiate and facilitate the learning process.

In Chapter 7 Stephen R. Wooten deals with commercial horticultural production in rural Mali. Wooten describes the livelihood diversification strategy adapted by the Bamana-speaking community in Mali who have diversified their farming activities to the production of vegetable and fruits catered to the local markets. Wooten stresses the importance and effectiveness of locally tailored developments, in which local people identify and mobilize site specific assets and institutions. Chapter 8, by Mirjam de Bruijin and Han van Dijk, discusses the political hierarchies and the associated rules that maintain and govern the hierarchy of the Fulbe in central Mali by trying to understand ecological (environmental) dynamics. They explain the increasing marginalization of the Fulbe due to a number of political developments including favorable policy for sedentary agriculture and the decentralization process (agriculture gaining importance towards pastoralism), and their influence as electorates in elections (less accessible for community council elections).

Part III, composing of the chapters 9-11, is concerned with global environmental politics and conservation in Africa. Chapter 9, by Jennifer E. Coffman, discusses the successes and failures of community-based wildlife resource management within the context of Kenya's Maasailand.. In Chapter 10 Rachel B. DeMotts traces the evolution of community-based conservation policies in Namibia as a case that is widely considered to be a model for the inclusion of local communities in conservation initiatives. DeMotts cites decentralization, aid and training as key components for the success of the conservation initiatives. In contrast, DeMotts takes the case of South Africa which approaches conservation efforts based on its trans-frontier conservation initiatives (including territories in Botswana, Lesotho, Tanzania), which allow only limited community participation. Chapter 11, by Phia Steyn, deals with three aspects: (i) the development of the oil industry in Nigeria and the associated environmental problems caused by oil production with particular reference to Ogoniland; (ii) the environmental and human rights struggle of Ken Saro-Wiwa and the Ogoni in the 1990s; and (iii) the environment-related political impact of the struggle against Shell International. The Ogoni launched a struggle in 1990 with the objective to convince Shell and the Nigerian government to pay closer attention to air, water and land pollution and to communal development programmes. The situation escalated in 1995, resulting in the trail and execution of Saro-Wiwa and eight of his combatants. Moreover,, Shell International also faced an international crises caused by a strong opposition to its decision to decommission its Brent Spar storage and loading buoy in the North Sea and to dispose it into the sea These events in 1995 led Shell International to conduct an internal investigation which fundamentally changed the views of the company towards environmental concerns. In subsequent years, Shell International has contributed significantly, both in financial and technical terms, to environmental development programs.

The ideological source of this book is the dependency theory and world system schools whose mainstream thought is the belief that Third World nations are in a perpetual state of domination by a world economic system created and maintained by Western nations. Two major points come to mind when we analyze this line of thought. First, whether this system of domination exists or not is a matter of opinion and not a fact. Second, assuming this ideology is correct, these schools (as well as this book) fail to present a holistic and pragmatic approach that can substitute neo-liberalism as the ideology behind the world economic system.

Isaac Hailemariam Desta, Bremen

Peter Gibbon, Stefano Ponte; *Trading Down. Africa, Value Chains, and the Global Economy,* 2006, Philadelphia: Temple University Press, ISBN: 1-59213-368-1, pages: xviii + 251.

The authors bring together the global value chain analysis, the convention theory and work on Africa's marginalisation in the global economy to elaborate Africa's option to scale-up production and services and to enter new, dynamic markets. Since the global value chain analysis has been mainly applied for developed countries and has neglected external dynamics, such as the international trading environment and barriers to enter markets, it is a novelty to combine these issues in an African context. The case studies comprise agricultural and labour-intensive products in eight African countries, thus mirroring the predominant production structure on the continent.

Chapter 1 examines recent transformations in global trade and corporation strategies. It is stated that retail activities have internationalised in the past decades and that retailers have concentrated – with few groups dominating world retail sales. The lead firms tend to outsource manufacturing activities but retain control over branding, supply chain management and innovations. Economies of scale are crucial to benefit from oligopolistic rents and African producers inability to realise economies of scale is one reason for their marginalisation in global value chains.

Chapter 2 investigates how African countries are affected by the new international trade regime. It is argued that liberalisation, privatisation and deregulation have changed the individual politically negotiated regulation system into a uniform judicially-regulated system. This also applies to the new trade regime of WTO where developing countries largely have to comply with the conditions defined by industrialised countries. African countries are differently affected by global business strategies, depending on their level of import liberalisation and the reduction of national regulation systems. Since many African countries had to liberalise their markets and to abandon national regulations systems, there are often no frameworks for managing price falls or price vulnerabilities of agricultural products, leaving the countries vulnerable to shocks. The lack of domestic regulation and ineffective quality systems have also lead to increased price competition and a deteriorating quality of products, which again resulted in lower prices obtained in international markets.

The *Chapters 3 to 6* deal in detail with an examination of the global value chain analysis and convention theory approaches to assess Africa's role in the global economy. The main features, governance and upgrading options in the global value chain are presented in Chapter 3. The rise of buyer-driven chains, the relationship between lead firms and first-tier suppliers, and between first- and second-tier suppliers are analysed in Chapter 4. Entry-barriers for African companies, which are, if at all, second-tier suppliers, are numerous and also a result of the failure of public institutions in African countries to negotiate accessible entry barriers. Chapter 5 discusses the entry barriers for first- and second-tier suppliers and reasons for the exclusion of African suppliers on the example of different products such as cocoa, coffee, cotton or citrus fruits. To remain competitive, first-tier suppliers constantly need to improve their functions and performance. This again, also implies higher requirements for Africa-based second-tier suppliers. The performance and upgrading options for selected commodity markets in different African countries are analysed, concluding that they look rather bleak. Economic coordination by private business elites as well as increased capacities of African states is regarded as crucial factors to improve the position of African companies in global value chains.

Chapter 6 discusses quality standards, conventions and governance in global value chains. It is stated that quality control and certification of products and processes are becoming more and more important. Control over where and how quality is generated along the chain has become crucial for governing the chain. Compliance with pre-determined quality requirements is a prerequisite for suppliers. Often, lead firms do not control whether their suppliers comply with products and processing requirements but outsource the supervision of quality control to agents, which undertake according certification and codification procedures, thus transferring the cost of quality control to suppliers.

The last *Chapter 7* summarises the main findings of the book and draws policy recommendations. According to the title of the book the authors state that most African countries have been "trading down", thus becoming more and more marginalised in the global trading system. An improved African position in global value chains would rely on increased foreign direct investment and, in the long run, enhanced capacities of public institutions and companies. In the short run, "trading down" could even be used as a practical business strategy: Successful African companies have focused on natural endowments as well as on economies of scale and specialisation. According to the authors, such a strategy, which has been successfully applied by companies from different African countries, would be promising considering increasing demand for resource-intensive mass products from big developing countries like China and India.

The publication by Gibbon and Ponte is a very interesting analysis of African countries' comparative advantages in today's trading environment. It is comprehensibly demonstrated that African countries were to a large extent not able to manage the challenges arising from new trade regimes, domestic market liberalisation and tightening demands of participating in global value chains. In their analysis of the increasing dominance of buyer-driven governed global value chains and their implications for African countries the authors do not pretend to know an all-embracing solution. However, by studying the reasons for African countries' marginalisation in the globalisation process in-depth, Gibbon and Ponte offer a valuable contribution to the discussion of how to improve African countries position in global value chains.

Mareike Meyn, Bremen

Philippe Burger; *Sustainable Fiscal Policy and Economic Stability*, 2003, Cheltenham, Northampton: Edward Elgar, ISBN: 1-84376-632-9, pages: 232 + viii.

The concept of sustainability is widely referred to in today's politics and economics. What is often missing in the discussion is a clear and stringent evaluation of the concept and the derivation of policy rules which are not only based on the broad and often misunderstood buzzword of sustainability but on the economic concept of sustainability. This gap is filled by Philippe Burger's book: "Sustainable Fiscal Policy and Economic Stability". The book employs the economic concept of sustainability to develop fiscal policy rules that are not exclusively focused on reducing budget deficits but consider the impact of fiscal policy on the private sector and overall economic stability.

After the introductory section, the author starts by spelling out the issue of fiscal sustainability in detail. Besides the expression of the mainstream theory, saying that governments should run sufficiently large primary surpluses in order to ensure a positive or zero net worth of the government, the author describes the origin of the concept and related theoretical concepts such as the Ricardian equivalence, the crowding out of private investment, and the 'golden rule' derived from growth theory. As two important assumptions underlying mainstream theory Burger identifies the inability of policy to influence real interest rates and the real growth rate in the long run. Only for these reasons governments need to run primary surpluses if real interest rates exceed real growth rates.

In the remaining chapters the author bases his analysis on a different and new approach of fiscal sustainability: a sectoral approach. The very basic idea behind this approach is that a primary deficit in one sector of the economy (e.g. the public sector) is necessarily reflected by a surplus in another sector (e.g. the private sector). Thus, the approach by Burger links the public budget to the budget of the private sector. The macroeconomic "general balance framework" allows to conclude that a shift of deficits from one sector to another may also lead to a shift of unsustainability between the sectors. A separate section discusses the relevance of uncertainty and expectations of agents, and concludes that changes in fiscal policy may have long run effects caused by sectoral linkages. Additionally, Burger concludes that the interrelation of uncertainty, sustainability and instability is high and so far underestimated in the literature.

Thus, Burger discusses these interrelations and their implications in chapter six. The main implication is that unsustainability caused by uncertainty may lead to economic instability. This transmission affects all sectors depending on their specific financial position. In times of economic instability and private sector financial unsustainability, Burger sees a potential role of the public sector to bear 'unsustainability', whereby the private sector temporarily shifts uncertainty to the public sector, so as to give the private sector time and financial space to adjust its financial position and balance sheets. The book then considers various scenarios under which fiscal sustainability should be restored or established and derives a menu of policy rules for fiscal policy. It turns out that the implications of the Burger-approach to fiscal sustainability are far more differentiated than the implication of the mainstream theory. This is in particular the case since Burger considers the effects of government actions on other sectors. Therefore, governments should ensure that their efforts to create fiscal sustainability do not lead to unsustainability of the financial positions of private agents, which, in turn, may cause instability. The book does not argue to simply relax the strict rule of mainstream theory but provides a set of rules for specific environments, which have not been considered yet. Therefore, the book steps on virgin soil in economics and contributes decisively to the extension of economic theory. Moreover, the author does not restrict its analysis to economic theory but derives detailed policy implication. Policy makers should consider the derived set of rules as helpful advice. The book is easily readable and the author amazes the reader by interesting and delighting citations of historical economists. The book should not only be used by policy makers and economic researchers but also by students interested in macroeconomic issues.

Tobias Knedlik, Halle (Saale)

Sanjeev Gupta; Robert Powell, Yongzheng Yang; *Macroeconomic Challenges of Scaling Up Aid to Africa. A Checklist for Practitioners,* 2006, Washington D.C.: IMF, ISBN: 1-58906-505-0, pages: 68.

The increase of aid to Africa in order to reach the Millennium Development Goals implies several macroeconomic changes and challenges for African countries, such as the possibility of an appreciation of the exchange rate which in turn would increase the prices for export goods as it has been recently the case in Malawi and Zambia. This IMF publication aims to address macroeconomic challenges of increased aid flows and debt relief by explaining the effects of absorbed and spent aid in order to help African policymakers to develop different scenarios of how higher capital inflows impact on their economy and what policies would need to be undertaken to use the aid efficiently.

The first Chapter gives an overview of the macroeconomic effects of increased aid to Africa, emphasising that these effects depend on the level and time period of increased aid, the form of additional finance (project aid, grants or loans), the sectors in which the resources will be spent and the absorption ability of these sectors as well as on governance capabilities of public institutions. Other relevant factors to assess scaling-up scenarios relate to the impact of increased aid inflows on exchange rate and growth, on private investment (crowding in or crowding out?), on the impact of public resources (such as expenditures and tax efficiency) and on monetary policy management. These are the key issues that need to be considered for preparing scaling-up scenarios and which are discussed in the single Chapters of the book.

The policy recommendations drawn are general, emphasising that the assumptions must be tailored to the specific circumstances in the according countries. However, the authors present five primary guidelines for scaling up aid. 1) To avoid the risk of an appreciated exchange rate and Dutch Disease effects it is recommended to increase the absorption ability by channelling aid flows to public infrastructure and to the consumption of domestic goods. 2) A gradual increase in aid is likely to be easier absorbed than a sharp increase and should be directed towards activities that boost economic growth in the short to medium run such as improved infrastructure. 3) Good governance and the fight against corruption are crucial to spend increased aid effectively. 4) To prevent aid dependency and to mobilise domestic efforts to increase public revenues it is recommended to address weaknesses in revenue administration and to increase institutional capacities. 5) The government does not only need to implement scaling-up policies but also to ensure a smooth transition period when aid is scaled down.

With their report the authors point out relevant factors that need to be evaluated to ensure the efficient use of increased aid and its positive impact on economic growth and socio-economic development. This important discussion was neglected by African action plans of the past years (NEPAD, UK Commission for Africa) which plead for more aid without discussing the absorption ability of countries and the possible destructive macroeconomic consequences.

Mareike Meyn, Bremen

David Fielding (ed.); *Macroeconomic Policy in the Franc Zone*, 2005, New York: Palgrave, ISBN: 1-4039-4952-2, pages: xix + 213.

The publication is a compendium of papers originated from a research project at the World Institute for Development Economics Research at the United Nations University (UNU-WIDER). Besides an introductory section the book consists of three parts, each of them consisting of two to three papers written by economic scholars. Most of the contributions focus on monetary and exchange rate policy or their respective implications on the real sphere of the economy.

The first part of the book consists of three articles and is titled "Convergence in the Franc Zone and Optimum Currency Area Theory". The first paper is an empirical analysis of the convergence progress in the UEMOA (Economic and Monetary Union of West Africa), which includes Senegal, Mali, Niger, Guinea-Bissau, Burkina Faso, Côte D'Ivoire, Togo, and Benin. Using econometric techniques the article finds that nominal convergence is low in the region, which is in contrast to earlier literature that focussed on descriptive statistics only. The second paper addresses the problem of divergent macroeconomic shocks, which have been identified as hindrances for optimum currency areas in the literature. The paper takes a purely econometric approach in search for homogeneity of macro developments among countries of UEMOA-CEMAC (Central African Economic and Monetary Community). The authors find some homogeneity among countries, which is, however, not in line with the country groupings in UEMOA or CEMAC. The third paper compares shocks in the Franc Zone with shocks of neighbouring countries in order to identify specifics of macroeconomic shocks under a fixed exchange rate regime. One important finding of the empirically analysis is that that monetary shocks are more important in explaining macroeconomic shocks in CEMAC than in UEMOA, but even more important in explaining macroeconomic shocks outside the Franc Zone.

The second part of the book is titled "The Positive and Normative Analysis of Monetary and Exchange Rate Policy" and consists of two papers. The first article deals with the credit policy of the Central Bank of West African

States. The econometric analyses have different outcomes. While there is some evidence for interest rate policy responding to inflationary pressure, other estimations cannot confirm these findings. What can be concluded from further analyses is that interest policy is geared to the UEOMA Zone and not to the country level. The second paper addresses the interest rate reaction function of the Central Bank of West African States. It seems that the Central Bank largely follows interest rate signal from France and the European Central Bank. Other significant factors are inflation rates, output gap, claims on governments, and foreign exchange reserves.

The third part of the book links monetary and exchange rate policy with poverty issues. The first of three papers of this section highlights the effects of the 1994 devaluation on growth and poverty. It concludes that in the pre-devaluation period savings increased due to expected real wage declines. After the devaluation, real wages declined in line with savings. As a result, poverty largely increased after the devaluation. Only in the agricultural sector profited from increased crop prices. The second article takes a longer term perspective and looks at determinants of growth in the region. It is found that standard models of growth theory fit in this specific case. The final paper asks how monetary policy affects the poor. The authors look at food and non-food prices finding co-integration among countries but also short-term asymmetries. It turns out that poor households bear the most of price volatility. The authors conclude that while monetary policy cannot target specific commodities prices, other measures, such as price subsidies, could help to reduce price volatility of basic commodities.

The book is especially enlightening since it does not try to favour on theoretical concept over another but discusses monetary end exchange rate policy issues from the perspective of a certain school of monetary theory developed for industrial countries. This is done in a highly sophisticated manner. The widely used econometric techniques are presented in a way that also allow non-technical economists and policy-makers to gain a deep inside in the macroeconomic development of the Franc Zone.

Tobias Knedlik, Halle (Saale)

United Nations Industrial Development Organization (UNIDO), ***Industrial Development Report 2004. Industrialization, Environment and the Millennium Development Goals in Sub-Saharan Africa. The new frontier in the fight against poverty*****, 2004, Vienna: UNIDO, ISBN: 92-1-106428-7, pages: xxiv + 215.**

The Industrial Development Report 2004 is divided into eight chapters focussing from different perspectives on the role of industrial development in Sub-Saharan Africa for reaching the Millennium Development Goals. Chapter one analyses economic constraints African countries face for industrial development and poverty reduction and sums up the challenges the continent faces. The second Chapter recaptures African countries' industrial experiences since independence, from import substitution over structural adjustment to today's challenges and opportunities, such as China's accession to the WTO. The third Chapter investigates the achievements and shortcomings of the Poverty Reduction Strategy Papers (the successor of the Structural Adjustment Programmes), focussing on the role the private sector plays currently in these programmes and drawing policy recommendations for a better inclusion of the private sector in national and international poverty reduction strategies. Chapter four discusses the relevance of sustainability for industrial development and the stage of environmental degradation in Africa. The role of new technologies for a sustained use of natural resources and innovative industrial policies are the topic of Chapter five while Chapter six focuses on recommendations for policy-maker in Africa to promote industrial development. The Chapters seven and eight review industrial trends and countries performances worldwide. One sub-chapter focuses on the competitive industrial performance of African economies since 2000 and compares it with the performance of other developing countries and transition economies.

The Report is highly informative, connecting competently the topics industrial development and poverty reduction. Both topics are discussed extensively and are analysed in the African context. Boxes that contain successful examples of industrialisation, technology transfer and poverty reduction in African countries as well as a statistical annex ranking the world's economies according to different industrial indicators add to the informative character of this UNIDO Report.

Mareike Meyn, Bremen

Martin Grandes, Nicolas Pinaud, N. (eds.); *Reducing Capital Cost in Southern Africa*, 2005, Paris: OECD Publishing, ISBN: 92-64-01401-2, pages: 204.

The book, which is partly a result of a OECD project, is subdivided into three analytical parts consisting of two to three papers each and including some comments and reviews of selected papers.

After 18 pages of forewords, acknowledgements, prefaces, etc. the book starts with an analysis of country risk, capital costs and growth in South Africa. The first paper is about "South African Country Risk: Backdrop and Challenges Ahead" and provides a broad overview over post-1994 developments on fiscal and monetary policy. It concludes that there is little danger of returning to an unsustainable policy path. The second paper takes the perspective of businesses and highlights what South African companies have done to minimise capital costs. The in-depth analysis shows that South African companies find their way to lower capital costs by going global. The high domestic capital costs are avoided by the listing of South African companies at international stock exchanges. The paper identifies high real interest rates as important reason for high capital costs in South Africa.

The second part of the book is titled "Monetary Policy, Country Risk and the Bond Market in South Africa" and consists of three papers. The first paper aims to determine the currency risk premium of South Africa, which is part of the total risk premium. One interesting finding is that the change of the monetary policy framework to inflation targeting resulted in increased currency risk premium. The high volatility of the Rand leads to the conclusion that currency mismatch and liability dollarization should be avoided in order to minimise the effects of volatility on the real sphere of the economy. The second paper tackles the issue of sovereign spreads. High spreads do not only indicate higher vulnerability of the economy but are also a source of higher capital costs. The reduction of South Africa's Net Open Forward Position (liabilities of the Reserve Bank due to interventions at forward currency markets) has led to decreased spreads. Further closing of the spread is expected from higher economic growth rates and increased foreign exchange reserves. The third paper of the section focuses on the bond market and describes current developments as well as the differences of the South African market compared to other markets, like the trade in only few corporate bonds and the dominance of loans in financing corporations.

The third part of the book widens the angle from the South African to the southern African perspective and looks at financial integration. The first paper links financial development in the region with economic growth. The paper finds strong evidence for a positive relationship between these two variables in the region and confirms the "demand following finance" hypothesis. The final paper of the book discusses the role of foreign finance in the southern African region. It shows the composition of capital flows from outside and within the region and discusses their respective impact on investment. The paper finds that while capital flows from outside the region are mainly focused on South Africa, South Africa is a source of capital into the region. The authors expect this development to continue and mention also potential problems occurring from South African FDI into the region.

The publication combines very different methodological approaches. While some papers by policy-makers and business practitioners provide stylised facts and broad outlooks, other papers written by economists provide a detailed theoretical and empirical analysis. It is, therefore the combination of very different contributions that readers may find interesting.

Tobias Knedlik, Halle (Saale)

Book Notes

Sven Wunder; *Oil Wealth and the Fate of the Forest, A Comparative Study of Eight Tropical Countries*, London And New York: Routledge Explorations In Environmental Economics 2003, ISBN 0-415-27867-8, pages: 432.

The book is a study of eight tropical oil-producing countries and examines the links between oil exploration, trade, macroeconomic conditions and economic policies affecting the environment and especially the fate of the forests in these countries. The main argument that is discussed and empirically tested is that oil revenues can – in some cases and under specific conditions - protect tropical forests indirectly. There are positive and negative factors that are associated with oil production (oil revenues) and economic development (macroeconomic effects), land use for agriculture and agricultural exports (urbanisation) and forest cover.

After the introduction we find chapters on the malady of prosperity, on the impacts of oil wealth on forests, on defining and measuring changing forest conditions, on country cases (Gabon, Venezuela, Cameroon, Ecuador, Papua New Guinea, on Mexico, Nigeria, and Indonesia) and a concluding chapter.

The core hypothesis of the book that oil and mineral wealth may help to protect forests - through macroeconomic impacts, sector-specific changes, land use and infrastructure effects - is more or less substantiated by the analytical study and the country cases.

The results are important. Agricultural production, agricultural exports and the required land use were held back in various countries by exploiting the oil wealth. Therefore, the positive indirect effects on the forests can be substantiated since people have not cleared land for agricultural production. Also, the international competitiveness of agriculture is affected by oil exports and by the related exchange rate effects which has other indirect (positive or negative) impacts on forests. Additionally, urbanisation effects from oil production may have helped to protect the forests to some extent. And there are many more indirect effects analysed in the book, with negative and positive effects on the forest cover. The author presents a kind of balance of all these effects.

The study is interesting as Resource Curse and Dutch Disease phenomena and issues are related in a thought-provoking manner to environmental concerns. Though there must not be a resource curse for the environment such effects can occur, especially at the local level where the oil production takes place and where land is cleared for the oil sector infrastructure. The book may give some hints for the protection of forests in oil-producing countries. Also for local resource control in oil-producing countries the book gives policy recommendations. The author is based at the Center for International Forestry Research (CIFOR), Indonesia.

Karl Wohlmuth, Bremen

Matthias Basedau/Andreas Mehler (eds.), Resource Politics in Sub-Saharan Africa, African Studies No. 14, Hamburg: The Institute of African Affairs/Institut für Afrika-Kunde (IAK), 2005, ISBN: 0947- 4900 and ISBN 3-928049-91-7, pages: 355.

The book contains several studies on the issue of the "resource curse" and on the role of oil for Africa's development. After the introduction, there is a part on "General Regional Aspects" highlighting the concept of the resource curse and Africa's dependence on oil. In the following part "Country Cases" we find cases of countries endowed with oil and diamonds such as Angola, Botswana, Congo Republic, Democratic Republic of Congo, Gabon, Nigeria (Niger Delta Region), Sao Tomé E Principe, and Sierra Leone). In the next part on "Prevention and Cooperation" there are two studies on trans-boundary cooperation (on water resources in the SADC region) and on international cooperation (on preventing illegal diamonds trade). In the final part "Conclusions" there is an analytical summary on resource politics beyond the resource curse. Although most of the country cases have to do with oil, also diamonds production and resource trade play a role in the studies on Angola, Sierra Leone and Botswana. Water comes in as a scarce resource in the context of the SADC region.

It is important that, once again, the issue of resource curse is taken up in the Sub-Saharan African context. The increasing relevance of oil in Africa and the involvement of new actors like China, India and Malaysia give such studies additional importance. It is also good that the editors consider diamonds and its role in illegal arms trade and in conflict escalation, and that so-called successful cases of avoiding a resource curse such as Botswana are questioned by giving a critical evaluation of the portrayed successes. An additional advantage of the book is its interdisciplinary dimension. Economists, political scientists and social scientists worked on these important issues with different methodological approaches.

The introductory and concluding studies by the editor and author Basedau are very informative. He organised the book around the topic of a political management strategy for avoiding a resource curse. In the country cases we find however quite different approaches of resources politics - historical analyses, strategic conflict analyses, political systems and development analyses, political economy analyses, economic analyses, etc.. This implies that the introduction and conclusions are very important and Basedau takes up the issues and summarises open questions of the various contributions by emphasising strongly the context of resource politics with respect to country-specific factors and resource-specific factors. Both, the country-specific factors and the resource-specific factors, matter and their interactions are important for the overall outcome in terms of resource politics in order to avoid a resource curse. Dynamic interplays and interactions of such factors have to be studied carefully. Based on the country cases and other literature Basedau comes to the conclusion that a methodological challenge is required to analyse these issues. Basedau favours a dynamic analysis of interplays and interactions in resource politics by showing that various possible outcomes have to be considered, depending on the situation before and after resource exploitation. In such a dynamic analysis, resource-specific conditions (resource type, geographic location, technical mode of exploitation, degree of dependence and abundance, revenue management, and involved actors) have to be considered side by side with country-specific conditions (level of development, relations between groups, behaviour of actors, level of violence, political system, and externalities). New research strategies and new analyses on intervention and prevention strategies are recommended.

Recapitulating, we can say that a good introductory and concluding chapter back up the quite heterogeneous case studies in an appropriate manner. Unfortunately, not all case studies went the way, as proposed by Basedau to analyse the context factors and the dynamic interplay of factors in detail. However, the editors did a good job by presenting the research results at this preliminary stage. Much more research and new methodological approaches are needed to come to better results - towards a deeper understanding of the resource curse in Africa and towards more developmental resource politics.

Karl Wohlmuth, Bremen

Tony Addison, Alan Roe (eds.); *Fiscal Policy for Development – Poverty, Reconstruction and Growth*, 2004, Basingstoke and New York: Palgrave Macmillan, in association with UNU/WIDER, ISBN: 1-4039-3480-0, pages: xviii + 336.

Fiscal policy is critical for the development of poor countries. Public spending on pro-poor services and public goods must be increased, tax revenues must be mobilized and macro-economic stabilization must be achieved without inhibiting growth, poverty reduction and post-conflict reconstruction. Fiscal crisis is common in developing countries – and seems to be present all the time in many African countries.

The book reports the results of a major UNU-WIDER research project that re-examines these complex and difficult issues. It is organized according to five major themes. Three of them relate to the high-level issues mentioned in the book's subtitle: economic growth, poverty reduction and post-conflict reconstruction. The other two topics are cross-cutting issues, namely the overall (macroeconomic) framework for fiscal policy and the management of public expenditures and revenues.

The book consists of thirteen chapters. After the introduction, chapter 2 ("The macroeconomics of fiscal policy in developing countries") analyses the general question of the circumstances under which fiscal and external deficits of low-income countries can be considered sustainable. Chapter 3 ("Fiscal policy design in low-income countries") suggests that real policy choice remains heavily circumscribed by the legacy of past fiscal laxity. In chapter 4 ("Fiscal effects of aid") the authors stress that foreign aid complicates governments' fiscal management. Chapter 5 ("Changing approaches to public expenditure management in low-income aid-dependent countries") deals with new approaches set by economists, management scientists and politicians with respect to revitalizing polices of the public sector. Chapter 6 explains the design of tax systems in developing countries in the light of tax reform advices it frequently given by the IMF and other multilateral donors.

Chapter 7 assesses recent theoretical and empirical evidence on the impact of fiscal policy – taxes, public expenditures and budget deficits - on growth in the long run. Chapter 8 supports the links between fiscal policy and private investment, a crucial issue given the importance of such investment to growth. Chapter 9 provides an overview of the manner in which poverty effects can be quantified and assessed. Chapter 10 is a discussion of the measurements of service delivery, a topic highly relevant to poverty reduction, given the widespread concern that too little public services benefit the poor. Evidence shows that lack of funds for education and health impedes social service delivery as it is the case in Ghana, Uganda and Tanzania.

Chapter 11 gives specific example on the impact of poor service delivery in India.

Chapter 12 notes that civil wars in low-income countries have done great damage to state institutions and especially fiscal institutions, e.g. in Angola and Liberia. Chapter 13 ("Fiscal policy, conflict and reconstruction in Burundi and Rwanda") focuses on the specific situation of Burundi and Rwanda. Both countries are extremely poor and have been plagued by ethnic conflicts. The author notes that the relationship between military expenditures and conflict is complex; however, fiscal policy must move beyond the conventional goals of macro-economic adjustment and stabilization and must pay more attention to poverty alleviation.

Achim Gutowski, Bremen

Peter Batchelor, Kees Kingma (eds.); *Demilitarisation and Peace-Building in Southern Africa – National and Regional Experiences*, 2004, Vol. II, The International Political Economy of new Regionalisms Series, Aldershot: Ashgate, ISBN: 0-7546-3315-2, pages: xvi + 237.

The *International Political Economy of New Regionalisms Series* presents innovative analyses of a range of novel regional relations and institutions. Going beyond established, formal, interstate economic organizations, the series provides interdisciplinary and international research and debate.

This volume is one of the products of a collaborative regional research project which started in 1997. Over a period of nearly four years, researchers attempted to understand and explain the processes and experiences of demilitarisation and peace-building in Southern Africa. The book presents overall conclusions concerning national and regional peace-building efforts and processes in the region as well as a number of studies on peace-building efforts and experiences in Southern Africa. Some chapters deal with specific countries (e.g. Mozambique, Zimbabwe, Angola, and South Africa), others with cross-cutting issues or regional peace-building issues.

The book has seven chapters. Chapter I examines the relationship between the state, conflict parties and violence in Mozambique since the end of civil war in 1992. Chapter II describes how the issues of land availability and land redistributions in Zimbabwe have been connected with war and conflicts since the arrival of white settlers a century ago. Chapter III provides an analysis of Angola's civil war since the early 1960s.

Chapter IV deals with the issues of internal security, law and order, particularly in Mozambique and South Africa. Chapter V analyses the challenges and problems involved with the privatisation of security services.

Chapter VI presents a study looking at potential intra- and interstate conflicts for environmental resources in Southern Africa on the example of water. Chapter VII assesses the effects peace organizations on processes of demilitarisation and peace-building in the region.

Achim Gutowski, Bremen

UNIDO (United Nations Industrial Development Organization), Industrial Development Report 2005. Capability Building for Catching-Up. Historical, Empirical and Policy Dimensions, Vienna: UNIDO, 2005, ISBN: 92-1-106431-7, pages: 178.

UNCTAD (United Nations Conference On Trade And Development), The Least Developed Countries Report 2004. Linking International Trade with Poverty Reduction, New York and Geneva: UNCTAD, 2004, ISBN 92-1-112581-2, ISSN: 0257-7550, pages: 362.

UNCTAD (United Nations Conference On Trade And Development), The Least Developed Countries Report 2006. Developing Productive Capacities, New York and Geneva: UNCTAD, 2006, ISBN 92-1-112701-7, ISSN 0257-7550, pages: 352.

These three reports are essential reading for development experts from donor organisations and research institutions. These annual and bi-annual reports combine analysis of developments with reporting on specific sector and country developments and give policy recommendations for the design of national and international strategies.

The Industrial Development Report 2005 asks how to narrow the gap in income and productivity between developed and developing countries and what strategies and policies are suitable for capacity building in developing countries to catch up. Building of institutions and of framework conditions for catching up processes are important aspects of the report. Structural adjustments towards catching-up and capacity building are discussed in various chapters. In Section One we find analyses of the critical factors for catching-up, of the role of knowledge systems, and of the issues and policies for innovation and standard setting. Building capacities in food safety is a concrete example of capacity building and innovation in industrial development processes that is discussed in detail. Section Two reviews world industry trends, including the measurement of industrial development trends and of performance indicators for industrial development. The report is useful as it analyses two important issues – catching up and capability building for catching up. This helps to understand the existence of different levels of industrial development. The Least Developed Countries Reports are useful as the group of now 50 Least Developed Countries (LDCs) is targeted bi-annually in analysis, giving important policy recommendations.

The Least Developed Countries Report 2004 assesses the links between trade and poverty reduction by observing that trade expansion does not contribute sufficiently to poverty alleviation in Least Developed Countries (LDCs). LDCs are exposed to economic shocks and suffer from a high degree of vulnerability in terms of changes in demand, price, and terms of trade, but also with respect to policy changes and changes of financial conditions and technological flows. It therefore makes sense to analyse the relationship between international trade and poverty changes in great detail and to discuss policies how to make trade more pro-poor. In order to reduce poverty by trade the linkages between trade and growth have to be strengthened. More inclusive types of production, trade and growth are needed and have to be developed. Civil conflicts play also a role in the weak link between trade, growth and poverty reduction and are discussed in detail. National and international strategies how to link trade in a more effective way to growth and poverty reduction are presented. A whole menu of policies is proposed for action at national and international levels. However, the realisation of such a package needs a coherent international development policy framework which does not exist yet. The tables in the Annex are useful as they allow to compare socio-economic structures and developments of the world's LDCs.

The Least Developed Countries Report 2006 focuses on the concept of "developing productive capacities". Productive capacities are defined as productive resources, entrepreneurial capabilities and production linkages. On this basis, the capacity of a country to produce goods and services is determined. Productive capacities are also preconditions for growth and poverty alleviation. The capacity to produce goods and services in an internationally competitive manner may be added as a fourth dimension of productive capacity. Not only the traditional factors like technical progress, capital accumulation and structural change are discussed but also the constraints to develop productive services like poor infrastructure, weak institutions and low and fluctuating demand for products. The increasing gap (or imbalance) between the accumulation of capital and technological development on the one side and the growth of the labour force on the other side is addressed as a major policy issue for LDCs. The report recommends a "paradigm shift" towards the development of productive capacity meaning that all policies and interventions have to be subordinated to this concept of development.

The Least Developed Countries Report 2006 is rich on strategies for developing productive capacities. It is emphasised that a focus on the real economy is more relevant than any financial or macroeconomic target. This paradigm shift has implications for policies and strategies. Agriculture (as an important source of domestic demand) comes up as the main sector for sustainable growth and poverty alleviation. Relying on rather old development theories (from Adam Smith on the effects of the division of labour to the more recent schools of thought on agricultural demand-led industrialisation and development) the report combines this inherited knowledge about sustainable growth with new development thinking on governance reforms. However, it does not become clear why all these attempts to stimulate growth have failed to restructure the economies of LDCs so far.

These reports are however relevant since they remind the international public that alternative development strategies should be discussed and are feasible if certain international and national preconditions are given.

Karl Wohlmuth, Bremen

Contemporary Perspectives on Developing Societies Series, Aldershot: Ashgate.

The *Contemporary Perspectives on Development Society Series* was founded to serve as an outlet for policy relevant research. Books published in this series provide an analysis of issues relevant to the Third World and its efforts to improve participation in the global economy. The series is published since 1997 with a special focus on Africa. The objective is to examine why post-colonial African states continue to struggle with respect to their political and economic development with no clear and generalisable framework to explain how the different governments – whether military of civilian – make decisions. Moreover, research focuses on broad socio-economic topics like political instability, environmental problems, famine, and hunger, desertification, rent-seeking and intra-state conflicts across the African continent. Two studies of the series are noted below:

Kelechi A. Kalu (ed.); *Agenda Setting and Public Policy in Africa*, 2004, Contemporary Perspectives on Developing Societies Series, Aldershot: Ashgate, ISBN: 0-7546-3708-5, pages: xiv + 267.

This book is a collaborative project by African scholars whose task is to identify and explain causes of poor governance in African states. It is divided into two sections. Section I includes five chapters that deal with general theoretical and analytical issues of policy making and management in Africa.

Section II is devoted to six chapters on specific countries and issues of public policy in Africa. The following contributions are included: Social factors relating to maternal mortality in Sub-Saharan Africa, the role of women in Africa's economic development, privatisation policy, challenges and prospects for sustainable development in Nigeria, Cameroon's economic policy and forest loss, the role of NGOs in public policy in Africa, and finally constitutionalism as public policy in Africa.

According to the author, Africa's problems can be categorized by the absence of people-driven, participatory institutional reforms, violence, suffocation of civil society and abject poverty. Productive transition and transformation in Africa must be based on a democratic culture and system of governance that holds leaders and citizens accountable for their public and private actions. Moreover, constitutions and participatory constitution-making are crucial for the success of African states. Africa's only alternative is to ensure effective, competent and sustainable public policy which is relevant to the continent, its issues and citizens.

Achim Gutowski, Bremen

Giovanni Andrea Cornia (ed.), Inequality, Growth and Poverty in an Era of Liberalization and Globalization, UNU-WIDER Studies In Development Economics, Oxford et al.: Oxford University Press, 2004, ISBN 0-19-927141-0, pages: 438.

UNU-WIDER, WIDER Perspectives on Global Development, Studies in Development Economics and Policy, (Contributors: Anthony B. Atkinson, Kaushik Basu, Jagdish N. Bhagwati, Douglass C. North, Dani Rodrik, Frances Stewart, Joseph E. Stiglitz, Jeffrey G. Williamson), Houndmills et al.: Palgrave Macmillan, 2005, ISBN: 1-4039-9631-8, pages: 259.

The contributions of these two books contain important research outcomes of UNU-WIDER and highlight important issues of global development and recent changes of globalisation and liberalisation trends; particularly on inequality, poverty and growth.

The first book (edited by G. A. Cornia) is a collection of papers on income distribution trends, on traditional and new factors in the world economy causing inequality, and on important country cases showing inequality changes in the context of globalisation and liberalisation. The main findings are highlighted in such a way that preliminary policy conclusions can be drawn. The changes in inequality that took place in the 1980s are discussed as well as old and new sources of inequality and the impacts of the inequality changes on poverty and growth. The editor and the authors analyse whether liberalisation and globalisation have changed the inequality of incomes and with it poverty and growth conditions. Important is the differentiation between traditional/structural and more recent/policy-based factors leading to the recent surge of inequality. The new factors (skills-biased technical change and specific policies towards stabilisation, liberalisation and globalisation) are regarded as more important than traditional factors. Capital account liberalisation has – according to the studies in the book - a strong role in recent changes of inequality, followed by domestic financial liberalisation, labour market deregulation, and tax reforms whereas trade liberalisation has ambiguous effects. There is, according to the authors, still need for research on the effects of the Washington Consensus since these policies can be far-reaching. Therefore the conclusions presented are rather tentative, and much more research on the framework of such policies in times of globalisation is recommended. The authors do not propose a consistent alternative reform package. Only implicitly we find some policy reform recommendations (although they may already be part of augmented Washington Consensus as discussed widely in contrast to the prescriptions of the traditional Washington Consensus). The implicit policy recommendations include more cautious policies on capital account liberalisation, more balanced fiscal policy reforms, coherent redistribution and social safety policies, new growth policies, and cautious labour market reforms. The country cases on India, Venezuela, Turkey, South Africa and Thailand cover some emerging economies. However, it does not become clear what the rationale of this country selection is.

The second book (edited by UNU-WIDER) is a collection of the WIDER Annual Lectures on important topics of global development that takes place since 1997. Because of the important topics of the lectures and the prominent role of the speakers and authors this is a useful collection of essays on global development and development economics. The lectures include essays on 1) institutional economics; 2) the road towards a Post-Washington Consensus; 3) trends in inequality; 4) globalisation and global Governance; 5) horizontal inequalities and conflict prevention; 6) winners and losers of two centuries of globalisation; 7) global labour standards and local freedoms; and 7) thoughts on new growth strategies.

Both books contain relevant information and useful analyses and the current globalisation trends give a key reference frame for the respective analyses. Both books highlight social and economic issues and necessary policy and governance reforms. Most important is the fact that the editors and contributors have in mind how to shape globalisation and development processes towards the benefit of the people, especially the poor. The books analyse specific policy issues in a clear but sophisticated way. UNU-WIDER should continue to work on such important researches and policy-oriented analyses.

Karl Wohlmuth, Bremen

Okon Akiba (ed.); *Constitutionalism and Society in Africa*, 2004, Contemporary Perspectives on Developing Societies Series, Aldershot: Ashgate, ISBN: 0-7546-3640-2, pages: ix + 172.

The purpose of the book is to analyse the evolving constellation of structural forces and their effects on the momentum of constitutionalism in Africa. It is intended to offer fresh insights in the way people conceive, reflect and study the problems of political transformation and constitutional government.

The structure of the book reflects the attempt to penetrate and explore the central ideas about how constitutionalism might be used to address problems of stability and institution building. The topics of the four sections are as follows: I. Rediscovering traditional African democratic values of government (chapters on the impact of imperialism on constitutional thought in Africa and on the study of constitutional government in Africa); II. Citizenship and civil liberties (chapters on citizens and citizenship and the historic origins and contemporary relevance of the great lakes crisis); III. Ethnicity and pluralism (chapters on ethnicity, the state and constitutionalism in Africa, and constitutionalism and political inclusion in Nigeria); IV. Democratic control of the military and civil conflict (chapters on how to bring military and security agencies under democratic control, and democratisation and its challenges).

At the time of independence, all African governments had constitutions that provided basics for the protection of human rights, separation of powers, and independent judiciary including parliamentary bodies. But within a few years the constitutions were abrogated, nullified or rewritten. In some cases single party structures were established, with the excuse that the Western constitutional model cannot be successful in Africa.

Finally, the issues raised in the book suggest many aspects for further research. Information concerning national experiences, including similarities and differences in political reform, could form the basis for new models on comparative constitutionalism.

Achim Gutowski, Bremen

Barry Carin, Angela Wood (eds.); *Accountability of the International Monetary Fund*, 2005, Voices in Development Management Series, Aldershot: Ashgate, ISBN: 0-7546-4523-1, pages: xi + 124.

The *Voices in Development Management Series* provides a forum in which grass root organisations and development practitioners can present their views perspectives together with academic development experts. Many volumes of the series contain debates between various voices in development. It permits the suite of neglected development issues such as gender issues and transport or the micro-credit needs of low income communities to receive appropriate public services.

The growing influence of the IMF and its role in developing countries has generated demands for greater accountability. In this context, accountability means that decisions should be predictable, equitable, based on sound judgement, follow clear and enforceable procedures, and have clear mechanisms for reporting. Decision makers should be responsible to clearly defined authorities.

The object of the book is to inform about the debate on the decision making processes of the IMF and the Fund's accountability towards various stakeholders. Questions arise such as: Who should be involved in the decision making process? How should decisions be taken? Who should be hold responsible for decisions? What degree of transparency should be applied for taken decisions? Against what criteria should decision makers be judged? What mechanisms and processes are needed to hold decision makers responsible?

The book consists of four chapters. Chapter I deals with the inability of developing countries executive directors to adequately represent the views of their constituency members at the board of the IMF. Chapter II explores what options and limitations exist for parliamentarians to become more involved in the executive board of the IMF, which is the legitimate link between civil society and governments. Chapter III argues that the demand for greater accountability arises from the perceived failure of the IMF to learn from its policy shortcomings and to take account of the risks to full policy implementation. Chapter IV discusses the problem that staff and management of the IMF are not held directly accountable for the outcomes of their policy advices.

Achim Gutowski, Bremen

Africa Institute of South Africa; *Africa Insight,* Pretoria: Africa Institute of South Africa, ISSN: 0256-2804.

The quarterly distributed journal *Africa Insight* by the Africa Institute of South Africa (AISA) provides insight into changes in Africa and covers various topics and countries. A book note section and a section about new publications from the AISA can be found in each journal. Noted is here one issue

Issue 2004, June-September, Vol. 34, no. 2/3, pages: 108.

This issue of the journal deals with the topic of sustainable development in Africa discussing among others the elections in Ghana, how South Africans understand democracy and Christianity, the Niger delta problem in Nigeria, the road from war to peace and national reconstruction in DR Congo, women's participation in subsidised housing in South Africa, higher education transformation in South Africa, public school education in South Africa, competitive intelligence in South Africa, the future of biotechnology, and sub-regional security efforts in Africa.

Africa Institute of South Africa; *The Social Sciences in South Africa since 1994 – Disciplinary and Transdisciplinary Areas of Study*, 2004, Research Paper no. 74, F. Hendricks (ed.), Pretoria: Africa Institute of South Africa, ISBN: 0-7983-0185-6, pages: 106.

The twelve papers collected in this volume deal with the subject of the enduring problems of intellectual freedom and institutional autonomy in South Africa. It tries to highlight some of the changes that have taken place in South African social sciences since 1994.

Its first object is to ensure that the voice of black scholars is heard. Secondly, the chapters demonstrate how little changed in academia in the decade of democracy and how high the challenges are that remain. Chapter 2 provides an overview of the evolvement of strengths and weaknesses of sociology since 1994. Chapter 3 outlines the contours of research in the field of rural and agrarian studies and links it to the politics of knowledge production in a racially divided society. White monopoly over the production of knowledge remains firmly entrenched as an abiding legacy of apartheid. Chapter 4 provides a critical overview of globalisation as an independent area of study. The author sketches the main challenges posed by globalisation to a national bounded social sciences discourse and suggests a range of research questions on how this challenge can be met in the South African context, in ways which allow local and national problems to be understood in global terms. Chapter 5 highlights the continuing reality of the white monopoly over intellectual production. It is highlighted that the differentiation between historically black and white institutions is relevant for the South African higher education sector.

Chapter 6 reviews changes in political sciences departments as a reflection of broader changes in the discipline. Chapter 7 focuses on the methodological and linguistic facts in the field of media studies at South African universities. Chapter 8 maps the changing focus in population studies in South Africa and the impact of AIDS on population trends. Chapter 9 and 10 provide an overview of the historical changes of this discipline. Chapter 11 provides a personal journey of the author into the discipline of anthropology.

Chapter 12 reflects on the discipline of psychology and cultural biases between black and white psychologists.

Achim Gutowski, Bremen

United Nations Industrial Development Organization (UNIDO); *Establishment of National Capability. Providing Instrumentation Support Services: Case Study,* 2005, Trade Capacity Building Working Paper Series 04/2005, Vienna: UNIDO, no ISBN/ISSN, pages: 41.

The booklet investigates the efficient use of national instrumentation resources on the example of the Malawi Bureau of Standards. Products and services need to comply with the quality management of the International Organization of Standardization (ISO) to become internationally tradable. Therefore, the provision of Quality Management Systems is becoming increasingly important for developing countries to increase their competitiveness. To ensure the according compliance of private and public companies, a national standardisation authority is needed that supervises the performance of quality systems and offers support services. Such an authority exists in many developing countries including Malawi but often faces manifold problems such as a lack of training for repair and maintenance of the instrumentation and poor quality assurance services.

The booklet starts with explaining the conception of the instrumentation support service centre and its relevance and impact for social and economic development. Thereafter, the experience of implementing an instrumentation support service centre in Malawi is described in detail, including an analysis of the socio-economic environment, the legal framework, and a strengths and weakness analysis of the Malawi Bureau of Standards. Also, the situation at the end of the project and future challenges to sustain the smooth operation of the Malawi Bureau of Standards are discussed.

With this publication the UNIDO gives comprehensive insights into the successful operation of one of its projects and provides important lessons for the replication of this project for other developing countries.

Mareike Meyn, Bremen

The United Nations University (UNU); *UNU and TICAD III, How can TICAD III contribute to support the Grand Design for Africa?*, 2003, policy brief, Tokyo: UNU, no ISBN, pages: 66.

This policy brief booklet is the product of research conducted by UNU. Over the last years the UNU, in cooperation with the African Diplomatic Corps in

Tokyo, has been preparing its contribution to the Third Tokyo International Conference on African Development (TICAD III).

At a workshop in Tokyo, a number of conclusions were drawn regarding the overall topics identified by the New Partnership for Africa's Development (NEPAD), namely the triangle "infrastructure, regional integration and capital flows" and the possible synergies between NEPAD and TICAD III.

NEPAD provides Africa with a "grand design" and gives a perspective on where Africa should be in 15 to 20 years. TICAD III provides the support needed to implement the ambitious plans of NEPAD.

Part II, consisting of four sections, includes working materials from an expert workshop. Section one discusses infrastructures and development in Africa from the view of an UNU/WIDER representative Section two, written by a representative from the International Monetary Fund (IMF) is about "African institutions building and regional integration: lessons from experience". Section three deals with "Enhancing capital flows, trade and cultural exchanges between Africa, Japan and Asia: the launching of an Africa-Japan-Asia Centre". Section four includes a contribution of the Japan Institute of International Affairs which holds the view "Africa is big enough for both NEPAD and TICAD". Comments and discussion parts follow every contribution. Various annexes close the booklet.

Achim Gutowski, Bremen

Journal of International Development; Addison, T. et al (eds.), *Aid to Africa*, Special Issue, 2005, Vol. 17, No. 8, ISSN: 0954-1748, pages: 121.

This edition of the Journal of International Development is a special issue on "Aid to Africa". The journal consists of six articles which emerged from a conference of the United Nations University, World Institute for Development Research in Helsinki on Sharing Global Prosperity. All papers address aid impacts on African economies, mainly by advanced empirical methods.

The first paper is an introduction into the topic. It notes that decreasing aid resulted in increasing poverty in Africa and demands more aid in order to meet the Millennium Development Goals (MDG). The article further states that aid is positively linked to economic growth, contributes to higher public spending, and that budgetary support can be effective. The efficiency of aid allocation depends on the quality of political institutions. Aid can therefore be a driving force to reach the MDG.

The second article focuses on the determinants of aid flows to Africa. The author's main finding is that policy regimes are important determinants of aid flows, at least in the sample of observation: Egypt, Morocco, Kenya, and Tanzania were the biggest aid recipients. The paper concludes that changes in the political environment could encourage larger aid flows.

The third paper is titled "Aid Heterogeneity: Looking at aid effectiveness from a different angle". It takes the example of Uganda for the conduction of time-series analysis in order to examine the impact of aid on public budget. Project and food aid were found to reduce public investment, but programme aid and technical assistance had positive effects on investments.

The fourth paper looks at Ghana and the fiscal effects of aid in this country. Aid to Ghana led to reduced public borrowing but increased spending. Thus, aid contributed to a better fiscal performance.

The fifth article contributes to the literature on aid and growth by explicitly accounting for aid transmission mechanisms, namely via investment, public spending, and import financing. This approach results in much larger aid contribution to growth as found in the literature so far. For African countries this means that a one percent increase in the aid to GDP ratio results in a 0.25 percent increase in growth.

The final contribution evaluates an innovative way of dealing with aid. Ghana agreed with its donors to package aid and so as to ensure continuous flows of aid for its poverty reduction programme. The paper finds that this approach could work, given that Ghana would not be pressed to use aid to reduce its public debt.

Tobias Knedlik, Halle (Saale)

Economic Research Forum (ERF), *The Economic Research Forum Newsletter*, 2005, Vol. 3 and 4, Cairo: ERF, no ISBN, pages: 49.

The Economic Research Forum (ERF) Newsletter is a free electronic bullet with the latest news of ERF's activities. It can be downloaded under www.erf.org.eg. The Newsletter is published four times a year.

This special issue of the newsletter refers to the XIIth conference of the ERF titled "Institutionalizing Reform", discussing the role of institutions in reform processes. The relevance of institutions has often been neglected by both economic theory and in policy making.

Researchers working on institutional reforms in Africa could obtain relevant insights when reading the ERF e-newsletter.

Achim Gutowski, Bremen

Unit 5: Profiles, News and Information

edited by Mareike Meyn

Ghana's Experience with the African Peer Review Mechanism (APRM). How the Mechanism can Assist the Country in Diversifying Primary Commodity Exports

APRM Secretariat, Midrand, South Africa

I Introduction

While the concept of peer review has precedents in the academic world, audits instituted by international organizations such as the International Monetary Fund (IMF) Article IV Consultations and the sector-specific peer reviews of the Organization for Economic Co-operation and Development (OECD), the African Peer Review Mechanism APRM (APRM) which was inaugurated under the auspices of the New Partnership for Africa's Development (NEPAD) by the Heads of State and Government Implementation Committee (HSGIC) of NEPAD in Abuja, Nigeria on March 26, 2002 is unique in its scope and breadth. It is an African-based self-monitoring mechanism intended to foster the adoption of policies, standards and practices that would lead to political stability, high economic growth rate, sustainable development and accelerated sub-regional and continental economic integration through sharing of experiences and reinforcement of successful and best practice, including identifying deficiencies and assessing the needs for capacity building. It is geared towards ensuring that the policies and practices of participating states conform to the agreed political, economic and corporate governance values, codes and standards contained in the (African Union) AU Declarations on Democracy, Political, Economic and Corporate Governance.

II The Idea Behind the African Peer Review Mechanism

The APRM is designed as a mechanism whereby countries voluntarily 'open their books' to be examined within a formal structure according to established guidelines. Teams of African experts in various spheres will assess and critique the countries' governance practice based on a number of key indicators in four thematic areas namely: political governance, economic governance, corporate governance and socio-economic development. This commonly agreed instruments for self – monitoring has at its epicentre the development and the dissemination of best practices among African Union (AU) members. The framework is aimed at encouraging and building responsible leadership through constructive peer dialogue and the sharing of information and common experiences in order to reinforce successful and exemplary practices among African countries.

Participation in the process is open to all member states of the AU. Accession entails signing up to the NEPAD Declaration on Democracy, Political, Economic and Corporate Governance, undertaking to submit to and facilitate periodic peer reviews and generally be guided by agreed parameters for good governance at both the political and economic levels. So far, a total of twenty five of the fifty-three African countries have signed the APRM Memorandum of Understanding (MOU) indicating readiness to be peer reviewed. Sudan and Zambia were the most recent additions and Sao Tome's request to accede has been formally accepted by the Forum. Ghana and Rwanda are currently the most advanced in the implementation of the APRM process at the national level as the Panel of Eminent Persons have had the opportunity to present the two reports to the participating Heads of State. Nonetheless, only Ghana has been "peer reviewed" and Rwanda is expected to be peer reviewed at the next meeting of the Forum.

III The APRM in Ghana

Ghana, together with eleven other countries signed the Memorandum of Understanding (MOU) for the APRM Review on 9th March, 2003. The country created a Ministry of Regional Cooperation and NEPAD in May 2003 to oversee the APRM process in Ghana. In keeping with the APRM principle for a participating country to have an independent self-assessment of its governance record, Ghana instituted a seven-member National Governing Council comprising highly qualified and esteemed personalities independent of the government. The Governing Council appointed four reputable national think-tanks and research institutions to undertake the Country Self-Assessment in each of the four thematic areas of the APRM, namely, Democracy and Good Political Governance; Economic Governance and Management; Corporate Governance; and Socio-Economic Development and to make appropriate recommendations to serve as guidelines in drafting a National Programme of Action. Ghana submitted its Self-Assessment Report and a Draft National Programme of Action to the APRM Secretariat in March 2005. On the basis of the self-assessment report, a 16- member fact finding Country Review Team (CRT) from 11 African visited Ghana from 04-16 April, 2005 to undertake the country review.

Following this mission, a Country Review Report was drafted, which together with the Rwanda Report, was presented by the APR Panel to the Committee of Participating Heads of State and Government (APR Forum) in Abuja, Nigeria on the 19th June 2005. The actual peer review by Heads of participating States and Government was conducted in Khartoum, Sudan on 20 January, 2006, where the President of Ghana presented the core findings in the report and actions to be taken to improve governance in Ghana. The other Heads of States engaged with the President, in a closed session, on pertinent issues relevant to good governance in Ghana.

IV Outcome of the Peer Review for Ghana

The Country review report presented by the Lead Panel Member for Ghana, Dr. Chris Stals, in Abuja showed that Ghana's best practice is evident in its effort to build and sustain peace and tranquility in a sub-region that is perpetually in turmoil. This is manifest in three peaceful elections and the orderly transfer of government from one political party to another. The country has also made efforts to broaden the space for national dialogue by instituting the Annual Governance Forum, the Peoples Assembly and the National Economic Dialogue. The Panel urged Ghana to ratify outstanding standards and codes as outlined by the APRM. It also expressed concern with the size of its 88-member executive and the presence of the ministry of parliamentary affairs, which blurs the line between the executive and legislature.

On economic governance and management, the report presented Ghana's economy as being relatively weak and highly vulnerable to external shocks, especially the vagaries of world trade and sub-regional political instability. It noted that Ghana has a weak internal capacity for economic management that relies so much on external resources and policy advice. Furthermore, corruption is impeding on good governance.

In sum, while Ghana's consolidated democracy and coordinated development goals is a hopeful indicator of enormous potential in a region marked by conflict and instability, peaceful democratic transition has yet to satisfy economic expectations, as the predominantly agricultural economy struggles to meet the needs of a rapidly expanding population.

Ghana has prepared a comprehensive Programme of Action to address the issues raised in the report. The President of Ghana, H.E. John A. Kuffour, indicated in the Khartoum Summit that Ghana needs $5 billion to address the weaknesses raised in the African Peer Review Mechanism (APRM) report. He noted however, that some actions are already in progress as per the implementation of the Ghana Poverty Reduction Strategy (GPRS) For Ghana, the APRM could thus be viewed as a major plank in the quest to build a democratic, accountable and transparent government and diversify the economy.

V How the APRM Can Assist Ghana's Diversification Attempts

The last two decades have seen steady and significant economic growth in Ghana in spite of considerable instability in macroeconomic performance and a growing dependence on aid and other foreign inflows. An average of 5 % GDP growth has been recorded for the best part of that period. While the growth performance may not be exceptional this has been significantly above average by African standards.

Despite the sustained per capita growth accompanied by some measured reduction in income poverty, levels of poverty remain high and the perception that poverty is worsening prevails strongly. Related to the issue of growth and poverty is the question of structural change. To a large extent, Ghana has not been able to alter its structure significantly. The economy of Ghana remains vulnerable to external shocks and internal disruption through uncontrollable events such as crop failures and adverse weather conditions. The past 45 years have also proven that it is no easy task to engineer structural change in, and greater diversification of the national economy in a very competitive global environment.

Like many other countries in Africa, Ghana continue to depend on a narrow range of export commodities, namely; cocoa, timber, and mineral resources - for a large proportion of its export earnings - and the country has had to contend with the problem of instability of primary commodity prices especially coping with large shocks. Peaks (or booms) in commodity prices are interspersed by longer troughs (or slumps), which have had a major impact on management of the economy via a variety of channels.

The APRM can make a major contribution towards Ghana's turn around in the quest for diversifying the economy. It could trigger a deliberate and dynamic transformation and diversification in the commodity sector through combined actions by government and entrepreneurs in the implementation of the Programme of Action.

Like the APRM Country Report for Ghana rightly diagnosed. Meeting the challenges of structural transformation and export diversification would require the following, in addition to macroeconomic stability:

- Appropriate policies for strengthening entrepreneurship and the private sector, including the design of efficient state-private sector cooperation and coordination mechanisms;
- Substantial increase in the stock and quality of human capital, including the technological capability of the labour force; and
- Creation of a more favourable climate for foreign direct investment.

While the Ghanaian governments should take action to eliminate bottlenecks and adopt appropriate strategies to enhance competitiveness and create new areas of comparative advantage, entrepreneurs should make conscious efforts to adopt modern business strategies and tailor production patterns towards higher-value-added and/or more processed products. In this regard, there is a need to move into higher technological areas such as the growing Business Processing Outsourcing and Information Technology (BPO/IT) industry. Ghana can create both a competitive advantage in this area and set the stage for a massive accelerated growth rate.

For further information please contact:

NEPAD/African Peer Review Secretariat
Drs. Bernard Kouassi and Afeikhena Jerome
Postal Address: P. O. Box 1234
Halfway House
Midrand 1685
South Africa
Tel.: +27 11 313 3352
Fax: +27 11 313 3440
E-mail; afeikhenaj@nepad.org
Webpage: http://www.nepad.org

YENEPAD: For What Future? From a Vision to the Implementation

Young Entrepreneurs for NEPAD (YENEPAD) Secretariat, Pretoria, South Africa

1 Introduction

The new Partnership for Africa's Development (NEPAD), the Africa Union's socio-economic renewal programme, is a watershed in the history of the African continent. The programme represents a unique commitment by Africans to lead decisively the social, economic and political transformation of the continent in partnership with the international community. (Nepad, 2005). To accelerate and focus development efforts, comprehensive integrated development plans and programmes covering various NEPAD priority areas must be developed. Many initiatives, organisations and institutions have been developed to support the whole NEPAD programme across the continent. YENEPAD, standing for YOUNG ENTREPRENEURS FOR NEPAD, is a platform for young African to be involved with the programme NEPAD. The organisation was launched in April 2002 and is registered with the South African Department of Social Development as a Non- Profit Organisation since February 2003. The present paper is an attempt to develop YENEPAD's contribution on the development of the African continent.

2.1 The Strategic Framework of YENEPAD

There are 15 YENEPAD founding members from eight African countries, who are supported by professionals from Universities and the private and public sector. The founding members, all Africans, were at the time of YENEPAD's creation enrolled as Postgraduate students in various fields, from social sciences to engineering. Various professionals, from higher learning institutions to the private sector, have been supporting the organisation since its creation. Their support is mostly intellectual, mentorship and network facilitator.

This group of scholars developed the vision, the mission, the objectives and the focus areas of YENEPAD. The main issues that pose challenges for the continent are: 1. HIV/AIDS and Malaria; 2. Good Governance; 3. Higher Education and Post Learning Schooling; 3. Job Creation, Famine and Poverty; 4. Health and Environment; 5. Drug Abuse Reduction; and 6. Globalization, Information and Communication Technologies (ICT). Every YENEPAD country representative will set up its own priorities to address the plights facing the population. The projects resulting from the mentioned issues aimed at constituting focal points of research in Africa.

2.2 Vision, Objective, Means

YENEPAD's vision is the peace, the development and the fulfilment of the potential of Africans. Its objective is to support and spread the ideas of the New Partnership for Africa's Development (NEPAD). This objective will be achieved through efficient projects undertaken in the ground. YENEPAD's means are the organization and the management of our activities, which include conferences, round tables whereby scholars, business leaders and other researchers having contributed in any aspect of the development of the continent, could be invited in order to share their experiences and expertise. Moreover, we carry out studies and make publications on issues related to the development of the African continent. Many papers have been presented in local, regional and international conferences. We are planning to publish a book on Millennium Development Goals (MDGs), and the involvement of African leaders (Ndedi, 2005). YENEPAD is part of institutions involved in the drafting of the Millennium Project 2020 Global Energy, sponsored by the Millennium Project of the American Council for the United Nations University of an international study to construct alternative global energy scenarios to the year 2020.

Another of our activities is the creation of documentation centres on education in the entire continent. We are in talks with some Universities, publishers in South Africa to document some Universities libraries in West Africa. Our organisation is in search of any institutions willing to support this initiative.

3 Focus Areas: Trade, Investment and Education

One of the main priorities of YENEPAD is to contribute to trade facilitation in Africa. It is our goal to provide a platform for discussion among relevant stakeholders and to identify the products and services that have a competitive advantage and a potential market, not only in Africa, but also in the world. Currently there is a lack of information between trade institutions, such as chambers of commerce, in Africa. The various initiatives developed below are supposed to fill the gap. YENEPAD plans to create web sites of certain chambers of commerce and business associations. These projects will be carried pertaining to the availability of funds raised.

A. Organization of Trade Fairs

YENEPAD is involved in many trade fairs organised around the continent. YENEPAD supplies information of different events to potential exhibitors. We are also developing an African Network among trade focal points and link the Johannesburg Chamber of Commerce with other chambers in Africa. These links are bearing fruits, as opportunities of imports substitution or replacement are developed.

B. Education and Post School Learning

The organisation is trying to link South African universities with universities across the continent. The University of Pretoria is already collaborating with universities in Uganda, Cameroon, Egypt, Tanzania, Ethiopia and Eritrea, partly through the endeavour of the organisation. We are also in the process on bringing UNISA (University of South Africa) to open its doors in Cameroon. Furthermore, YENEPAD signed a two-year protocol of agreement with the Pretoria Good Governance Academy (PGGA) for short courses on good governance to members of the organisation.

4 Achievements

The marginalisation of the African continent has often been regarded as a normal situation. During many decades, projects have been launched in order to get out of this situation without any success. NEPAD has been conceived by African Heads of State as a development framework that should enable the continent to get out of this marginalisation. All this can be only achieved if the talks are translated into actions. NEPAD and affiliated organisations can only be efficient and effective if projects are implemented on the ground. The following projects have already successfully been undertaken by YENEPAD:

- YENEPAD launched an initiative of creation of websites of various national branches in co-operation with the organisation Virtualactivism based in the USA. YENEPAD initiated a project aimed at distributing of information bulletin on latest development of NEPAD (such as Peer Review Mechanism, E-schools, and the African Agricultural Development Programme. Each issue of the around 10-pages information bulletin is e-mailed to more than 1000 addresses, most of them are YENEPAD members. Another initiative is in view, the development of a database and document centre in all our national offices on various issues.
- We attended many events in Africa and abroad. Among them the participation of at the conference organised by IDEP (African Institute for Economic Development and Planning) and AFEA (African Finance and Economics Association) under the theme "NEPAD and the future of economic and politic policies in Africa" in Dakar, 10-11 November 2005 and the 11th General Assembly of CODESRIA (Council for the Development of Social Science Research in Africa) on "African development" in: Maputo, 6-11 December 2005.
- YENEPAD is member of the African Representation of the World Bank, the Global Development Network (GDN), the KM4DEV Forum and Knowledge Management Forum launched by GDN, and part of the Canadian Communication Initiative.
- Currently, YENEPAD Consulting is carrying a study on "Millennium Project on 2020 Alternative Global Energy Scenarios" producing an annotated bibliography of global energy scenarios and related reports. To achieve this, the design of a Delphi questionnaire is carried in order to collect views of a large group of experts and to allow the exchange of ideas between these experts with the objective of forming a consensus on alternative energy scenarios in 2020. The results of all three phases of this international study will be published in the "2006 State of the Future" with YENEPAD as one of the contributors.

For further information:

Young Entrepreneurs for NEPAD (YENEPAD), University of Pretoria,
Mr. Alain A. Ndedi
P O BOX 30069
Pretoria
South Africa
Tel: +237 12 440 2353
Fax: +237 123208674
Email: yenepad@aim.com
Website: http://yenepad.virtualactivism.net

References

Ndedi, A, A. (2004): "Entrepreneurship and Black Economic Empowerment (BEE) in South Africa". Article presented during the Africa Week Conference at the University of Pretoria, 1-3 September 2004.

Ndedi, A, A. (2005): "NEPAD and the Millennium Development Goals (MDGs): the challenges of African governments". Paper presented during the African Week conference held at the University of South Africa, 18th October 2005.

Ndedi, A, A. (forthcoming): "NEPAD and the Millennium Development Goals: Opportunities and Challenges", Unisa Press. Pretoria, South Africa.

Ndjuide, K, R. (2005): "APRM and the Challenges of the Implementation of Economic Governance Standards: a Critical Assessment". Paper presented during the conference entitled "NEPAD and the Future of Economic Policy in Africa". 9th to 12th November 2005 (Dakar).

A New Initiative to Strengthen Capacity Development in East Africa

The East Africa Regional Technical Assistance Center, Dar es Salaam, Tanzania

I Background

The East Africa Regional Technical Assistance Center (EAST AFRITAC) was established in October 2002 by the IMF and a group of multilateral and bilateral donors in response to calls by African countries for more support in macroeconomic management capacity building. The center is located in Dar-es-Salaam (Tanzania) and its main goal is to contribute toward strengthening the capacity of beneficiary East African countries. The countries served by East AFRITAC initiative are: Eritrea, Ethiopia, Kenya, Rwanda, Uganda and Tanzania. Improving their central government institutions' organizational and technical performance in the fiscal, monetary, financial and related statistical areas will be the basis for achieving a stable macro-economic environment and for attaining development goals laid out in these countries poverty reduction strategies.

A key feature of the East AFRITAC is the strong ownership of policies and activities by stakeholders. Specifically, strategic direction is provided by a Steering Committee (SC), with representation from member countries, donors and regional organization observers. The SC provides strategic guidance to the center, reviews its work plans, and assesses progress in technical assistance delivery. This governance structure is designed to ensure that the initiative delivers an assistance that is demand driven, responsive to the needs of countries, closely linked to poverty-reducing strategies (PRS) of member countries and well coordinated with the technical assistance provided by other donors.

East AFRITAC works closely with, and in support of regional institutions offering technical assistance, training, and advisory services. Such institutions include the Macroeconomic and Financial Management Institute of Eastern and Southern Africa (MEFMI) and the African Capacity Building Foundation (ACBF) both located in Harare (Zimbabwe).

II Assistance Provided by East AFRITAC

Since its inception in October 2002, East AFRITAC provided technical assistance and training in a wide range of areas in the field of macro-economic management. The assistance is delivered through technical assistance missions by AFRITAC resident advisors complemented by short-term expertise drawn from within and outside the region and coupled with in-country and regional workshops and seminars.

In the public financial management component, the assistance included: improving budget preparation methodology and introducing a Medium Term Expenditure Framework (MTEF), treasury reforms focusing on cash management and banking arrangements, improving Ministry of Finance's capacity to manage intergovernmental fiscal affairs, and strengthening the accounting, budget execution and reporting functions. For example, East AFRITAC has assisted Ethiopia in introducing a strengthened treasury system including a system for effective transfer and management of funds to local governments. In the broader area of setting the reform agenda in the context of Poverty Reduction Strategy Papers (PRSPs), East AFRITAC worked with a number of the countries on the content of their public financial management reform programs and action plans.

Within the revenue administration component, the assistance carried-out in cooperation with the authorities and with other providers contributed to a better knowledge of the challenges faced by the East-AFRITAC countries in their revenue modernization efforts. Establishment of modern (integrated and function-based) revenue administrations should facilitate staff specializations in key areas, eliminate fragmentation, and enhance revenue mobilization. East-AFRITAC assisted Kenya and Uganda to implement fully integrated domestic tax administrations and also advised on the separation of operational policy from field delivery. East AFRITAC has assisted Kenya and Uganda to implement fully integrated domestic tax administrations.

In the monetary operations areas, East AFRITAC conducted monetary operation assessment missions in Eritrea, Ethiopia, Kenya, and Uganda, in each case, outlining a medium-term prioritized reform strategy. Assistance was provided to develop the domestic debt and money markets in Rwanda and Tanzania. Assessments of reserve management practices were conducted in Ethiopia, Kenya and Rwanda and in each case a plan of action was provided to implement best practices. In Kenya, East AFRITAC provided critical assistance in the review of the strategic approach to payment system reform, outlining the structure of a payment systems unit and an implementation plan for a real-time gross settlement system. assistance was also provided to Tanzania on the implementation of their real-time system and to Rwanda on outlining the steps necessary to ensure that the legal environment is supportive of the reform initiatives.

Activities in the banking supervision area, largely focused on upgrading skills in core supervisory activities, namely on-site inspections and off-site surveillance. In support of the shift from traditional to a risk-based supervision approach, East AFRITAC helped four countries draw up an implementation framework for risk-based supervision and mobilize dedicated teams of supervision staff to oversee the change process. East AFRITAC also contributed towards better supervision practices in Eritrea through the development of an on-site inspection manual and an off-site surveillance system, and in Rwanda through the development of a new format for inspection reports. In Uganda, East AFRITAC helped in drawing up the supervisory framework for non-bank financial institutions and the regulatory framework for the national pension fund. Hands-on technical assistance was also provided on country-specific issues such as dealing with problem banks and non-performing loans, implementing anti-money laundering measures, and introducing the CAMEL (Capital adequacy, Asset quality, Management, Earnings, and Liquidity) rating system for banks.

Macroeconomic statistics activities focused mainly on improving the quality of the annual national accounts estimates and developing short-term economic indicators. Four countries (Kenya, Rwanda, Tanzania, and Uganda) are currently benchmarking and rebasing their national accounts estimates. By the end of 2006, five of the six countries in East AFRITAC will have shifted to the 1993 System of National Accounts and will publish a revised series of national accounts estimates based on more firm data and using more robust compilation methodologies. Assistance on quarterly national accounts was provided to Uganda and Tanzania, as was the construction of a monthly producer price index for manufacturing in Ethiopia, Kenya, and Rwanda.

Finally, seminars and workshops activities have also formed a major and integral part of East AFRITAC activities. Regional workshops were conducted in response to demand from the majority of member countries along topics similar to those covered by the technical advice, thereby reinforcing the impact of hands-on technical assistance. The regional seminars also served to share experiences among countries and as a means of peer review. Mostly, the seminars were organized jointly with regional organizations, chief among these the African Capacity Building Foundation (ACBF) and the Financial Management Institute of Eastern and Southern Africa (MEFMI). In some cases, in-house workshops or in-country workshops proved most effective, as they were tailored to the country's circumstances and exposed a larger number of persons than those working directly with East AFRITAC to the key issues.

III Medium Term Perspectives

With the key reforms already underway, medium term needs for this group of countries will focus more and more on:

- The performance of the budget, both in providing a clearer link to government policy objectives and priorities, and in achieving more cost effective value for money oriented in-year resource management focused on achieving outputs stated in the annual budget.
- Improving both tax policy and revenue administration. Establishing lean management structures that are organized along functional lines, have separated operations policy from field delivery, and focused on the compliance and service needs of the large, medium and small taxpayer segments.
- Fundamental reform of the financial sector to substantially increase competition in the banking sector. More market determined exchange rates and enhanced capacity to conduct foreign operations and to manage foreign reserves. Improved functioning of the primary market and development of a secondary market for governments' debt instruments. Strengthened cash management / liquidity forecasting system
- Establishing a supervisory and regulatory framework that enables sound financial institutions to compete and thus increase efficiency in financial intermediation.
- Enhanced capacity to collect, process and publish timely and reliable economic data for analysis and effective macroeconomic and fiscal management.

IV Conclusions

All the beneficiary countries recognize that strong domestic institutional capacity is a precondition for economic and social development and for sound public policy making. For markets to function efficiently and for the private sector to develop and thrive, effective institutions are essential. They are also critical for ensuring that economic policies and reforms are "home grown" and have true domestic ownership. This provides a strong motivation for East AFRITACs to continue to assist in institutional capacity building in its areas of expertise. Its physical presence in the region; proximity to country counterparts; an ability to respond quickly to requests for assistance and the provision of integrated advice across its areas of expertise and the knowledge of cross-regional issues should help it contribute to capacity-building efforts in this region.

For further information please contact:

East Africa Regional Technical Assistance Center (AFRITAC)
Mr. Bassirou A. Sarr
Center Coordinator
PPF Tower, 6th Floor,
P.O. Box 10054
Dar es Salaam, Tanzania
Tel: +255-22-2134342
Fax: +255-22-2137827
E-mail: bsarr@imf.org
Website: http://www.eastafritac.org

Sustainable Capacity in Economic Modelling Towards Responsible and Effective Economic Policy in Africa

The African Institute for Economic Modelling (AFRINEM), University of Pretoria, South Africa

I Background

Arguably the primary challenge for African countries is the formulation and implementation of effective and responsible economic policies, targeted at the unique and relevant policy challenges of the continent. What immediately comes to mind are the challenges regarding regional integration and improved intra-Africa trade; the need for increased diversification in the face of rising international commodity prices; as well as the design and implementation of sustainable growth strategies towards poverty alleviation and development?

These challenges emphasize the need for improved capacity amongst policy makers in African countries in economic modelling, as credible and evidence-based tools to facilitate responsible and effective economic policy.

The African Institute for Economic Modelling (AFRINEM) has been established 2003 to provide in this need and is a direct consequence of the execution of a United Nations/DESA funded project: "Research Network for Development Policy Analysis".

The aim of the project was to enhance the capacity of policy makers in 15 African countries[1] to formulate and implement development policies. The project utilised internationally accepted policy-analysis techniques and economic modelling, both on national and regional levels.

The project met all of its objectives and substantially managed to improve interaction and cooperation between modellers and policy makers. The

---

1 Angola, Ethiopia, Ghana, Kenya, Lesotho, Malawi, Namibia, Senegal, Sudan, Swaziland, Tanzania, Togo, Uganda, Zambia, Zimbabwe.

result was an independent network with expertise on economic modelling in Africa. However, when the project reached the end of its 2-year period in 2003, not only the participating teams indicated a definite demand to extend the project through further technical and stylized training, but huge interest were shown by other countries to join the program. AFRINEM is the result of that demand and serves as the institutional home for the continuation of the activities – establishing the first, albeit indispensable steps towards ownership of economic modelling on the African continent. Furthermore, AFRINEM's vision and goals support the New Partnership for African Development by facilitating the sound fundamentals for sustainable growth and development.

II Objectives

The objectives of AFRINEM include:

- To strengthen the capacity of institutional, national and regional policy makers and other stakeholders involved in the promotion and development of sustainable macroeconomic policy through training;
- To build institutional and national capacities in econometric modelling for the analysis and forecasting of trends and policy alternatives at the national level – each country will have its own national macroeconomic model;
- To build the capacity of national and regional statistical offices for the generation of standardized, timely and reliable national and regional data;
- To utilize experts of developing countries in Africa for capacity building in macroeconomic analysis and forecasting;
- To build an African network for exchanging economic information to better adjust to global economic changes through annual conferences, policy dialogues and African LINK[2] meetings;

---

2 An initiative analogue to the United Nation's Project LINK. Project LINK is a world-wide network of participants in more than 60 countries in the industrial and developing world, and it is internationally recognised as a leading centre of quantitative international economic analysis. The activities of Project LINK are co-ordinated jointly by the Project LINK Research Centre at the University of Toronto and the Department for Economic and Social Policy Analysis and Information of the United Nations. Project LINK's principal achievement has been

- To obtain more efficient and timely assistance from international agencies and donors by providing up-to-date assessments of economic conditions at both national and regional levels; and
- To support policy makers by producing periodic publications of national and regional economic outlooks based on the research conducted through a multi-country model and research centre.

III Methodology

What distinguishes AFRINEM from other capacity building initiatives in Africa, is the fact that its approach has proven to be successful. The work on the United Nations project demonstrated that the AFRINEM team understand the process and its challenges, thoroughly.
The secret of AFRINEM's success is:

- A holistic approach in the design of the training programmes, combining in-depth theoretical lectures, practical applications, presentations from participants and policy dialogue;
- A hands-on approach, where careful attention is paid to best-practices techniques – especially within the African "limited data" context;
- The emphasis on the application of the models to generate credible, effective and timely forecasts, as well as reputable and relevant policy analyses;
- The models are customized to capture the unique characteristics and constraints within each individual economy;
- Given the nature of the model-building process, training is spread over a 2-year period; the models are systematically and thematically developed during a series of workshops. Continuity in participation and continuous technical support are essential for the success of this approach;
- Care is taken in developing a network amongst modellers and policy makers. For example, an electronic network has been developed for continuous interaction between all participants, trainers and consultants; and finally
- The notion is "from Africa to Africa": utilising and developing the expertise, skills and experience of Africans.

---

to integrate independently developed national econometric models into a world econometric model (LINK).

IV Capacity Building Programmes

4.1 Modelling Workshops and Programmes

- The Introduction to Macroeconomic Modelling and Forecasting Workshop is a single workshop, which covers the main issues surrounding model selection and model building, and addresses the specifics of modelling the various sectors of the economy (real sector demand and supply, monetary, public and foreign sectors). The emphasis is to allow practitioners to gain hands-on experience in full model building and application processes. A South African prototype model is used to facilitate these processes.

With respect to the full modelling programmes, a distinction is made between a Core Modelling and an Advanced Modelling Programme.

- The **Core Modelling Programme** facilitates the development of a customized macroeconomic model that comprises a series of 5 workshops, 1-week duration each, spread over an 18-month period. Participants are required to attend the full series of workshops, which are outlined in the workshop menu below
- The **Advanced Modelling Programme** focuses on customized model refinements and the development of specific sectors for specialised application. The Advanced programme presents the opportunity for established modellers and teams to attend a selection of workshop(s) from the menu according to their field of specialisation.

The Core and Advanced programmes are structured to overlap to ensure constructive interaction between various groups in support of the "training of trainers", constructive policy dialogue on common issues, and the expansion of the network between modellers and policy makers.
The training programmes are designed to combine a number of activities:

- Training in econometrics and modelling;
- Technical support on a continuous basis, that is throughout and in between workshops;
- Annual conference participation;
- Regular publications; and
- Bi-annual policy dialogues in the form of African LINK meetings.

Workshop menu

Workshop	Topic	Emphasis
1	An Introduction to Macro-economic Modelling and Forecasting	Specification and development of a demand-side model
2	Monetary sector specification and development	Issues of inflation targeting and associated policy rules
3	Foreign sector specification and development	Intra-Africa trade; market openness and diversification
4	Fiscal sector specification and development	Public Finance and Tax policy issues
5	Supply-side modelling	Determining the long-run growth potential of economies related to investment, employment and poverty alleviation issues

4.2 Short courses in Econometrics

Econometrics for the Practitioner[3]

This course is of an applied nature and focuses on the hands-on experience in estimation, interpretation and evaluation of economic relationships. The course is presented in two parallel sections that run simultaneously: theory and empirical applications. The aim is to reconcile economic theory with practice, thereby empowering students with analytical skills and a hands-on approach to decision-making processes. The course begins with a basic introduction to the concepts of regression, ordinary least squares estimation, the classical linear regression model and statistical inference. The course also includes the discussion of the practical implications of employing non-stationary data in estimation, the detection of unit roots in the underlying data-generating processes and concepts of co-integration and error-correction modelling. The course furthermore includes the process of diagnostic testing and the interpretation of test results.

Course fee: ZAR 9 500 per delegate

3 For detailed information and course content refer to: www.up.ac.za/up/web/en/academic/economics/Academic/Short_courses/index.html.

Econometrics in depth: Theory and Practice[2]

This course begins with an introduction to the objectives, principles and methodology of econometrics. This is followed by a review of introductory statistics. Attention is then devoted to the basics of regression analysis. The estimation of single equations is studied along the lines of both two variable and multiple regression models. Attention is also paid to the analysis of the problems that arise when the basic assumptions of the classical linear regression model are violated, how to test for it as well as remedies for it. Considerable attention is devoted to applications on current economic issues and examples drawn from the applied econometric literature. Compared to the course Econometrics for the Practitioner, this course is theoretically more challenging (equal to the Honours level course in Econometrics) and covers the selected topics in depth.

Course fee: ZAR 9 500 per delegate

Econometrics in depth: Using Cointegration[2]

This course addresses appropriate modelling techniques for time series data when unit roots are present in the data (i.e. data is non-stationary) - a problem that applied economists encounter in almost all economic time-series applications. To ignore the fact that data may be non-stationary and to proceed to estimate a regression model containing non-stationary variables, at best ignores important information about the underlying statistical and economic processes generating the data, and at worst leads to nonsensical (or spurious) results. Therefore, to begin with, an initial understanding of the common technical characteristics of time series data is provided. Thereafter, the concept of stationarity is formally defined, together with a discussion of its implications for ordinary least squares estimation. Consequently, attention is then focused on the advanced econometric techniques of co-integration and error-correction models, with emphasis on their empirical application. To conclude, the notion of multivariate co-integration is discussed and applied.

Course fee: ZAR 7 500 per delegate

Panel Data Econometrics for the Practitioner[2]

In this course "panel data" refers to the pooling of observations on a cross-section of countries, households, firms, etc. over a number of time periods. We use panel data techniques for example to control for individual heterogeneity or to study the dynamics of adjustment. Panel data allows for more informative results, more variability, more degrees of freedom and more efficiency. This course is of an applied nature and focuses on the hands-on experience in estimation, interpretation and evaluation of economic relationships, within a panel data context. The course comprises more or less equal components of the statistical theory of panel data with practical examples and empirical applications. The application software used is E-Views 5 or 5.1. The section on stationary panel data techniques concludes with a discussion of seemingly unrelated regression models. In the non-stationary panel data section we discuss unit root testing in the panel context, estimation of non-stationary panels and tests for co-integration.

Course fee: ZAR 9 500 per delegate

4.3 Short course in Economic Analysis

A short course in Economic Analysis is also presented.

Economic Indicators: Monitoring the SA Economy[2]

The course starts with an overview of the different types of economic indicators that users of economic information are confronted with and how these relate to the operation of the overall economy. The central focus is on extracting meaningful information on the macroeconomic performance of the South African economy from the myriad of information available in the daily press and specialist data collection institutions. Students are introduced to the most prominent sources of readily available South African data (e.g. data from Stats SA, the South African Reserve Bank, the Treasury, etc.). Detailed guidance is provided on ways of extracting raw data from these and other sources of economic data. A further component of the course deals with the basic economic and statistical manipulation techniques for these different categories of data. Attention is awarded to interpreting this information in order to compile an informed opinion on the state of economic performance. Furthermore, practical training is provided on ways of presenting this information in the business environment to assist in the process of decision making.

Course fee: ZAR 7 500 per delegate

V Research

In general AFRINEM conducts topical research and provides a quantitative framework and platform for policy dialogues.

- Hosting bi-annual African LINK meetings;
- Assisting in the development of individual and regional country models;

- Generating forecasts and conducting policy analyses;
- Regular publications; and finally
- Developing and operating a multi-country African model, that is an African LINK model.

Africa

AFRINEM serves as the institutional home for the former "Research Network for Development Policy Analysis" network.

The vision for continued activities is:

- To utilise the established network of expertise, models and framework on to conduct relevant and topical research on African economic policy issues; and
- To continuously upgrade and the expertise on econometric techniques, macro modelling and policy analysis

South Africa

With specific reference to the South African case, we developed a range of economic models. More specifically a macro-econometric model, which represents South Africa at the United Nations' Project LINK, a Computable General Equilibrium model, as well as a Gravity model capturing global and intra-Africa trade linkages on an industry level. The suit of models also incorporates a farm model of the SA agricultural economy developed by the Department of Agricultural Economics, Extension and Rural Development at the University of Pretoria.

One of the flagship publications of the Department is the bi-annual Forecasting and Policy Analysis Report on the South African economy, including

- A series, focusing on key economic policy issues;
- A forecast of the South African economy against the backdrop of recent national policy and international economic developments; and underlying the policy analysis and forecast,
- A discussion of the economic challenges for South Africa.

VI A Dedicated Programme in Poverty and Growth: The Economics of Social Protection

The Minister of Social Development, Dr Zola Skweyiya has initiated a wide-ranging research and capacity building collaboration with the Department of Economic at the University of Pretoria, focused on the Economics of Social Protection in 2005. AFRINEM is responsible for the execution of the project and specifically to generate evidence-based research utilizing internationally accepted policy-analysis techniques and economic modelling. This project seeks to consolidate the policy innovations with respect to social protection, in particular social assistance, that have been made in the SADC region over the past few years by enhancing the capacity to development appropriate strategies and by increasing implementation capacity in the region. Two critical elements underpinning both these objectives (a) increased research and training in the Economics of Social Protection, and (b) exchanges visits and information sharing between the public officials work in the area of social protection in the SADC member states.

In addition to extensive capacity building programmes, the partnership envisages improved policy coordination through the design and implementation of an Integrated National Strategy on Social Development, ensuring sustainable growth in support of employment creation and poverty alleviation. The outputs produced by this project will provide direct inputs into policy formulation and performance evaluation, thereby contributing to the promotion of growth and development.

The process will involve social partners, policy makers, scientists and all key individuals in research and policy design in the Economics of Social Protection and interested parties are invited to contact AFRINEM for a schedule of activities and associated projects.

Objectives:

- To share experiences and information on the design, implementation and evaluation of social protection programmes;
- To enhance the research, implementation and policy/programme development capacity of dedicated teams in the region on the Economics of Social Protection;
- To promote regional cooperation with respect to the complementarities between social protection, economic growth and social development;

- To update and develop a set of relevant indicators on the complementarities between social protection, economic growth and social development;
- To assist in the design of integrated national strategies that leverage these complementarities in ways that mobilize the economically active population, empower the working force population, reduce poverty and accelerate growth;
- To specify streamlined and effective incentives for the business, labour and civil society sectors to take advantage of the social investment opportunities in these complementarities; and
- To promote critical debate among key stakeholders on these issues.

For further information:

The African Institute for Economic Modelling (AFRINEM), University of Pretoria, South Africa
Prof. Charlotte du Toit
Department of Economics - University of Pretoria
P.O. Box, Postal code
Tel: +27-12-420 2413/3522
Fax: +27-12-362 5207
E-mail: charlotte.dutoit@up.ac.za
Web site: www.afrinem.up.ac.za

Scaling-up of Energy Services Access in East Africa to Achieve the Millennium Development Goals

Stockholm Environmental Institute (SEI), Stockholm, Sweden

I Background

In August 2005 the Ministers of Energy in the East African Community (EAC) endorsed a document titled "Scaling up Modern Energy Services in East Africa to alleviate poverty and meet the Millennium Development Goals."[1]

This document outlines priority energy services that need to be scaled up in Kenya, Tanzania, Uganda and Rwanda[2] in order to meet the Millennium Development Goals (MDGs). The EAC has taken on the challenge of developing a regional strategy and implementation framework, leading to an investment portfolio to achieve these targets – a process that is supported by the United Nations Development Programme (UNDP).

Particularly four energy targets are identified in the "Scale-up document":

Target 1: Enable the use of modern fuels for 50% of those who at present use traditional biomass for cooking. Support efforts to develop and adopt the use of improved cook stoves, means to reduce indoor air

---

1 The "Scale-up document" is available to download at: www.enable.nu.

2 Rwanda is not yet a member of the EAC but is included in the regional energy scale-up initiative driven by similar motives to tackle the urgency of scaling up energy and sees the benefits of sharing thoughts, experience and practice in moving forward together with the EAC member states.

pollution, and measures to increase sustainable biomass production.

Target 2: Access to reliable modern energy services for all urban and peri-urban poor.

Target 3: Electricity for services such as lighting, refrigeration, information and communication technology, and water treatment and supply for schools, clinics, hospitals and community centres.

Target 4: Access to mechanical power within the community for all communities for productive uses.

The East African region has a population of close to 100 million people and is characterised by high poverty levels. Their energy sources are derived mainly from traditional biomass consisting of fuel wood, charcoal and agricultural waste (contributing to more that 70% of the region's energy mix).

Modern energy sources such as electricity or liquefied petroleum gas are available only for a minority. Currently less than 5% of East Africa's rural population and 40% of its urban population (12% overall) have access to electricity.

The targets of the energy scale-up initiative would improve access to energy services for about 48 million people in the region. The largest challenge in terms of number of end users and in terms of energy demand comes from meeting cooking and heating needs.

The endorsement of the document by the ministries of energy marked the beginning of the next phase: to define the process and further develop the regional strategy and the implementation framework, including the institutional framework for moving forward.

Several activities necessary to develop a regional strategic framework for East African countries to meet objectives for scaling up access to modern energy services through the development of MDG-based investment programmes have been identified, including the following:

- Agreement on an implementation framework to meet the four targets including planning capacity at relevant administrative levels
- Strategies to mobilise financial resources to implement the formulated energy policies; and
- Learning from the Economic Community of West African States (ECOWAS) experience in defining a regional energy strategy.[3]

---

3 EAC and ECOWAS share common goals in promoting MDG-based strategies to address scaling-up of modern energy services in their respective member states. ECOWAS has made political commitments to this regard and in January 2006

In order to foster the processes envisaged in the Scale-up document, the Energy Committee of the EAC in December 2005 decided to develop a regional strategic framework for the Scale-up Initiative. Furthermore, the EAC decided to communicate its engagement in energy issues for development by presenting the Scale-up initiative as its regional energy programme at the Commission for Sustainable Development, CSD-14 held in New York 1 – 12 May 2006.

II A Regional Workshop in Support of the Scale-up Initiative

In support of the Scale-up Initiative, the ENABLE[4] team[5] together with UNDP facilitated a three day consultative regional workshop hosted by the EAC to complement the ongoing processes of advancing the regional scale-up document into a corresponding work plan and investment programmes.

The workshop brought together 48 participants from the Eastern African region and from Europe, representing various sectors (health, education, water, agriculture, environment, finance and planning), organisations (public, private and NGOs) and donors. 16 participants came from Kenya, 13 from Tanzania, 7 from Uganda, 3 from Rwanda and 1 from South Africa. Nine of the participants came from Europe and were part of the facilitating team or donor representatives. A majority of the participants (18) from the region represented the public sector. Seven of the participants represented the pri-

---

adopted a regional policy on access to energy services for populations in rural and peri-urban areas for poverty reduction in line with achieving the MDGs in member states. It is envisioned that EAC and its member states could lean first-hand from the experience of another African sub-regional economic community undertaking a regional MDG-based energy investment planning exercise on the respective roles of the regional entities in promoting access to energy services .

4 ENABLE is supported by the European Commission's Directorate General for Energy and Transport (DG TREN), as a COOPENER action through the Intelligent Energy Europe (IEE) programme. It commenced in January 2005 and is due to be completed in June 2007. The COOPENER actions of the IEE programme aim to support and stimulate the activities of the European Energy Initiative (EUEI) for Poverty Eradication and Sustainable Development.

5 The Coordinator of ENABLE is IT Power (UK) and the European partners are the Stockholm Environment Institute (Sweden) and Transenergie (France). The partners in sub-Saharan Africa are IT Power East Africa (Kenya), TaTEDO (Tanzania), Africon Uganda (Uganda), QuinTsens (Senegal) and ASER, the Rural Electrification Agency of Senegal.

vate sector in the region and 6 came from NGOs in the region. There were 7 representatives from donors present in the region, with local UNDP staff constituting the bulk of this group of participants.

Workshop Objectives

The overall objective of the workshop was to identify and analyse the processes and resources that are needed in order to implement the regional energy scale-up initiative and recommend actions that need to be taken in East Africa at regional, national and local levels.

The purpose of the workshop was to offer direct support to the EAC Energy Committee and particularly its meeting that was held 16 – 17 March 2006 by engaging major stakeholders in the region to identify the principal elements of a regional energy access strategy and investment programmes that would be part of an EAC work plan.

Principally, the participants were tasked to discuss how to reach the energy services targets based on three different types of energy carriers:

- Electricity - key for providing services such as lighting, access to communication tools (radio, telephones, internet)
- Cleaner fuels for household uses - heating and cooking services
- Mechanical power – for productive purposes such as pumping and milling

III Workshop Structure and Methodology

The workshop was an objective-oriented and interactive "working" workshop, with structure and facilitation to identify the processes and resources needed to implement the Scale-up Initiative by designing an EAC work plan, including a prioritisation of interventions.

Preconditions for Success

The workshop was designed to provide the participants with opportunities for real engagement to be innovative and produce results. At the same time the boundaries of the discussions and the intentions from the sponsor's perspective was clearly communicated.

Generally there are certain conditions that need to be met in order to arrive at the expected results of a consultative workshop (see Box 1). These preconditions were present which is also reflected in the results of the workshop and the consecutive actions that have been taken since.

Box 1: Preconditions for Success

- A controversial and highly complex issue that does not have a known answer
- Clear and transparent boundary defined by the process-owner
- Engaged and informed participants that bring a diversity of perspectives and interest to the discussion
- A structured method that supports the discussions and allows the participants to engage themselves and take responsibility
- A process-owner or sponsor that has not committed him or herself to a pre-conceived result

Boundaries for the Discussions

The boundaries defined for the workshop where intended to focus the outputs on relevant and useful input to the ongoing East African energy access initiative. Thus, for each session, question and prioritisation the participants were tasked with keeping the following criteria in mind:

- The four targets from the scale-up strategy
- High Impact, Low-Cost and Scalable solutions (HILCS)
- Not interventions at the "project" level but focus on programmatic and political activities
- Creativity and innovation without loosing sight of the four targets

Structure

The workshop was structured around five sessions. In four of the sessions the topics for discussion was pre-decided by the organisers and in the fifth session the topic for discussion was open for suggestions by the participants.

The participants were seated around six tables with about seven participants around each table.

Session 1

In the first session consisted of the opening and introduction to the objectives and scope of the workshop and an exercise to focus the attention on the topic of the workshop and instil an appreciation of the role that energy has in achieving the MDGs.

Sessions 2, 3 and 4

Half a day was devoted to each of the sessions 2, 3 and 4, each covering one of the energy scale-up targets. The sessions were introduced by a short presentation[6] on the challenges related to the target. Thereafter, discussions on a set of pre-determined questions (see Box 2) in smaller groups generated proposals for actions that need to be taken to achieve the targets.

Box 2: Working Group Rotating Questions

- What cross-sectoral institutional collaboration activities are necessary, to formulate and implement policies and programmes to achieve the target?
- What types of training and awareness raising activities are needed to achieve the target?
- What types of information collection and processing tools and methods are needed for planning, implementation and monitoring to achieve the target?
- What actions can minimize the cost of achieving the target?
- What actions will encourage private sector engagement in achieving the target? (financing, supply of energy goods and services)
- What actions relating to regional cooperation will contribute to the achieving the target?

The material generated in each session was organised and presented on six large panels. Figure 1 provides a schematic overview of the structure and phases of the workshop methodology.

6 The presentations can be downloaded from www.enable.nu.

Figure 1: Schematic of the Workshop steps

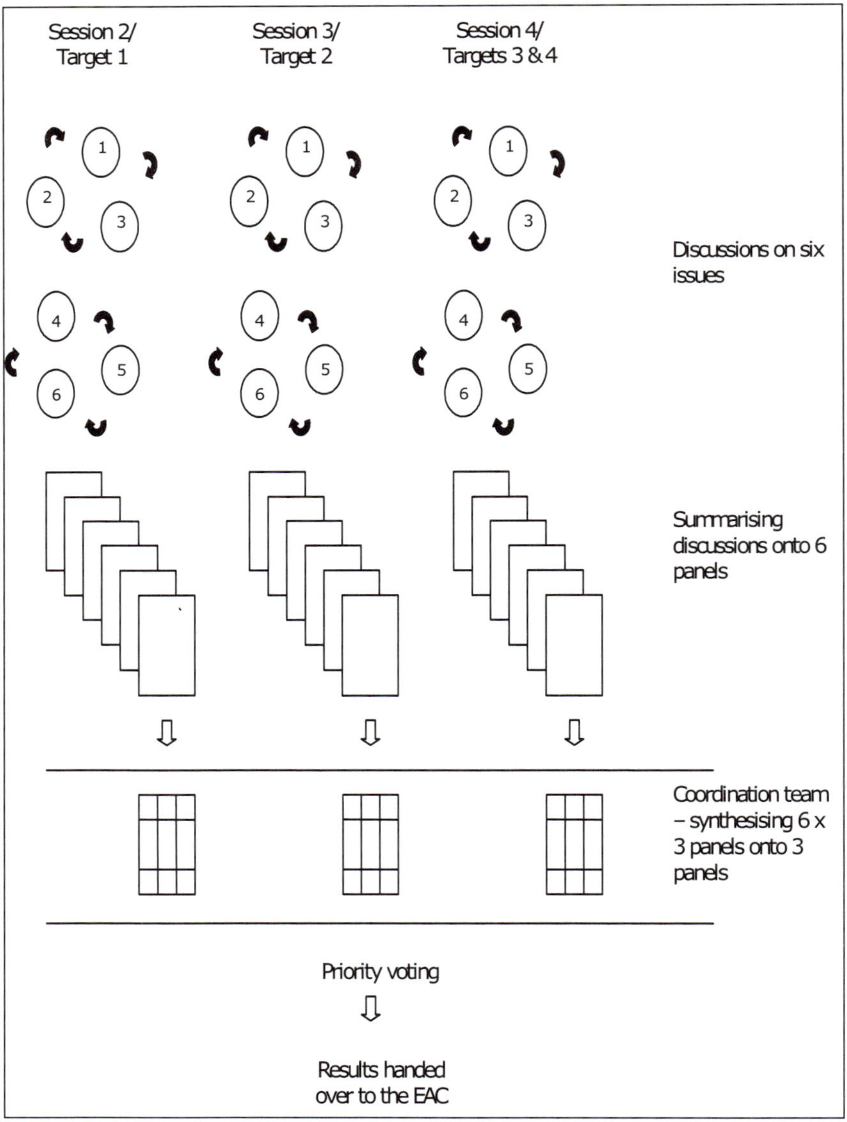

Source: Author's presentation.

Parallel coordination team

During sessions 3, 4 and 5 a smaller coordination team worked in parallel to the main sessions with the task to further synthesise the results generated in the main sessions The coordination team was asked to generate a matrix with actions grouped into appropriate themes and assigning these to either the regional, national or local level. The themes were left to the coordination team to identify whereas the responsibility or action level was pre-determined to be regional, national and local.

Prioritisation

When the coordination team had completed the three panels that synthesised each of the discussion sessions and the identified actions and identified at which level (regional, national, local) the action would be most relevant, the participants were asked to give priority to the actions that would lead to high impacts, low cost and scaleable solutions.

IV Results

The main output from the workshop was a set of thematically clustered interventions that participants saw as necessary to achieve each of the targets. In the workshop, the thematically clustered interventions were structured according to level of interventions (regional, national or local). Subsequently the proposed interventions were prioritised by the participants with reference to the perceived positive feasibility and effectiveness.

A thematic clustering of the proposed interventions that received priority votes by the workshop participants is presented in Table 1:

Table 1: Thematic Clusters (Generated from ENABLE Analysis)

Votes	Clustered action theme
31	Stakeholder involvement in planning, implementation and monitoring
21	Mobilising actors to be involved in reaching the targets
17	Regional approaches
15	Public-private partnerships
14	Technology development
13	Political support and governance issues
11	Planning, monitoring and evaluation tools

Continuation on the next page.

Continuation of table 1 from the previous page.

Votes	Clustered action theme
11	Cross sector collaboration/coordination in planning and implementation
9	Strategic analysis and studies
9	Financial instruments
8	Professional Information Dissemination and knowledge management
8	Public information dissemination
4	Harmonisation of standards

Key Messages

Emerging from the priority themes are a number of key messages. The key messages that emerge from the analysis of the proposed prioritised actions is presented below in descending order of priority.

1. Involve and strengthen the capacity and authority at the district and municipal levels to plan for, implement and monitor actions to achieve the targets.

The strongest message that comes out of the workshop is that the local stakeholders at district and municipal levels, including administration, and women and men need to be given the mandate, the tools and the powers to be more involved in planning, implementing and monitoring activities that aim at achieving the four energy access targets. This also reinforces the message coming out of previous national consultations carried out within the ENABLE project.

2. Mobilise the involvement of more actors to be involved in reaching the targets

Another clear message is to encourage and make use of existing and potential actors in providing energy services and in manufacturing technologies and fuels necessary to reach the targets. This is specifically proposed to be locally based actors such as rural energy service companies, artisans and community based organisations.

3. Utilise the opportunities that lie within regional cooperation including sharing costs and resources in developing and implementing common regional strategies to achieve the targets.

The participants clearly identified the need to seize the existing opportunities imbedded in active regional cooperation to achieve the targets faster and at a lower cost. Such opportunities lie within sharing investment costs, research and development costs, carrying out studies and developing plans as well as creating a larger market for services, fuels and appliances.

4. Develop public-private partnerships and strengthen involvement of credit and financial institutions as well as carbon trading schemes in reaching the targets.

Participants identified and prioritised the need to engage financial institutions in achieving the targets and to create stronger commitment and links with these. Joint initiatives and partnerships are called for.

5. Apply an energy efficiency approach in meeting the targets and develop an appropriate mix of energy efficient technologies and fuel alternatives to meet the targets.

The participants perceived it to be a priority to apply an energy efficiency approach in meeting the targets so as to use available energy resources efficiently and thereby be able to reach out to more end-users. Another prioritised action is to diversify and develop an appropriate mix of gaseous, liquid and energy efficient biomass technologies to meet the cooking and heating related targets.

6. Take actions to get strong commitment from governments in reaching the targets.

Government awareness and commitment is an identified and prioritised action in order to achieve the targets. Such commitment can be shown by allocating funding towards actions needed to meet the targets, by instituting proper regulatory and legal frameworks as well as rhetorically recognising and communicating the importance of the targets for sustainable development and poverty reduction.

7. Develop tools and methods to facilitate energy planning and carry out needs assessments and to monitor and evaluate initiatives to achieve the targets.

The development and application of a range of tools and methods, ranging from needs assessments, to monitoring and evaluation tools are identified and prioritised by the participants in the undertaking to achieve the targets. Participants also recognised the need to build capacity within institutions and amongst individual to apply these tools and methods.

8. Take actions to integrate analysis of the implications of energy services from a cross-sectoral perspective and take action to enhance cross-sector dialogue and coordination.

Cross sector coordination and dialogue is important in effectively meeting the targets according to the participants. The message is that cross sector coordination regarding accelerated energy services delivery needs to be enhanced from the central government level down to the district level.

9. Carry out studies and assessments to improve the information available to be able to take strategic decisions relevant to meeting the targets

A number of strategic studies and assessments are seen as necessary by the participants in order to meet the targets. The message is to use existing institutions to generate and provide relevant information for strategically planning the approach to meeting the targets.

10. Use appropriate taxation instruments and subsidies to reach the targets

The identified activities are related to changes in the use of taxes such as removing taxes and levies as well as providing tax incentives; end-user financing; financing of energy service and energy technology suppliers; diversifying and mobilising funding sources to specifically achieve the targets

11. Put in place systematic knowledge management systems targeting professionals and decision makers regarding approaches to achieve the targets

Participants recognise and prioritise the need to establish and enhance professional knowledge management to effectively achieve the targets. This relates to sharing of best-practices, information that is relevant for the development of energy markets and information on energy end-users.

12. Take actions to raise the public awareness on energy and its role and potential for sustainable development and poverty reduction should be taken

The participants also recognise and prioritise the need to raise public awareness on energy issues amongst energy end-users. Proposed topics include awareness on productive use of modern energy services, consequences of indoor air pollution and energy efficiency.

13. Take actions to harmonise standards on a regional and national level to support the achievement of the targets

Finally, standards need to be harmonised across the region and at national level to facilitate market development and to reduce costs.

Messages Emerging from the Open Space Session

In addition to the results and key messages resulting from the discussions around the six questions pre-determined by the workshop organisers the participants were given the opportunity to freely suggest topics and questions that they felt had not been treated sufficiently under the framework of the predetermined questions.

The messages emerging from this session are presented below. These were not, however, included in the prioritisation exercise carried out by the participants.

- A SWOT (Strengths, Weaknesses, Opportunities and Threats) analysis of EAC government to scale up provision of modern energy to rural areas should be made.

Significant efforts for scaling up modern energy services to rural areas have been made with different degrees of success – some reasons for failures include the low income situation in target communities. The lessons from these failures and successes should be taken into consideration when moving forward.

- Gender issues should be mainstreamed in any plans to achieve the targets.
  Concrete steps include assuring gender balance on planning committees, analysing the planned energy services from a gender perspective and gender issues in energy planning and building capacity amongst women to participate more actively in initiatives to achieve the targets.
- Environmental concerns need to be integrated in any plans to achieve the targets by enforcing the application and building the capacity to carry out strategic environmental assessments

Corruption, which negatively affects the efficiency and effectiveness with which the targets are met, needs to be addressed systematically. This is proposed to be done by establishing proper monitoring and follow-up mechanisms, liberalising the market and introducing more competitiveness, increasing the level of transparency and accountability of utilities and by having regulatory authorities that can properly enforce laws and regulations that curbs corruption.

- The environmental and economic effects of population growth and immigration need to be taken into account when planning for and implementing programmes to achieve the targets.
  Practical actions to consider here are more continuous monitoring of population pattern changes, strengthening of environmental laws and institutions dealing with enforcement of such laws should be strengthened. Also the external effects of having access to more energy services need to be considered such as implications of energy service to draw larger amounts of water and its impact on institutions, ecosystem services and changes on livestock and food production.
- Increase public awareness of the risks associated with utilisation of energy as well as the options to reduce e.g. indoor air pollution and to reduce energy consumption through he use of more energy efficient appliances.
- How sustainable are modern energy services?
- The need for sustained maintenance, adaptability and creation of productive markets was raised under this topic as an important preconditions for sustainability.
- Creation of productive markets
- The importance of using the opportunities of improved modern energy services to create added value in production was discussed under this topic. Associated to this was information to end-users about such opportunities as well as assistance to energy entrepreneurs through access to financing.
- Integrate the targets in the district development plans and establish energy sector representation at district and lower levels.
- This group discussed the need for capacity building on energy and environment issues and properly integrating this in district development plans.
- Establishment of a regional e-network of champions for energy/implementation programmes.

- The purpose of such a network would be to share best practices and to share knowledge and experience in how the targets can be met. One of the group participants volunteered to facilitate the start up of such a network.
- Individual households to reach the targets
- This group discussed the need to properly assess the needs and priorities at the household level. How households could increase their incomes in the process of meeting the targets was discussed.

V Conclusions

The workshop successfully brought out a consensus on the major elements that need to be considered in the eventual strategy, EAC work plan, and investment programmes and the priority activities associated with these elements (which essentially constitute a draft framework for the regional strategy and implementation framework). To achieve a broad agreement on a programme framework the workshop deliberately focused on energy access content based on the four regional energy targets. Broader issues such as process, timing, institutional roles, etc. were not sufficiently addressed for the purposes of a regional strategy.

The results of the workshop fed directly into the 10th meeting of the EAC Energy Committee which was held back to back. The EAC further synthesised the results and formulated 14 recommendations to the EAC Council of Ministers and Head of State. The Council of Ministers considered and approved the recommendations on the 29th of March, 2006. The recommendations in themselves are reflective of and provide the basic framework for a regional strategy and for the work plan that will be eventually adopted by the EAC Energy Committee.

The next step is the development of a regional strategy that will include the following elements:

1. The context, background and underlying analysis used in developing the regional strategy
2. A strategic approach for meeting the targets. This strategy will identify key objectives, targets and MGD indicators as well as a discrete set of programmes with clear goals that together will enable EAC to meet its targets.

3. An implementation plan to execute the strategy including a regional action plan and set of investment programmes.
4. The institutional framework necessary to implement the plan including roles and responsibilities between the EAC regional body and individual government entities.
5. An investment plan that will provide ballpark quantification of near, medium and long term funding requirements.
6. A funds mobilising strategy including donors, cross sectoral government ministries and carbon and development finance.

Agreement of the detailed outline of the strategy document will be approved by the EAC in the beginning of June 2006. A draft version of the regional strategy will be a core document to be shared by stakeholders including donors, public sector, private sector, NGOs and beneficiaries.

Approval of the strategy document by Heads of State will give it the legitimacy and weight needed to put key funding activities in place.

For further information:

Stockholm Environmental Institute (SEI)
Mr. Anders Arvidson
Post Box 21 42
103 14 Stockholm
Tel: +46-8-412 14 14
Fax: +46-8-723 03 48
E-mail: anders.arvidson@sei.se
Web site: www.sei.se

Renewable Resources for Industrial Development and Export Diversification: The Case of Bioenergy from Sugar Cane in Southern Africa

Cane Resources Network for Southern Africa (CARENSA) &
Stockholm Environment Institute (SEI)
Stockholm, Sweden

I Background

This article is based on the work programme of the Cane Resources Network for Southern Africa (CARENSA), a four-year thematic research network that was supported under the European Commission's Fifth Framework Programme for Research. The primary objectives of the network were to synthesize existing research, develop performance benchmarks, and establish market scenarios for cane resources in support of sustainable development and improved global competitiveness for the sugar industry in southern Africa. The scientific and administrative coordinator for CARENSA was the Stockholm Environment Institute (SEI), while the other partners were associated with universities, research institutes, or policy-making bodies.[1] The structure of the network was based on a model of North-South-South collaboration, with four European partners, four African partners, three international organisations, and one partner each in Brazil and India, which are the world's largest producers of sugar cane. The activities of the network included workshops, field visits, stakeholder meetings, exchanges, and participation in international conferences and symposia. The participants included representatives from governments at various levels, academia, research institutes, foun-

1 The article was written by Francis X. Johnson from the Stockholm Environment Institute, Jeremy Woods from the Centre for Energy, Policy and Technology, Vikram Seebaluck from the University of Mauritius and Helen Kerr Watson from the University of Kwazulu Natal.

dations, NGOs, consulting companies, manufacturers, traders, community groups, and even interested citizens.[2]

II Introduction: Bioenergy, Sugar Cane and the SADC Region

Biomass accounts for the greatest share of primary energy consumption among all renewable sources and represents the main source of energy in sub-Saharan Africa. However, nearly all of this biomass is consumed for traditional uses in cooking, heating, and for small industries, in the form of fuelwood, charcoal, and residues from agricultural and industrial production. Adoption of more efficient and higher quality "modern" bio-energy options is an important element in the global transition to clean and sustainable energy. Modern bio-energy can facilitate the creation of rural livelihoods, reduce dependence on imported energy sources and offer new development paths.

On average, biomass in tropical and sub-tropical climates is five times as productive, in terms of photosynthetic efficiency, compared to biomass produced in temperate regions. Sub-Saharan Africa has significant bioenergy potential due to low population density in many areas, large areas of suitable cropland and pasture land, and the low productivity of existing agricultural production systems. The lack of employment opportunities in rural areas and the high labour intensity of bioenergy - relative to other energy supply options - suggest excellent opportunities for rural development.

Harnessing the potential of modern bioenergy requires regional coordination with respect to economic policy, trade, resource practices, and regulations. A large region encompassing fourteen countries that is undergoing a

---

2 In addition to the four organisations mentioned above, the other nine CARENSA partners are: Agricultural University of Athens, Greece (AUA); Interuniversity Research Centre on Developing Countries, Italy (CIRPS); Biomass Users Network, Zimbabwe (BUN); Centre for Energy, Environment, and Engineering, Zambia (CEEEZ); International Sugar Organisation (ISO); Food and Agricultural Organisation (FAO), United Nations (FAO); Winrock International India (WII); National Reference Centre for Biomass, Brazil (CENBIO); Southern African Development Community (SADC).

All references are taken from the CARENSA work programme and can be found on the website (www.carensa.net).

Thanks are extended to the European Commission (EC) Research Directorate, which has provided financial support and scientific guidance. The authors are responsible for the contents of the report, which should not be construed as representing the views held by their respective organisations or the views of the EC.

process of economic integration - the Southern African Development Community (SADC) - is therefore of special interest. The broader regional economic context has become more important with the recent rise in oil prices. The process of economic integration in SADC can both facilitate - and benefit from - the expanded production of modern biomass and biofuels. The domestic benefits will include health improvements, reduced regional emissions, and creation of rural livelihoods. The macroeconomic impacts include foreign exchange savings and reduced dependence on imported sources of energy. There is also significant potential for greenhouse gas (GHG) emission reductions from expanded use of modern bio-energy, with the latter earning credits in carbon markets.

As the world's most commercially significant energy crop, the sugar cane plant has special significance for bioenergy expansion, offering new development opportunities, export markets, and rural livelihoods. Global and regional markets are emerging for the many co-products[3] of the sugar cane plant, particularly bioethanol and co-generation of steam and electricity, as well as non-energy bio-products such as yeasts and bio-plastics. The advances in Brazil and elsewhere have demonstrated the considerable economic potential of cane resources. The following sections outline the opportunities and key challenges for southern Africa in developing sugar cane as a renewable resource for industrial development, including export markets for bioethanol.

III Agricultural Overview

Sugar cane (Saccharum officinarum) is a member of the grass or Gramineae family that concentrates sucrose in its stalks. It has high photosynthetic efficiency, i.e. it converts solar energy to biomass at a relatively high rate. It grows only in tropical and sub-tropical regions, with the result that over 90% of sugar cane is grown in the developing world. Sugar cane re-emerges when cut, thus enabling several harvests to be obtained from one planting. The number of re-plantings increases with mechanisation; since harvesting is still largely manual in southern Africa, the number of re-plantings is generally lower than elsewhere in the world, which saves considerable costs.

In southern Africa, the cane is generally burnt before harvest to remove the extraneous residues, known as "cane trash." In other parts of the world,

---

3 The many products other than crystalline sucrose (sugar) that can be made from sugar cane are generally referred to as "co-products."

the practice of burning cane has been ended, generally in combination with a switch to mechanical harvesting, thereby creating the possibility to use cane trash for cogeneration. Mechanical harvesting of green cane results in lower sucrose recovery in the sugar factory, but on the other hand enhances energy generation in the boiler house by making additional fuel available. The growth of bioenergy markets and environmental concerns will most likely stimulate a similar transition in southern Africa.

The potential to expand cane production in the SADC region depends on alternative land uses, vegetative cycles, soil properties, and climate conditions, as well as the potential effect of such expansion on the availability of water and other key resource inputs. Under such considerations, the potential for expansion is quite limited in Mauritius, South Africa, and Zimbabwe - which are the three countries that currently account for two-thirds of SADC's sugar cane production. Environmental issues such as salinization are key limiting factories in other countries, such as Swaziland. Other countries such as Angola and the Democratic Republic of Congo that do have suitable land and climate seem unlikely to expand in the near-term due to political instability. Madagascar has some expansion potential, although concern over deforestation may limit some options. The countries that appear to have the greatest potential for expansion are Malawi, Mozambique, and Zambia.

An alternative crop that is being considered in some future scenarios is sweet sorghum, which is a sorghum variety that has higher relative sugar content than grain sorghum, making it suitable for ethanol production as well as being a source of fibre. It has a much shorter growing period than cane - about 4 months - and has much lower water requirements and drought resistance properties. It does not have good properties for crystalline sugar production and consequently is not yet grown for commercial uses. It is grown from seeds rather than plantings, making it a more flexible alternative compared to sugar cane and more suited to small-scale farming.

IV Industrial Configurations

Assessment of the industry side can be divided into four main components: the set-up of the sugar factory, the configuration of the ethanol distillery, the cogeneration plant, and any other co-product facilities. The cogeneration plant uses bagasse from the sugar factory as its primary input fuel; bagasse is the fibrous residue left after juice extraction from the cane plant. Ethanol can be made from directly from sugar cane juice - in which case there would be no sugar production at all - or from a major by-product of sugar production - molasses. A cogeneration plant can be installed if the sugar factory processing capacity is adequate and energy-efficient enough to generate sufficient surplus bagasse and if there were markets for surplus heat and electricity. In today's market, where sugar production is still highly valued, ethanol-only operations are unusual, although there remain some "autonomous" distilleries in Brazil. Distilleries also rely on the availability of bagasse-based energy to minimise or eliminate external energy requirements and thereby maintain a good energy balance.

Cane is grown on a large, medium and small scale, predominately as permanent monoculture for commercial sugar production. In southern Africa, large estates are normally used and often owned by the same company that owns the factory. However, small growers and in some cases medium-size commercial growers also supply cane to sugar factories, and receive some technical support. The smaller scale of sugar production in SADC countries is among the reasons why it has been difficult to establish bio-ethanol production at competitive cost. The experience in Brazil suggests that economies-of-scale for bio-ethanol production require a cane supply between 1 and 2 million tonnes per year; most producers in SADC operate near the lower end of this range.

For a cogeneration plant, the current state-of-the-art for commercial applications is the Condensing Extraction Steam Turbine (CEST), which can produce much more surplus electricity when compared to the back-pressure turbines commonly used at most existing factories. The CEST systems are most widespread in Mauritius, where they have been installed at nearly all factories, and export surplus electricity to the grid during the harvest season. An option for the future is the Biomass Gasifier/Gas Turbine system (BIG-GT), which can quadruple the electricity being generated from the CEST system. In southern Africa, installation of CEST systems would diversify the fuel mix in the electric power sector, which is heavily dependent on hydro, or coal in the case of South Africa.

For ethanol production, the Brazilian designs offer the best technical configuration, including the preparation of feedstock (juice and/or molasses). The present tendency for distillery configuration is the so-called "annexed" distillery, which offers advantage of flexibility in allowing various combinations of sugar and ethanol production. In the near-term, southern African operations would need such flexibility. In the longer-term, the optimisation of ethanol production may suggest options for ethanol-only operations. Furthermore, the development of an export market for bio-ethanol from the SADC region would require some autonomous production of ethanol because the current levels available would be too low to reach sufficient scale, and the high investment cost for sugar factories means that new factories are unlikely to be built. Alternatively, other feedstocks could be made available, such as cassava, sweet sorghum, maize, and cellulosic[4] materials.

Fuel ethanol can be blended with gasoline at levels varying from 10% to 25% with little or no effect on fuel economy and with relatively minor adjustments, if any (depending on the share) to the engine. Rising oil prices and falling prices for sugar exports make ethanol production more commercially attractive than production of sugar in SADC countries, and will stimulate a shift from exporting sugar to ethanol production (for domestic use and/or export). Since typical ignition-spark engines are optimised for petrol, the substitution of ethanol results in lower output, generally between 65% and 80%. At or above the minimum efficient scale, and in the absence of import tariffs, bio-ethanol from SADC countries appears to be competitive with petrol when oil prices rise above 45-55 USD per barrel. With current import tariffs in the EU and U.S., the competitive price is 60-70 USD per barrel.

V Market Scenarios and Strategies

Brazil has become the world leader in bio-ethanol markets, while cogeneration has been pursued fairly intensively in India, Mauritius, Brazil and other countries. The long experience with sugar cane in southern Africa presents similar development opportunities, but thus far the sugar market has dictated the direction of the industry; efforts at bioenergy development from cane have been quite limited. Only Malawi and Zimbabwe have attempted to follow the Brazilian model for bio-ethanol, although their smaller production scale and the lack of a regional market have kept the price significantly higher than that of Brazil. The total cane production in SADC is less than 4% of the world total, making it rather small compared to Brazil and India, which account for about half of total world production. The lack of market power has contributed to the tendency of African sugar producers to rely wherever possible on preferential sugar markets in the EU and elsewhere.

There are many different market issues that will impact the future direction of the sugar industry in southern Africa and its potential for becoming a major producer of renewable energy. The changes in the sugar industry through reforms in EU sugar policies as well as WTO trade reforms will most likely result in some consolidation of the industry; the lower sugar prices resulting from the removal of preferential markets will cause shifts to the regions with better conditions and higher agricultural productivity. At the

4 Conversion technologies for cellulose-to-ethanol are not sufficiently mature to be cost-competitive.

same time, rising oil prices and energy security issues are providing incentives for expanded bio-energy production in the sugar sector. Market scenarios therefore depend on three key factors: (1) future demand for sugar, (2) future demand for biofuels, and (3) future demand for alternative sources of electric power. The emerging nexus between sugar policy reform and incentives for bio-energy production is important for sugar producers worldwide and not just in southern Africa.

Demand for electricity is expected to grow considerably in some areas within SADC, with growth rates of 3-5% annually, and the need for new power capacity will be come more acute by 2015. The sale of surplus electricity from sugar factories in the region would generally require installation of cogeneration plants similar to the CEST systems currently used in India, Mauritius, and Brazil. Where economies-of-scale are reached and there are policies and regulations in place for independent power production, electricity co-generated by CEST systems at sugar factories can be available at a reasonable price, generally in the range of 5-7 US cents per kWh. Power from reliable and continuous sources would add diversity to the fuel mix for electric power in SADC, which is currently overly dependent on hydro, or coal in the case of South Africa.

The potential for bio-ethanol production in SADC countries exceeds what would be required domestically for blending in all countries except South Africa, and thus indicates opportunities for export markets. The current global ethanol market is one in which Brazil exerts extreme market power, as the world's only major swing producer between sugar and ethanol. The expansion of the ethanol market could help to create many medium-size players and make the industry more competitive in the long-term. The geographical diversification will contribute to a transition towards ethanol as a global bio-energy resource rather than a regional one. Consequently, the entrance of new players in this market is generally welcomed by Brazil because its industry would benefit from South-South technology transfer, and from market opportunities that would emerge at the global scale.

VI Social-Economic Impacts

The socio-economic impacts were investigated by juxtaposing the small-scale production found in some areas with the medium-to-large-scale processing found in most countries. Case studies were conducted on small-scale production and sale of ethanol in the form of illicit spirits in several low-income peri-urban settlements near Harare, Zimbabwe. The second set of assessments addressed socio-economic impacts of medium-to-large-scale sugar cane in Malawi, Mauritius, Swaziland and Zimbabwe, where sugar, co-generation, and bio-ethanol production are represented to some degree.

The case studies highlight an essential tension between the large-scale centralised approach favoured by governments and large business vs. the possible benefits that could accrue to the rural poor from a smaller-scale decentralised approach. One of the most important measures of socio-economic impacts is the total number of jobs created, which is much higher than for other energy options and is concentrated in the agricultural side of the sugar cane agro-industry sector, which is much more labour-intensive. The quality of jobs, however, will differ considerably and with mechanisation there will be fewer total jobs, but they will be of higher quality and less seasonal.

The localised illegal activities in micro-production of ethanol demonstrated social problems but also business opportunities. The supply and demand for potable spirits could potentially be turned into opportunities for small-scale production for other markets, such as for household cooking or business applications. Instead of criminalising the activities of these poor producers who have extremely limited income-generating alternatives, it may be more effective to take a more positive stance that develops regulations and standards to assist these small industries to move into the mainstream economy. New organisational structures could emerge that integrate small-holder production, and possibly pre-processing, with large-scale conversion and marketing. Such systems would bring some of the benefits of scale, financing and market access to be small-holders so as to return a fair share of the value generated to the rural population. The important role of women in the localised production also showed that expansion of small-scale options has a positive gender impact.

The mature sugar industries are dominated by economies of scale, which in turn imply large-scale, high capital cost infrastructure. Such capital-intensive infrastructure was costly to upgrade, particularly during the falling world sugar prices in the 1980s and 90s. The region's industry is therefore saddled with outdated factories that need improved efficiency so that surplus energy can be made and sold. The investments in physical infrastructure would have to be matched by various investments in the soft infrastructure, e.g. education, health, training, and thus socio-economic benefits would accrue. Initially, the number of jobs would increase, but as operations became more mechanised, the number of jobs would fall on the agricultural side of the sugar cane sector. However, mechanisation would improve the overall quality of jobs and reduce the number of seasonal workers in favour of a more stable workforce that can help to build communities.

VII Environmental Impacts

The production and processing of sugar cane, as with any agro-industrial activity, has significant impacts on air, water, soil, flora, fauna, and human activity as well as on the global climate. These impacts arise throughout the crop production and industrial processing chain even where processing is remote from production. Furthermore, the relative importance ascribed to the primary product e.g. crystalline sugar, versus co-products such as ethanol and electricity, has implications for the way a future sugar cane-based renewable energy industry might be configured. A framework was developed to assess and measure the impacts of alternative sugar cane co-product scenarios, focusing mainly on ethanol and co-generation. Most sugar cane producing countries have local standards for emissions and apply the ISO 14000 management standards. Other impacts, such as those due to fertiliser use and agricultural run-off are not readily available outside South Africa and Mauritius. As with most environmental impact assessments, local conditions will be quite important, since ecosystem functions, biodiversity, and other localised impacts vary widely.

There are a number of health and environmental incentives for improving efficiency in the sugar industry and in expanded markets for bio-ethanol. For example, the planned phase-out of lead in petrol in the region illustrates how several development objectives can converge - health, energy, and environment - since ethanol can substitute for lead as an octane enhancer. In general, the environmental impacts of new production are much greater than the marginal impacts due to modifications in the product mix (e.g. expanded production of bio-ethanol) based on existing sugar cane production. The reason for the difference is that the key impacts occur on the agricultural side rather than the industry side of the operations, due to the significant amount of land preparation and infrastructure provision required for a permanent crop such as sugar cane. In the case of sweet sorghum, such impacts would be lower, since it requires less water, has a shorter growing season, and can be operated at smaller scales where appropriate. Land impacts in southern Africa, however, are likely to be less in comparison to other regions of the world, due to low population density and the significant amount of pasture land that is available for agricultural expansion.

There are two major exceptions to the rule that the significant impacts are found on the agricultural side. The first exception relates to the large wastewater stream resulting from ethanol production, known as vinasse or stillage, which can be toxic to water supplies if not discarded properly or used for further production of biogas, biofertilisers that can be returned back to the soil, and other products. Disposal regulations now exist in most countries, but their enforcement level varies. The second exception relates to the overall efficiency of the factory in terms of energy, water, and other resource inputs, which is almost always negatively correlated with the age of the factory. An inefficient factory will use up much more bagasse, water, etc. than is needed, and the result can be much higher economic and environmental costs.

VIII Implementation and Investment

The countries of southern Africa can benefit from the experiences of Mauritius, India, and Brazil with respect to electricity and ethanol from sugar cane. In addition to scaling up production, implementation strategies can be based on South-South technology transfer platforms so as to benefit the global development of bio-energy resources. Sugar cane and other crops with high energy potential offer a potential comparative advantage to southern Africa in the industrial development of bio-energy. By comparison, bio-energy efforts underway in northern temperate climates, where biomass is much less productive, are predicated on high capital inputs and advanced technology, which can compensate somewhat for the natural disadvantage but may not be sustainable in the longer-term. However, significant investment will be needed to upgrade facilities in order to harness the cane resource and stimulate industrial development.

A significant amount of capital investment would be needed to upgrade factories and install state-of-the-art equipment. The establishment of a new estate and sugar factory processing 2 million tc (steam/cane) per year would cost 200-300 million USD; the capital costs for an ethanol distillery are in the range of 50-80 million USD; the costs of a cogeneration plant are about 1000-1200 USD per installed kW or about 70-84 million USD for a 70 MW plant. Further costs for transport infrastructure and storage would also be incurred. It will be difficult to attract such investment to the region, where poor infrastructure and high interest rates often pose formidable barriers. However, additional investment could be leveraged through carbon finance, i.e. to leverage other investments using the market value of expected GHG emission reductions in existing carbon markets.

The only established export market is currently for raw or refined sugar, which is still governed by preferential agreements. Export markets for bioethanol are small and generally aimed only at the potable ethanol market or the industrial market[5] rather than the fuel ethanol market. Large-scale export

---

5 The potable market includes those buyers who provide ethanol to producers of spirits and alcoholic beverages. The industrial market includes applications in chemical, pharmaceutical, and other industries. Both the potable and industrial

to the U.S. or the EU faces trade barriers in the form of agricultural tariffs and/or domestic producer credits. For countries with ports, transport costs are extremely low in comparison to the total cost. In landlocked SADC countries, costs are higher although not insurmountable. Due in part to the low cost of shipment by sea, import tariffs and non-tariff barriers to trade present a much more significant barrier than transport and distribution costs. In Brazil, efforts are underway to reduce transport costs even further by building a pipeline, or adapting oil pipelines where feasible.[6] Reduction in tariffs and other trade barriers along with the loss of preferential sugar markets will create incentives for South-to-North exports of bio-ethanol, since production costs of ethanol from sugar cane are lower than is the case in temperate regions where feedstocks such as corn and wheat are used.

Programmes and policies for the development of cane as a bioenergy resource for the SADC region should start by replicating the successful undertakings/projects that have been realised elsewhere, particularly the Brazilian fuel ethanol experience, the Mauritius efforts in cogeneration, and Indian programmes in cogeneration and co-product development. Sharing of knowledge and expertise will facilitate a transformation of the traditional sugar sector into a sugar cane processing "biorefinery" complex with a number of end-products. Continuous improvements are very important to remain competitive and should be enhanced by R&D support from OECD countries. Above all, it would depend on availability of markets and the political commitment of the countries towards sustainable energy for development; common decisions and targets could be formulated at the level of SADC.

IX Conclusions

The exploitable bio-energy potential of the Sub-Saharan African region is significant. Economic integration in southern Africa through the Southern African Development Community (SADC) makes the southern African region particularly appealing for bio-energy expansion, given the efforts at lowering trade barriers and the harmonization of standards and regulations in the SADC region. The sugar sector is the most promising area for bio-energy development, offering opportunities both for domestic markets and international markets, particularly for bio-ethanol and co-generated electricity. The

---

markets require higher quality or purity and therefore command a price premium.

6 Ethanol mixes easily with water, unlike oil, and thus pipelines must be separate or have dehydration capability.

region has a fairly strong industrial base in the sugar industry, but expansion of sugar production is unlikely to be rewarding, given the decisions in recent years to reduce preferential market access to ACP countries. The cultivation of other highly productive crops such as sweet sorghum for bio-energy may provide valuable supplementary and/or complementary strategies to those pursued for cane.

Bio-energy expansion can create rural livelihoods, reduce costly energy imports, stimulate economic integration, reduce GHG emissions, and offer new development paths. Bio-ethanol can replace significant shares of petrol in many countries and export markets could also be developed. Co-generated electricity from sugar factories can help to diversify the fuel mix in the power sectors of the region. Harnessing this bio-energy potential will require significant increases in investment, technology transfer, and international cooperation. Because of its high efficiency and its concentration in the developing world, the cane resource and other highly efficient bioenergy sources should be viewed as global resources for sustainable development and should command much greater focus and concerted policy action through north-south and south-south cooperation. The transition to cane as a bio-energy resource in southern Africa would promote sustainable development and improve global competitiveness for the sugar industry and the general economy in the region.

For further information please contact:

Stockholm Environment Institute (SEI)
Climate and Energy Resources Programme
Mr. Francis X. Johnson
Lilla Nygatan, 1
Box 2142,
S-103 14 Stockholm,
Sweden
Tel: +46 8 412 1400
Fax: +46 8 723 0348
E-Mail: francis.johnson@sei.se
Web site: http://www.sei.se/

Contents Volume 11
African Development Perspectives Yearbook 2005/2006
Africa – Escaping the Primary Commodities Dilemma

Unit 2: International Trade in and Production of Primary Commodities: Interventions to Improve the Position of Countries and Firms in the Global Value Chain

edited by Tobias Knedlik and Mareike Meyn

Unit 3: Global Raw Materials Markets and Diversification Efforts of Commodity Producers in SADC Countries

edited by Philippe Burger and Tobias Knedlik

Overview
African Development Perspectives Yearbook Volume 13 (2008):
New Growth and Poverty Alleviation Strategies for Africa

I Objectives and Contents

Volume 13 continues the discussion that took place in recent volumes of the African Development Perspectives Yearbook on ways to revitalise African economies. This is done by focussing on new growth and poverty alleviation strategies for sustainable African economic development in the era of globalisation. The dependence of the vast majority of African countries on raw materials exports, the natural resource curse, the difficulties to diversify production and exports towards manufactured goods and services, and the prospects for escaping the primary commodities dilemma in Africa were the issues that were dealt with in the volumes 11 and 12 of the Yearbook. In this volume 13 the focus is on new growth and poverty alleviation strategies that will be highlighted in various units.

We will discuss in volume 13 the issues of growth and poverty alleviation as two sides of the development process in Africa. Africa has - after decades of stagnation - experienced in recent years some acceleration of growth, but the regional effects and the local outcomes in Africa were quite different as were the benefits to the population in terms of income distribution, human development and poverty alleviation. The growth process in Africa was not stable and was not sustainable. It has to be analysed in detail, as growth still is the most powerful mechanism to alleviate poverty. However, we know that generalisations do not make sense, and therefore we will review cases from various regions of Africa.

The discussion will also centre on actions to be taken at local, national, regional and international levels to move to a more sustainable path of growth and development. Public and private sector strategies will be discussed, as well as the factors that impede internally and externally sustainable growth. National, regional and international policies that affect poverty, income distribution and human development will be analysed. Main orientation for all the contributions is the policy and institutional change needed in African countries in the coming years so as to reach sustainable growth and effective poverty alleviation.

The contributions will highlight cases of new growth and poverty alleviation strategies for African countries that lead to lessons to be learned by other countries. Most important is it to analyse how growth processes can be shaped so as to reach poor producers and households at the local and regional levels. Local growth, employment and poverty alleviation strategies will be emphasised. Growth and poverty alleviation policies will be studied by functions, institutions and strategies, and with regard to all relevant levels and dimensions of action.

To study all the relevant aspects in detail, the Research Group on African Development Perspectives in Bremen has invited by the way of an International Call for Papers leading African and international researchers, development practitioners, experts from international research centres and international organisations, and also representatives from nongovernmental organisations and from the donor community to contribute to this volume of the Yearbook. The response to this Call for Papers was great, and the invited contributors are now drafting their papers.

II Units and Procedures

We have invited contributions for the following Units:

Unit 1: New Growth and Poverty Alleviation Strategies for Africa – How to reach the Millennium Development Goals? (Editors: K. Wohlmuth/Invited A. Jerome/NN)

Unit 2: Growth, Employment, Poverty Alleviation and Institutional Development in Selected African Countries – Lessons from Country Cases (Editors: K. Wohlmuth/NN)

Unit 3: New Growth and Poverty Alleviation Strategies – The Case of South Africa (Editors: P. Burger/M. Meyn)

Unit 4: Local Growth, Employment and Poverty Alleviation Strategies in Selected African countries – Learning from Successful Initiatives (Editors: K. Wohlmuth/NN)

Unit 5: Book Reviews and Book Notes: Books, research papers and documents that are relevant to the theme will be reviewed and can still be sent to the Research Group. Editor: A. Gutowski

Unit 6: Profiles, News and Information: Profiles, News and Information that are relevant to the theme will be covered, and reports of this type can still be sent to the Research Group. Editor: Invited T. Urban

III Abstracts, Manuscripts and Inquiries

Books for Review and Contributions for Profiles, News and information can still be sent to the Co-ordinating Editor of the African Development Perspectives Yearbook:

Prof. Dr. Karl Wohlmuth
Research Group on African Development Perspectives
University of Bremen
Department of Economics (FB 7)
Institute for World Economics and International Management (IWIM)
P.O. Box 330 440
D-28334 Bremen
Germany

Telephone:	+49-421-218-3074/-2138
Fax:	+49-421-218-4550
E-mail:	wohlmuth@uni-bremen.de
Internet:	http://www.iwim.uni-bremen.de

African Development Perspectives Yearbook

Research Group on African Development Perspectives University of Bremen

Karl Wohlmuth; Elke Grawert; Robert Kappel; Markus Wauschkuhn; Hans-Heinrich Bass; Bankole Oni; Achim Gutowski

Africa's Reintegration into the World Economy

The marginalisation of Africa with regard to international trade, international investment, international technology flows and international firm cooperation is the outcome of historical factors, especially of the colonial period, but also of the policies pursued after independence. Africa's marginalisation is also the result of highly inadequate economic reforms during the 1980s that failed to stimulate internationally competitive production of goods and services in primary production, in manufacturing and in services. Volume 8 of the African Development Perspectives Yearbook focusses on the causes of Africa's inadequate integration into the world economy, and on the strategies to regain an international status for Africa's production and trade sectors. Cases of successful integration of companies and countries into the world market as well as lessons for a better integration are the main thrust of the book. It is now time to demonstrate that world market integration is in reach for African producers, especially when considering the rich history of trading within Africa and between Africa and other world economic regions. Content: Africa and Globalisation; Policies to Reintegrate Africa into the World Economy; Country Cases of Africa responding to Globalisation Trends; Globalisation and Gender in Africa; Regional Development and Globalisation; News and Booknotes.

Bd. 8, 2001, 992 S., 50,90 €, br., ISBN 3-8258-4781-0

Karl Wohlmuth; Achim Gutowski; Tobias Knedlik; Mareike Meyn; Sunita Pitamber (Eds.)

African Entrepreneurship and Private Sector Development

This volume IX of the African Development Perspectives Yearbook on "AFRICAN ENTREPRENEURSHIP AND PRIVATE SECTOR DEVELOPMENT" presents analyses, policy papers, development projections and proposals for reform with regard to the role of African entrepreneurs, as they are now more and more exposed to a more market-oriented economy and to a new policy of the governments to support private sector development in Africa. This is how Africa is responding to the globalisation trend. Major policy problems facing entrepreneurs in Africa in the era of globalisation are analysed and solutions for macro policies and micro policies are outlined. This is done in the Yearbook with regard to issues as industrial policy, support for small and medium enterprises, financing small enterprises, investment promotion and regulation, and redirecting macro policies so that they are more pro-market. Cases of successful entrepreneurship in Africa are reviewed, and the role of networks and clusters for the success is analysed. Issues of women entrepreneurship are discussed with regard to empowerment, education and employment policies. The country cases reviewed in the Yearbook highlight the role of entrepreneurs in African societies, and the impact of the new policy trend towards private sector development. However, also the complexities of policy formulation and adaptation in the era of globalisation are discussed. Book Reviews and Book Notes are presented, and News and Information follow with up-to-date entries. This volume does not only present facts, trends and analyses, but also builds the foundation for a comprehensive strategy of policy reforms in Africa in the era of globalisation that are directed towards private sector development. Complementary to this volume IX is volume X on "PRIVATE AND PUBLIC SECTORS: TOWARDS A BALANCE". Both volumes are of use for all those working in African countries as officials, executives, managers, researchers, and policy-makers, but also for all those in the world-wide donor community that are actively supporting Africa's development at the regional, country, local and project levels. Development practitioners, government officials, business executives, and development researchers as well as media people will experience this volume 9 and also the complementary volume 10 as indispensable sources of insight, reference and inspiration.

Bd. 9, 2004, 696 S., 69,90 €, br., ISBN 3-8258-7406-6

LIT Verlag Münster – Berlin – Hamburg – London – Wien – Zürich

Fresnostr. 2 48159 Münster

Tel.: 0251 – 62 032 22 – Fax: 0251 – 23 19 72

e-Mail: vertrieb@lit-verlag.de – http://www.lit-verlag.de